The Ancient Near E

Blackwell Sourcebooks in Ancient History

This series presents readers with new translations of the raw material of ancient history. It provides direct access to the ancient world, from wars and power politics to daily life and entertainment, allowing readers to discover the extraordinary diversity of ancient societies.

Published

The Ancient Near East
Edited by Mark W. Chavalas

Roman Games
Alison Futrell

Alexander the Great
Waldemar Heckel and J. C. Yardley

The Hellenistic Period
Roger Bagnall and Peter Derow

The Ancient Near East

Historical Sources in Translation

Edited by Mark W. Chavalas

Blackwell
Publishing

BLACKWELL PUBLISHING
350 Main Street, Malden, MA 02148-5020, USA
9600 Garsington Road, Oxford OX4 2DQ, UK
550 Swanston Street, Carlton, Victoria 3053, Australia

First published 2006 by Blackwell Publishing Ltd

1 2006

Library of Congress Cataloging-in-Publication Data

The ancient Near East : historical sources in translation / edited by Mark W. Chavalas.
p. cm. — (Blackwell sourcebooks in ancient history)
Includes bibliographical references and index.
ISBN-13: 978-0-631-23580-4 (hardcover : alk. paper)
ISBN-10: 0-631-23580-9 (hardcover : alk. paper)
ISBN-13: 978-0-631-23581-1 (pbk. : alk. paper)
ISBN-10: 0-631-23581-7 (pbk. : alk. paper) 1. Middle East—History—To 622—Sources. I. Chavalas, Mark W. (Mark William), 1954– II. Series.
DS62.2.A63 2005
939'.4—dc22

2005013796

A catalogue record for this title is available from the British Library.

Set in 10/13pt Stone Serif
by Graphicraft Limited, Hong Kong
Printed and bound in Singapore
by C.O.S. Printers Pte Ltd

The publisher's policy is to use permanent paper from mills that operate a sustainable forestry policy, and which has been manufactured from pulp processed using acid-free and elementary chlorine-free practices. Furthermore, the publisher ensures that the text paper and cover board used have met acceptable environmental accreditation standards.

For further information on
Blackwell Publishing, visit our website:
www.blackwellpublishing.com

Contents

Contents in Detail

11 Neo-Assyrian and Syro-Palestinian Texts II   331

Brent A. Strawn, Sarah C. Melville, Kyle Greenwood, and Scott Noegel

12 Neo-Babylonian Period Texts from Babylonia and Syro-Palestine   382

Benjamin Studevent-Hickman, Sarah C. Melville, and Scott Noegel

Acknowledgments

This project literally began at the ground floor. I was asked by Al Bertrand of Blackwell to preview an upcoming volume on ancient Persia. I naively suggested to him that Blackwell might consider publishing a primary source reader for the ancient Near East, as there was nothing of the sort for this field of study. Blackwell were far ahead of me in this regard, as they had heard from a number of scholars of the need of such a book. Not knowing what I was getting into, I accepted the challenge of editing such a work. The first challenge was the issue of translations. It was agreed that clearing permissions for previously published translations would be too costly to get the project off the ground. However, it was not feasible to use translations that were out of copyright, since they were much too out of date to be useful. Thus, it was decided to conscript an army of scholars to make new translations and provide historical commentary and bibliographies. What was also difficult was the realization that a number of ancient languages are involved in this project, including Sumerian, Akkadian (various dialects), Aramaic, Hittite, Hebrew, Greek, and various other West Semitic languages. Furthermore, a number of different writing systems are involved that the translaters had to deal with. Needless to say, no one person could do justice to all of this material.

There have been so many individuals who have helped in this little volume, either as contributors to the volume itself, or by giving advice or encouragement. Aside from the contributors (many of whom gave very useful advice on the choice of documents or persons to use), I want to thank Benjamin Foster, Daniel Snell, Billie Jean Collins, Wayne Pitard, Daniel Fleming, Marc Van De Mieroop, Steve Tinney, Joan Westenholz, Seth Richardson, and Paul-Alain Beaulieu, among others. I also want to thank Al Bertrand and Simon Alexander of Blackwell for their help and encouragement. Special thanks go to Blackwell for allowing me to reproduce a map from D. C. Snell, ed., *A Companion to the Ancient Near East* (Oxford: Blackwell, 2005).

Lastly, but most importantly, I want to thank my wife Kimberlee and my six children for their patience and forbearance over the past few years that I have labored over this project.

Abbreviations

The following symbols are used to clarify the translated text:

"[. . .]" = irretrievable, damaged text; "⌜xxx⌝" = damaged or partially damaged, but reconstructed, text.

< > signifies an insertion by the contributor; i.e., the word was omitted by the scribe, but should have been there.

ABAT2	H. Gressman, ed., *Altorientalische Bilder zum Alten Testaments*, 2d ed. (Berlin: de Gruyter, 1927)
ANET	J. B. Pritchard, ed., *Ancient Near Eastern Texts Relating to the Old Testament*, 3d ed. (Princeton: Princeton University Press, 1969)
ARM	Archives royales de Mari
ASJ	*Acta Sumerologica*
AT	Siglum for tablets found at Alalakh (Tell Atchana)
BE	The Babylonian Expedition of the University of Pennsylvania
CAD	*The Assyrian Dictionary of the Oriental Institute of the University of Chicago* (Chicago: University of Chicago Press, 1956–)
CAH	*The Cambridge Ancient History*, 3d ed. (Cambridge: Cambridge University Press, 1971)
CANE	J. M. Sasson, ed., *Civilizations of the Ancient Near East* 4 vols. (New York: Scribners, 1995)
CDA	Jeremy A. Black, Andrew R. George, and J. N. Postgate, *A Concise Dictionary of Akkadian*, 2d ed. (Wiesbaden: Harrassowitz, 2000)
CHD	H. Guterbock and H. A. Hoffner, Jr. eds, *The Hittite Dictionary of the Oriental Institute of the University of Chicago* (Chicago: University of Chicago Press, 1980–)
COS	W. W. Hallo and K. L. Younger, Jr. eds, *The Context of Scripture*, 3 vols. (Leiden: Brill, 1999–2003)

CT	*Cuneiform Texts from Babylonian Tablets in the British Museum* (London: Trustees of the British Museum, 1896–)
CTH	E. Laroche, ed., Catalogue des textes Hittites (Paris: Klincksleck, 1971)
CTMMA	Cuneiform Texts in the Metropolitan Museum of Art
DOTT	D. W. Thomas., ed., *Documents from Old Testament Times* (London: Nelson, 1958)
History	Marc Van De Mieroop, *A History of the Ancient Near East, ca. 3000–323* BC (Oxford: Blackwell, 2004)
KAH 2	O. Schroeder, *Keilschrifttexte aus Assur historischen Inhalts*, vol. 2 (Leipzig: Hinrich, 1922)
KAI	H. Donner and W. Röllig, Kanaanaïsche und Aramäische Inschriften, 3 vols (Wiesbaden: Harrassowitz, 1962–4)
KBo	*Keilschrifttexte aus Boghazköi*
KUB	*Keilschrifturkunden aus Boghazköi*
lit.	literally
NERT	W. Beyerlin, *Near Eastern Religious Texts Relating to the Old Testament* (Philadelphia: Westminster Press, 1978)
obv.	obverse
NB	*nota bene* (note well)
PRU	Palais royal d'Ugarit. Mission de Ras Shamra
RANE	B. Arnold and B. Beyer, eds., *Readings from the Ancient Near East: Primary Sources for Old Testament Study* (Grand Rapids: Baker, 2002)
rev.	reverse
RGTC	Répertoire géographique des textes cuneiforms
RIMA	A. K. Grayson et al., *The Royal Inscriptions of Mesopotamia: Assyrian rulers of the third and second millennia* BC *(to 1115* BC*)* (Toronto: University of Toronto Press, 1987)
RIMB	G. Frame, *Rulers of Babylonia from the Second Dynasty of Isin to the End of the Assyrian Domination (1157–612* BC*)* (Toronto: University of Toronto Press, 1995)
RIME 2	D. Frayne, *Early Periods, II: Sargonic and Gutian Periods (2334–2113* BC*)* (Toronto: University of Toronto Press 1993)
RIME 3/1	D. O. Edzard, *Gudea and His Dynasty* (Toronto: University of Toronto Press, 1997)
RIME 3/2	D. Frayne, *Ur III Period (2112–2004* BC*)* (Toronto: University of Toronto Press, 1997)
RIME 4/2	D. Frayne, *Old Babylonian Period (2003–1595* BC*)* (Toronto: University of Toronto Press, 1990)
RS	Museum siglum of the Louvre and Damascus (Ras Shamra)
SDAS	Seventh-Day Adventist Theological Seminary
TCL	Textes cunéiformes. Musée du Louvre
TSSI	J. C. L. Gibson, *Textbook of Syrian Semitic Inscriptions*, 2 vols. (Oxford: Clarendon, 1971–82)
TUAT	*Texte aus der Umwelt des Alten Testaments*
var.	variant

Notes on Contributors

Bill T. Arnold is Director of Hebrew Studies and Professor of Old Testament and Semitic Languages, Asbury Theological Seminary. He is the author of *Who Were the Babylonians?* (Atlanta: Society of Biblical Literature, 2004); *1 and 2 Samuel* (NIV Application Commentary; Grand Rapids: Zondervan, 2003); and coauthor of *A Guide to Biblical Hebrew Syntax*, with John H. Choi (Cambridge: Cambridge University Press, 2003). His PhD is from Hebrew Union College.

Richard Averbeck, Trinity International University, is the co-editor of *Life in the Ancient Near East.*

Gary Beckman is Professor of Hittite and Mesopotamian Studies and Chair of Near Eastern Studies at the University of Michigan. He is an editor of the *Journal of the American Oriental Society* and the *Journal of Cuneiform Studies.* His primary research interest is in the reception of Babylonian and Assyrian culture among the Hittites.

Mark W. Chavalas is Professor of History at the University of Wisconsin-La Crosse. His research interests include the study of Syria and Upper Mesopotamia in the Bronze and early Iron Ages.

Yoram Cohen, Tel Aviv University, is an Assyriologist specialising in the Late Bronze Age. He is the author of *Taboos and Prohibitions in Hittite Society.*

Jeff Cooley, Xavier University, concentrates on the study of the Middle Babylonian period.

Eva von Dassow teaches the history of the ancient Near East at the University of Minnesota. Her research focuses on social history, historical method, and the representation of language in writing.

Petra Goedegebuure has as a main field of interest the application of the results of discourse and functional linguistics to the Anatolian and West-

Semitic languages, with emphasis on reference tracking and pragmatic notions such as Topic and Focus. She is affiliated with Leiden University.

Kyle Greenwood is a PhD candidate at Hebrew Union College where he is writing his dissertation on Middle Assyrian royal theology. He is also Adjunct Faculty of Bible at Indiana Wesleyan University, Cincinnati Campus.

Joost Hazenbos is currently at the University of Leipzig. Among his works is *The Organization of the Anatolian Local Cults during the Thirteenth Century* B.C.

Harry A. Hoffner, Jr. is The John A. Wilson Professor of Hittitology Emeritus at the University of Chicago. He is founding and senior editor of the *Chicago Hittite Dictionary* and the author of many books on the Hittites.

Theo van den Hout is Professor of Hittite and Anatolian languages at the Oriental Institute of the University of Chicago. He is executive editor of the *Chicago Hittite Dictionary* and managing editor of the *Journal of Ancient Near Eastern Religions*.

Frans van Koppen is a PhD candidate in Assyriology at the University of Leiden.

Glenn Magid is a PhD candidate at Harvard University.

Sarah C. Melville is an Assistant Professor of Ancient History at Clarkson University. Her publications on women in the Ancient Near East include a monograph, *The Role of Naqia Zakutu in Sargonid Politics* (1999), and two recent articles.

Piotr Michalowski, University of Michigan, is the editor of the *Journal of Cuneiform Studies*, and has published many works on the Sumerian language and civilization.

Kathleen Mineck is a doctoral candidate in Hittitology at the Oriental Institute of the University of Chicago. She is also a parttime staff member of the *Chicago Hittite Dictionary*.

Christopher Morgan is a PhD student at Hebrew Union College, and teaches at Asbury Theological Seminary.

Scott Noegel is Associate Professor of Biblical and Ancient Near Eastern Studies, University of Washington.

Brian B. Schmidt is Associate Professor of Hebrew Bible and Ancient Mediterranean West Asia in the Department of Near Eastern Studies at the University of Michigan, Ann Arbor. He holds a DPhil from the University of Oxford. His research interests include the history of Canaanite and Israelite religious and cultural traditions.

Brent A. Strawn (PhD, Princeton Theological Seminary, 2001) is assistant professor of Old Testament at the Candler School of Theology and in the Graduate Division of Religion at Emory University.

Benjamin Studevent-Hickman is a PhD candidate in Assyriology at Harvard, where he is writing his dissertation on the organization of labor in the Ur III period.

Illustrations

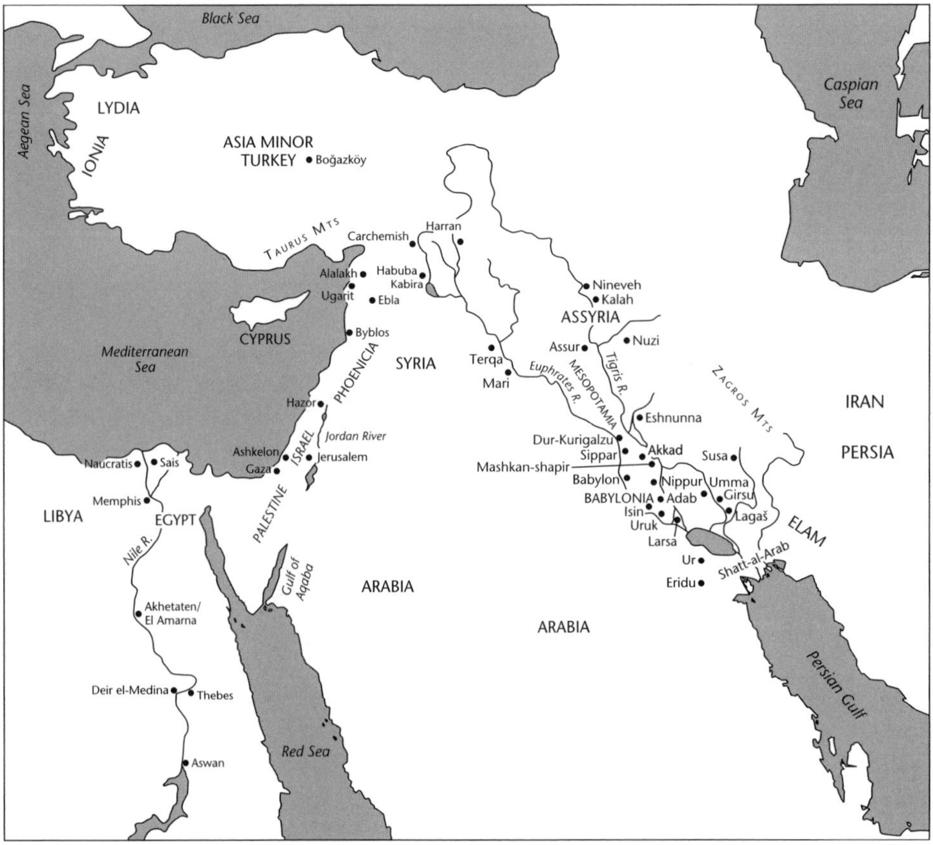

Map 1 The Near East

Introduction

Mark W. Chavalas

This volume is a primary source book that has excerpts of Mesopotamian and other ancient Near Eastern (specifically Hittite and Syro-Palestinian) historiographic texts and other primary source materials that further an understanding of ancient Near Eastern history. It is intended as a supplemental book for a textbook that surveys ancient Near Eastern history; for example, Marc van de Mieroop's work, *A History of the Ancient Near East, ca. 3200–323* BC (Oxford: Blackwell, 2004); and D. C. Snell, ed., *A Companion to the Ancient Near East* (Oxford: Blackwell, 2005). This present work surveys the period in Mesopotamia from the earliest historical and literary texts (ca. 2700 BC) to the Achaemenid Period. Because of space, it was decided to forego a study of Hellenistic historians who comment on ancient Near Eastern history (e.g., Berossus, ca. 250 BC), as well as pertinent biblical documents that concentrate upon Mesopotamian topics.

It is essential for students of history to read primary sources in translation; hence, the rationale for this book. In other words, we have written this book with the intention that it will be considered a readable and affordable analogy of ancient Near Eastern historical texts in translation. Although one finds source books like this one for a number of areas of history, there are no books of this kind for historical texts in Mesopotamia in English. This is in part because of the difficulty of translating the material. One cannot simply edit old translations, as they are out of date quickly in this rapidly changing field. Thus, I enlisted scholars to make new translations of excerpts of Mesopotamian (and nearby ancient Near Eastern) historical texts. The translator has also provided historical-critical commentary on the text in question, and has provided a bibliographic list for further reading on the subject.

One of the great Mesopotamian scholars of the last century, A. L. Oppenheim, called for an anthology such as this in the introduction to his landmark (with E. Reiner) *Ancient Mesopotamia: Portrait of a Dead Civilization*, 2d ed. (Chicago: University of Chicago Press, 1977), calling for a "critical discussion of the literary, stylistic, and emotional setting of each translated piece" (p. 3). I add that the historical context is as important to relate.

As previously stated, this work is geared for a one semester undergraduate course on ancient Near Eastern or Mesopotamian history. Though there are 13 chapters, it can be used in a 15-week course, as most educators will begin the course with a brief survey of prehistoric developments, and end the course with thematic issues (e.g., religion, literature, medicine, and gender). We also hope that it has been written in a manner that will make it accessible to those in the general public who are interested in history in general and the ancient Near East in particular.

Though there are a number of other works in English that could be used as supplementary texts in a course on Mesopotamian civilization, they do not precisely fill the need of a volume on historical texts in translation. They include B. Foster, *From Distant Days* (Bethesda: CDL, 1995), a collection of Akkadian literary texts in translation, which include a few of the historiographic texts proposed for our volume. S. Dalley's *Myths from Mesopotamia* (Oxford: Oxford University Press, 1998) is also an excellent supplement for a Mesopotamian civilization course, but has no explicitly historiographic material. J. B. Pritchard's classic two-volume abridged work *Ancient Near Eastern Texts Relating to the Old Testament,* 2 vols. (Princeton: Princeton University Press, 1971, 1975, 1992) includes documents from Egypt, while providing little historical commentary. W. W. Hallo and K. L. Younger's *The Context of Scripture* (Leiden: Brill, 1997–2002) is an excellent but massive undertaking, and is not appropriate to use as a college textbook. More recently, J. Glassner, *Mesopotamian Chronicles* (Atlanta: Society of Biblical Literature, 2003), has published an excellent anthology of Mesopotamian historical chronicles that is narrower in scope than our present volume.

The decipherment of the cuneiform writing script is barely 150 years old, and sometimes it is impossible for the modern student to fathom the enormous difficulties involved, not only in the decipherment of the cuneiform writing system, but the ongoing task of translating the dead languages of Akkadian (and then Sumerian) into modern languages has presented severe problems for the reconstruction of Mesopotamian history and civilization. Even to this day the scholar of Mesopotamian history (often called an "Assyriologist") encounters new values for cuneiform signs, let alone fundamental issues concerning the transcription, transliteration, and translation of the document in question. In fact, Assyriologists have often concentrated in working out philological difficulties so that historical reconstruction and historiographic reflection have often been relegated to an afterthought, and the learned information has not been made available to a wider public. Furthermore, because of its philological emphasis, the discipline of Mesopotamian studies has traditionally been empirical in its approach, and has been somewhat immune until recently to new-fangled ideas of historical research. Some researchers have often indiscriminately equated all sources as potentially historical. This is why the recent upsurge in the translation and publication of primary source materials is so critical to an understanding of Mesopotamian history. The reader will quickly see that the selection of sources here are concerned with "history from above," or history from the standpoint of the rulers, a very traditional way of approaching the subject. One can easily make the case for an ancient Near Eastern sourcebook concerning "history from below," or history from the standpoint of the common person, a subject to which the cuneiform record is well suited. That, however, could be the topic of another book!

For purposes of studying the chronology of the ancient Near East, the reader is referred to J. Brinkman's appendix to A. L. Oppenheim, *Ancient Mesopotamia: Portrait of a Dead Civilization*, 2d ed. (Chicago: University of Chicago Press, 1977), pp. 335–48. For the study of the nature of Mesopotamian historiography, see Marc van de Mieroop's *Cuneiform Texts and the Writing of History* (London: Routledge, 1999).

Note

Each contributor in this volume was given the discretion whether to use the form BC or BCE and to determine which citation and bibliographic format to use. Moreover, many personal names in ancient Near Eastern languages have variant English spellings. Once again, I have in some cases allowed the contributor to determine which spelling to employ.

1

Sumerian Early Dynastic Royal Inscriptions

Glenn Magid

The history of ancient Sumer is reconstructed largely from documentary evidence. Cuneiform texts have been unearthed at numerous archaeological sites in southern Iraq, the heartland of Sumerian civilization. They owe their survival to the materials on which they were inscribed: most often clay, occasionally stone, and, rarely, metal. Extant texts, numbering in the tens of thousands, constitute only a small portion of the ancient scribal output. To date, only a fraction of them have been published.

Sumerian texts fall into several types: those that were employed in the training of scribes (e.g., word and sign lists), those that were consulted and compiled by a variety of specialist practitioners (e.g., lists of omens, medical remedies, and astronomical observations), those that formed the archives (and included, e.g., inventories and records of purchases, sales, and loans) of private persons (like merchants and high officials) and public institutions (like palaces and temples), and those that served the propaganda needs of the society's elite members (e.g., myths, epics, and royal inscriptions), to name some of the most important ones. Of all of these types, archival texts provide the most "objective" data for the reconstruction of Sumerian social and economic history. Reconstructions of Sumerian political history draw more heavily on texts of the "literary"/propagandistic type. One in particular, the so-called Sumerian King List (SKL) – of which numerous and variant examples are attested – furnishes the names and reign lengths of kings in a number of Sumerian and non-Sumerian dynasties. Though the SKL presents a highly and deliberately distorted view of dynastic history (historically contemporaneous dynasties are treated as sequential, and some dynasties – most conspicuously Lagash's – are omitted altogether), properly analyzed it provides a basic chronological framework for Sumerian history. The details of that history, to the extent they may be reconstructed, are assembled largely from another corpus of "literary"/propagandistic evidence: royal inscriptions.

Below is a selection of pre-Sargonic royal inscriptions from five southern (Sumerian) kingdoms (Ur, Uruk, Nippur, Umma, and Lagash) and one northern (Akkadian) kingdom (Kish). In the Early Dynastic period the southern and northern portions of the Mesopotamian alluvium had distinct types of social, political, and economic organization. The south, predominantly Sumerian, was divided into a number of petty kingdoms; the north, predominantly Akkadian, formed a single kingdom centered on the city of Kish. A variety of evidence suggests that Kish was politically dominant in the south in the first and second phases of the period (ED I and II). Royal inscription Ki 3.1 speaks succinctly to the inequality of power relations between the two regions. The text records an offering from Mesalim, king of Kish, to Ningirsu (city-god of Girsu, and chief god of the kingdom of Lagash). That a Kishite king made this offering at all underscores the closeness of political ties between Kish and Lagash. Additional details about Ki 3.1 reveal that Kish was the more powerful of the two. For one, Mesalim is called "Ningirsu's temple-builder," that is, the builder of Ningirsu's temple (in Lagash), a striking epithet for a non-Lagashite king to assume. Mesalim is also designated by the term for "king" (*lugal*; from the Sumerian terms for "man" (*lú*) and "big" [*gal*]). In contrast, the ruler of Lagash, Lugalsha'engur, is designated by the more modest term for "city ruler" (*ensi*$_2$; etymology uncertain). Consider, as well, that Ki 3.1 was found in Girsu (indicating that Mesalim dedicated it there), and that it was inscribed on a weapon of war (a stone mace-head). This last suggests that Kish–Lagash relations were established and perpetuated through force of arms. La 5.1 supplies additional evidence of the extent of Kishite power. The very same Mesalim, king of Kish, is credited with fixing the (original?) border between the neighboring kingdoms of Umma and Lagash ("at the command of (*the goddess*) Ishtaran, he measured the field and set up a (*boundary-*)stone there").

The northern type of kingship – territorial and autocratic – was aspired to by a number of southern rulers. A few would-be imperialists succeeded in establishing short-lived hegemonies over neighboring Sumerian kingdoms, even in extending their influence into the north. In their inscriptions, these rulers took the symbolic title *lugal-Kiš*, "King of Kish" (see Ur 5.2 (not in this volume); elsewhere in their inscriptions, Eanatum of Lagash and Lugalkiginedudu of Uruk also took this title). A similarly self-aggrandizing title, *lugal-kalam*, "King of the Land" (see Uruk 4.1 and Um 7.1) denoted hegemony – at least the pretense to it – over all of Sumer.

The inscriptions from Ur, all discovered in different graves in the so-called "Royal Cemetery" pose a number of interpretive challenges. Ur 2 marks the cylinder seal on which it is inscribed as being the property of Pu'abi *nin*. Though conventionally translated as "queen" the basic meaning of *nin* is "lady." The lavishness of Pu'abi's burial – which included dozens of sacrificed attendants – favors the assumption that she was a queen, but definitive proof (such as the name and title of her husband) are lacking. That Ninbanda, in Ur 5.3 (not in this volume), was a "queen" (*nin*), is confirmed by the fact that her husband, Mesanepada, is called "king" (*lugal*) in Ur 5.1 and 5.2 (and also in the SKL). Yet, it is not clear whether Ninbanda should be interpreted as a personal name. The terms *nin+banda*$_3$ mean "young lady/queen." Ninbanda may have been the queen's throne name, but it is equally plausible that *nin+banda*$_3$ was her title, or the name or title of a junior wife of the king. Further complicating the matter, Ur 5.2 identifies a certain *NU.GIG* (capital letters indicate an uncertain reading) as the spouse of Mesanepada. There are several possible solutions to the conflicting testimony of Ur 5.3 and 5.2. The simplest one is that *nin+banda*$_3$ and *NU.GIG* refer to one and the same person, Nugig being her name and "young lady/queen" her title. Alternatively, *nin+banda*$_3$ and *NU.GIG* may have been two different persons, possibly the junior and senior wives of the ruler. A third possibility is that *NU.GIG* was not the ruler's actual wife, but rather a well-known type of priestess (*nu-gig*). If so, then Ur 5.2 would constitute the earliest evidence for a ritual that is otherwise attested only later in Mesopotamian history: the annual "sacred marriage" between the king and the goddess (embodied in the person of her priestess). Such an interpretation is highly tentative, however. Finally, it should be noted, the copper bowl on which Ur 5.4 (not in this volume) ("Ninbanda, the queen") is inscribed was found in the grave of Mesanepada's father, Meskalamdug. Did father and son share a spouse? Did their spouses share a title? Or was the bowl simply dedicated by the son's spouse to her father-in-law? We cannot be sure.

The inscriptions from Uruk speak to the complex geopolitics of the ED IIIb period. Lugalkiginedudu (Uruk 1.1) and Enshakushana (Uruk 4.1) both made overtures at empire-building. Though Lugalkiginedudu conquered Ur, and ruled both Uruk and Ur for a period, his claims to sovereignty over Sumer ("king of all the lands") are surely inflated. Several royal inscriptions inform us that Entemena, ruler of Lagash, concluded a treaty (*nam-šeš*, literally, "brotherhood") with Lugalkiginedudu. Uruk 1.1 and 4.1 also highlight the special role of Nippur. As the religious (though never political) capital of ancient Sumer, it was from Nippur and its high god that Lugalkiginedudu and Enshakushana sought legitimacy for their imperial ambitions, and to them that they duly paid homage. Note that Enshakushana was ordered to do battle with Kish, but Lugalkiginedudu was granted the kingship of Ur. The notion that the conquest of Ur was a bloodless one, indeed, that Enlil simply "had (*Lugalkiginedudu*) exercise lordship" there, harmonized with Sumerian conceptions of dynastic history (as reflected, later, in the SKL), and resolved the religious/ideological contradictions that an actual conquest of Sumerians by Sumerians raised.

Ki 1, one of the oldest surviving royal inscriptions, sheds light on the complex interplay between myth and history in ancient Mesopotamia. Mebara(ge)si, elsewhere known as Enmebaragesi, is one of several postdiluvian kings to whom the SKL attributes a fantastically long reign (900 years; long, indeed, but far short of the antediluvian reigns). Enmebaragesi is best known, from the Sumerian literary tradition, as the father of Agga, the king who laid siege to Uruk and was vanquished by Sumer's most famous hero, Gilgamesh, king of Uruk. Ki 1 illustrates an important principle of historical reconstruction: the historian of ancient Mesopotamia imputes different degrees of credibility to different kinds of sources. Enmebaragesi's place in history – as opposed to legend – is assured by his one surviving royal inscription.

The royal inscriptions from pre-Sargonic Lagash are among the most detailed sources for reconstructing Sumerian history, albeit a narrow slice of it. Spanning the reigns of nine kings (ca. 150 years), the Lagash dynasty is the most richly documented of all the Sumerian dynasties. In addition to dozens of royal inscriptions (many in numerous copies), excavations at Girsu yielded an archive of roughly 1,700 administrative texts. The archive derives from a massive estate that was controlled by at least the last three queens of the Lagash dynasty. Together, the royal inscriptions and the archive offer rich, at times overlapping, insights into the political, economic, and social history of the kingdom. In their inscriptions, the kings of Lagash enumerate building and renovation projects on behalf of various local and "national" gods (see the beginning of La 1.6 and 4.2). Throughout Mesopotamian history, temple-building was a quintessential expression of kings' piety to the gods, and an important means of soliciting divine favor. As proof of having received such favor, kings often elaborated on real or exaggerated military triumphs in their inscriptions. In the royal inscriptions from Lagash, one conflict in particular – an ongoing border dispute with Lagash's upstream neighbor, Umma – is a recurring leitmotif. Already at the beginning of the dynasty, its founder, Urnanshe, battled the allied armies of Umma and Ur (La 1.6), and defeated Pabilgaltuk, ruler of Umma. Urnanshe does not explicitly refer to a "border conflict," but a number of his successors do. (La 5.1 credits Mesalim, king of Kish, with fixing the border in question.) La 1.6 is unique in naming several high-ranking prisoners of war. The only surviving inscription of Urnanshe's son and successor, Akurgal, does not mention the border conflict. Yet, La 5.1 informs us that a certain Ush, ruler of Umma, initiated hostilities with Lagash sometime before the reign of Lagash's third king, Eanatum. This episode should probably be situated in Akurgal's reign.

The most vivid account of the Lagash–Umma border conflict is found on Eanatum's "Stele of the Vultures" (La 3.1; named for its relief depiction of vultures circling over a heap of enemy corpses). In the inscription, Eanatum sketches the history of the conflict, charging Umma with violating an agreement over the use of an agricultural area called Gu'edena that belonged to Ningirsu (i.e., to the kingdom of Lagash). Upon defeating the leader of Umma – Enakale (see La 5.1) – Eanatum makes him swear that he will "use the field of Ningirsu as an (*interest-bearing*) loan." During the reign of Eanatum's brother and successor, Enanatum I, Umma is assessed of the staggering debt of 11,833,454 gallons (4,478,976,000,000 liters) of barley (La 5.1). Though practically untenable, we need not assume that this assessment was hyperbolic. Throughout Mesopotamian history, the standard rate of interest on barley was 33 1/3 percent. Compounded annually, an initial loan of 136,961 gallons (518,400 liters) of barley (La 5.1) would have approached this sum in roughly 50 years, a span of time that accords with the chronology of the Lagash–Umma conflict. It has been argued that the "Stele of Vultures" recounts Eanatum's second major war with Umma, the first – commemorated in other inscriptions – having been prosecuted early in his reign. As La 5.1 attests, Eanatum campaigned widely in both Sumer and Akkad.

La 4.2 extends the narrative history of the Lagash–Umma conflict into the reign of Enanatum I. Enanatum accuses Urluma, ruler of Umma (identified in Umma 4.1 as the son of Enakale, for whom see above), of falsely claiming Ningirsu's property as his own. The reference at the end of La 4.2 to Enanatum's son and successor, Enmetena, is unusual. The fact that Enmetena, himself, took credit for defeating Urluma (La 5.1: "Enanatum, ruler of Lagash, battled with him in Ugiga . . . Enmetena . . . defeated him") suggests that his father may have died in battle. Enmetena also boasts of routing the next Ummaean ruler, Il (Urluma's nephew and one-time temple-administrator of Zabalam, an important cult center in the kingdom of Umma).

There is no record of a continuing conflict between Lagash and Umma under Enmetena's successors, Enentarzi and Lugalanda. Under the last ruler of pre-Sargonic Lagash, UruKAgina, the course of the conflict changed profoundly. In his seventh regnal year, Lagash was finally and soundly defeated by an upstart hegemon, Lugalzagesi, ruler of Umma, conqueror of Uruk, and claimant to the title "king of the Land" (i.e., Sumer; see Um 7.1). A lament from Girsu, reciting the litany of devastation wrought by Lugalzagesi on Lagash, concludes with the plea that Nisaba, "the god of Lugalzagesi," hold the Ummaean ruler, not UruKAgina, responsible. Signficantlly, UruKAgina is referred to here – and in a couple of other inscriptions – as the "king of Girsu," a title that underscores his vastly diminished powers.

The last of the inscriptions under consideration is the so-called "UruKAgina Reform" text (La 9.5). The text opens with a list of building projects that UruKAgina conducted on behalf of different gods. It then recounts a number of alleged abuses from bygone days. Inter alia, UruKAgina inveighs against the state, of yore, for levying grain taxes on certain priests, against funereal professionals for extracting hefty fees from mourners, and against wealthy persons for exploiting poor ones (by forcing them to dig wells and do other irrigation work on their fields). Most damningly, however, he indicts his own predecessors for appropriating the property of the gods – their plough animals, their choice fields, and their grain. This last accusation – a particularly striking one – is widely regarded as evidence that UruKAgina was a usurper. In this light, the Reforms are seen as a special plea for legitimacy. While it is true that UruKAgina was not in direct succession to the throne (in archival texts dating to his immediate predecessor's reign he is identified as a type of high-ranking official), there is no evidence that he came to power on the heels of a coup, and some evidence to the contrary. Be that as it may,

UruKAgina's royal Reform was not necessarily empty rhetoric. There is no direct evidence that UruKAgina's social reforms were ever enforced, but there is some evidence that he took measures to restore the property of the gods. The archival texts from Lagash derive from an institution that was called "House(hold) of the Woman" (i.e., the queen) in texts dating to the reigns of Enentarzi and Lugalanda. In texts dating to UruKAgina's reign it was renamed "House(hold) of (*the goddess*) Ba'U." Moreover, fields and other forms of moveable and immovable property that had hitherto been explicitly designated, in the archival texts, as property of the queen, were newly designated as property of the goddess. On the surface, such data seem to imply that UruKAgina did, as he claims, enact a substantial reform. A close comparison of all of the archival texts, however, yields little evidence that the "House(hold) of Ba'U" and the "House(hold) of the Woman" differed in anything other than in name. This raises the question whether the most far-reaching of UruKAgina's purported reforms was merely symbolic, or whether it entailed a substantial reconfiguring of political and economic power in the state, one benefiting temples to the detriment of the palace. The general scholarly consensus favors the first of these views, but the evidence is inconclusive.

The UruKAgina Reform text is the earliest example of a justice decree, a type of edict that Mesopotamian kings customarily issued at the beginning of their reigns. Common themes in such decrees were the fixing of certain prices, the remission of debts, and the pledge to protect widows and orphans. Many of the UruKAgina Reforms redress the problem of excessive taxation. In the closing section of the Reforms, UruKAgina cancels the obligations of debt slaves. (Such a measure, if enacted, would have had profound social and economic consequences. Not surprisingly, there is very little evidence, from any period of Mesopotamian history, that royal debt cancelations were actually and widely enforced. Note that the Lagash texts furnish an earlier example of the freeing of debt slaves: in one of his inscriptions, Enmetena claims to have canceled the debts of his own subjects, and to have freed the citizens of other cities – Uruk, Larsa, and Padtibira – from the obligation to perform conscript labor.) At the end of the Reforms, UruKAgina promises Ningirsu that he will not let the widow and orphan fall prey to the powerful.

Pre-Sargonic Royal Inscriptions

A. Ur

1. Pu'abi

(Ur 2, Cooper) *Pu'abi, the queen.* Possible alternatives: (a) *Pu'abi, queen,* (b) *(This cylinder seal belongs to) Pu'abi, the queen.*

2. Mesanepada

(Ur 5.1) *Mesanepada, king of Ur, son of Meskalamdug, king of Kish, dedicated (this lapis lazuli bead) to (the god) Lugalkalama** (a more literal rendering, reflecting the underlying Sumerian syntax, would foreground the dative clause *[To Lugalkalama, Mesanepada]*).

B. Uruk

3. Lugalkiginedudu

(Uruk 1.1) *When (the god) Enlil favorably summoned him (Lugalkiginedudu) and combined the kingship and the lordship for him, Enlil, king of all the lands, had Lugalkiginedudu exercise lordship in Uruk, had him exercise lordship in Ur. In great joy, Lugalkiginedudu dedicated (this stone vessel), for (the sake of) his (own) life, to Enlil, his beloved king.*

4. Enshakushana

(Uruk 4.1) *For (the god) Enlil, king of all the lands, Enshakushana, lord of Sumer and king of the "Land" (i.e., Sumer) – (who), when the gods ordered him, destroyed Kish and seized Enbi'eshtar, the king of Kish – returned to(?) the leader of Akshak and the leader of Kish, whose cities were destroyed, their [. . .] in their(?) [. . .], (but) he dedicated their statues, their precious metals and lapis lazuli, their wood, and their treasure to Enlil, for Nippur.*

C. Nippur

5. Nammah

(Nippur 1) *Pakalam, spouse/wife of Nammah, the ruler of Nippur, dedicated (this stone vessel) to (the god) RUkalama.*

D. Umma

6. Urluma

(Umma 4.1) *For (the god) Enkigal, Urluma, king of Umma(!), son of Enakale, king of Umma(!), built (his) temple.*

E. Kish

7. Mebaragesi

(Ki 1, Cooper) *Mebara(ge)si, king of Kish*

Possible alternatives: (a) *Mebarasi, (the) king of Kish,* (b) *[For(?) (the god(?)) . . .] Mebarasi, (the) king of Kish, [dedicated(?) (this stone vessel(?))]* (the inscription derives from fragments of two different stone vessels. The first preserves only the PN, on either side of which there may have been additional text in the original. The second preserves both the PN and the royal title, after which [though not preceding, if Steible and Behrens's transcription is correct] there may have been additional text in the original. It is unclear what the full text of the originals was, and whether they were the same.)

8. Mesalim

(Ki 3.1) *Mesalim, king of Kish, (the god) Ningirsu's temple-builder, placed (this stone mace-head) (for) Ningirsu. Lugalsha'engur is the ruler of Lagash.*

F. Lagash

9. Urnanshe

(La 1.6) *[Urnansh]e, [king of Lagash, son of Gunidu], son of Gursar (or, citizen of Gursar), built the Bagara (temple) out of baked brick. In(?) the Bagara, he dug the . . . SAR. The name(?) of the temple is "Bagara, Endowed with Justice(?)." The name(?) of the shrine is "Bagara, Endowed with Justice(?)."*

He built the Ibgal (shrine); built the temple of (the goddess) Nanshe; built the sanctuary of (the city of) Girsu; built the Kinir (sanctuary); built the temple of (the goddess) Gatumdug; built the Tirash (sanctuary); built the Ningar (sanctuary); built the temple of (the goddess) Ninmarki; built the Edam (sanctuary); built the ME-gate; built the Abzu'e (sanctuary); and built the wall of Lagash. He dug the Saman-canal and dug the Asuhur(-canal). He fashioned (a statue of the goddess) Ninmarki; fashioned (a statue of the goddess) Ninesh . . . ; fashioned (a statue of the goddess) Ningidri; fashioned (a statue of the god) Shulsha; fashioned (a statue of the god) Kindazi; fashioned (a statue of the god) Gushudu; fashioned (a statue of the goddess) Lama'u'e; and fashioned (a statue of the god) Lugalurtur.

[The leader(?)] of Lagash waged war with the leader of Ur and the leader of Umma.

The leader of Lagash defeated the leader of Ur; took Mu[. . .], the . . . , captive; took Amabarasi and Kishibgal, the commanders, captive; [took] Papursag, son of U'u [captive]; took [. . .], the commander, captive; and heaped up a burial mound (for them).

He defeated the leader of Umma; took Lupad and Bilala, the commanders, captive; took Pabilgaltuk, ruler of Umma, captive; took Urpusag(!), the commander, captive; took Hursagshemah, the chief merchant, captive; and heaped up a burial mound (for them).

The leader of Umma.

10. Eanatum

(La 3.1) *[. . .] He reduced(?) their sustenance field(s)(?). A grain rent was imposed on them. The king of Lagash [. . .]. The leader of Umma spoke angrily with him and defied Lagash. Akurgal, king of Lagash, son of Urnanshe, [king of Lagash . . . The leader of Umma spoke] angrily [with him] and defied Lagash on account of its (Lagash's) own property. At(?) PirigZA[. . .]girnunshaga (the god) Ningirsu spoke (saying) "Umma has [. . . ed] my pasture(?), my own property, the fields of the Gu'edena."*

[. . .] Ningirsu, warrior of (the god) Enlil [. . .] Ningirsu planted the [seed] of (i.e., that would engender) Eanatum in the [womb] and [. . .] rejoiced over [Eanatum]. (The goddess) Inanna took him by the arm and named him Eana'Inanna'Ibgalkaka'atum ("In the Eana (temple) of Inanna of the Ibgal (shrine) he is worthy") and sat him on the fine lap of (the goddess) Ninhursag. Ninhursag [offered him] her fine breast. Ningirsu rejoiced over Eanatum, the womb-implanted seed of Ningirsu. Ningirsu laid his span on him. His cubits being five (in height) he laid on him. (In all he stood) five cubits and one span (tall) (approximately 9 feet 2 inches / 2.79 meters). With great joy Ningirsu [gave him] the kingship [of Lagash . . .]

Eanatum, the strong one, declares, " . . . !" For Eanatum he (Ningirsu(?)) [established] (as his) name the name which Inanna had given him: Eana'Inanna'Ibgalkaka'atum. [. . .] (Addressing) a timeless (conflict)(?), Eanatum, the strong one whose name was chosen by Ningirsu, Eanatum who [declared(?)], " . . . !" proclaimed, "Where is the ruler of Umma recruiting? With (other) leaders [. . .] he consumes the Gu'edena, the beloved field of Ningirsu. I will strike him down!" [. . .]

He followed after him. Towards the sleeping one, towards the sleeping one, he approaches (his) head. Towards Eanatum, the sleeping one, [his] beloved king [Ningirsu approaches his head . . .] "Umma, it being Kish . . . At your right side Utu (the sun-god) will rise, and a . . . will be bound to your forehead. Eanatum [. . .] you will kill there. Their myriad (literally, 3,600) corpses will reach the base of heaven. [In] Umma [. . . the people of his own city] will raise arms against him. He will be killed inside Umma. You will [. . .]"

He did battle with him. Someone shot an arrow at Eanatum. He was shot through(?) with the arrow, and he broke(?) the arrow. He cried out before it. The [. . .]-man [. . .] Eanatum released a deluge like an evil rainstorm in Umma. [. . .] Eanatum, being a man of just words, measured the boundary [from(?) . . .], left it towards the side of Umma, and set up a (boundary-)stone on it. The leader of Umma [. . .] He defeated [Umma(?)] and heaped up 20 burial mounds for it. Eanatum, the one over whom (his personal god) Shulutul cried sweetly, Eanatum [. . . ed] Eanatum destroyed the foreign lands [for Ningirsu]. Eanatum restored his beloved field, the Gu'edena to Ningirsu. [. . .] The Dana field, the Kihara of Ningirsu [he . . . ed] In the Emah (temple) of [(the goddess) Nanshe] he set up a stele. [. . .] of Ningirsu Eanatum, the [. . .] of Ningirsu – (Shulutul) is his (personal) god. The fields [(named) . . . Eanatum], whose [name] was chosen by Ningirsu, restored [to Ningirsu].

To the leader of Umma Eanatum gave the great battle net of Enlil, and made him swear by it. The leader of Umma swore the (following) oath to Eanatum: "By the life of Enlil, king of heaven and earth, I shall (only) use the field of Ningirsu as an (interest-bearing) loan. I hereby declare (its) irrigation channels . . . For [evermore I shall not transgress the boundary of Ningirsu. I shall not alter its irrigation channels and canals. I shall not rip out its (boundary-)stones. If I do transgress, may the great battle net of Enlil, king of heaven and earth, by which I have sworn, fall upon Umma." Eanatum was also very wise. He smeared kohl on the eyes of two doves, adorned their heads with cedar (resin), and released them towards Nippur, to Enlil, king of heaven and earth, in the Ekur (temple), (saying): "Having (thus) spoken], having (thus) pled to Enlil, my lord, if any leader of Umma, in violation of the agreement, should renege against or oppose the agreement, or should overturn the agreement, may the great battle net of Enlil, by which he has sworn, fall upon Umma!"

(The same oath is sworn before, and doves are released to, the mother-goddess Ninhursag, in Kesh; the god of wisdom, Enki, in Abzu; the moon-god, Su'en, in Ur; the sun-god Utu, in Larsa; and the netherworld-goddess Ninki. With the exception of Ninki, the aforementioned gods are summoned to release their battle nets (downwards) in the event a leader of Umma violates the agreement. In contrast, Ninki is summoned to release snakes (upwards) to bite the trespasser's feet.)

Eanatum, king of Lagash – the one granted strength by Enlil, fed fine milk by Ninhursag, given a good name by Inanna, granted wisdom by Enki, chosen in (her) heart by Nanshe, the powerful lady, Ningirsu's subjugator of foreign lands, beloved of (the goddess) Dumuzi'abzu, whose name was chosen by Ninhursag, beloved friend of (the god) Lugalurub, beloved spouse of Inanna – [defeated] Elam and Subar, lands of wood and treasure [. . .] defeated [. . .], defeated Susa, [defeated] the ruler of Uru'a, who stood with the (city-)emblem at the head (of his army), [defeated . . .], smashed (the city of) Aru'a, . . . Sumer, defeated (the city of) Ur. [. . .]

[Eanatum] who restored the [Gu'edena to Ningirsu], Eanatum [. . .] of Ningirsu, who erected (the stele on which this text is inscribed) for Ningirsu [. . .] The name of this stele – it is not a man's name – he declared: Ningirsu'enmenlumanamti'i'pirigedena ("Ningirsu, the lord, crown of Luma (=Eanatum), is the life of the Pirigedena canal"). (For Ningirsu) Eanatum set up the (boundary-)stone of the Gu'edena, the beloved field of Ningirsu, which Eanatum had restored to Ningirsu.

11. Enanatum I

(La 4.2) *For (the god) Hendursag, chief herald of the Abzu, Enanatum, ruler of Lagash – the one granted strength by Enlil, fed fine milk by (the goddess) Ninhursag, chosen in (her) heart by (the goddess) Nanshe, ensigal-priest of (the god) Ningirsu, specially summoned by (the goddess) Inanna, whose name was chosen by Hendursag, son borne of (the god) Lugalurub, son of Akurgal, ruler of Lagash, beloved brother of Eanatum, ruler of Lagash –*

When he built the Ibgal (shrine) for Inanna, made the Eana the preeminent (temple) in all the lands for her, and decorated it for her with gold and silver; built his palace of Urukug for Hendursag and decorated it for him with gold and silver; restored (the god) Nindar's temple for him; built Ningirsu's and Ba'u's(?)] Giguna (temple) for them; built Lugalurub's palace of Urub for him, and decorated it for him with god and silver; built (the goddess) Amageshtinana's Esagug (temple) for her, built a brick well for her, and [. . .]; [built Ningirsu's] Eshdugru (shrine) [for him]; (then) [he . . .]

[When Enlil(?)] relinquished control of Umma to Ningirsu and placed it in Enanatum's charge, Urluma, ruler of Umma, [recruited (soldiers from) the foreign lands] and transgressed the boundary-channel of Ningirsu. "Antasura is mine! I shall exploit it as my (rightful) property(?)," he said. At the hill of Urgiga he stood his ground.

Ningirsu spoke angrily (saying): "Urluma, ruler of Umma, has said, 'Antasura is mine!' He who has marched into my own inner sanctum must not raise arms against Enanatum, my powerful male!"

Enanatum beat back Urluma, ruler of Umma, to the boundary-channel of Ningirsu. At the . . . of the Lumagirnunta(-canal) he . . . ed his . . . and stripped(?) him of his cloak.

Enanatum, the one who built the temple of Hendursag – his (personal) god is Shulutul.

He (Enanatum) had (this inscription) inscribed on the copper standard and the . . . of the copper standard set on (a pole made of) wood.

[. . .] Shulutul, loyal [. . .] of Enmetena (son and successor of Enanatum) checked it. He (Hendursag(?)) is the owner of the standard.

12. Enmetena

(La 5.1) *Enlil, king of all the lands, father of all the gods, by his firm command, fixed the border (between the god) Ningirsu (i.e., the kingdom of Lagash) and (the god) Shara (i.e., the kingdom of Umma). Mesalim, king of Kish, at the command of (the goddess) Ishtaran, measured the field and set up a (boundary-)stone there.*

Ush, ruler of Umma, acted haughtily. He ripped out that (boundary-)stone, and marched toward the plain of Lagash. Ningirsu, warrior of Enlil, at his (Enlil's) just command, made war with Umma. At Enlil's command, he threw his great battle net over it and heaped up burial mounds for it on the plain.

Eanatum, ruler of Lagash, uncle of Enmetena, ruler of Lagash, fixed the border with Enakale, ruler of Umma; made the (boundary-)channel extend from the Nun canal to the Gu'edena; left a 1,411 yard / 1,290 meter length of Ningirsu's field, toward the side of Umma, and established it (as) an ownerless field. At that (boundary-)channel he inscribed (new boundary-)stones, and restored the (boundary-)stone of Mesalim. He did not cross into the plain of Umma. On the (boundary-)levee of Ningirsu – the Namnundakigara – he built a shrine of Enlil, a shrine of (the goddess) Ninhursag, a shrine of Ningirsu, and a shrine of (the god) Utu.

The leader of Umma consumed 136,961 gallons (518,400 liters) of barley of (the goddess) Nanshe and barley of (the god) Ningirsu as an (interest-bearing) loan. It bore interest. (A total debt of) 44.78976 [mult] 10^{11} liters accrued. Because he could not repay the barley, Urluma, ruler of Umma, made irrigation water flow in the boundary-channel of Ningirsu and the boundary-channel of Nanshe; torched and tore out their (boundary-)stones; destroyed the . . . shrines of the gods that had been built on the Namnundakigara; recruited (soldiers from) the foreign lands and crossed the boundary-channel of Ningirsu.

Enanatum, ruler of Lagash, battled with him in Ugiga, Ningirsu's beloved field. Enmetena, beloved son of Enanatum, defeated him. Urluma fled, but he (Enmetena) killed him in Umma. His (Urluma's) asses – forming 60 teams – were abandoned on the bank of the Lumagirnunta canal. The bones of their attendants were strewn about the plain. He (Enmetena) heaped up their burial mounds in five places.

At that time Il – being (a high) temple administrator of (the city of) Zabalam – fell back from Girsu to Umma. Il assumed the rulership of Umma. He made irrigation water flow in the boundary-channel of Ningirsu and the boundary-channel of Nanshe, in the (boundary-)levee of Ningirsu – toward the bank of the Tigris river in the area of Girsu – and in the Namnundakigara of Enlil, Enki, and Ninhursag. Of Lagash's barley he paid back (only) 18.6624 [mult] 10^8 liters.

When, on account of those (boundary-)channels, Enmetena, ruler of Lagash, sent representatives to Il, Il, ruler of Umma, the field thief, speaking wickedly, said: "The boundary-channel of Ningirsu and the boundary-channel of Nanshe are mine! I will divert the (boundary-)levee from Antasura to Edimgalabzu." (But) Enlil and Ninhursag did not give (it) to him.

Enmetena, ruler of Lagash, whose name was chosen by Ningirsu, at the just command of Enlil, at the just command of Ningirsu, and at the just command of Nanshe, built that (boundary-)channel from the Tigris river to the Nun canal. The foundations of the Namnundakigara he constructed in stone for him (Ningirsu), and restored it to Ningirsu, the lord who loves him, and Nanshe, the lady who loves him.

Enmetena, ruler of Lagash, given the scepter by Enlil, given wisdom by Enki, chosen in (her) heart by Nanshe, ensigal-priest of Ningirsu, who heeds the commands of the gods – may his (personal) god, Shulutul, stand forever before Ningirsu and Nanshe (advocating) for the life of Enmetena.

The leader of Umma who crosses the (boundary-)channel of Ningirsu and the (boundary-)channel of Nanshe to take fields by force – be he an Ummaean or a foreigner – may Enlil smite him! After Ningirsu throws his great battle net on him may he crush (him) from on high with his mighty hands and mighty feet! May the people of his city, after raising arms against him, kill him in his city!

G. *Umma*

13. Lugalzagesi

(Um 7.1) *For Enlil, king of all the lands – to Lugalzagesi, king of Uruk, king of "the Land" (i.e., Sumer), išib-priest of (the god) An, lumah-priest of (the goddess) Nisaba, son of U'u, ruler of Umma and lumah-priest of Nisaba, the one looked on favorably by An, king of all the lands, the ensigal-priest of Enlil, the one given wisdom by Enki, whose name was chosen by (the god) Utu, great vizier of (the god) Su'en, general of Utu, provider for (the goddess) Inanna, son borne of Nisaba, fed fine milk by (the goddess) Ninhursag, man of (the god) Messanga'unuga, raised by (the goddess) Ningirim, lady of Uruk, chief steward of the gods –*

When Enlil, king of all the lands, gave kingship of "the Land" to Lugalzagesi, pointed the eyes of "the Land" toward him, set all of the lands at his feet, from sunrise to sunset (i.e., east to west) subordinated (them) to him – at that time, from the Lower Sea (i.e., the Persian Gulf), (along) the Tigris and Euphrates rivers to the Upper Sea (i.e., the Mediterranean), he (Enlil) put their paths in order for him. From east to west Enlil let him have no rival. Under him, all the lands lay in lush pastures. "The Land" made merry under him. All the sovereigns of Sumer and the rulers of all the lands . . . to him at Uruk.

At that time, under him, Uruk passed the days in rejoicing; Ur, like a bull, raised its head; Larsa, beloved city of Utu, made merry; Umma, beloved city of Shara, raised its mighty horns; the territory of Zabalam cried out like a ewe separated from its lamb; and Kidingir raised its neck.

Lugalzagesi, king of Uruk, king of "the Land", . . . brings sumtpuous food offerings and pours sweet water, in Nippur, for his lord Enlil.

. . . "May Enlil, king of all the lands, say a prayer for me to An, his beloved father! May he (An) add life (to) my life! Under me, may the lands lie in lush pastures; may the population become as widespread as the grass; may the teats of heaven function well; may the people look upon a good land (only). May they (An and Enlil) not change the good fate they have decreed for me! May I always be the . . . shepherd!

For his life he (Lugalzagesi) dedicated (the object on which this text is inscribed) to Enlil, his beloved lord.

Bibliography

Charvat, P., "The Growth of Lugalzagessi's Empire," in G. Komoroxcy, ed., *Festschrift Lubor Matous* (Budapest: Eotvos Lorand Tudomanyegyetem, 1978), 43–9.

Cooper, J., *Reconstructing History from Ancient Inscriptions: The Lagash-Umma Border Conflict* (Malibu: Undena, 1983).

Cooper, J., *Sumerian and Akkadian Royal Inscriptions I: Presargonic Inscriptions* (New Haven: American Oriental Society, 1986).

Foster, B., "A New Look at the Sumerian Temple State," *Journal of the Economic and Social History of the Orient* 24 (1981), 225–41.

Jacobsen, T., "Early Political Development in Mesopotamia," *Zeitschrift für Assyriologie* 52 (1957), 91–170.

Larsen, M. T. (ed.), *Power and Propaganda: A Symposium on Ancient Empires* (Copenhagen: Akademisk Forlag, 1979).

Steible, H., and H. Behrens, *Die Altsumerischen Bau- und Weihinschriften* (Wiesbaden: Steiner, 1982).

2

Old Akkadian Period Texts

Benjamin Studevent-Hickman
and Christopher Morgan

I. Texts from the Old Akkadian Period (Studevent-Hickman)

The events of the Old Akkadian period fundamentally transformed the social, religious, and economic structure of southern Babylonia forever. Under King Sargon the city-states of Sumer were forced into a single polity. This violated the very idea of the divinely owned city-state and forced a reckoning of radically different ideologies. Rebellions were a constant problem for the Sargonic kings in Sumer and elsewhere; given that fact, one must marvel at their ability to maintain what has been called the first empire. The ancients themselves certainly did: The Sargonic kings were paradigmatic rulers for future regimes, and many elaborate traditions evolved around their persons.

Old Akkadian royal inscriptions have a simple structure and are generally not very long. They consist of three parts: the royal titulary, a narration of the event commemorated, and a curse against anyone who should alter the inscription (especially by erasing the name of the king and inserting his own). Many were copied in Old Babylonian scribal schools at Nippur on *Sammeltafeln*, large tablets containing several separate inscriptions. These copies also bear colophons indicating where the various sections of an inscription were written on the original object.

Many features of Sargonic religious and political ideology are immediately clear from the Old Akkadian inscriptions. First, the phrase "king of the world" (literally "king of Kish"), which had already taken on greater ideological significance in the Early Dynastic period, was used extensively for the titulary (see *History* 64).[1] Second, the kings made every effort to assure their audience that Enlil, the head of the Sumerian pantheon, had authorized both their kingship and their accomplishments. Finally, the inscriptions reflect an obvious attempt to exhalt Semitic deities of war, above all the goddess Ishtar, who was synchronized with the Sumerian goddess Inanna, and the god Ilaba (or Aba),[2] the personal god of the dynasty.

A. Sargon: ca. 2334–2279 BCE

14. The creation of the Akkadian Empire

Battles for hegemony were common among the city-states of Early Dynastic Sumer, and some of them were quite successful. When Sargon came to power, the seat of hegemony was in Uruk. There, Lugalzagesi (a former governor of Umma) had consolidated power and united much of Sumer for the first time. To be sure, his efforts paved the way for Sargon campaigns there.

Several of Sargon's inscriptions record the campaign against Lugalzagesi in southern Babylonia. The example below is attested exclusively by Old Babylonian copies.

Sargon, the king of Akkad, the bailiff of Ishtar, the king of the universe, the anointed one of An, the king of the land, the governor of Enlil. He vanquished Uruk in battle and smote fifty governors and the city by the mace of the god Ilaba.[3] *And he destroyed its fortress and captured Lugalzagesi, the king of Uruk in battle. He led him to the gate of Enlil in a neckstock.*

Sargon, the king of Akkad, vanquished Ur in battle and smote the city and destroyed its fortress.

He smote Eninmar and destroyed its fortress. He smote its territory and Lagash as far as the sea.

He washed his weapons in the sea.

He vanquished Umma in battle and smote the city and destroyed its fortress.

Sargon, king of the land, to whom Enlil has given no rival, to him he (i.e., Enlil) gave the upper and lower sea. Indeed, from the lower sea to the upper sea the inhabitants of the land Akkad hold governorships. Mari and Elam stand before Sargon, king of the land. Sargon, king of the land, restored the territory of Kish and made them occupy it.[4]

Whoever should remove this inscription, may Enlil and Shamash uproot his foundation and obliterate his progeny (lit. "his seed") . . . Anyone who should neglect this statue, may Enlil neglect him (lit. "his name"). Let him (Enlil) destroy his weapon. May he not stand before Enlil.

(This) inscription was written on the socle in front of Lugalzagesi.

B. Manishtusu: ca. 2278–2264 BCE

15. The standard inscription of Manishtusu

Following the Sumerian King List, scholars have long thought that Rimush succeeded Sargon to the Akkadian throne. However, a recently published copy of that document places Manishtusu in this position, and there is other evidence to support this (Steinkeller 2003, esp. 278–9). The question of Sargon's successor is far from resolved, of course; suffice it to say that this latest development provides a humbling reminder of just how little we know about this period. Manishtusu is presented first here.

Only a handful of inscriptions have survived from the reign of Manishtusu, the son of Sargon. The lengthiest and best-attested is known as the "Standard Inscription." It records a campaign against Anshan, one of the two major powers in the land of Elam, and Sherihum, which lie south of there. As it stands, the inscription suggests that troops from these polities still or once again needed to be removed from the south. If nothing else, this blocked vital access to trade routes to the east. The curse that follows the text is not unusual.

Manishtusu, king of the universe. When he smote Anshan and Shirihum, he made warships[5] cross the lower sea. The (troops of the) thirty-two cities on the other side of the sea assembled for war, and he vanquished (them) and smote their cities. He felled their rulers and captured their fugitives as far as the silver mines.[6] He quarried the black stone of the mountains on the other side of the lower sea and loaded (it) into the boats and moored (them) at the wharf of Akkad. He made a statue of himself (lit. "his statue") and gave it as a votive to Enlil. By Shamash and Ilaba I swear: "Verily these are indeed not lies!"

C. *Rimush: ca. 2263–2255 BCE*

16. Rimush's campaign to Elam

After quelling a rebellion of Sumerian cities, Rimush, the brother of Manishtusu, turned his attention to Elam. Several of his inscriptions record campaigns there. The longest of these is presented below.

The inscription includes several toponyms known to be major centers of power in Elam, specifically the region northeast of Babylonia. It also includes the name of several kings of these cities. Given our limited knowledge of Elamite history, these attestations are extremely valuable.[7] According to the colophon, this section of the inscription is written on the left side of a statue of the king.

The curse formula near the end of the text is a bit more explicit and emphatic than usual. According to the colophon, it was written on the socle of a statue.

Rimush, king of the universe. He vanquished Abalgamash, the king of Parahshum, in battle. (The troops of) Zahara and Elam gathered in Parahshum, and he vanquished (them) and fell 16,212 men. He took 4,216 prisoners captive and took Emahsini, the king of Elam, captive. He took all . . . of Elam captive and took Sidgau, the general of Parahshum, captive. He took Shargapi,[8] the general of Zahara, captive. Between

Awan and Susa, in the "middle river", He heaped destruction upon them around the city.[9] *He slew the cities of Elam and destroyed their walls and uprooted the foundation of Parahshum in the land of Elam. Rimush, king of the universe ruled over Elam. Enlil made it possible: In the third year that Enlil gave him the kingship, (there were) in total 9,624 men, including the fallen, including the prisoners. By Shamash and Ilaba I swear: "Verily these are indeed not lies!"*

At the time of this battle he made a statue of himself (lit. "his statue") and devoted it to Enlil, his helper.[10]

Whoever should remove this inscription, may Enlil and Shamash uproot his foundation and obliterate his progeny . . . As for anyone who removes the name of Rimush, king of the universe, and places his name on the statue of Rimush and declares "(It is) my statue!"; may Enlil, the owner of this statue, and Shamash uproot his foundation and obliterate his progeny. May the two of them not grant him a male (heir). May he not stand before his god.

When he smote Elam and Parahshum, he brought back thirty minas of gold, 3,600 minas of copper, and 360[11] *male slaves and female slaves and presented them as a votive to Enlil.*

D. Naram-Sin: ca. 2254–2218 BCE

17. The inscription from the Basetki Statue: the deification of Naram-Sin

The greatest transformation in the notion of kingship in Mesopotamia took place during the reign of Naram-Sin: He deified himself. The event is commemorated by several inscriptions, where it is connected to his "nine battles in one year," a phrase generally assumed to refer to the Great Rebellion. It is also reflected by the presence of the divine determinative, which was subsequently written before Naram-Sin's name.

By far the best-known version of the inscription is found on the base of a huge copper statue discovered in the village of Basetki, some 40 miles (64 kilometers) northwest of Mosul. The statue is now famous. In 2003 it disappeared from the Baghdad Museum during the invasion of Iraq by the United States and other forces. In the same year it was miraculously recovered intact. The statue was already broken when it was first discovered. It appears to be a *lahmu*, a benevolent protective deity and attendant of the god Enki/Ea.[12] The inscription itself is very short; it is amazing that such a momentous event could be conveyed so concisely.[13]

Naram-Sin, the mighty one, the king of Akkad. When the four regions (of the world) revolted against him as one, by the love which Ishtar showed him, he was victorious in nine battles in one year and captured those kings who had risen up (against him). Because he fortified the foundations of his city, which was in the line of danger,[14] *(the residents of) his city asked of Ishtar in the Eanna, of Enlil in Nippur, of Dagan in Tuttul, of Ninhursag in Kish, of Enki in Eridu, of Sin in Ur, of Shamash in Sippar, of Nergal in Kutha, that he be the god of their city, Akkad, and they built his temple within Akkad.*

Whoever removes this inscription, may Shamash and Ishtar and Nergal, the bailiff of the gods – all of these gods – uproot his foundations and obliterate his progeny.

E. *Shar-kali-sharri: ca. 2217–2193* BCE

18. A letter concerning the Gutians

The reign of Shar-kali-sharri, the son of Naram-Sin, marks the demise of the Akkadian empire despite the fact that other ruler succeeded him. Next to nothing is known about his military campaigns outside year names, which suggest an increasing threat of foreign invasion.

The most palpable threat was posed by the Gutians, an ethnolinguistic group from the Zagras region (see Hallo 1957–71). A letter from Babylonia, probably from Girsu or Adab, provides an intimate look at their actions in the countryside and the effects these had on the operation of the state and the relationships between officials. Two basic translations are possible, one of them requiring a slight emendation. Each of these is offered below; together they reveal just how much our understanding of Mesopotamian history can hinge on the smallest detail of a translation.

Version one (following Michalowski 1993):

Thus says Ishkun-Dagan to Lugalra:

"Work the field and protect the flock! This time, do not say '(Because of) the Gutians, I could not work the field'! Install maqqatu[15] *every half-mile and work the field! If the troops attack, you should raise help and bring the flock to the city. If you say 'The Gutians took away the flock!' I will not say anything. I will (still) give you the silver. Now, I swear by the life of Shar-kali-sharri: If the Gutians take away the flock and you have to pay (for it) yourself, I will give you the silver when I arrive in the city. But (even if) you do not guard the flock, I will (still) ask you for the regular yield (of the aforementioned field) . . . You (should) know this.*

Version two (following Kienast and Volk 1995):

Thus says Ishkun-Dagan to Lugalra:

"Work the field and protect the flock! And this time, do not say '(Because of) the Gutians, I could not work the field!' Install maqqatu every half-mile and work the field! If someone notices the troops, let them resist (the Gutians) for you so you may bring the flock to the city. You have said, 'The Gutians took away the flock!' and I have not said anything. (In fact) I have given you silver! But now, I swear by the life of Shar-kali-sharri: If the Gutians take away the flock, you shall indeed pay (for them) yourself! When I come to the city, I will <not> give you the silver. But (even if) you do not guard the flock, I will (still) ask you for the regular yield (of the aforementioned field) . . . You (should) know this.

II. Late Traditions Concerning Sargon and Naram-Sin (Morgan)

A. Sargon of Akkad

The exploits of Sargon of Akkad became legendary, and later generations passed down accounts of his life and reign in the scribal tradition. Few texts contemporary with his reign have been discovered: our knowledge of this figure arises nearly exclusively from the study of later texts. Centuries after the time of Sargon, scribes of the Old Babylonian period copied a number of Sargonic inscriptions and deposited them in Nippur, an important Mesopotamian religious center. It is assumed that these Old Babylonian copies faithfully reproduce original texts; thus, these inscriptions are considered useful for historical reconstruction.

These inscriptions – or more accurately these copies – represent but a fraction of the texts relating to Sargon. While these ancient copies are presumably reproductions of authentic Sargonic texts, other Sargonic traditions have no such direct link with the ruler. These late traditions are found in omens, chronicles, and legends and must be critically evaluated in an effort to glean whatever kernel of historical memory they may preserve.

The translations below represent two late, legendary traditions concerning Sargon. The "Sargon Birth Legend" is known from three Neo-Assyrian fragments from Nineveh and one Neo-Babylonian fragment from Dilbat. The English below represents a composite translation – a detail missing in one source may be supplied by another.

The legend "Sargon, King of Battle" is known from Amarna, Assur, and Nineveh.[16] The English below derives from the Amarna recension. It is a testament to Sargon's greatness that, even a millennium and a half after the era bearing his name, he remains the principal character of legends with widespread currency.

19. The Sargon Birth Legend

The Sargon Birth Legend has been described as an example of *narû*-literature.[17] The genre takes its name from the *narû*, a memorial stele set up by a king in commemoration of his achievements. This type of composition opens with a first-person introduction, continues with a first-person account of significant events or achievements, and concludes with a blessing/curse formula (blessings on those who honor the ruler's stele and heed its message, curses on those who would deface the stele). The brief text of the Sargon Birth Legend exhibits a similar structure: introduction (lines 1–12), events/achievements (lines 13–21), and blessing/curse (lines 22–33).

It is unlikely, however, that the Sargon Birth Legend was ever inscribed on a *narû*. To distinguish such literature from authentic inscriptions, the more appropriate designation "pseudo-autobiography" has been proposed.[18] As the term suggests, scholars view these late traditions with some skepticism, and they come to differing conclusions regarding the usefulness of such traditions for modern historical reconstruction.

Yet it is possible that later writers drew upon ancient traditions when composing these legends, and the careful reader must remain alert to the possibility that an underlying kernel of historical truth may await discovery even in legendary materials.[19] In other words, pseudo-autobiographical texts may preserve authentic historical memories of persons whose stories they purport to tell. Nonetheless, scholars and students must approach these texts critically, and modern historical reconstructions based on data of this sort will remain somewhat tentative.

The Birth Legend describes the infant Sargon imperiled as his mother sets him adrift on a river in a reed basket (lines 5–8), one example of the infant-exposure motif that pervades ancient literature. The motif appears in the literature of the Hittites, the Israelites,[20] and the Greeks, among numerous other peoples.[21] In several instances the parallels are striking – the child is placed in a small vessel, set upon waters, then rescued.[22] These details are clearly not to be taken at face value. The Sargon Birth Legend represents one expression of a stock literary motif often used in world literature to introduce a figure of some importance.

While the lateness of the tradition and its legendary character limit the usefulness of this text for modern historical purposes, it does not necessarily follow that the tradition is completely devoid of value for knowledge concerning the figure of Sargon. Though the traditions surrounding Sargon's birth offer contradictory details – in the Birth Legend Sargon's father is unknown, in the Sumerian Sargon Legend his father is named La'ibum, and in the King List his father is an anonymous gardener – they each offer a portrait of a man with humble origins.[23] This understanding of Sargon's origins may find support in his very name: in the Akkadian language, "Sargon" means, "the king is legitimate." Such a name, assumed upon rise to kingship, would counter assertions that a man of lowly birth held no legitimate claim to the throne. Thus, while the details of the Birth Legend cannot be taken literally, they correspond with a tradition of humble beginnings, a tradition perhaps indirectly evidenced in Sargon's name itself.

The text presents the water-drawer Aqqi rescuing the helpless infant Sargon from the river, then adopting the child (lines 8–11). Adoption was fairly common in the ancient world and took place for a variety of reasons. In some cases specific legal contracts formalized adoption agreements between natural and adoptive parents, while in other cases legal documents do not appear to have been involved. The adoption of Sargon by Aqqi represents a class of adoption in which an abandoned or orphaned child is discovered and subsequently taken in.[24]

According to the Birth Legend, Sargon becomes a gardener for Aqqi (line 11), but eventually the amorous goddess Ishtar grows fond of him (lines 12–14). He rises to kingship, a result of Ishtar's favor. The tradition linking

Sargon with Ishtar may reflect a close relationship between the king and the cult of Ishtar, though the nature of the relationship remains unclear.[25] Ishtar was, however, revered by the kings of the Sargonic dynasty.

Lines 14–21 relate Sargon's accomplishments in rather vague terms, presenting him as a king who repeatedly crosses mountains and navigates seas. Dilmun (line 19) has been identified as Bahrain.[26] With its strategic location on the Persian Gulf, Dilmun served as a port of entry for goods destined for Mesopotamia. Dilmun is often mentioned alongside Magan and Melukkha, and ancient literary texts had a tendency to romanticize these areas.[27] The city of Der (line 20) was situated east of the Tigris, and Sargon may have encountered this city in route to his invasion of Elam. The Sargon Geography, a late tradition describing Sargon's empire, also associates the king with these sites.[28]

The final lines of the text (lines 22–33) address a future king in terms of blessing. These lines emphasize Sargon's greatness by challenging future kings to achieve greatness by walking in his footsteps. The implications are clear: only a truly great king can do as Sargon has done, and any king who does what Sargon has done will be remembered as truly great.

I am Sargon, the mighty king – king of Akkad.
My mother was a high priestess; I did not know my father.
My father's brother occupies the mountains.
Azupiranu is my city, situated on the bank of the Euphrates.
My mother, the high priestess, conceived me; in secrecy she bore me.
She placed me in a reed basket; she sealed my opening with bitumen.
She gave me to the river, from which I could not come forth.
The river carried me; to Aqqi the water-drawer it brought me.
Aqqi the water-drawer brought me forth when he dipped his bucket.
Aqqi the water-drawer raised me as his adopted son.
Aqqi the water-drawer made me his gardener.
While I was a gardener, Ishtar loved me and
I reigned as king for [. . .] years.
Humankind I ruled and [governed (?)].
With copper pickaxes I cut through mighty mountains.
I ascended high mountains.
I traversed the hills.
I sailed around the sea[lands] three times.
Dilmun [submitted to me].
To Greater Der I . . .
I removed [sto]nes.
Any king who arises after me
[Let him reign as king for . . . years.]
Let him rule humankind!
Let him [cut through] mighty mountains with [copper] pickaxes.
Let him ascend the high mountains.
[Let him traverse the foothills.]
Let him sail around the sea lands three times.

[. . .]
(30) Let him go up to greater Der.
[. . .]
[. . .] from my city, Akkad
[. . .] like arrows [. . .]

Column ii of this composition contains text of uncertain relation to the Sargon Birth Legend. Numerous animals, seemingly restless, appear in a context replete with rhetorical queries. Due to the fragmentary state of the text, its connection (if any) to the Birth Legend cannot be determined.

20. Sargon, King of Battle

The King of Battle Legend may serve as an example of the need to view late traditions with a critical eye. The text itself is fourteenth century, found in the Egyptian city of Amarna. The general setting of the story seems most at home in Old Assyrian times (nineteenth century), an era characterized by Assyrian merchant activity in Anatolia. The narrative claims as its protagonist Sargon of Akkad, a figure of the twenty-third century. We have reason to question the credibility of this late tradition.

The tablet containing our text has major breaks in the upper corners and damage along the left side and bottom of the obverse. On the reverse, the top and left side are damaged. Consequently, many readings remain incomplete, and scholars have offered various interpretations of these partial lines. A comparison of several English translations will reveal the degree to which the meaning of various portions of the text remains ambiguous.

Nevertheless, the substance of the document seems clear enough. Sargon yearns for battle (lines 1–6), but his soldiers advise against it, complaining of the difficulties they will face (lines 7–12). A messenger speaks on behalf of some merchants stationed in Anatolia, relating their oppression and urging the king to come to their aid (lines 13–20). The merchants themselves then enter the palace, and Sargon agrees to engage in a campaign to help them. He is again reminded of the grave difficulties that lie ahead (lines 21–7). Sargon and his soldiers march through difficult terrain (lines 28ff.).

On the reverse of the tablet, the scene shifts to the court of Nur-Daggal, ruler of Purushanda. Nur-Daggal takes comfort in the fact that Sargon has not yet attacked, and he expresses the hope that flooding and difficult terrain will hold Sargon back. His warriors ask rhetorically what king has ever come against their lands (lines 3′–7′). Before Nur-Daggal has a chance to respond, in an instant Sargon sweeps down upon the city (7′–12′). Sargon is crowned, and Nur-Daggal is brought before him. Nur-Daggal, astonished by the onslaught, speculates that Sargon's god must have given him aid. Nur-Daggal grovels before the great Sargon, perhaps even swearing allegiance as a vassal (13′–23′). When Sargon and his soldiers depart after three years, they carry the fruits of the land with them as the spoils of war (24′–8′).

In the King of Battle Legend, Mesopotamian traders complain of unfavorable conditions in Anatolia and plead for relief from Sargon. The setting reflects the nineteenth century (some four centuries following Sargon of Akkad), a time when Assyrian merchants participated in a well-organized system of trade in Anatolia. The Cappadocian Texts from this period provide extensive documentation of certain Assyrian merchants' activities in an area outside the ancient city of Kanesh. These merchants established a permanent settlement known as a *kārum* – an Assyrian word originally meaning "port" or "quay," which eventually came to signify a commercial district.

The goods the Assyrian merchants sold in Anatolia did not originate in Assur. The merchants purchased imported tin and textiles in Assur and transported them to Anatolia by means of donkey caravans, thus participating in a trade network of wide geographical scope. The tin originated east of the Tigris, likely in the central parts of present-day Afghanistan, while Babylonia to the south served as the source of the textiles. Once in Anatolia, the Assyrian merchants would exchange their goods for silver, gold, and other precious metals which would be used upon return to Assur to pay expenses and purchase more imported goods for sale in Anatolia.

The Cappadocian Texts, unearthed at Kanesh, offer a wealth of information with respect to the region and period in general. They reveal, for example, that three cities – Purushanda, Kanesh, and Wahshushana – seem to have been major political centers in the nineteenth century. It is Purushanda and its ruler Nur-Daggal that serve as the objects of Sargon's campaign in the King of Battle Legend. Though the precise location of Purushanda is not yet known, it appears in the texts as a major seat of power in Anatolia. Its ruler is known as "great prince" while other rulers are simply called "prince," a nomenclature reflecting the city's political preeminence.

The King of Battle Legend does not represent history in any modern sense of the word. This legend places Sargon of Akkad in a setting most appropriate centuries later, the Old Assyrian period in which organized Assyrian merchant activity in Anatolia thrived. Furthermore, at this time Purushanda seems to have been a most influential city. This is not to imply that Purushanda was not influential in an earlier era, or that there were not precursors to the type of merchant activity so thoroughly documented in the Cappadocian Texts. To the contrary, both were certainly the case. Nevertheless, the student of history must view the claims of the King of Battle Legend with skepticism.

The situation becomes even more complex when one takes into account that the setting of King of Battle more accurately reflects the period of Sargon I of Assyria. Though the legend clearly understands its protagonist as Sargon of Akkad (e.g., lines 17, 20′), it is possible that a campaign of Sargon I of Assyria (or some other king) has been attributed to the earlier and more famous ruler. It is also possible that the legend has no basis at all in any historical campaign: King of Battle may be a literary creation crafted to prod an irresolute monarch to action, an anachronistic tale serving as a reminder that a great king responds decisively in times of crisis.

In fact, a number of important literary themes appear in the legend. The king's decisiveness in the face of his soldiers' misgivings serves to underscore Sargon's bravery, and in defending the defenseless merchants, he performs one of the duties of the ideal Mesopotamian monarch. Sargon faces and overcomes seemingly insurmountable obstacles, a testament to the king's determination. The legend's antagonist, Nur-Daggal, is humbled at a moment when he and members of his court are speaking arrogantly.[29]

We may conclude that though the King of Battle Legend has as its central character the historical figure of Sargon of Akkad, it is best understood as a work of literature. Despite this, the document likely finds inspiration in Sargonic traditions that, quite broadly speaking, have a factual basis – traditions regarding Sargon's greatness, bravery, and influence in distant lands.

[.............] of Ishtar, [he who ???] the foundations (?) of A[kkad.........]
[.............] battles, the king in the mid[st of Akkad (?)...........]
[......Sargon] speaks of battle. Sargon [.........]
[......... . with] his furious weapon. The palace of Sargon [.........]
[He speaks to his warriors], he declares –
"My warriors, (against) Ka[nesh ... ..].
[............ .] I seek battle. They have subjugated [.........]
[.............] he has brought. Sargon is despised [............]
[. . .] the thrones. The road, my lord, [that you wish] to travel
[is a difficult path], a treacherous [w]ay. The road to Purushanda
[that you wish to travel,] the road of which I complain,
is a task of (seven double-miles).[30] When will we
[.........] we sit down on a chair. Will we soon rest
[....... when] our arms have become exhausted,
(when) our knees have grown weary from walking the paths?
[Then] he opens [his mouth][31] and speaks,
the messenger of the merchants declares,
[By your god, Zabab]a, who travels the ways, who takes to the road,
who watches over the world
[. . .] of the thrones, that from the rising of the sun to the setting of the sun
[. . . th]at the merchants' hearts retch, coated with bile, vomiting
[on the gro]und.[32] What can Kish snatch from the midst of Akkad?
We invoked [Sarg]on, king of the world:
"Come down to us! We face opposition, (and) we are not warriors.
(The cost of) provisions for the road, O king, impose (on us),
that which we shall pay, O king.
As for the one who will stand at his battle, let the king pay.
[Let] the warriors of Sargon [. . .] gold; let them give him shafts of silver.
Our [lord], we shall go. Treachery is committed
in the very place where your god Zababa rests!
The merchants gathered; they entered the palace. After they entered,
the merchants did not confront the warriors. Sargon opens his mouth, he speaks.

The King of Battle [declares]: "Purushanda, which is acclaimed – let me see its valor!
What is its direction? Which is its mountain?
Where is its Anzu?[33] *Which (is its) Kililtu*[34]*?"*
"The road that you wish to travel is a difficult path, a treacherous way.
Purushanda, where you wish to travel, the road of which I complain,
is a task of seven double-miles."
[. . .] the enormous mountain, whose stones are lapis lazuli,
with gold in its confines.
[. . .] the apple tree, the fig tree, the boxwood, the urzinnu tree,
a depth of seven abzu.
[. . .] the place where the servants had fought one another.
The haft[35] *of its peak is seven double-miles. The brambles*
[. . .] all of it is seven double miles. The trees, the thorn bush, the area of
[. . .] the thorns[36] *of the trees are sixty cubits, is seven double-miles.*
The thorny bushes . . .

(Bottom of tablet obverse broken. Top of tablet reverse broken.)

[........] Nur-D[aggal] opens his mouth and speaks [to his warriors]
He declares, "Sargon has not yet come against us.
May the riverbank and the flooding detain him,
(together with) the mighty mountain. May the reeds become a forest,
a thicket, a wood, binding themselves together into knots."
His warriors answer him – they declare to Nur-Daggal, "Which kings,
more recent or long ago, what king came and saw our lands?" Nur-Daggal
had not even finished responding when Sargon surrounded his city,
making the Gate of the Princes 2 iku wide.
[He kno]cked it down. He made a breach in the highest point of its wall.
He struck down all his drunken men.
[Sarg]on, before the gate, approached his throne. Sargon opens his mouth
[and sp]eaks. He declares to his warriors, "Now, as for Nur-Daggal,
favorite of Enlil!
[Let him ro]use himself! Let him bow himself down. Let me see!
He was crowned with a crown of precious stones on his head;
a footstool of lapis lazuli below. Fifty-five officials
[. . .] sat before him, who like him sat on a throne of gold;
the king sits like a god.
Who is exalted like the king? They made Nur-Daggal sit before Sargon.
Sargon opens his mouth
and speaks to Nur-Daggal. He [declares], "Come Nur-Daggal, favorite of Enlil.
How could you say,
'Sargon has not yet come against us. May the riverbank, the flooding,
and the mighty mountain detain him.
May the reeds become a forest. May it produce a thicket, a wood, knots.'"
Nur-Daggal opens his mouth
and speaks to Sargon. "Perhaps, my lord, your god
Zababa, the warrior of the trans-Euphrates, informed you
and brought the troops across for you. What land of all the lands rivals Akkad?

[What] king rivals you? Your adversary does not exist.
The military campaign is their enemy.
The kiln [fire] burns the hearts of your enemies.
They have feared, and I am petrified. Restore to them
[. . .] the field and the pasture land – lords, who are allies, over it.
[. . .] we will return to his place. Let him carry its fruit –
apples, figs, plums, vines,
(25′) [. . .] pistachios, olives, sweet pomegranates (?).
Never shall we return to his place.
[. . .] let him carry. Let the city be treated harshly.
Let him take good things as he goes.
[. . . .] remaining. Who accompanied Sargon?
They departed the city,
having remained three years and [. . .].
Tablet One of "King of Battle" is complete.

B. Naram-Sin of Akkad

As with Sargon of Akkad, the figure of Naram-Sin continued to capture the imaginations of many generations of Mesopotamians. While traditions far removed from his time present Sargon's reign quite positively and portray the dynasty's founder as a mythic hero, the same cannot be said of all late traditions concerning Sargon's grandson and eventual successor, Naram-Sin. There is considerable irony in the fact that Naram-Sin's inscriptions extol him extravagantly, eventually going so far as to proclaim him a god, yet in later periods he is sometimes remembered for his ineptitude. The translations below represent divergent views of Naram-Sin's reign. The Great Revolt describes in some detail the rebellion against Naram-Sin as a means of emphasizing the king's might and military prowess. The Cutha Legend offers a very different portrait of Naram-Sin, presenting him as a somewhat tragic figure whose hubris nearly brings about the downfall of his kingdom.

In fact, the reign of Naram-Sin did not end so disastrously as some late traditions suggest, and the historical Naram-Sin would become the most important monarch of the Sargonic dynasty. Two sons of Sargon, first Rimush and then Manishtusu but please see the discussion on pp. 18–19, had consolidated and governed Sargon's empire for nearly a quarter-century following their father's death. Upon the death of Manishtusu, his son Naram-Sin – grandson of Sargon of Akkad – began a lengthy reign.

Naram-Sin enlarged the sphere of Akkadian influence by campaigning to the north, south, east, and west. He erected stelae in far-off lands, boasting of the uniqueness of his accomplishments. After successfully checking a challenge to Akkadian power, likely the rebellion inspiring traditions preserved in The Great Revolt, Naram-Sin's subjects hailed him as divine. The king passed the empire on to his son and successor, Sharkalisharri, who maintained the Sargonic dynasty for another 25 years.

Clearly, late traditions ascribing the demise of the empire to Naram-Sin are in error.[37] It was he who presided over the Sargonic empire at its greatest, he whose subjects thought him fit for divinity. Naram-Sin expanded the realm, proving himself a worthy heir to his famous grandfather's throne. The Sargonic dynasty with its empire did not crumble on his watch: its collapse awaited the close of his successor's reign.

21. The Great Revolt

As our knowledge of Sargon's inscriptions stems from copies made by Old Babylonian scribes, so also we may gain some knowledge of Naram-Sin's reign from the activity of these ancient copyists. Scribes in the important religious center Nippur copied stelae deposited there by kings of the Sargonic dynasty, among them the stelae of Naram-Sin. Of interest here is the presence at Nippur of two fragmentary copies referencing events described in The Great Revolt.

These texts, copied from texts originating in Naram-Sin's time, provide important corroborating evidence for the content of texts produced in later periods. They reveal that in The Great Revolt we are dealing with a tradition that has historical foundation. This is not to say that the text is devoid of legendary material or that no literary license has been taken: a reading of the text will reveal both legendary and literary features. Nevertheless, the tradition preserves a genuine historical memory of an episode that served as the defining crisis of Naram-Sin's reign.

In addition to the Nippur copies, four other versions exist. From Eshnunna we have an Old Akkadian fragment of some rendering of The Great Revolt, an exercise by a student who has not yet mastered the scribal art. Two Old Babylonian tablets, one from Mari and the other of unknown provenance, offer a version closely related to the Nippur copies. The translation below reflects the text of the latter – it is an essentially complete Old Babylonian tablet[38] closely following the Nippur copies. An Old Babylonian version from Sippar (?) describes a confederation of 18 rulers who oppose Naram-Sin as well as a description of a battle in which the Gutian king emerges victorious. One scene in this version characterizes Naram-Sin's enemies as superhuman. Finally, one Old Babylonian tablet of unknown provenance describes a series of nine revolts, followed by a tenth decisive battle. This final version presents Naram-Sin as divine.

While the tablet translated below is in good condition and essentially complete, it does not contain a comprehensive account of the rebellion and its consequences. The contents may be described as follows: an invocation to the great god Enlil and the warrior of the gods, Ilaba[39] (line 1); Naram-Sin is identified by name and royal titles (lines 2–9); the rebellion is described (lines 10–15); Naram-Sin relates the previous kindness of the Sargonic dynasty toward Kish (16–20); Naram-Sin swears that Kish was, in fact his ally and not his enemy (lines 21–3); the city of Kish nonetheless rebels, making

Iphur-Kish king (lines 24–8); the tablet closes with a catalogue of 10 kings who join the revolt against Naram-Sin (29–38).

Noticeably absent from this particular text is any description of the ensuing battle(s) and the ultimate outcome. To learn more we must consult the other versions, all of which unfortunately are broken or become fragmentary at precisely this point. The traces of the text that remain legible reveal that Naram-Sin triumphs, but the details of his triumph are largely lost. Naram-Sin's victory must have been hard fought, to say the least. One tradition has him fighting 10 battles before ostensibly achieving final victory; another has him facing off against 18 kings and suffering substantial casualties before the tide turns in his favor.

That the odds seemed stacked against Naram-Sin appears certain. The king's success at thwarting the rebellion must have resembled a superhuman accomplishment, and it is likely this success that led to his deification shortly thereafter.

Two features of the text deserve brief comment: the king's titles and his declaration of innocence. Naram-Sin's titles emphasize his connection with some of the more celebrated gods of the pantheon: the fierce Enlil, the august An, the warring goddess Ishtar. The goddess Anunitum, whom the Babylonians associated with childbirth, is here coupled with Ishtar.[40] The heroic Ilaba is likely a clan god of the Sargonic rulers, a deity who all but disappears with the passing of the dynasty. Among other epithets, Naram-Sin is termed "protector of the sources of the Irnina Canal, the Tigris and Euphrates." As the divinely appointed protector of this long and important watercourse, Naram-Sin can claim divine legitimation for controlling the Tigris/Euphrates region.

In fashion characteristic of royal tales, The Great Revolt contrasts Naram-Sin's innocence with his adversaries' guilt.[41] Despite the beneficence of the Sargonic dynasty toward Kish, described in detail in lines 16–20, the city has responded treacherously – Kish has repaid evil for good. An assembly has gathered and raised to kingship Iphur-Kish, a man whose name (no doubt assumed upon elevation to the royal office) means "Kish assembled," but Kish's defiance does not represent an isolated event. Numerous others join the rebellion, and to the king it seems that all the world is in revolt against him.

(For) Enlil, his strength, (and) Ilaba, the warrior of the gods – his clan god:
Naram-Sin, the mighty king – the king of Akkad,
the king of the four quarters of the world,
who glorifies Ishtar and Anunitum,
(5) anointed priest of Anu, military governor of Enlil,
ruler of Ilaba,
protector of the sources of the Irnina canal – that is, the Tigris and Euphrates,
who sends forth the power of . . .
against all the kings.
(10) When the four quarters of the world
together revolted against me –

Kish, Cutha, Tiwa, Urumu,
Kazallu, Giritab, Apiak,
Ibrat, Dilbat, Uruk, and Sippar
(15) together revolted against me.
At the time when Sargon my forefather
defeated Uruk,
he established freedom for the people of Kish,
shaved off the hairstyles that identified them as slaves,
(20) (and) broke their fetters.
O Ishtar, Ilaba, Shullat, and Hanish
Shamash and Umshum,
Kish was not an enemy – it was an ally to me!
(Yet) between Tiwa and Urumu,
(25) at Ugar-Sin between the temples Esabad and Gula,
Kish assembled.
Iphur-Kish, a man from Kish,
the son of Ṣumirat-Ishtar the lamentation priestess,
they installed as king.
Puttimadal king of Simurrum,
(30) Ingi king of the land of Namar,
Rish-Adad king of Apishal,
Migir-Dagan king of Mari,
Hupshumkipi king of Marhashi,
Duhsusu king of Mardaman,
(35) Manum king of Magan,
Lugal-Anne king of Uruk,
Ir-Enlila king of Umma,
Amar-Enlila king of Nippur.

22. The Cutha Legend

We may begin by noting two important contrasts between The Great Revolt and the Cutha Legend. First, texts describing The Great Revolt offer a literary account of an event with a genuinely historical foundation. Although the versions vary in their descriptions of the rebellion and its participants, they preserve the essence of an authentic historical memory – at some point in Naram-Sin's reign he faced a widespread uprising, an uprising posing so great a threat to the survival of the kingdom that its suppression seemed a superhuman act. The Cutha Legend has no such basis in fact:[42] it is, rather, a tale told for a didactic purpose, a story with a moral.

The second contrast involves the characterization of Naram-Sin. If The Great Revolt belongs to a collection of texts that applaud Naram-Sin's prowess, the Cutha Legend belongs to a group of texts presenting a decidedly different appraisal of this king's reign. While the Cutha Legend does not go so far as The Curse of Agade, a text blaming Akkad's destruction at the hand of Gutian invaders on Naram-Sin's sacrilege, it nonetheless characterizes the king as a proud figure whose flagrant disregard for divine instruction endangers his reign and the well-being of his kingdom. By the Cutha Legend's end, Naram-Sin has learned his lesson. The king addresses future monarchs and commends something of a compliant stance toward both the gods and enemies: Naram-Sin has become a mere shadow of his former warlike self.

Though we have already touched on the ahistorical nature of traditions attributing Akkad's demise and downfall to Naram-Sin,[43] we may hypothesize something of the process by which this attribution came to be made. Subsequent generations recalled the Sargonic dynasty's strength and rapid decline, as well as the names of its two principal dynasts, Sargon and Naram-Sin. Over time the period of dynastic strength became associated with the former, and (naturally) the period of dynastic decline/demise with the latter. Whatever the origin of these less flattering traditions, they do not describe the historical situation at the time of Naram-Sin.

The Cutha Legend is not an historical document; rather, it represents an example of *narû*-literature, more commonly termed in recent scholarship "pseudo-autobiography."[44] Such works generally follow a tripartite division:

1. A first-person introduction (lines 1–3)
2. A first-person narrative of events (lines 4–148)
3. A blessing/curse formula. The Cutha Legend incorporates a brief blessing formula (lines 179–80) at the close of a larger unit of instructional material (149–80).

The word *narû* is Akkadian for "stele," and the structure and content of *narû*-literature resembles that of authentic royal inscriptions etched on such stones. *Narû*-literature, however, is fictional; the terms "pseudo-autobiography" or "fictional autobiography"[45] more aptly express the character of these works.

Though an awareness of the general three-part division of the text is informative, a more detailed outline will reveal more clearly the contents of the Cutha Legend. The following sketch presents the smaller units as they are situated within the work's larger structural framework, and particular attention is given to the legend's narrative. Students less familiar with the language and content of ancient literature may find it useful to reference this outline as they work through the translation below.

I. Introduction – Naram-Sin identifies himself and invites future generations to read his document (lines 1–3)

II. The Narrative (lines 4–148)

A. The story of Enmerkar (lines 4–30)
   1. Enmerkar is identified, his fate given – he has disappeared (4–6)
   2. After a time, Enmerkar lost divine favor (7–9)
   3. Enmerkar had gathered diviners to consult the gods (10–14)
   4. The diviners spoke, their message unfavorable (?) (15–22)
   5. Shamash issued a particularly severe judgment (23–7)
   6. Naram-Sin laments that Enmerkar left no record (28–30)

B. The creation of Naram-Sin's enemies (31–62)
  1. The enemies created and divinely nurtured (31–6)
  2. The enemies explicitly identified (37–48)
  3. The enemies march on in seemingly unstoppable advance (49–62)
C. Naram-Sin tests his enemies – human or superhuman? (63–71)
  1. Instructions to a soldier (63–8)
  2. The soldier's report – they bleed (69–71)
D. Naram-Sin consults the gods, then defies them (72–87)
  1. Naram-Sin gathers diviners to consult the gods (72–7)
  2. Naram-Sin told not to attack (78)
  3. Naram-Sin defies the oracle, attacks nonetheless (79–83)
  4. The armies of Akkad suffer three devastating losses (84–7)
E. Naram-Sin's depression, intercession by the god Ea (88–107)
  1. Naram-Sin declares himself a royal failure (88–96)
  2. The god Ea intercedes for Naram-Sin (97–103)
  3. Naram-Sin participates in the New Year Festival (103–7)
F. Naram-Sin again consults the gods (108–23)
  1. Naram-Sin again gathers diviners to consult the gods (108–13)
  2. The king receives a favorable response (114–19)
  3. Naram-Sin pursues and captures enemy soldiers (120–3)
G. Naram-Sin, the obedient king (124–48)
  1. The king resolves not to act without consulting the gods (124–5)
  2. The king is told to spare the captives (126–45)
  3. Naram-Sin obeys (146–8)

III. Instruction and Blessing (149–80)
A. A call to read the record Naram-Sin has left behind (149–55)
B. Counsel to future rulers (156–74)
C. Final blessing (175–80)

Divination is a recurring activity in the narrative: with the aid of professional diviners, both Enmerkar (lines 11ff.) and Naram-Sin (lines 72ff., 108ff.) seek to discern the will of the gods. It was believed that the gods communicated with humankind by means of omens. An unsolicited omen might simply appear, such as the birth of a two-headed animal or the appearance of a comet. A person could also seek an omen by consulting diviners – those schooled in the art of divination. The technical term for the principal form of divination referenced in this text is extispicy. A sheep was slaughtered for the purpose of examining its entrails, and specific features of the liver so observed were believed to communicate particular messages from the gods.

We find in the narrative perhaps two[46] references to other means of divination. Lines 78 and 81 refer to dreams, the former suggesting that Naram-Sin sought, but did not receive, divine sanction for a military campaign both through extispicy and through nocturnal communication. Lines 128–45 show some form of celestial divination in which Venus relays a rather lengthy message to the Akkadian monarch. In each of these cases, the second form of divination serves to confirm instruction received through extispicy.

Before turning to the text itself, three literary themes warrant some attention: the transformation taking place within the character of Naram-Sin, the necessity of obedience to the gods, and the king's obligation to pass his acquired knowledge on to future generations.

The Cutha Legend chronicles a series of events that bring great personal transformation to the character of Naram-Sin. We learn of the king's cleverness when enemies arise, foes powerful enough to make Naram-Sin wonder if they are flesh and blood. The king devises a test to see if his opponents are mortal. Upon receiving the news that they bleed (and thus, he surmises, they may die), he immediately sets his mind on battle. Though Naram-Sin seeks an omen sanctioning his plans for military action, the king receives no such authorization from the gods. At this point Naram-Sin makes a fateful decision – relying on his own shrewdness and strength, the king resolves to act nonetheless. It is an act of sheer hubris that spells disaster for the kingdom, and the enemy annihilates three consecutive battalions dispatched by Naram-Sin. Naram-Sin enters a deep depression in which he characterizes himself as a royal failure. At the New Year festival, he resolves to amend his ways and to act only in accordance with the known will of the gods. Naram-Sin again inquires of the gods and receives permission to pursue and capture 12 fleeing enemy soldiers, but the gods prohibit him from meting out any punishment to them. This time the king carefully observes the gods' will; he has learned his lesson well. The change taking place within Naram-Sin may best be seen by contrasting lines 79–83 with lines 124–5.

The two remaining themes correspond to the twofold didactic purpose of the Cutha Legend: on the one hand, the legend warns rulers to seek the divine will and to act accordingly; on the other, it urges kings to leave behind a record for future generations. The central narrative portion of the legend clearly illustrates the hazards of transgressing the divine will. After divination, Enmerkar presumably behaves in some manner that brings down a severe judgment and a curse upon himself and his descendants. Naram-Sin too solicits an omen, only to ignore it and cause the death of 270,700 of his troops. Plainly the gods do not look kindly upon those who defy their counsel. Naram-Sin, however, receives a second chance when the god Ea intercedes for him in the heavenly realm, and the king's resolve to obey the gods prevents the kingdom's collapse.

Finally, the legend reminds rulers that they have a responsibility to pass their knowledge on to future generations. The famed Enmerkar failed to do so, possibly because the curse of the god Shamash was carried out so swiftly that Enmerkar had no occasion to record his experiences. Naram-Sin would not repeat this mistake: he entreats future readers to learn from his example and to follow his instructions.

The following is a translation of the composite text of the Cutha Legend, a compilation in which various fragmentary copies of the text are compared and assembled to present a more complete version. The composite text includes seven Neo-Assyrian manuscripts and one Neo-Babylonian fragment.[47]

(1)[48] *[Open the tablet box and] read the stele*
[that I, Naram-Sin,] a descendant of Sargon
[inscribed and left behind for] perpetuity.

[The king of Uruk] disappeared.
(5) [Enmerkar] disappeared.
[Enmerkar, king of Uruk, ru]ler of the land.[49]
[Some period of time] passed.
[Some period of time] went by.
[Ishtar (?) . . . chan]ged her decision.[50]
(10) . . . and he rode.
[Enmerkar consulted] the great gods –
[Ishtar, Ilaba,] Zababa, Annunitum
[Shullat, Hanish, Shamash] the hero.[51]
[He summoned the diviners] and gave orders.
(15) They sacrificed[52] *the lambs, [seven (lambs) for seven (diviners).]*[53]
[He set up] the holy reed altars.
[The diviners] spoke thus:
....
.... face.
(20) and like....
[upon] the earth . . . may your corpse lie flat.
The great gods had not [yet finished speaking][54]
Enmerkar........ Shamash brought a severe judgment.
His judgment, the decision that he ma[de], (was that) his ghost, the ghos[ts] . . .
(25) the ghost(s) of his family, the ghost(s) of his descendants,
the ghost(s) of his descendants' descendants –
(This was decreed by) Shamash the hero,
the lord above and below, the lord of the Anunnaki, the lord of the ghosts –
that they should drink contaminated water and not drink pure water.
The one whose wisdom and weapons bound, defeated, and killed those troops
did not write on a stele, he did not leave (one) behind for me, and
(30) he did not make a name for himself, and I did not pray for him.

A people with partridge bodies, raven-faced humans,
the great gods created them.
On the earth that the gods created was their[55] *city.*
Tiamat suckled them.
(35) Their maternal goddess, Belet-ili, beautified them.
In the midst of the mountains they grew, they reached manhood,
they acquired (their) proper size.
Seven kings, brothers, renowned for beauty,
their troops numbered 360,000.
Anubanini, the king, was their father. Their mother was queen Melili.
(40) Their eldest brother was their leader – Memanduh was his name.
Their second brother – Medudu was his name.

Their third brother – . . . tapish (?) was his name.
Their fourth brother – Tartadada was his name.
Their fifth brother – Baldahdah was his name.
Their sixth brother – Ahudanadih was his name.
Their seventh brother – Hurrakidu was his name.
They rode in the shining mountains, and
the soldier seized them, but they struck their thighs.[56]
At the beginning of their approach, they advanced against Purushanda.
Purushanda was wholly scattered.
Puhlu was wholly scattered.
Puranshu was wholly scattered.
Indeed,.....[57]
The powers of Umman-manda are struck down (?), the camps of Shubat-Enlil,
and in the midst of Subartu, all of them [wandered about (?)].
They scattered (those in) the seas, and they approached Gutium.
They scattered Gutium, and they approached the land of Elam.
They scattered Elam, and they reached the plains.
They killed those at the crossing, and cast (them) into . . .
Dilmun, Makkan, Meluhha, in the midst of the sea, as many as they were, they killed.
Seventeen kings, with 90,000 of [their] troops,
with them they ha[d come] to their aid.

[I] summoned a soldier and gave (him) orders.
[I handed ov]er a [dagger] and a pin.
"Attack with the dagger, [prick] with the pin.
[If blood comes out,] they are human like us.
[If blood does not come out,] they are spirits, fiends from the underworld,
demons, lurking ghosts, the work of Enlil."
The soldier delivered his report:
"I attacked with the dagger,
I pricked with the pin, and blood came out."

I summoned the diviners and gave orders.
I sacrificed[58] *seven lambs for the seven (diviners).*
I set up the holy reed altars.
I inquired of the great gods –
Ishtar, [Ila]ba, Zababa, Annunitum,
Shullat, Hanish, Shamash the hero.
The key of the great gods did not permit me to go,
nor did a divine communication in my dream.[59]

Thus I said to myself, thus indeed I (spoke):
"What lion practiced divination?
What wolf inquired of an interpreter of dreams?
Let me go like a bandit, following the counsel of my own heart.
Let me disregard (the counsel) of the god; let me take responsibility for myself.

At the arrival of the first year,
I sent out 120,000 troops, and not one from among them returned alive.

At the arrival of the second year,
I sent out 90,000 troops, and not one from among them returned alive.
At the arrival of the third year, I sent out 60,700 troops,
and not one from among them returned alive.

I was disturbed, perplexed, anxious, distressed, (and) dejected.
Thus I said to myself, thus indeed I (spoke):
"What have I left behind as the legacy of my reign?
I am a king who has not looked after his land,
and a shepherd who has not looked after his people.
How can I keep proceeding? How can I save the country?[60]
Dread of lions, death, fate, famine
dismay, chills, losses, hunger,
[starva]tion, insomnia – every sort (of calamity) descended upon them.
Above, in the ass[embly], the flood was devised.
Below, on the [earth, the flo]od came.
Ea, lord [of the deep, opened his mouth] and said,
speaking to [the gods], his [broth]ers,
"O great gods, [what have you do]ne?
You spoke and I un[leashed a flood],[61]
and to bring about that which . . . you . . ."
[At the arriv]al of the New Year festival in the fourth y[ear],
with the earnest prayer that Ea [. . .] of the [great] gods,
[I offered] the holy New Year's sacrifices.
[I soug]ht the holy omens.

I summoned the diviners and ga[ve ord]ers.
I sacrificed[62] *seven lambs for the seven (diviners).*
I set up the h[oly] reed altars.
I inquired of the great gods –
Ishtar, [Ilaba, Zababa, Annuni]tum,
Shullat, [Hanish, Shamash the her]o.
[Thus the divin]ers [said] to me:
"If [.........] carries
[........] there is
[........] hangs down in it
[........] the battle-axe will cause [blood] to flow
[........] will dro[wn(?)] in blood.

Twelve soldiers from among them fled from me.
I pursued after them, I hastened, I went faster.
As for those soldiers, I overtook them.
As for those soldiers, I brought them back.

Thus I said to myself, thus indeed I (spoke):
"Without divination, I will not inflict punishments."
I sacrificed[63] *a lamb concerning them.*
The key of the great gods [said,] "Spare them."
Shining Venus thus appro[ached] me from heaven,

"To Naram-Sin, descendant of Sargon:
Cease! You shall not destroy the accursed people!
In the future, Enlil will raise them up for evil.[64]
They await the furious heart of Enlil.
The city of those soldiers will be [demolished].
They will burn and besiege the dwelling places.
The city will pour out their blood.
The earth will reduce its store, the date palm its yield.
The city of those soldiers will die.
City will fight [against city], household against household,
fath[er against son, brother against] brother,
[young man] against young man, friend against companion.
They will not speak truth(fully) with one another.
People will be taught falsehood and . . .
They will kill that enemy city.
As for that city, an enemy city will seize it.
For one [mina of si]lver, (a person) will receive a seah of barley."
There was no mighty king in the land [. . .]
I brought them [to] the great [gods] as tribute,[65]
I did not bring them for my hand to kill.

Whoever you are, a governor, or a prince, or any other,
whom the gods shall call to carry out the office of kingship:
I made you a tablet box, I inscribed for you a stele.
In Kutha, in the Emeslam temple,
in the shrine of Nergal I left (it) behind for you.
Read this stele,
and heed the message of this stele!
Do not be disturbed; do not be perplexed.
Do not fear; do not tremble.
Let your foundations be firm!
As for you, do your work in the embrace of your wife.
Fortify your walls.
Fill your moats with water.
Your chests, your grain, your silver, your possessions, your goods,
gather in to your fortified city.
Bind your weapons together, and lean (them) against the corners.
Curb your boldness, look out for yourself!
Should he wander throughout your land, do not go out to him.
Should he loose the livestock, do not approach him.
Should he consume the flesh of your so[ldie]rs,
should he kill, and ret[urn...] –
you maintain self-control, you keep yourself in check.
Answer them thus: "My lord."
For their wickedness, return good.
For (their) good, (return) gifts and more![66]
Do not approach them.
Let wise scribes

read your stele.
You who have read my stele,
you have saved your country.[67]
You who have blessed me, may a future (king)
(180) bless you!

Bibliography

Black, Jeremy A. *Gods, Demons, and Symbols of Ancient Mesopotamia: An Illustrated Dictionary*. Austin: University of Texas Press, 1992. (A useful resource for those unfamiliar with the Mesopotamian pantheon.)

Farber, Walter. "Witchcraft, Magic, and Divination in Ancient Mesopotamia." In *Civilizations of the Ancient Near East*. Jack M. Sasson, Editor in Chief. New York: Charles Scribner's Sons, 1995, 3: 1895–1909.

Foster, Benjamin R. *From Distant Days: Myths, Tales, and Poetry of Ancient Mesopotamia*. Bethesda: CDL, 1995. (Translation of the Brith Legend and the King of Battle, pp. 165–70. Translation of the Cutha Legend, pp. 171–7.)

Franke, Sabina. "Kings of Akkad: Sargon and Naram-Sin." Translated by Andrew Baumann. *Civilizations of the Ancient Near East*. Jack M. Sasson, Editor in Chief. New York: Charles Scribner's Sons, 1995, 2: 831–41.

Frayne, Douglas R. *Sargonic and Gutian Periods*. Toronto: University of Toronto Press.

Gadd, C. J. "The Dynasty of Agade and the Gutian Invasion." *The Cambridge Ancient History*. 3d ed. Cambridge: Cambridge University Press, 1971, 1/2: 417–63.

Gaster, T. *Myth, Legend, and Custom in the Old Testament*. New York: Harper & Row, 1969. (See pp. 224–30 for the infant exposure motif.)

Gelb, I. J. and B. Kienast. *Die Altakkadischen Königsinschriften des dritten Jahrtausends v. Chr.* Freiburger altorientalische Studien 7. Stuttgart: Franz Steiner, 1990, 170–4 and pls. 1–3, 11–12.

Gurney, O. R. "Corrections to Previous Articles." *Anatolian Studies* 6 (1956): 162–4.

——. "The Sultantepe Tablets (continued), the Cuthaean Legend of Naram-Sin." *Anatolian Studies* 5 (1955): 93–113.

Hallo, W. W. "Gutium." In *Reallexikon der Assyriologie*. 3 (1957–71): 708–20.

Hallo, W. W. and W. K. Simpson. *The Ancient Near East: A History*. 2d ed. New York: Harcourt Brace, 1998, 52–65.

Jeyes, Ulla. *Old Babylonian Extispicy: Omen Texts in the British Museum*. Istanbul: Nederlands Historisch-Archaeologisch Instituut, 1989.

Kienast, B. "Sargonic Incriptions." In COS 2: 243 (no. 2.89), and 2: 244 (no. 2.90).

Kienast, B. and K. Volk. *Die sumerischen und akkadischen Briefe des III. Jahrtausends aus der Zeit vor der III. Dynastie von Ur*. Freiburger altorientalische Studien 19. Stuttgart: Steiner, 1995, 89–94.

Koch-Westenholz, Ulla. *Mesopotamian Astrology: An Introduction to Babylonian and Assyrian Celestial Divination*. Copenhagen: Museum Tusculanum Press, 1995.

Kuhrt, Amélie. *The Ancient Near East: c. 3000–330 BC*. New York: Routledge, 1995, 44–55.

Leichty, Erle. *The Omen Series Šumma Izbu*. Locust Valley, NY: Augustin, 1970. (A study of the omen series dealing with the interpretation of anomalous births.)

Lewis, Brian. *The Sargon Legend: A Study of the Akkadian Text and the Tale of the Hero Who Was Exposed at Birth*. Cambridge: ASOR, 1980.

Longman, Tremper, III. *Fictional Akkadian Autobiography: A Generic and Comparative Study*. Winona Lake, Ind.: Eisenbrauns, 1991. (A thorough examination of the genre, with a translation of the Cutha Legend on pp. 228–31.)

Michalowski, P. *Letters from Early Mesopotamia*. Ed. Erica Reiner. Writings from the Ancient World Series, Society of Biblical Literature 3. Atlanta, 1993, 27–8 (no. 22).

Oppenheim, A. Leo. *The Interpretation of Dreams in the Ancient Near East*. Philadelphia: American Philosophical Society, 1956.

Orlin, L. *Assryian Colonies in Cappadocia*. The Hague: Mouton, 1970.

Redford, Donald. "The Literary Motif of the Exposed Child." *Numen* 14 (1967): 209–28.

Roberts, J. J. M. *The Earliest Semitic Pantheon: A Study of the Semitic Deities Attested in Mesopotamia before Ur III*. Baltimore: Johns Hopkins University Press, 1972. (A more technical examination of the pre-Ur III Semitic pantheon.)

Starr, Ivan. *The Rituals of the Diviner*. Malibu: Undena, 1983.

Steinkeller, P. "An Ur III Manuscript of the Sumerian King List." In *Literature, Politik und Recht in Mesopotamien: Festschrift für Claus Wilcke*. Orientalia Biblica et Christiana 14. Wiesbaden: Harrassowitz, 2003, 267–92.

——. "Early Political Development in Mesopotamia and the Origins of the Sargonic Empire." In *Akkad: The First World Empire*. Ed. M. Liverani. Padova: Sargon, 1993, 107–29.

Stone, Elizabeth C. and David I. Owen. *Adoption in Old Babylonian Nippur and the Archive Mannum-mesu-Lissur*. Winona Lake, Ind.: Eisenbrauns, 1991.

Veenhof, Klaas R. "Kanesh: An Assyrian Colony in Anatolia." *Civilizations of the Ancient Near East* [*CANE*]. Jack M. Sasson, Editor in Chief. New York: Charles Scribner's Sons, 1995, 2: 859–71.

Westenholz, A. Review of Frayne, Douglas R. *The Royal Inscriptions of Mesopotamia, Early Periods, II: Sargonic and Gutian Periods (2334–2113 BC)*. University of Toronto Press 1993. *Bibliotheca Orientalis* 58: 1/2 (January–March 1996): 116–23.

——. "The Old Akkadian Period: History and Culture." In Walther Sallaberger et al. *Mesopotamien: Akkade-Zeit und Ur III-Zeit*. Orbis Biblicus et Orientalis 160/3. Freiburg: Universitätsverlag Freiburg, 1999, 17–117.

Westenholz, Joan Goodnick. *Legends of the Kings of Akkade*. Winona Lake, Ind.: Eisenbrauns, 1997.

Notes

1 Also see Steinkeller 1993: 120–1. For arguments favoring a more literal translation of the phrase, see Westenholz 1996: 121; cf. 1999: 37–8.

2 The reading of the name is not certain. The divine determinative may also be read as the Akkadian word for god (*ilu*), hence the problem.

3 Literally "and 50 governors by the mace of Ilaba and the city he smote." See Kienast 2003: 243 n. 1.

4 The line is difficult. See Gelb and Kienast 1990: 162 (under 97–102) for discussion.

5 The type of boat is unknown.

6 Following the comments of Westenholz 1996: 118, 120.

7 One should know that several kings of Awan are mentioned in a damaged section of the Sumerian King List. More informative is a text from the Old

Babylonian period, which lists 12 kings of Awan and 12 kings of Shimashki, both major centers of influence in Elam (see Gelb and Kienast 1990: 317–20). Unfortunately, little else is known about these kings.

8 The reading of the name is not certain.

9 Or "in the area" (Westenholz 1996: 121). The Akkadian term translated as "destruction" refers to a mound, often of corpses.

10 Or "for his well being."

11 Following Gelb and Kienast 1990: 211; cf. Westenholz 1996: 118.

12 The figure, whose name means "hairy," has also been called the "Nude Hero." He appears frequently on Old Akkadian seal impressions.

13 Cf. the translation and discussion of the inscription in *History* 64.

14 Or "during the time of distress."

15 The meaning of the term is not known. According to the only other attestation, maqqatu, themselves, may be cultivated.

16 In addition, Hittite fragments of this legend have been discovered.

17 H. G. Güterbock, "Die historische Tradition und ihre literarische Gestaltung bei Babyloniern und Hethitern bis 1200," *Zeitschrift für Assyriologie* 42 (1934): 19.

18 A. K. Grayson, *Assyrian and Babylonian Chronicles*, Texts from Cuneiform Sources (Locust Valley, NY: Augustin, 1966ff.), 1–3.

19 Güterbock, for example, responds to charges of over-criticism by stating, "I do agree with those who argue that even a legend must be based on some historical fact." H. G. Güterbock, "Sargon of Akkad Mentioned by Hattušili I of Hatti," *Journal of Cuneiform Studies* 17 (1964): 1–6.

20 The account of the birth of Moses (Exod 2: 1–10) represents a well-known example of this motif.

21 The theme is found in the literature of many languages.

22 See Donald B. Redford, "The Literary Motif of the Exposed Child," *Numen* 14 (1967): 209–28. Of particular interest are the parallels discussed on p. 226.

23 See Hallo and Simpson 1998: 52. On the other hand, Brian Lewis sees the claim that Sargon's mother's had priestly status as a claim of noble descent. *The Sargon Legend: A Study of the Akkadian Text and the Tale of the Hero Who was Exposed at Birth*, American Schools of Oriental Research Dissertation Series (Cambridge: ASOR, 1980), p. 37.

24 See Lewis 1980: 50; Marten Stol, "Private Life in Ancient Mesopotamia," *Civilizations of the Ancient Near East* (New York: Charles Scribner's Sons, 1995), 1: 485–501, particularly pp. 491–2 on childlessness.

25 W. W. Hallo and J. J. A. van Dijk, *The Exaltation of Inanna* (New Haven: Yale, 1968), pp. 1–11.

26 Daniel T. Potts, ed., *Dilmun: New Studies in the Archaeology and Early History of Bahrain* (Berlin: Dietrich Reimer, 1983).

27 See D. T. Potts, "Distant Shores: Ancient Near Eastern Trade with South Asia and Northeast Africa," *Civilizations of the Ancient Near East* (Charles Scribner's Sons: New York, 1995), 3: 1451–63.

28 Wayne Horowitz, *Mesopotamian Cosmic Geography* (Winona Lake, Ind.: Eisenbrauns, 1998), ch. 4, "The Sargon Geography," pp. 67–95.

29 Compare the figure of Belshazzar in Daniel 5.

30 See line 27.

31 Restoration follows Westenholz 1997, p. 114.

32 Restoration follows Westenholz 1997, p. 114.
33 A mythical bird.
34 Meaning unclear. Perhaps a female demon taking the form of an owl. See *CAD kililu*.
35 Meaning uncertain.
36 Westenholz 1996: 120.
37 The Curse of Agade, for instance.
38 Although a complete tablet, not the total account. See below.
39 Ilaba is understood here as a "protector." See Piotr Michalowski, "New Sources Concerning the Reign of Naram-Sin," *Journal of Cuneiform Studies* 32/4 (1980): 233–46.
40 In the mythology of Mesopotamia, Ishtar is both a goddess of love and war. This text expresses these two themes by bringing together Ishtar (war) and Anunitum (fertility).
41 Compare, for example, the Tukulti-Ninurta epic, in which Tukulti-Ninurta is presented as blameless, while his opponent, Kashtiliash, is characterized as a transgressor.
42 This does not mean that the text makes no historically accurate references. For instance, Anubanini – mentioned in line 39 of the text – is a figure from Naram-Sin's era known from other sources. See discussion in Tremper Longman 1991: 110–11, 113–17. Landsberger suggests that some of the personal names in the Cutha Legend, as well as certain country and city names, come from a *Vorlage* dealing with the deeds of Naram-Sin. B. Landsberger, "The Sin of Sargon and Sennacherib's Last Will," (Tadmor, Landsberger, Parpola) *State Archives of Assyria Bulletin* 3/1(1989): 44.
43 See in ch. 2 the section "Late Traditions Concerning Sargon and Naram-Sin" (Morgan).
44 See also comments on the Sargon Birth Legend, a brief text with a similar structure.
45 Taken from a title by Tremper Longman III, 1991.
46 The meaning of the second half of line 78 remains somewhat uncertain.
47 The manuscripts and composite text are presented in Westenholz 1996: 332–68.
48 The line numbers below follow J. G. Westenholz, "'Naram-Sin and the Enemy Hordes': The 'Cuthean Legend' of Naram-Sin," Composite Text (Winona Lake, Ind.: Eisenbrauns, 1997), 300–68.
49 Restoration follows Gurney: 163.
50 This seems to refer to the decision by a deity concerning the land, a decision that would alter the fortunes of the land.
51 Deity names reconstructed from lines 76–7.
52 Lit. "touched."
53 Reconstruction from lines 73, 109.
54 Lines 21–2, following Westenholz 1997, 305.
55 Text: "his city."
56 This line likely implies that the enemy troops rallied themselves.
57 The meaning of this line is uncertain.
58 Lit. "touched."
59 Considerable uncertainty surrounds the function of the "key" and the sense of the word translated here "a divine communication in my dream." Clearly, however, the gods respond negatively to Naram-Sin's inquiry.

60 This translation follows B. Landsberger, "The Sin of Sargon and Sennacherib's Last Will" (Tadmor, Landsberger, Parpola), *State Archives of Assyria Bulletin* 3/1 (1989): 42–3.

61 Restoration follows Gurney 1956: 164.

62 Lit. "touched."

63 Lit. "touched."

64 Or "honor them for an evil (purpose)."

65 Following Westenholz 1997: 326–7.

66 Following Westenholz 1997: 330; Landsberger 1989 (see note 60): 44.

67 Cf. line 93. See Landsberger 1989: 42–3.

3

Late Third Millennium BCE Sumerian Texts

Richard Averbeck, Benjamin Studevent-Hickman, and Piotr Michalowski

I. Gudea Historical Texts (Averbeck)

Gudea was an important ruler (*énsi*) of ancient Lagash, a Sumerian city-state in southern Mesopotamia, between the fall of the previous empire of Agade (ca. 2350–2193 BC; located further north in the Tigris and Euphrates alluvium) founded by the Semite Sargon the Great, and the establishment of the Ur III Empire (2112–2004 BC) founded by the Sumerian Ur-Nammu (2112–2095 BC; based at Ur, along the southern course of the Euphrates river). Lagash and Girsu (the actual administrative center of Gudea) are located north of Ur in the region between the Tigris to the north and the Euphrates to the south. The reference to the Tigris River at the beginning of Gudea Cylinder A suggests that the Tigris rather than the Euphrates was the main source for the irrigation of the Lagash region.

The most recent research on the subject suggests that, for a period of time between the end of the Agade Empire and the beginning of the Ur III Empire, there appear to have been a number of rival city-states that vied for prominence in the lower Tigris and Euphrates area. The three most prominent ones in chronological order were (1) the Lagash II dynasty under the rule of Urbaba (the father-in-law of Gudea) and Gudea himself, referred to as the Lagash II dynasty to distinguish it from the Pre-Sargonic dynasty at Lagash that ended about two centuries earlier, (2) Uruk, located northeast of Ur on the Euphrates, under the rule of Utu-hegal, to whom both the immediate successor of Gudea at Lagash, Ur-Ningirsu II, and the later founder of the Ur III kingdom, Ur-Nammu, were in submission, and finally (3) the Ur III dynasty under Ur-Nammu, who rebelled against his overlord, Utu-hegal, and took control of the region so that even Ur-abba of Lagash (the second successor of Gudea) submitted to him. The first two of these remained city-states that only became predominant in the immediate region of the city, but the third became a full-fledged empire with influence and control far beyond even the southern Tigris and Euphrates alluvium.

The internal sequence and duration of Gudea's reign still remains to be established in detail, but we have discovered 17 Gudea period year names (e.g., the first one reads "The year Gudea became ruler"), so he ruled at least that long. We also know that after his death he was honored as a god through libation offerings at the "place of libations." Today, as in ancient times, Gudea is by far the most well-known ruler of ancient Lagash because of the archaeological recovery of his many diorite statues (most of them housed in the Louvre Museum, in Paris; see selections from certain of them below) and the two large clay cylinders inscribed with a lengthy hymn describing and lauding Gudea's building of a new Eninnu temple for the main god of Lagash, Ningirsu (called Gudea Cylinders A and B, and also housed in the Louvre). The latter is one of the longest and most impressive extant literary masterpieces in the repertoire of Sumerian literature.

There is no reason to doubt that, in historical fact, Gudea was a consummate builder. He commissioned, participated in, and perhaps sometimes even designed temples. Statue B has Gudea sitting, holding a slab on his lap with what appears to be the ground plan of the temple on it. The tools for making the plan (i.e., a stick with a scale of measurements and a stylus) are also represented there. From other inscriptions we also know of his activities in building a city wall, a gate and its façade, and fashioning such things as a mace and a decorative chariot. Moreover, the fact that he has intentionally left behind so many written evidences of his works for the gods and human posterity shows that Gudea had a definite sense of his place in history. Both his history and his historiography are tied largely to building projects. Even when he makes reference to his victory over the cities of Anshan and Elam (see Statue B below), he ties it in with the building of the Eninnu temple by recording that he donated the booty to the temple.

23. Gudea Statue I

We begin with Gudea Statue I, known as "the small sitting statue" (it is only 18 inches/45 centimeters high), because it refers specifically to some of the major temples that Gudea (re)built during his reign for his major gods, and underlines the fact that he built temples for other gods as well. Except for the name given to the statue, the same inscription appears on Statue P, which is also a small sitting statue about the same size as Statue I.

(i 1–ii 13) When Ningirsu, the mighty warrior of Enlil, had established a sacred place in the city for Ningishzida, the son of Ninazu, the beloved of the gods, and had established the irrigated field plots; (and) when Gudea, the ruler of Lagash, the righteous man who loves his god, had built the Eninnu, his white Anzu-bird, and the EPA, his temple of seven regions, for his king Ningirsu;

(ii 14–iii 10) (then) he built for Nanshe, the lordly queen, his queen, the Sirara temple, her mountain which rises up over the (other) houses; (and) he built temples for

the (other) great gods of Lagash; (and) he built a temple in Girsu for Ningishzida, his (personal) god.

(iii 11–iv 7) Any man whom, like my god, his god, Ningirsu, will have called him out of the (crowd of) people, let him not look with scorn(?) at the temple of my (personal) god, (but rather) let him proclaim its name, (and) let that man be my friend (and) proclaim my name.

(v 1–8) He (Gudea) shaped this stone into a statue (and) named it "Life is given to Gudea, the man who built the temple," (and) he brought (it) into the temple for him (Ningishzida).

24. Gudea Statue B

Gudea Statue B is especially important to our historical concerns for several reasons. First, it recounts in narrative fashion the construction of the same temple as that recounted in hymnic poetic form on the Gudea Cylinders, the Eninnu of Ningirsu. Second, Gudea's fourth year formula reads: "The year the brick of Ningirsu was set in the brick mold." This no doubt refers to the year of the building of the Eninnu, which would put it early in Gudea's reign. Gudea Statue I (see above) puts the construction of this temple before the others it mentions.

Third, the section that recounts the locations far and wide, from which Gudea gathered and brought the needed materials for building the temple (Statue B v 21–vi 76), corresponds to essentially the same places mentioned in the parallel passage in Gudea Cylinder A xv 6–xvi 32. It is interesting to take note of the fact, however, that the two lists are arranged differently. In Statue B the locations are arranged in geographical order running from the northwest (the Amanus mountains in northern Lebanon) to the southeast (Anshan and Elam), while in Gudea Cylinder A they are arranged in a manner that keeps the different kinds of building materials together (wood, stone, bitumen, and metals, in that order). This may be due to that fact that Gudea Cylinder A is concerned with all the details of the construction process, while Gudea Statue B is more concerned with commemoration of the event in a more general way.

(i 1–20) From the temple of his king Ningirsu, for this statue of Gudea – the ruler of Lagash, the man who built the Eninnu – the regular offering is to be one quart of beer, one quart of bread, half a quart of meal, and half a quart of fine emmer flour. Any (future) ruler who revokes this command (for these offerings), who withholds the functions of Ningirsu, may his command regarding his regular offering from the house of Ningirsu be revoked, may his words be restrained.

(ii 1–iii 14) For Ningirsu, the mighty warrior of Enlil, Gudea, whose name endures – the ruler of Lagash, the shepherd called (chosen) in the heart by Ningirsu, regarded with favor by Nanshe, strengthened by Nindara, the man who is subject to the command by Baba, the son born by Gatumdu, given prominence and an exalted scepter by Igalim, provided abundantly with life by Shulshaga, the one whose head was raised high in glory in the assembly by his (personal) god Ningishzida – on the

day when Ningirsu looked at his city with favor (and) called Gudea to be the faithful shepherd in the land, when he (Ningirsu) took him by the hand from the midst of the human multitude (lit. 216,000 men); (then) he sanctified the city, cleansed it with fire, established the brick mold, (and) selected the brick by extispicy.

(iii 15–v 11) The impure man who is frightening, the man inflamed with venereal disease, (and) the woman in (her impure) birth period went out of the city. No woman lifted a work basket, (but only) the cultic functionaries (or best warriors) built for him. He built the temple of Ningirsu in a pure place like Eridu. Whip did not crack, lash did not strike, (and) no mother struck her son (child). The governor, inspector, overseer, (and) foreman who stood over the work, the striking instrument in their hand(s) was (like) soft combed wool. In the city cemetery no hoe was used, no corpse was brought there, no cult singer brought his harp there, no one intoned lamentation music, (and) no (hired female) mourner wailed a lament. Within the boundaries of Lagash no one who had a legal complaint brought a(nother) man to the tribunal, (and) no debt collector entered a(nother) man's house.

(v 12–20) He (Gudea) made the long enduring important things (of the temple) shine in (their) splendor for Ningirsu; he built for him the Eninnu, his white Anzu-bird; he restored it to its (rightful) place (in the temple complex); (and) in its midst he installed his beloved gigunu (terrace garden?) with the scent of cedar.

(v 21–vi 63) On the day when he (began to) build the temple of Ningirsu, his beloved king (Ningirsu) opened the way for him from the upper sea to the lower sea. From the Amanus (mountains), the mountain range of cedars, he made rafts out of cedar logs thirty yards long, cedar logs twenty-five yards long, (and) box-wood logs twelve and a half yards long, (and) brought (floated) them (down the river) from that land. He made for him the Sharur(-weapon = "the leveler of all"), his storm flood of battle. He made for him the Shargaz(-weapon = "the killer of all"), the copper mace with seven eyes. He made for him his copper peg-shaped(?) basket(?), and his copper crab-shaped(?) basket(?). He fashioned those cedars into great doors, decorated them with precious metal flowers(?), and brought them all into the Eninnu for him. He used (the logs) as roof beams in the lofty temple, his place where cold water is poured out.

From the city Ursu (and) the mountain range of Ibla he made rafts out of logs from junipers, large firs trees, and plane trees, mountain woods, (and) he used them for roof beams for him (Ningirsu) in the Eninnu.

He brought great stones from Umanum, the mountain range of Menus, and from Basalla, the mountain range of the Martu, fashioned them into steles, (and) erected them in courtyard of the Eninnu for him. He brought large blocks of alabaster from Tidanum, the mountain range of Martu, fashioned them into ferocious lions for him (Ningirsu), (and) installed them as (protective) door bolts(?) in the temple.

He mined copper in Abullat, the mountain range of Kimash, and fashioned it into the Shita(-weapon) that no region can endure.

He brought ebony wood from the land of Meluhha and used it to build for him, (and) he (also) brought blocks of hulalu-stones from there (and) fashioned them into a Shita(-club) with three lion heads for him. He brought gold ore from the mountain range of Hahum and used it to plate the Shita(-club) with three lion heads for him. He brought gold ore from the land of Meluhha and fashioned it into a quiver for him, (and) he (also) brought . . . from there. He brought oak wood from Gubin, the land of oak wood (and) fashioned it into the Sharur (= "leveler of all") bird (weapon) for him.

He brought a massive amount of bitumen from Madga, the mountain range of the Luruda(?) river and used it to build the retaining wall of the Eninnu, (and) he (also) brought Haum clay from there. He loaded stone slabs for him from the mountain range of Barme into great ships and brought them back(?) for the foundation of the Eninnu.

(vi 64–76) He struck the cities of Anshan and Elam with weapons and brought their spoil into the Eninnu for Ningirsu. On the day when Gudea, the ruler of Lagash, had (finished) building the Eninnu for Ningirsu, he made it (the booty) a permanent donation (to the temple).

(vi 77–vii 57) A ruler had never built a temple fashioned in this manner for Ningirsu, (but) he (Gudea) surely did built it. He inscribed the (or "his") name (on the temple), made the long enduring important things (of the temple) shine in (their) splendor, and acted faithfully on the spoken word of Ningirsu.

He brought a diorite stone from the land of Magan (and) shaped it into this stone statue. "I built his temple for my king; life is my reward" he named it for him (Ningirsu) and brought it into the Eninnu for him. (Then) Gudea gave (the following) command to the statue: "O Statue, when you speak to my king (say this): 'On the day when I built for him the Eninnu, his beloved temple, I remitted debts and washed all hands (of such obligations). For seven days no grain was ground, the slave girl was equal with her mistress, (and) the slave stood at his master's side. The unclean person in my city laid down (only) outside; I turned all evil back from their houses. I paid close attention to the laws of Nanshe and Ningirsu: the orphan was not given over to the wealthy man; the widow was not given over to the powerful man; (and) in the house with no (male) heir its daughter became its heir.'" He installed the statue with this command.

The statue is (made of) neither precious metal nor lapis lazuli; from neither copper nor tin nor bronze did the man sculpt it. Being of diorite stone (only), let it stand at the place of libations! Let no man arrogantly destroy it.

(vii 58–xi 30) "O statue, your eye is (that) of Ningirsu. The statue of Gudea, the ruler of Lagash, the man who built the Eninnu of Ningirsu, the man who removes it from the Eninnu; who rubs out its inscription; the man who demolishes it; the man who, at the beginning of the new year, Ningirsu, my king, will have proclaimed in the public assembly (as) his god, but my judgment has altered; who revokes my gifts; who deletes my name from my collection of songs (and) put there his name; who cuts of its (the statue's) prescribed offerings in the courtyard of my king Ningirsu; who does not recognize that since ancient days, since seed sprouted, a ruler of Lagash who will have built the Eninnu for his king Ningirsu, being a man who makes the long enduring important things (of the temple) shine in (their) splendor, no man shall change his spoken command (or) alter his judgment; the man who changes the command of Gudea, the ruler of Lagash (or) alters his judgment; let An, Enlil, Ninhursag, Enki, who speaks rightly, Sin, whose name no man can explain, Ninigirsu, the king of weapons, Nanshe, the lady of the boundary regions, Nindara, the master warrior, the mother of Lagash, holy Gatumdu, Baba (= Bau), the firstborn lady of An, Inanna, the lady of battle, Utu, the king of the shining sky, Hendursag, the herald of the land, Igalim, Shulshagana, Nin-MAR.KI, the firstborn of Nanshe, Dumuzi-abzu, the lord of the Kinunir, (and) my (personal) god Ningishzida – let them change his destiny.

On that very day let him be slain like an ox; let him be seized by his ferocious horns like a wild bull; let him sit down in the dust rather than on his throne that a man has set up for him; let understanding be taken away from the one who thinks he can rub out its inscription, (and) let his name be removed from the house of his (personal) god and from the tablet; let his (personal) god have no regard for his public wounds; let the rain from heaven be held back; let the ground water be held back; let him have years of need; let there be famine during his reign; that man, like a man who inflicts evil on a righteous man, let that (man's) end be like a flood from heaven(?) (and) let him never be set free. Let the land know the majesty of the broad chested one of the gods, the lord Ningirsu.

Commentary on Gudea Historical Texts

Gudea Statue I

(i 1–ii 13) Ningirsu was the chief deity of Lagash, but Enlil was the head of the Sumerian pantheon overall, to whom Ningirsu was subject. The term "king" in the Gudea texts refers to Ningirsu, since Gudea was a "ruler," not a "king." Ningishzida was Gudea's personal god, whose support he relied upon before all the other gods. The Anzu-bird was the thunderbird of the clouds who was considered to be the emblem of Ningirsu and the Eninnu temple of Ningirsu in Lagash. The EPA was the central chapel within the Eninnu.

Gudea Statue B

(i 1–20) Within the cultic procedures of the temple as a whole there was to be regular offering for this statue as well.

(ii 1–iii 14) The procedures for building the temple are given in great detail in Gudea Cylinder A.

(iii 15–v 11) The concern for eliminating impurity and social unrest stands out here. The time and place of the building of the temple were to be treated as sacred.

(v 21–vi 63) Here in Gudea Statue B the arrangement of the places from which materials were gathered, from the upper to the lower sea (i.e., from the upper eastern coast of Mediterranean Sea to the Arabian Sea down below the Persian Gulf), seems to run from the northwest to the southeast, from the Amanus mountains in northern Lebanon to Meluhha and Madga down the coast of the Persian Gulf and into the Arabian Sea. The summary of the collection given in Gudea Cylinder A xv 6–xvi 24 seems to be arranged more according to the materials themselves (i.e., generally from wood, to stone, to bitumen, and then to metals), rather than according to the regions from which they were brought.

(vi 64–76) The defeat of Anshan and Elam stands out here as an important historical reference to Gudea's conflicts with the people to the east, in modern-day Iran. Lagash, and Sumer as a whole, is located where Kuwait is today.

(vi 77–xi 30) The concern for the honoring of Statue B in terms of its regular offerings, protection from being effaced by a later ruler, and other commands of Gudea outlined on the statue shows his concern for his on-going posterity.

Bibliography (I)

For the history of Gudea and his dynasty see especially now the summary of the scholarly debate and conclusions in Douglas R. Frayne, *Ur III Period (2112–2004 BC)*, The Royal Inscriptions of Mesopotamia, Early Periods 3/2 (Toronto: University of Toronto Press, 1997), 5–7, and the scholarly literature cited there. For a good overall synthesis of the period from the end of Agade to the beginning of Ur III see Amélie Kuhrt, *The Ancient Near East c. 3000–300 BC* (London: Routledge, 1995), 44–70. A full modern transliteration and English translation of the Gudea texts with good introductions and some notes can be found in Dietz Otto Edzard, *Gudea and His Dynasty*, RIME. In addition to Edzard's volume, the translations from the Gudea Statues presented here take into consideration Horst Steible, *Die Neusumerischen Bau- und Weihinschriften*, Freiburger Altorientalische Studien 9 (Stuttgart: Steiner, 1991). For clear pictures of the Gudea Statues and helpful discussions of their artistic features see Flemming Johansen, *Statues of Gudea Ancient and Modern*, Mesopotamia 6 (Copenhagen: Akademisk Forlag, 1978).

II. Texts from the Ur III Period: ca. 2112–2004 BCE

The collapse of the Akkadian Empire brought chaos to Babylonia. Gutian invaders dealt the final blow, but it appears that their efforts were less successful in the south, where pockets of Sumerian resistance were strongest. According to the Sumerian King List (SKL), kingship was ultimately transferred to Uruk and subsumed under Utu-hegal, and this is supported by later copies of his inscriptions. The governor of Ur at this time was Ur-Namma (also called Ur-Nammu), a military general of Utu-hegal and perhaps his brother.[1] Under circumstances that remain unclear, Ur-Namma assumed kingship in Ur. This is third time in the SKL that hegemony was exercised from there, hence the phrase "Ur III."

The Ur III period is sometimes called the "Sumerian Renaissance," and for good reason. Sumerian again became the language of the administration, and Sumerian literary compositions were created and preserved on an unprecedented scale. With this came the establishment of the scribal school (Sumerian *eduba*, literally "house of the tablet") in the political and religious centers of the land.[2] Although there is evidence for Ur-Namma's hand in these developments, the real inspiration appears to have come from his son Shulgi, one of three kings in Mesopotamian history who claimed to have mastered writing.

Several texts from or dealing with the Ur III period are offered below. They provide a broad look at the political, socio-economic, and religious dimensions of the Sumerian state during its heyday.

Inscriptions of the Ur III Kings

Outside administrative texts, royal inscriptions are our primary source of contemporary evidence for the Ur III state. Like other royal inscriptions from ancient Mesopotamia, they record the military campaigns and building projects undertaken by the Ur III kings in a highly religious and congratulatory language. Most commemorate building and agricultural projects and are very short. They appear in various forms as foundation deposits; extremely common are brick inscriptions, many of which were made by carving a stamp in reverse and pressing it into the moist mud brick of the structure commemorated. The basic collections of Ur III inscriptions are Frayne 1997 and Steible 1991; Hallo's discussion of their typology remains indispensable (1962).

Bibliography (II introduction)

Flückiger-Hawker, E. *Urnamma of Ur in Sumerian Literary Tradition.* Orbis Biblicus et Orientalis 166. Fribourg, Switzerland: University Fribourg, 1999.

Sallaberger, W. "Ur III Zeit." In *Mesopotamien: Akkade-Zeit und Ur III-Zeit.* Ed. P. Attinger and M. Wäfler. Orbis Biblicus et Orientalis 160/3. Fribourg, Switzerland: University Fribourg, 1999, 119–390.

Frayne, D. R. *Ur III Period (2112–2004* BC*).* RIME

Hallo, W. W. "The Royal Inscriptions of Ur: A Typology." *Hebrew Union College Annual* 33 (1962): 1–43.

Steible, H. *Die neusumerischen Bau- und Weihinschriften.* Freiburger altorientalische Studien 9/1–2. Stuttgart: Steiner, 1991.

A. Ur-Namma: ca. 2112–2095 BCE *(Studevent-Hickman)*

25. The restoration of the temple wall named Etemennigur ("the temple 'platform clad in ominousness'")

Ur-Namma enjoyed a relatively peaceful reign, which allowed him to undertake massive agricultural and building projects.[3] His role as the royal builder par excellence is well attested in both the textual and iconographic records.[4]

Understandably, one of Ur-Namma's first priorities was the renovation of the temple complex of Ur's patron deity, the moon-god Nanna (Akkadian Su'en). Within the larger complex stood the Etemennigur, the temenos or platform for the ziggurat. Two versions of an inscription commemorating its renovation are preserved: one on cones recovered from the temenos wall as foundation deposits, another on the mud bricks themselves. A translation of each appears below.

The cone inscription (Frayne 1997: 31–4; Steible 1991: 97–8):

> *For Nanna (the wild calf of An, the eldest son of Enlil, his [Ur-Namma's] master), Ur-Namma (the mighty man, the king of Ur) built his [Nanna's] Etemennigur.*

The brick inscription (Frayne 1997: 35; Steible 1991: 104–5):

> *For Nanna (the eldest son of Enlil, his [Ur-Namma's] master), Ur-Namma (the mighty man, the lord of Uruk, the king of Ur, the king of Sumer and Akkad) built the Etemennigur, his [Nanna's] beloved temple, [and] restored it.*[5]

These inscriptions raise several issues of interest to scholars. Nanna is called the "wild calf" of An, the chief god of the heavens – indeed, the heavens themselves. Nanna's association with a bull is well attested and self-evident: the crescent moon looks very much like a bull's horns. His relationship to Enlil, the chief god of Nippur, is also an important datum not only for the ancient Mesopotamian religious tradition but also for the political realities that underlay them.

The titulary is a constant source of interest, particularly when it varies in copies of the same inscription. In the first inscription Ur-Namma is called simply "the king of Ur." In the second he is also called "the lord [Sumerian *en*] of Uruk" and "the king of Sumer and Akkad." "Lord of Uruk" has a complex religious and political tradition (Steinkeller 1999); the fact that it appears here but not in the first inscription may suggest that Utu-hegal has died (see above), allowing Ur-Namma to adopt the title. "King of Sumer and Akkad" suggests hegemony over all of Babylonia, and it is well known that kings needed the approval of Enlil in Nippur to validate this form of kingship. This inevitably involved a trip to Nippur, and such a trip is attested for Ur-Namma in a hymn very much concerned with his legitimation (Flückiger-Hawker 1999: 204–27, see esp. lines 103–14). Since he adopts this epithet in the second of these inscriptions, he may have gone to Nippur during the renovation of the Etemennigur (Frayne 1997: 12). Indeed, some scholars divide his inscriptions chronologically based on the absence or presence of this title (Hallo 1957: 77–83). While none of these matters can be confirmed with certainty, they illustrate well the subtleties of these texts and the information potentially available when they are considered within the larger sociopolitical and religious context of Sumerian kingship.

Bibliography (II A)

Canby, J. V. *The "Ur-Nammu" Stela*. University Museum Monograph 110. Philadelphia: University of Pennsylvania Museum of Archaeology and Anthropology, 2001.

Frayne, D. R. *Ur III Period (2112–2004 BC)*. RIME, 31–5 (no. E3/2.1.1.11 and E3/2.1.1.12).

Hallo, W. W. *Early Mesopotamian Royal Titles: A Philologic and Historical Analysis*. American Oriental Series 43. New Haven: Yale University Press, 1957.

Sallaberger, W. "Ur III Zeit." In *Mesopotamien: Akkade-Zeit und Ur III-Zeit*. Ed. P. Attinger and M. Wäfler. Orbis Biblicus et Orientalis 160/3. Fribourg, Switzerland: University Fribourg, 1999, 119–390.

Steible, H. *Die neusumerischen Bau- und Weihinschriften*. 2 vols. Freiburger altorientalische Studien 9/1–2. Stuttgart: Steiner, 1991, 2: 97–8 (Urnammu 4) 2: 104–5 (Urnammu 10).

Steinkeller, P. "On Rulers, Priests and Sacred Marriage: Tracing the Evolution of Early Sumerian Kingship." *Priests and Officials in the Ancient Near East: Papers of the Second Colloquium on the Ancient Near East – The City and its Life Held at the Middle Eastern Culture Center in Japan (Mitaka, Tokyo) March 22–24, 1996*. Ed. K. Watanabe. Heidelberg: Winter, 1999, 103–37.

B. Shulgi: ca. 2094–2047 BCE (Studevent-Hickman)

26. The construction of the Eninnu ("Fifty House") for Ningirsu

Shulgi is often considered to be the real architect of the Ur III state and the major catalyst for its progress in the literary arts. We are much better informed about this king; indeed, the major accomplishments of each of his nearly 50-year reign are known from year names (*History* 61 Box 4.1). Shulgi devoted his early efforts primarily to cultic establishments and building projects for the crown. The second half of his reign saw the first real expansion of the state outside Babylonia. Military campaigns were largely confined to the east and were clearly successful. As with Ur-Namma, Shulgi's ambitions and successes were reflected in the titulary, where he adopted the phrase "king of the four corners."

Like Ur-Namma's inscriptions, Shulgi's are generally quite short and equally formulaic. One inscription commemorates the building of the Eninnu, Ningirsu's temple in the province of Lagash. The inscription was discovered during excavations in Girsu, the capital city of the province, and was written with minor variants on several media, including cones, a foundation tablet, and copper canephors.

> *For Ningirsu (the mighty hero of Enlil, his [Shulgi's] master), Shulgi (the mighty man, the king of Ur, the king of Sumer and Akkad) built the Eninnu, his [Ningirsu's] beloved temple.*

Though short the inscription raises two important points. First, Shulgi's name bears the divine determinative. Like Naram-Suen, Shulgi deified himself, and all indications suggest he did so between his tenth and twenty-first regnal years (Sallaberger 1999: 152 with n. 99), coincidentally enough at the onset of the aforementioned expansion and various other reforms he introduced in the administration (Steinkeller 1987; cf. Sallaberger 1999: 148). Second, the Eninnu had been built recently by Gudea, a local ruler of Lagash well known for his statues and cylinders (*History* 67).[6] The date of Gudea and his dynasty is among the more hotly debated topics in Sumerian history, his reign overlapping that of Ur-Namma or coming slightly before it (Flückiger-Hawker 1999: 2–4 with bibliography). As in Japanese tradition, Sumerian temples were restored on a regular basis, so perhaps this illustrates the period between the time Gudea built the temple and the time Shulgi renovated it.

Bibliography (II B)

Edzard, D. O. *Gudea and His Dynasty*. RIME 3/1, 1997.

Flückiger-Hawker, E. *Urnamma of Ur in Sumerian Literary Tradition*. Orbis Biblicus et Orientalis 166. Fribourg, Switzerland: University Fribourg, 1999.

Frayne, D. R. *Ur III Period (2112–2004 BC)*. RIME 3/2, 1997, 120–2 (E3/2.1.2.11 and E3/2.1.2.12).

Sallaberger, W. "Ur III Zeit." In *Mesopotamien: Akkade-Zeit und Ur III-Zeit.* Ed. P. Attinger and M. Wäfler. Orbis Biblicus et Orientalis 160/3. Fribourg, Switzerland: University Fribourg, 1999, 119–390.

Steible, H. *Die neusumerischen Bau- und Weihinschriften.* 2 vols. Freiburger altorientalische Studien 9/1–2. Stuttgart: Steiner, 1991, 2: 167–8 (Shulgi 15), 2: 176 (Shulgi 23).

Steinkeller, P. "The Administrative and Economic Organization of the Ur III State: The Core and the Periphery." In *The Organization of Power: Aspects of Bureaucracy in the Ancient Near East.* Ed. M. Gibson and R. D. Biggs. Chicago: University of Chicago Press, 1987, 19–41.

Suter, C. E. *Gudea's Temple Building: The Representation of an Early Mesopotamian Ruler in Text and Image.* Cuneiform Monographs 17. Leiden: Brill, 2000.

Van De Mieroop, M., *A History of the Ancient Near East ca. 3000–323 BC.* Oxford: Blackwell, 2004.

C. Amar-Suen: ca. 2046–2038 BCE (Studevent-Hickman)

27. The construction of the *gipar* and the installation of the *en*-priestess for Nanna of Karzida

Amar-Suen is probably best known as the son of Shulgi,[7] but his reign was not without its own accomplishments. Aside from building projects and military campaigns to the east, Amar-Suen initiated several reforms in the administration, including the use of a unified calendar in the political and religious centers of the state.

Amar-Suen's best-attested accomplishments were in the cultic domain, at least according to his royal inscriptions. Four of the nine regnal years are named for the installation of various en-priestesses in Sumer, a highly symbolic religious and political act generally connected to the Akkadian king Sargon, who installed his daughter En-hedu-ana into the office at Ur (*History* 62; cf. ch. 2 in this volume). An inscription commemorating the construction of the *gipar*, the residence of the enpriestess, and her installation is translated below. In this case the act is for Nanna of Karzida, presumably in the town of Gaesh. According to the name of Amar-Suen's ninth year, he installed the en-priestess of Nanna of Karzida three times (Sigrist and Gomi 1991: 326). Evidence for two of these is available from administrative texts (Sallaberger 1999: 164).

> *For Nanna of Karzida, his beloved master, Amar-Suen–the one whose name was revealed in Nippur, the caretaker of the temple of Enlil (the true god, the sun-god of his land),[8] the mighty king, the king of Ur, the king of the four corners – [did the following]: For a very long time no gipar was built in Karzida, and no en-priestess lived in it. Amar-Suen, the beloved of Nanna, built the resplendent gipar for him [and] installed his [Nanna's] beloved en-priestess in it. Amar-Suen [thus] lengthened [his] days [and] dedicated it for his life.*

Bibliography (II C)

Beckman, G. "'My Sun-God': Reflections of Mesopotamian Conceptions of Kingship among the Hittites." In *Ideologies as Intercultural Phenomena: Proceedings of the Third Annual Symposium of the Assyrian and Babylonian Intellectual Heritage Project Held in Chicago, USA, October 27–31, 2000*. Ed. A. Panaino and G. Pettinato. Melammu Symposia 3. Milan: University of Bologna, 2002, 37–43.

Boese, J. and W. Sallaberger. "Apil-kin von Mari und die Könige der III. Dynastie von Ur." *Altorientalische Forschungen* 23 (1996): 24–39.

Frayne, D. R. *Ur III Period (2112–2004 BC)*. RIME 3/2, 1997, 262–4 (E3/2.1.3.16).

Sigrist, M. and T. Ozaki (GOMI). *The Comprehensive Catalogue of Published Ur III Tablets*. Bethesda, MD: CDL Press, 1991.

Steible, H. *Die neusumerischen Bau- und Weihinschriften*. 2 vols. Freiburger altorientalische Studien 9/1–2. Stuttgart: Steiner, 1991, 2: 229–30 (Amarsuen 6), 2: 236–8 (Amarsuen 11), and 250–1 (Amarsuen 21).

D. Shu-Suen: ca. 2037–2029 BCE (Studevent-Hickman)

28. The construction of the Eshagepada ("temple revealed by the heart") for the god Shara

Aside from reforms in the administration, Shu-Suen is best known for his efforts to keep Amorite invaders out of Sumer. Two of his year names (Shu-Suen 4 and 5) commemorate the building of a wall or string of fortresses called "Muriq Tidnim"; that is, "the one that keeps out the Amorites." We know surprisingly little about this project, but it appears to have finished one started by Shulgi, whose thirty-seventh and thirty-eighth regnal years commemorate the construction of the "wall of the land." Aside from Shu-Suen's year names, the only contemporary evidence for this project is a royal inscription commemorating the completion of the temple of the god Shara in the province of Umma.[9] A translation of that inscription appears below; a discussion of the Muriq-Tidnim wall in terms of the larger military strategy of the Ur III kings is in preparation by P. Michalowski.

For Shara (the noble one of An, the beloved son of Inanna, his [Shu-Suen's] father), Shu-Suen (the purification priest of An, the anointed priest – clean of hand – of Enlil and Ninlil and of the great gods, the king whom Enlil affectionately revealed in his heart as shepherd of the land, the mighty king, the king of Ur, the king of the four corners) built the Eshagepada, his [Shara's] beloved temple, for his [Shu-Suen's] life when he built the Amorite wall Muriq-Tidnim [and] turned back the paths of the Amorites to their land.

Bibliography (II D)

Edzard, D. O. "Deux lettres royales d'Ur III en sumérien 'syllabique' et pourvu d'une traduction accadienne." In *Textes littéraires de Susa*. Ed. R. Labat and D. O. Edzard.

Mémoires de la délégation archéologique en Iran, Mission de Susiane 57/Suse Ville Royale 11. Paris: P. Geuthner, 1974, 9–34.
Frayne, D. R. *Ur III Period (2112–2004 BC)*. RIME 3/2, 1997, 327–8 (E3/2.1.4.17).
Steible, H. *Die neusumerischen Bau- und Weihinschriften*. 2 vols. Freiburger altorientalische Studien 9/1–2. Stuttgart: Steiner, 1991, 2: 260–2 (Susuen 9).

E. Ibbi-Suen: ca. 2028–2004 BCE (Studevent-Hickman)

29. The construction of the "great wall" around Nippur and Ur

The last king of the Ur III state was Ibbi-Suen, the son of Shu-Suen. By the third of his 25 regnal years the state had clearly begun to disintegrate. Texts from the best-attested archives suddenly ceased, and several cities under Ibbi-Suen's control no longer used his year names to date their records. Around this time commodities in Ur and elsewhere grew outrageously expensive, making the end all the more palpable (Jacobsen 1953; Gomi 1984).

Foreign invaders were certainly a catalyst to the fall of Ur and led to its ultimate destruction. Both Amorite and Elamite incursions penetrated the Sumerian heartland in the early stages of Ibbi-Suen's reign. For this reason, perhaps, he surrounded both Nippur and Ur with massive walls. It appears they were completed around the same time: together they give Ibbi-Suen's sixth year its name. The wall at Ur is the only building project from Ibbi-Suen's reign commemorated in a royal inscription, making this the last building inscription from the Ur III period.

> *Ibbi-Suen (the god of his land, the mighty king, the king of Ur, the king of the four corners), by the beloved greatness of Suen, set out to enlarge Ur. To that end, to fortify the land [and] to subdue the lower and upper [lands], he surrounded his city with a massive wall . . . [and] revealed the place for its foundation deposit. As for the wall, its name is Ibbi-Suen-gugal-namnuna ("Ibbi-Suen is the canal inspector of princeliness").*

Bibliography (II E)

Frayne, D. R. *Ur III Period (2112–2004 BC)*. RIME 3/2, 1997, 368–9 (E3/2.1.5.1).
Gomi, T. "On the Critical Economic Situation at Ur Early in the Reign of Ibbisin." *Journal of Cuneiform Studies* 36 (1984): 211–42.
Jacobsen, T. "The Reign of Ibbi-Suen." *Journal of Cuneiform Studies* 7 (1953): 36–47.
Steible, H. Die neusumerischen Bau- und Weihinschriften. 2 vols. Freiburger altorientalische Studien 9/1–2. Stuttgart: Steiner, 1991, 2: 279–81 (Ibbi-Suen 1–2).
Wilcke, C. "Drei Phasen des Niedergangs des Reiches von Ur III." *Zeitschrift für Assyriologie* 60 (1970): 54–69.

F. Royal hymns of the Ur III kings (Studevent-Hickman)

One of the real innovations of the Ur III period is the so-called royal hymn. The genre has been defined in various ways; often one will see references to

Type A and Type B hymns (Klein 1981: 21–49). Type A texts are essentially divine hymns on behalf of a given king. In Type B hymns the king *is* the object of the praise, which is often delivered in the first person. For identification purposes only, royal hymns bear generic titles formed by the name of the king in question followed by a letter of the alphabet (e.g., Ur-Namma A, Shulgi D, etc.).

Royal hymns were very popular in the Old Babylonian period, being adopted above all for the kings of Isin, the seat of kingship after the fall of the Ur III state (Römer 1965). The overwhelming number of copies of Ur III royal hymns date to this period. Though written and preserved well after the fall of the Ur III state, they nevertheless provide valuable insights into the lives of the Ur III kings and the traditions that grew up around them. Two of the more famous hymns are offered in translation below; other hymns and many other Sumerian literary compositions are available online from the Electronic Text Corpus of Sumerian Literature <http://etcsl.orinst.ox.ac.uk/>.[10]

Bibliography (II F)

Jacobsen, T. *The Harps That Once . . . : Sumerian Poetry in Translation.* New Haven: Yale University Press, 1987.

Klein, J. *Three Šulgi Hymns: Sumerian Royal Hymns Glorifying King Šulgi of Ur.* Ramat-Gan: Bar-Ilan University Press, 1981.

Römer, W. H. P. *Sumerische "Königshymnen" der Isin-Zeit.* Documenta et monumenta Orientis antiqui 13. Leiden: Brill, 1965.

30. Shulgi's journey to Nippur

One of Shulgi's most famous claims appears in the royal hymn known as Shulgi A.[11] In this composition the king claims to have traveled from Nippur to Ur and back in a single day. At roughly one-hundred miles each way, this was a truly unbelievable feat, indeed, one of Shulgi's year names commemorates the event or one very similar to it.[12]

Shulgi's quickness and endurance are the focus of the hymn from the very beginning. The text opens with the so-called -me-en or "I am" section typical of the Type B royal hymn; even here several of the epithets foreshadow the journey.

I am the king. From the womb I have been a hero.
I am Shulgi. From the time I was born I have been a mighty man.
I am the lion with a ferocious look born by the dragon.
I am the king of the four corners.
I am the keeper, the shepherd of the black-headed ones.[13]
I am the noble one, the god of all the lands.
I am the child born of Ninsun.
I am the one revealed by the heart of holy An.

I am the man of a fate decreed of Enlil.
I am Shulgi, the beloved of Ninlil.
I am the one nurtured faithfully by Nintu.
I am the one given wisdom of Enki.
I am the mighty king of Nanna.
I am the roaring lion of Utu.
I am Shulgi, whose charms are revealed of Inanna.
I am the mule suitable for the road.
I am the horse, [its] tail wagging on the campaign trail.
I am the stallion of Shakan, prepared for the race.
I am the scribe of Nisaba, exceeding in wisdom.

The Ur III kings, like other kings from ancient Mesopotamia, claimed extremely close relationships to the gods of the pantheon in their titularies. The phrase "child born of Ninsun" raises two important points. First, it may be a reference to Shulgi's own divine status. In another Shulgi hymn, Ninsun adopts him, thus making him a god.[14] Second, as the son of Ninsun, Shulgi becomes Gilgamesh's brother. The Ur III kings routinely stressed their ties to Uruk, among other things calling themselves the "brothers of Gilgamesh." Without a doubt this reflects the fact that the Ur III state has its roots there: Ur-Namma, the founder of the dynasty, started as a military general of Utuhegal, who established kingship in Uruk after the Gutian period (see above).

After the requisite phrases in which he expounds his love of wisdom and truth, Shulgi boasts of his accomplishments in preparing the roads of his kingdom. According to the hymn, he established rest stops and other amenities for travelers. It is in this context that his initial desire to make the trip from Nippur to Ur is unveiled.

To establish my name forever, that it never fall from speech,
to build my fame in the land,
to proclaim my glory in all the lands,
I built up my mighty strength as a runner, and, to exercise this speed,
my heart made me to go from Nippur to the brickwork of Ur altogether as if it were a single mile.
I am the lion that never tires in its youthfulness [but] stands firm.
I put the . . . garment on my hips [and]
like a dove flying . . . did I wave my arms.
Like the Anzu-bird raising its eyes to the mountains did I open my stride.
[The residents of] my cities established in the countryside stood [alongside].
The black-headed people, numerous as ewes, did show [their] admiration.

According to this passage, the journey from Nippur went rather smoothly; one even gets the image of the Boston Marathon or the Tour de France, given all the onlookers. Things went equally well in Ur. Upon arriving, Shulgi entered the Ekishnugal, the temple complex of Nanna, and performed the appropriate sacrifices and rituals. The trip back to Nippur would not go as smoothly. As is common in Sumerian literature, the moment things turn is introduced by the phrase "at that time":

I indeed rose like a . . . bird
[and] returned to Nippur in my jubilation.
At that time, a storm [began to] rage [and] the west wind swirled.
The north wind and the south wind howled together.
With the seven winds lightning consumed everything in the heavens.
The raging storm did shake the earth.
Ishkur[15] *indeed thundered in the vast heavens.*
The [storm] clouds of heaven did mingle[?] with the waters of earth.
Their small stones [and] their big stones
pelted my back, [but],
since I am the king, I did not fear. I was not scared.
Like an impending lion I showed my ferocity[?].
Like a wild donkey I ran . . .

But he does make it back to Nippur, apparently before sunset.

[Before] Utu set his sights on his house,
I indeed completed a fifteen-mile stretch.
My . . . priest gazed upon me.
In one day I verily perform the . . . festivals[?] in Nippur and Ur.

At the completion of his journey Shulgi enjoyed a banquet with the gods Utu and Inanna. Predictably, his journey ended in the Ekur, the temple of Enlil in Nippur, where he performed a variety of acts symbolizing the legitimacy and consolidation of his kingship. The text ends with a short praise to Shulgi typical of the royal hymns:

Shulgi, who continual destroys the foreign lands [and] strengthens the land,
the purification priest of heaven and earth [who] has no rival;
Shulgi, the one nurtured by the noble son of An.
Nisaba be praised!

As is often the case in literary compositions, Nisaba, the goddess of writing and the scribal art, receives the final praise.

Bibliography (II F: 30)

Klein, J. *Three Šulgi Hymns: Sumerian Royal Hymns Glorifying King Šulgi of Ur.* Ramat-Gan: Bar-Ilan University Press, 1981.

Sigrist, M. and T. Gomi. *The Comprehensive Catalogue of Published Ur III Tablets.* Bethesda: CDL, 1991.

31. The death of Ur-Namma

One of the most unusual texts dealing with the Ur III kings is the so-called "Death of Ur-Namma," which is preserved in Old Babylonian copies from Nippur and Susa. It adopts elements from broad range of genres in Sumerian literature – above all lamentation literature (see Flückiger-Hawker 1999: 85–91; cf. Kramer 1967: 104). However, the text is categorized by scholars as a royal hymn; hence the title Ur-Namma A.

The text opens with the setting in which Ur-Namma died:

Evil entered Ur [and] brought the faithful shepherd out of it.
It brought the faithful shepherd Ur-Namma out of the city.
[The god] An altered the holy command he had established, it was an empty promise[?];
In deceit Enlil overturned the fate he had established.
Ninmah established lamentations . . .
Enki sealed off the great door of Eridu.
Nudimmud entered the bedroom [and] lay down.
Nanna grew exceedingly angry at the holy[?] command of An.
Utu does not rise in the sky; the day hangs in despair.
The mother, living in misery for her son,
the mother of the king, holy Ninsumun, says "O My heart!"
Because of the fate she determined [for?] Ur-Namma,
because it brought out the faithful shepherd,
they wept bitter tears in the broad square, the place where there is celebration.
The happiness of humanity had come to an end, [and] they do not sleep well.
They pass the day in lamentation of their faithful shepherd.

For reasons that are entirely unclear, both An and Enlil reneged on pronouncements they had made, and it appears that the other deities could do little but react to this news. Ur-Namma died, and this had an instant and devastating effect on the abundance of the land (note Hallo 1991). The portion of text narrating his death is unfortunately plagued by lacunae, but we do learn about his fate when his body is brought back to Ur:

Ur-Namma, the king of the land, approached the "House of Fury"[16]
He approached Ur and Ur-Namma entered the "House of the Siege"[?].
The noble one lay down in his palace.
Ur-Namma, the one beloved by the troops, can no longer raise his head.
The wise one of all the lands lay down, a stillness enters.[17]
The pride of the land has fallen; it is cut down like a mountain.
Like a grove of apples[?], it is [now] barren; its appearance is changed.
. . .
Ur-Namma, the son of Nin-sumun, went in his prime.[18]
The troops who went with the king returned lamenting.
Their boat was sunk in a land as foreign to him as Dilmun.[19]

The passage suggests that Ur-Namma was brought back to Ur to be buried. As it happens, there is considerable textual and archaeological evidence to support the fact that several – if not all – of the Ur III kings were buried there. What is more revealing is the nature of the burial itself. This is outlined in the following section:

His donkeys dwelt with him; the donkeys were buried with him.
His donkeys dwelt with Ur-Namma; the donkeys were buried with him.
He crossed the . . . of the land; the pride of the land was changed.[20]
The road he took to the netherworld was desolate.
. . . the chariot was covered; the road was difficult [so] he could not proceed [easily].

This description raises several important points concerning the ancient Mesopotamian concepts of death and the afterlife. First, there was indeed a life after death in the Mesopotamian conceptual framework: Virtually everyone went to the netherworld, a dismal place known above all as the "land of no return." Second, Ur-Namma takes a journey to get there, a motif that is well documented for humans and deities alike. Finally, it is clear from this passage that Ur-Namma was buried with his retinue and, as we learn later, various other accoutrements. This is precisely what one finds in the many graves that have been excavated in Mesopotamia, and in some cases the items that accompany the deceased can be quite lavish.[21] The purpose of these goods remains a topic of debate among scholars, but the "Death of Ur-Namma" provides some possible answers:

He gives gifts to the seven porters of the netherworld . . .
the famous kings who had died.
The dead purification priest . . . priest, and en-priestess who had been selected by extispicy . . .
informed the people of the king's arrival, [and] a din was established in the netherworld.
They informed the people of Ur-Namma's arrival and a din was established in the netherworld.
[Whereupon] the king slaughtered oxen and sacrificed sheep.
On Ur-Namma's account they sat at the largest table.
The food of the netherworld is bitter; the water of the netherworld is brackish.
The faithful shepherd learned the proper order of the netherworld.
Ur-Namma learned the proper order of the netherworld.
The king sacrificed the offerings of the netherworld
Ur-Namma sacrificed the offerings of the netherworld.
Blemishless bulls, blemishless goats, [and] grain-fed sheep, as many as [could be] led in.

As the first few lines suggest, the items that accompany the dead in their burials may be intended to serve as gifts in the netherworld (see Tinney 1998 for this specific connection). Indeed, a large section of the text that follows is devoted to the various gifts that Ur-Namma gave to the deities there. In many cases the meanings of the terms used for these items are unclear, but a few examples may be offered here:

A mace, a large bow [with] quiver and arrow, a skillfully made flint[?] dagger,
and a speckled leather bag which was at [his] hip,
the shepherd, Ur-Namma, sacrificed to Nergal, the Enlil of the netherworld,[22] *in his [Nergal's] palace.*
A dagger, a leather bag made [for] the saddle, [and] a . . . mace (the lion of heaven),
a leather shield lying against the ground (the strength of heroism), [and] an ax (a cherished item of Ereshkigal),
the shepherd Ur-Namma sacrificed to Gilgamesh, the king of the netherworld, in his [Gilgamesh's] palace.
A container in which he had poured oil, a bowl perfectly [made],
a heavy garment, a fleecy garment, a . . . garment of queenship . . .
the shepherd Ur-Namma sacrificed to Ereshkigal, the mother of Ninazu, in her palace . . .

The list goes on to include other netherworld deities, among them Dumuzi, Namtar (the vizier of Ereshkigal), Hushbisag (the wife of Namtar), Ningishzida, Dimpi(me)kug, Ninazimua, and Geshtinana (Dumuzi's brother). Of particular interest is the presence of Gilgamesh, whose connection to the Ur III kings was noted above.

After the accounting of Ur-Namma's gifts the text returns to Ur-Namma's conditions in the netherworld:

After the king put . . . [the sacrifices] of the netherworld in order,
after Ur-Namma put . . . [the sacrifices] of the netherworld in order . . .
they enthroned Ur-Namma on the great dais of the netherworld.
They established a dwelling place in the netherworld for him.
By the command of Ereshkigal,
the troops . . . who were killed by the weapon,
and all the captives who were known[?],
were given to the king.[23]
. . . .
For his beloved brother Gilgamesh,
he himself judges the cases of the netherworld and makes the decisions of the netherworld.

As it appears, Ur-Namma himself was fitted with a palace by the order of Ereshkigal, Nergal's wife and the chief goddess of the netherworld. Moreover, he was given a position alongside Gilgamesh, who serves as the judge of the dead lords (Sumerian *en*) there.

But Ur-Namma's attention to matters in his new home is short-lived. Within a few days the lamentations of his people reached him, and he is forced to contemplate the joys of life among the living, joys he will no longer experience:

When seven days, even ten, had passed.
The wailing of Sumer reached my king.
The wailing of Sumer reached Ur-Namma.
Since he had not finished the wall of Ur,
since he had verily build the new palace [but] did not [get to] enjoy it,
since the shepherd did not perfect his house,
since he could no longer take pleasure of his wife in his lap,
since he no longer bounced his sons on his knee,
since he no longer developed the charms of the young sisters he raised . . .
O My lord, his heart sinking, weeps bitter tears.
The faithful shepherd utters a silent [lament] for himself:
"When I, myself, did these things,
standing before the gods and providing for them,
[my work] emerging in abundance for the chief deities;
when I set up treasures for them, beds spread with lapis and straw[?],
no god stood with me; my heart was not soothed.
I am . . . an auspicious sign [was] as distant as the heavens.
[Now] what have I received in serving . . . standing by day?
In standing by night [and] not sleeping my days are never ending."

The text goes on to describe how Ur-Namma cannot return to Ur from the netherworld. As a result, his wife – now a widow – wails for him, and it appears that a similar fate befalls her.

But what is more striking about the above passage is the view of the world Ur-Namma so boldly articulates. Much like Job or Ecclesiastes, Ur-Namma is upset because all of the good deeds he has performed for the gods are pointless – the gods do not ultimately look with favor upon him but let him die a premature death. True, divine abandonment is the source of catastrophe in ancient Mesopotamia, but it is extremely rare to find an individual not taking responsibility for having upset the gods.

Ultimately, Inanna hears what has happened to Ur-Namma, and is visibly upset:

Inanna, the fierce storm, the eldest child of Suen . . .
Making the heavens rumble [and] the earth quake.
Inanna destroyed the cattle pen and devastated the sheepfold [saying]:
"Let me curse An, the king of the gods.
When Enlil has raised someone, who [can] alter that command?
Who has altered the magnificent utterance of An, the king?
When designs have been verily established in the land, [and] they have not been observed,
there can be no abundance for the gods at the place where the sun rises,
the holy gipar, my sanctuary of the Eanna . . . like a mountain.
O that my shepherd would bring in his allure! I must not enter it.
That my mighty one could grow for me like fragrant herbs in the steppe.
That he could hold firm for me like a riverboat in a calm harbor."
Inanna indeed observed[?] his lament.

Irrational – perhaps better inappropriate – behavior is typical of Inanna, the goddess of love and war. In this case, she appears to be upset because she will no longer enjoy the sacred marriage ceremony with Ur-Namma (Flückiger-Hawker 1999: 180).[24] This forms yet another connection between the Ur III kings and the religious and political dynamics of rulership in ancient Uruk.

The end of the text is heavily damaged. It includes a short passage apparently extoling Ur-Namma for his various building activities (e.g., canals he had excavated, the tracts of land he created by draining areas of the marshland, etc.). These, we must presume, are what led to his relatively comfortable surroundings in the netherworld – a compromise, perhaps, for the unfairness Ur-Namma experienced while alive.

Bibliography (II F: 31)

Flückiger-Hawker, E. *Urnamma of Ur in Sumerian Literary Tradition.* Orbis Biblicus et Orientalis 166. Fribourg, Switzerland: University of Fribourg, 1999.

Hallo, W. W. "The Death of Kings: Traditional Historiography in Contextual Perspective." In *Ah Assyria . . . : Studies in Assyrian History and Ancient Near Eastern Historiography Presented to Hayim Tadmor.* Jerusalem: Magnes, 1991, 148–65.

Jacobsen, T. "The Sacred Marriage of Iddin-Dagan and Inanna." In *The Context of Scripture.* Ed. W. W. Hallo. 3 vols. Leiden: Brill, 2003, 3: 554–9 (no. 1.173).

Kramer, S. N. *The Sacred Marriage Rite: Aspects of Faith, Myth, and Ritual in Ancient Sumer.* Bloomington: Indiana University Press, 1969.

——. "The Death of Ur-Nammu and His Descent to the Netherworld." *Journal of Cuneiform Studies* 21 (1967): 104–122.

Steinkeller, P. "On Rulers, Priests and Sacred Marriage: Tracing the Evolution of Early Sumerian Kingship." *Priests and Officials in the Ancient Near East: Papers of the Second Colloquium on the Ancient Near East – The City and its Life held at the Middle Eastern Culture Center in Japan (Mitaka, Tokyo) March 22–24, 1996.* Ed. K. Watanabe. Heidelberg: Winter, 1999, 103–37.

Tinney, S. "Death and Burial in Early Mesopotamia: The View from the Texts." In *Treasures from the Royal Tombs of Ur.* Ed. R. L. Zettler and L. Horne. Philadelphia: University of Pennsylvania, Museum of Archaeology and Anthropology, 1998, 26–8.

32. The death of Shulgi

The Ur III period is perhaps best known for the massive number of administrative and legal texts it generated. As of this publication, some 65,000 texts covering roughly 40 years of bureaucratic activity have been published, and there may be twice to three times as many in museums and private collections still waiting to be examined. For the most part these texts were used to calculate payments in goods and services by provincial officials (Steinkeller 1987; Sharlach 2004). When pieced together, they provide unbelievable detail concerning the social and economic conditions of southern Babylonia at this time.

On rare occasions a single administrative text can provide exceptional information. One text from Puzrish-Dagan, modern Drehem, records the work of several female slaves for a very special occasion:

[20][25] minus 1 female slaves,
2 female slaves at two-thirds output,
for seven days.
Their (total) output: 142 1/3 female slaves for one day,
on the day that Shulgi ascended into heaven . . .
Month: "The festival of Mekigal" [month 11]
Year: Harshi and Kimash were destroyed [Shulgi 48]

The critical phrase is "on the day that Shulgi ascended into heaven," which raises two important issues. First, the phrase provides an important witness to the Mesopotamian belief that deified kings did not die; rather, they ascended to heaven and took up residence there as stars. Second, it provides a valuable datum for the precise date of Shulgi's death. A separate text dated to the second day of the same month records a libation place at Shulgi's grave (Michalowski 1977). Since this text was drawn up after the work was completed, and since this text is also dated to the eleventh month of Shulgi's forty-eighth year, it follows that Shulgi died on either the first or second day of the month.[26]

Bibliography (II F: 32)

Frayne, D. R. *Ur III Period (2112–2004 BC)*. RIME 3/2, 1997.
Hallo, W. W. "The Death of Shulgi." In COS, 2003, 3: 315 (no. 3.143).
Michalowski, P. "The Death of Shulgi." *Orientalia* NS 46 (1977): 220–5.
Sallaberger, W. "Ur III Zeit." In *Mesopotamien: Akkade-Zeit und Ur III-Zeit*. Ed. P. Attinger and M. Wäfler. Orbis Biblicus et Orientalis 160/3. Fribourg: Steiner, 1999, 119–390.
Sharlach, T. M. *Provincial Taxation and the Ur III State*. Leiden: Brill, 2004.
Steinkeller, P. "Mesopotamia in the Third Millennium." *Anchor Bible Dictionary*. Ed. D. N. Freedman. New York: Doubleday, 1992, 4: 724–32.
——. "The Administrative and Economic Organization of the Ur III State: The Core and the Periphery." In *The Organization of Power: Aspects of Bureaucracy in the Ancient Near East*. Ed. M. Gibson and R. D. Biggs. Chicago: University of Chicago Press, 1987, 19–41.
Wilcke, C. "König Šulgis Himmelfahrt." In *Festschrift László Vajda*. Ed. C. Müller and H.-J. Paproth. Münchner Beiträge zur Völkerkunde 1. Munich: Hirmer, 1988, 245–55.

33. Lamentations

In the Sumerian worldview the city was the property of the divine family and the temple was its dwelling place (Steinkeller 1992). If the death of Ur-Namma brought instant despair to the Sumerian people, one can only imagine the trauma they would feel should one of their beloved cities be destroyed. Several texts from the early Old Babylonian period detail precisely that. These so-called "city laments" or "lamentations" describe in vivid detail the various dimensions of the experience in a highly charged and poetic language.[27] To date laments for Sumer's four major cities have been preserved: Nippur, the religious capital and home of Enlil (Tinney 1996); Eridu, in Sumerian tradition the oldest city and the home of Enki (Green 1978); Uruk, which was of particular concern to the Ur III kings and the home of An and Inanna (Green 1984); and Ur, itself, discussed in more detail below.

Aside from narrating the destruction of a given city these laments share several other features in content and structure. As for content, a city is destroyed because the chief deities of the pantheon, An and Enlil, have decreed for it an ominous fate. With this the gods – above all the patron deity of the city – abandon it. In line with this reasoning, the enemies who destroy the city are portrayed as agents of the gods; above all, they are described as a storm or flood. Generally speaking, the city is restored at the end of the composition. As for structure, the laments are clearly subdivided into sections called *kirugus*. The *kirugus* in turn are echoed by *gishgigal* or antiphones, which summarize the preceding section or repeat a catchphrase from it. The sections vary in size and, accordingly, emphasis from lament to lament.

The structure of the laments reveals further details concerning their Sitz im Leben or "setting in life." From this and other evidence we know that laments were sung within the cult and accompanied by a harp (Sumerian *balag*).[28] Indeed, the insertion of the phrase *kirugu* may indicate a gesture of submission by a performer or the congregation itself. As for their purpose, the laments may have been used to soothe the heart of the deity "to prevent the recurrence of the disaster in the future" (Klein 2003; 535).[29]

The laments are associated above all with the first dynasty of Isin, whose kings made considerable efforts to present themselves as the legitimate heirs of the Ur III state. To be sure, these compositions played a major role in that process: in two cases, the laments of Nippur and Uruk, king Ishbi-Erra of Isin is responsible for the restoration of the city. Although the city laments are associated above all with the Old Babylonian kings, it is clear that their roots extend well into Sumer's early literary and religious tradition.[30]

Lamentation over the destruction of Sumer and Ur

Two of the five city laments focus on the city of Ur. The first one, known in its complete form for over 60 years, took the name "The Lamentation over the Destruction of Ur" (Römer 2004; Kramer 1940); the second took the name "The Lamentation over the Destruction of Sumer and Ur" or, by virtue of the other lament, "The Second Lamentation over the Destruction of Ur" (Michalowski 1989).[31] Each of these compositions follows a similar structure: After the decrees of An and Enlil, the various gods of Sumer abandon their cities, which are subsequently destroyed. The focus then turns to Ur and Nanna's interaction on behalf of his city.

The text traditionally known as "The Lamentation over the Destruction of Sumer and Ur" (i.e., the second Ur lament) is presented below. It consists of over five hundred lines attested by manuscripts from both Nippur and Ur. Several sections are omitted because they are either repetitive or largely damaged. The translation follows the composite text of Michalowski's edition (1989).

The lament opens with an extremely long section composed of infinitive phrases, thus outlining the purposes and effects of the pronouncements of An and Enlil.

To overturn [the course of] time, to destroy the [cosmic] design,
the storm consumed everything like a flood.
To overturn the rites[32] *of Sumer,*
to lock up the peaceful reign in its home,[33]
to destroy the city, to destroy the temple,
to destroy the cattle pen, to level the sheepfold,
to prevent the cattle from the cattle pen,
to prevent the sheep from increasing in the sheepfold,
to make the river carry brackish water,[34]
to make the fields produce bitter grass,
to make the wilderness produce "mourning grass,"
to make the mother not [even] look for her child,
to make the father not say "O my wife!",
to make [him] not enjoy the concubine in [his] lap,
to make [her] not raise [even] the youngest on [her] knee,[35]
to make the wetnurse not utter a lullaby,
to alter the dwelling place of kingship,
to diminish[?] the oracles,
to remove kingship from the land,
to look upon the many lands,
to destroy the [cosmic] design by order of An and Enlil:
When An frowned upon all the land,
when Enlil looked upon the foreign lands,
when Nintu scattered her creation,[36]
when Enki changed the Tigris and Euphrates,
when Utu cursed the roads and [campaign] trails,
to destroy the rites of Sumer, to alter the [cosmic] design,[37]
to distance the rite of kingship, the reign of Ur,
to defile the [things] of the princely son in his Ekishnugal,[38]
to fracture the people of Nanna (numerous as ewes),
to alter the food offerings of Ur, the shrine of the greatest food offerings,
to make the people not live in their [own] dwellings, [but rather] to give them over to an evil place
[and] make the Shimashkians and Elamites – foreigners – take residence [in] their dwellings,
to make the enemy seize the shepherd in his own palace,
to take Ibbi-Suen to the land of Elam in fetters . . .

With even a cursory glance at this section two things are immediately clear. First, the composition is very specific to Ur. Not only does it mention Ur's perennial enemies to the east, namely the Shimashkians and Elamites, but it also mentions the last king of the dynasty, Ibbi-Suen, who was taken to Elam when the capital was destroyed. Second, it bears a striking resemblance to the "Death of Ur-Namma" translated above. Several of the motifs – even the exact phrases – of that composition appear here, including the description of the joys of family, the abundance in the land or lack thereof, and even the roles of the gods in the disaster.

The introduction continues with vivid but rather repetitive description of the general decrepitude to befall the city and the land before turning to the deeds and pronouncements of Sumer's primary deities.

After Ur has stood [as] a great . . . ox (noble on its own) –
the seedling city of lordship and kingship built on virgin soil –
to quickly subdue it [with] a rope like an ox, to bring its neck to the ground:
An, Enlil, Enki, and Ninmah determined its fate.
Who [can] overturn its fate, something that cannot be altered?
Who [can] oppose the pronouncement of An and Enlil?
An terrified Sumer in its dwelling place; the people were afraid.
Enlil brought a bitter storm; silence was established in the city.
Nintu blocked off the womb of the land.
Enki stopped up the water in the Tigris and Euphrates.
Utu removed the prouncements of righteousness and just rulings.
Inanna granted battle and strife to a rebellious land.
Ningirsu poured Sumer to the dogs like milk.[39]
Rebellion fell upon the land, something which no one known.
It was something which had not been seen, something unspeakable, something that could not be grasped.
All the lands were confounded in their fear.
The gods of the city turned away; the shepherd fell away.
The population breathed in fear.
The storm immobilized them; daylight would not return for them.[40]
With no daylight returning form them to their dwelling,
this is what Enlil, the shepherd of the black-headed ones, did:

Even here the roles of the gods bear a striking resemblence to the "Death of Ur-Namma." But here is where the lament distinguishes itself. Enlil has a specific agent: He calls the Gutians (later the Amorites and Elamites as well) from the mountains to destroy the city. The description of the carnage continues and becomes both vivid – there are corpses in the Euphrates – and, again, slightly repetitive. With this the first *kirugu* ends, its antiphone repeating the second line of the composition ("the storm consumed everything like a flood"). By doing so it stresses the image of the enemy as a storm.

The text turns to various short descriptions of the destruction that takes place in Sumer. Above all these are concerned with the shrines, which, for obvious reasons, are most deeply affected by divine abandonment. The shrines involved include, among other, the Hursagkalama (the temple of Zababa at

Kish to the north), the Urukug (Bau's temple in Girsu), and even Enlil's own complex in Nippur. In each of these brief descriptions the patron deity takes a "foreign path," abandoning his or her city and "beloved dwelling" (i.e., the temple) and lamenting over them with the bitter cry: "O the destroyed city, my destroyed temple." Interestingly, in the case of Eridu the people plead for Enki's help, but the section is badly damaged and the details of their pleas are not available.

Enlil makes a second round of destructive pronouncements near the midpoint of the composition. The final city in his tour is Ur.

In Ur no one went for food, no one went for water.
Its people wandered[?] like water poured into a well.
Having no strength, they do not [even] travel.[41]
Enlil installed[42] *a pestilent famine in the city.*
He installed a city destroyer and a temple destroyer in the city.
He installed something no weapon could withstand in the city.
He installed impropriety and shiftiness in the city.
In Ur, like a single planted reed, he was establishing fear.[43]
Its people, like fish seized with the hand, gasped for breath.
[People] small and great were spread about; no one [could] rise.
At the "royal station," which was atop the portico, there was no food.
The king, who [usually] ate fine food, [could] take only a morsel.
As the day grew dark[44] *. . . they knew hunger.*
There was no beer in the brewery, there was no malt.
There was no food for him in his palace; it was unsuitable.
No grain filled his magnificent storehouse; he [could] not bear his life.[45]
From the large granary to the small granary of Nanna there was no grain.
. . .
The boat of the first fruits did not bring first fruits to the father who begat him [Nanna].
Its food offerings could not enter for Enlil [in] Nippur.

Here the lament raises two important points. First, it provides a poetic description of the famine that gripped the city. As noted above, we know from administrative texts and royal letters that hard times fell upon Ur vis-à-vis the availability of food. Second, it preserves a significant detail concerning the function of the Ur III bureaucracy. Several of the state's core provinces had an official month in which to supply goods and services to the state (Sharlach 2004, see above). Above all these items were used for the maintenance of the temples not only in Nippur but also in Uruk and Ur. Since the system was highly integrated, even the smallest disruption would have had major consequences for shipments of offerings to Enlil in Nippur. In this case, of course, the extent of the damage is far greater, but it nonetheless reveals an important component of the Ur III economic and religious framework. With the condition of Ur deteriorating fast, Nanna takes it upon himself to confront Enlil directly by describing the situation and by pleading with him to return. Enlil's response is far from comforting:

"There is mourning in the midst of the haunted city. Reeds of tears are growing there.
. . .
In its midst [the people] pass the day in lament.
O my son, noble one . . . Why are you in tears?
O Nanna, noble one . . . Why are you in tears?
There is no revoking the verdict, the command of the assembly.
The pronouncement of An and Enlil knows no overturning.
Ur was indeed given kingship, but it was not given an everlasting reign.
From [the time] the land was established ages ago until the people were multiplied,
who has seen a reign of kingship that has emerged for preeminence?
Its kingship, its reign, was long [but] grew tired.
My Nanna, do not grow tired [yourself], [but] leave your city!"

And so, like the other deities, Nanna abandons his city; indeed, all the gods of Ur leave, and the city prepares for the onslaught by the Elamites. The destruction commences, and once again Nanna approaches Enlil. This time Enlil responds favorably:

"My son, the city that was [indeed] built for you in prosperity and joy is your reign.
The destroyed city, the great wall, the walls with leveled ramparts . . . all these were aside from the reign.
That which was arranged for you there, a reign of dark days . . . was created[?] for you.
Take a seat in your Etemennigur, righteously built!
Let Ur be [re]built in joy; let the people lie down before you!
Let it have substance in its foundation! Let Ashnan[46] *dwell there with it!*
Let there be joy in its branches! Let Utu rejoice there!
Let an abundance of grain overflow its table!
Let Ur, the city [for which] An decreed fate, be restored for you!"
Enlil, proclaiming his blessing, stretched his neck to the heavens:[47]
Let the land be organized [from] south [to] north for Nanna!
For Suen, let the road of the land be set in order!
Like a cloud, like one hugging the earth, they will lay hands on him!
By the order of An and Enlil, let them set a righteous hand on him."[48]

With this Ur is finally restored and Nanna returns from exile. Nanna's joy is best expressed by the lament itself:

Father Nanna went into his city Ur [with his] head raised.
The young man Suen entered the Ekishnugal.
Ningal[49] *refreshed herself in her holy inner chamber.*
In Ur she entered the Ekishnugal.
. . .
[Nanna proclaims:]
"O bitter storm! Retreat, O storm! Return to your home, O storm!
O storm, destroying temples, retreat, O storm! Return to your home, O storm!
Let the storm, which passed through Sumer, pass to [another] land![50]

Let the storm, which passed through the land, pass to [another] land!
Let it pass through the land of the Tidnum![51] *Let it pass to [another] land!*
Let it pass through the land of the Gutians! Let it pass to [another] land!
Let it pass through the land of Anshan! Let it pass to [another] land!
Let it level Anshan like a blowing destructive wind!
Let An not [again] alter the rites of heaven, the [cosmic] design, for a firm land!
Let An not alter the judgments and decisions for a proper society!
Let An not alter travel on the roads of the land!
Let An and Enlil not alter it! Let An not alter it!
Let Enki and Ninmah not alter it! Let An not alter it!
Let An not alter [the ability of] the Tigris and Euphrates to carry their water!
Let An not alter the rain cloud in the sky and various grain in the earth!
Let An not alter the canals with their water and the fields with their grain!
Let An [not alter] the marshes carrying fish and fowl!
Let An not alter [the ability of] new reeds and new shoots to grow in the canebrake!
Let An and Enlil not alter it!
Let Enki and Enlil not alter it!
[Let An not alter] the well[?] and orchard yielding honey and wine!
[Let An not alter] the "high plain" yielding the . . . plant!
[Let An not alter] the long life in the palace!
Let An not alter the sea land yielding abundance!
Let An not alter the population in the land [from] south [to] north!
Let An and Enlil not alter it! Let An not alter it!
Let Enki and Ninmah not alter it! Let An not alter it!
The cities constructed, the people multiplied[?]!
In all of heaven and earth the people cared for[?]!
O Nanna, your kingship is sweet! Return to your [rightful] place!
In Ur let a sweet and abundant reign be long of days!
Let the people lie down in fine grass! Let them reproduce!
. . .
O Nanna! O your city! O your temple! O your people!

Further reading

Michalowski, P. *The Lamentation over the Destruction of Sumer and Ur.* Mesopotamian Civilizations 1. Winona Lake, Ind.: Eisenbrauns, 1989.

Sharlach, T. *Provincial Taxation and the Ur III State.* Cuneiform Monographs 26. Leiden: Brill, 2004.

Bibliography (II F: 33)

Edzard, D. O. *Die "Zweite Zwischenzeit" Babyloniens.* Wiesbaden: Harrassowitz, 1957.

Green, M. W. "The Eridu Lament." *Journal of Cuneiform Studies* 30 (1978): 127–67.

——. "The Uruk Lament." *Journal of the American Oriental Society* 104 (1984): 253–79.

Klein, J. "Lamentation over the Destruction of Sumer and Ur." In COS, 2003, 2: 535–9 (no. 1.166).

Kramer, S. N. *Lamentation over the Destruction of Ur.* Assyriological Studies 12. Chicago: Oriental Institute Publications, 1940, 611–19.

Michalowski, P. *The Lamentation over the Destruction of Sumer and Ur.* Mesopotamian Civilizations 1. Winona Lake, Ind.: Eisenbrauns, 1989.

Powell, M., "The Sins of Lugalzagesi", *Wiener Zeitschrift für die Kunde des Morgenlandes* 86 (1996): 307–14.

Römer, W. H. P. *Die Klage über die Zerstörung von Ur.* Alter Orient und Altes Testament 309. Münster Ugarit-Verlag, 2004.

Steinkeller, P. "Mesopotamia in the Third Millennium." In D. M. Freedman (ed.), *Anchor Bible Dictionary.* New York: Doubleday, 1992, 4: 724–32.

Tinney, S. *The Nippur Lament: Royal Rhetoric and Divine Legitimation in the Reign of Isme-Dagan of Isin (1953–1935 BC).* Occasional Publications of the Samuel Noah Kramer Fund 16. Philadelphia: Samuel Noah Kramer Fund, University of Pennsylvania Museum, 1996.

Notes

1 Flückiger-Hawker 1999: 1 n. 1 with bibliography for and against this claim. Pages 1–11 provide a concise and informative introduction to the figure of Ur-Namma in English, including discussions of dating and chronology, Ur-Namma's family, and the reading of his name.

2 The establishment of the *eduba* under Shulgi is mentioned in one of the so-called "royal hymns" of Shulgi (see below), which is known from later copies. It should be noted that there is very little contemporary evidence for these literary developments (Sallaberger 1999: 129–31); most of it is from Old Babylonian copies.

3 Among these are the famous ziggurats or temple towers. The one in Ur is largely preserved, although it has suffered considerable damage in recent years.

4 For the former, see Sallaberger 1999: 137–9. For the latter, note the famous Stele of Ur-Namma, which may depict him holding various tools (Canby 2001: pls. 3, 31), and the many canephors, where the king holds the ceremonial basket of earth (*History* 71, Figure 4.2).

5 Literally "returned it to its place." This is the stock phrase for restoration, the sense being to return something to its former condition.

6 The texts have been collected in Edzard 1997; see Suter 2000 for more on the iconographic and architectural aspects of Gudea's activities.

7 More specifically, he appears to have been the son of Shulgi and Taram-Uram, the daughter of Apil-kin, ruler of Mari (Boese and Sallaberger 1996: 24–39). Such "dynastic marriages" were a common way to avoid confrontation and to preserve political stability.

8 Literally "the Utu." For more on the use of the sun god as the head noun in a construct chain, see Beckman 2002.

9 Later evidence includes an Old Babylonian copy of a letter to the king from one of his servants, who was commissioned for the project (Edzard 1974).

10 Note also Jacobsen's collection of Sumerian literature in translation, which is a standard in the field (1987).

11 See <http://etcsl.orinst.ox.ac.uk/cgi-bin/etcslmac.cgi?text=c.2.4.2*, text 2.4.2.01>. Links to earlier additional bibliography appear at the bottom of the composite text.

12 The seventh year of Shulgi's reign is called "The king traveled roundtrip from Ur to Nippur" (Sigrist and Gomi 1991: 320). The verb used in this year name clearly indicates a round trip against Klein's doubts (1981: 181). Note, however, that the towns appear reversed in the two sources.
13 A common epithet for the residents of Sumer.
14 See Klein 1981: 37 n. 64, with bibliography and relevant passages.
15 The Sumerian storm-god.
16 The identity of these places is unknown. Flückiger-Hawker notes that they may be "rooms in the palace complex . . . where the residents were brought to die or to be laid out (in state)" (1999: 166).
17 Or "strife is coming."
18 Literally "with his allure."
19 Modern Bahrain.
20 Or "the pride of the land was changed."
21 Note in particular the so-called Royal Tombs of Ur.
22 Meaning the chief deity of the netherworld. Personal names of deities can appear as head nouns in construct chains. Kramer suggests that this usage goes back to the myth "Enlil and Ninlil," where Enlil himself goes to the netherworld (1967: 111 n. 8).
23 Literally "they [indefinite] gave them to the hand of the king."
24 For a recent translation of a sacred marriage text, see Jacobsen 2003. The classic study of the event is Kramer 1969; see more recently Steinkeller 1999 with bibliography and further considerations.
25 This restoration is based on the total output.
26 For further discussion, see Sallaberger 1999: 161–3; Frayne 1997: 110; cf. Wilcke 1988.
27 For fairly accessible discussions – especially of the city lament as a genre – see Tinney 1996: 11–25; Michalowski 1989: 1–9; cf. Green 1984: 253; Edzard 1957: 50–8.
28 The term may be an onomatopoeia.
29 Elements of the ershahunga, a genre loosely translated "lament to appease the heart" and devoted exclusively to bringing the people back into good graces with the deity, are clearly present in the city laments.
30 Note in particular the comments concerning the compositions known as "The Curse of Akkad" (Michalowski 1989: 8–9) and "The Sins of Lugalzagesi" (Powell 1996).
31 Not everyone follows these distinctions. For example, a recent publication of the first composition called it the "Lamentation over the Destruction of Sumer and Ur" (Klein 2003).
32 Sumerian *me*. The term denotes the implements of civilization (cultic offices, crafts, etc.).
33 Or "to return the peaceful reign to its home." The phrase parallels the idea of restoration found especially in royal inscriptions (see above), but that makes little sense in this context.
34 Or "for the river to carry . . ." avoiding the causative in English.
35 Note the chiastic structure of these four lines. It is also possible to translate the last two with "the concubine" and "the youngest" as the grammatical object, hence "to make the concubine not enjoy [his] lap . . ."
36 Nintu is the birth goddess, hence living things.

37 Resuming line 1, thus forming an inclusio before turning specifically to Ur.
38 The phrase refers to Nanna and his temple complex in Ur. In Michalowski's translation Nanna himself is defiled, which would be very strange (1989: 37 l. 29).
39 Or "Ningirsu poured Sumer out completely like milk." The translation selected reflects the parallelism to the preceding line.
40 Or "the storm does not let them return," following Michalowski (1989: 41 line 70). This and the following line are difficult, particularly given the fact that "storm" and "daylight" are the same term in Sumerian. The translation offered here is highly speculative, but it fits the imagery provided in the following section.
41 Literally "they do not seize the path."
42 Reading the verb as "to live" (i.e., "to make live") versus Michalowski's "to afflict," from the verb "to seize" (1989: 55 passim).
43 The phrase actually appears in the negative but makes little sense this way.
44 Lit. "the sun grew covered," perhaps a reference to an eclipse.
45 The phrase is nearly identical to the earlier phrase translated "Its people . . . gasped for breath."
46 Or Nisaba, the grain goddess.
47 I.e., to the god An.
48 Perhaps a ceremonial move. Michalowski translates "Like a cloud hugging the earth, they shall submit to him. By order of An and Enlil (abundance) shall be bestowed!" (1989: 67 lines 473–4).
49 That is, Nanna's wife.
50 Or "It has indeed passed to another land!" (also for the following lines).
51 Another designation for the Amorites (see above).
52 Usually rendered: "From the beginning of (the reign of) King Amar-Sin until (the year named) 'The Year King Ibbi-Sin chose (prince) Enamgalana to be the high priest of (the goddess) Inana of Uruk by means of extispicy' (= Ibbi-Sin year 4, 13 years later), Ninlil came regularly to Tumal."

G. *Royal letters of the Ur III kings (Michalowski)*

The kings of the Ur III dynasty controlled Sumer and Babylonia for only one century (2112–2004), but they left a large imprint on the literature of later times. Most of what we know as Sumerian literature comes from rooms used for schooling children from a handful of cities from the eighteenth century BC. By this time the Sumerian language was no longer spoken and was reserved for educational and scholarly purposes. Alongside hundreds of poetic literary compositions copied by school children, many of which originated in Ur III times, one finds only a small number of texts written in prose, including a group of letters written to and from three of the five rulers of the Ur III dynasty.

Of the 23 surviving letters fewer than half are attested in from the main centers of Babylonian education. The remaining epistles are documented primarily from modern museum collections and have no established provenance. An analysis of the number of manuscripts and site distribution suggests that only six or seven of the royal letters were regularly used in the mainstream curriculum of cities such as Nippur and Ur.

The letters are limited to a few general topics. The three most commonly copied items form an epistolary exchange between Prime Minister Aradmu and King Shulgi (letters 34 and 35). The most powerful official of the state reported from a journey he had undertaken to the eastern border provinces to put in order taxes and settle matters with a royal appointee, Apillasha. The prime minister wrote back with indignation, implying that the officer had become a semi-independent ruler, whose provocative actions insulted the Crown. The king, however, sided with Apillasha, recognizing his need for freedom of action to keep the dangerous and volatile border provinces under control. In a letter that is still being reconstructed, and therefore is not included here, Aradmu wrote back to the king, attempting to placate his master and justify his accusations.

During the thirty-sixth year of his reign, Shulgi finished building a wall, or line of fortifications, that was meant to provide protection and a staging area for offensive actions against Amorite enemies in the mountains and valleys east of Babylonia and Sumer. Less than a quarter century later, his second successor, Shu-Sin, rebuilt and extended the fortifications and renamed them "The Wall that Keeps the Tidnum-(Amorites) at a Distance." A number of letters are concerned with these building activities. The letter translated here (no. 36) is from the correspondence between Shulgi and Puzur-Shulgi, governor of a place called Badigihursaga, situated at the western end of the wall, and possibly the man in charge of the fortifications. This part of the royal correspondence seems to have been used for making several new school exercises so that some of them just seem to be variants on one another. The building of the later version of the wall is the subject of a pair of letters between an important officer, Sharrum-bani, and King Shu-Sin (letters 37 and 38). Sharrum-bani had been appointed to rebuild the fortifications, but he encountered hostile Amorites in the mountains and proceeded to fight them. The king was unhappy with this state of affairs and relieved him of his duties, charging that he had diverted attention from his main task.

The third main topic of the royal letters is the relationship between the last king of the dynasty, Ibbi-Sin, and Ishbi-Erra, an officer in his employ who seceded from Ur and set up his own kingdom in the city of Isin, thus contributing to the downfall of the Ur III state. Of the four letters dealing with this topic only one was copied often, and it is included here (no. 6). By the time this letter was purportedly written, the state of Ur was reduced to the environs of the capitol and a few outlying loyal pockets such as the area of Kazallu. An officer named Puzur-Numushda (in some versions named Puzur-Shulgi), who was in charge of the city, cites a message he had received from Ishbi-Erra demanding his surrender. The epistle is highly rhetorical; the argument is organized around the prediction and confirmation of various acts undertaken by the usurper king over a number of years.

Vivid though these letters may be, they must be approached with caution. Scholars have been tempted to use them as direct historical sources, but it is difficult to gauge which, if any, of these texts were actually composed in Ur

III times. Some now argue that they were all composed later, others view them as authentic. Many of the people and events can be verified by analysis of Ur III archival and historical documents; it is therefore more probable that the truth may lie somewhere in the middle. One can posit that a small core goes back to real letters from the court at Ur, but that they were undoubtedly modified for schooling purposes: the language was updated and some of the contents changed. Other letters, composed in a similar mode, were then added by students and teachers over the years. One should add that these translations are preliminary at best, and that many passages could be rendered in a different manner.

34. Aradmu to King Shulgi

Say to my liege: thus speaks Aradmu, your servant:

You commanded me, while I was on an expedition to Subir, to put in order the taxes on the border-zone provinces, to learn the state of your provinces, to counsel with Apillasha, the high commissioner, and thus make him obedient, so that he could bring them (i.e. the people of Subir) (correct) daily instructions(?).

When I had arrived at the gate of the establishment, no one inquired about my liege's well-being, no one rose from (his) seat for me, did not prostrate himself (before me), (and all) this made me nervous.

When I drew nearer, (I discovered that Apillasha) was dwelling in a travel tent constructed by means of finely combed fleece (panels) with pegs inlaid with gold, silver, carnelian, and lapis-lazuli covering an area of thirty sar (c. 1080 sq. m.). (He) was gratifying (himself with gifts of) precious stones and metals as he was seated on a throne set up inside a screened enclosure of the finest cloth with his feet set on a golden footstool. He would not remove his feet in my presence! Choice guards stood to his right and left, five thousand on each side. (He ordered) six grass-fed oxen and sixty grass-fed sheep placed (on tables) for a meal; he finished my liege's cleansing rites. A man (now) brought me in through the very gate at which I had not been greeted.

When I finally came in, someone brought me a chair with red gold encrusted knobs and told me: "Sit!" I answered him: "When I am on my liege's orders I stand – I do not sit!" Someone heaped two grass-fed oxen and twenty grass-fed sheep unto my table, but even though I had given no offense, my liege's guard(s) overturned my table. I was absolutely terrified!

It is now the evening of the fifth day of the fifth month. My liege thus commanded me; now the evening of the first day of the third month has passed and I have sent you a messenger. It is midday, and war is brewing! My liege must know (about this)!

35. King Shulgi to Aradmu

To Aradmu speak: thus says Shulgi, your lord:

(Apillasha), the one to whom you were dispatched, is he not your own trusted subordinate? Did he not receive (his) orders from your very own hands? Indeed, how could you misunderstand the true meaning of all that he has been doing? As far as I am concerned, you were to make the territories secure as my representative, you were to

make safe the people and keep them obedient, and having arrived in the citi(es) of the territory, you were to discern their plans, and inform their (local) dignitaries of their orders, so that my battle cry should cover the land(s), that my mighty battle weapons subdue the foreign lands, and that my "storm" cover the land!

"Forget the murderer in open the steppe and thief in the field(?); until you have reached Apillasha, my high commissioner, let them flee before you, so that you can face him (as soon as possible)!(?)" So I commanded you!

(As to your accusations), if my high commissioner had not elevated himself just like me, if he had not sat in a screened enclosure, had not set his feet on a golden footstool, had not by his very own authority appointed and removed governors from the office of governor, royal officers from the position of royal officer, had not (punished anyone) by death or blinding, (and) had not elevated, by his own authority, those of his own choice (to positions of power) – how else could he have maintained order in the territory? If you (truly) love me you will not be so set against him!

You have made yourself so important so that you no longer understand your (own) soldiers! Now you have experienced their/his independence and his valor!

If you are (indeed) both my loyal servants, you will both listen carefully to my written instructions. Both of you – come to an understanding and secure the foundations of the land! It is urgent!

36. Puzur-Shulgi to King Shulgi

Say to my liege: thus speaks Puzur-Shulgi, general of Bad-Igihursaga, your servant:

Is it not for the sake of his own well-being that my liege fashions gold and silver (objects) for the gods? My liege, for the well-being of the troops and his land has built the great fortifications of Igihursaga against the vile enemy for the well-being of the people and the land.

But now the enemy troops have mustered (for battle). One man was brought before me as a fugitive – was coming and going – he spoke to me and went out (as a spy/scout). I now know the enemy secret signals. The enemy has concentrated (all) his forces for battle, but my forces are insufficient (to keep them off). It is impossible to strengthen the wall against them, nor (properly) guard it. In the sector under the responsibility of Puzur-Numushda, governor of Ullumtura, the section that had been widened to fifty nindan collapsed in the middle; in the sector under the responsibility of Lugal-melam, overseer of the Sheshshektum canal, five nindan of his section can be breached; in the sector under the responsibility of Kakugani, governor of the central territory(?), a thirty-five nindan section, its face and base are damaged, (and) in the part under the responsibility of Takil-ilishu, canal inspector of the Abgal and Me-Enlila waterways, forty nindan of his section does not have its perimeter yet laid out(?).

I do not know ahead of time when the enemy will come against it (the wall). The enemy has concentrated (all) his forces for battle and his troops are encamped in the mountain valleys. If my lord is agreeable, he will immediately dispatch to me seventy-two hundred workers to move earth for me. He will (also) send me right away six hundred Sudalunutum troopers. I am resolved; I shall unseat them (i.e. the enemy)! Let this be known, for his (the enemy's) sins have been grievous from days of old! I am the true servant of my lord Shulgi – do not let me perish! My liege must know (about this)!

37. Sharrum-bani to King Shu-Sin

Say to Shu-Sin, my liege: thus speaks Sharrum-bani, the royal commissioner, your servant:

You commissioned me to (re)construct the great fortifications of Muriq-Tidnim. He (var: you) presented the matter to me as follows: "The Amorites have repeatedly raided the territory." You ordered me to rebuild the fortifications, to cut off their (infiltration) route, to prevent them from swooping down on the fields through a breach (in the defenses) between the Tigris and Euphrates. As soon as I left (for my commission) I was mustering forces from the banks of the Abgal canal to the territory of Zimudar.

When I had constructed the wall to a length of 269 km., after having reached the area between the two mountain ranges, the Amorite camped in the mountains focused on me because of my building activities. (The leader of) Simurum came to his aid and went out against me between the mountain ranges of Ebih to battle. And therefore I – not having seen the (promised) corvée laborers – went out to confront him in battle.

If my liege is agreeable, he will reinforce my laborers and my fighting forces. Although I have not been able to reach the (main) fortification tower(?) of the land, [I have received] news. I sent an envoy inland, (informing you) that the political balance of the territory has been altered, but I have not neglected to build the fortifications – (to the contrary), and I have been both building and fighting. (The envoy I sent) now advises me: "because the royal commissioner comes from a grand family, he has been installed (over the land), and should not do anything to alter the very political balance of the territory."

As soon as I dispatched my envoy to you, I immediately dispatched (another) envoy to Lu-Nanna, the governor of Zimudar. He sent 7200 workers for your (project). I now have enough corvée laborers, but not enough fighting men! Once my king gives the orders to release the workers (for military duty), when (the enemy) raids, I shall be able to fight him!

He (Lu-Nanna?) dispatched someone to the nobles of your land and they presented their case to me as follows: "We are incapable of guarding all the cities by ourselves, why should you be given (our) troops?" They then sent my messenger back to him.

Ever since my liege commanded me, night and day I have been fulfilling (these) orders as well as fighting (the enemy). Because I am obedient to my liege's command I continue to fight; force shall not prevail (over me), I shall not be overcome by force of arms (?). My liege must know (about this)!

38. King Shu-Sin to Sharrum-bani

Say to Sharrum-bani: thus speaks Shu-Sin, your liege:

The envoy whom I sent to you, . . . above and beyond . . . At daybreak my instructions that I had provided, . . . you were not to exceed. After you went away, before . . . As for me, whatever (you) say to me . . . After you set out for to the center of the territory, you approached the territory and after spending the night . . . Its nobles . . . If by yourself . . . their understanding . . . his . . . Their nobles then staged an ambush against you. When their people had been expelled(?), like them the territory . . . If their officers . . . are of one mind you will not be able to root them out from their hiding places. The enemy, all gathered together . . . When their cities have been handed over, until they come out from these fortifications, let no one get through. Once their (fighting) men had been killed, their women/workers of the citi(es) of your territory, who had been captured, were not to be [harmed?]. Thus you were ordered. Why did you not do as I (told you)?

But although you were not authorized to execute and blind people nor to destroy cities, I gave you (other/this) authority. When earlier (my) father (King) Shulgi had built Bad-igihursaga, were you all not (with him)? Is my throne not the throne of Shulgi? Lu-Nanna, the governor of Zimudar is to come to you and he will bring 60 soldiers. He is to send them [from among his own conscripts]. Babati, the royal minister, in accordance with instructions(?) that I have already given to him, is to build the fortifications. But you, with the workers that have been entrusted to you – dig the moat! You are both enjoined not to change the political climate of the territory. You will both not release the workers until the territory is secured! Then have envoys bring news of the territory to me each morning! It is urgent!

39. Puzur-Numushda to King Ibbi-Sin

To Ibbi-Sin, my liege, speak: Thus says Puzur-Numushda, governor of Kazallu, your servant:

The envoy of Ishbi-Erra came before me and presented his case as follows: "My liege Ishbi-Erra has sent me to you with (this) message: 'My master Enlil has promised to make me shepherd of the land. Yes, it was to me that Enlil promised (that I shall be able) to deliver to (the goddess) Nininsina the banks of the Tigris and Euphrates, the Abgal and Me-Enlila watercourses, their cities, their (city gods) and their armies, from the land of Hamazi to the Magan Sea, to settle their war captives and in their cities, [11]to make (the city of) Isin the storehouse of Enlil, and make it renown! Why do you do me wrong? I have sworn by the name of my personal god Dagan that I shall conquer (the city of) Kazallu! Since Enlil has promised me the cities of the land, I shall build all their (i.e. the city gods) shrines in Isin, I will celebrate their regular festivals; I shall set up my own statues, my own emblems, my own priestesses and ecstatics, in their gipar complexes, so that my subjects might perform their rites before (the god) Enlil in the Ekur (temple in Nippur) and before (the god) Nanna in the Ekishnugal (temple in Ur). And as for you – the one in whom you put your trust (i.e. Ibbi-Sin), I shall remove from his land! Isin's wall I shall rebuild (and) name it Idil-pa-shunu.'"

It was just as he said: Isin's wall he rebuilt and named it Idil-pa-shunu; he captured Nippur, appointed his own guard, and captured Nig-dugani, the chief temple administrator of Nippur. (His ally) Zinnum took the ruler of Subir prisoner (and) plundered Hamazi. Nur-ahum, governor of Eshnunna, Shu-Enlil, governor of Kish and Puzur-Tutu, governor of Borsippa were returned to their individual posts(?). The land trembles like a reed fence from his clamor, Ishbi-Erra goes everywhere at the head of the troops.

It was just as he said: he captured the banks of the Tigris, Euphrates, the Abgal and Me-Enlila watercourses. He appointed(?) Iddin-Malgium (to high office), but Girbubu, governor of Girkal, rebelled against (Iddin-Malgium), cut off his belt, and took him prisoner.

(Ishbi-Erra's) clamor is has become loud (indeed, and now) he has made cast his eyes in my direction. I have no ally, no one who could compete with him! Although he has not yet been able to defeat me, when he finally moves against me, I will have to flee! My liege must know (about this)!

Bibliography (II G)

Sources: A full edition of all the letters will appear shortly, Piotr Michalowski, *The Royal Correspondence of Ur*. Winona Lake, Ind.: Eisenbrauns, 2005.

Other materials: On Sumerian literary letters, see W. W. Hallo, "Letters, Prayers, and Letter-Prayers," in Gutman, Israel, ed., *Proceedings of the Seventh World Congress of Jewish Studies: Studies in the Bible and the Ancient Near East*. Jerusalem : World Union of Jewish Studies, 1981, 17–27; for the Ur III royal letters, see Piotr Michalowski, "Königsbriefe (in English)," *Reallexicon der Assyriologie*, vol. 5, 1981, 51–9. For studies that utilize the letters as historical documents, see Claus Wilcke, "Zur Geschichte der Amurriter in der Ur-III Zeit," *Die Welt des Orients* 5 (1969): 1–31; and idem, "Drei Phasen des Niedergangs des Reiches von Ur III," *Zeitschrift für Assyriologie* 60 (1970): 54–69. The argument for the fictitious character of the letters has been made by Fabienne Huber, "La correspondence royale d'Ur: un corpus apocryphe," *Zeitschrift für Assyriologie* 91 (2001): 169–206.

H. Sumerian King List (Michalowski)

The Sumerian King List (SKL) describes the cycle of hegemonic cities in early Mesopotamian history. The repetitive listing of cities, "dynasties," and kings was designed to bolster the fiction that only one urban power center ruled the land at any one time, hence it has also been called the "Chronicle of a Single Monarchy." Although to us it may appear as a monotonous list of names and figures, this compositional form actually served two related didactic purposes: the study of cuneiform by means of personal names and the inculcation of a broadly perceived notion of political history. By the time Mesopotamia came to be governed by territorial states centered around one city, that is the houses of Agade, Ur, or Babylon, there came into being a notion of a "turn of reign" that was predestined for each dynasty. In the SKL this idea was projected into the past when competing city states ruled the land, infusing history with distortion. The notion was made explicit in an often cited passage from the Lamentation over the Destruction of Sumer and Ur, a poem that described in detail the final collapse of the Third Dynasty of Ur. The great god Enlil provides this explanation to Nanna, the chief deity of Ur:

Ur was indeed given kingship, but it was not given an eternal reign;
From time immemorial, since the land was founded, until the people multiplied,
Who has ever seen a reign of kingship that would take precedence (for ever)?
The reign of kingship has been long indeed but had to exhaust itself.

In the past, scholars have differed on the time and place of the origin of the SKL. It is now evident that it goes back at least to the time of Shulgi of Ur, and perhaps earlier to the period when Mesopotamia was first united under the rule of the kings of Agade (Akkad). It therefore has a long and complex redactional history and the reception and understanding of the text differed as the composition was transmitted and adjusted to contemporary ideas. At present, the SKL can be reconstructed from 15 Old Babylonian school copies, mostly dating to the eighteenth century BC. No two are the same, and there are many variants; some recensions begin after the flood, dynasties are listed in different order, certain expressions differ, as do the lengths of reign of individual kings.

The differences can be significant; for example, there is no agreement between any versions as to the number and identity of the Gutian Kings. The present translation is a conflation of many sources that is only meant to illustrate the general tenor of the composition. The recently published early version that was written during the reign of Shulgi, the second king of the Third Dynasty of Ur, gives us a glimpse of the complex history of the composition, as it differs in significant detail from the versions known from Old Babylonian times. The paragraph divisions are modern.

40. Text

After kingship had descended from the heavens, (the seat of) kingship was in (the city of) Eridu. In Eridu Alulim became king and reigned for 28,800 years. Alalgar reigned for 36,000 years. (In sum) two kings reigned for 64,800 years. Eridu was abandoned and its kingship was taken to (the city of) Badtibira.

In Bad-tibira, Enmeluana reigned for 43,200 years; Enmegalana reigned for 28,800 years, Dumuzi, the shepherd, reigned for 36,000 years. (In sum) three kings reigned for 108,000 years.

Then Badtibira was abandoned and its kingship was taken to (the city of) Larak. In Larak, Ensipaziana reigned for 28,800 years. (In sum) 1 king reigned for 28,800 years.

Then Larak was abandoned and its kingship was taken to (the city of) Sippar. In Sippar Enmendurana became king and reigned for 21,000 years. (In sum) 1 king reigned for 21,000 years.

Then Sippar was abandoned and its kingship was taken to (the city of) Shuruppak. In Shuruppak, Ubar-Tutu became king and reigned for 18,600 years. (In sum) 1 king reigned for 18,600 years.

In five cities eight kings reigned for 385,200 years. Then the flood swept over (the land).

After the flood had swept over (the land and) kingship had (once again) descended from the heavens, (the seat of) kingship was in (the city of) Kish. In Kish, Gishur became king and reigned for 1,200 years. Kullassina-bel reigned for 900 years. Nangishlishma reigned for 670 (?) years. Endarahana reigned for 420 years, 3 months, and 3½ days, Babum . . . reigned for 300 years, Pu'annum reigned for 840 years, Kalibum reigned for 960 years, Kalumum reigned for 840 years, Zuqaqqip reigned for 900 years, Atab reigned for 600 years, Mashda, the son of Atab, reigned for 840 years, Arwi'um, the son of Mashda, reigned for 720 years. Etana, the shepherd, who flew to the heavens and made fast all the foreign lands, became king and reigned for 1,500 years. Balih, the son of Etana, reigned for 400 years, Enmenuna reigned for 660 years, Melam-Kish, the son of Enmenuna, reigned for 900 years. BarSALnuna, the son of Enmenuna, reigned for 1,200 years. Samug, the son of BarSALnuna, reigned for 140 years. Tizqar, the son of Samug, reigned for 305 years. Ilku'u reigned for 900 years. Ilta-

sadum reigned for 1,200 years. Enishibbaragesi, who subjugated the land of Elam, became king and reigned for 900 years. Aka, the son of Enishibbaragesi, reigned for 625 years. (In sum) 23 kings reigned for 23,310 years, 3 months, and 3½ days. Then Kish was defeated and kingship was taken to the Eana (precinct of Uruk).

In the Eana, Meski'aggasher, the son of (the god) Utu, became king, became sovereign, and reigned for 324 years. Meski'aggasher entered the sea and came out in the highlands. Enmerkar, the son of Meski'aggasher, king of Uruk, who built Uruk, became king and reigned for 420 years. Lugalbanda, the shepherd, reigned for 1,200 years. Dumuzi, the fisherman, whose city (of origin) was Ku'ara, reigned for 100 years (one text adds: "he captured Enishibbaragesi single-handed"). Gilgamesh, whose father was a ghost, the king of Kulaba, reigned for 126 years. Urlugal, the son of Gilgamesh, reigned or 30 years. Utulkalama, the son of Urlugal, reigned for 15 years. La-basher reigned for 9 years. Ennundarahana reigned for 7 years. Meshe, the metal smith, reigned for 36 years. Melamana reigned for 6 years. LugalkiGIN reigned for 36 years. (In sum) 12 kings reigned for 2,310 years. Then Uruk was defeated and kingship was taken to Ur.

In Ur Mesanepada became king and reigned for 80 years. Meskiag-Nanna, the son of Mesanepada, became king and reigned for 36 years. Elulu reigned for 25 years. Balulu reigned for 36 years. (In sum) four kings reigned for 177 years. Then Ur was defeated and kingship was taken to Awan.

In Awan, . . . became king and reigned for . . . years. . . . reigned for . . . years . . . reigned for 36 years. (In sum) 3 kings reigned for 356 years. Then Awan was defeated and kingship was taken to Kish.

In Kish, Susuda, the fuller, became king and reigned for 200 years. Dadase reigned for 81 years. Mamagal, the boatman, reigned for 360 years. Kalbum, the son of Mamagal, reigned for 195 years. TUGe reigned for 360 years. Mennuna, the son of TUGe, reigned for 180 years. Enbi-Eshtar reigned for 290(?) years. Lugalmu reigned for 360 years. (In sum) eight kings reigned for 3,195 years. Then Kish was defeated and kingship was taken to Hamazi.

In Hamazi Hatanish reigned for 360 years. (In sum) 1 king reigned for 360 years. Then Hamazi was defeated and kingship was taken to Uruk.

In Uruk Enshakushana became king and reigned for 60 years. Lugalure/ LugalkinisheDU.DU reigned for 120 years. Argandea reigned for 7 years. (In sum) three kings reigned for 187 years. Then Uruk was defeated and kingship was taken to Ur.

In Ur Nane became king and reigned for 54 years. Meski'ag-Nanna, the son of Nane, reigned for 48 years (?) . . . , the son of Meski'ag-Nanna, reigned for 2 years. (In sum) three kings reigned for . . . years. Then Ur was defeated and kingship was taken to Adab.

In Adab Lugalanemundu became king and reigned for 90 years. (In sum) one king reigned for 90 years. Then Adab was defeated and kingship was taken to Mari.

In Mari Anbu became king and reigned for 30 years. Anba, the son of Anbu, reigned for 17 years. Bazi, the leatherworker, reigned for 30 years. Zizi, the fuller, reigned for 20 years. Limer, the anointed priest, reigned for 30 years. Sharrum-iter reigned for 9 years. (In sum) six kings reigned for 136 years. Then Mari was defeated and kingship was taken to Kish.

In Kish Ku-Ba'u, the woman tavern keeper, who made firm the foundations of Kish, became king; she reigned for 100 years. (In sum) one king reigned for 100 years. Then Kish was defeated and kingship was taken to Akshak.

In Akshak Unzi became king and reigned for 30 years. Undalulu reigned for 6 years. Urur reigned for 6 years. Puzur-Nirah reigned for 20 years. Ilshu-Il reigned for

24 years. Shu-Sin, the son of Ilshu-Il, reigned for 7 years. (In sum) six kings reigned for 93 years. Then Akshak was defeated and kingship was taken to Kish.

In Kish Puzur-Sin, son of Ku-Ba'u, became king and reigned for 25 years. Ur-Zababa, the son of Puzur-Sin, reigned for 400 years. Simudar reigned for 30 years. Us.i-watar, the son of Simudar, reigned for 7 years. Eshtar-muti reigned for 11 years. Imid-Shamash reigned for 11 years. Nannija, the jeweler, reigned for 7 years. (In sum) seven kings reigned for 491 years. Then Kish was defeated and kingship was taken to Uruk.

In Uruk Lugalzagesi became king and reigned for 25 years. (In sum)1 king reigned for 25 years. Then Uruk was defeated and kingship was taken to Agade.

In Agade Sargon, whose father was a gardener, the cupbearer of Ur-Zababa, became king, the king of Agade, who built Agade, reigned for 56 years. Rimush, son of Sargon, reigned for 9 years. Manishtushu, the elder brother of Rimush, son of Sargon, reigned for 15 years. Naram-Sin, the son of Manishtushu, reigned for 56 years. Shar-kali-sharri, the son of Naram-Sin, reigned for 25 years. Then who was king, who was not king? Irgigi was king, Nanum was king, Imi was king, Elulu was king. (In sum) four kings reigned for 3 years. Dudu reigned for 21 years. Shu-Durul, the son of Dudu, reigned for 15 years. (In sum) 11 kings reigned for 181 years. Then Agade was defeated and kingship was taken to Uruk.

In Uruk Urnigin became king and reigned for 7 years. Urgigir, the son of Urnigin, reigned for 6 years. Kuda reigned for 6 years. Puzur-ili reigned for 5 years. Ur-Utu reigned for 6 years. (In sum) five kings reigned for 30 years. Uruk was defeated and its kingship was taken to the troops/land of Gutium.

Among the troops/land of Gutium, at first no king was famous. They were their own kings and reigned thus for 3 years. Then Inkishush reigned for 6 years. Zarlagab reigned for 6 years. Shulme reigned for 6 years. Silulumesh reigned for 6 years. Inimabakesh reigned for 5 years. Igesha'ush reigned for 6 years. Jarlagab reigned for 15 years. Ibate reigned for 3 years. Jarla reigned for 3 years. Kurum reigned for 1 year. Apil-kin reigned for 3 years. Laerabum reigned for 2 years. Irarum reigned for 2 years. Ibranum reigned for 1 year. Hablum reigned for 2 years. Puzur-Sin, the son of Hablum, reigned for 7 years. Jarlaganda reigned for 7 years . . . reigned for 7 years. Tiriga reigned for 40 days. (In sum) 21 kings reigned for 124 years and 40 days. Then the army of Gutium was defeated and kingship was taken to Uruk.

In Uruk Utu-hegal became king and reigned for 7 years, 6 months, and 7 days (the numbers vary widely). (In sum) one king reigned for 7 years, 6 months, and 7 days. Then Uruk was defeated and kingship was taken to Ur.

In Ur Ur-Namma became king and reigned for 18 years. Shulgi, the son of Ur-Namma, reigned for 48 years. Amar-Sin, the son of Shulgi, reigned for 9 years. Shu-Sin, the son of Amar-Sin, reigned for 9 years. Ibbi-Sin, the son of Shu-Sin, reigned for 24 years. (In sum) five kings reigned for 108 (text: 117) years. Then Ur was defeated, and its kingship was taken to Isin.

In Isin, Ishbi-Erra became king and reigned for 33 years. Shu-ilishu, the son of Ishbi-Erra, reigned for 20 years. Iddin-Dagan, the son of Shu-ilishu, reigned for 21 years. Ishme-Dagan, the son of Iddin-Dagan, reigned for 20 years. Lipit-Eshtar, the son of Ishme-Dagan, reigned for 11 years. Ur-Ninurta reigned for 28 years. Bur-Sin, the son of Ur-Ninurta, reigned for 21 years. Lipit-Enlil, the son of Bur-Sin, reigned for 5 years. Erra-imitti reigned for 8 years. Enlil-bani reigned for 24 years. Zambaya reigned for 3 years. Iter-pisha reigned for 4 years. Urdukuga reigned for 4 years. Sin-magir reigned for 11 years. (In sum) 14 (text: 13) kings reigned for 213 years.

A total of 39 kings reigned for 14,409 years, 3 months and 3, 4 times in Kish. A total of 22 kings reigned for 2,610 years, 6 months and 14½ days, 5 times in Uruk. A total of 12 kings reigned for 396 years, 3 times in Ur. A total of 3 kings reigned for 356 years, once in Awan. A total of 1 king reigned for 420 years, once in Hamazi. A total of 6(?) kings reigned for 136(?) years, once in Mari. A total of 6(?) kings reigned for 99(?) years, once at Akshak. A total of 11 kings reigned for 197 years, once in Agade. A total of 21 kings reigned for 125 years and 40 days, once among the army of Gutium. A total of 11 kings reigned for 159 years, once in Isin.

There are 11 royal cities. A grand total of 134 kings, who altogether reigned for 28,876 years . . .

Bibliography (II H)

Sources: The classic edition is by Thorkild Jacobsen, *The Sumerian King List*. Chicago: University of Chicago Press, 1939. Sources published since that time are listed in D. O. Edzard, and C.-A. Vincenze, "The Tall Leilan Recension of the Sumerian King List." *Zeitschrift für Assyriologie* 85 (1995): 236–8. The earliest known version is in Piotr Steinkeller, "An Ur III Manuscript of the Sumerian King List." in W. Sallaberger, K. Volk, and A. Zgoll, eds., *Literatur, Politik und Recht in Mesopotamie. Festchrift für Claus Wilcke*. Wiesbaden: Harrassowitz, 2003, 267–92.

Other materials: William W. Hallo, "Beginning and End of the Sumerian King List in the Nippur Recension." *Journal of Cuneiform Studies* 17 (1963): 52–6; Piotr Michalowski, "History as Charter: Some Observations on the Sumerian King List." *Journal of the American Oriental Society* 103 (1983): 237–48; Claus Wilcke, "Genealogical and Geographical Thought in the Sumerian King List." 557–71, in H. Behrens, D. Loding, and M. T. Roth, eds., *DUMU-E$_2$-DUB-BA-A. Studies in Honor of Åke W. Sjöberg*. Philadelphia: Samuel Noah Kramer Fund, University Museum, 1989; Jacob Klein, "A New Nippur Duplicate of the Sumerian King List in the Brockmon Collection, University of Haifa." *Aula Orientalis* 9 (1991): 123–30; Jean-Jacques Glassner, *Mesopotamian Chronicles*. Atlanta: Society of Biblical Literature, 2004, 117–26.

I. Bringing Ninlil to Tumal (Michalowski)

This short text, probably derived from the early version of the Sumerian King List, has been considered to be a chronicle of royal works at the sacred precinct of the god Enlil in the city of Nippur, and at Tumal, a ceremonial center sacred to his wife Ninlil, located south of the city. During the Ur III period Tumal was not only an important place of worship but also a major royal residence.

The composition was used in school instruction, and was often included in a short collection of letters and miscellanies that originated in Ur III and early Isin times. The text is fairly stable with only a few variants. It begins with Enishibbaragesi ("Enmebaragesi"), a legendary king of Kish who was an important adversary in Ur III royal lore, and ends with the fourth year of Ibbi-Sin, the last king of Ur. There is an additional notation mentioning Ishbi-Erra of Isin, an officer in the service of Ibbi-Sin who took over Nippur and Isin early in the reign of his master and established a separate kingdom, whose actions led to the downfall of the Ur III state. Note that the word "abandoned" could also be translated as "fell (into ruin)."

Scholars have described the text as an "inscription," or as a "chronicle," and have viewed it as a significant, if short, historiographic text. It is more probable that this is a self-serving little school composition that was meant to memorialize an Ur III official, Lu-Inana, who may have never even existed. This would fit into the context of the letter collections; the use of names and places within a repetitive pattern could be seen as a pedagogical device.

The interpretation of the composition is dependent on the translation of the third paragraph from the end. All existing modern renditions interpret the phrase as a continuation of the established pattern; this traditional rendering is provided in a footnote. This is incorrect, however, as the verb is in the first person and thus everything leading up to this must be the words of Lu-Inana, who had served Ninlil during the reign of the last three kings of the Third Dynasty of Ur, or at least until the fourth year of its final king Ibbi-Sin. The text then ends with two remarks; the first informs us of the name of the aforementioned servant of the god Enlil, and the second is a postscript adding the name of Ishbi-Erra, the usurper who contributed to the downfall of Ur. We know that he probably took over Nippur during Ibbi-Sin's eighth year, so we are not informed as to what happened in the intervening four years.

It is difficult to place most of the cult places of Enlil mentioned here; they are known only from lexical lists and cultic litanies. Two of them are also attested in a Middle Babylonian metrological text that lists some of the temples in Nippur. The last one named, Ekur ("Temple-Mountain") was the temple tower of Enlil, in a sense the central shrine of Sumer. It had a long history before Ur-Namma rebuilt it as a stepped temple tower (ziggurat).

41. Tumal inscription

King Enishibbaragesi (of Kish) built the Irinanam, the temple of Enlil. Aka, son of Enishibbaragesi, made Tumal flourish and brought Ninlil into Tumal. For the first time the Tumal was abandoned.

Mesanepada (of Ur) built the Burshushua, the temple of Enlil. Meskiagnuna, son of Mesanepada, made Tumal flourish and brought Ninlil into Tumal. For the second time Tumal was abandoned.

Gilgamesh (of Uruk) constructed Dunumunbura, the dais of Enlil. Urlugal, son of Gilgamesh, made Tumal flourish and brought Ninlil into Tumal. For the third time Tumal was abandoned.

Nane (of Ur) built the Sublime Garden, the temple of Enlil. Meskiag-Nanna, son of Nane, made Tumal flourish and brought Ninlil into Tumal. For the fourth time Tumal fell was abandoned.

Ur-Namma (of Ur), built the (temple tower) Ekur. Shulgi, son of Ur-Namma, made the Tumal flourish and brought Ninlil into Tumal. For the fifth time the Tumal was abandoned.

From the beginning of (the reign of) King Amar-Sin until (the year named) "The Year King Ibbi-Sin chose (prince) Enamgalana to be the high priest of (the goddess) Inana of Uruk by means of extispicy" (=Ibbi-Sin year 4, 13 years later), I regularly brought Ninlil to Tumal.[52]

Written according to the words of Lu-Inana the chief leatherworker of Enlil.

Ishbi-Erra (of Isin) built Ekurigigal, the storehouse of Enlil.

Bibliography (II I)

Sources: The first full edition was provided by Fadhil A. Ali, "Sumerian Letters: Two Collections from the Old Babylonian Schools." University of Pennsylvania: Philadelphia PhD dissertation, 1964, 99–104; updated by Edmond Sollberger, "The Tummal Inscription." *Journal of Cuneiform Studies* 16 (1962): 40–7. A new edition was recently published by Joachim Oelsner, "Aus den sumerischen literarischen Texten der Hilprecht-Sammlung Jena: Der Text der Tummal-Chronik, in W. Sallaberger et al., eds., *Literatur, Politik und Recht in Mesopotamien. Festschrift für Claus Wilcke.* Wiesbaden: Harrassowitz, 2003, 209–24. A translation appears in Andrew R. George, *The Babylonian Gilgamesh Epic: Introduction, Critical Edition and Cuneiform Text.* Oxford: Oxford University Press, 2003, 105; and a composite text and translation is in Jean-Jacques Glassner, *Mesopotamian Chronicles.* Atlanta: Society of Biblical Literature, 2004, 156–9. A new edition by P. Michalowski is forthcoming.

4

Old Babylonian Period Inscriptions

Frans van Koppen

I. Isin-Larsa Period

The term Isin-Larsa Period is commonly used to designate the period in Mesopotamian history subsequent to the fall of the Third Dynasty of Ur and preceding the rise of Babylon in absolute data (according to the Middle Chronology), the period from 2002 BC, when the reign of Ibbi-Sin of Ur had come to an end, until the conquest of Larsa by Hammurabi in 1763 BC. The term refers to two important capital cities of southern Mesopotamia of the period, but these were in no way the only political centers, as the fragmentation of power was a salient feature of the aftermath of the Ur III Period.

Ishbi-Erra, the founder of the Isin dynasty, established an independent state in Isin well before the last years of Ibbi-Sin of Ur and secured control over the ideologically important cities Ur, Uruk, and Nippur once the rule of Ur had come to an end. From ideological forms to administrative structures the Isin state patterned itself on the Ur III model, and initially its kings managed with success to have their influence felt far beyond the confines of their state. But the weight of the rulers of Yamutbal, of Amorite stock and residents of Larsa with control over territories along the lower reaches of the Tigris River, increased steadily. A case could be made that the conquest of Ur by Gungunum of Larsa (1926 BC) marks a shift of balance, as it severed trade between Isin and the Persian Gulf and set off the decline of Isin, but the struggle between the two states nonetheless continued for over a century. Other political centers now manifest themselves, like the dynasty of Sin-kashid of Uruk, and we see states in the northern part of the alluvium, like Kazallu and Babylon, participate in coalitions with southern rulers. The history of these northern states remains undesirably obscure, as very few sources other that year names are available; only in Eshnunna has a series of dedicatory inscriptions been found.

Towards the end of the period a new equilibrium came about: Rim-Sin of Larsa successfully unified the southern alluvium by incorporating the kingdoms of Uruk and Isin in his realm, whereas Ipiq-Adad II of Eshnunna and his successors created a powerful state in the North that thwarted all ambitions of other rulers of that area, those of the kings of Babylon in particular. It would take intervention from outside, in the form of the elimination of the kingdom of Eshnunna by an Elamite invasion, before the balance would shift again, this time in favor of Babylon.

A. Isin

42. Inscription of Ishme-Dagan, fourth king of the First Dynasty of Isin (ca. 1955–1937 BC)

(In Sumerian [12 lines], on bricks from Nippur.)

When Enlil had taken Ninurta, his strong hero, as bailiff for Ishme-Dagan, king of the land of Sumer and Akkad, he (Ishme-Dagan) fashioned for him (Ninurta) his 50-headed mace, set up for him his beloved weapon on (a structure of) baked bricks.

This inscription commemorates the fashioning of a divine weapon and the construction of its socle of baked bricks. The 50-headed mace is a well-attested weapon of Ningirsu and Ninurta, two closely related deities, perhaps even local variants of the same god (Cooper 1978: 130, 154–62). This particular specimen seems to have survived Ishme-Dagan's reign for quite some time, for it may well be the same mace that appears later as one of the destinations for offerings distributed in Eshumesha, the temple of Ninurta in Nippur.

The donation of this weapon is also mentioned in royal hymns of Ishme-Dagan (Frayne 1998: 39) and narrated at some length in a fragmentary text of that king, where it is said that the mace was fashioned in the capital Isin and brought to Nippur, where it was set up in Eshumesha, in the "gate facing Shugalam, the place where fate is determined" (RIME 4.1.4.15). In other Old Babylonian hymns, the temple Eshumesha is sometimes said to be "facing Shugalam," and later on the "House facing Shugalam" became the name of a specific part of Ninurta's temple (George 1993: 105). The meaning of the word is not clear (Falkenstein 1966: 140), but the gate "facing Shugalam" was presumably the place where oaths were administered with the help of the god's weapon. An identical gate was part of Ningirsu's temple in Girsu, where Shugalam, "the place yielding judgment," housed Ningirsu's Sharur-weapon (Falkenstein 1966: 140–1).

Some bricks carrying this inscription were picked up at Nippur in the nineteenth century, and many more were found *in situ* in a brick platform excavated during the early campaigns at that site; this may well be the remnants of the socle built by Ishme-Dagan (Tinney 1996: 5).

The occasion for this gift is the appointment of Ninurta as Ishme-Dagan's "bailiff." This word translates Sumerian *maškim*, a term used for worldly officials, but also for supernatural beings, both benign benefactors as well as demonic opponents. Here it expresses Ninurta's quality as exclusive advocate and supporter of the king, a motive recurring in the royal hymns of Ishme-

Dagan. The inauguration of this relationship may well have to do with Ishme-Dagan's conquest of Nippur (Frayne 1998: 26–9).

Bibliography: RIME 4.1.4.7 = *COS* 2.94.

43. Inscription of Lipit-Ishtar, fifth king of the First Dynasty of Isin (ca. 1936–1926 BC)

(In Akkadian [36 lines], on headless cones from Isin.)

I am Lipit-Ishtar, reverent shepherd of Nippur, true farmer of Ur, unceasing (provider) for Eridu, fitting en-priest of Uruk, king of Isin, king of the land of Sumer and Akkad, favorite of Ishtar. I, Lipit-Ishtar, son of Enlil, fashioned, on the day when I established justice in the land of Sumer and Akkad, a storehouse for contributions (?) to Enlil and Ninlil, in Isin, my royal city, in the gate of the palace.

A remarkable number of exemplars of this inscription have survived; they were presumably picked up from the surface of the site of ancient Isin. Some more were excavated by a team of the University of Munich in the 1970s and 1980s. Most of the excavated exemplars contain a slightly abbreviated text, omitting the phrase "in the gate of the palace," and were found in a section of the city where other epigraphic finds suggest the presence of depots for cultic usage. All exemplars with the longer text, translated above, presumably commemorate the building of another storehouse for Enlil and Ninlil, this time one connected with a palace, presumably the one built by Lipit-Ishtar (W. Sommerfeld in Hrouda 1992: 154–8).

The king praises himself as caretaker of all sanctuaries of his realm. Another key aspect of royal ideology is the king's role of guardian of justice, featuring prominently in year names, inscriptions and hymns of many kings of Isin (Kraus 1984: 16–30). Lipit-Ishtar's statement to have established justice for his land refers to a royal act from the beginning of his reign. This act comprised various social measures, such as the liberation of enslaved citizens and the relief of tax obligations, and perhaps the promulgation of the king's law code as well. Lipit-Ishtar clearly considered this act his most laudable feat and refers to it in all his inscriptions. Hence, its mention in this text does not imply that this particular royal donation was somehow linked with the establishment of justice.

Bibliography: RIME 4.1.5.3 = *COS* 2.95.

44. Inscription of Ur-dukuga, thirteenth king of the First Dynasty of Isin (ca. 1831–1828 BC)

(In Sumerian [24 lines], on cones from Isin.)

For Dagan, the great lord of foreign lands, the god who created him – Ur-dukuga, shepherd who brings everything for Nippur, great farmer of An and Enlil, provider for

Ekur, who supplies abundance for Eshumesha and Egalmah, who returned the regular offerings for the great gods that were diminished from the sanctuaries, strong king, king of Isin, king of the land of Sumer and Akkad, favorably regarded husband of Inanna, built for him the Edurkigara in Isin, his shining, beloved place of residence.

The cult of Dagan, an important god of the Middle Euphrates region, flourished in Isin at the time of the first kings of the Isin Dynasty, perhaps because the founder of the dynasty, Ishbi-Erra, came from the city of Mari. Later rulers are mostly silent about his cult, but Ur-dukuga here commemorates the building of a temple for this god, whom he, quite significantly, praises as his creator (Richter 1999: 193–6).

Many epithets of Ur-dukuga in this inscription refer to the ruler's care for Nippur and its sanctuaries. With the prestigious Sumerian centers of Ur and Uruk outside of his realm, he, like other kings of the later Isin Dynasty, focused almost exclusively on Nippur for ideological legitimation (Sallaberger 1997: 161). Ekur is the temple of Enlil in Nippur, Eshumesha Ninurta's temple in the same city, and Egalmah the temple of Ninisina in Isin, or perhaps, on account of their pairing, the shrine of Gula as Ninurta's wife in Nippur (George 1993: 88–9). Ur-dukuga's title of husband of Inanna invokes the ancient sacred marriage rite, but it is not clear if, or how, this ritual was performed without the participation of Inanna of Uruk.

Bibliography: RIME 4.1.13.1 = *COS* 2.97.

B. Larsa

45. Inscription of En-ana-tuma for the life of Gungunum, fifth king of the Larsa Dynasty (ca. 1932–1906 BC)

(In Sumerian [24 lines], on cones from Ur.)

For Utu, offspring of Nanna, . . . son of Ekishnugal, given birth by Ningal, her lord, for the life of Gungunum, the strong man, king of Ur – En-ana-tuma, zirru-priestress, en-priestress of Nanna in Ur, daughter of Ishme-Dagan, king of the land of Sumer and Akkad, built his Ehili, built for him his shining storehouse and dedicated it for the sake of his life.

Ishme-Dagan of Isin installed his daughter En-ana-tuma as high-priestess of Nanna in Ur, where she remained in office when, late in the reign of Ishme-Dagan's successor Lipit-Ishtar, control over the city fell into the hands of Gungunum of Larsa. During the reign of the latter, En-ana-tuma had inscriptions written "for the life" of Gungunum. In these Gungunum holds the title of "king of Ur," clearly an expression of the significance of this conquest, whereas the late Ishme-Dagan is called "king of the land of Sumer and Akkad." Later in his reign, Gungunum assumed this title as well, probably after his recognition by the Nippur priesthood.

En-ana-tuma was the *en*-priestess of Nanna; that is, the priestly wife of a male deity, an office exclusively occupied by princesses and of major political significance. Her second title was that of *zirru*-priestess, originally a term for a god's servant, but later understood as a variant of the high-priestess office (Steinkeller 1999: 121–2, 128). She resided in the Giparu, a large building consisting of the temple of Ningal, Nanna's divine consort, and the residence of the *en*-priestess (Charpin 1986: 192–220). Ishme-Dagan reinstated the office of *en*-priestess after it was interrupted at the end of the Ur III period, and inscribed bricks of En-ana-tuma, as well as a statue of the princess erected in one of the rooms of the Ningal temple (RIME 4.1.4.13), are evidence for his renovations of the Giparu.

The cult of Utu is poorly attested in Ur (Richter 1999: 434–6). The epithets in this inscription show that he was here primarily seen as a junior member of the pantheon, the son of Nanna of the temple Ekishnugal and his wife Ningal. His temple, Ehili, "House of Luxuriance," has not been discovered, and might well have been a simple chapel in one of their temples.

Bibliography: RIME 4.2.5.2 = *COS* 2.98.

46. Inscription of Kudur-mabuk for the life of Warad-Sin, thirteenth king of the Larsa Dynasty (ca. 1834–1823 BC)

(In Sumerian [50 lines], on cones from Ur.)

For Nanna, lord who appears gloriously in the shining sky, first son of Enlil, his lord, I, Kudurmabuk, father of the Amorite land, son of Simti-shilhak, who looks out for Enlil, who is heard by Ninlil, who reverences Ebabbar, provider for Ekur, constantly attending Ekishnugal, who brings joy to the heart of Nippur – when Nanna complied with my prayer and delivered the evildoers who had desecrated (?) Ebabbar in my hand, I restored Mashkan-shapir and Kar-Shamash to (the fold of) Larsa. Nanna, my lord, it is you who did it, as to myself, what am I? For this reason, so I can pray fervently to Nanna, my lord, I built for him Ganunmah, the house of silver and gold, the storehouse of heavy treasure of Suen, that was built long ago and had become dilapidated, for the sake of my life and the life of Warad-Sin, my son, the king of Larsa, and restored it to its place. May Nanna, my lord, rejoice at my deeds and may he grant me a destiny of life, a good reign and a throne of firm foundations! May I be the beloved shepherd of Nanna, may my days be long!

Kudur-mabuk was a powerful tribal chief of Yamutbal, the country at the Tigris, who interfered in Larsa at a time when the city went through a phase of weak rule and external pressure. Here he removed Ṣilli-Adad from the throne, after a reign of less than one year, drove Larsa's enemies back and restored order, installing his son Warad-Sin as king in Larsa while taking up residence for himself in the city of Mashkan-shapir, the stronghold on the Tigris and chief city of the land of Yamutbal.

This inscription commemorates the renovation on the Ganunmah, the treasury of Nanna and Ningal in Ur, and a large number of exemplars were recovered during the excavation of this building. Kudur-mabuk does not qualify himself as a king, a title reserved for his son Warad-Sin, but invokes his good works for the main cult centers of the kingdom. He credits his successful takeover of rule to Nanna, and acknowledges that his capture of Kar-Shamash and Mashkan-shapir, two cities on the Tigris that were ruled by some Ṣilli-Ishtar, an "enemy of Larsa and evil-doer against Yamutbal" (RIME 4.2.13a.1), was in fact the work of Nanna.

Bibliography: RIME 4.2.13.10 = *COS* 2.101A.

47. Inscription of Shep-Sin for the life of Rim-Sin, fourteenth king of the Larsa Dynasty (ca. 1822–1763 BC)

(In Sumerian [12 lines], on a stone vessel of unknown provenance.)

For Martu, his lord, for the sake of the life of Rim-Sin, king of Larsa, Shep-Sin, son of Ipqusha, the chief physician, the servant who venerates him, dedicated a stone cup of black obsidian, its lip inlaid with gold, its bottom with silver.

Private individuals often consecrated objects to a god for the health of their master and placed them in the god's temple. This piece is a 4 inch (9 centimeter) high cup of rock crystal with a gold band around the top and a silver band around the base, as described in the text, and was offered for the life of Rim-Sin, the second son of Kudur-mabuk, who reigned for 60 years as last king of Larsa. The inscription states that the cup is made of "black *zú*-stone"; *zú*-stone is commonly translated as obsidian, but the material of the piece, rock crystal, shows once more that ancient Mesopotamian petrological terminology is quite often incompatible with modern classification.

Bibliography: RIME 4.2.14.2004 = *COS* 2.102D.

C. *Eshnunna*

48. Inscription of Ipiq-Adad II, king of Eshnunna (ca. 1850 BC)

(In Akkadian [11 lines], on bricks from Ishchali.)

To Ishtar-Kititum, Ipiq-Adad, strong king, king who widens (the territory) of Eshnunna, shepherd of the black-headed (people), beloved of Tishpak, son of Ibal-pi-El, gave Neribtum as a present.

The reign of Ipiq-Adad II was a turning point in the history of the kingdom of Eshnunna. During his long reign, of at least 36 years, he brought the rule of various independent monarchs in the Diyala region to an end and extended his influence far beyond this area, conquering Arrapha in the north and Rapiqum on the Euphrates. As a contemporary, and opponent, of Aminum, presumably the elder brother of Shamshi-Adad, his exploits are discussed in the Mari Eponym Chronicle (Birot 1985), but besides this, knowledge of his reign remains scanty.

Bricks carrying this inscription were found *in situ* in pavements of the courtyards and elsewhere in a secondary context in the Kititum temple of Ishchali, the modern name of the site of ancient Neribtum (T. Jacobsen in Hill et al. 1990: 91). Previously, Neribtum had been the seat of a local king, by the name of Sin-abushu, who was defeated by Ipiq-Adad. In this inscription, Ipiq-Adad's name is preceded by a divine determinative and the king holds titles that honour his exploits and express his relation with Tishpak, the city-god of Eshnunna. The text celebrates the donation of the town to Ishtar-Kititum; that is, a local manifestation of Ishtar, who was also the patron deity of the kings of Eshnunna. Previously, the divine lord of the city of Neribtum was Sin, and this grant presumably implies that Ishtar-Kititum was appointed as divine mistress of the town in his place (Charpin 1999: 179).

Bibliography: RIME 4.5.14.3 = *COS* 2.103.

D. Uruk

49. Inscription of Sin-kashid, king of Uruk (ca. 1850 BC)

(In Sumerian [seven lines], on bricks and tablets from Uruk.)

Sin-kashid, strong man, king of Uruk, king of Amnanum, built his royal palace.

Sin-kashid detached the city of Uruk from the realm of Larsa and founded a dynasty that ruled in this city for about 50 years. He belonged to the royal lineage of the Amnanum tribe, a claim often repeated in his inscriptions, and this particular ancestry made his political ties with the royal house of Babylon, of the same lineage, particularly strong. He married a daughter of Sumula-El of Babylon (RIME 4.4.1.16), and the relationship between the two royal houses are discussed in detail in the letter of Anam translated elsewhere in this volume.

One of his more important building enterprises was the construction of his palace, the so-called "House – Abode of Rejoicing" (RIME 4.4.1.5). This building was scientifically examined by the German archaeological mission at Uruk, and countless inscribed bricks, small baked tablets, and cones were found inside its walls. Many of these had been found previously and are nowadays kept in numerous collections.

Bibliography: RIME 4.4.1.2 = *COS* 2.104.

Bibliography

Birot, M., 1985. Les chroniques "assyriennes" de Mari, *Mari: Annales de recherches interdisciplinaires* 4: 219–40.

Charpin, D., 1986. *Le clergé d'Ur au siècle d'Hammurabi (XIXe–XVIIIe siècles av. J.-C.)*, Hautes Études Orientales 22, Geneva: Librairie Droz.

Charpin, D., 1999. Review of *OIP* 98, *Revue d'Assyriologie* 93: 178–80.

Cooper, J. S., 1978. *The Return of Ninurta to Nippur*, Analecta orientalia 52, Rome: Pontifical Biblical Institute.

Falkenstein, A., 1966. *Die Inschriften Gudeas von Lagaš – I. Einleitung*, Analecta orientalia 30, Rome: Pontifical Biblical Institute.

Frayne, D. R., 1998. New light on the reign of Išme-Dagān, *Zeitschrift für Assyriologie* 88: 6–44.

George, A. R., 1993. *House Most High: The Temples of Ancient Mesopotamia*, MC 5, Winona Lake, Ind.: Eisenbrauns.

Hill, H. D., Jacobsen, T. and Delougaz, P., 1990. *Old Babylonian Public Buildings in the Diyala Region*, Oriental Institute Publications 98, Chicago: Oriental Institute Publications.

Hrouda, B. (ed.), 1992. *Isin – Išan Baḥrīyāt IV. Die Ergebnisse der Ausgrabungen 1986–1989*, Bayerische Akademie der Wissenschaften, Philosophisch-Historische Klasse Abhandelungen – Neue Folge Heft 105, Munich: Beck.

Kraus, F. R., 1984. *Königliche Verfügungen in altbabylonischer Zeit*, Studia et documenta ad iura orientis antiqui pertinentia 11, Leiden: Brill.

Richter, T., 1999. *Untersuchungen zu den lokalen Panthea Süd- und Mittelbabyloniens in altbabylonischer Zeit*, Alter Orient und Altes Testament 257, Münster: Ugarit-Verlag.

Sallaberger, W., 1997. Nippur als religiöses Zentrum Mesopotamiens im historischen Wandel, 147–68, in G. Wilhelm (ed.), *Der orientalische Stadt: Kontinuität, Wandel, Bruch. 1. Internationales Colloquium der Deutschen Orient-Gesellschaft 9.10. Mai 1996 in Halle / Saale*, Saarbrücken: Saarbrücker Druckerei und Verlag.

Steinkeller, P., 1999. On Rulers, Priests and Sacred Marriage: Tracing the Evolution of Early Sumerian Kingship, in K. Watanabe (ed.), *Priests and Officials in the Ancient Near East. Papers of the Second Colloquium of the Ancient Near East – The City and its Life Held at the Middle Eastern Culture Center in Japan (Mitaka, Tokyo) March 22–24, 1996*, Heidelberg: Winter, 103–37.

Tinney, S., 1996. *The Nippur Lament: Royal Rhetoric and Divine Legitimation in the Reign of Išme-Dagan of Isin (1953–1935* B.C.*)*, Occasional Publications of the Samuel Noah Kramer Fund, 16, Philadelphia: Samuel Noah Kramer Fund, University of Pennsylvania Museum.

II. Old Babylonian Period

The term "Old Babylonian Period" can be used with different meanings in mind. For some writers it refers to the whole period from the end of the Ur III Dynasty until the fall of Babylon, but for others the term emphasizes the role of the city and kings of Babylon in shaping the course of events in Mesopotamia, and they reserve it for the period when the dynasty of Babylon held its position of influence, the founding of which is usually associated with the reign of king Hammurabi (1792–1750 BC).

The rise of Babylon was an outcome of an epoch of rapid and turbulent changes in the political organization of Mesopotamia and is documented by a rich array of historical sources. Around 1800 BC the upper Mesopotamian kingdoms of Yahdun-Lim of Mari and Shamshi-Adad of Ekallatum competed for supremacy and interacted, with hostile as well as friendly intent, with the kingdom of Eshnunna, the unmatched power of lower Mesopotamia. The union of the kingdoms of Ekallatum and Mari gave birth to the short-lived empire of Shamshi-Adad, but upon the death of its founder the old ruling families returned to their thrones, a situation that allowed the kings of Aleppo and Eshnunna to increase their influence in upper Mesopotamia. In the South, Eshnunna was tied by common interests with Larsa and its aging king, Rim-Sin, and Babylon found itself enclosed by this alliance well into the reign of Hammurabi.

When Eshnunna fell to the Elamites the situation radically changed. Hammurabi proved himself a cunning and decisive strategist and came outas the champion of the war with Elam. In a quick succession of events he established Babylon as the unrivalled power of lower Mesopotamia and increased his influence in upper Mesopotamia. However, the political unity of Mesopotamia proved short-lived, for his son Samsuiluna (1749–1712 BC) faced widespread rebellions that in due course resulted in the establishment of the Sea Land Dynasty somewhere in the South. Also the environmental decline of the southern alluvium aggravated in this period of disorder, finally leading to the abandonment of urban centers and the northward migration of the population.

The later history of the First Dynasty of Babylon is still shrouded in undesired obscurity. The competition between Babylon and Aleppo over influence in upper Mesopotamia slowly gave way to the establishment of new indigenous political structures in that area. New players manifested themselves elsewhere as well, such as the Kassites who offered their military services to the kings of Babylon and ruled semi-independently over territories in the Babylonian periphery, or the Hittites in Anatolia, whose kings of the Old Hittite Period persistently pushed forward into Syria and upper Mesopotamia. Their efforts were crowned by Murshili's celebrated raid on Babylon (1595 BC), and in doing so he dethroned Babylon's last king, Samsuditana, and brought a formal end to the Old Babylonian period.

A. Mari royal inscriptions

50. Inscription of Yahdun-Lim, king of Mari (ca. 1810–1794 BC)

(In Akkadian [nine exemplars with varying line arrangements; total length 143 to 157 lines], on bricks from Mari.)

For Shamash, the king of heaven and earth, the commander of the gods and mankind, his share is justice, truth is bestowed on him as a grant, the shepherd of the black-headed (people), the exalted god, the judge of all that lives, who hears appeals, who listens to prayers, who takes petitions, who gives a life of happiness and long days to those who revere him, the lord of Mari, – Yahdun-Lim, son of Yagid-Lim, the king of Mari and the land of Hana, who opens rivers, who builds walls, who inserts memorials that mention his name, who sets prosperity and affluence for his people, who makes everything available in his land, the strong king, the exalted youth, – when Shamash had heard his appeal and had listened to his words, (since) Shamash loves Yahdun-Lim, he went at his side and where, since the distant day when the god created the city of Mari, no king who resides in Mari had reached the seas, had reached the mountains of cedar and boxwood, the great mountains or had cut its trees – Yahdun-Lim, son of Yagid-Lim, the mighty king, the bull among kings, with his power and might came to the shore of the sea and made his great royal offering to the ocean. And his troops bathed with water in the middle of the ocean. He entered the mountains of cedar and boxwood, the great mountains and cut these trees: boxwood, cedar, cypress and elammakum-wood. He erected his monument and set himself a name. And he made his power manifest. He subdued that land at the shore of the ocean. He made it reside at a (single) command. He made it follow behind him. He imposed a permanent tribute on them and they carry their tribute to him.

In that same year, La'um, the king of Samanum and the land of Uprapum; Bahlu-kulim, the king of Tuttul and the land of Amnanum; Ayalum, the king of Abattum and the land of Rabbum – these kings became hostile against him, and the troops of Sumu-epuh, the king of the land of Yamhad, came to them for military support. In the town of Samanum, the masses of the Yaminites assembled as one against him. He caught these three kings of the Yaminites with his strong weapon. He killed their troops and their support troops. He inflicted a defeat on them. He heaped up their corpses in a pile. He destroyed their walls and turned them into ruins and wasteland. The town of Haman of the masses of the Haneans, which all the "fathers" of the Haneans had built, he destroyed and turned it into ruins and wasteland. He caught its king Kasurihala. He took away their land and unified the Bank of the Euphrates.

He built for the sake of his own life a temple, a building that is perfect of construction and completed in craftsmanship, befitting his divinity, for Shamash, his lord, and made him reside in his great abode. He called the name of that temple: Egirlazanki, the "house of celebration of heaven and earth."

May Shamash, the resident of this temple, bestow on Yahdun-Lim, the builder of his temple, the king beloved of his heart, a strong weapon that conquers the enemy, a long reign of happiness and years of affluence (and) rejoicing for lasting days.

He who will desecrate this temple, will plan bad and undesirable acts against it, will not strengthen its foundations, will not erect what has collapsed and will interrupt its offerings, will erase my written name or will have it erased, will write down his unwritten name or will have it written down or, because of the curses, will instruct somebody else (to do so) – this man, be it a king, or a governor or a mayor or whatever human being, may Enlil, the commander of the gods, make the kingship of this man smaller than that of all kings; may Sin, the eldest brother among the gods, his brothers, curse him with a big curse, may Nergal, the lord of the weapon, break his weapon so that he cannot confront warriors, may Ea, the king of destiny, make his destiny a bad one, may bride Aja, the great mistress, forever be the one who pleads against him in front of Shamash! May Bunene, the great vizier of Shamash, cut of his throat, pluck his seed and may his offspring and his name not escape from Shamash!

These bricks were installed in the foundations of the temple of Shamash at Mari and commemorate the renovation of this building by Yahdun-Lim. In the historical portion of the text, Yahdun-Lim narrates the heroic exploits of his reign: his campaign to the shores of the Mediterranean Sea and into the hilly forests and the defeat of the Yaminites. The first action evokes the legendary works of Gilgamesh and was one of the most emblematic deeds on hand for a Mesopotamian king to distinguish himself as the ideal hero.

Building with cedars patently displayed the feat at home, and the burnt remnants of cedar beams in the Shamash temple show how Yahdun-Lim put the profit of his expedition to use.

Yahdun-Lim's motive for campaigning in the West was to assist to his ally, the king of Qatna, but his inscription does not elaborate this aspect. This engagement on behalf of Qatna provoked the anger of Sumu-epuh, the king of Yamhad (with Aleppo as his capital) who rivalled Qatna for power in the Syrian area. Sumu-epuh succeeded in turning three kings against Yahdun-Lim, each of them described as the ruler of a town and a particular tribe. They are collectively called the "kings of the Yaminites": the text employs here a short form (dumu-*mi-im*) of the better-known form "sons of Yamina" (dumu-meš-*ia-mi-na* and variants). The Yaminites were a prevalent ethnic group in the Middle Euphrates region, roughly of the area between Emar and Mari, and made up an important part of the population of the kingdom of Mari. Yahdun-Lim and Zimri-Lim, however, claimed leadership of the Sim'alites, another important and ramified ethnic group, especially in the area of the Habur headwaters, and their repeated conflicts with the Yaminites were no doubt stirred by rivalry for power between these two groups. The inscription of Yahdun-Lim carries on with a description of his subjugation of the Haneans. The notoriously elusive term *Hana* is the name of a land, more specifically that around the city of Terqa, but appears commonly in Mari texts to describe people. In this usage, the term "Haneans" can most of the time be taken to refer to a particular way of life ("nomads"), but sometimes to particular ethnic groups as well. Which nuance the term carries in the present text remains unclear.

Bibliography: RIME 4.6.8.2 = *COS* 2.111.

B. Dadusha Stele

51. Inscription of Dadusha, king of Eshnunna (ca. 1800–1779 BC)

(A stone stele found in the vicinity of Tell Asmar [ancient Eshnunna] in Akkadian [220 lines divided over 17 columns].)

(I) Adad, the warrior, the son of Anum, whom the great gods in a lordly way have given the ultimate power, the massive roar that makes heaven and earth tremble, to lift the head up high, who lets terrifying bolts of lightning (and) destructive stones (II) angrily rain down on the enemy land, the lord, whom by his own command is given wealth from east to west, made the massive flood superb in the land – for Adad, the perfect warrior, who renews the destinies of his reign for all time,

(III) Dadusha, the son of Ipiq-Adad, the strong king, whose name has been called magnificently from his creation in the womb to carry out the rule over the totality of the land, the beloved of Tishpak, the deliberate king, whom Adad, his god, majestically decreed to throw down his enemies with a strong weapon, the king of Eshnunna, eternal seed, whom lord Shamash (IV) led to his heart's desire (?) and (for whom) he majestically determined the destruction of the land of his opponents, Dadusha, supreme chief of kings, who binds

his enemies, who places the punishment of his strong weapon on the land of his opponents, who acquires fame for great victories on the battlefield, the son of Ipiq-Adad, am I.

When Anum and Enlil (V) with a magnificent order instructed me in a lordly way to execute kingship over the universe forever and govern the totality of the peoples, (when) at the declaration of warrior Tishpak and Adad, my god, the skill of battle, that of throwing down all evil and of lifting up the head of Eshnunna, was majestically given to me – at that time Qabarā, where none of the princes, my predecessors (VI) who have ruled in Eshnunna, nor of the kings who exist in the whole world, where no king at all had ventured to besiege it, to this land that hated me and failed to bow down respectfully upon the evocation of my honourable name I sent ten thousand first rate troops. With the strong weapon of warrior Tishpak and Adad, my god, (VII) I passed through its territory like the wild kašūšum (divine destruction). His allied forces and all his warriors, none of them offered me any resistance, his widespread cities Tutarra, Hatkum, Hurarā, Kirhum and his extensive settlements I swiftly seized with my strong weapon. I truly had their gods, their booty and their precious wealth brought to Eshnunna, my royal capital. (VIII) After I had laid waste to its surrounding territories and crushed his extensive land, I majestically approached Qabarā, his main city. In ten days I seized this city by means of a surrounding siege wall, by heaping up earth, with the help of a breach, an attack and my great strength. I swiftly bound its king Bunu-Ishtar by the blaze of my strong weapon and I truly had his head quickly brought to Eshnunna. (IX) The determination of the kings who supported him and his allies dissolved altogether and I truly set them in deadly silence. I brought in a lordly way his vast booty, the heavy treasure of this city, gold, silver, precious stones, fine luxuries and everything else that this land possessed, to Eshnunna, my royal capital, and (X) I truly exhibited it to all people, young and old, of the upper and lower land. All that remained in this land, this city, its vast territory and its settlements, I truly gave as a gift to Samsi-Addu, the king of Ekallatum. Up above in the land of Subartum, from the land of Burunda and the land of Eluhti (XI) to the mountain of Diluba and the mountain of Lullum, this land I truly crushed angrily with my strong weapon. I truly achieved that the kings who exist in the whole world will forever keep on praising me. In the course of the same year I built Dur-Dadusha, my frontier city, on the banks of the Tigris and I truly brought my good name into existence for all eternity.

(XII) Because [. . .] an eternal name [. . . a stele (?)] (XIV) I truly erected for all time in Etemenursag, the temple of Adad, the god who raised me, (XII) upon which is ***(1)*** *the image of my heroism, a slayer majestically endowed with the splendour of battle to overwhelm the enemy land;* ***(2)*** *above him radiantly appear Sin and Shamash, who strengthen my weapon to prolong the years of my reign;* ***(3)*** *above the wall of Qabarā is* ***(4)*** *Bunu-Ishtar, the king of the land of Urbel (i.e. Arbil), whom I angrily bound with my strong weapon, (XIII) on whom he (the royal figure) treads from above, standing in a lordly way;* ***(5)*** *below him wild warriors carefully hold the bound – its lapidary quality has no rival, precisely executed in skilful labour of craftsmanship, surpassing words of praise, in order to stand day after day in front of Adad, my god who created me, to support my well-being and renew the destiny of my reign.*

(XIV) Adad, give Dadusha, the prince who reveres you, a strong weapon that binds his enemy, everlasting life, years of wealth and affluence as a gift! So that the land will always and forever keep on instructing my words of praise, that the old tells the young (XV) of my heroic [deeds], for this purpose I had a stele inscribed with an eternal name.

Who instructs with evil intentions and obliterates my figure, removes it from its position, hides it at a place where the eye will not behold it, will throw it in the water,

Figure 1 The Dadusha Stele (after Miglus 2003)

will bury it in the ground, destroy it with fire, (XVI) *erase my inscribed name, write his name, or, on account of the curse, instructs somebody else, saying: "erase [. . .] his (?) written name and write my name!" – may Anum, Enlil, Sin, Shamash, Tishpak, Adad, my god, and the great gods bitterly and full-heartedly curse this king and may they never allow the mention of his name to exist in the land!* (XVII) *May the Annunaku (gods), those of heaven and earth, angrily swear to destroy his descendants – he himself and all of his family! May Ninurta, the caretaker of Ekur (temple) not allow him to acquire offspring that will mention his name! May his treasure constantly get out of reach!*

The stone stele that carries this inscription was found by accident in 1983, when a well was drilled outside of Tell Asmar (Eshnunna). This elongated stone monument (180 cm high, 37 cm wide and 18,5 cm thick) is inscribed on the two narrow sides, while the front side is decorated with four registers of relief scenes, the centre of which has suffered damage during discovery. It was removed in antiquity from its original position to the find spot, for the text indicates that the stele once stood in the temple of Adad, king Dadusha's personal deity, in Eshnunna.

The building of the frontier stronghold Dur-Dadusha was, according to the text, the formal occasion for the creation of this monument, but the king's military exploits stand unmistakably in the centre of the narrative and the relief scenes. The text expresses that the stele was meant as an everlasting public testimony of the king's heroic deeds, and the account of the defeat of Bunu-Ishtar and the conquest of Qabarā was no doubt appreciated as a prime example of royal valour. This war is also described in other sources: The stele hints that Shamsi-Addu of Ekallatum played a part in the project, and the contemporary letters from Mari and Shemshara show that it was in fact a joint enterprise of the kings of Ekallatum and Eshnunna, who were at that time united by treaty. Moreover, a stele of Samsi-Addu immortalizing the same events has survived as well (RIMA I A.0.39.1001).

The campaign took place in 1980 BC, the penultimate year of Dadusha's reign, and it is likely that the king of Eshnunna did not participate in person; the letters report that Shamsi-Addu and his sons led the troops against several fortified cities throughout the summer of that year, until Qabarā was conquered in the fall. The kingdom of Bunu-Ishtar was located in the plains east of the Tigris, between the Upper and the Lower Zab. The text calls Bunu-Ishtar the "king of Arbil", a title that expresses the importance of this ancient cult centre in his kingdom, but the city of Qabarā, located near a strategic crossing over the Lower Zab, seems to have been the main citadel of his realm.

A unique feature of this monument is the correlation between the text and the images, for the inscription contains a description of some scenes of the relief (numbers between brackets refer to the translation). The upper of the four relief registers contains two figures facing each other. The text allows to identify the figure of the left as **(1)** an "image of heroism" of king Dadusha, in the position of a "slayer". The figure in adoration opposite of him is unidentified, but may represent the crown prince, or perhaps a general. Above these two figures appear the moon crescent and sun disk as the symbols of the gods **(2)** Shamash and Sin. The king treads on the slain king **(4)** Bunu-Ishtar, while below them the **(3)** wall of Qabarā appears. Below the representation of the city are two registers (separated by depictions of mountain ranges) with scenes of **(5)** members of the army subduing and guarding the enemy soldiers. The bottom register depicts the decapitated heads of subjugated kings being attacked by vultures.

Bibliography: Ismaïl and Cavigneaux 2003.

C. *Ekallatum royal inscriptions*

52. Inscription of Shamshi-Adad, king of Ekallatum (1796–1775 BC)

(In Akkadian [three columns on each side, total length 135 lines], on stone tablets from Assur. The city and the god Assur carry the same name, but are here, for the sake of clarity, distinguished as Assur, resp. Ashur.)

Shamshi-Adad, king of the universe, builder of the temple of Ashur, unifier (?) of the land between Tigris and Euphrates by the command of Ashur who loves him, whom Anum and Enlil called by his name for greatness from the kings who went before – the temple of Enlil, which Erishum, son of Ilushumma, had built, (that) temple had become dilapidated and I cleaned it away and built in the midst of my city Assur the temple of Enlil, my lord, an awe-inspiring dais, a large sanctuary, the seat of Enlil, my lord, which was fashioned perfectly with skillful work of the building trade. I roofed the temple with cedars. I erected doors of cedarwood, whose stars are of silver and gold, in the rooms. I coated the walls of the temple with a plaster of silver, gold, lapis lazuli, carnelian, cedar oil, fine oil, honey and butter. I constructed the temple of Enlil, my lord, and called its name Eamkurkura, "House: wild bull of the lands," the temple of Enlil, my lord, in the midst of my city Assur.

When I built the temple of Enlil, my lord, the market (prices) of my city Assur (were): for one shekel of silver two kor of barley, for one shekel of silver 15 minas of wool, for one shekel of silver two seahs of oil were truly bought on the market of my city Assur.

At that time I truly received the tribute of the kings of Tukrish and the king of the Upper Land in the midst of my city Assur. I truly set up my great name and my memorials in the land of Lebanon on the shore of the Great Ocean.

When the temple will become dilapidated, may (then) whoever among the kings, my sons, who will renovate the temple, anoint my foundation inscriptions and memorials with oil, may he bring a sacrifice and put them back in place. Who will not anoint my foundation inscriptions and memorials with oil, will not bring a sacrifice and will not put them back in place, but instead will alter my memorials by taking out my name and writing his own name, will bury (them) it the ground (or) throw (them) in the water – may Shamash, Enlil, Adad and Sharru-matim pluck the offspring of that king, may he with his army fail to block the path of his enemy king, may Nergal with superb force appropriate time and again his treasure and the treasure of his land, may Ishtar, mistress of battle, break his weapon and the weapon of his army, may Sin, the god of my head, be his evil demon forever!

This inscription commemorates the building of the temple of Enlil in Assur and was written on a number of stone tablets, most of which were found, in a secondary context, in the area of the temple of Ashur. It has long been open to question to what building this inscription refers. Excavations have shown that Shamshi-Adad rebuilt the Ashur temple on a grand scale, and like this established a layout that was maintained until the final destruction of the temple. His name is found on numerous bricks and other objects from the building with the text "Shamshi-Adad, builder of the temple of Ashur," a title repeated in the beginning of this inscription. The main body of the inscription, however, concerns a temple for Enlil. This has often been taken as an indication that Shamshi-Adad dedicated the Ashur temple to Enlil, a southern Mesopotamian god that was later on closely linked with Ashur (Menzel 1981: 65), but a study of the ground plan of the Ashur temple (Miglus 1990) has suggested that the building was originally conceived as a double temple for Ashur and Enlil.

Shamshi-Adad was a king of Ekallatum and conquered Assur early in his reign. The old institutions of the city-state were no doubt profoundly affected by the integration into his kingdom, and this inscription shows that the new political situation also had its effect on the cult. Enlil features prominently in the life of Shamshi-Adad, for example in the name of his capital city Shubat-Enlil, "seat of Enlil," and it can be expected that he promoted this cult in the sacred city of Assur as well. The city population saw this no doubt as an outright deed of sacrilege, for Puzur-Sin, a native king of Assur who reigned soon after the Shamshi-Adad dynasty, scornfully describes their evil deeds and celebrates the restoration of old customs (RIMA I A.0.40).

Shamshi-Adad refers to an earlier building of Erishum I, a ruler of Assur of the twentieth century BC, whose own building inscription tells of his work on a temple of Ashur by the name of "House: wild bull" (RIMA I A.0.33.1), evidently the same name as given, in a longer form, by Shamshi-Adad to the Enlil temple. Shamshi-Adad emphasizes his use of cedar in building the temple, describes the decoration of the doors and the treatment of the walls. The text here lumps together two different actions: precious metals and stones were put as foundation deposits under the walls and aromatics and sweets were mixed with the mortar. This inscription dates to the final phase of the reign of Shamshi-Adad when, after the conquest of Mari, he claimed rule over the region between Tigris and Euphrates. The text summarizes the highlights of his reign: the tribute of Tukrish and the Upper Land indicate his recognition as overlord of the countries in the Zagros Mountains, and his monuments on the shore of the Mediterranean Sea, and the cedar beams used to build the Enlil temple are a testimony for his power over distant regions in the west. The list of ideal, cheap prices for the basic staples is an element that is known from other royal inscriptions as well and conveys the idea that the king brought about economic prosperity for the people.

Bibliography: RIMA I A.0.39.1 = *COS* 2.110.

D. Babylon

53. Inscription of Hammurabi, king of Babylon (1792–1750 BC)

(In Akkadian [81 lines], on cones from Sippar.)

When Shamash, the great lord of heaven and earth, the king of the gods, with a content face joyfully looked at me, Hammurabi, the prince, his favorite, granted me an eternal kingship, a reign of long days, set firm for me the foundations of the land that he had given to me to rule, ordered with his pure mouth that cannot be altered to settle the people of Sippar and Babylon in a dwelling of peace, instructed me to built the wall of Sippar, to raise its head – at that time I, Hammurabi, the strong king, the king of Babylon, the pious one who listens to Shamash, beloved of Aja, who gladdens the heart of Marduk, his lord, with the supreme force that Shamash has given to me, with the levy of the masses of my land, I truly raised with earth the foundations of the walls of Sippar high as a great mountain. I truly built that supreme wall. What since distant days no king among the kings had built, I truly built for Shamash, my lord. The name of that wall is: "May Hammurabi have no rival at the command of Shamash." In my good reign that Shamash has called, I truly exempted the troops of Sippar, the eternal city of Shamash, from corvée duty for the sake of Shamash. I truly dug its river. I truly established eternal water for its region. I truly accumulated prosperity and affluence. I truly established joy for the people of Sippar. They pray for my health. I truly did what pleases Shamash, my lord, and Aja, my mistress. I truly set in the mouth of the people to pronounce every day my good name like a god, something that will never be forgotten.

This inscription is set on cones with either the Akkadian or the Sumerian version of the text and commemorates the king's work on the wall of Abu Habbah, one of the two towns called Sippar and later distinguished as Sippar-Yahrurum. The building of the wall is mentioned in the twenty-third and twenty-fifth year name of Hammurabi and this inscription can be dated to about the same time. City walls in this part of Mesopotamia functioned as defense works as much as dikes against flooding, and the dredging of rivers mentioned in the text can be seen as part of the same operation. Hammurabi also claims to have given up his tax income from the citizens of Sippar, in money or in labour, for the benefit of the Shamash temple.

Bibliography: RIME 4.3.6.2 = *COS* 2.107A.

54. Inscription of Samsuiluna, king of Babylon (1749–1712 BC)

(In Sumerian [94 lines], on clay cylinders from Khafajah and Babylon.)

Samsuiluna, the strong king, the king of Babylon, the king of Kish, the king who brings the four corners of the world in agreement, the king who slew by the instruction of Enlil the totality of those who hate him, the shepherd whose favorable omen and support are made by Inanna, who bound the hand of all those who turn away from him, who made all evil ones disappear from the land, who brings out the bright daylight for the numerous people, foremost heir of Hammurabi, the lord who extended the land, the king who subdued the land of Idamaraṣ from the border of Gutium as far as the border of Elam with his strong weapon, who conquered the widespread people of the land of Idamaras, who demolished the totality of the fortresses of the land of Warûm that had rebelled against him, who achieved his victory, who manifested his power, who released after two months had passed the people of the land of Idamaraṣ whom he had taken as booty and the prisoners of the troops of Eshnunna as many as he had taken, who took action for them for the sake of their life, who built the various fortresses of the land of Warûm that had been destroyed, who assembled its scattered people, who restored them to their place – at that time, in order to settle the people who live on the bank of the Turul River and the Ṭaban River in a dwelling of peace, no intimidator to acquire (and) to have the whole land sing the praise of his might and heroism, Samsuiluna, the strong man, built in the course of two months Dūr-Samsuiluna on the bank of the Turul River. He dug its moat. He piled up its earth. He formed its bricks. He built its wall. He raised its head high as a mountain. On account of this, An, Enlil, Marduk, Enki and Inanna determined as his destiny to outfit him with a strong weapon that has no equal and with a life like that of Nanna and Utu. They bestowed it on him. The name of that wall is: "Enlil has made the land of those who hate him bow down before Samsuiluna."

This inscription commemorates the building of the fortress town of Dūr-Samsuiluna, the ruins of which were partly excavated at Khafajah Mound B by the University of Chicago in 1937–8. They investigated part of a rectangular fortified enclosure and two of the buildings inside it, one of which most likely had a public function. A clay cylinder with this text was found under the floor of a gateway in the city wall, and a fragment of another cylinder, this time with the Akkadian version of the text, is reported from the same site as well. Another cylinder with the Sumerian version of the text comes from a house in Babylon, where a library and archival texts from the second half of the reign of Samsuiluna were found (Pedersén 1998: 330–2). The purpose of this piece in the archive is not clear, nor has the identity of the inhabitants of this house been established, but the find confirms that these objects also circulated among the contemporary public.

The inscription recounts the conquest of Idamaraṣ a land east of the Tigris, and Warûm, the adjoining land situated in the basin of the Diyala River with Eshnunna as its capital city, and the lenient treatment of their populations. Dūr-Samsuiluna was built in Samsuiluna's twenty-third year, as is known from the following year name, and the actions described in the text may be linked with the war with Eshnunna recorded in his twentieth year name.

Bibliography: RIME 4.2.7.8 = *COS* 2.108.

55. Inscription of Ammiditana, king of Babylon (1683–1647 BC)

(Preserved as a copy on a clay tablet of uncertain date. Bilingual text; the translation follows the Akkadian version [beginning and end broken, 37 lines preserved].)

[Beginning broken . . . the gods] commanded with their pure mouths [. . .] me to lift my head high (and) no leader to rise against my lordship. Shamash and Marduk, who love my reign, have made my kingship surpassing in the world corners and wholly bestowed the black-headed people on me to rule. I guided the land of Sumer and Akkad aright. I [settled] the widespread people in a dwelling of peace. I [gladdened] the heart of the land. In those days, with the wisdom that Ea had given to me, in order to proudly shepherd the widespread people of my land in pasturage and watering place [. . .] (one word) (and) let them rest in the river meadows, I created Dūr-Ammiditana above the Sharbit River on (its) east and west side. I built their great walls. I rooted them as firm as a mountain. I exalted my supreme name forever. The wall [. . . Remainder broken]

This tablet contains the text that was inscribed on some public monument, such as a stele or a statue, in two languages, with the Sumerian and Akkadian versions in separate columns side by side. The same layout is found in a few fragments of original monuments of Hammurabi and in clay tablet copies of lost monuments of Abieshuh, Ammiditana, and Ammisaduqa. This layout was reserved for monuments that were displayed in the public domain, while building inscriptions on cones and cylinders, which were buried in the foundations of temples and other buildings, were written in one language only.

This text can be attributed to Ammiditana on account of the name of the fortress. The description of its site shows that it was situated at a point where a river arm branched off from the main riverbed and flowed from north to south. The fortress occupied both of its banks. A contemporary letter describes Dūr-Ammiditana as lying "on the mouth of the Silakum River" (van Soldt 1990 83), thus confirming the suggestion that the name Šarbit of the present text is a variant name of the better-known Silakum River.

Bibliography: RIME 4.3.9.2.

Bibliography

Ismaïl, B. K. and Cavigneaux, A., 2003. Dādušas Siegesstele IM 95200 aus Ešnunna. Die Inschrift, *Baghdader Mitteilungen*, 34: 129–156 and plates 1–7.

Menzel, B., 1981. *Assyrische Tempel*, Studia Pohl: Series Maior 10, Rome: Pontifical Biblical Institute.

Miglus, P. A., 1990. Auf der Suche nach dem "Ekur" in Assur, *Baghdader Mitteilungen* 21: 303–20.

Miglus, P. A., 2003. Die Siegesstele des Königs Dāduša von Ešnunna und ihre Stellung in der Kunst Mesopotamiens und der Nachbargebiete, 397–419. In R. Dittmann, C. Eder and B. Jacobs (eds.), *Altertumswissenschaften im Dialog. Festschrift für Wolfram Nagel*, Alter Orient und Altes Testament 306, Münster: Ugarit Verlag.

Pedersén, O., 1998. Zu den altbabylonischen Archiven aus Babylon, *Altorientalische Forschungen* 25: 328–38.

van Soldt, W. H., 1990. *Letters in the British Museum. Altbabylonische Briefe in Umschrift und Übersetzung* 12, Leiden: Brill.

5

Miscellaneous Old Babylonian Period Documents

Frans van Koppen

I. Old Babylonian Year Names

It was customary in Mesopotamia, from the late Early Dynastic period to the early Kassite period, to designate each year with a formula that mentions an event of the preceding year or, less often, with one referring to an era that had started with an event of the more distant past. Used in all kinds of legal and administrative records and surviving in large numbers, these so-called year names are an invaluable source of historical information. Nonetheless, they present challenges, not only in identifying and ordering them, but also in decoding their message and understanding the native attitudes that governed the choice of a particular event and the words used to describe it.

Year names are royal literature. Whenever sufficient sources are available, correlations between the year names, inscriptions, and hymns of the same ruler often appear. They discuss the same events and now and again share specific language, thereby encouraging the idea that these texts lean on a common source: the discourse of the royal court. Year names were coined by the palace and then passed on to the outside world, but how they were made public is little known. Here year names were widely used for everyday purposes, and were familiar to a large segment of the population. Thus the year name, as the most widely disseminated piece of royal discourse, can be seen as a powerful tool to convey particular images of kingship to the people.

Year names commemorate recent events that the ruler and his circles deemed most laudable. The opening years were traditionally spoken for, the first dealing with the king's accession, the second, since Hammurabi, with the "establishment of justice"; that is, the enactment of a redress measure. Subject matter for other year names is threefold: pious work for the gods, good deeds for the people, and defeat of the enemies. The king's deeds are invariably related to the gods. Each ruler could celebrate deeds of every category, but there is a gradual change in emphasis throughout the reign of the Babylonian dynasty. Hammurabi's conquests initiated a "heroic" phase that lasted until the end of the reign of Samsuiluna and is characterized by a predilection for military deeds. These rulers also commemorate works for the people and for the gods, but it was this last category in particular that became very prominent in the year names of their successors, to the virtual exclusion of mention of foreign or military actions.

Form and substance of the year names of the First Dynasty of Babylon changed over time: the short, unadorned descriptions of a single event from the early period gave way to statements of considerable length and complexity at the time of later rulers. But this impression might rely too much on fragmentary evidence, for elaborate formulas could be abbreviated to the barest minimum. This point can be made with the name of Hammurabi's fourteenth year, surviving in a long form (translated below) but appearing elsewhere in forms as short as three words. The alleged growth of the length of year names is therefore in part the effect of a scribal trend to write out more of the year name formula in the date of documents than was conventional before. Nevertheless, it is clear that the style and word choice of year names changed markedly during the reign of Hammurabi. His later year names, and those of his successors, draw on a highly literary language and include subordinate clauses that refer to divine support or attributes of the king, features that were unknown before. The point of change in this seems to be the name of his thirtieth year, commemorating a crucial military victory and a decisive moment of his career.

Below the year names of Hammurabi (1792–1750 BC) are translated. They were composed and promulgated in a set formula, but the complete text of this formula has only rarely survived. The best witnesses are the so-called "promulgation documents": tablets with no more than the full form of a year name, in Sumerian only or in Sumerian and Akkadian versions, which were most likely used to communicate the formula to some unknown audience at the beginning of the year. At least some of them can be considered as the original message of the palace, but others might be secondary copies. All other attestations of year names are found in the work of local scribes; that is, legal and administrative records and date lists. Their scribal output can be used to reconstruct the complete, original text of the year name and, with a closely related yet different approach, to study how a local audience received, adapted, and reproduced the message of the palace.

In everyday records, scribes normally use a short form of the full formula, and different abbreviations for the same formula occur. Most variants are easily recognizable as alternative short forms of the same lengthy text, but some differ considerably from the rest and may represent local interpretations of the formula and the events. Date lists enumerate year names of the recent past in chronological order, usually in abbreviated form, and served practical needs. Some, however, may have been written with different aims in mind, such as lists with very lengthy versions (date list O below), or lists of year names of the more distant past.

The translation is based on the comprehensive survey of M. J. A. Horsnell (1999), but does not adopt the full forms of year names reconstructed in this book. Instead, we follow a well-preserved date list, possibly written shortly after Hammurabi's reign, with all year names in short forms, which we will complement, if available, with longer forms from other sources; that is, the dates of everyday documents, promulgation documents and other date lists. In some cases, versions from several sources are given. On occasion these versions are incomplete sentences, which are then marked as "(. . .)." Sigla and abbreviations for text editions follow Horsnell 1999.

56. The year names of Hammurabi (date list K)

Ha 1 The year: Hammurabi, the king.
Ha 2 The year: he established justice in his country.
Ha 3 The year: the throne of Nanna of Babylon.
(Date list C) The year: he fashioned the magnificent dais-throne (for) Nanna of Babylon.
Ha 4 The year: the "cloister."
(Date list C) [The year:] he built the wall of the "cloister."
Ha 5 The year: the lord, who decides about heaven and earth.
Ha 6 The year: the dais of Ninpirig.
(Date list C) [The year:] he fashioned [a dais for Ninpirig].
Ha 7 [The year:] Uruk (and) Isin.
(TCL 1 81) The year: he took Uruk and Isin.
Ha 8 [The year:] the country on the bank of the Shumudar River.
Ha 9 [The year:] the "Hammurabi" River.
(CT 48 70) The year: the "Hammurabi (is) affluence" River.
Ha 10 The year: the surroundings of Malgium.
(TCL 1 83) The year: he destroyed the city and surroundings of Malgium.
Ha 11 The year: Rapiqum.
(CT 33 26b) The year: he took Rapiqum.
Ha 12 The year: [the throne] of Zarpanitum.
(VS 8 114) The year: he fashioned the throne (for) Zarpanitum.
Ha 13 The year: the royal stand.
(VS 13 32) The year: he fashioned for him/her mountains and rivers.
Ha 14 [The year:] the throne of Inanna of Babylon.
(Promulgation document A) The year when Hammurabi, the king, fashioned the magnificent dais-throne, perfected with gold and silver, eye-chalcedony, chalcedony of gír.múš-type and lapis lazuli, shining like radiance, for Inanna of Babylon to complete her chariot (outfit).
Ha 15 The year: seven statues.
(FLP 1340) The year: he placed seven <statues> in their positions.
Ha 16 [The year:] the throne of Nabium.
(VS 8 135) The year: he fashioned the throne (for) Nabium.
Ha 17 [The year:] the throne of Inanna of Ilip.
(BE 6/2 71) The year when Hammurabi, the king, elevated the statue of Inanna of Ilip.
Ha 18 [The year:] the dais for Enlil.
(CT 8 43c) The year: he fashioned a magnificent dais (for) Enlil.

Ha 19 [The year:] the magnificent wall of Igihursaga.

(MHET 2/2 202) The year when Hammurabi, the king, built the magnificent wall of Igihursaga.

Ha 20 [The year: the throne] of Adad.

(CBTBM II BM 22553) The year: he fashioned a throne for Adad of Babylon.

Ha 21 [The year: the wall of the city of Ba]ṣum.

(CT 47 38) The year: Hammurabi, the king, built the wall of the city of Baṣum.

Ha 22 [The year: the statue of Hammu]rabi.

(Date list F) The year: the statue "Hammurabi, king of justice."

Ha 23 [broken]

(Date list L) The year: the fundaments of the wall of Sippar.

Ha 24 [broken].

(VS 13 28) The year: he dug the Tilimda-Enlil River and the Euphrates River.

Ha 25 [broken].

(VS 22 2) The year when he built the great wall of Sippar.

Ha 26 [The year:] the great daises.

(MHET 2/2 218) The year: he fashioned great daises of gold for Shamash, Adad and Aya.

Ha 27 [The year: the magnificent] standard.

(VS 9 27) The year: he fashioned a magnificent standard of gold, which goes in front of the troops, for the great gods.

Ha 28 The year: Enamhe.

(MHET 2/2 230) The year: he built the temple of Adad.

Ha 29 [The year:] the statue of Shala.

(ARN 65) The year: Hammurabi, the king, fashioned a statue for Shala.

Ha 30 The year: the army of Elam.

(Date list O) The year when Hammurabi, the king, the forceful one, beloved of Marduk, (with) the magnificent power of the great gods, overthrew the army of Elam which, from the border of Marhashi, had raised Shubartum, Gutium, Eshnunna and Malgium (as) their main army group, and made the foundations of the land of Sumer and Akkad firm.

Ha 31 The year: the country of Yamutbalum.

(Date list O) The year when Hammurabi, the king, who marches with confidence in An and Enlil in front of the [troops], whom the great gods have given magnificent [power], conquered [the country] of Yamutbalum [and (its) king] Rim-Sin, . . . (a main clause of one line unclear), and made Sumer and Akkad dwell at [his command].

Ha 32 The year: the army of Eshnunna.

(Date list O) [The year when Hammurabi, the king, the hero, who attains victory for Marduk], slew in battle the army of Eshnunna, Shubartum (and) Gutium with (his) strong weapon and conquered Mankisum and the banks of the Tigris River up to the country of Shubartum.

Ha 33 The year: the "Hammurabi (is) prosperity for the people" River.

(Date list O) The year when Hammurabi, the king, dug the "Hammurabi, the prosperity for the people, is the favorite of An and Enlil" River and established eternal water of affluence for Nippur, Eridu, Ur, Larsa, Uruk (and) Isin, restored the land of Sumer and Akkad which had been scattered to their place, threw down the army of Mari and Malgium in battle, made Mari and its surroundings and many cities of Shubartum dwell in friendship at his command . . . (one short clause unclear).

(Riftin 69) The year: Hammurabi subjugated the country of Shubartum, Ekallatum, Burunda and the country of Zalmaqum, (from) the banks of the Tigris River as far as the Euphrates River.

Ha 34 The year: An, Inanna (and) Nanaya.
(TS 35) The year when Hammurabi, the king, whom An, Inanna and Nanaya made shine like the light of the skies, renovated Eturkalama.
Ha 35 The year: the wall of Mari.
(TCL 11 151) The year when Hammurabi, the king, at the command of An and Enlil, destroyed the walls of Mari and Malgium.
Ha 36 The year: Emeteursag.
(Date list O) The year when Hammurabi, the king, [renovated] Emeteursag, [built] the ziqqurat, the [magnificent] seat of Zababa and Inanna, whose top is raised high as heaven, (and) . . . (one word) greatly increased the divine splendor of Zababa and Inanna.
Ha 37 The year: the army of the Turukkeans.
(Date list O) The year when Hammurabi, the king, with the great power of Marduk, threw down the army of the Turukkeans, Kakmum and the land of Shubartum in battle.
Ha 38 The year: Eshnunna (with) great waters.
(Promulgation document N) The year when Hammurabi, the king, at the command of An and Enlil, (with) wisdom which Marduk gave him, destroyed Eshnunna (with) great waters (and) . . . (clause consisting of a place name and a verbal form unclear).
Ha 39 The year: the totality of the enemy.
(Larsa date list) The year when Hammurabi, the king, with the strong power that Enlil gave to him, slew the totality of the enemy of the land of Shubartum.
Ha 40 The year: Emeslam.
(TCL 11 176) The year when Hammurabi, the king, raised the head of Emeslam high as the mountains.
Ha 41 The year: Tashmetum.
(ARN 72) The year when Hammurabi, the king, Tashmetum, his prayers, red gold and choice stones (. . .).
Ha 42 The year: the wall of Kar-Shamash.
(N 1236) The year when Hammurabi, the king, raised a big wall on the bank of the Tigris high as the mountains and called its name Kar-Shamash.
Ha 43 The year: Sippar, eternal city [of Shamash].
(Date list O) [The year when Hammurabi, the king,] set the [wall of Sip]par with [a large amount of earth].
(summary) 43 years of Hammurabi.

II. Old Babylonian Letters

A. Letters from Mari

The vast royal archive from the palace of Mari covers a period of just 20 years, the last phase of occupation of the building, when it served as the main residence of Yasmah-Addu and Zimri-Lim. The archive consists of administrative material concerning the royal household and a very large body of letters, representing the "passive" share of the king's correspondence; that is, letters sent to him by his royal correspondents and, most of all, his servants posted in other centers of the kingdom and abroad. His archive also contains letters that were never dispatched, letters forwarded by other recipients and intercepted letters of the king's enemies. The letter archive was found in a state as created by the officials of Hammurabi, who classified and packed the tablets for transport to Babylon in the wake of the conquest of the city. This plan did not come to fruition and the tablets were buried when the palace burned down shortly afterwards. Part of the royal correspondence, however, had been evacuated before, which explains the absence of letters from particular senders.

The two rulers who received the letters operated under very different circumstances. Zimri-Lim, the last king of Mari, ruled over the kingdom of the "Bank of the Euphrates" that stretched along this river and its tributaries, but managed to extend his political influence much further, imposing himself as overlord of other kings in Northern Mesopotamia. His predecessor Yasmah-Addu was installed as vice-king in Mari by his father Shamshi-Adad, in the same way that his brother Ishme-Dagan ruled in Ekallatum on the Tigris. With Shamshi-Adad closely supervising all actions of his co-regents, Mari played only a minor role in political decision-making, and the correspondence of Yasmah-Addu is largely made up of letters with instructions and admonitions from other members of the ruling family. In the time of Zimri-Lim, however, Mari had become the seat of an important autonomous ruler who received petitions of his allies and vassals and a constant flow of reports of his diplomatic and military envoys from abroad to guide his responses in international affairs.

Authors of letters narrate historical events in order to convey particular messages to the king. Fellow kings, subservient vassals as well as equal partners, tried to win the king of Mari for their case and often overtly express their ambitions. Royal envoys aspired above all to convey their excellence as loyal servants of their master. One of their key tasks was to inform the king about whatever came to their notice, and they did so in "full reports" of all matters deemed important, recounting their own observations and qualifying the reliability of hearsay. These letters can include elements of the sender's own opinion and recommendations about future actions as well. Such reports were only put into writing when they could not be delivered verbally, and the arrival of the king in person on the scene often marks the end of a series of letters sent from one place.

Long-distance communication took place by means of messengers. The letter, and its sealed envelope, was above all intended to authenticate the messenger and what he had to tell, besides serving as a tool to record the substance of his message. The messenger played a vital role in contacts between kings, but his part in transmitting reports about the king's servants was no doubt less important. Even so, the surviving letter corpus can hardly be considered a complete record of the king's communications. Furthermore, a message between two informed partners presupposes knowledge of circumstances that is unavailable to the modern reader. Letters are rarely dated, and always survive as a single manuscript, where the state of preservation of the tablet, the lucidity of the writer and modern grasp of vernacular and idiom set further limits to understanding. Despite these obstacles, the study of the Mari letters and related text corpora has progressed to the point that this period can justifiably be considered the best-known years of ancient Mesopotamian history (Charpin and Ziegler 2003).

Only the last years of the so-called kingdom of Upper Mesopotamia, a political configuration inextricably bound up with the life of its creator Shamshi-Adad, are covered by the sources from Mari. During the eight years when his son Yasmah-Addu occupied the royal palace (1782–1775 BC), the kingdom reached the zenith of its power and waged war in east and west, but also disintegrated at breathtaking pace upon its master's death.

57. Letter of Yasmah-Addu to the god Nergal

(Tablet from the Mari palace. Partly broken; originally ca. 60 lines.)

Speak to fearsome Nergal, who has ordered me (to do) so: thus (says) Yasmah-Addu, your servant and your worshipper. Ever since my birth nobody who has sinned against god is still present. Everybody respects the order (?) of god. Long ago Ila-kabkabu and Yagid-Lim concluded a solemn treaty sworn by god and Ila-kabkabu committed no crime against Yagid-Lim, (but) Yagid-Lim committed a crime against Ila-kabkabu. You learned (this) and questioned him. [Then] you went at the side of Ila-kabkabu, and Ila-kabkabu destroyed his fortress and captured his [son] Yahdun-Lim. [When] Shamshi-Adad [ascended the throne of his father's house, he did not commit a crime against] Yagid-Lim [because of] the misdeeds of Yagid-Lim [which he had committed against] Ila-kabkabu [. . .] (Break in the text) [His son] Sumu-Yamam drove Yahdun-Lim away from Mari [because of his misdeeds] which he (i.e., Yahdun-Lim) had committed against Shamshi-Adad and because he keeps . . . (one word) of god. Sumu-Yamam started to act exactly like his father Yahdun-Lim. And he [did] inappropriate things by himself and destroyed your temple, which former kings had built, and built (there) the house of his wife. You came and questioned him. Then his servants killed him. You learned (this) and restored the whole Banks of the Euphrates in the hand of Shamshi-Adad. [Because] of the misdeeds of Sumu-Yamam [which] he had committed [against] Shamshi-Adad, you restored [the city of Mari] and the Bank of the Euphrates [in his hand]. He took me and installed me as [king] of Mari. (Some fragmentary lines; Yasmah-Addu describes his good rule and states his request:) Former [kings] wished for a wide land; I wish for life and offspring! (End of the text fragmentary)

This tablet is badly damaged but repetitions help to restore many of the breaks. The text states in the opening line that it is an answer to a message of the underworld-god Nergal, quite likely the god venerated in the city of Ṣuprum, the original capital of Yagid-Lim, situated on the opposite river bank from Mari. The tablet is carelessly written and is probably a draft for the tablet that was sent to the deity. It is not clear how messages were presented to a god, but one can imagine that they were read to the divine statue or his human agent and that the tablets was deposited in the sanctuary.

Yasmah-Addu states a general principle about moral behavior and elaborates this with an account of the relations between his family and the "Lim-Dynasty," with the intention of showing that he rightfully rules over Mari. This highly prejudiced story offers important information about a period in the history of the city for which contemporary sources are scarce.

Bibliography: ARM 1 3 = Durand 2000 no. 931.

58. Letter of Shamshi-Adad to Yasmah-Addu

(Tablet from the Mari palace, 63 lines.)

Speak to Yasmah-Addu: thus (says) Shamshi-Adad, your father. I wrote down on this tablet of mine a copy of the tablet that I wrote to Ishi-Addu and am herewith sending it to you. Hear it and write sweet words, in the manner of the words (of) the copy of his tablet that I sent to you, on a tablet and send it to him. (small open space on the tablet)

Speak to Ishi-Addu: thus (says) Shamshi-Adad, your brother. I heard that you gladly dispatched my daughter-in-law on a safe way back to me, that you treated [my servants] when they stayed with you well, [and that] they were not hindered at all. [My heart is very] happy.

[Concerning the message you sent] me in all sincerity, saying: "Sumu-epuh attacks me constantly!" – let him attack for one month, two months even, until this ambition will be achieved! That (matter) is not important: your land that is situated near his frontier must be assembled in strongholds. As for the entire army of the man of Eshnunna that will come up to me, apart from his troops that have already come up before, his entire army is right now coming up; one has spotted these troops [on their way]. Previously I sent my brother the following message: "Once this ambition will be achieved, if you ask so, I shall send you a [general] with my troops; if you will ask so, a son of mine shall come to you, if you will ask so, I shall come to you myself." This message I sent my brother in the past. Now my brother has asked for me to come. As my brother has asked for me to come, once this ambition will be achieved I will come with my troops to my brother and will achieve the ambition of my brother. At the moment I have just sent a message to Sin-teri, and he will gather all the Haneans and with all his forces attack the large cattle herds of Sumu-epuh and the Rabbayu.

As for the man of Haššum, the man of Ursum and the man of Karkemis about whom my brother sent me a message, I have assembled previously the man of Haššum, the man of Ursum and the man of Karkemis and spoken to them, saying: "I shall find out the intention of the words of Sumu-epuh; if there is to be enmity, we shall fight together!" I have already informed my brother of this. [Now that] I have heard the message of my brother, [I again sent a message] and the man of Haššum, the man of Ursum and the man of Karkemis will declare war on Sumu-epuh. They trusted away the hand (i.e., canceled alliance). The man of Haššum dispatched his people to me and they are now at my disposal. And the man of Ursum asked me for thousand troops: I will give him two thousand troops. I will make them ready to go and . . . (one word). They will cause Sumu-epuh difficulties and turn his attention away from you.

Ishi-Addu of Qatna and Shamshi-Adad had concluded a treaty and clinched their pact through a marriage of a daughter of Ishi-Addu with Yasmah-Addu. In the present letter, Shamshi-Adad capitalizes on his son's good connections with the royal house of Qatna to soften the blow of what must have been bad news for Ishi-Addu. Their alliance served strategic purposes, for both kings found a common enemy in Sumu-epuh of Aleppo, and the pact stipulated military assistance of the partner in case of an attack. Ishi-Addu had appealed to Shamshi-Adad for this very reason, but Shamshi-Adad could not afford to use his forces in support of his partner. He needed them right now for another purpose, indistinctly referred to as "this ambition" in the letter, that involved the army of the king of Eshnunna. This is no doubt the celebrated joint campaign of Shamshi-Adad and Dadusha against Qabrā.

Shamshi-Adad explains his decision by playing down the severity of the attacks on Ishi-Addu's realm and by pompously reaffirming his commitment to the alliance. This rhetoric contrasts sharply with the little help that Shamshi-Adad could actually provide at that time: he ordered one of his officers to make a symbolic attack, and rallied the small states north of the kingdom of Aleppo to commence hostilities. Serious intervention on behalf of Qatna could only follow after the end of the Qabrā campaign.

Bibliography: ARM 1 24+ = Charpin and Durand 1985: 309 = Durand 1997 no. 330.

59. Letter of Shamshi-Adad to Yasmah-Addu

(Tablet from the Mari palace, 42 lines.)

Speak to Yasmah-Addu: thus (says) Shamshi-Adad, your father. Concerning the sons of Ya'ilanum who are with you, as it seemed that peace might have followed later, I told you to keep them in hand. Now there is no peace at all with Ya'ilanum; I am in fact planning to conquer it. Give orders that the sons of Ya'ilanum, each one of them who is with you, must die tonight. Guards, worries and provisions will not be necessary anymore. One must prepare graves for them and they must die and be buried in the graves. And Sammêtar, his blood-relative, [he will] not [live], but don't detain his maids! Two pack donkeys and one servant [. . .] are standing ready for them and [have them conducted] to me. Furthermore, one mina of gold and two minas of silver are in the hand of the maids of Sammêtar. The servant Mannana must not say [improper things to you], don't [believe him]! The servant Mannana must not come near [his maids.] He must only take care of their headdresses and cloths. Take away their gold and silver and have these maids conducted to me. There are (also) two female singers, Nawra-sharur and the maids of each of them (i.e., the sons of Ya'ilanum). Detain these women with you, but have the maids of Sammêtar conducted to me! I have sent you this tablet of mine on the fifteenth day of the month of Tīrum.

This letter was written during the joint campaign of Shamshi-Adad and Eshnunna against Qabrā and other Zagros kingdoms. One of these was the land of Ya'ilanum, named after a person who was perhaps the eponymous founder of its ruling house. Family members of the king of Ya'ilanum were held as hostages to be released if the country would surrender, but the chance for peace had gone by and Shamshi-Adad now orders their execution. Yasmah-Addu was participating in this campaign and stayed somewhere where these hostages were kept. He received instructions about what to do with these princes and their wives (their "maids"). The wives of a man called Sammêtar should receive a special treatment, for reasons not disclosed by the letter, and Yasmah-Addu must beware of a particular servant of Sammêtar who was staying with them.

Bibliography: ARM 1 8 = Durand 1998 no. 679.

60. Letter of Shamshi-Adad to Yasmah-Addu

(Tablet from the Mari palace, 43 lines.)

Speak to Yasmah-Addu: thus (says) Shamshi-Adad, your father. When the army gathered in Qabrā, I sent Ishme-Dagan with the army to the land of Ahazum and I myself returned to the City (i.e., Assur). But while the army was gathering in Qabrā, the land of Ahazum heard about the gathering of forces in Qabrā and took a decision. All the troops of that land and the Turukkeans who are with them gathered together and took position against Ishme-Dagan in the town of Ikkallum in the land of Ahazum. Ishme-Dagan set out for that town and, (approaching it) at a distance of less than 300 cubits, all the troops of that land and the Turukkeans who have gathered with them [came out] in front of Ishme-Dagan to [give] battle. [They did] battle [and he defeated them]. He rounded up the people of that land and the Turukkeans who had gathered with them. Not a single man escaped. And that very day he seized the whole land of Ahazum. This victory is great for the land! Be happy! Here your brother has achieved victory while you are lying there among women. Now then, be a man when you will go with the army to Qatna! Just like your brother has set a great name, you as well must set yourself a great name during the campaign of Qatna!

This famous letter was sent by Shamshi-Adad to inspire his son with a tale of heroism of his brother Ishme-Dagan. The story took place in the spring of the year that followed the conquest of Qabrā. The army of Shamshi-Adad had been engaged in a prolonged campaign to conquer the country of Ahazum, situated in the Zagros foothills, and the episode told in this letter might well have been one of the decisive victories in this war. Shamshi-Adad brings it up as an example for Yasmah-Addu, who was at that time preparing himself for a military operation in support of Qatna.

Bibliography: ARM 1 69+ = Charpin and Durand 1985: 313 = Durand 1998 no. 452.

61. Letter of Shamshi-Adad to Yasmah-Addu

(Tablet from the Mari palace, 43 lines.)

Speak to Yasmah-Addu: thus (says) Shamshi-Adad, your father. Mashiya has come to me. You have dispatched with him only 30 men to guard the booty! Thirty men for guarding a booty of a thousand (prisoners), for what is this sufficient? Let [x] hundred troops, sons of the land, take supplies for 15 days. Make them ready to go with La'um and dispatch them quickly to me to guard the booty. I do not allow you any delay for these troops to arrive. The booty is waiting in Ha[labit]. Let these troops go there when you see fit.

Something else: You sent me the following message through Mashiya: "I want to make as many troops as can be done ready to go with me and move on to Tuttul. The rumor of my coming will be heard in the land of Yamhad!" This message you sent me. The word you sent me is excellent! Troops who are (staying) in Mari, Ṣuprum, Saggaratum or Terqa, get these men ready to go with you! It is (today) day 15 of the month of Ayarum: the assembly of troops (will take) 5 days and the trip itself 5 days. Arrive by the end of the month of Ayarum in Tuttul. Sumu-epuh will hear the rumors of your coming and will give up his conquests: Dūr-Adad, my fortress and many other towns that the enemy has attacked. Then that country will calm down. Speak as follows to the sons of Yamina: "In order to avoid that pasture (rights) come to end, come up to support the land!" Stay there for 15 days; your return trip (will take) 5 days. Come back to Mari on the twentieth of the month Addarum, five days before the harvest. Send (then) the troops to harvest. Act in accordance with my message!

Shamshi-Adad instructs his son in two matters: he must provide an adequate escort for a prisoner convoy waiting for transport, and carry out his campaign against Yamhad; that is, the kingdom of Sumu-epuh of Aleppo, according to a strict timetable. No direct confrontation is planned, but the mission is to retake the border fortresses of Dūr-Adad and Dūr-Samsī-Addu (here called "my fortress") by surprise. The action takes place in spring just before the harvest, an unusual season for campaigns as the troops are needed on the fields. Shamshi-Adad therefore expects little resistance and sets a tight agenda so that the troops will be back again in time for the harvest. The campaign should last 30 days only, to begin 5 days after the date of his letter. Yasmah-Addu is also ordered to force the Yaminite pasturalists of the border region between Aleppo and the kingdom of Upper Mesopotamia to take sides.

Bibliography: ARM 1 43 = Durand 1998 no. 492.

62. Letter of Shamshi-Adad to Yasmah-Addu

(Tablet from the Mari palace, 28 lines.)

Speak to Yasmah-Addu: thus (says) Shamshi-Adad, your father. In Amursakkum, where the Turukkeans are staying, Dadanum with 2,000 Nurrugeans is occupying one side of the siege lines by himself. The enemy approached in front of Dadanum to break through the fortifications by engaging in battle with Muharrirum, and they killed him (i.e., Muharrirum). They also killed five soldiers with him. Soon after they drove the mob back and killed 50 enemies. Ishar-Lim is staying with him and Ishar-Lim is well, the troops are well. The two flanks are secure. The army is building up the siege lines (and) digging out a ditch. One will surround the whole town with siege lines. It is to be feared that you will worry because you might hear unofficially that a man of name is killed: don't worry at all! The army is well. I have sent you this tablet of mine on the twenty-sixth day of the month of Niqmum.

The clash with the Turukkeans was one of the important events in the last years of Shamshi-Adad. This conflict was the unforeseen effect of the war of Shamshi-Adad and Dadusha against the principalities of the Zagros foothills some years before. These campaigns had in fact further destabilized a region where the pressure of another conflict, that between the Guteans and Turukkeans further eastwards, was already badly felt. This opened the way for the advance of mountain population groups into the lowlands, where these migrants, indiscriminately called Turukkeans, finally forced Shamshi-Adad to abandon his conquests. Meanwhile many of them had been integrated into his army or resettled in other parts of the kingdom, where they at last rose in rebellion against their new lord.

One particularly alarming episode took place in the very heart of the kingdom, near the capital Shubat-Enlil, but the army managed to fence the hostile Turukkeans inside the city of Amursakkum in an attempt to starve them into submission. Ishme-Dagan led these operations, and Yasmah-Addu was kept informed when called upon to supply various needs, or when incidents occurred that concerned his interests. The incident reported in this letter seems to have taken place when Ishme-Dagan was not at the site. Yasmah-Addu is updated on details of the siege in order to contradict rumors that important persons, such as the generals Ishar-Lim or Dadanum, had been killed. The sortie was made against a section of the lines where auxiliary forces from Nurrugum were stationed, and although one of the commanders was killed, nothing should upset his mind.

Bibliography: ARM 1 90 = Durand 1998 no. 497.

63. Letter of Ishme-Dagan to Yasmah-Addu

(Tablet from the Mari palace, 20 lines.)

Speak to Yasmah-Addu: thus (says) Ishme-Dagan, your brother. I am well, the troops are well. I act to protect the troops. Now I have Mashum [carry out] my strategy and I have burned down the surrounding area of Amursakkum for a distance of one double-hour (ca. 6 miles / 10 kilometers) [. . .] (one word) and I have destroyed the provisions of the enemy. Something else: I am dining on pears from Nawila; they are delicious! Herewith I have some pears and pistachios from the Sindjar Mountains, the first fruits of the year, brought to you.

The siege of Amursakkum did not go according to plan, and Ishme-Dagan had complained in a previous letter that the Turukkeans still managed to break through the siege lines to get food. He sent this letter to inform his brother about his method of solving this problem once and for all. This brief message is evocative of Ishme-Dagan's boastful character and the immense hate for the enemy: his sardonic postscript about his own menu, along with the delivery of some table delicacies, was no doubt meant to emphasize his superiority over the starving Turukkeans in Amursakkum.

Bibliography: ARM 4 42 = Durand 1998 no. 499.

64. Letter of Shamshi-Adad to Yasmah-Addu

(Tablet from the Mari palace, 31 lines.)

[Speak to Yasma]h-Addu: [thus (says) Sham]shi-Adad, your [father]. [Herewith] I have a tablet that [was written] for the man of Eshnunna brought to you. Like I have instructed Sin-teri for you, keep that tablet until Malgium will be taken. Once Malgium has been taken and the heart has gladdened, have either Ili-ite or Belshunu bring this tablet to Eshnunna and send him the following message: "Your brother gave me this tablet in my hand and said to me as follows: 'Once Malgium has been taken and the heart of my brother has gladdened, have this tablet brought to Eshnunna.'" "Those who treats a soldier well are regarded among his lords (and) receive large gifts." (proverb) Now you, once the heart of my brother has gladdened, take good care of your desire! Ask for the sons of the king who were taken in Qabrā and say as follows: "Well, they may be sons of a king, but what are they really? Dogs! Give these men and gladden the heart of your brother!" Send [this] message to Eshnunna.

Following the death of Dadusha, his son Ibal-pi-El II ascended the throne of Eshnunna. The relation between Eshnunna and Shamshi-Adad had gone through long phases of animosity and even open warfare before the strategic partnership with Dadusha was concluded, and a new king in Eshnunna required that the terms be set once more. At the same time the two kingdoms, in concord with Hammurabi of Babylon, set out against the small kingdom of Malgium on the Tigris.

It is not said what kind of tablet Yasmah-Addu must keep with him, but it might well have contained a proposal in support of an agreement between the two royal houses. Negotiations for this treaty were protracted for a long time, and Shamshi-Adad might have hoped that the exuberance that comes after a simple and profitable victory would influence the young ruler to follow in his father's steps and renew the alliance. Shamshi-Adad had a fancy for using proverbs in his letters, and quotes one here to express the idea that ample praise for the young king's first military achievement might well win him over. Another topic of concern is the delivery of the princes who have been staying at the court of Eshnunna ever since the capture of Qabrā. Shamshi-Adad needs them, perhaps to make a diplomatic gesture towards their home country, and orders his son to bring about their release.

Bibliography: ARM 1 27 = Durand 1997 no. 317.

65. Letter of Ishme-Dagan to Yasmah-Addu

(Tablet from the Mari palace, 29 lines.)

Speak to Yasmah-Addu: thus (says) Ishme-Dagan, your brother. I am well; send me constantly messages about your wellbeing. The troops that were staying with Ishar-Lim in Malgium are well. They have just come up to me. The man of Malgium has spent 15 talents of silver for them. They have divided the 15 talents in these three parts: the man of Eshnunna [has received 5 talents] and they have given 5 talents to the man of Babylon. The troops have come back and I will perform a complete clearing. And this clearing will be very thorough! The population (?) is gathered. And now the king (i.e. Shamshi-Adad) will send men in charge of clearing to you, and you will likewise clear your country.

The king of Malgium averted a siege and conquest of his city by paying a huge ransom (ca. 1000 pounds / 450 kilograms of silver) to the three powers assembled before his gate. With this the employ of the army came to an end and the census could be carried out. A census, Akkadian *tebibtum*, literally "clearing," was meant to review what manpower was available to the palace and to verify and, when necessary, reallocate their land holdings.

Bibliography: ARM 1 129 = Durand 1998 no. 544.

When the kingdom of Upper Mesopotamia broke down under the assault of Aleppo and Eshnunna soon after the death of Shamshi-Adad, Ishme-Dagan at first stayed in control of Ekallatum, but Yasmah-Addu had to give way to Zimri-Lim, a member of the family of Yahdun-Lim, who would reign in Mari for 13 years (1774–1762 BC).

66. Letter of Zimri-Lim to Tish-Ulme, king of Mardaman

(Tablet, with envelope, from the Mari palace, 22 lines.)

Speak to Tish-Ulme: thus (says) Zimri-Lim. The whole land has returned to its hereditary division and everybody has ascended the throne of his father's house. And this is what I heard: "The whole land of Idamaraṣ that holds strongholds pays attention to Zimri-Lim only!" Now send me a message! I shall come and I shall swear a solemn oath on your behalf! Give me the town and I shall give it back to its rightful owner. Then I shall set you up with all your belongings where you tell me. Have an answer to my tablet quickly brought to me.

Legend of the seal impressed on the envelope: Zimri-Lim, beloved of Dagan, governor of [. . .], king of Mari and the land of Hana, son of Hadni-[Addu].

King makes offering in return for surrender of the town to a king he supports.

This letter, never dispatched, was found in Mari still enclosed in its envelope. It dates from the very beginning of Zimri-Lim's rule, before he started to designate himself as a son of Yahdun-Lim, and the seal legend contains the name of his real father. The text addresses a plural audience, the city administrators of the old regime, with an offer to surrender the town to a king who is supported by Zimri-Lim. Tish-Ulme was later the king of Mardaman, and this letter might well have been intended for a group present in that town. Members of the old royal families tried elsewhere, like in Mari, to recover the throne when the kingdom of Shamshi-Adad collapsed, and Zimri-Lim set out to restore the erstwhile state of affairs. He posted many of these letters, and another exemplar, with virtually the same content but addressed to another ruler, has survived as well.

Bibliography: Birot 1989 = Durand 1997 no. 247.

67. Letter of Zimri-Lim to Hatnu-Rabi, king of Qaṭṭarā and Karanā

(Tablet from Tell al Rimah. Only obverse preserved; originally ca. 55 lines.)

Speak to Hatnu-rabi: thus (says) Zimri-Lim. Previously I have indeed sent you, once and even twice, a full report that the troops of the man of Eshnunna have come up against me. Now, herewith I have you brought this tablet of mine. Since three days I have gone to help my own territory in the face of the man of Eshnunna. If these troops will withdraw before me, then they will withdraw. If this is not the case and they will not withdraw before me, then I will fight with my own troops. I will not withdraw. Ever since I have been sending you (pl.) messages to come and help me, your support troops have not come to me. I will now tear out the claw of the man of Eshnunna from my territory with my own troops. And I will deal with him so that he will never come up against my territory again. Something else: I heard unofficially that you (pl.) are laying siege to Qarni-Lim. (Rest of the text fragmentary.)

threats

King states he has asked for Hatnu-rabi help to send troops in order to face Eshnunna troops that have come into his territory & if he does not help them, he & his troops will take them on themselves

This letter dates from the beginning of the conflict with Eshnunna and was found in the palace of the addressee in Qaṭṭarā (modern Tell al Rimah). Eshnunna pushed northwards on two fronts: it sent one army up the Euphrates in the direction of Mari, and another along the Tigris to the Sindjar zone. In that region Eshnunna found an ally in Qarni-Lim, king of Andarig, and came into conflict with Zimri-Lim's vassals, but no direct confrontation with Mari took place. On the other front, however, a clash was unavoidable and Zimri-Lim pressed his vassals for troops. They were not forthcoming in this, and his solemn vow in this letter was no doubt another attempt to convince them.

Bibliography: Dalley et al. 1976 no. 2.

68. Letter of General Yassi-Dagan to Zimri-Lim

(Tablet from the Mari palace, 93 lines.)

Speak [to my lord: thus (says) Yassi-Dagan], your servant. [Ever since the day] my lord left for the Banks of the Euphrates, the allied kings and the whole land have become prejudiced against my lord and their opinion turned around. Previously I have addressed these kings, saying: "Certainly, my lord will take the lead of the Haneans, arrive here quickly and tear out the claw of the man of Eshnunna from this land and will rescue the land!" I spoke like this to them and I appeased their heart. Now these kings have heard of my lord's departure for the Bank of the Euphrates, they became upset and their opinion turned around, saying: "Where then is your lord who will come here, rescue us and repel the man of Eshnunna? He has left for the Bank of the Euphrates!" This is how these kings discussed with each other.

Moreover, lord Sasiya seeks to destroy Hatnu-rabi and his country and has caused the attitude to my lord to turn around. He addressed the kings as follows: "Where then is Zimri-Lim whom you all seek as your father and whom you follow when he parades around in his coach? Why did he not show up now and rescue you?" Sasiya spoke like this to Bunu-Ištar, Hatnu-rabi, Šarrum-kima-kalima, Zimriya and the (other) kings. And they do not take notice of the (hidden) plan of that man! It looks as if he talked honestly with them, but he made it all up! And they started to slander my lord to Sasiya; [do they] not [know] that he talks deceitfully to them and is keeping peace with the man of Eshnunna? This man holds it against my lord that my lord left for the Bank of the Euphrates, saying: "Zimri-Lim has sworn an oath with Qarni-Lim and the man of Eshnunna, and that's why he fails to come to us. He departed and went away to his country!" This man is prejudiced against my lord for these and other reasons. They are spreading malicious talks about my lord, saying: "Tablets of Zimri-Lim go all the time to Šallurum (army commander of Eshnunna), saying: 'Come over with your lord, or else I want to come to my lord and meet with my lord. My lord (i.e., Ibal-pi-El of Eshnunna) is lord of their lord (i.e., Zimri-Lim himself; "their" stands for his vassals)!', and these tablets go forth from Šallurum to Nidnat-Sin, the general of the man of Babylon." And they reported (?) about the fact that my lord has sent in the past a message with a shepherd to Qarni-Lim, and that it was written in the tablet that he was carrying: "Speak to Qarni-Lim, thus (says) Zimri-Lim. As for the secret message that I sent you with a shepherd: carry this plan out quickly!" They heard about this tablet and started to smear my lord. It looks as if my lord has made peace with the man of Eshnunna: the whole land has become afraid.

Now these kings have gone to Sasiya, as did the guard officers of the whole land, one with each of them, and we – me, Yaphur-Lim and one guard officer with him – followed. They arrived with Sasiya and Sasiya, leaving out all asides, focused entirely on my lord, saying: "What it this that Zimri-Lim has decided? Last year he came up into the country and the kings accepted him as their father and leader and he gave troops to Hatnu-rabi. He (i.e., Hatnu-rabi) conquered some towns of mine, stole sheep and piled up bodies everywhere in my land. Later the man of Eshnunna came up, but Zimri-Lim departed and went away to his country. He did not rescue us at all! Now he has come up again, swore an oath with the man of Eshnunna and went back to his land." These things and more Sasiya talked about and holds against my lord. They spoke to him that he should go to Karanā, but he refused, saying: "He (i.e., the king of Eshnunna) is united with Hatnu-rabi, the aggressive (?) 'finger' (i.e., partner in a treaty) and I will fight. I will not go to Karanā. Here I will have extispicy performed and if the predictions are positive, I will fight with the man of Eshnunna or else, if the predictions are negative, I will not fight. I will send a message to Hammurabi and additional troops will come up from the man of Babylon. And Zimri-Lim will arrive here and we will fight." This is how that man addressed (them), but these words of his that he spoke are dishonest, (for) he keeps peace with the man of Eshnunna!

Now the kings and the whole land are on fire against my lord. And Bunu-Ištar stood up and said as follows to Sasiya: "Zimri-Lim has withheld his best troops and sent us weak troops and we will all die with them!" He repeatedly called the Haneans "crows." (?)

The kings and the whole country are looking out for my lord. If only my lord, before deciding to come, would have straightened out (?) the Haneans with my lord, so they could have come here, then the man of Eshnunna would have withdrawn already long ago and this land would have returned behind my lord. Now my lord must confer with his servants and have extispicy performed about his considerations, and in keeping with positive predictions my lord must come here when he wants to come. If otherwise, then my lord must send a message to the merhûm (official in charge of transhumance), so that the merhûm may take the lead of 1,000 or 2,000 Haneans and come here and, once the season will become nice again and the hand will warm up, we shall fight with the man of Eshnunna!

It is to be feared that my lord will say as follows: "My servant Yassi-Dagan is staying there, but fails to inform me of all the information he hears." All information that I have heard before I have already sent to my lord. Now, as to Hatnu-rabi, my lord must not be concerned about these things, but he must be concerned about the Bank of the Euphrates! I have sent my lord a message in accordance with my status of servant. My lord must reflect about it and do what can be done in accordance with his status of great king!

This long letter was written at the end of winter, quite likely of the year that followed the events described in the previous document. Yassi-Dagan gives his master a full report about the state of mind of his vassals in the Sindjar region. They are frustrated and sceptical about the ability and willingness of their lord to remedy their problems. Their main complaint is that Zimri-Lim has so far failed to accomplish anything substantial, no doubt because he is tied down by the attack against his own kingdom. Their dissatisfaction is increased by the suspicion that Zimri-Lim secretly plans to make peace with the king of Eshnunna and his ally Qarni-Lim, and an intercepted letter of Zimri-Lim to Qarni-Lim is taken by many as proof that these rumors are really true.

Yassi-Dagan argues that this situation was engineered by Sasiya, king of the Turukkeans, and that he did so with the intention of breaking up the coalition to accomplish his own plans; that is, to deal with his enemy Hatnu-rabi, king of Qaṭṭarā and Karanā. In the kings' assembly, Sasiya accuses Hatnu-rabi of attacks against his land and refuses to assist the city of Karanā against some unspecified danger. Sasiya's indignation is, according to Yassi-Dagan, just an act, for he has struck his own deal with Eshnunna, something that none of the other kings seems to know. But Yassi-Dagan is not shy to comment on the king's responsibility for this situation either and blames the king, in guarded terms, for letting things get out of hand.

Bibliography: Kupper 1990 = Durand 1998 no. 545.

69. Letter of Qarni-Lim, king of Andarig, to Zimri-Lim

(Tablet from the Mari palace, 36 lines.)

Speak to Zimri-Lim: thus (says) Qarni-Lim, your brother. The day that I have this tablet of mine brought to you, a report (with) confirmation about the man of Eshnunna reached me. Since three days his whole army is staying in Assur. Atamrum and Yagih-Addu have taken their lead. They are approaching Qaṭṭarā and aim for the center of my land. My brother must get with the main body of his troops on his way to Qaṭṭarā! And my brother must prepare 500 troops with light equipment and they must take supplies for three days and quickly enter into Andarig, so that I can unite forces with my brother and we will counter our enemy. (If not, then) it is to be feared that they could suddenly lay siege to me in my city. The whole land belongs to my brother. My brother must send a message to Sasiya, Bunu-Ištar, Šarriya, Haya-Sumu and the (other) kings. They all must assemble and my brother must not be lenient in saving me! I will counter (the enemy) in my city. My brother must be strong (?) and save me! Instruct my servants in function (with you) and dispatch them quickly to me!

Request for Zimri-Lim's help from ally

This letter followed shortly after the previous document. A major event of the recent past was already heralded by the shepherd's tablet mentioned in the letter of Yassi-Dagan: Qarni-Lim of Andarig had joined the ranks of Zimri-Lim's coalition. He now rightfully feared the revenge of Eshnunna, for this year the king of Eshnunna concentrated his full force on the Sindjar frontier. He asks Zimri-Lim to secure the city of Qaṭṭarā, a road station separating him from the army of Eshnunna, and to reinforce his own capital for the coming assault.

Bibliography: ARM 28 168.

70. Letter of General Ibal-pi-El to Zimri-Lim

(Tablet from the Mari palace, 33 lines.)

Speak to my lord: thus (says) Ibal-pi-El, your servant. I heard that Yarih-Abum has been excused by the man of Eshnunna. My lord knows that that house is full of treachery. It is to be feared that it will deceive my lord until it will capture Andarig. Once it will have captured Andarig, it will aim for Kurda. Soon after it will cross the Sindjar Mountains, and the whole land of Shubartum will shout "long live my lord!" at him. This house has started to act just like Shamshi-Adad. It resets its frontiers all the time. It has captured Ekallatum and now taken up position against Qaṭṭarā and Allahad. And (each) city it will take it will make its very own. That house is full of treachery! We shall march against it before things get out of hand and time runs out!

The Haneans are ablaze to fight and the kings of Idamaraṣ are assembled with their troops and are looking out for my lord. The sugāgum-cheichs have come together and have sent a message with Anniti-El and Hanzan to my lord. My lord must confer with his servants and get on his way!

This letter was written at about the same time as the previous one. Ibal-pi-El had learned of the failure of Zimri-Lim's envoy with the king of Eshnunna and draws on an historical example to predict future events for his argument that a military confrontation is the only remaining option.

Bibliography: Charpin 1992 = Durand 1998 no. 442.

71. Letter of Inibšina, ugbabtum-devotee of Adad and daughter of Yahdun-Lim, to Zimri-Lim

(Tablet from the Mari palace, 27 lines.)

Speak to my Star: thus (says) Inibšina. Some time ago, Šelebum, the assinnum, gave me a directive and I sent you a message. Now a qammatum-woman of Dagan of Terqa came to me and spoke to me as follows: "The peace offers of the man of Eshnunna are treacherous. Below straw runs water. I will pack him into the net that I knot. I will destroy his city. And his treasure, which is from ancient times, I will have utterly defiled." This she said to me. Now watch yourself and don't enter the city without a directive! I heard the following: he always acts irresponsibly of his own accord. Don't act irresponsibly on your own accord!

The divine messages that were expressed by prophets and communicated to the king can often be linked with political events of the day. The present example occurred after the end of hostilities with Eshnunna, when negotiations for a peace agreement were in progress. This particular oracle was also communicated by Sammêtar, the vizier of Zimri-Lim, but his rendering varied significantly from the one above: "Below straw runs water. They will send you messages for peace. They will dispatch their gods to you. And they will plot another 'wind' (i.e. trick) in their heart. The king must not touch his throat if he has not asked god" (ARM 26/1 199). Both texts share the phrase about water and straw and refer to the peace offer of Eshnunna, but give their own explanation of the oracle. Sammêtar, at that time in charge of the treaty negotiations, gives specific technical instructions how the king should proceed in the negotiations, and Inibšina stresses the impending doom of Eshnunna. She adds a warning for the king not to leave the palace without soliciting a sign of approval with the help of extispicy, for she has been told that he was apt to do so without it.

Bibliography: ARM 10 80 = ARM 26/1 197 = Durand 2000 no. 1203 = Heimpel 2003: 251–2.

72. Letter of Hammi-ištamar to Zimri-Lim

(Tablet from the Mari palace, 39 lines.)

Speak to my lord: thus (says) Hammi-ištamar, your servant. I have heard the tablet that you had brought to me. My lord sent me a message concerning the troops. All the troops are assembled. And my lord had a very long letter brought to me. May the god not bring the evil enemy to the Bank of the Euphrates! May your god and Dagan, the lord of the land, break the weapon of the Elamites! When they indeed will come to the Bank of the Euphrates, will they not stand out like beads of a necklace where one is white and another black? It is said: "this town is a son of Sim'al, that town is a son of Yamina" – is it not like the flood of a river where what is upstream evens out downstream? Why has my lord sent me this message? My lord must not get angry with me because I have not yet arrived with lord! My lord knows that the sugāgum-cheichs and the Haneans are staying with me in Samanum. And, because they have not met with their brothers who are living in the town for a long time, their stay has been drawn out. My lord must not get angry with me so long as I allow them what they are entitled to!

Hammi-ištamar was the leader of the Uprapu clan of the Yaminites. He had been ordered to participate with his men in a military campaign against Elam, but evidently failed to show up in time at the gathering point. Zimri-Lim sent him an angry letter, and Hammi-ištamar now explains why his men where held up. The king had expressed his concern that the Yaminites ('the sons of Yamina'), to which the Uprapu belong, would desert the Sim'alites, to which Zimri-Lim belongs, and collaborate with the invaders, like they had done at the time of the war with Eshnunna. Hammi-ištamar answers this accusation with two metaphors. The first shows that the Elamites were considered alien, a message that would no doubt reassure the king that no pact with the Yaminites would be possible. The meaning of the second is not fully apparent, but it probably implies that the whole land, regardless of its ethnic diversity, would act as one in the face of a common enemy.

Bibliography: Durand 1990 = Durand 1998 no. 733.

73. Letter of Nur-Sin to Zimri-Lim

(Tablet from the Mari palace. Half of the tablet missing; 10+19 lines preserved.)

Speak to my lord: thus (says) Nur-Sin, your servant: Abiya, the āpilum of Adad of Aleppo, came to me and said as follows: "Thus (says) Adad: 'I have given the whole land to Yahdun-Lim. And with my weapons he did not meet any opposition. (But) he left me and I gave the land that I had given to him to Shamshi-Adad. Shamshi-Adad [large break] I brought you back and restored you to the throne [of your father's house]. I have given you the weapons with which I defeated the sea. I anointed you with the oil of my splendour. Nobody will stand in your way. Hear one word: When somebody who is involved in a lawsuit calls out for you, saying "I am duped!" then be present and judge his case. Treat him right. This is what I wish from you: when you will go out on a campaign, don't leave without a sign. If I am present in my sign, go out on a campaign. If this is not the case, don't leave the gate.'" This is what the āpilum said to me. Herewith [I have the hair and hem of the āpilum brought to my lord.]

Zimri-Lim at the end of his reign acquired some property in the kingdom of Aleppo. Nur-Sin, his principal envoy to negotiate the deal, informed his lord with this letter of an oracle that had come to his attention. In it the god presents himself as a universal power who determines the fate of kingship and orders the king to honor his obligation to defend the weak, and to abide by the omens he receives through extispicy. Nur-Sin sends some personal attributes of the prophet to Zimri-Lim for verification of the omen.

Bibliography: Durand 1993 = FM 7 38.

B. *Letters from Southern Mesopotamia*

74. Letter of Anam, king of Uruk, to Sin-muballiṭ, king of Babylon (1812–1793 BC)

(Tablet from Uruk. Two columns on each side, total length more than 150 lines.)

This tablet was found in the palace of Sin-kashid in Uruk, where it had been buried under the floor with many other tablets by later users of the building. The letter is addressed to the king of Babylon, and the present tablet is either a letter that was never sent, or a copy for reference purposes. In view of the significance of the matters discussed, and the literary merits of the text, the second option seems the likelier of the two. The text is set shortly after an expedition of the Babylonian army through the land of its ally Uruk, evidently with the purpose of intimidating their mutual enemy, the kingdom of Larsa. After the conclusion of the campaign, Sin-muballiṭ wrote an angry letter about questions of protocol and the negative attitude of Uruk towards Babylon. Anam writes an elaborate answer in defense, countering the king's grievances and the reports about Uruk's disloyalty, which are quoted verbatim in the letter.

Speak to Sin-muballiṭ: thus (says) Anam, regarding the army of Amnan-Yahrur that arrived with me and about which your heart was grieved, and about which you stated before your servants: "Why did they not enter into the city?" Ishtar and Marduk may keep you healthy for many days!

When the army arrived in front of the city gate, the "fathers of the troops" who go ahead of the army came in before me and gave me their report, saying: "At the time when our lord gave us instructions, he instructed us that the 'fathers of the troops' come in before you and be informed of your strategy. It was not said that the troops be brought into the city. The troops will spend the night at the rear of the walls in the desert. In the morning the troops will move on to wherever they are going. The (soldiers for) garrison duty that we will take up and everything that we are ordered to bring we will leave behind in the walled cities and once we have dealt with various matters it will be time for our return to you." The "fathers of the troops" gave me this report and I have acted in accordance with the order that you had given them at the time, (nothing but) your own instructions!

What is more: once my heart was persuaded and I agreed with them not to have the troops enter (the city), saying: "The army that has come here is forceful. (Once) the troops of Amnan-Yahrur, the troops of Uruk and the troops of Yamutbalum are mixed together, [if just one] son of Babylon will boast about his strength to a son of Yamutbalum . . . [then there will be trouble!"]. (break of some lines) Truly, Uruk and Babylon are one house and can speak openly. Just like a son of Yamutbalum and a son of the Upper Land . . . [are unable to get along,] something you know well yourself, like fallow (?) land is not suitable for tax collection, why would the heart have confidence (in this)? The one who will see this will go off and make (news of) killing (a) (in) the city, which he has seen, reach the enemy and cause the evil foe to lift his knees (to attack). Twice my heart pondered about these (matters) and I agreed (again) with them not to have the troops enter (the city). And the considerations that were in my mind have perhaps occurred to Marduk-muballiṭ (a Babylonian official) as well, and he might for that reason have ordered the "fathers of the troops" not to have the troops enter into the city. For these (matters) the "fathers of the troops" came in before me and I placed the considerations that were in my mind before them and we came to an agreement.

When the troops went to . . . (two place names), they moved upstream to Kisurra. They executed the order with which you had instructed them. They reinforced the garrisons in the fortresses. Ishtar and Marduk, who are at your side, made the expedition of your troops successful! They (only) came across regular tasks. His troops moved down (?) (again) to my land or to Isin, (and) crossed over to the region of Amnan-Yahrur, to his own land.

And about the report of Abdi-Addu: "It is true: the troops have not entered into the city! Why did neither he (i.e., Anam), nor Dingir-mansum or else Ilum-eriš go out with their 10 courtiers and why did [they not admire] the troops which you (i.e. King Sin-muballiṭ) have dispatched?" About this report [. . .] because of thousand or two thousand troops . . . (break of some lines) Your troops were surely assembled in one place at Dūrum, at the crossing over [the . . . river] . . . Because of this procedure neither [Ilum-eriš] nor Dingir-mansum [knew] where the troops were. We have not seen the troops with our own eyes. Ali-[. . .], the commander of troops, came over to me. Dingir-mansum went forth and stood in front of the city gate. "A pin, a broken saddle, a harmed foot of a donkey, but nothing serious happened" (proverb). Now then, whoever said this and caused ill-feeling – his saddle may be really broken, the foot of his donkey may be really harmed! – he should say out loud the word of this serious error! And the army that had come here and stays in the environs is close to the city gate: Ilum-eriš and his servants, as many as there are, admire him (i.e., the commander). All of Uruk is happy about the way you act and they bless you, because your name is good.

And the word about the report of Abdi-Ami is: "Why did this enormous army come here? Will they not load (?) Uruk in a basket and go away again?" As regards these (malicious words) that are being said – ever since the kings of Uruk and Babylon are one house – except for the present moment when my heart and your heart were grieved – and, by what I have heard from the mouth of my father and my grandfather, whom I have known personally, ever since the time of Sin-kashid and since the time I witnessed myself until now, the army of Amnan-Yahrur has indeed arrived here two or three times for military assistance to this house. (An army of) one, two, five (or) ten thousand, with all their equipment, has indeed come here and stayed for one, two or three years in this city. And Sabium, the king, the lord of his city, has indeed come here with thousand troops. What (aggression) has ever come about in Amnan-Yahrur against Uruk? – He (i.e., Abdi-Ami) has no argument at all! That is why, wherever the Amnanite tongue is spoken, Ishtar and Marduk who keep you healthy . . . (break of some lines) . . . [In fact, a large army is necessary, because] . . . For each walled city the garrison should be strengthened to thousand (soldiers) each and it should be kept in readiness. I have written this to you time and again since the very beginning. Enough of it! Why is this being said? The servant who told you this, who seeks to make mutual enemies of Uruk and Amnan-Yahrur, exaggerated this for no reason!

God knows that I truly trust in you, like a man trusts in Ishtar, ever since the day we made our acquaintance! And my head lies certainly in your lap! As regards these (malicious words) – so that our hearts can be open to each other and my plan and your plan can be just one – (like) everywhere you know, where an oath is required if ever peace and good relations (are present), where the heart does not become confident until the throat is touched and where the oath is yearly renewed – already for three or four years the troops of Amnan-Yahrur are permanent in this house, (but) the offer of an oath was never taken in the mouth or written to you. As regards these (malicious words) – because this house speaks openly with you and loves the mention of your name, you are in the position to turn these (malicious words) to good!

Why have these (malicious words) been taken in the mouth and been said? Like the report of what Ipqu-Adad had said, that was brought and put before you on the same day – so will he who has heard this bring it and put it before the enemy and the knees of the evil foe will be swift (to attack)! These utterances! If they can be proven then they should be said out loud and the error should be identified! If this is not the case and they can't be proven, then the heart must not be grieved for no reason!

Anam deals with three grievances of Sin-muballiṭ. The first is that the army was not allowed to enter the city. Anam gives two arguments in defense of this decision: it was the order of Sin-muballiṭ himself, and free circulation of troops of different nationalities would have been hazardous: incidents of violence that result from it would lead the enemy to believe that the solidarity of the coalition was weak.

Abdi-Addu, a Babylonian official, had reported to his master Sin-muballiṭ that the army was deprived of the opportunity to parade in front of the Uruk noblemen. Anam says in explanation of this blunder that he did not know where the army had lined up, and adds in his defense that Abdi-Addu should not overstate the incident, because one of his officials had inspected the troops when they had come close to the city.

Sin-muballiṭ had also received notice that Abdi-Ami, probably a servant of the king of Uruk, had voiced doubts about the good intentions of the large Babylonian army before the walls of Uruk. Anam reacts to this issue with a retrospective of the history of the relation between the two royal houses, emphasizing that it has always been mutually beneficial. He insists that the size of the army was necessary for the tasks at hand and sets Abdi-Ami's remark aside as the dissenting opinion of a malicious servant.

In conclusion, Anam raises two topics: the need for a formal treaty of alliance between Uruk and Babylon to prevent this kind of rumor from again resulting in needless friction between them, and preventing the risk of such rumors, which travel fast and benefit only the enemy.

Uruk had maintained strong ties with Babylon from the time when it became independent. The common ethnic background of their ruling houses no doubt played a role in this: the early kings of Uruk identified themselves as leaders of the Amnanum, and the kingdom of Babylon is here called the "region (*erṣetum*) of Amnan-Yahrur," a combination of the two main ethnic groups on its territory. Babylon was clearly the more powerful of the two kingdoms, and the present letter shows that Uruk was not always willing to have faith in its dominant partner. Nothing else is known about this incident, but the reluctance to respond properly to the visit of the army and the rumors that reached the king of Babylon show that there was serious doubt in Uruk whether the Babylonians had come in peace or as enemies. Anam decided to play it safe and kept the city gates closed. But support of Babylon was vital if Uruk wanted to stay independent of Larsa, and, once the threat had passed by, relations needed to be repaired again. Anam's way of doing this, by denying all feelings of hostility on Uruk's part and by offering tortuous alternative explanations of what has happened, is preserved in this remarkable document.

Bibliography: Falkenstein 1963: 56–71.

75. Letter of King Samsuiluna of Babylon (1749–1712 BC) to Etel-pi-Marduk

(Tablet of unknown provenance, 24 lines.)

Speak to Etel-pi-Marduk: thus says Samsuiluna. The king, my father, is sick and I have just now ascended the throne of [my father's] house in order to guide the land aright. And, in order to support the producers of state revenue, I have exempted the arrears of [. . .], field managers [and (?) . . .]. I have broken the tablets with debt obligations of soldiers, "fishermen" and civilians. I have established justice in the land. Nobody may hold any demands against the households of soldiers, "fishermen" and civilians in the region that you administer (?)! When you see this tablet of mine, you and the eldest of the region that you administer must come up and meet with me.

This letter was sent to the head administrator of an unknown region and it seems likely that many copies of the same text were distributed throughout the kingdom. Samsuiluna states that he has come into power when his father is still alive but no longer able to "guide the land aright." It was custom that a change of regime was accompanied by a justice measure, and the letter announces that the debts of state producers and military fief holders towards the palace and all consumptive loans have been remitted. The addressee must protect these groups against illegal debt collection.

Bibliography: TCL 17 76

76. Letter of Marduk-mušallim to his superior

(Tablet from Abu Habbah, 48 lines.)

This letter was found in Sippar-Yahrurum together with a series of letters of King Ammiṣaduqa of Babylon (1646–1626 BC) to Marduk-mušallim and Marduk-lamassašu, all with warnings against marauding groups of Kassites and instructions to guard the city and surroundings. The two officials quarreled about the execution of the royal orders, and in the following letter Marduk-mušallim complains to his (anonymous) senior about the behavior of his colleague.

Speak to my superior: thus (says) Marduk-mušallim. As I have informed my lord in my tablet, the tablet of the king with instructions that is brought to us says:

"The city gate must not be opened as long as the sun does not rise. When the sun stands (on the horizon; i.e., dusk) it must be closed. The labour force that works outside must be questioned. The guards must be strong. The Manahean (troops) must not come down from the city wall. One must quickly move the large and small cattle that pasture in the territory of Sippar-Yahrurum to the countryside. The enemy troops must not strike! If the enemy troops will strike, you (pl.) will not be pardoned; it will be settled with your lives."

Thus we are informed. By the actions of Marduk-lamassašu, the barber, the city gate is opened before the sun rises and closed too late. I close the city gate myself by (the light of) a torch and enter. I protest, but he says (to the gatekeepers): "Do not follow his (i.e., Marduk-mušallim) orders!" In order to avoid a brawl, I give up in this matter time and again, but, out of fear for you, my lord, I keep it close in mind. If now an error should occur, who will then be able to clear the liability? It will be discussed! They will for sure examine us!

The generals were negligent this year. They did not get their troops ready and they are now not available. And the troops are still staying in their villages and busy doing (other things). Thus I informed you, my lord, in my tablet. That tablet of mine, saying "Herewith I send a message (that) clears (my) liability," I had a servant of my lord bring to my lord, (but) my lord did not hear (it) at all. Now, what has been done on the twenty-second day of the eighth month is not suitable for the king or you, my lord, to hear: large and small cattle grazed in the city gate, the gatekeeper did not close (the gate) until one-third part of a night watch had passed. My lord may ask Gimil-Marduk, the messenger who brought the cash boxes here. I have offered you, my lord, warnings all the time. Should this year some grave error occur, then I have sent a message for my lord to hear.

Marduk-mušallim first repeats the orders that are also known from the original letters of Ammiṣaduqa: the city gates and walls must be guarded and the herds grazing in the environs must be moved to a secure position. People who work outside of the city must be asked upon return whether they have seen the enemy somewhere. Their comments are then passed on to the king, who includes them in his next letter of warning. Marduk-mušallim's rendering of the royal orders adds that failure to protect the city is a capital offense. This element does not appear in the original royal letters and might stand for Marduk-mušallim's understanding of the gravity of the order, but there is no reason to doubt his judgment.

His colleague Marduk-lamassašu (who bore the honorary title of "barber"), however, did not take things seriously and was lax in executing the directives. Marduk-mušallim had already once before written a letter to his superior about these and other misdemeanours, with the intention of showing that he should not be held responsible if something bad happened. The failing response and new incidents of insubordination require that he does so once more by writing this letter.

Bibliography: CTMMA I 69.
Falkenstein 1963: 1–82.

Bibliography

Birot, M., 1989. La lettre de Zimri-Lim à Tiš-Ulme, 21–5, in M. Lebeau and P. Talon (eds.), *Reflets des deux fleuves. Volume de mélanges offerts à André Finet*, Akkadica Supplementum 6, Leuven: Peeters.

Charpin, D., 1992. De la vallée du Tigre au "triangle du Habur": un engrenage géopolitique?, 97–102, in J.-M. Durand (ed.), *Recherches en Haute Mésopotamie. Tell Mohammed Diyab campagnes 1990 et 1991*, Mémoires de N.A.B.U. 2, Paris: Société pour l'étude du Proche-Orient ancien.

Charpin, D., and Durand, J.-M., 1985. La prise du pouvoir par Zimri-Lim, *Mari: Annales de recherches interdisciplinaires* 4: 293–334.

Charpin, D., and Ziegler, N., 2003. *Mari et le Proche-Orient à époque amorrite. Essai d'histoire politique*, Florilegium marianum V, Mémoires de N.A.B.U. 6, Paris: Société pour l'étude du Proche-orient ancien.

Dalley, S., Walker, C. B. F., and Hawkins, J. D., 1976. *The Old Babylonian Tablets from Tell al Rimah*, London: British School of Archaeology in Iraq.

Durand, J.-M., 1990. Fourmis blanches et formis noires, in F. Vallat (ed.), *Contribution à l'histoire de L'Iran. Mélanges Jean Perrot*, Paris: Editions Recherche sur les civilisations, 101–8.

——, 1993. Le mythologème du combat entre le dieu de l'orage et la mer en Mésopotamie, *Mari: Annales de recherches interdisciplinaires* 7: 41–61.

——, 1997. *Documents épistolaires du palais de Mari* I, LAPO 16, Paris: Cerf.

——, 1998. *Documents épistolaires du palais de Mari* II, LAPO 17, Paris: Cerf.
——, 2000. *Documents épistolaires du palais de Mari* III, LAPO 18, Paris: Cerf.
Falkenstein, A., 1963. Zu den Inschriftfunden der Grabung in Uruk-Warka 1960–1961, *Baghdader Mitteilungen*, 2.
Heimpel, W., 2003. *Letters to the King of Mari*, MC 12, Winona Lake, Ind.: Eisenbrauns.
Horsnell, M., 1999. *The Year-names of the First Dynasty of Babylon*, Hamilton: McMaster University Press.
Kupper, J.-R., 1990. Une lettre du général Yassi-Dagan, *Mari: Annales de recherches interdisciplinaires* 6: 337–47.

6

Late Bronze Age Inscriptions from Babylon, Assyria, and Syro-Palestine

Frans van Koppen, Kyle Greenwood, Christopher Morgan, Brent A. Strawn, Jeff Cooley, Bill T. Arnold, Eva von Dassow, and Yoram Cohen

The Kassite Period designates the period of time in the history of Mesopotamia that followed upon the First Dynasty of Babylon (1594 BC) and ended with the ultimate fall of the Kassite Dynasty, when in 1155 BC the last king of the Kassite Dynasty, Enlil-nadin-ahi, was defeated and Babylon was conquered by the Elamites. The era is named after the dynasty that for most, if not all, of this time occupied the throne of Babylon, the sequence of 36 kings known as the Kassite Dynasty. Alternatively, the same period may be called the Middle Babylonian Period, but this concept includes, in the usage of many authors, one or more of the post-Kassite dynasties that ruled after the reign of Enlil-nadin-ahi.

Despite the length of this period and the wealth and power of Babylonia at that time, limited historical information is available, and the chronological and geographical diversity of what is at hand is generally inadequate. Even the exact length of the Kassite period remains unclear, as the date for the end of the Old Babylonian period, and all earlier dates in Mesopotamian history, are based on astronomical data that are most often interpreted to yield the so-called Middle Chronology, whereas the dates for the later Kassite kings are based on the chronographical data of the Assyrian King List. While this tradition is quite reliable, the astronomical dating of the Dynasty of Babylon is subject of much debate, whereby certain authors favor lower dates than those of the conventional Middle Chronology. As a consequence, the time-span in which the early kings of the Kassite Dynasty are to be set remains undecided.

The ascent of the Kassite Dynasty is as a matter of fact not documented and is situated in what is usually called a "Dark Age." The king lists enumerate a sequence of rulers and their lengths of reign that stretches into the Old Babylonian Period, but the reliability of the information regarding the early kings cannot be confirmed with other sources. Kassites appear in Old Babylonian times primarily as mercenaries, and an unproven hypothesis is that it was their leaders who, after the defeat of Samsuditana of Babylon, filled the vacuum and assumed power in the capital and maybe elsewhere. The first figure to appear in some detail is the king commonly known as Agum-kakrime, who authored a long inscription of disputed authenticity translated below. A landmark in early Kassite history was the conquest of the Sea Land, which, for the first time since the reign of Samsuiluna of Babylon, brought about the enduring political unification of the Mesopotamian alluvium. Recently, evidence has come to light that indicates that these early Kassite rulers also extended their influence in the Persian Gulf, and Kassite rule was for a long time recognized on the island of Bahrain.

The first well-documented Kassite king is Kurigalzu I (ca. 1400 BC) who defeated Elam and installed a dynasty of his choice. By now Babylonia again belonged to the great powers of the time, and it is in this guise that his successors participated in the international Amarna correspondence. The florescence of the Kassite period was also marked by wide-ranging building programs, canal digging, and regional agricultural growth, and essential steps towards the canonization of Babylonian literature may have been taken at this time as well.

Few details about the political history for the Kassite Dynasty after the Amarna Age are yet available, but by the time of Kashtiliash IV the growing power of Assyria had turned against Babylonia, and Tukulti-Ninurta I of Assyria conquered Babylon in 1225 BC. The Kassite rulers who ascended the throne after this Assyrian interlude proved again to be vigorous rulers, but they once more faced the menace of a foreign foe: a new dynasty in Elam entertained different attitudes towards Babylon than its predecessors and repeatedly invaded the Mesopotamian lowlands. Shutruk-Nahhunte conducted a famous campaign in 1158 BC, during which he deposited Zababa-shuma-iddina and carried off countless Mesopotamian monuments to Susa, and a few years later his successor Kutir-Nahhunte undertook another campaign that brought the Kassite Dynasty to a close.

I. Kassite inscriptions (van Koppen)

77. The Agum-kakrime inscription

The "Agum-kakrime" Inscription – so called after the king's name as it appears in the first line; note, however, that it is partly broken and should perhaps be restored differently – follows the traditional pattern of royal inscriptions, starting with the king's name, genealogy, and epithets, and ending with an invocation to the gods to bless the king. The middle part is a long first-person account of how the king brought Marduk, the principal god of Babylon, back to his city and refurbished his temple Esagil. This event has been interpreted as referring to the recovery of the cult statue that was taken away by the Hittites from the sack of Babylon, an episode that marked the end of the Old Babylonian period (1595 BC). If so, then the king who commissioned this inscription was an early ruler of the succeeding Kassite Dynasty, and his testimony a key source for an otherwise poorly documented period.

Nonetheless, the question of the authenticity of this composition remains unresolved. It is solely known from manuscripts of a much later date than the events it purports to portray, the king's name is not attested elsewhere and contemporary evidence for the exile of Marduk is lacking. For these reasons, the text has long been dismissed as an authentic historical source and has instead been considered as a later, pseudonymous composition. But no proof for this opinion is available either: in fact, certain features, such as the Marduk theology reflected by the text, fit a second millennium BC date of composition better than a later date. Hence the view that the text is a genuine royal inscription of the sixteenth or fifteenth century BC preserved in much later copies has gained popularity.

The text is preserved on an almost complete eight-column tablet (originally more than 350 lines) and a fragmentary duplicate, both from the library of Ashurbanipal at Nineveh (seventh century BC), and was, according to the postscript on the tablet, classified as secret lore. The text contains a detailed description of the attire of Marduk's cult statue and the furnishing of his cult rooms. It was this subject matter that made the text particularly interesting for the Neo-Assyrian court and explains why it was then considered a piece of classified information. It was presumably copied from a statue or some other monument erected by Agum-kakrime in Esagil, but whether the text as known from Ashurbanipal's library accurately reproduces this monumental inscription, or else is the product of editorial reworking, remains undecided.

> *I am [Agum]-kakrime, son of Urshigurumash, pure offspring of Shuqamunu, named by Anu and Enlil, Ea and Marduk, Sin and Shamash, strong man of Ishtar, the most valiant of the goddesses. I am a king of intelligence and understanding, king of concord and reconciliation, the son of Urshigurumash, descendant of Abi[rattash], the fierce hero, son of Kashtiliyashu, firstborn heir of Agum the Great, pure offspring, royal offspring, who holds the reins of the peoples, the mighty shepherd. I am a shepherd of widespread people, a hero, a shepherd who fastens the base of his father's throne. I am the king of Kassites and Akkadians, king of the wide land of Babylon, who settles the land of Eshnunna with widespread people, king of the land of Padan and Alman, king of the land of the Guteans, a barbarous people, king who makes the four corners of the world settle down, favorite of the great gods.*

The text opens with an elaborate representation of the king, linking him with the gods, the royal lineage and his people. Shuqamunu was a patron deity of the Kassite Dynasty and precedes the main deities of the Mesopotamian pantheon. Names and epithets of four predecessors of Agum-kakrime appear, tracing his decent back to Agum the Great, the legendary founder of the dynasty. Agum-kakrime is portrayed as their legitimate successor and as a caring "shepherd" of his people, the Kassites and Akkadians, the second term referring to the native population of Babylonia. Agum-kakrime did not rule over all of Babylonia, for in his days the southern part was the domain of the First Sea Land Dynasty. The passage about Eshnunna presumably refers to some political achievement of the ruler, who also claims control over more eastern territories, the Zagros countries of Padan and Alman, and over the Guteans, a people in the same mountainous area.

When the great [gods] ordered with their pure mouths the return of Marduk, lord of Esagil [and] Babylon, to Babylon, then Marduk set out to return to Tintir. I carefully planned [the return] of Marduk, [who loves] my [reign], set out to take Marduk back to Babylon, assisted Marduk, who loves my reign, and questioned king Shamash through the lamb of the diviner. I sent (an embassy) to a faraway land, the land of the Haneans, and they took Marduk and Zarpanitum by the hand. I brought Marduk and Zarpanitum, who love my reign, back to Esagil and Babylon. I brought them back in the house that Shamash had confirmed to me in the examination.

In Mesopotamian thinking the absence of a deity from his temple is a manifestation of divine disapproval of worldly rule, while the return of the god signals divine support for the king. Thus the restoration of Marduk's cult was an important public endorsement of the young dynasty. The "great gods" instruct Marduk to return to Babylon; this motive is markedly different from the telling of the same story in a later literary text, the so-called Marduk Prophecy from the time of Nebuchadnezzar I, where Marduk decided to return on his own accord. Agum-kakrime brought Marduk and his consort Zarpanitum back from the land of the Haneans, the country around the city of Terqa that was ruled by a local dynasty, while the Marduk Prophecy situates Marduk's exile with the Hittites. No explanation for this disagreement can be offered. Agum-kakrime stresses that his assistance to Marduk and the place where the god should reside were approved by the gods through divination.

I had craftsmen settle (there), [ordered] the smith, gold smith and stone cutter and [renewed] their [attire]. I gave four talents of red gold for the wardrobe of Marduk and Zarpanitum, I clothed Marduk and Zarpanitum in a great wardrobe, a wardrobe of red gold, I gave lapis lazuli from the mountain, green obsidian from Marhashi, eye-chalcedony, chalcedony of muš.gír-type, chalcedony with a white stripe, chalcedony with multiple white stripes, eye stones from Meluhha, alabaster, precious "lean stone" (and) "pure stone," whatever is choice in its mountain, for the sanctuaries of Marduk and Zarpanitum. I adorned the top of their great godly wardrobe, I set upon his head a lofty horn crown, a lordly crown befitting a god, full of awesome splendor, of lapis lazuli and gold, and I set on the top of his crown eye-stones of chalcedony of

> *muš.gír-type, stones of choice, and I adorned the top of his crown with chalcedony, muš.gír-stone, obsidian from Marhashi, lapis lazuli (and) chalcedony with a white stripe.*

In this passage the royal donations for the decoration of the cult statues are described in great detail; the statues were covered in garments with sewed-on or otherwise applied golden adornments and precious stones (Oppenheim 1949), and crowned with the typical horned crown of the gods, again set with costly stones.

The next part of the text is unfortunately badly preserved; it seems to touch on other ornaments and attributes of the cult statue and starts with the "Furious Snake" (*mušhuššu*), the emblem animal of Marduk, which was presumably represented by a statue, or perhaps a piece of jewelry on Marduk's statue. After that follows a description of more pieces of jewelry, again of gold and precious stones, and of some obscure action with, perhaps, the pedestal of the statue. Then the acquisition of wood from the "pure mountain" is mentioned, presumably used to make the doors of the cult room:

> *I had big doors, double doors of cedar wood made and set them in place at the cult rooms of Marduk and Zarpanitum. I bound them with long bands of bronze. I fixed their pivots with straps of refined copper. I covered them with "Venomous Snake" (bašmu), "Hairy One" (lahmu), "Bison" (kusarikku), "Big Weather-Beast" (ugallu), "Mad Lion" (uridimmu), "Fish-Man" (kulullû) (and) "Carp-Goat" (suhurmāšu) of lapis lazuli, dušû-stone, carnelian and alabaster. I had their purification carried out and set the pure doors in place at the cult rooms of Marduk and Zarpanitum.*

This passage describes the doors that gave access to the innermost part of the temple, the rooms where the cult statues of Marduk and Zarpanitum were normally kept. The doors depicted monsters who, according to mythology, had once been subjugated by Marduk and as his war trophies ever since serve in the function of apotropaic door keepers (Wiggermann 1992). The doors were ritually purified for service in the sanctuary, and similar rituals were performed in the whole temple before the gods were brought into their sanctuary:

> *Then I had the snake charmer purify all of Esagil. After the purification of the entire house . . . (large break) . . . I brought them in "Gate of Radiance," the cult rooms of Marduk. I performed their great offerings. I organized provisions for the "House of Abundant Tribute." I gave their gifts to my Lord and Mistress . . . (some lines fragmentary) . . . I gave cups of gold, cups of silver, cups of lapis lazuli, a big . . . of silver to Marduk. I gave gifts of silver and gold to the gods of Esagil. After I had assigned good and sweet things for Esagil . . . (some lines fragmentary, followed by a large break and some more fragmentary lines).*

This enumeration of gifts and offerings ends with the dedication of several individuals, one of them a craftsman and another an exorcist, and their possessions to Marduk. They were presumably the specialists whose work for the cult renovation was mentioned before and who were now permanently transferred from the royal household to the service of the god. The text now switches to the third person, presumably as the dedication is meant as a permanent memorial for the king's pious works:

> *Nur-[. . .] together with his house, his field and his garden; Iqisha-[. . .], the excorcist, together with his house, his field and his garden; Marduk-muballit, the smith, together with his house, his field and his garden – for king Agum, who built the cult room of Marduk, renovated Esagil, brought Marduk into his place of residence, he freed these craftsmen together with houses, fields and gardens (as) gifts for Marduk and Zarpanitum.*

The text ends with a blessing of the king. The main gods of the Mesopotamian pantheon, already familiar from the opening passage, are again invoked with the request to bless the king and his descendants. Other topics from the opening passage, dynastic continuity, and the prosperity of the people, appear here once more: the king's good deeds may effect prosperity and rich harvests for his people, and the gods may grant his lineage eternal rule.

> *May king Agum's days be long, may his years lengthen! May his reign be pervaded with prosperity! May the lead-ropes of the wide heaven be opened for him, may the clouds [bring forth] rain! May [at the command of] Šamaš [. . .] the orchards eternally bring forth sweet fruits! For the good king Agum, who built the cult rooms of Marduk (and) freed the craftsmen – may Anu and Antum bless him in heaven! May Enlil and Ninlil in Ekur ordain him a destiny of life! May Ea and Damkina, who reside in the great Apsû, give him a life of long days! May Dingir-mah, mistress of the great mountains, perfect his pure offspring! May Sin, the light of heaven, renew (his) royal offspring for all time! May valiant Šamaš, ruler of heaven and earth, fasten the base of royal throne for all time! May Ea, lord of the deep, perfect his wisdom! May Marduk, who loves his reign, the lord of the deep, perfect his state of abundance!*

Herewith the original inscription has come to an end. On the Ashurbanipal library tablet, after a double ruling of the tablet, a later scribal postscript follows, which underlines that the text is reserved for an initiated audience only:

> *. . . of Agum. May the informed reveal (it) to the informed, (but) the uninformed should [not] see. (That) is a taboo of Šullat and Haniš, Šamaš and Adad, the austere gods, the lords of divination.*

A colophon of Ashurbanipal concludes the text of the tablet.

Bibliography: Brinkman 1976 D^{b}.3.1 = Stein 2000: 150–165.

78. Inscription of Kurigalzu I

Most royal inscriptions of the Kassite Dynasty are short texts in Sumerian recording the building of a temple or palace and stamped or inscribed on bricks and other objects. More than two-thirds of this corpus concern a king by the name of Kurigalzu. Two kings of this name ruled over Babylonia, the first as a son of Kadashman-Harbe, some decades before the Amarna period (ca. 1400 BC), and the second as a son of Burna-Buriash shortly after the Amarna period (1332–1308 BC). The texts never give the genealogy of the king, but it would seem that most of them can be ascribed to Kurigalzu I (Clayden 1996).

Kurigalzu was an energetic builder: He founded a new royal residence, Dūr-Kurigalzu, and had all over Babylonia temples restored. For many cult centres this work was the first episode of royal sponsorship after centuries of neglect since the end of Old Babylonian rule. However, since his numerous building inscriptions do not concern matters of political history, another dedication will here be considered.

With the defeat of the Sea Land Dynasty and the annexation of its realm, the predecessors of Kurigalzu I had extended their influence over the whole Mesopotamian alluvium. Kurigalzu's father battled with Elam, as is indicated by an Elamite year name, and this conflict was continued by Kurigalzu, who in the end overthrew his Elamite opponents and set his client dynasty in place (Vallet 2000).

(Text is in Akkadian [9 lines], on a stone tablet from Nippur.)

Kurigalzu, the king of Karduniyaš, conquered the palace of the city of Šaša in Elam and gave (this object) for the sake of his life as a gift to Ninlil, his lady.

This small tablet of agate is bored lengthwise and might have been used as a piece of jewellery for a person or a statue. It is inscribed on both sides. On one side an inscription of the mother of king Shulgi of Ur is set: "For Inanna, her mistress, for the sake of the life of Shulgi, strong man, king of Ur, Watartum, his mother [dedicated (this object)]" (RIME 3/2.1.2.66 = BE 1 15). The other side was inscribed much later, when part of the tablet had come off, with this dedication of Kurigalzu. This object was a piece of the treasury from an unknown Babylonian temple that had been taken to Elam, but was recovered by Kurigalzu and dedicated to Ninlil of Nippur. Here it was found as part of a hoard of the Parthian period. Šaša in this text is perhaps a variant form of the name Susa.

Bibliography: Brinkman 1976 Q.2.63 = BE 1 43 = Stein 2000: 130.

Bibliography

Brinkman, J. A., 1976. *Materials and Studies for Kassite History*, vol. 1. *A Catalogue of Cuneiform Sources Pertaining to Specific Monarchs of the Kassite Dynasty*, Chicago: Oriental Institute of the University of Chicago.

Clayden, T., 1996. Kurigalzu I and the Restoration of Babylonia, *Iraq* 58: 109–21.

Oppenheim, A. L., 1949. The Golden Garments of the Gods, *Journal of Near Eastern Studies* 8: 172–93.

Stein, P., 2000. *Die mittel- und neubabylonische Königsinschriften bis zum Ende der Assyrerherrschaft. Grammatische Untersuchungen*, Jenaer Beiträge zum Vorderen Orient 3, Wiesbaden: Harrassowitz.

Vallat, F., 2000. L'Elam du IIe millénaire et la chronologie courte, *Akkadica* 119–20: 7–17.

Wiggermann, F. A. M., 1992. *Mesopotamian Protective Spirits: The Ritual Texts*, Cuneiform Monographs 1, Groningen: STYX & PP.

II. Middle Assyrian Period Texts

A. Ashur-uballit I (Greenwood)

79. Restoration of the Ishtar Temple

The clay tablet holding this text was discovered inside the Ishtar Temple of Ashur. The tablet is broken on the bottom edge, so an unknown amount of text is missing between lines 11 (obverse) and 12 (reverse).

The text consists of three parts. In lines 1–11 we find the standard genealogical information. Within lines 12–19 the purpose of the inscription is disclosed. Ashur-uballit declares the shrine of Ishtar repaired to its rightful condition. The text concludes by following the standard formula for dedication inscriptions.

Translation

(1–11) Ashur-uballit, the viceroy of the god Ashur, the son of Eriba-Adad; Eriba-Adad, the viceroy of the god Ashur, the son of Ashur-bel-nisheshu; Ashur-bel-nisheshu, the viceroy of the god Ashur, [the son] of Ashur-nirari; Ashur-nirari, [the viceroy] of the god Ashur.

(12–19) I roofed it with beams and I placed doors on it. From its foundation to its parapet I renewed it. I restored it to its sacred condition. I settled Ishtar kudnittu, *the mistress, inside that temple and I deposited my foundation cone.*

(20–5) When that temple falls in ruins and a later prince rebuilds it, may Ashur, Adad and Ishtar kudnittu *hear his prayer. May he return my foundation cone to its place.*

Commentary

(1–11) Although the text is broken below line 11, it is likely that the genealogy continues through Puzur-Ashur.

(12–19) Despite the lacuna in the text (in which the structure was undoubtedly mentioned), the provenance of the discovered tablet and the context of the inscription make it fairly certain that the structure was the shrine of Ishtar. Both the beams and doors were composed of wood, possibly from the famous cedars of Lebanon.

Ishtar, the preeminent female deity of ancient Mesopotamia, was the goddess of war, sex, and fertility. Her name is known today through the biblical character Esther and the Christian holy day Easter. With respect to astronomy, she is associated with the planet Venus, the morning and evening star. In ancient literature she is best known for her descent into the netherworld. After seeking and gaining admittance, she is killed by her sister, Ereshkigal, the queen of the netherworld, leading to the demise of all sexual reproduction on earth. Eventually, she is saved by her lover, Tammuz. Upon her ascent, the myth suggests a type of resurrection of all the dead.

In ancient Near Eastern cultic practice, graven images of a deity were paraded through the city during the *isinnu* and *akitu* (New Year's) festivals, then placed within the shrine. In this milieu the statue and the deity were one and the same, each possessing anthropomorphic qualities. The priest, or in this case the viceroy, would perform the rituals necessary to give life to the deity. One such ritual involved the daily care of the deity, in which the priest/viceroy would present the statue-god with actual food and drink. Although the statue could not consume the meal, its mouth would nonetheless be opened by the priest/viceroy so the deity could accept the offering.

Bibliography

For a history of the period see A. T. Olmstead, *History of Assyria* (New York: Scribner, 1923), 33–44; and H. W. F. Saggs, *The Might that Was Assyria* (London: Sidgwick & Jackson, 1984), 35–45. For an English translation, see A. Kirk Grayson, *Assyrian Royal Inscriptions*, vol. 1 (Wiesbaden: Harrossowitz, 1972), 43–4. For an English translation of Ishtar's descent, see Benjamin R. Foster, *From Distant Days: Myths, Tales and Poetry of Ancient Mesopotamia* (Bethesda: CDL, 1995), 78–84. For an introduction of ancient Mesopotamian mythology and cultic practices see Thorkild Jacobsen, *The Treasures of Darkness: A History of Mesopotamian Religion* (New Haven: Yale University Press, 1976); and F. A. M. Wiggermann, "Theologies, Priests, and Worship," in CANE, 1857–70.

B. Adad-Nirari I (Greenwood)

80. The campaigns of Adad-nirari I against Mitanni

During the fifteenth century BCE Mitanni, known as Hanigalbat in most Akkadian sources, emerged as a dominant force in the ancient Near East. At its peak the empire stretched from the Mediterranean Sea in the west to the Lower Zab River in the east. Some of the significant cities controlled by the Hurrians included Tarsus, Carchemish, Qadesh, Emar, Ashur, and Nuzi. Both Assyria and Babylon submitted to Mitanni, becoming vassal states. With the organization of Thutmose III's Egyptian war machine and the rise of the Hittites from the north, Mitanni's supremacy was in jeopardy. Mitanni was able to postpone its decline by entering into a marriage alliance with Thutmose IV of Egypt, which, in essence, established the northern border of Egypt at Byblos and the southern border of Mitanni at Qadesh. When Shuppiluliuma ascended to the Hittite throne ca. 1380 BCE, using both diplomatic and military means he rendered Mitanni powerless, leaving the door open for Assyria to reemerge as one of the great powers.

Once Assyria had regained control of its own territory it sought to extend that territory. Ashur-uballit I (1362–1327) was the first Assyrian king both willing and able to exploit Mitanni's weakness via military conflict, but our knowledge of these events is limited to Hittite sources. Under Adad-nirari I (1327–1274), however, Assyria increased the intensity and scope of its campaigns against Hanigalbat. The account of these campaigns appears in royal inscriptions as the first detailed record of any Assyrian military operation, describing geographical summaries and actual battle narratives.

Because of the amount of scribal activity required in Ashur, scribes often sought to reduce their labor by adhering to one of two standard introductions. This text represents one such formulaic introduction. This particular formula was used on approximately five texts, all of which were found in Ashur.

Translation

(1–7) Adad-nirari, king of the universe, heir of Arik-din-ili, the king of Ashur, son of Enlil-nirari, the king of Ashur. Adad-nirari, the king of the universe, strong king, the king of Ashur, the son of Arik-din-ili, the king of Ashur, the son of Enlil-nirari, the king of Ashur.

(7–17) When Shattuara, the king of Hanigalbat, rebelled against me and committed hostilities, at the command of Ashur, my lord and ally, and by the great gods, my good advisors, I seized him then brought him to my city Ashur. I made him swear an oath, then I released him. Every year, as long as he was alive, I received his tribute in my city Ashur.

(18–37) After him, his son, Wasashatta, revolted, rebelled against me, and committed hostilities. He went to Hatti for help. Hatti took his bribes, but he did not lend his aid. With the mighty weaponry of the god Ashur, my lord, and with the support of Anu, Enlil and Ea, Sin, Shamash, Adad, Ishtar, and Nergal, the omnipotence of the gods, the terrifying gods, my lords, I seized by conquest the cities of Taidu – his great royal city – Amasakku, Kahat, Shuru, Nabula, Hurra, Shuduhu, and Washukanu. I took the possessions of those cities, his forefathers' accumulations, and his palace treasure and brought them to my city Ashur.

(38–54) I conquered, burned, and destroyed the city of Irridu and I sowed kudimmu *plants over it. The great gods gave me – and I ruled in its entirety – from the cities of Taidu to Irridu, from the city of Eluhuat and Mt. Kashiari, the fortress-city of Sudu, and the fortress-city of Harranu to the bank of the Euphrates. I imposed the hoe, shovel, and corvée on the remainder of his people. As for him, his palace wife, his sons, his daughters, and his people, I removed them from Irridu. I brought them captive and bound along with their possessions to my city Ashur. I conquered, burned, and destroyed Irridu as well as the cities of the district of Irridu.*

Commentary

(1–7) The opening lines of dedicatory inscriptions proclaim ownership. Although all five texts with this introductory formula were found in Ashur, one text can be linked with certainty to the city of Taidu (see below). Presumably, the texts were written in Ashur on a transportable stone then taken to the designated building for the dedication ceremony. It is interesting that in that particular text space was left so the name of the specific structure being commemorated could be filled upon arrival to its designated location.

(7–17) The first campaign of Adad-nirari into Hanigalbat was in retaliation for hostilities committed against the Assyrian king. The particular acts of aggression perpetrated by Shattuara, the grandson of Tushratta, are unclear. One suggestion is that these hostilities involved attacking Assyrian merchants or messengers, or plundering border cities. Whatever the exact nature of these acts, it is evident from the concluding lines that the consequence for committing them was vassalage. Shattuara, forcibly taken to Ashur, was given an ultimatum: submit or be destroyed. According to Adad-nirari's account – and supported by Hittite documents – Shattuara chose the latter.

(18–37) The offense committed by Wasashatta was seeking the aid of Hatti to free itself from the oath of his father. Hatti gladly received Mitanni's gift, but, being in a state of internal instability, was unable to provide the requested services. This rebellion prompted Adad-nirari's second campaign against Hanigalbat.

The gods invoked by the king include all the major deities of the Assyrian pantheon. This is the only place in all the Middle Assyrian royal inscriptions in which the name of each major deity is invoked at the outset of battle. In a single text from Tukulti-Ninurta I each of these deities is mentioned, but not in the successive fashion done here.

The cities that came under Assyrian attack were located in approximately a 60-mile radius 150 miles northwest of Ashur. On a modern map they are located in extreme northeastern Syria, near Al-Qamishi and Nusaybin.

(38–54) In these concluding lines Adad-nirari summarizes the extent of devastation he inflicted upon Hanigalbat during his second campaign. Irridu, located near Carchemish, approximately 275 miles (443 kilometers) west by northwest of Ashur, became the westernmost city to succumb to Assyrian forces. The geographical area described in this account encompasses the entire region of Hanigalbat, from the foothills of the Zagros Mountains to the Euphrates River, and all areas in between.

As a rebellious vassal, the fate of Wasashatta was much more severe than that of his father. First, his cities were plundered. Second, he and his family were deported to Ashur along with all his 'people', either Irridu citizens or Hurrian troops. Since it was both inefficient to transport entire populations and unproductive to leave viable fields untended, other people were left behind to cultivate the land (cf. 2 Kgs 25: 8–12). Finally, his city was destroyed. The *kudimmu* plant, which produced a kind of salt or lye, was planted on ruin mounds in a symbolic act to pronounce the site barren and uninhabitable.

Bibliography

On the history of Mitanni see Gernot Wilhelm, "The Kingdom of Mitanni in Second-Millennium Upper Mesopotamia," in CANE 2, 1243–54. For a detailed study of the relationship between Assyria and Mitanni see Amir Harrak, *Assyria and Hanigalbat: A Historical Reconstruction of Bilateral Relations from the Middle of the Fourteenth to the End of the Twelfth Centuries* B.C., Texte und Studien zur Orientalisk 4 (Hildesheim: Olm, 1987). For a history of Assyria during the reign of Adad-nirari I see A. T. Olmstead, *History of Assyria* (New York: Scribner, 1923), 45–61; and H. W. F. Saggs, *The Might that Was Assyria* (London: Sidgwick & Jackson, 1984), 46–57. An English translation can be found in A. K. Grayson, *Assyrian Royal Inscriptions* (Wiesbaden: Harrossowitz, 1972), vol. 1, 59–61.

C. *Tukulti-Ninurta I (Morgan)*

81. The Tukulti-Ninurta I Epic

One of the many fascinating figures in the history of the ancient Near East is that of Tukulti-Ninurta I. His early military successes, bold campaigns into new territories, and tragic end have ensured that the memory of this Middle Assyrian ruler has become legendary.[1] Significant achievements in his relatively lengthy reign (1244–1208 BCE) include consolidation of his rule over territories inherited from his father Shalmaneser, extension of Assyrian rule into the Nairi lands to the north, the defeat of the Babylonian king Kashtiliash and subsequent plunder of Babylon, and the founding of the new capital Kar Tukulti-Ninurta (the Quay of Tukulti-Ninurta).

The defeat of the Kassite Kashtiliash marked a climax in Tukulti-Ninurta's reign. There had long been skirmishes in areas where Assyria and Babylonia had competing interests. Tukulti-Ninurta's control over the Zagros region, however, represented a direct threat to Babylonia's welfare. The flow of much needed resources – wood, metal, and stone – was redirected to Assyria. Kashtiliash attacked Assyria, a move that would ultimately prove devastating for Babylonia.

Kashtiliash was defeated in battle and taken from his land in chains. Tukulti-Ninurta destroyed the walls of Babylon, killed many of its inhabitants, plundered the city, and transported the statue of the god Marduk from Babylon to Assyria. The Assyrian king then took control of Babylonia, adopting its royal epithets as his own.

Having greatly increased the size and influence of his empire, Tukulti-Ninurta engaged in a series of massive building projects. He restored his father's palace, constructed another palace, then ultimately founded a new capital across the Tigris from Assur.

Despite Tukulti-Ninurta's celebrated victory over Kashtiliash, triumph would not characterize the close of his reign. Tukulti-Ninurta exercised control over Babylonia for only seven years,[2] after which a rebellion elevated Adad-shuma-uṣur, a son of Kashtiliash, to the Babylonian throne. A revolt took place within Assyria, perhaps precipitated in part by the economic burdens of maintaining the massive empire and financing the king's large-scale building activity. There are also hints within the texts of military defeats and rebellion. In a conspiracy led by his own son, Tukulti-Ninurta was assassinated in the capital that bore his name.

The Tukulti-Ninurta Epic details the most famous event of Tukulti-Ninurta's reign, his encounter with Kashtiliash. It artfully describes the provocation, the battle, and the plunder of the land. The Epic, originally an expansive literary masterpiece, is preserved only in fragmentary form. Readers unaccustomed to the study of incomplete texts may find breaks and ambiguous readings perplexing, particularly when they interrupt a sense of continuity within the narrative. Large portions of the text have been destroyed, and scholars have offered differing interpretations as to the proper arrangement of the fragments that have come down to us. A glance at the translations below will reveal the extent of the damage to even the surviving portions of the Epic, and the reader should keep in mind that the texts translated here were chosen specifically because they represent the largest and most well-preserved of the Epic's fragments.[3]

Despite the text's less that ideal condition, it nonetheless offers a literary account of the confrontation between the Assyrian king Tukulti-Ninurta and his Babylonian counterpart Kashtiliash. The Epic describes the conflict in striking poetic language. The selections below highlight several important scenes in the Epic's presentation both of events leading up to the battle and of the contest itself. The selections below appear at four separate points within the narrative, which for the sake of convenience I have designated Selections 1, 2, 3, and 4.[4] The column numbers, line numbers, and text identifications of these selections are those of Machinist.[5]

(Selection 1) Tukulti-Ninurta brings his complaint against Kashtiliash to Shamash, the god of justice. Tukulti-Ninurta maintains his own innocence while charging that Kashtiliash has violated the terms of an old treaty established by their ancestors [Column II: A obv. 1–24].

(Selection 2a) Tukulti-Ninurta makes his accusation directly to Kashtiliash, accusing the latter of unprovoked crimes against Assyria. The Assyrian king declares that nothing short of combat will settle the score and expresses confidence that the one who has remained faithful to the treaty will emerge victorious [Column III: A obv. 1–20].

(2b) Kashtiliash is frightened, for he recognizes his unfaithfulness to the treaty's provisions. He contrasts his own guilt with the pious reverence displayed by Tukulti-Ninurta, and portentous omens and dreams convince him that his defeat draws near [Column III: A obv. 21–57].

(Selection 3a) Tukulti-Ninurta sends a messenger to Kashtiliash, mocking the Babylonian king for postponing the battle. Tukulti-Ninurta reminds Kashtiliash that the armies are near one another and that the fight cannot be delayed indefinitely. Tukulti-Ninurta, having already encroached into Babylonian territory, challenges Kashtiliash to fight rather than flee [Column IV: A rev. 5–28].

(3b) With verbal bravado, Kashtiliash responds to the challenge while preparing an ambush. The Assyrian army, however, takes note of his preparations and thwarts his plan. Bloodshed follows, and some of the Babylonian's allies and nobles are killed [Column IV: A rev. 29–48].

(Selection 4a) The Assyrians urge Tukulti-Ninurta to attack again. Their army, they maintain, is experienced in battle. They obsequiously remind the king of his greatness, remarking that the Babylonian king daily conspires against the Assyrian's reign. Once again, Kashtiliash's guilt is stressed: Kashtiliash acted belligerently in a time of peace [Column V: A rev. 9–30].

(4b) The battle takes place, and the great gods lead the charge on Tukulti-Ninurta's behalf. One by one, the deities unleash their arsenal against the Babylonian king and his army [Column V: A rev. 31–40].

(4c) Tukulti-Ninurta leads the bloodthirsty Assyrian warriors, who bravely enter the battle from which they will emerge victorious [Column V: A rev. 41–52].

The Epic understands the battle between Tukulti-Ninurta and Kashtiliash as an ordeal, an exercise whose divinely influenced outcome reveals guilt or innocence. The Epic emphasizes Tukulti-Ninurta's blamelessness (Selection 1: 13ff.) and places an acknowledgment of Kashtiliash's guilt on his own lips (Selection 2b: 25ff.). The gods fight for Tukulti-Ninurta (Selection 4b), and a favorable outcome for Assyria is assured. In this way the text argues in a not-so-subtle fashion from military victory to moral superiority.

Selection 1

(Column II: A obv. 1–24)......................

....

In the territory of the land of [Assyria] he rendered a judgment
not to reveal the secr[et]

They went [. . .] very much [. . .]
(5) Those who brought the [. . .] of the king of the Kassites,
the merchants were bound in the evening . . .
They brought [the]m before Tukulti-Ninurta, lord of all people, bound together.
The king brought [them] to the place of Shamash, he did not act treacherously.
He provided h[el]p, he did a favor for the lord of Babylon.
[. . .] he freed the merchants, those carrying the money bags.
(10) He made [them] stand [be]fore Shamash,
he anointed their heads with oil.
The [tablet (?) of the kin]g of the Kassites, which he had impressed with his seal,
he set [be]fore Shamash [. . .], he continually addressed his plea to the gods.
"O Shamash, lord [. . .], I abided by (?) your oath, I feared your greatness.
He who has not [. . .] transgressed before your [. . .], but I kept your command.
(15) When our ancestors made a pact [bef]ore your divinity,
they established an oath between them, they invoked your greatness.
You are the warrior who does not change,
the judge of our [fat]hers from of [old],
and you are the god who maintains order,
now observing our loyalties!
Why has the king of the Kassites long frustrated your plan and your command?
(20) He did not fe[ar] your oath, he transgressed your judgment,
he plotted malice.
His filled up the measure of his sins before you. O Shamash, judge me!
[But as for the one wh]o committed no offense against the king of the Kassites,
[act favorably toward him.][6]
[. . .] great. Grant victory [. . .] to the one who keeps the oath.
[As for the one who does not obey] your instruction,
destroy(?) [his] people in the defeat of battle."

Selection 2

2a (Column III: A obv. 1–20) ....
[And in the bord]ers of your territory [. . .]
Why did you turn back and [. . .] the road where n[o escape] . . .
and (why did) you fear, without combat [. . .].
(5) You have plundered all my land; the pl[under].
You carried off the armies of Assur, before the battles you [. . .]
In a premature death, [the troops] are constantly laid to rest [. . .].
At an unexpected time, [their wives] became widows.
I raise the tablet with the oath between us, and I read it to the Lord of Heaven [. . .].
(10) You continue in the sin which you [. . .] both of us on the battlefield,
saying "Your father was set free,[7] *I did not avenge [. . .]."*
In which you plundered my unarmed people, our abuse [. . .] forever.
When we come together for battle, let [. . .] be judge between us.
We will [meet] on that day,[8] *as a righteous person who plunders [the property] of a criminal.*
(15) Peace will not be made without hostility, all the [. . .]
There can be no harmony without combat before [. . .].

Until I display your baldness behind you and you [go] to an untimely death.
Until my eyes have seen retreats in your battle time and again, slaughter [. . .].
Now come to me in a battle of soldiers,[9]
and let us exa[mine] the facts together.
(20) In this festival of battle, may he who transgressed the oath not rise up.
Let [them ca]st down his body.

2b (Column III: 21–57) Tukulti-Ninurta, having relied on keeping the oath, planned for battle,
while Kashtiliash's spirits fell, because he transgressed the instruction
of the gods.
He was afraid because of the cry of complaint to Shamash[10]
and the appeal to the gods;
he was frightened and concerned.
The command of the great king paralyzed his body like an evil spirit.[11]
(25) Kashtiliash thought, "I did not listen to the Assyrian.
I disregarded the messenger.
I did not appease him earlier. I failed to agree to his good plan.
Now I have seen[12] *– the sin of my land is grievous.*
A mortal punishment has overwhelmed me; death grips me.
The oath of Shamash troubles me, it holds back the hem of my garment.
(30) You have brought evidence against me, an unalterable tablet
sealed by my an[cestors].
They [. . .] before me, whose command cannot be changed,
the pact of my ancestors, which was not breached [. . .].
The just judge, who does not change, the warrior,
brought evidence against me and [. . .].
and the plundering caused by my ancestors [. . .].
(35) I placed my people into a merciless hand, an [inescapable] clutch.
I gathered [my people] into a narrow pit with no escape.
My sins are numerous before Shamash, [my] guilt [is great.]
Who is the god who will spare my people from [calamity]?
The Assyrian is constantly attentive to all the gods, he [. . .].
(40) [. . .] the lords of our oath [. . .] of heaven and earth.
I will not look within a sheep [for an omen],
the favorable omens[13] *for my army [have disappeared?] from the land [. . .].*
[. . .] the patterns on the intestines [. . .].
They will never es[tabl]ish the permanence of the foundations of [my house].
(45) Every one of my dreams is constantly terrifying [. . .].
Assur, the king of th[e world], frowns on me [. . .]
"Quickly, let me know [. . .]
To what portentous omen shall I [. . .]
"Let me know for co[mbat] [. . .]
(50) How long [. . .]

....

Let me take refuge [. . .]
He will conquer me and [. . .]
A fire,[14] *a destructive wind [. . .]*
(55) He has confined me and [. . .]

And death [. . .]
He grew weary [. . .].

Selection 3

3a (Column IV: A rev. 5–28) Again he [. . .]
He did not submit [to Tukulti-Ninurta]
He does not face him [. . .]
Again he [. . .]
He was placed in [. . .]
He decided [. . .]
Tukulti-Ninurta gave orders [. . .]
A messenger to Kashtiliash to [. . .]
How long will [your troops] flee?[15]
You constantly reposition your army with [your] command [. . .].
For which day do you keep [the weapons] of com[bat?]
And which day do your weapons await? [. . .]
I am dwelling in your land. [. . .] the shrine of [. . .].
I ransacked your cities, as many as there were, and I [. . .] your people.
Has your characteristic arrogance ever [made] your battle [successful]?
We will show you the rage and slaughter that you desire.
Perhaps now you have courage, because it is the month of the spring flood – the water will be your aid!
And you have pitched your camp in difficult terrain, Girra is your support.
In the hot season, when the flood has crested, at the shining of the god [. . .]
In what difficult terrain will you put your trust that you might save your people?
My army is not situated many leagues from you.
And you – all your chariots are prepared, your army is assembled.
[Come u]p to me fiercely, you who strive to do battle,
[Di]splay your weapons,
find fulfillment in the battle for which your passion burns.
3b (Column IV: A rev. 29–48) [Kashti]liash, dismayed and enraged, issued the command for conflict.
"Tukulti-Ninurta, let your army stay put
until such time as Shamash determines.
Do not begin your battle until the proper time for my combat arrives!
This is the day the blood of your people
will drench the steppes and meadowlands,
And like Adad I will send a devastating flood upon your camp!"
He delayed the message so as to deceive (?) until he sent out his troops.
(His) chariots were held back from fighting
until he prepared his battle (plans).
He commanded his army, but Girra held it back like a dangerous revolt (?).
He brought his camp across secret places, seizing the road.
The mighty warriors of [Assur] saw the preparations of the Kassite king.
They were not clad in armor; like a lion they ki[ll . . .]
The matchless weapon of Assur meets the onslaught of [his] for[ces].
And Tukulti-Ninurta, the furious, merciless storm, made [their blood] flow.

The warriors of Assur [struck] the army of the Kassite king like a fierce serpent.
A mighty battle, an irresistible onslaught [they brought] against them.
Kashtiliash turned back [...........] to save himself.
(45) The weapon of Enlil, the Lord of all Lands, which surrounds the enemies, shattered [his troops].
[. . .] of combat, his allies, were slaughtered like oxen. [His] nobles [. . .]
The governor of all lands, to destroy the war[riors]
[. . .] the forefinger of the Lord of all Lands [. . .]

Selection 4

4a (Column V: A rev. 9–30) ....
(10) His warriors in [. . .]
"My lord, from the begi[nning] of your [re]ign [. . .]
B[at]tle and conflict have been our festival; jo[y]
You instruct us to prepare for the mêlée [. . .]
With the auspicious sign of your lordship, let us advance like men!
(15) In your royal reign, no king has stood as your peer.
Your supremacy is established over all the land, sea, and mountains.
With the fury of your scepter, you established all regions in every direction.[16]
You extended the strength of your land to innumerable regions; you established boundaries.
Kings know of your heroism; they live in fear of your battle.
(20) And like slander, a blasphemy which is attached following it, they bear your fearsomeness.[17]
Now plan against the Kassite king,
scatter his troops before the appointed time for battle.
Terrify the forces he has encamped; burn [his cha]riots.
How much longer will he plot evil against us?
Conspiring maliciously against us, he constantly plans murder!
(25) Daily he plots the destruction of the land of Assur, his finger is pointed (toward it).
He constantly makes preparation to take the power of the Assyrian's kingship.
Let us join battle – may he who advances live, may he who retreats die.
While I was peaceful, he brought our friendly discourse to an end.[18]
Plan for battle!
[. . .] with you, when they previously encouraged you at the place of battle.
(30) And our lord, you will receive a victorious name over the Kassite king by the command of Shamash."

4b (Column V: A rev. 31–40) Battle lines were drawn up; hostilities commenced on the battlefield.
There was a great tumult, the soldiers trembled amongst themselves.
Assur went out front, he kindled a devastating fire upon the enemies.
Enlil whirls in the midst of the enemy, he made smoke rise from the flame.
(35) Anu set his merciless mace against the wicked.
The heavenly light, Sin, fixed upon them the paralysis of war.
Adad, the hero, poured out a wind and flood on their fighting.
Shamash, the lord of judgment,

blinded the armies of the lands of Sumer and Akkad.
Valiant Ninurta, preeminent among the gods, shattered their weapons,
and Ishtar whipped with her jump rope,[19] *causing their warriors to go mad.*

4c (Column V: A rev. 41–52) After the gods, his helpers, the king at the forefront began the battle.
He shot an arrow, (and) with the weapon of Assur,
which can dispel an aggressive attack, he felled a corpse.
The warriors of Assur shouted, "Forward to the battle!"
They face death.
They cry, "O Ishtar, have mercy!"
They praise the mistress amid the tumult.
They are enraged and furious. They become strange in form like Anzu.[20]
They are aggressive, (they go) fiercely into the chaos of battle without armor.
They had removed breastplates, cast off garments.
They gathered up (their) hair, they polished (their) lances with bran(?).[21]
Wild, heroic warriors played with sharpened[22] *weapons*
[And] mighty winds rushed together like quarreling lions,
[And] the confusion of the whirlwind swirls in the battle.
[And] death was, in the eyes of the warriors,
like finding refreshment on a day of thirst.

82. A letter from Tukulti-Ninurta I to Tudhaliya IV[23]

This brief and heavily damaged letter likely represents a communication from Tukulti-Ninurta I to the Hittite king Tudhaliya IV.[24] The text was unearthed at Boğazköy, the site of the ancient Hittite capital Hattusha.

Tukulti-Ninurta responds to the Hittite's complaint of Assyrian incursions into Hittite territory. Border skirmishes and raiding occurred with regularity in the ancient world, and in the Epic it is the Assyrian king who complains of raids by the Babylonians (Selection 2a, lines 5–6, 12).

Always eager to maintain his own innocence,[25] Tukulti-Ninurta flatly denies that the Assyrians have engaged in such behavior. The Assyrians, he declares, have not snatched even a twig from Hittite soil. Tukulti-Ninurta seeks to assure Tudhaliya that they are allies, though lines 12 and 13 seem to hint that Tukulti-Ninurta senses a change in Tudhaliya's demeanor towards him. In fact, though Tukulti-Ninurta terms Tudhaliya his "brother" (indicating that he views him as a monarch of equal status), the relationship between the two monarchs was often openly hostile.

....
....
[. . .] of the kingdom, indeed (was there) any sin
[. . .] I committed against the land of my brother?
[. . .]-ili remained a friend of my brother.
[. . .] time and again they have plundered your land.
[. . .] time and again they have plundered your land!

[. . .] no one sinned against your land.
[. . .] no one removed so much as a twig from within the borders of your land.
(10) [. . .] he has done to me. My father was your enemy,
[but] I am my brother's ally.
[why] did you change your mind?
[And why] have you done such to (our) good relationship?[26]

Bibliography

The Middle Assyrian Period and Tukulti-Ninurta I

Charpin, Dominique. "The History of Ancient Mesopotamia." CANE 2: 817–21.
Grayson, A. K. "Mesopotamia, History of (Assyria)." *The Anchor Bible Dictionary*. D. N. Freedman, ed. (New York: Doubleday, 1992) 2: 738–40.
Hallo, W. W. and Simpson, W. K. *The Ancient Near East: A History*. 2d ed. New York: Harcourt Brace College, 1998.
Kuhrt, Amélie. *The Ancient Near East: c. 3000–330* BC. New York: Routledge, 1995: 348–65.
Munn-Rankin, J. M. "Assyrian Military Power." 2/2: 274–306 of the *Cambridge Ancient History*. 3d ed. Cambridge: Cambridge University Press, 1975.

Kar Tukulti-Ninurta

Dittman, R. "Kar-Tukulti-Ninurta." *The Oxford Encyclopedia of Archaeology in the Near East*. Eric M. Meyers, ed. in chief. (Oxford: OUP, 1997) 3: 269–71.

Further English translations of the Epic and other texts from Tukulti-Ninurta's reign

Grayson, A. K. *Assyrian Rulers of the Third and Second Millennia* B.C. RIMA, 1987.
——. *Assyrian Royal Inscriptions*. 2 vols. Wiesbaden: Harrassowitz, 1972.
Foster, Benjamin R. *Before the Muses*. 2 vols. Bethesda: CDL, 1993.
——. *From Distant Days: Myths, Tales, and Poetry of Ancient Mesopotamia.*
King, L. W. *Records of the Reign of Tukulti-Ninib I*. London: Luzac, 1904.
Luckenbill, D. D. *Ancient Records of Assyria and Babylonia*. New York: Greenwood, 1926.

Detailed Studies on the Tukulti-Ninurta Epic

Machinist, Peter Bruce. "Literature as Politics: The Tukulti-Ninurta Epic and the Bible." *Catholic Biblical Quarterly*. 38: 455–82.
——. "The Epic of Tukulti-Ninurta I: A Study in Middle Assyrian Literature." PhD dissertation, Yale University, 1978.

83. The construction of a new capital

The text below, inscribed on an alabaster tablet found in the ziggurat at Kar-Tukulti-Ninurta, describes the king's building activity at this site. Of particular interest are the royal titles used to describe the king and the report concerning the building of the new capital.

The expansion of the royal titulary may be observed by comparing the titles used by the king before and after his victory over Kashtiliash. An earlier tablet from Assur begins:

> *Tukulti-Ninurta, king of the world, mighty king, king of the land of Assyria, chosen by Assur, viceroy of Assur, the just shepherd, beloved of the goddess Ishtar, the one who made all the land of Qutu submit, the son of Shalmaneser, viceroy of Assur, the son of Adad-Narari, viceroy of Assur . . .*[27]

Here Tukulti-Ninurta is described using traditional royal epithets. He boasts of the conquest of the Qutu lands in the early part of his rule, and underscores his legitimacy by drawing attention to his genealogical link with previous rulers. Following the defeat of Kashtiliash (see the Epic above), however, Tukulti-Ninurta adopts Babylonian royal titles as his own. Lines 1–26 below, a lengthy list of royal epithets, include the Babylonian title "King of Sumer and Akkad." A tablet describing the construction of a new palace in Assur provides another example:

> *Tukulti-Ninurta, king of the world, king of the land of Assyria, king of the four quarters, the Sun god of all people, mighty king, king of the land of Karduniash (a reference to Babylon), king of Sumer and Akkad . . .*[28]

Lines 88–109a detail the construction of Kar-Tukulti-Ninurta (the quay, or harbor, of Tukulti-Ninurta). This new capital bearing the name of the monarch is located two miles north of Assur, east of the Tigris River. The site was excavated in 1913–14 by Walter Bachmann, and Reinhard Dittmann resumed work there in 1986.

Lines 109b–118 include a description of the building of the ziggurat at Kar-Tukulti-Ninurta, the base of which measures 33 yards (30 meters). The ziggurat is associated with the Assur Temple, which Tukulti-Ninurta gave the name Ekurmesharra – in Sumerian, "House, mountain of all the *Me's*."[29] *Me's* were traditional rules thought to govern all aspects of worship and civilization which the ancients understood to be divinely ordained.[30]

The text goes to some lengths to underscore the fact that the new capital, Kar-Tukulti-Ninurta, was constructed on virgin soil. The king built the city at a location where "no house or dwelling had previously existed, [where] no ruin mound or debris was piled up, [where] no bricks were laid" (lines 95–8). Tukulti-Ninurta provided means of access to the city and dug a canal that provided fish and otherwise met the population's hydraulic needs. The venture required a massive labor force and a tremendous outlay of resources, and the economic impact of this project may have contributed to the discontent that eventually resulted in the king's assassination.

Monarchs in ancient Mesopotamia wanted future generations to remember their names and deeds, and a curse formula was often used in an attempt to discourage neglect or willful destruction of either the edifice itself or the written record of the king who built it. This tablet closes by expressing confidence that the gods Ashur, Enlil, and Shamash will hear the prayer of the one who looks attentively after the temple and ziggurat Tukulti-Ninurta has built (lines 119–25a). It imposes a curse on those who would efface the king's name or damage his work (lines 125b–46).

(1–26) I am Tukulti-Ninurta, king of the world, the mighty king, king of the land of Assyria, king of the land of Sumer and Akkad, king of the four quarters, chosen by the gods Ashur and Shamash, reverent prince, the king who is the favorite of the god Enlil, the one who shepherded his land in green pastures with his benevolent staff, the preeminent purification priest, nominated by the god Anu, the one who in his fierce heroism subdued princes and all kings, the faithful shepherd, the god Ea's heart's desire, the one who has established his names over the four quarters in victory, the exalted priest, beloved of the god Sin, who properly directed people and settlements with his just scepter, the valiant hero, the handiwork of the god Adad who, in his sovereign reign, provided copious abundance, the mighty male, favorite of the god Ninurta, the one who has encircled all quarters with his mighty power, the competent one, fierce, beloved of the goddess Ishtar, the one who received tribute from lands east and west, the son of Shalmaneser, king of the world, king of Assyria, the son of Adad-Nirari, king of the world, king of Assyria.

Lines 27–56a describe Tukulti-Ninurta's early victories, while lines 56b–68 describe the Assyrian king's triumph over Kashtiliash of Babylon. Lines 69–87 list lands paying tribute to Tukulti-Ninurta.

(88–109a) Then the god Ashur my lord requested of me a cult center across (the river) from my city,[31] *which was chosen by the gods, and he commanded me to build his temple. At the command of the god Ashur, the god who loves me, on the other side (of the river) from Assur, my city, I indeed built a city for the god Ashur on the opposite bank of the Tigris, in the barren steppes and meadows where no house or dwelling had previously existed. No ruin mound or debris was piled up there, no bricks were laid. I named it Kar-Tukulti-Ninurta. I sliced straight through the hills, I hewed out high mountain passes with chisels. I channeled a stream that brings abundance, making secure the life of the land. I transformed the environs of my city into irrigated land. From the abundant yield of the waters of that canal I prepared perpetual offerings for the god Ashur and the great gods, my lords.*

(109b–118) Then I built in my city – Kar-Tukulti-Ninurta, the cult center that I constructed – a pure temple, an awe-inspiring sanctuary for the dwelling of the god Ashur, my lord. I named it Ekurmesharra. Within it I completed a great ziggurat as the cult platform for the god Ashur, my lord, and I deposited my inscriptions.

(119–125a) May a later ruler restore this ziggurat and temple of the god Ashur, my lord, when they become dilapidated. May he anoint my inscriptions with oil, may he offer sacrifices, and may he return (them) to their proper places. The gods Ashur, Enlil, and Shamash will listen to his prayers.

(125b–146) He who does not restore the ziggurat and the temple of Ashur my lord; who removes my inscriptions and inscribed name; who destroys it by inattention,

neglect, or disrepair; who plans any evil matter or makes trouble for this ziggurat and for this temple of the god Ashur my lord; may the gods Ashur, Enlil, and Shamash – the gods who are my help – lead him into distress and sorrow. Wherever battle and conflict are found, may they break his weapons. May they bring about the defeat of his army. May they hand him over to a king who is his adversary and make him live in bondage in the land of his enemies. May they overthrow his reign, and may they destroy his name and his progeny from the land.

D. *Tiglath-pilesar I (Greenwood)*

84. Campaigns of Tiglath-pilesar I against the Arameans and Babylonia

This 7-line excerpt comes from a 94-line building inscription that elucidates Tiglath-pilesar's work on and around his palace at Ashur. The selection chosen here is interesting on two levels. First, it contains some of the earliest Mesopotamian information on the Aramean tribes, outlining the geographical region of this people group. Second, it contains the first account of Assyria's defeat of Babylonia under Tiglath-pilesar.

Translation

(34–6) I have crossed the Euphrates 28 times against the ahlamu *Arameans – twice in one year. I secured their defeat from Tadmar of the land of Amurru and Anat of the land of the Suhu to Rapiqu city of Karduniash. I brought their spoils and their property to my city, Ashur.*

(37–40) I marched to the land of Karduniash. I conquered the cities Dur-Kurigalzu, Sippar of Shamash, Sippar of Annunitu, Babylon and Upi, the great shrine of Karduniash, including their fortresses. I massacred them in great number. I plundered countless amounts of their booty. I conquered the palaces of Babylon belonging to Marduk-nadin-ahhe, the king of Karduniash, and I burned them with fire. Twice I drew up a battle line of chariots against Marduk-nadin-ahhe, the king of Karduniash, and I defeated him.

Commentary

(34–6) At the turn of the first millennium BCE the Arameans, whose Aramaic language would eventually become the *lingua franca* of the ancient Near East, were independent, semi-nomadic pastoralist tribes, loosely unified by geography rather than ethnicity. The *ahlamu* seem to have been one of the nomadic Aramean tribes.

Previous Assyrian campaigns under Tiglath-pilesar were conducted through the highlands of southern Anatolia. During this particular expedition, he boasts of victories in the very heart of the Aramean territory. Despite Tiglath-pilesar's confidence in the defeat of these peoples, the fact that he had to wage battle against them 28 times indicates the persistent threat they posed to the Assyrian Empire. In fact, in the waning years of his reign a damaged

Assyrian chronicle suggests that the Arameans had captured Nineveh, a city that had increased in prominence during the Tiglath-pilesar era.

(37–40) The account of the fall of Babylonia at the hands of the Assyrians is substantiated by the Synchronistic History. The purpose of the campaign does not appear to have been one of subjugation, since Marduk-nadin-ahhe was not brought back to Ashur to swear vassalage to Assyria. Nor did Tiglath-pilesar attempt to establish himself as the king of Karduniash. Instead, the raid seems to have been little more than a firm statement on the sovereignty of Assyria.

Bibliography

For bibliography on the history and historiography of Assyria for this period, see under "Tiglath-pileser I's subjugation of the Nairi lands" (§85 in this chapter). For studies on the Arameans see Paul E. Dion, "Aramaean Tribes and Nations of First-Millennium Western Asia," in Jack M. Sasson (ed.), *Civilizations of the Ancient Near East* (New York: Scribners/Macmillan, 1995), vol. 2, 1281–94; and William M. Schniedewind, "The Rise of the Aramean States," in Mark W. Chavalas and K. Lawson Younger (eds.), *Mesopotamia and the Bible: Comparative Explorations* (Grand Rapids: Baker Academic, 2002), 276–87. An English translation of the entire text may be found in A. K. Grayson, *Assyrian Royal Inscriptions* (Wiesbaden: Otto Harrassowitz, 1976), vol. 2, 24–9; and James B. Pritchard (ed.), *Ancient Near Eastern Texts Relating to the Old Testament*. 3rd ed. (Princeton: Princeton University Press, 1969), 275.

85. Tiglath-pilesar I's subjugation of the Nairi lands

For the first time in Assyrian royal inscriptions we are presented with a real example of military annals. It diverges from previous military records in that combat events are narrated in chronological order. Although Tiglath-pilesar's annals do not yet date or number the years of particular campaigns, they move in that direction by clearly indicating the events of a new year with certain literary features.

The text itself is found on over three dozen exemplars, almost exclusively from Ashur. The inscription was written on clay octagonal prisms, each side containing approximately 100 lines of text. This particular excerpt contains 89 lines from columns iv and v.

Translation

(43–70) At that time, by the exalted might of Ashur, my lord, with the authoritative consent of Shamash, the warrior, with the support of the great gods by which I have just authority in the four quarters and have neither competitor in battle nor rival in combat, Ashur, my lord, commissioned me to march to the Nairi lands, whose distant kings on the Upper Sea coast in the west, have not known submission. I passed through treacherous roads and narrow passes – whose interior no king had previously

known – blocked roads and closed remote mountain regions: the mountains of Elama, Amadanu, Elhish, Sherabeli, Tarhuna, Terkahuli, Kisra, Tarhanabe, Elula, Hashtarae, Shahishara, Ubera, Miadruni, Shulianzi, Nubanashe, and Sheshe. Sixteen rugged mountains became smooth terrain in my chariot because I hacked that difficult terrain with bronze mattocks. I felled the Urumu trees of the mountains. I constructed bridges for the passage of my chariots and troops.

(71–87) I crossed the Euphrates. The king of Tummu, the king of Tunubu, the king of Tualu, the king of Dardaru, the king of Uzula, the king of Unzamunu, the king of Andiabu, the king of Piladarnu, the king of Adurginu, the king of Kulibarzinu, the king of Shinibirnu, the king of Himua, the king of Paiteru, the king of Uiram, the king of Shururia, the king of Abaenu, the king of Adaenu, the king of Kirinu, the king of Albaya, the king of Ugina, the king of Nazabia, the king of Abarsiunu, the king of Dayenu – a total of 23 kings of the Nairi lands – mustered their chariotry and their troops within their lands. They advanced in order to wage warfare, battle and combat.

(87–100) I attacked them with the fury of my fierce weaponry. I brought about the slaughter of their vast armies like a deluge of Adad. I laid out like sheaves the corpses of their warriors in the plains, on the heights of the mountains, and in the vicinity of their cities. I seized 120 of their wooden chariots in the midst of battle. I pursued the 60 kings of the Nairi lands, including those who had come to their aid, at the tip of my arrow as far as the Upper Sea.

(101–8) I conquered their great towns. I removed their booty, their property, and their possessions. Their cities I burned with fire, leveled, and demolished. I turned them into a mound and ruin heap. I brought back multitudinous herds of horses, mules, and donkeys and innumerable livestock from their pastures.

(108–21) I personally captured alive all of the kings of the Nairi lands. I showed mercy on those kings and spared their lives. I released them from their captivity and bondage in the presence of Shamash, my lord. I made them swear by my great gods an oath of permanent vassalage. I seized their royal male progeny as hostages. I imposed upon them a tribute of 1,200 horses and 2,000 cattle. I released them to their lands.

(122–32) Sheni, the king of Dayenu, had not been submissive to Ashur, my lord, so I brought him into captivity and bondage to my city. I showed him mercy and released him alive from my city, Ashur, in order to proclaim the glory of the great gods. I ruled the vast Nairi lands in their entirety and subjugated all their kings at my two feet.

Commentary

(43–70) In the inscriptions of Tiglath-pilesar I the Nairi lands refer to a broad geographical region in the southern Anatolian mountains, ranging from Lake Van in the east to the Mediterranean (Upper Sea) in the west. Although the extent to which Tiglath-pilesar marched cannot be known precisely at this time, two rock inscriptions provide physical evidence for the extent of his campaigns. The first is in the Melazzert region northwest of Lake Van. The second is found near the source of the Tigris River, where the Sebeneh-Su River emerges from a tunnel.

(71–87) Tiglath-pilesar's campaigns were not limited to the northern frontier. His westward thrust took him across the Euphrates River. There is a great deal of uncertainty surrounding the identity of "the 60 kings of the

Nairi lands," 23 of whom are listed here. However, all current evidence indicates Tummu and Dayenu represented the southeastern and northwestern extremes of Nairi, respectively.

(87–100) In the next four paragraphs Tiglath-pilesar recounts the destruction inflicted upon the Nairi lands by his Assyrian military forces. In a highly literary fashion his account moves from the general to the specific. Using imagery of the storm-god Adad, Tiglath-pilesar begins his description with what happened on the rural and suburban battlefield, from the mountains of the Zagros, Anti-Taurus, and Taurus to the upper-Mesopotamian plains. As his spoils of battle in the wilderness setting, Tiglath-pilesar apprehended ten dozen combat chariots.

(101–108) The king focuses his narration slightly, moving from the outskirts of populated areas to the very heart of the urban centers. Tiglath-pilesar's characterization of utter annihilation of the towns must be understood in light of royal propaganda. The use of hyperbole was a significant feature in ancient Near Eastern conquest accounts. Therefore, extensive archaeological excavations are required in making concrete determinations regarding the extent of military destruction.

The acquisition of foreign animals by an Assyrian king is not unique to this text. These monarchs were known to have received many exotic animals from afar including apes, crocodiles, and the Bactrian camel. Other texts mention hunts for bears, hyenas, lions, tigers, leopards, deer, wild goats, and a sea-horse.

(108–21) Tiglath-pilesar narrows his focus even further, honing in on the kings of the very cities he destroyed. As his ancestor Adad-nirari had done with Shattuara, the king of Mitanni, Tiglath-pilesar forcibly takes the Nairi kings back to his palace in Ashur. Upon their arrival the foreign kings would have been greeted by texts and images declaring the irresistible power of Assyria. At the palace the kings would have declared their allegiance to Assyria. As sworn vassal rulers, they were then released to their homelands.

The vast amount of tribute received from the Nairi kings indicates Tiglath-pilesar had economic, as well as military, motives for northwestward campaigns. In one text he explicitly states his intention for amassing hoards of livestock; namely, to increase grain production.

(122–32) Finally, Tiglath-pilesar pinpoints one specific king who warranted special mention. The act of resistance against Ashur is not specified, but it is probably on par with that of Wasashatta against Adad-nirari. That is, Sheni was one of the kings originally brought to Ashur and released as a vassal, but shortly thereafter rebelled by seeking to renege on his oath.

Bibliography

For a history of the period see A. T. Olmstead, *History of Assyria* (New York: Scribner, 1923), 62–9; and H. W. F. Saggs, *The Might That Was Assyria* (London: Sidgwick &

Jackson, 1984), 58–69. On the historiography of Assyrian royal inscriptions see Hayim Tadmor, "History and Ideology in the Assyrian Royal Inscriptions," in F. M. Fales (ed.), *Assyrian Royal Inscriptions: New Horizons in Literary, Ideological, and Historical Analysis*. Orientis Antiqui Collectio 17 (Rome: Isitituto Per L'Oriente, 1981), 13–33; A. K. Grayson, "Assyrian Royal Inscriptions: Literary Characteristics," in Fales, 35–47; and K. Lawson Younger, Jr., *Ancient Conquest Accounts: A Study of Ancient Near Eastern and Biblical History Writing* (Sheffield: Sheffield Academic Press, 1990). An English translation of the entire text may be found in A. K. Grayson, *Assyrian Royal Inscriptions* (Wiesbaden: Harrossowitz, 1976), vol. 2, 3–20.

III. Middle Babylonian Texts

A. *Text from the reign of Nebuchadnezzar I (Cooley)*

Perhaps the most significant Babylonian monarch of the Middle Babylonian Period, Nebuchadnezzar I's (Akkadian *Nabû-kudurrī-uṣur*, "Oh Nabu, guard my heirs") reign of 22 years was celebrated long after his death. Though he engaged the Assyrians militarily on a few occasions, the best-documented event of his reign, and the feat for which he was later famous, was his campaign against Elam. At the end of the Kassite Period the Elamites had conducted a series of raids into Babylonia. On one of these raids they captured a number of the cultic statues. Among those was that of Marduk, the patron deity of Babylon itself. Nebuchadnezzar I's campaign (or possibly campaigns) against Elam not only successfully routed the Elamite army, thus securing Babylonia from further incursions from the east, but also succeeded in returning Marduk's statue to Babylon.

86. The Shitti-Marduk Stele

The stele (often called a *kudurru*) is a four-sided limestone block 26 inches (65 centimeters) high, 8.5 inches (21.5 centimeters) wide, and 7 inches (17 centimeters) deep. Two sides contain the text, while a third is covered with protective emblems associated with various deities. After its manufacture, the stele was deposited in the Shamash Temple in Nippur where it was ultimately discovered by excavators in the late nineteenth century.

The text itself is written in Akkadian in high literary style. Indeed, this text is considered by several scholars to be the high point of the literary art in the Middle Babylonian period, containing various chiastic structures and wordplays.

The Shitti-Marduk stele records Nebuchadnezzar's emancipation of the tribal towns of Bit-Karziabku (a Kassite tribe) from the service of a neighboring region, Namar, which was granted in recognition of Shitti-Marduk's (the tribal leader of Bit-Karziabku) valor in combat during the Elamite campaign.

Text

Historical circumstances for the granting of the emancipation

(1–11) When Nebuchadnezzar – the reverent prince, the finest, the offspring of Babylon, the pre-eminent of kings, the heroic governor, the regent of Babylon, the Sun of his land, who makes his people flourish, who protects the borders, who insures the heirs, the righteous king who renders just verdicts, the heroic man whose might is always devoted to waging war, who bears a furious bow, who does not fear war, who felled the powerful Lullubu Land with (his) weapon, who conquers the Amurru Land, who loots the Kassites, the finest of kings, the prince, the beloved of Marduk –

(12–16) (When) Marduk, King of the Gods, ordered him to avenge Akkad, he raised his weapons. From Der, the sanctuary of An, he launched an attack 30 leagues (deep). In Tammuz he took to the road.

(17–21) The radiant heat burned like fire and it was as if the roads were blazing like flames. There was no water in the watering-pastures and the watering places were cut off. The very finest of the horses stood (still) while the legs of the heroic soldier buckled.

(22–4) (But) the finest king was marching, the gods bearing him! Nebuchadnezzar advances – he has no equal! He does not fear the hardships of field – he extends the daily marches!

(25–34) Shitti-Marduk, lord of the house of Bit-Karziabku, whose chariot was on the right flank of the king, his lord, did not delay and he kept control of his chariot. The potent king sped and he reached the bank of the Ulai River. The kings met and they both waged war. Fire ignited between them. The sun's face was obscured by their dust. Dust storms whirled about, the storm pranced. During the storm of their battle the soldier in the chariot could not see (his) second who was with him.

(35–41) Shitti-Marduk, lord of the house of Bit-Karziabku, whose chariot was on the right flank of the king, his lord, did not delay and he kept control of his chariot. He did not fear combat and he descended on the enemy. Into his lord's enemy's (positions) he penetrated deeply. At the command of Ishtar and Adad, the lords of combat, he routed Hultelutish, the king of Elam. He (Hultelutish) disappeared.

(42–3) So the king, Nebuchadnezzar, stood triumphantly. He seized Elam. He looted its property.

(44–9) After he returned triumphantly and contentedly to Akkad, Shitti-Marduk, lord of the house of Bit-Karziabku, whom the king, his lord, noticed among the enemies and combatants, informed the king, his lord, Nebuchadnezzar about the towns of Bit Karziabku, the territory of Namar in their entirety, which, though they (the towns of Bit-Karziabku) were free under a previous king, through hostilities they entered into the service of Namar not under treaty.

(50–1) So the king asked his experts and, as previously, the towns were emancipated from the service of the whole of Namar.

Stipulations of emancipation

(51–2) The work supervisor of either the king or of the governor of Namar, or the herald is not to enter a town.

(53–4) A horse overseer is not to lead stallions and mares into the towns.

(55–6) The tax of the king of Namar on cattle or sheep is not to be collected. Neither a pin's worth nor homer is to be given.

(57) A donkey is not to be given to the customs official.

(58–9) A riding horse trainer is not to enter the towns nor is he to seize any of the riding horses.

(60) Orchards or date trees are not to be felled.

Column 2

(1) The fortress of the towns of Bit-Shamash and Shanbasha is not to be (re)built.

(2) A bridge is not to be built, a road is not to be constructed.

(3–5) The armies of Nippur, Babylon or the army of the king, as many as are stationed in the towns of Bit-Karziabku, are not to order the seizing of a man in the town or in open country.

(6–9) Nebuchadnezzar, king of the universe, has freed all the towns of Shitti-Marduk, son of Karziabku of the district of Namar, from all of the service of Namar entirely forever.

(9–10) He ordered the armies stationed in those towns as the special aid of the governor of Namar and the herald.

Witnesses

(11) At the emancipation of those cities:
(12) Nazi-Marduk, son of Shaddakme, lamentation priest of Akkad
(13) Arad-Nana, son of Mudammiq-Adad, provincial governor of the land
(14) Marduk-kudurri-uzzer, court official of Bel
(15) Tubia-enna, servant
(16) Mukkutissah, son of Sapri, palace gate official
(17) Shamash-nadin-shumi, son of Atta-iluma, governor of Ishin
(18) Bau-shumi-iddina, son of Hunna, governor of Babylon
(19) Uballissu-Gula, son of Arad-Ea, provincial official
(20) Marduk-mukin-apli, son of Tabu-mile, manager of the equipment storehouse
(21) Arad-Gula, son of Kalbi, governor of Ushti
(22) Tab-ashab-Marduk, son of Esaggil-zeru, governor of Halman
(23) Enlil-nadin-shumi, son of Habban, governor of Namar
(24) and Nabu-kudurri-uzzer, the herald of Namar – they (all) stood (by in attendance).
(25) The scribe who inscribed this stele was Enlil-tabni-bullit, the diviner.

Curses

(26–38) Forevermore, if one of the sons of Habban or some other man who should be installed in the governorship of Namar, or administrative officials of Namar, whether unimportant or important, having not feared the king nor his gods, again imposed the service on the towns of Bit-Karziabku, which the king has freed from the service of Namar, or if he has erased the name of a god or the king and has inscribed another, or if he has ordered either a twit, deaf man, a half-wit or a blind man to demolish this stele with a rock, burn it with fire, throw it into the river, bury it in an unseen field

– that man may the great gods, as many as whose names are mentioned in heaven and earth angrily curse him. May god and the king glare at him furiously.

(39–40) May Ninurta, king of heaven and earth, and Gula, bride of the Eshharra Temple, destroy his heir, ruin his progeny.

(41–5) May Adad, canal inspector of heaven and earth, lord of deep water and rain, fill his canals with silt. May he set upon him starvation and famine. May poverty, want, and misfortune be bound to his side day and night. May he beg from even the poor of his town.

(46–52) May Shumalia, lady of pure mountains, who lives at the peaks, who treads the springs, may Adad, Nergal and Nana, the gods of Namar, may Nirah, the spectacular god, member of the temple of Der, may Sin and the Lady of Akkad, the gods of the house of Habban, may these great gods with a raging heart always plot evil against him.

(53) May another man own the house which he built.

(54–7) Because of the dagger at his neck and the knife in his eye, may he implore his captor and may he not accept his supplication. May he quickly cut his life off.

(58) May his hands enter the mud through a fissure in his house.

(59–60) May he drag on in difficulty as long as he lives and may his progeny be lost as long as there is a heaven and an earth.

Commentary

(I: 1–11) The verbose titulary of Nebuchadnezzar, which functions as the introduction to the text as a whole, serves to highlight the king's lineage, piety, righteousness, power as both conqueror and protector, as well as his special relationship with Marduk.

The Lullubu, Amurru, and Kassites, though actual peoples, are probably listed here as stereotypical enemies of Babylonia rather than indicating any specific military undertaking.

(12–21) Nebuchadnezzar sets off on his campaign, which he considers to have been divinely ordained, in the unexpected summer month of Tammuz (June–July). His timing made for a miserable forced march for his army because of the unbearable heat and the dried-up water sources. But this unorthodox timing also afforded Nebuchadnezzar the element of surprise when confronting the Elamite forces.

Der is located on the eastern edge of the Tigris–Euphrates flood plain and is the last Babylonian settlement before entering Elamite territory. He claims to have traveled 30 double-hours (the equivalent to ca. 201 miles / 324 kilometers) from Der, which would place his army too far into Elamite territory for the most-accepted modern identifications of the Ulai River (perhaps the modern Saimarreh and Karkheh Rivers), unless the distance includes the return trip to Der. On the other hand, if the Ulai is associated with the modern Karun River instead, the distance would be more accurate but the assumed site of the battle would have to be relocated.

(25–41) Nebuchadnezzar and his army reach the Ulai River (the classical Eulaeus) probably at a point just north of Susa (assuming the identifcation of the Saimarrah and Karkheh Rivers with the Ulai), where they join battle with the Elamite forces commanded by Hultelutish. The battle is fierce and the armies kick up so much dust that their vision is impaired. In the midst of combat, Shitti-Marduk, commanding his chariot, pushes into the enemy lines and is integral to their collapse. Hultelutish flees the battlefield.

(42–51) The victorious Nebuchadnezzar pillages Elam, and Shitti-Marduk's heroism gives him access to the king, which, presumably, he had not had previously. Shitti-Marduk explains the predicament of his tribal territory; that it is subservient to the territory of Namar (possibly on the Diyalah River ca. 124 miles / 200 kilometers NNE of Babylon). Nebuchadnezzar rewards Shitti-Marduk for his bravery by emancipating his tribal towns from the service of Namar.

(43–II: 10) By this list of stipulations, we can determine generally what was meant by Bit-Karziabku's former service to Namar. It included various forms of taxation, including the seizure of livestock, agricultural products, and the forcible drafting of men into military service.

(11–25) The list of witnesses comprises government and religious officials from the territories under Nebuchadnezzar's control, including representatives from Namar.

(26–60) The list of curses acts in conjunction with the divine emblems inscribed on the stele to protect both the emancipation and the stele itself. In the case that someone does renege on the emancipation, or efface, destroy, alter, steal, or dispose of the stele, various gods are to afflict the responsible individual according to their own cosmic domain.

The Eshhara Temple (literally, the "Temple of the Universe") is a structure associated with the worship of Ninurta.

Bibliography

Brinkman, J. *A Political History of Post-Kassite Babylonia, 1158–722* BC. Analecta Orientalia 43. Rome: Pontifical Biblical Institute, 1968.

Frame, G. "A Bilingual Inscription of Nebuchadnezzar I." in *Corolla Torontonensis: Studies in Honor of Ronald Morton Smith*. Edited by E. Robbins and S. Sandahl. Toronto: Tsar, 1994, 59–72.

——. RIMB, 1995, 11–35.

Hurowitz, V. "Some Literary Observations on the Šitti-Marduk Kudurru (BBSt. 6)." *Zeitschrift für Assyriologie* 82 (1992): 30–59.

King, L. *Babylonian Boundary Stones and Memorial-Tablets in the British Museum*. London: British Museum, 1912.

Lambert, W. G. "Enmeduranki and Related Matters." *Journal of Cuneiform Studies* 21 (1967): 126–38.

——. "The Reign of Nebuchadnezzar I: A Turning Point in the History of Ancient Mesopotamian Religion." *The Seed of Wisdom: Essays in Honour of T. J. Meek*. Edited by W. McCullough. Toronto: University of Toronto Press, 1964, 3–13.

——. "The Seed of Kingship," in *Le Pallais et la royauté: Archéologie et civilisation*. Compte rendu de la Rencontre Assyriologique Internationale 19. Edited by P. Garelli. Paris: P. Geuthner, 1974, 432–40.

B. *The Weidner Chronicle (Arnold)*

The so-called "Weidner Chronicle" received its name in the 1920s when E. F. Weidner drew attention to it, although the tablet had been discovered years earlier during the German excavations at Ashur.[32] This Neo-Assyrian copy recovered from Ashur was supplemented later by four Neo-Babylonian fragments.[33] Our understanding of this text was expanded dramatically in 1986, when Iraqi archaeologists from the University of Baghdad excavating the Shamash Temple at Sippar (E-babbara) discovered a Neo-Babylonian library of almost exclusively literary texts, which included a nearly complete copy of this composition.[34] The Sippar copy was done by a skilled scribe, named Marduk-eṭir, who carefully marked his text wherever his *Vorlage* contained breaks or cracks. This translation is thus a composite relying primarily on the Sippar copy, but filling gaps where possible from the other fragments.

All of these copies come from the first millennium, although scholars generally assume the chronicle was composed in the late second millennium BCE (late Kassite or Isin II date), on the basis of internal content and ideological perspective. What was originally taken as a mythological preamble to the chronicle proper, must now, in light of the Neo-Babylonian copy from Sippar, be taken as a fictive, hypothetical letter from one Old Babylonian king to another. Although the names at the beginning are damaged, enough traces remain to suggest the kings imagined to have been involved in the correspondence are Damiq-ilišu of Isin writing either to Apil-Sin of Babylon or Rim-Sin of Larsa. The author is concerned with the city of Babylon, and specifically, with the supply of fish offerings for Esagil, Marduk's temple. The concept of one Old Babylonian ruler advising another to support the Marduk ideology of Babylon reflects the Kassite/Isin II period.[35]

In the first portion of the text, before the chronicle proper, the author describes a night vision in which the goddess Gula appears (lines 14–32), and announces that Marduk has requested a supreme position for his royal city, Babylon. After an impressive litany of leading deities grant supremacy to Marduk (Ea, Anu, and Enlil), Gula announces that no one can compete with Marduk for supremacy, and warns that any king who chooses to rebel will lose his position (lines 34–8). In a transition to the chronicle proper, the author refers to "the conduct of each former king" (line 40). The text then systematically lists 13 kings in chronicle fashion and critiques each reign in light of the care with which that king tended to the sacrifices at Esagil (lines 41–rev.38).

The events described in the chronicle range from the Early Dynastic period to the reign of Sumulael, near the beginning of the First Dynasty of Babylon (1880–1845 BCE). The author in the late second millennium has thus used kings from great antiquity, from his perspective, as illustrations of rulers who failed to heed the advice proffered in the opening section. On the one hand, the chronicle is of little value for reconstructing historical events of early Mesopotamian history due to its tendentious and propagandistic agenda, and in this regard, it offers nothing like the objectivity of the Neo-Babylonian Chronicle Series (see elsewhere in this volume). On the other hand, as an early exemplar of the chronographic genre, the Weidner Chronicle is extremely significant for the glimpse it provides of Mesopotamian historiosophy, and its ideological perspective makes it a primary text on the idea of history in antiquity.[36]

87. Text

(obv 1–9)[37] *Say to [Apil(?)]-Sin, ki[ng of Babyl]on(?), thus speaks Damiq-ilišu(?), king of Isin: [. . .] like . . . [. . .] . . . his reign. I myself wrote to you a matter for reflection, a matter [. . .]. But you did not give it serious consideration. You did not heed the charge I gave you, nor did you pay attention. You have not attended to the special instruction, which [. . .]; instead you have changed over to something else. In order to do an act of kindness for you, [I have . . .] to you, but you did not take it to heart. For your own well-being, I have advised(?) you for a very long time to strengthen the discipline of your army, but you have not set your hand to it. His sh[rines](?) where I sought advice [. . .] and have ceased. Now let me tell you of my journey [. . .], learn it quickly!*

(obv 10–13) I offered a sacrifice to Ninkarrak,[38] *my lady, the mistress of E-gal-mah, and I prayed to her, I entreated her with supplications, I told her the thoughts that were always in my heart. Thus I said: "Hand over to me the people of Sumer and Akkad [. . .] all the lands [. . .]. Let the peoples of both the highlands and the lowlands bring their heavy alloys into E-gal-mah."*

(obv 14–26) Sacred Gula, the exalted mistress, stood before me in the watches of the night. Then [she heard] my words and swore to me firmly, and blessed me. "You shall establish an abode in the subterranean waters, in the underground waters . . . [. . .]. You shall lift up your head to the distant heavens, into . . . [. . .] above, the divine aegis. [After]wards(?), Marduk, King of the Gods, who . . . [. . .] . . . all of heaven and earth . . . over . . . [will . . . the peo]ple of Sumer and Akkad to his city, Babylon. [. . .] . . . He went quickly to his father, Ea, divine craftsman, sage counsellor of heaven and earth, to the bīt apsî[39] *. . . "May [Bab]ylon, the city firmly chosen in my heart, be exalted over the entire world! Let Esagil, the exalted shrine, [be . . .] unto the borders of all heaven and earth . . . [. . .]. [May] the lord of lords, who inhabits the shrine, from the rising of the sun to its setting, . . . [. . .]. May he continuely shepherd human beings like sheep [. . .]! Let the city be honored, of all countries . . . [. . .]!" Lord Nudimmud*[40] *[granted] everything he spoke to him. From heaven's foundation unto its zenith, he established him . . . [. . .].*

(obv 27–40) Next, Anu and Enlil, the great gods, looked favorably on him and [. . .]. "Let him be chief ruler(?) of both the highlands and the lowlands [. . .]. May the great gods of heaven and earth tremble because of his great sanctuary [. . .]. With regard to Esagil, Ekua, the palace of heaven and earth, lift up its top like the heavens [. . .]. May its foundation be [established . . .] like the heavens and the earth forever after [. . .]. As a result of your offering, I assign the thing you requested and [I grant you] long life [. . .]. Apart from the fact that the decision was announced in my dream, [. . .] a favorable decree for . . . [. . .]. For the gods of that city, the great gods of heaven and earth . . . [. . .] daily, monthly, and yearly provisions (lit. life of renewal) . . . [. . .] . . . no god will oppose him, whose heart(?) . . . [. . .]. At his

command, hostile gods clothed in dirty [garments . . .] are bound . . . Whoever commits sacrilege against the gods of that city, his star shall not stand in heaven . . . [. . .]. His kingship will come to an end, his scepter will be taken away, his treasury will become mounds and [ruins]. [. . .] . . . his . . . , and the king of all heaven and earth said,(?) "The gods of heaven and earth . . . [. . .]. And the behavior of each former king, which I keep hearing about . . . [. . .].

(obv 41–rev 13) Akka, son of Enmebaragesi . . . [. . .]. Enmekar, king of Uruk, ravaged the populace . . . [. . .] . . . The wise man, Adapa, son of . . . [. . .] . . . heard in his pure sanctuary and he cursed Enmekar . . . [. . .] . . . he/I granted to him kingship of all the lands, and his rites . . . [. . .] . . . he/I beautified like the "writing of the heavens" (i.e., constellations), and in Esagil . . . [. . .], the king, overseer of all heaven and earth for his 3,020 . . . years[41] *[. . .]. In the reign of Puzur-Nirah, king of Akshak, the freshwater fisherman of Esagil [. . .], they used to catch fish for the meal of the great lord Marduk,*[42] *but the lieutenant of the king took away the fish. The freshwater fisherman . . . [. . .]. After seven days had passed,*[43] *the freshwater fisherman was catching fish . . . [. . .]. In the house of Kubaba, the tavern keeper,*[44] *they mea[sured out(?)]*[45] *large jars of beer . . . [. . . to Esag]il they presented. At that time . . . [broken place*[46]*] was restored for Esagil . . . fish . . . [. . .]. Kubaba gave bread to the fisherman, (and) she gave (him) water. The fish she se[nt quickly(?) . . .] to Esagil [. . .]. Marduk, the king, prince of the Apsu,*[47] *looked favorably at her and said, "Let it be so!" To Kubaba, the tavern keeper, he assigned royal sovereignty of all lands.*

(rev 14–19) Ur-Zababa [ordered] Sargon, his cupbearer(?), to abolish the wine libations for Esagil. Sargon did not abolish the wine but rather took great care and sent quickly to Esagil. Marduk, king of all heaven and earth,[48] *looked favorably at him and gave him sovereignty of the four corners (of the world). He exercised the role "Provisioner of Esagil." All those who sat upon royal thrones [brought] their tribute to Babylon. Yet he [neglected(?)] the word that Bel had spoken. He dug up the soil of its pit, and in front of Akkad he built a city and na[med] it Babylon. Enlil changed what he had said of him, and from east to west*[49] *they (his subjects) rebelled against him. He imposed sleeplessness upon him.*[50]

(rev 20–2) Naram-Sin ravaged the populace of Babylon, and twice he (Marduk) called up the Gutian armies against him. [He/They put to flight(?)] his people as with a donkey-goad [and] he (Marduk) gave his royal sovereignty to the Gutian armies. The Gutians, who were a disgruntled people, showed no divine reverence. They did not know how to carry out[51] *the rituals and observances correctly.*

(rev 23–7) Utu-hegal, the freshwater fisherman, caught fish as donation-offerings in the region of the sea edge. Until such fish is offered to the great lord Marduk, it should not be offered to another god. But the Gutians took from his hand fish that had been boiled but not yet offered. By his exalted command, he (Marduk) deprived the Gutian army of his land's sovereignty, and gave it to Utu-hegal. But Utu-hegal, the freshwater fisherman, carried out crimes against his (Marduk's) city,[52] *and so his corpse was carried away at the river dam.*

(rev 28–9) Then he (Marduk) gave sovereignty over all lands to Šulgi, son of Ur-nammu. But he (Šulgi) did not complete his rituals perfectly (and) he sullied his purification rites, and his sin(?) . . . [. . .].

(rev 30–1) Amar-Sin, his son, exchanged the large oxen and the (sheep) sacrifices of the New Year Festival of Esagil. (Death) by a goring ox was foretold for him, but he died(?) from the "bite" of his shoe.

(rev 32–40) Šu-Sin, for the well-being of his life, [made(?)] Esagil like the "writing of the heavens" (constellations). [. . .][53] . . . Šulgi committed, Ibbi-Sin, his son . . . his penalty. [. . .] . . . an earlier king who came before . . . of your heart, and over his father, Ea, the heaven and earth . . . did not create. Anu and Ištar . . . his exalted son, the great lord Marduk, [king(?)] of the gods, whom the gods [made(?) pri]nce. His grandson, Nabu, who . . . will name him king. To his descendant, king Sumu-la-EL, whom Anu na[med], that you may protect yourself(?), and . . . all of it . . . dwelling . . . , until a perpetual dynasty [is] in your hands.

(colophon) Tablet of Marduk-eṭir, son of Eṭir-[. . .] . . . ; worshipper of Nabu. Return if lost.

Bibliography

Al-Rawi, Farouk N. H. "Tablets from the Sippar Library I: The 'Weidner Chronicle': A Supposititious Royal Letter concerning a Vision." *Iraq* 52 (1990): 1–14.

Arnold, Bill T. "The Weidner Chronicle and the Idea of History in Israel and Mesopotamia." *Faith, Tradition, and History: Old Testament Historiography in Its Near Eastern Context.* Edited by Alan R. Millard, James K. Hoffmeier, and David W. Baker. Winona Lake, Ind.: Eisenbrauns, 1994, 129–48.

Arnold, Bill T. *Who Were the Babylonians?* Society of Biblical Literature Archaeology and Biblical Studies, 10. Atlanta: Society of Biblical Literature, 2004.

Black, Jeremy A., and Anthony R. Green. *Gods, Demons, and Symbols of Ancient Mesopotamia: An Illustrated Dictionary.* Austin: University of Texas Press, 1992.

Christian, Viktor, and Ernst F. Weidner. "Das Alter der Gräberfunde aus Ur." *Archiv für Orientforschung* 5 (1928): 139–50.

Finkel, Irving L. "Bilingual Chronicle Fragments." *Journal of Cuneiform Studies* 32 (1980): 65–80.

Goldstein, Jonathan. *Peoples of an Almighty God: Competing Religions in the Ancient World.* Anchor Bible Reference Library. New York: Doubleday, 2002.

Grayson, A. K. *Assyrian and Babylonian Chronicles.* Texts from cuneiform sources 5. Winona Lake, Ind.: Eisenbrauns, 2000.

Güterbock, Hans-Gustav. "Die historische tradition und ihre literarische Gestaltung bei Babyloniern und Hethitern bis 1200." *Zeitschrift für Assyriologie* 42 (1934): 1–91.

Weidner, Ernst F. Review of Stephen Langdon, *The Weld-Blundell Collection, Vol. II: Historical Inscriptions. Archiv für Orientforschung* 3 (1924): 198–9.

C. *Apocalyptic Texts (Strawn)*

88. Marduk Prophecy

There are at least five Akkadian texts that are commonly designated as apocalypses. In general, apocalyptic is not an easy genre to define (see Collins 1979) and not all scholars agree that the Akkadian texts in question are, in fact, apocalyptic.[54] The issue is complicated by the fact that these texts are often called "prophecies" in the secondary literature. This adds to the confusion, since what commonly passes today as "prophecy" – namely, prediction of future "endtime" events, often with ominous and climactic overtones – is more akin to the ancient genre of apocalyptic than it is ancient prophecy. So, if one thinks of Michel de Nostradame, better known as Nostradamus (1503–66 CE) when one thinks of prophecy, then it might be appropriate to use that term for the Akkadian apocalypses. It must be stressed, however, that the kind of prophecy that one finds in the Old Testament / Hebrew Bible is of a different, though not completely unrelated, sort.[55] Moreover, various ancient Near Eastern texts have been recovered (especially from Mari and Nineveh) that indicate that Mesopotamia also had prophets and prophecy like that found in Israel, both prior to and contemporary with the biblical prophets (see Parpola 1997; Nissinen et al. 2003).

Two main aspects that seem to separate the Akkadian "apocalypses" from prophetic texts proper – biblical or otherwise – is their cyclical view of history (see Hallo 1966; *NERT*, 71, 118–19; contrast Grayson 1975: 21 and n. 34) and the fact that they appear to contain *vaticinia ex eventu* ("post-event prophecies") – that is, the prophecies are written *after* the events they describe but purport to be prior to them and are thus "prophetic" in the modern, predictive sense. Of course, scholars have said the same about several biblical prophetic texts – that they, too, may be after the fact – and insofar as biblical prophecy also operates with sometimes vague predictions of the (mostly imminent) future, we must reckon with the fluidity between the genres of apocalyptic and prophecy, with our analyses thereof, and with the fact that we are probably faced with a continuum-like relationship between the two (Longman 1991; Walton 1990: 222; cf. Hanson 1979). Even so, in comparison with biblical prophetic texts, the Akkadian texts tend toward the apocalyptic pole of the continuum and bear the most similarity to Daniel (esp. 8: 23–5 and 11: 2–45), the Old Testament's only full-blown apocalyptic book.

When it was first published (Grayson and Lambert 1964), the Marduk Prophecy was presented as the fourth in a group of four texts recovered from Ashur, Nineveh, and Babylon. The first, known as Text A (*ANET*, 606–7; Grayson and Lambert 1964: 12–16; *NERT*, 118–19; Longman 1991: 240–2), describes a sequence of rulers who rule for different lengths of time, alternating between being "good" or "bad." Scholars have questioned whether the second text, Text B, is really apocalyptic at all or, instead, prophetic.[56] This text bears strong connections to astrological omen literature – a point that holds true to some extent for all of the apocalyptic texts. The third text is the Šulgi Prophecy (*NERT*, 119–20; Longman 1991: 236–7), since it is placed in the mouth of Šulgi, an important king of the Ur III period (reigned ca. 2094–2047). It describes some unfortunate historical events and is basically "a survey of Babylonian history in the guise of a prophecy" (Ringgren 1989: 382). Since this initial publication, additional fragments have been added to both the Marduk and Šulgi texts (Borger 1971) and two new compositions have come to light that are of the same genre: the Uruk Prophecy (Hunger and Kaufman 1975; *RANE*, 217; Longman 1991: 237–8) and the Dynastic Prophecy (Grayson 1975: 24–37; Longman 1991: 239–40; *COS* 1.150: 481–2). Like Text A, the Uruk Prophecy describes various (unnamed) kings' reigns: a series of bad kings followed, at last, by a good king and his son, who will rule Uruk. The son's dynasty "will be established forever" and "the kings of Uruk will exercise rule like the gods" (Longman 1991: 238). The Dynastic Prophecy may have continued the same kind of king-schema into the Seleucid period, but the state of the manuscript precludes certainty.

The Marduk Prophecy, which belonged to the same series as the Šulgi Prophecy (see the colophon), is like the other texts insofar as it predicts the rise of a good king who will set matters aright. This text has several distinctive elements, however, that make it of particular importance for the student of ancient Near Eastern history and literature.

1. The Marduk Prophecy is the *only (fictive) divine autobiography* that is extant; in it the god Marduk speaks in the first person. Here, then, is a case of a god "foretelling" the future, including specific political events.

2. The first part of the text, which in the other texts would describe a "bad" time attributed to wicked kings, is given *sufficient historical detail* that the text can be dated with a good degree of confidence. In this case, the bad time is marked by three different occasions in which the god Marduk (i.e., his cult statue) was taken from Babylon to an enemy city. Such removals were common in ancient Near Eastern warfare, since divine statues were considered valuable (ideological) booty. The first of these removals was to Hatti, the second to Assyria (Ashur), and the third to Elam. Each of these occasions can be dated on the basis of other corroborating texts. So, the three removals of the cult statue correspond to victories by Mursili I of Hatti (reigned 1620–1590), Tukulti-Ninurta I of Assyria (reigned 1243–1207), and Kutir-Naḫḫunte of Elam (reigned ca. 1155–1150), respectively (see Block 2000: 123). These data suggest that the good king who will arise and set things right is none other than Nebuchadnezzar I (ca. 1125–1104), the fourth king in the second dynasty of Isin (so Borger 1971; *NERT*, 121; Foster 1995: 215; Walton 1990: 218; Block 2000: 123; Longman 1991: 138–41; etc.). Several factors support this, including the fact that the text mentions events prior to Nebuchadnezzar's reign but not, apparently, after it. Moreover, the king that will arise is said to be one who will smite Elam, destroy its cities, and lead Marduk back from there to Babylon and its temple – things that Nebuchadnezzar did, in fact, do (see Roberts 2002 [1977]). Lastly, it was apparently in the reign of Nebuchadnezzar I that Marduk's rise to the pinnacle of the pantheon was finally complete (*NERT*, 121; Grayson 1975: 16; Longman 1991: 141).[57] The correlation of these items demonstrates that the Akkadian apocalypses – that is, non-historiographic texts (and this is true whether the text in question is apocalyptic or not) –

can still be used and useful for history and historical reconstructions. Even so, scholars continue to debate the nature and function of the Marduk Prophecy. Is the last section that discusses (presumably) Nebuchadnezzar I's anti-Elamite campaign a *vaticinum ex eventu*, or is it truly predictive? And what is the text's function in either scenario? In the former, the Marduk Prophecy might be seen to serve as theological propaganda supporting Nebuchadnezzar's rule and foreign policy; in the latter, it may have been intended as political propaganda to spur on, or generate support for, the king's action against Elam.

3. The mention of *theology* leads to a discussion of this significant component of the Marduk Prophecy. Some theological insights have already been mentioned above (see also Roberts 2002), but perhaps most important is that the text portrays Marduk's departures, not as defeats by an enemy, but as self-willed exiles of sorts (Walton 1990: 219).[58] Marduk is described as the lord of his own fate and of certain historical events, not to mention the other gods and, indeed, "all" (III: rev. 21). Even when Marduk sojourned in what, in human terms, was enemy territory, he acted in ways positive to that area or to his home city of Babylon. The first departure is described as little more than a "business trip" (Roberts 2002: 85) in which Marduk establishes Babylonian trade among the Hittites. The description of the second trip, to Assyria, is broken, but the parts that exist suggest that it, too, was peaceful, especially since Marduk claims to have blessed Ashur (I: rev. 12). The third trip, to Elam, is not depicted with quite the same sanguinity, but it, too, is at Marduk's command. Hence, the absence of the god along with its associated calamities is presented in this text as the free choice of the deity in question.[59] While this is very much a theological understanding of history, it is no less important due to the significant light it casts on what the ancients believed happened in the historical events they both witnessed and enacted.

Text[60]

(Col. I: 1–6) O divine Ḫarḫarnum, Ḫayyashum, Anum, Enlil, Nudim[mud], Ea, ⌜Muati⌝?, Nabium:[61] *Let the great gods learn my secrets. Once I am r[e]ady,*[62] *I will utter my speech.*

(7–12) I am Marduk, the great lord: a watcher watching, roaming the mountains; a careful watcher, wandering the lands. I am he who, from sunrise to sunset, roams back and forth in all lands.

(13–22) I commanded: I went to the land of Hatti. I investigated Hatti. I set up the throne of my divinity in its midst. For 24 years I dwelt in its midst. I established [the t]rade (routes) of the citizens of Babylon [i]n its midst. Its [. . .], its goods, and its valuables [to? Si]ppar, Nippur, [and Babylo]n, I oversaw?.

(23–38) [A king of Babylon?] arose and [. . .] grasped [my hand?[63]*] and [. . . B]abylon, ⌜which⌝ (. . .) was at peace?. The market? of the cit[y of Babylon?] was good and the crown of my [divini]ty (. . .) I returne[d.*[64] *Concerning Babylon, I said:] "Brin[g your tribute, O] ⌜la⌝[nds, to Babylon . . .]."*

(Gap.)[65]

(rev. 3–17) (. . .) Baltil was good? (. . .) After I prepar[ed][66] the people of Enlil with it [. . .] I gave [it?] wings like a bird. All [the land]s I fille[d.] (. . .) I blessed the land of Ashur. (. . .) [I returne]d.[67] Concerning Babylon, I said: "Br[i]ng your tribute, O lands, to Babylon [. . .]."

(rev. 18–25) I am Marduk, the great lord: I am Lord of fates and de[cisio]ns. Who has undertaken su[c]h a journey (as this)? As I went, (so) [I] returned. I commanded: I went to the land of Elam – all of the gods went (with me) – I myself commanded (it). The offerings of the temples I myself withheld. I made the gods Šakkan and Nisaba go away up to he[a]ven.[68] (Col. II: 1–18) Širis[69] made the heart of the land sick. People's corpses block the gates.[70] A brother eats his own brother. A friend strikes his own friend with a weapon. Nobles' sons extend their hands[71] to commoners' sons. The scepter[72] becomes [sh]ort. Evil lies across the land?. Kings [. . .] diminish the land. Lions ⌜b⌝lock the road. Dogs [go rabid] and bite people. ⌜Those⌝ they b[it]e do not live: they die. I (had) completed my ⌜d⌝ays ⌜and⌝ fulfilled my years. My heart desired my city, Babylon, and E-kur-sagila.[73] [. . .] I summoned all the goddesses [and] I commanded: "Bring yo[ur] tribute, O lands, to Babylon [. . .]."

(II: 19–35) A king of Babylon will arise: he will restore the wondrous temple, E-kur-sagila [and] draw up the plans of heav⌜en⌝ and ear[th] in E-kur-sagila. Its height, he will change. He will institute relief[74] for my city Babylon. He will take my hand[75] and bring [me] to my city Babylon ⌜and E⌝-kur-sagila forever. He will restore the ship [Ma]tush [and] will fi[ll] its [ru]dder with gold alloy. Its [side]s he will [. . .] with gold. He will cause the ⌜s⌝ailors who serve [it] to enter [in]to it. They will face each other on the [rig]ht and left.

(Gap and fragmentary lines.)[76]

(Col. III rev. 5–20) the god Nin[girs]u will rule. The rivers will carry fish. Field (and) meado[w] will be full of produce. [W]inter grass will endure until summer, summer grass until winter. The country's harvest will succeed. The marketplace will thrive. He[77] will keep evil in line. He will help clear up those who are troubled. He will illuminate evil. Clouds will constantly be present.[78] Brother will lov[e] his brother. A son will hono[r][79] his father as if (he were) a ⌜god⌝. Mother [will . . . her] daughter. A bride will mar[ry; she] ⌜will honor⌝[80] [her husband]. Compassion toward the peo[ple . . .] A youth will [. . .] his produce. That prince will [ru]le [all] lands.

(rev. 21–30) And I, the ⌜god⌝ of all, will be at peace with him. He will destroy Elam; its cities he will ruin. The city (and) its swamps he will smother?. He will make the great king of the city Der arise in the absence of his dwelling place. His devastating circumstances he will transform. His evil [. . .]. He will grasp his hand. He will fo[re]ver cause him to enter into De⌜r⌝[81] and E-kur-UD-galkalamma.[82]

(Gap and fragmentary lines.)[83]

Bibliography

Arnold, B. and Beyer, B., eds. RANE, 2002, 207–17.
Beyerlin, W. NERT, 1978, 188–22.

Biggs, Robert D. "More Babylonian 'Prophecies.'" *Iraq* 29 (1967): 117–32.
——. "Babylonian Prophecies, Astrology, and a New Source for 'Prophecy Text B.'" In *Language, Literature, and History: Philosophical and Historical Studies Presented to Erica Reiner*. Ed. F. Rochberg-Halton. New Haven: American Oriental Society, 1987, 1–14.
——. "The Babylonian Prophecies and the Astrological Traditions of Mesopotamia." *Journal of Cuneiform Studies* 37 (1985): 86–90.
Block, Daniel Isaac. *The Gods of the Nations: Studies in Ancient Near Eastern National Theology*. Jackson: Evangelical Theological Society, 1988. Esp. 169–76 for a translation of the Marduk Prophecy. 2d ed. Grand Rapids: Baker, 2000. (Does not include the translation.)
Borger, Rykle. "Gott Marduk und Gott-König Šulgi als Propheten: Zwei prophetische Texte." *Bibliotheca orientalis* 28 (1971): 3–24.
Collins, John J., ed. *Apocalypse: The Morphology of a Genre*. Semeia 14. Missoula: Society of Biblical Literature, 1979.
Foster, Benjamin R. *From Distant Days: Myths, Tales, and Poetry of Ancient Mesopotamia*. Bethesda: CDL, 1995, 215–17.
Grayson, A. K. *Babylonian Historical-Literary Texts*. Toronto: University of Toronto Press, 1975.
Grayson, A. K. and W. G. Lambert. "Akkadian Prophecies." *Journal of Cuneiform Studies* 18 (1964): 7–30.
Hallo, W. W. "Akkadian Apocalypses." *Israel Exploration Journal* 16 (1966): 231–42.
Hanson, Paul D. *The Dawn of Apocalyptic: The Historical and Sociological Roots of Jewish Apocalyptic Eschatology*. Rev. ed. Philadelphia: Fortress, 1979.
Hunger, Hermann and Stephen A. Kaufman. "A New Akkadian Prophecy Text." *Journal of the American Oriental Society* 95 (1975): 371–5.
Kaiser, O., ed. *Texte aus der Umwelt des Alten Testaments*. Gütersloh: Gütersloher Verlagshaus, 1984–, 65–9.
Longman, Tremper, III. *Fictional Akkadian Autobiography: A Generic and Comparative Study*. Winona Lake, Ind.: Eisenbrauns, 1991.
——. "The Dynastic Prophecy (1.150)." In COS, 1999–2003, 1: 481–2.
——. "The Marduk Prophecy (1.149)." In COS, 1999–2003, 1: 480–1.
Nissinen, Martti. "Neither Prophecies nor Apocalypses: The Akkadian Literary Predictive Texts." In *Knowing the End from the Beginning: The Prophetic, the Apocalyptic, and Their Relationships*. Ed. Lester L. Grabbe and Robert D. Haak. London: T. & T. Clark, 2003, 134–48.
Nissinen, Martti, with contributions by C. L. Seow and Robert K. Ritner. *Prophets and Prophecy in the Ancient Near East*. Atlanta: Society of Biblical Literature, 2003.
Parpola, Simo. *Assyrian Prophecies*. State Archives of Assyria 9. Helsinki: Helsinki University Press, 1997.
Ringgren, Helmer. "Akkadian Apocalypses." In *Apocalyptisicm in the Mediterranean World and the Near East: Proceedings of the International Colloquium on Apocalypticism, Uppsala, August 12–17, 1979*. 2d ed. Ed. D. Hellholm. Tübingen: Mohr (Siebeck), 1989, 379–86.
Roberts, J. J. M. "Nebuchadnezzar I's Elamite Crisis in Theological Perspective." In *Essays on the Ancient Near East in Memory of Jacob Joel Finkelstein*. Ed. Maria de Jong Ellis. Memoirs of the Connecticut Academy of Arts and Sciences 19. Hamden: Archon, 1977, 183–7. Reprinted in J. J. M. Roberts, *The Bible and the Ancient Near East: Collected Essays*. Winona Lake, Ind.: Eisenbrauns, 2002, 83–92.

Walton, John H. *Ancient Israelite Literature in its Cultural Context: A Survey of Parallels Between Biblical and Ancient Near Eastern Texts*. Grand Rapids: Zondervan, 1990.

IV. Second Millennium BCE Syro-Palestinian Texts

A. Alalakh

89. Idrimi (AT 3) (von Dassow)

In the early fifteenth century BCE, Idrimi, who claimed descent from Aleppo's old royal dynasty, gathered an army and seized power at Alalakh, a city located on the lower Orontes River. Alalakh had formerly been a dependency of Aleppo, and now it became the capital of the small kingdom Idrimi carved out, occupying a territory corresponding largely to what is nowadays the Hatay province of Turkey. But Idrimi could keep the kingship he acquired only at the price of submitting to a greater king, Parattarna, ruler of Mittanni. Having sworn allegiance to Parattarna, Idrimi marched northward into Anatolia, in the direction of Hittite territory, perhaps at his overlord's behest. He despoiled several towns and enriched himself and Alalakh with booty and captives of war. Parattarna, meanwhile, also obtained the allegiance of Pilliya, king of Kizzuwatna, the land immediately north of Idrimi's kingdom, located in the area later called Cilicia.

In the wake of these events, Pilliya and Idrimi made the treaty presented here (AT 3), a "binding agreement" that was concluded under the aegis of their common overlord, Parattarna. This treaty was recorded in cuneiform, in the Akkadian language, on a tablet found in the fortress at Alalakh. The tablet bears the seal of Pilliya, and presumably a copy of the same treaty, sealed by Idrimi instead, was kept by Pilliya in Kizzuwatna. It is a parity treaty, meaning that the two parties deal with each other as equal partners and the terms of the agreement are equivalent for both. The treaty is exclusively concerned with the extradition of fugitives between the two kingdoms. Both the fugitives and the extradition agreement should be understood as a reflection of conflict: whether or not the towns Idrimi despoiled on his Anatolian campaign were actually located in Kizzuwatna, this war, as well as others not recorded in the extant sources, no doubt forced many people from their homes. Territorial boundaries were shifted, too; a dispute between Alalakh and Kizzuwatna over the jurisdiction of Alawari, a town located between the two kingdoms, was only resolved in the time of Idrimi's and Pilliya's successors. This extradition treaty, then, marks the conclusion of warfare, and proclaims the parties' agreement to repair some of the dislocations wrought upon each other's people and (human) property through armed conflict.

The stipulations of the agreement speak of "fugitives," without making distinctions in regard to the status of persons or in regard to how they found themselves in the other side's territory. Subjects of each king, who may have fled to the other king's land during war, are classified under a single term together with escaped slaves, and future escapees are lumped together with persons already displaced: all are "fugitives" (Akkadian *munnabtu*), and all are to be returned to their "lords" (Akkadian *bēlu*), whether that lord is simply the king or someone else having legal rights over the subject. Communities in each kingdom are prohibited from knowingly concealing fugitives or escapees from the other kingdom, just as the two kingdoms are enjoined from keeping each other's fugitive subjects in their possession. No kingdom or household willingly tolerated the loss of its members to another.

As always, the gods were invoked to oversee this agreement. The deities named in the curse section of AT 3 are the storm-god, the sun-god, and Ishḫara, a goddess akin to Ishtar. The names of the storm-god and sun-god are written in logograms, so their names could be read in any language: in the West Semitic language of Syria, the storm-god and sun-god were Addu and Shapsh, and in Hurrian, the language of Mittanni, they were Teshup and Shimigi. Because both Kizzuwatna and Alalakh were largely Hurrian-speaking, although a West Semitic dialect was also spoken at Alalakh, the Hurrian reading is the more likely one.

Translation

(1) Tablet of a binding agreement.

(2–5) When Pilliya and Idrimi swore an oath by the gods and made this binding agreement between each other:

(6–7) They shall (thereafter) always send back fugitives between each other.

(8–11) Should Idrimi seize fugitives belonging to Pilliya, he shall send them back to Pilliya.

(12–15) And should Pilliya seize fugitives belonging to Idrimi, he shall send them back to Idrimi.

(15–17) And anyone who seizes a fugitive shall return him to his lord.

(18–23) If it is a man, then he (= the fugitive's lord) shall pay 500 (shekels of) copper as his ransom, and if it is a woman, then they shall pay 1,000 (shekels of) copper as her ransom.[84]

(23–9) And if a fugitive belonging to Pilliya enters the territory of Idrimi, and no one seizes him, but his lord seizes him, then he (= the fugitive's lord) shall not pay a ransom to anyone.

(29–35) And if a fugitive belonging to Idrimi enters the territory of Pilliya, and no one seizes him, but his lord seizes him, then he (= the fugitive's lord) shall not pay a ransom to anyone.

(36–9) And in whatever city they report a fugitive, the mayor with five nobles shall swear by the gods.[85]

(40–3) On whatever day Parattarna has sworn an oath by the gods with Idrimi, from that day (forward) fugitives are ordered to be returned.

(44–7) Whoever transgresses the words of this tablet, may Teshup, Shimigi, Ishḫara, and all the gods destroy him.

Bibliography

Copy and edition of AT 3: D. J. Wiseman, *The Alalakh Tablets* (London: British Institute of Archaeology at Ankara, 1953), 31–2 and pl. 4.

Other translations include the following: R. S. Hess, in *The Context of Scripture* vol. 2, ed. W. W. Hallo (Leiden: Brill, 2000), no. 2.129; E. Reiner, in *Ancient Near Eastern Texts Relating to the Old Testament* (Princeton: Princeton University Press, 1969), 532. The translation presented here is based on the author's personal collation of the tablet.

B. Emar (Cohen)

The city of Emar on the Euphrates became part of the Hittite empire in the wake of Šuppiluliuma's conquests. It was governed by the Hittite viceroy and his officials residing in Carchemish. However, the Emar royal house continued to hold some influence over the city, especially regarding its internal affairs, as the document below demonstrates. The city was destroyed at the beginning of the twelfth century, along with the other Bronze Age urban centers, probably by the Arameans.

None of the many textual finds from the city would fit into the category of what we define as historiography, because most are either school texts, administrative documents, or rituals. However, occasionally some historical details about the city's affairs can be glimpsed at. The following royal donation is such an example, demonstrating how historical narratives can be embedded within an administrative text. The contents of these documents may be compared with land grants found in the contemporary city of Ugarit.

90. An attack of Hurrian troops on the city

This document informs us of how a certain diviner at Emar received a royal donation in reward for his divinatory skills.[86] First comes a description of the field that is being given as a gift and then the historical narrative where it is told why Mašruḫe the diviner received his gift. It seems that Mašruḫe predicted the city would be saved, in spite of the fact that it lay under a siege. Who exactly the Hurrian forces behind the attack on the city were is still a matter of controversy.

(21–8) A field (is situated) in the marshes at the (canal-) gate of [such and such a place]. Its length 2 ikū measures; its width 1 ikū measure. Its upper side (borders the field of) the sons of Dagan-ma; its lower side – the city. One side (borders the field of) Pilsu-Dagan (the king of Emar), son of Ba'al-kabar; the other side – the city and the sons of Dagan-ma. The field belongs to king Pilsu-Dagan.

(29–40) When the Hurrian troops surrounded the walls of Emar, Mašruḫe was then the diviner of the king and the city. Now, his divination (about the enemies being defeated) came true. Therefore, the king Pilsu-Dagan has given him this very field as

his gift. In the future, whoever shall contest the field, shall pay [one] thousand shekels of silver (as a fine) to the god Ninurta.

Then follows the witness list headed by the king of Emar and curses directed against anyone contesting the deed.

Bibliography

Source: *ASJ* 12: 7.
Edition: Tsukimoto 1990: 189–93.

Adamthwaite, M. R., 2001. *Late Hittite Emar: The Chronology, Synchronisms and Socio-political Aspects of a Late Bronze Age Fortress Town*, Ancient Near Eastern Studies [formerly Abr-Nahrain], Suppl. 8. Leuven: Peeters.

Durand, J.-M., 1998. *Les documents épistolaires du Palais de Mari* Tome II. Paris: CERF: 624.

Tsukimoto, A., 1990. Akkadian Tablets in the Hirayama Collection, I. *Acta Sumerologica* 12, 177–227.

Vita, J. P., 2002. Warfare and the Army at Emar. *Altorientalische Forschungen* 29, 113–27.

Notes

1 For example, Tukulti-Ninurta has been viewed as the inspiration for both the biblical figure of Nimrod and the Greek Ninos. See E. A. Speiser, "In Search of Nimrod," *Eretz-Israel* 5 (1958): 32–6; and H. Lewy, "Nitokris-Naqi'a," *Journal of Near Eastern Studies* 11 (1952): 264–86.
2 The precise length of time Tukulti-Ninurta ruled Babylonia is uncertain. See *CAH*, 2/2: 288–90, for a discussion.
3 For English translations of the shorter, more poorly preserved segments, of the Epic, see Bibliography, p. 139.
4 In the scheme, Selection 1 is separated from Selection 2 by highly fragmentary text and/or gaps within the narrative. Selection 2a, however, is followed directly by 2b, which is separated from 3a by highly fragmentary text and/or gaps within the narrative, etc.
5 P. B. Machinist, "The Epic of Tukulti-Ninurta I" (PhD dissertation, Yale University, 1978).
6 Machinist, 77.
7 Machinist, 262.
8 Machinist, 414, n.173.
9 Literally "a battle of servants." See Machinist, 274, *CAD* A/II, 248–9.
10 Shamash, the sun god, is often portrayed as the god of justice.
11 Lit. an *alu* – a type of evil demon.
12 For the perfective sense of the preterite, see Machinist.
13 Literally "omen of well-being."
14 A fire, or the fire god Girra.

15 For the meaning "to flee" for this verb, see Machinist, 297.

16 Lit. "to the four winds, all of the regions."

17 I understand this line to imply that just as one cannot free one's self from slander or blasphemy once uttered, neither can the kings of line 19 rid themselves of the fear of Tukulti-Ninurta. Cf. B. R. Foster, *Before the Muses*, 2d ed. (Bethesda: CDL, 1996), 226 n. 1; Machinist, 341–3.

18 The first half of this line is difficult. See Machinist, 345–7; Foster (see note 17), 226, 230.

19 Foster, 227.

20 Anzu is a mythological creature resembling an eagle (See *CAD* A/II, 153–4).

21 For the interpretation offered here, see Machinist, 361–2.

22 See Machinist, 362–3.

23 Ernst Weidner, *Die Inschriften Tukulti-Ninurtas I. und seiner Nachfolger*, Archiv für Orientforschung Beiheft 12 (Graz: Archiv für Orientforschung Beheift 12, 1959). p. 40, #36. *KUB* 3: 73.

24 On the association of this letter with Tukulti-Ninurta, see Weidner, 40.

25 See comments on the Tukulti-Ninurta Epic regarding battle as ordeal. Innocence leads to military victory; guilt results in defeat.

26 Meaning unclear. Cf. A. Hagenbuchner, *Die Karrespondenz der Hethiter.* 2 Teil. (Heidelberg: Carl Winter, 1989), 276.

27 Weidner #10; *KAH* 2: 49.

28 Wiedner #5; *KAH* 2: 58.

29 A. R. George, *House Most High: The Temples of Ancient Mesopotamia* (Winona Lake, Ind.: Eisenbrauns, 1993), 117.

30 See F. A. M. Wiggermann, "Theologies, Priests, and Worship in Ancient Mesopotamia," CANE 3, 1865.

31 That is, Assur.

32 Ernst F. Weidner, review of Stephen Langdon, *The Weld-Blundell Collection, vol. II: Historical Inscriptions, Archiv für Orientforschung* 3 (1924): 198–9; Viktor Christian and Ernst F. Weidner, "Das Alter der Gräberfunde aus Ur," *Archiv für Orientforschung* 5 (1928): 139–50, esp. 139–40. The tablet itself is now lost; for transcription and translation, we are dependent upon an excavation photograph preserved in the Berlin Museum. See Hans-Gustav Güterbock, "Die historische tradition und ihre literarische Gestaltung bei Babyloniern und Hethitern bis 1200," *Zeitschrift für Assyriologie* 42 (1934): 1–91, esp. 47–57.

33 Güterbock 1934: esp. 47–57; A. K. Grayson, *Assyrian and Babylonian Chronicles* (Texts from cuneiform sources 5; Winona Lake, Ind.: Eisenbrauns, 2000), 145; Irving L. Finkel, "Bilingual Chronicle Fragments," *Journal of Cuneiform Studies* 32 (1980): 65–80.

34 Farouk N. H. Al-Rawi, "Tablets from the Sippar Library I: The 'Weidner Chronicle': A Supposititious Royal Letter Concerning a Vision," *Iraq* 52 (1990): 1–14.

35 Bill T. Arnold, *Who Were the Babylonians?* Society of Biblical Literature Archaeology and Biblical Studies 10 (Atlanta: Society of Biblical Literature, 2004), 62–72 and 78–85.

36 Bill T. Arnold, "The Weidner Chronicle and the Idea of History in Israel and Mesopotamia," in *Faith, Tradition, and History: Old Testament Historiography in Its Near Eastern Context*, ed. Alan R. Millard, James K. Hoffmeier, and David W.Baker (Winona Lake, Ind.: Eisenbrauns, 1994), 129–48, esp. 138–48. It has recently

been suggested that this chronicle is perhaps the first Babylonian attempt at connected history, an attempt made possible by the rise of Marduk to supremacy during the Kassite/Isin II period; see Jonathan Goldstein, *Peoples of An Almighty God: Competing Religions in the Ancient World*, Anchor Bible Reference Library (New York: Doubleday, 2002), 31–3.

37 The line numbers used here correspond to those of the Sippar copy, although this composite translation relies on all six copies and fragments of the text.

38 One of the several names for Gula, a healing goddess, whose principle temple was E-gal-mah at Isin; see Jeremy A. Black and Anthony R. Green, *Gods, Demons, and Symbols of Ancient Mesopotamia: An Illustrated Dictionary* (Austin: University of Texas Press, 1992), 101.

39 Ancient Babylonians believed a freshwater ocean beneath the surface of the earth (*abzu* or *apsû*) was the abode of the wise god Ea (or Enki). The É-abzu (*bīt apsî*), or "Abzu temple," was Ea's temple in the city of Eridu; see Black and Green, *Illustrated Dictionary*, 27.

40 An alternative name for Ea.

41 The original Neo-Assyrian version from Ashur has "the firstborn son [of Esagil(?)]" here instead of this reference to 3,020 years.

42 The original Neo-Assyrian version has "the Lord of the fish" for "the great lord Marduk."

43 The original Neo-Assyrian version has eight days.

44 Queen Kubaba (or Ku-Bau) is known from the Sumerian King List as the sole ruler of the Third Dynasty of Kish, which also mentions that she was a former tavern keeper.

45 Reading a D-stem preterite of *mašāḫu.*

46 A scribal *terminus technicus* (*ḫīpu*) to mark the exact spot of a damaged portion of the examplar being copied.

47 The original Neo-Assyrian version has simply "the great lord Marduk."

48 The original Neo-Assyrian version has "son of the prince of the Apsu" in place of "king of all heaven and earth."

49 Lit. "from the rising of the sun (the god Šamaš) until the setting of the sun (Šamaš)."

50 The original reflected in the Sippar copy was "broken" (*ḫīpu*) at this point, but Weidner's Assyrian version and one of the Neo-Babylonian fragments restores it.

51 Assuming a Št infinitive of *ešēru* (*šutēšuru*), although two of the copies have "complete perfectly" (*šuklulu*). Note also that the Sippar copy marks this line as copied from a "broken" original (*ḫīpu*).

52 Lit. he "laid his hands on his city with evil intent." The translation attempts to reflect a wordplay in the Akkadian: Utu-hegal *carried* evil intent, so the river *carried* him away.

53 The beginning of the next two lines were "broken" (*ḫīpu*) in the text preserved by the Sippar copy.

54 See Marti Nissinen *Prophets and Prophecy in the Ancient Near East*, with contributions by C. L. Seow and R. K. Ritner. Atlanta: Society of Biblical Literature, 2003, for an attempt to distinguish these texts from both prophecy and apocalyptic by labeling them "literary predictive texts."

55 A situation similar to that of the Akkadian apocalypses also obtains for Egyptian "prophecies" (e.g., Neferti, Ipuwer, etc.).

56 The same is true for the text known as LBAT 1543. See Robert D. Biggs, "More Babylonian 'Prophecies'". *Iraq* 29 (1967): 117–32; A. K. Grayson, *Babylonian Historical-Literary Texts*. Toronto: University of Toronto Press, 1975: 15.

57 The classic study is W. G. Lambert, "The Reign of Nebuchadnezzar I: A Turning Point in the History of Ancient Mesopotamian Religion," in *The Seed of Wisdom: Essays in Honour of T. J. Meek*, ed. W. S. McCullough (Toronto: University of Toronto, 1964), 3–13.

58 "Exile" is really too strong a word; as J. J. M. Roberts, *The Bible and the Ancient Near East: Collected Essays*. Winona Lake, IN: Eisenbrauns (2002: 85) has pointed out, they are presented as little more than "trips."

59 Marduk's departure is not a case of divine *defeat* (at the hands of other gods), therefore, but of divine *abandonment* – a theme known in other ancient Near Eastern and biblical texts (see D. I. Block, *The Gods of the Nations: Studies in Ancient Near Eastern National Theology*. 2nd ed., Grand Rapids: Baker, 2000; Tremper Longman III, *Fictional Akkadian Autobiography: A Generic and Comparative Study*. Winona Lake, IN: Eisenbrauns, 1991: 134–5). This is important, since other texts imply that Marduk may have been defeated or tricked by another deity (see Roberts 2002).

60 Particularly broken sections (partial or whole lines) are excluded from the translation and are indicated by ellipses (. . .). The Ashur texts are not included.

61 The first two deities in the list are not well known and are primordial or olden gods, B. R. Foster, *From Distant Days: Myths, Tales, and Poetry of Ancient Mesopotamia*. Bethesda: CDL, 1995: 215 n. 1.

62 Lit. "After I have girded my loins."

63 This is an idiom for leading – in this case, taking the god's statue back to its temple.

64 Marduk's return from Hatti is attributed to Agum-kakrime, an early Kassite king, in the inscription that bears his name (I: 44–II: 27). See Longman 1991: 133–4, and esp. 221–4 (for a translation).

65 This section would have recounted the departure to Assyria.

66 Lit. "girded the loins."

67 Marduk's return from Assyria is attributed to Tukulti-Aššur in Chronicle P iv: 12–13 (Longman 1991: 134).

68 Šakkan is god of cattle, Nisaba, goddess of grain. Their departure probably signals famine (*COS* 1.149: 481 n. 4).

69 The god of beer.

70 Note the shift to the durative (translated with the English present here) at this point in the text, though it must be admitted that in some cases the tense of the verb is not certain, because it is written with a logogram. The fairly extensive use of logograms in the Marduk Prophecy is similar to omen literature and lends "an esoteric cast to the composition" (*COS* 1.149: 480 n. 2).

71 Probably to beg.

72 That is, the royal reign.

73 The name of Marduk's temple in Babylon.

74 That is, freedom from obligations (perhaps tax relief).

75 See above note 63.

76 At this point, R. Borger, "Gott Marduk und Gott-König Šulgi als Propheten: Zwei prophetische Texte." *Bibliotheca orientalis* 28 (1971): 10 inserts the Ashur texts

(cols. III–V). The material is quite fragmentary and seems to echo, reduplicate, or be a version of at least some of the material from col. III. It is not translated here. See Longman 1991 and Block (1988 edition, Jackson: Evangelical Theological Society): 169–76 for English translations that follow Borger's edition.

77 This "he" refers to the "coming" king (Nebuchadnezzar I; see the introduction), not the god Ningirsu in line 5.

78 Providing both shade and, even more importantly, rain.

79 Lit. "fear"; in religious contexts, the term means "worship."

80 See previous note.

81 A site in northern Babylonia.

82 Another temple name.

83 The next section (col. IV: rev. 1–14), which is very broken, appears to list offerings made to "the ghost (or: wind)." It is apparently ritual instructions for priests or the like who work with the text. After this section is another scribal line followed by two lines that read as follows:

(rev. 15) (The text) "O divine Ḫarḫarnum, Ḫayyashum . . ." – completed.
(rev. 16) (The text) "I am divine Šulgi" (comes next).

On the bottom of the tablet is the following:

"(The text) is written according to the writing board; copy of Babylon; checked." Then there is a stamp: "Palace of Assurbanipal, king of the world, king of Assyria."

Line rev. 16 indicates that the next tablet in the series is the Šulgi prophecy, which begins with "I am divine Šulgi."

84 The term here translated "ransom" is *mištannu*, a word of debated etymology that occurs in no other extant ancient Near Eastern text. Some compare Hebrew *mišneh* and render the term as "equivalent" (or the like) while others propose an Indo-Iranian etymology (whereby *mištannu* would be cognate to Greek *misthos*, "pay") and translate "reward" (see James M. Lindenberger, "How Much for a Hebrew Slave? The Meaning of *mišneh* in Deut 15: 18," *Journal of Biblical Literature* 110 [1991], 479–98). The same 3ms. suffix is appended to *mištannu* in both the stipulation specifying a man and that specifying a woman; this does not decisively indicate that the antecedent must be the payee rather than the fugitive, because gender distinctions are not infrequently collapsed in Akkadian texts from Hurrian-speaking areas. Whichever etymology one prefers, the term denotes a payment the fugitive's lord is to make to the person who has seized the fugitive, in effect ransoming the individual.

85 They are to swear that they did not knowingly conceal the fugitive, in order to exonerate themselves from culpability for his or her presence in their community.

86 Only the second half of the document is given here. The first part concerns land purchased by the diviner, and has no direct relevance to the land grant.

7

Correspondence from El-Amarna in Egypt

Eva von Dassow and Kyle Greenwood

Introduction (von Dassow)

The Amarna letters are the remains of an archive of correspondence between the rulers of Egypt and various great and small rulers of Western Asia, dating to the mid-fourteenth century BCE. Most of the letters in this archive were written during the reigns of Amenhotep III and his son Amenhotep IV, also known as Akhenaten. They are called the "Amarna Letters" because they were found at Tell el-Amarna, which is the site of Akhetaten, the short-lived new capital founded by Akhenaten, located midway between Memphis and Thebes. About 350 letters belonging to this archive have been found. They are designated by the siglum EA (for el-Amarna) followed by a number (EA 1, 2, 3, etc.), their numbering having been established in the first comprehensive edition of the corpus.[1]

The Amarna letters are written in the cuneiform script, on clay tablets. Most of them are written in dialects of Akkadian, because Akkadian was the common language of international correspondence and diplomacy during the second millennium BCE. In fact, there was evidently a cuneiform school at Akhetaten, where Egyptian scribes learned the Akkadian language and learned to write in the cuneiform script; tablets of the type used to teach cuneiform, as well as fragments of Akkadian literary texts, were found at Akhetaten along with the international correspondence. While the letters sent to Egypt from Mesopotamian rulers are written in good Akkadian, those sent from kingdoms outside Mesopotamia, as well as letters written at the Egyptian court itself, are written using dialects that scholars call "peripheral Akkadian." Such "peripheral Akkadian" dialects tend to exhibit interference from the native languages of their senders; an extreme example is provided by the letters from Egypt's Canaanite vassals, which are written in what appears to be a hybrid of the Canaanite and Akkadian languages. Meanwhile, a few of the letters are written in Hurrian, the principal language of Mittanni, or in Hittite, the principal language of Ḫatti and neighboring parts of Anatolia. The cuneiform scribes of the Egyptian court had to become multilingual in order to handle Pharaoh's foreign affairs!

The selection of Amarna letters included here samples Egypt's correspondence with other "great kings," who were Pharaoh's peers, and with Egypt's vassals in the Levant. Foremost among the great powers were Assyria, Karduniash (the Kassite kingdom of Babylon),[2] Mittanni, and Ḫatti. The great kings addressed each other as "brothers," a designation that denotes equal rank rather than genealogical relationship. So, for example, the Kassite king of Babylon and the king of Egypt call each other "brother." Alliances linking the great kingdoms were typically secured through diplomatic marriages, a practice that gave some substance to the rhetoric of fraternal relationship; but marital links were one-way only, for while Egyptian rulers accepted other kings' daughters as wives, they gave no fellow king an Egyptian royal daughter as wife (see EA 4, below). The great kings made rich gifts to each other, and in their letters, rather than addressing what we might consider political affairs, they often seem obsessed with quibbling over the quantity and value of the gifts exchanged. Indeed, they tend to focus on this topic so much that the mutual exchange of gifts appears to constitute the essence of their alliances. In one of the letters included in this selection (EA 1, below), Pharaoh mocks the Kassite king of Babylon for marrying off his daughters in order to obtain gifts of gold.

Vassal rulers also had to provide goods to their overlord, but in their case the goods were requisitioned as tribute rather than presented as gifts. When addressing their overlord, whom they often dignified with epithets like "my sun" (comparable to "your majesty"), vassal rulers referred to themselves as "servants," although when addressing each other they would refer to themselves as kings. The rulers of the small Syro-Canaanite states subject to Egypt were designated by the title "mayor" (Akkadian *ḫazannu*) in the context of their relationship to Egyptian imperial rule. Egypt controlled its territories in the Levant through officials, sometimes called "commissioners," who were stationed in Gaza in the south, Kumidi in the north, and Ṣumur on the coast. From among the numerous Syro-Canaanite vassal states whose correspondence was kept in the archive at Amarna, the letters from Amurru, Gubla (Byblos), Jerusalem, and Shechem are sampled here.

The letters in this selection are organized geographically by Egypt's correspondents, great kingdoms first (1), and then vassal kingdoms (2), northern Levant (A) followed by southern Levant (B; this follows Knudtzon's arrangement; see n. 1, above); under the geographic rubrics the letters are organized chronologically so far as possible (thus the order sometimes departs from the numerical sequence established by Knudtzon). The geographic order is as follows: Karduniash (EA 1, 3, 4), Assyria (EA 15, 16), Mittanni (EA 17), Ḫatti (EA 41), Gubla (EA 74, 116, 137), Amurru (EA 170, 165), Shechem (EA 254), and Jerusalem (EA 287).

Here is a key to the names of people and places encountered in these letters.

Kings of Egypt

Kings of Egypt are usually called by their throne names (prenomen), not their birth names (nomen), in international correspondence, such as the Amarna letters, and in other cuneiform texts.

Nibmuareya, or Nimmuarea (Egyptian Neb-maat-re) – Amenhotep III
Napḫurureya (Egyptian Nefer-kheperu-ra-waenra) – Amenhotep IV, a.k.a. Akhenaten
Ḫuriya ((Ankh-)kheperu-ra?) – probably Smenkhkare

Kings of other "great powers"

Kadashman-Enlil – king of Karduniash, contemporary of Amenhotep III
Burra-Buriyash (also spelled Burna-Buriyash) – successor of Kadashman-Enlil, contemporary of Akhenaten
Ashur-uballit – king of Assyria, newly resurgent as Mittanni weakened
Tushratta (also spelled Tuisheratta) – king of Mittanni, contemporary of Amenhotep III and Akhenaten, until assassinated in a *coup d'état*
Suppiluliuma – king of Ḫatti, conqueror of Mittanni

Small kings or "mayors," vassals of Egypt

Abdi-Ashirta (also spelled Abdi-Ashrati) – ruler of Amurru, contemporary of Amenhotep III and Akhenaten
Abdi-Ḫeba – ruler of Jerusalem
Aziru – son and successor of Abdi-Ashirta, contemporary of Akhenaten
Lab'ayu – ruler of Shechem, in central Canaan
Milk-ilu – ruler of Gezer, in south-central Canaan
Rib-Hadda (also spelled Rib-Addi) – ruler of Gubla (Byblos), a loyal Egyptian vassal and a loquacious correspondent, whose pleas for support were largely neglected by Pharaoh, and who eventually died in exile

Egyptian officials in Canaan

Addaya, Amanappa, Ḫanni, Ḫatip, Pawuru, and Yanḫamu

Countries and states

Amurru – a country located between the upper Orontes and the Mediterranean; Amurru marked the northern limit of Egypt's empire in the Levant until Aziru defected to Ḫatti, whereupon Amurru marked the southern limit of the Hittite Empire

Ḫanigalbat – the core territory of the Mittanni Empire, adjacent to Assyria
Ḫatti – the core territory of the Hittite Empire, in central Anatolia
Karduniash (also Karaduniash) – the Kassite name for the realm of Babylon, comprising Sumer and Akkad
Mittanni – the Hurrian-dominated realm centered on the upper Euphrates and Ḫabur
Nuḫashe – a country located between the Orontes and the Euphrates

Population groups and social groups

Ḫapiru, or ʿApiru – persons who, for one reason or another, had become fugitives or outcasts from their communities (whether states or tribes); Ḫapiru were often portrayed as outlaws, and they sometimes formed militias or mercenary bands
ḫupšu – "free peasants," the main population of sedentary communities
maryannu – "nobles," the elite who had the privilege of using war chariots
Suteans – pastoral nomads, comparable to Bedouin, who lived outside the jurisdiction of states and empires, and who were often seen as lawless bandits

Other persons and places that appear in these letters are identified in notes to the texts, if adequate information is known about them and if the text itself does not provide such information.

NB: on many of the tablets, horizontal rulings separate sections of the text, and these are rendered as paragraph divisions in the translations.

I. Great Kingdoms

A. Karduniash (von Dassow)

Three letters from the correspondence between Egypt and Karduniash are included here: EA 1, 3, and 4. In EA 1, Amenhotep III (called by his prenomen, written Nibmuareya) writes to Kadashman-Enlil, king of Karduniash, answering a previous letter (which is not preserved in the extant Amarna corpus). Apparently Kadashman-Enlil had complained that he had no reliable information about the situation of his sister, who had long ago been sent as a bride to the king of Egypt, so he was not about to fulfill the latter's request to have his daughter in marriage too. Pharaoh responds to this complaint, and then to other complaints concerning the treatment of Kadashman-Enlil's messengers at the Egyptian court as well as a perceived insult to his prestige. Since EA 1 was found at Amarna, it may either be a letter that was never sent to Babylon, or the archive's copy of a letter that was sent; given the impolitic tone of some of Pharaoh's remarks, one might imagine that the text of EA 1 was revised in the version sent to Babylon, but on the other hand the great kings of this period did sometimes say very rude things to each other in their letters!

Regardless of the problems addressed in EA 1, everything seems to have been worked out in EA 3, in which Kadashman-Enlil tells Amenhotep that his daughter is now marriageable and the Egyptian king has only to send for her. The Kassite king has new complaints, however, about the treatment of his messengers and the quality of the gifts exchanged. He also makes an issue of the social requirement that "brother" kings invite each other to festivals and house-warming parties. Since in later years Burra-Buriyash, the next king of Karduniash, continued to tweak Pharaoh on the subject of long-distance journeys between their kingdoms (in EA 7, not included here), it may be that the Kassite kings were using this rhetorical tactic to test the Egyptian king's reach – to see how rapidly he could send a delegation (or, by implication, a military expedition) to Babylon – for it was in their interest to ascertain the limits of Egypt's capabilities.

EA 4, probably also from Kadashman-Enlil to Amenhotep III, reverses the question of giving royal women in marriage: the Kassite king now complains of Pharaoh's refusal to reciprocate and give him his daughter. Actually, any pretty Egyptian woman would do, he says, but Pharaoh has sent him no one. Having framed the issue this way, the Kassite king proceeds to demand that a shipment of as much gold as possible be sent to him as soon as possible, in the month of Du'ūzu or the month of Abu – that is, July or August, the worst time of year to travel between Egypt and Mesopotamia! – or else, once he has completed his current project, he will no longer need the gold and would even send it back, no matter what the quantity, without giving the Egyptian king his daughter after all.

91. EA 1: Amenhotep III rebuts Kadashman-Enlil II (Greenwood)

This is one of the few examples of Pharaoh's outgoing correspondence that was found at the site of Akhetaten.

The tone is confrontational. It is a series of rebuttals of comments made by Kadashman-Enlil in previous correspondence, which makes it difficult at times to keep straight who is speaking to whom. The body of the letter can be divided into two main sections. The first, lines 10–46, deals with the specific issue of the welfare of the Babylonian king's sister. The second, lines 52–98 (lines 47–51 are missing), deals with broader diplomatic issues. A common thread running throughout the letter is Amenhotep's dissatisfaction with a certain pair of envoys sent by Kadashman-Enlil.

Translation

(Address, 1–3) Say to Kadashman-Enlil, the king of Karduniash, my brother, on behalf of Nibmuareya, the Great King, the king of Egypt, your brother:

(Salutation, 3–9) All is well with me. May it be well with you! May it also be very well with your household, with your wives, with your children, and with your magnates,

your horses, your chariots, and throughout your lands. It is well with me. It is well with my household, with my wives, with my children, with my magnates, my horses, my chariots and the numerous troops. In my lands it is very well.

(10–25) Now I have received word, which you sent to me regarding her, which said, "Herewith, you request my daughter as your wife, while my sister, whom my father gave you, is there with you. Nobody has seen her. Is she dead or alive?" These were the very words you sent to me on your tablet. Did you ever send a dignitary who knows your sister, who could speak with her and identify her? So, let him speak with her! The men whom you sent are nobodies. One was the [. . .] of Zaqara, the other was an assherder from [. . .] land. There is not one among th[em w]ho [knows h]er, who is close to your father, and wh[o could identify her]. Furthermore, the envoys who [were with you, let them speak]. He has given [. . .] into his possession [t]o retr[ieve] it for her mother.

(26–36) Regarding what you wrote: "While your wives were gathered in your presence, you said to my envoys, 'Here is your lady standing in front of you.' But my envoys did not recognize her. That was my sister who was with you," about whom you, yourself, have written, "My envoys did not recognize her." So, you say, "Who can identify her?" Why will you not send a dignitary who will speak the truth to you about the welfare of your sister who is here? Then you may believe the one who enters to see her quarters and her relationship with the king.

(36–46) Regarding what you wrote: "Perhaps who my envoys saw was the daughter of a commoner or a Kaskean, or the daughter of a Ḫanigalbatean. Who can believe them? The one with you who [. . .] did not open her mouth. Someone could not possibly believe them." These were your words. But if your [sister] were dead, why would we cover up her de[ath and] substitute someone [else? As] Amen [lives, your sister is alive].

(47–51) Text damaged.

(52–62) Regarding what you wrote: "M[y] daughters [w]ho are married to lo[cal] kings, when my envoys [go] there, they speak with th[em and br]ing me a greeting gift. The one with you [. . .]." These were your words. Perhaps the kings of [your re]gion are quite wealthy. Your daughters could obtain something from them and send it to you. And what does your sister, the one who is with me, have? She should get something so I can send it to you. It is good that you give your daughters to obtain the good things of your region.

(62–77) Regarding the words of my father that you wrote: Forget it! You did not speak his words. Furthermore, "Establish a friendly brotherhood between us." These are your words, which you wrote. Now you and I are brothers, both of us. But I became angry on account of your envoys because they said to your face, "They did not give anything to those of us who travel to Egypt." Of those who come to me, do any one of them come [and not] receive [more] silver, gold, oil, garments, or every type of goods [than i]n any other country? He speaks dishonestly to the one who sends him. The first time the envoys had gone to your father, their mouths told lies. The next time they went, they told you lies. But I have said myself, "Whether [I gi]ve them anything or not, they will talk anyway." So I promised them I would not give them anything else.

(78–88) Regarding what you wrote: "You spoke to my envoys as follows, 'Your master does not have any troops.' And, 'It was not a beautiful girl that was given to me.'" These were your words. This is not true. Your envoys tell you these things. Whether they have troops available or not will be discovered for me. Why should I ask him whether or not you have horses? Do not listen to your two envoys, whom you

sent, whose mouths are dishonest. I swear they have shown you disrespect by telling lies in order to escape your grasp.

(88–95) Regarding what you wrote: "He placed my chariots among the chariots of the mayors. You did not view them separately. You carried them off to the lands under you. You did not view them separately." They have requested all my horses and chariots, even the chariots and horses of my own country.

(95–8) Regarding what you wrote in order to aggrandize yourself and to put oil on the [head] of a girl, you sent me one gift of fine oil.

Commentary

(1–3) The directive, "say to *PN*," was given to the scribe responsible both for taking dictation from the sender and for reading the letter to the recipient. Generally, scribes were the only literate members of ancient Near Eastern society; kings did not read or write their mail themselves.

One particular aspect of the diplomatic language employed at Amarna is the use of familial language. Political equals addressed one another as "brother." This "brotherhood" comprised Egypt, Assyria, Babylonia, and Ḫatti. Vassals, on the other hand, referred to themselves as "sons" and to Egypt as "father."

The proper names in the Amarna letters are sometimes different than what one is accustomed to seeing. Karduniash was a synonym for Babylonia, beginning in the Kassite period. Nibmuareya is a hypocoristicon for Amenhotep III, known as "The Magnificent."

(3–9) As one would expect in cordial correspondence, the body of the letter begins with a salutation, assuring the sender's well-being to the recipient.

The specific groups to whom wellness is wished may be grouped under two headings: (1) the king's household and (2) the king's military. The list concludes with a general blessing for the entire homeland.

(10–25) This paragraph sets the tone and structure for the letter: "You said *X*, but I say *Y*." In an earlier letter, Amenhotep had requested Kadashman-Enlil's daughter as a wife. Kadashman-Enlil appears to show some reservation in heeding the request, however, because the welfare of his sister, who had been sent to Egypt through one of these diplomatic marriages, is unknown. Amenhotep remarks sarcastically that "nobody" has seen her, because Kadashman-Enlil has sent only "nobodies" to find her. Perhaps Kadashman-Enlil's efforts would be more fruitful, the pharaoh posits, if he would send someone who actually knows what his sister looks like. So the rhetorical question is posed, "Did you ever send a dignitary who knows your sister?" In Amenhotep's judgment, the answer is a resounding negative because only "nobodies" were sent.

Unfortunately, the tablet is broken at the point where Amenhotep insults the search party. It may be that the assherder was, in actuality, a caravan leader, in which case the other individual would have been a trading agent. The fact that there are two individuals in the convoy is consistent with the practice of sending messengers in pairs (cf. lines 78–88). Zaqara is a personal name, perhaps related to the Mesopotamian dream-god, Zaqar.

A few terms introduced in this paragraph deserve comment. The word translated as *dignitary* is a high-ranking government official sent for diplomatic purposes. An *envoy*, by contrast, is a specialized messenger, whose role is more in line with that of an ambassador. Finally, it has been suggested that the word translated *mother* may best be understood as "nurse"; that is, the woman who would accompany a bride being given in marriage.

(26–36) The second main paragraph continues the theme from the first. Kadashman-Enlil has written that even though Amenhotep, in the presence of many witnesses, has presented a woman to the Babylonian envoys as the sought-after sister, the envoys could not positively identify her. According to the pharaoh, the misunderstanding is not the fault of Egypt. Rather, it is the fault of Babylonia for failing to send competent envoys who could easily recognize the sister. His position is that the Kassite king should send knowledgeable dignitaries, who would be able to recognize the sister and realize that she has comfortable living arrangements and is being treated well.

(36–46) In this paragraph, Kadashman-Enlil suggests that Amenhotep staged a charade in the palace to make the Babylonian think that his sister was still alive and well. Since the alleged imposter never spoke, Kadashman-Enlil asserts that his envoys could not have made the determination that the woman was even Babylonian. She could have been an Egyptian commoner. She could have been from the Kaska lands, a resilient and troublesome tribal people from the northeastern hill country. She could have been a Ḫanigalbatean; that is, someone from Mitanni. In the judgment of Amenhotep, however, there is no rational explanation for trying to pull off such a scheme. Although the text is broken, we can be almost certain that the mention of Amenhotep's namesake, the Egyptian god Amen, is within the context of an oath, swearing to the veracity of the pharaoh's statement.

(52–62) The third issue Kadashman-Enlil has raised against Amenhotep is that other countries with whom Babylonia has engaged in diplomatic marriages have been much more generous and less troublesome than Egypt. Although this can neither be confirmed nor denied on the basis of the extant evidence, one gets the impression that someone is bluffing. Either Kadashman-Enlil is not forthright regarding the success of other diplomatic marriages or Amenhotep is less than sincere with his support.

(62–77) The mention of Amenhotep's father, Thutmose IV, and Kadashman-Enlil's father, Kurigalzu I, indicates prior diplomatic ties between Babylonia and Egypt. This is further illustrated in EA 3, 9, and 11. Apparently, Amenhotep is incensed with Kadashman-Enlil for putting words in the mouth of Thutmose IV.

From this text it appears that one of the purposes of the diplomatic missions was simply to check on the welfare of the princess and collect gifts for their superior. Kadashman-Enlil's complaint, as recounted by Amenhotep, is that his envoys did not receive proper payment from Egypt.

By this point in the letter Amenhotep's frustration with the Babylonian envoys has reached its peak. The envoys have shown a history of alleging miserly pharaohs, a rumor Amenhotep is firm in dispelling. Once again he blames incompetent envoys for the current situation, making it clear that if Babylonia wants to see any more gifts Kadashman-Enlil had better send trustworthy emissaries. However, at the core of the dialogue between Amenhotep and Kadashman-Enlil is diplomatic maneuvering and political strategy. Both Karduniash and Egypt are engaged in gamesmanship revolving around maintenance of their prestige as "great powers."

(78–88) Amenhotep raises two more concerns from one of Kadashman-Enlil's prior letters. First, the pharaoh disputes the legitimacy of the envoys' comment that Karduniash does not have any available troops. According to Amenhotep, the envoys put words in his mouth. While only about 75 years earlier Egypt under Thutmose III was the most aggressive war machine in the ancient Near East, it was no longer the case. Instead, Amenhotep placed the emphasis of his reign on building projects, leading only one military campaign into Kush during his fifth regnal year, and this for preventative reasons. Nevertheless, the Egyptian king assures the Kassite that his reconnaissance capabilities are sufficient for determining the truth of the matter.

The second concern, the report that a beautiful girl was given to Amenhotep, is raised, but we cannot be certain precisely what Amenhotep disputed. Did he dispute the fact that the girl was beautiful? Did he dispute the fact that a girl was given at all? The pharaoh does not address this aspect of the envoys' report. Instead, he ignores the issue in order to further address the military matter.

(88–95) The exact translation and sense of this paragraph are open to debate. One explanation is that Kadashman-Enlil is complaining against having his horses and chariots paraded before Pharaoh along with those of the "mayors," the rulers of vassal territories. This public and indiscriminate display showed disrespect to Babylonia's status among the brotherhood of equals. In light of the fact that Amenhotep just assured the Kassite monarch that he would determine the availability of Babylonian troops, an alternate explanation might be considered. The second explanation, then, is that not only had Egypt ascertained the existence of Babylonian troops, but also Egypt had sent some of its chariots and horses to the aid of Egypt's vassals. This is further supported by the repeated pleas for Egyptian military assistance made by vassal rulers (e.g., EA 51, 53, 55, 59, 68, 70), which might have weakened Egypt's military potency. Amenhotep's reply is an indication of the unstable political atmosphere in the ancient Near East during this period.

(95–8) The act of anointing the head of a girl was the initial act of betrothal, akin to the modern practice of giving an engagement ring. Although Kadashman-Enlil was reluctant to send his own daughter to Egypt, he was not too reticent to request the same from Amenhotep.

The word translated as *fine* is unattested as such in Akkadian. A variant reading, which has the meaning *we are distressed* is also possible, producing the translation "You sent me one gift of oil. We are *distressed* (about this)."

Further reading

On treatments of the Amarna letters see E. F. Campbell, *The Chronology of the Amarna Letters: With Special Reference to the Hypothetical Coregency of Amenophis III and Akhenaten* (Baltimore: The Johns Hopkins University, 1964); Raymond Cohen and Raymond Westbrook (eds.), *Amarna Diplomacy: The Beginnings of International Relations* (Baltimore: The Johns Hopkins University, 2000); Richard S. Hess, *Amarna Personal Names*, American Schools of Oriental Research Dissertation Series 9 (Winona Lake, Ind.: Eisenbrauns, 1993); and Nadav Na'aman, "Amarna Letters," in D. N. Freedman (ed.), *Anchor Bible Dictionary (ABD)* (New York: Doubleday, 1992), vol. 1, pp. 174–81. For a history of Babylonia during the Amarna period see Margaret. S. Drower, "Syria c. 1550–1400 B.C.," in I. E. S. Edwards, C. J. Gadd, N. G. L. Hammond, and E. Sollberger (eds.), *The Cambridge Ancient History (CAH)*, vol. 2, part 1: *History of the Middle East and the Aegean Region c. 1800–1380*, 3d ed. (Cambridge: Cambridge University Press, 1973), pp. 417–525 (esp. pages 483–93); C. J. Gadd, "Assyria and Babylon c. 1370–1300," *CAH* 2: 2 (Cambridge: Cambridge University Press, 1975), pp. 21–48; A. K. Grayson, "Mesopotamia, History of (Babylonia)," in *ABD*, vol. 4, pp. 761–2; and H. W. F. Saggs, *The Babylonians* (Berkeley / Los Angeles: University of California Press, 2000), pp. 113–27. For Egyptian history during the period see Cyril Aldred, "Egypt: The Amarna Period and the End of the Eighteenth Dynasty," *CAH* 2: 2, pp. 49–97; William C. Hayes, "Egypt: Internal Affairs from Thuthmosis I to the Death of Amenophis III," in *CAH* 2: 1, pp. 313–416; William J. Murnane, "Egypt, History of (Dyn. 18–20)," in *ABD*, vol. 2, pp. 348–53; and Nicolas Grimal, *A History of Ancient Egypt*, translated by Ian Shaw (Oxford, UK: Blackwell, 1999), pp. 199–225. The most comprehensive English translation of the Amarna texts has been produced by William L. Moran, *The Amarna Letters* (Baltimore: The Johns Hopkins University, 1992).

92. EA 3: Kadashman-Enlil II to Amenhotep III (Greenwood)

This moderately damaged letter is primarily a complaint to Pharaoh regarding inequitable treatment. He complains about the length his envoys are detained, the amount of his goodwill gift, and not being invited to the *isinnu* festival in Egypt. In the end, Kadashman-Enlil makes diplomatic concessions by extending an invitation to Amenhotep III to attend an *isinnu* festival in Babylonia.

Translation

(Address, 1–3) [Sa]y to Nibmuareya, the king of Egypt, my brother, on behalf of Kadashman-Enlil, the king of Karduniash, your brother:

(Salutation, 4–6) It is, [indeed], well [with me]. May it be very well with you, your household, [your wives], and your children, [as well as with] your [en]tire country, your chariots, your horses, and your magnates.

(7–8) As for my daughter, the girl whom you requested for marriage, she has matured into a marriageable woman. Send an entourage to take her.

(9–14) Previously, my father would send an envoy to you and you would not detain him for long. You would send him off in a tim[ely fash]ion and my father would deliver a beautiful goodwill gift. But when it was I who sent you an envoy, you detained him for six years.

(14–18) In those six years you have merely sent as a goodwill gift 30 minas of gold that looks like silver. That gold was refined in the presence of Kasi, your messenger, so he witnessed it.

(19–22) When you arranged a great isinnu *festival, your envoy did not send the word to come, eat and drink. Nor did you send my gift for the festival. You have sent me these 30* minas *of gold. My [gi]ft [is not equival]ent to what [I have given you] every ye[ar.]*

(23–9) [Look wh]at I have done to [my palace]. I have made a large [. . .]. Your [del]egates have s[een it and are content]. [No]w I have arrang[ed] the entrance of the palace. Come with me [yourself to eat and] drink. [I did not do wh]at you, yourself, did.

(30–4) [25 men and] 25 women – 50 peo[ple] in all [who reside with me] – I have sent [to you]. I have also sent to you [. . . o]f 10 wooden chariots [and 10 teams of hors]es as your gift.

Commentary

(1–3) As we saw in EA 1, this introduction is the standard format in the Amarna Letters. In EA 3 the sender is Kadashman-Enlil, while the recipient is Amenhotep III.

(7–8) Diplomatic marriage was the subject of discussion for virtually every letter between Egypt and Karduniash, culminating in two extensive lists of dowry from Amenhotep IV in exchange for the daughter of Burra-Buriyash II (EA 13, 14). One letter (EA 4) is evidence of a prior request by a Babylonian king for a bride from Egypt. The Pharaoh responded, "From ancient times, no daughter of the king of Egypt has been given to anyone." About four centuries later, a Libyan dynasty ruling Egypt applied a different policy in relation to Israel (1 Kgs 3: 1–3).

In both Mesopotamia and Egypt, marriage was arranged by the father of the bride. A young woman became nubile when she reached her teenage years, presumably upon the passage through puberty.

(9–14) In all likelihood, Kadashman-Enlil is referring to his predecessor, Kurigalzu I, who is cited by his grandson, Burra-Buriyash II, in EA 9 and EA 11 to remind Egypt of its diplomatic history with Babylonia. Another complaint regarding the detention of foreign envoys into Egypt was sent by Tushratta of Mitanni (EA 28). In each of these instances, the great kings seem insulted that Egypt would dare strain diplomatic relations with such gamesmanship.

(14–18) Although gold was said to be as plentiful as dirt in Egypt (see, for example, EA 16; also EA 22 and 27), it was clear that the Mesopotamian kings were not happy with its grayish color, due to its high silver content. The amount of the goodwill gift, which is equal to about 30 pounds, was generous compared to the 2 *minas* Burra-Buriyash II received (EA 9), but only a fraction of the 20 talents (1,200 *minas*) Tushratta sent Akhenaten IV (EA 16).

(19–22) *Isinnu* may denote one of two kinds of events. First, the *isinnu* festival was a Mesopotamian cultic celebration in honor of a deity, as well as a communal celebration displaying the beauty of the temple. Second, it may be used in a general sense to mean any type of festival. According to one Egyptian papyrus, goodwill gifts were typically received on a specific day each year. Therefore, the festival may be in reference to the Egyptian New Year's festival, which has been linked to this annual day of diplomatic gift exchange.

(23–9) One of the great achievements of the Kassites was their building program. Kadashman-Enlil's father, Kurigalzu I, was responsible for the construction of Dur-Kurigalzu, a fortress city of temples and palaces whose 170-foot (52-meter) tall ziggurat can still be seen today on the western outskirts of Baghdad. These building projects may have been funded by commerce with Egypt.

(30–4) Egypt was not known for its equine initiative, so it imported most of its horses and related equipment. The Kassites, on the other hand, specialized in horse breeding and chariot building. The chariots sent as gifts were probably the light, two-wheeled battle chariots. It is also interesting to note that when Egypt sent chariots as a goodwill gift, they were usually overlaid with gold (e.g., EA 14, 34).

The purpose of sending the 50 people is unclear. If taken with the preceding sentences, they may have been associated with the *isinnu* festival. Evidence from other letters, however (EA 17, 19), suggests that men and women were acceptable as goodwill gifts, possibly as royal attendants.

Bibliography

All pertinent bibliography may be found under §91 above, "EA 1: Amenhotep III rebuts Kadashman-Enlil II."

93. EA 4: From the king of Karduniash to the king of Egypt (von Dassow)

The top of EA 4 is broken, so the address and greeting formulae are lost, and with them the names of the sender and addressee of the letter. This tablet clearly belongs to the correspondence between Karduniash and Egypt, and it was most likely sent by Kadashman-Enlil to Amenhotep III. Accordingly, the address and greeting are restored on the basis of EA 2 and 3, Kadashman-Enlil's other letters to Amenhotep III.

(Address and salutation (three or more lines are missing))

[To Nibmuareya, king of Egypt, my brother, speak: thus (says) Kadashman-Enlil, king of Karduniash, your brother. For me and my country all is very well. For you, your household, your wives, your sons, your horses, your chariots, your magnates, and your country, may all be very well.]

[n lines +](1′–3′) (too fragmentary for translation)

(4′–22′) [Moreove]r, you, my brother, when I wrote [to you] about marrying your daughter, as regards not giv[ing (her) you wrote to me], saying, "Never has a daughter of the king of Egypt been given to anyone." Why is [she not given]? You are king – you do as you please. If you were to give (her), who would [say] anything? When they told me this, I wrote to [my brother] thus, saying, "(Surely) beautiful women, adult(?) daughters [of . . .], are available. Send me one beautiful woman as if she [were your daughter]! Who would say, 'She is not the king's daughter'?" (But) you, in accord with your refusal, did not send me (anyone). Did you not seek brotherhood and friendship, when you wrote to me about marriage so that we might become close relations to each other? And I myself, for this very same reason, for brotherhood and friendship, wrote to you about marriage in order that we might become close relations to each other. Why has my brother not sent me one woman? Perhaps, (since) you have not sent me a woman, just like you I should withhold a woman from you, and not send her? (But) my daughters are available; I shall not withhold (one) from you.

(23′–35″) Perhaps, when I wrote [to you] about marriage, and when I (also) wrote to you about animals [. . .] . . .

(bottom edge of tablet broken away; several lines missing)

[. . .] your grandees(?) said to me [. . .]. Now, as to my daughter whom I am sending [you, . . .] you do not obtain her "seed" [. . .] as to the animals, s[end me] whatever I asked of you.[3]

(36″–50″) And as to the gold I wrote to you about, [send] as much as is a[vailable], a great quantity, before your messenger [comes] to me; now, quickly, during this summer, either in the month of Du'ūzu or in the month of Abu, send it to me, so I can accomplish the project I have undertaken. If you send me the gold I wrote you about this summer, in Du'ūzu or Abu, I shall give you my daughter. So you do me a favor and send me [as much(?)] gold as you [can(?)]. Otherwise, if you do not send me the gold in Du'ūzu or Abu, and I do not (use it to) accomplish the project I have undertaken, why do me the favor of sending it? Once I have finished the project I have undertaken, why should I want gold? Then you could send me 3,000 talents of gold – I would not accept it; I would return it to you.[4] *And I wouldn't give you my daughter in marriage.*

wants gold in return for his daughter

B. Assyria

Only two letters from Assyria to Egypt are preserved in the extant Amarna corpus, EA 15 and 16. Many more letters must have been exchanged between the two countries, however, during the interval that elapsed between the sending of EA 15, late in Akhenaten's reign, and EA 16, which was sent later in the reign of Akhenaten or possibly in the reign of one of his successors (see n. 6, below). While EA 15 marks the moment when Assyria first joined the club of "great powers," having emerged from the shadow of Mittanni, EA 16 reflects Assyrian confidence after a period of successful interaction with

Egypt. In EA 15, Ashur-uballit, king of Assyria, introduces himself to Pharaoh, declaring that his predecessors had not been in contact with Egypt and opening diplomatic relations by sending gifts. In EA 16, Ashur-uballit appears to have already become adept in the protocol of demanding better gifts, even citing past presents made to one of his predecessors (despite the denial of previous contact in EA 15). He also develops a new variation on the theme of complaining about the treatment of his messengers, but its interpretation remains uncertain. His complaint is that the messengers have to stand around in the "open sun" and thereby die (of sunstroke; Akkadian *ṣētu* refers to the sun's heat and the illness resulting from it). Possibly the messengers "die in the open sun" during the long, hot journeys between Assyria and Egypt, or waiting around in Egypt, or, perhaps, they "die in the open sun" standing in attendance during Akhenaten's open-air worship of the solar deity, Aten.[5]

94. EA 15: Assyrian diplomacy (Greenwood)

Although it will not be evident in translation, this particular letter is one of the few examples in the Amarna archive in which the usual Babylonian dialect of Akkadian is not used. In fact, this is the only letter that is written in the Assyrian dialect.

The brevity of this letter might be explained by the fact that it is Assyria's first serious attempt at forming a diplomatic relationship with Egypt. Up to this point in its history, Assyria had been recognized only as a geographical locality. It was not until the appearance of Ashur-uballit I that Assyria emerged as a sovereign political entity, let alone one of the great powers of the ancient Near East. Therefore, it was important in this age of international exchange that Assyria declare its arrival on the world stage, which was the primary function of this letter.

Translation

(1–3) Say to the king of E[gypt] on behalf of Ashur-uball[it], the king of [As]syria, as follows:

(4–6) May it be well with you, your household, yo[ur] country, your chariots and your troops.

(7–15) I have sent my envoy to you to visit you and [your country]. Until now, my predecessors have not sent word. Today, I have personally sent word to you. [I] have delivered one quality chariot, two horses [and] one date-stone of genuine lapis lazuli [as] your goodwill gift.

(16–22) As for the [en]voy whom I sent to visit you, do [n]ot detain him. [L]et him visit, then let him depart. Let him see your [ho]spitality and the [ho]spitality of your country, then let him depart."

Commentary

(1–3) Under the leadership of Ashur-uballit I Assyria emerged as an independent political power. Perhaps the most dramatic event of his reign took place within the Amarna context. As an act of international diplomacy, Ashur-uballit gave his daughter in marriage to the Kassite ruler, Burra-Buriyash II. The accession of their son, Kara-hardash, to the Babylonian throne was less than popular, leading to a palace rebellion and Kara-hardash's murder. Ashur-uballit avenged the death of his son by invading Babylon and replacing the usurper with Kurigalzu II.

(4–6) The salutation by Ashur-uballit is a condensed version of the standard Babylonian greeting. Ashur-uballit hits the main points, household and military, but omits some of the particulars, like wives, children, and magnates. There is also no mention of his own well-being. One might posit that the introduction is so brief because the diplomatic relationship is just now being initiated. However, in the only other Assyrian letter in the Amarna archive (EA 16), the salutation is even shorter, expressing well-being for only "you, your household, and your country." Due to the paucity of Assyrian correspondence, it is impossible to arrive at any definitive reasons for this feature.

(7–15) The reception of a foreign delegation was tantamount to its recognition as a member of the "brotherhood." That is, by allowing an Assyrian envoy to enter its country, Egypt would further advance the diplomatic process, acknowledging Assyria as its equal. This interaction between Assyria and Egypt did not go unnoticed in Karduniash, which not only maintained that Assyria was its vassal, but also demanded that Egypt send the Assyrian delegation home "empty-handed" (EA 9).

Almost exclusive to the Assyrian letters to Egypt is the placement of the gift list within the body of the letter. In the letters from Karduniash, Mitanni and Ḫatti, the gift list is practically a postscript, mentioned only after all matters of substance have been addressed. This is not too surprising, however, since the primary intent of Ashur-uballit's correspondence is to foster goodwill, which is certainly accomplished via goodwill gifts.

Among the gifts presented to Amenhotep, the date-stone is the most noteworthy. Lapis lazuli has been mined for the past 7,000 years in what is now northeastern Afghanistan, approximately 150 miles (241 kilometers) northeast of Kabul. Along with turquoise and carnelian, this deep-blue stone was one of the most precious gems of the ancient world.

(16–22) The concern of Ashur-uballit is not just the well-being of his envoy; it is also for the diplomatic relationship between Assyria and Egypt. As the host country, Egypt has the prerogative of determining whether the envoy is engaged in espionage or whether he should be treated as a dignitary. Should Amenhotep decide upon the former, efforts toward an Assyrian–Egyptian alliance would be strained. But, if Amenhotep accepts the envoy graciously, allowing him to visit and leave after a brief time, the diplomatic process could move forward. As we saw in EA 3, any unwarranted delay is damaging to the diplomatic relationship.

Bibliography

For a history of Assyria for the present period see Pinhas Artzi, "The Rise of the Middle-Assyrian Kingdom, According to El-Amarna Letters 15 and 16: A Contribution to the Diplomatic History of Ancient Near East in the Mid-Second Millennium B.C.E.," in *Bar Ilan Studies in History*, edited by Pinhas Artzi (Ramat-Gan, Israel: Bar Ilan University Press, 1978), pp. 25–41; A. K. Grayson, "Mesopotamia, History of (Assyria)," in *Anchor Bible Dictionary*, vol. 4, edited by D. N. Freedman (New York: Doubleday, 1992), pp. 732–55 (esp. pp. 737–8); A. T. Olmstead, *History of Assyria* (New York: Charles Scribner's Sons, 1923), pp. 33–44; and H. W. F. Saggs, *The Might That Was Assyria* (London: Sidgwick & Jackson, 1984), pp. 35–45. Bibliographies on Egypt and the Amarna letters may be found under EA 1 in this volume.

95. EA 16: From Ashur-uballit, king of Assyria, to the king of Egypt, probably Akhenaten (von Dassow)

(Address, 1–4) To Napḫurureya,[6] [great king], king of Egypt, my brother, [speak]: thus (says) Ashur-uballit, king of the land of Ashur, great king, your brother.

(Salutation, 5) For you, for your household and your country, may all be well.

(6–8) When I saw your messengers, I was very joyous. Your messengers will indeed reside in hospitality in my presence.

(9–12) As your greeting-gift I send you a beautiful royal chariot of my yo[king], and two white horses also of my yoking,[7] one chariot not yoked (to a team), and one genuine lapis lazuli seal.

(13–18) Is it from a great king, a gift such as this? Gold is dust in your land – one gathers it up. Why should it linger before you? I intend to build a new palace. Send me gold enough for its decoration and its furnishing.

(19–21) When my ancestor Ashur-nadin-aḫḫe wrote to the land of Egypt, they sent him 20 talents of gold.[8]

(22–5) When the Ḫanigalbatean king wrote to your father, to the land of Egypt, he sent 20 talents of gold to him.[9]

(26–31) [Now], I am [equal] to the Ḫanigalbatean king, but to me you send (only) [. . .] gold, and it does not suffice for the expense of my messengers' journey there and back.

(32–4) If in good faith your intention is friendship, send me much gold. And (here) it is your house – write to me, so that what you desire may be taken (to you).

(35–6) We are distant lands. Should our messengers go back and forth in such a way?

(37–42) As to your messengers having been delayed in reaching you, the Suteans, their guides, were dead(?); until I wrote and they took for me the Suteans, the guides, I detained them.[10] My messengers must not be delayed in reaching me.

(43–55) Why are my messengers made to stand around in the open sun, so that they die of sunstroke? If there is benefit to the king in standing in the open sun, then let him stand there and die of sunstroke, and let it benefit the king. But if not, why should they die of sunstroke? The messengers whom we [send to each other, . . .] they (should) sustain the messengers. They make them die of sunstroke!

C. *Mittanni*

EA 17 is the earliest of about a dozen extant tablets that Tushratta, king of Mittanni, sent to Egypt. In this letter, Tushratta (here spelled, atypically, Tuisheratta) reopens relations with Egypt after a lapse following the assassination of his brother Artashumara, who had been first in line to the throne of Mittanni. Tushratta introduces himself to Amenhotep III (Nibmuareya) by explaining that he was young at the time of the assassination (implying that he had nothing to do with it), and has now punished those responsible; moreover, he has recently won a battle against the invading Hittites, spoil from which he presents to the king of Egypt. His *bona fides* being thus established, he invites renewed friendship with his "brother," recalling the past friendship between his father Shuttarna II and Amenhotep III. Shuttarna had secured the alliance by giving Amenhotep his daughter Kelu-Ḫeba, Tushratta's sister, as a bride, and with this letter Tushratta sends her a greeting and gifts too.

Amenhotep III evidently responded favorably to this overture, for soon enough Tushratta sent his own daughter, Tadu-Ḫeba, to become another bride of the Egyptian king. Several of Tushratta's letters reflect the progress of negotiations preparatory to the marriage (EA 19, 20, and 21), and a very long tablet itemizes the enormous number of precious items sent with Tadu-Ḫeba as wedding gifts (EA 22). Later on, Tushratta even acceded to a request to send the statue of the goddess Shaushka, the Hurrian goddess of war, on loan to Egypt (EA 23). But Tushratta always seemed to find that his generosity and friendship were not adequately reciprocated, and the imbalance only got worse after Akhenaten succeeded Amenhotep III on the throne. Tushratta's letters to Akhenaten repeatedly implore him to honor promises his father made, and to maintain brotherly love and friendship with Mittanni (i.e., send embassies bearing gifts); he even wrote to Tiye, the queen mother, begging her to intercede with her son in this matter (EA 26). To no avail: Egypt needed Mittanni's friendship much less than Mittanni needed Egypt. Meanwhile, as the Hittite Empire expanded at Mittanni's expense – a development to which Akhenaten paid too little heed, for soon it was at Egypt's expense too – strife beset the Mittannian royal house. Tushratta was assassinated by a rival for the throne, and relations between Mittanni and Egypt ceased for good.

96. EA 17: From Tushratta, king of Mittanni, to Amenhotep III, king of Egypt (von Dassow)

(Address and salutation, 1–10) To Nibmuareya, k[ing of the land of Egypt], my brother, speak: thus (says) Tuisheratta, king of the land of Mittanni, your brother. For me all is well. For you, may all be well; for Kelu-Ḫeba, my sister, may all be

well; for your household, for your wife, for your children, for your magnates, for your army, for your horses, for your chariots, and for your country itself, may all be very well.

(11–20) When I sat on the throne of my father, I was young, and UD-ḫi[11] *had done a bad deed to my land, for he had killed his lord. And because of this, he would not permit me friendship with (any)one who loved me. However, I have not been neglectful regarding these bad deeds that had been done in my land, for I have killed the murderers of Artashumara, my brother, together with their households.*

(21–9) Since you were friendly with my father, and because of the foregoing, I am writing to speak to you, so that my brother may hear these (words) and rejoice. My father loved you, and you, moreover, loved my father. In accord with (this) love, my father gave my sister to you. And who else was with my father like you?

(30–5) [. . .], moreover, of my brother [. . .] . . . all the land of Ḫatti. When the enemy entered into my land, Teshub, my lord, gave him into my hand, and I defeated him; among them there was none who returned to his land.[12]

(36–8) Herewith I send you one chariot, two horses, one manservant, and one maidservant, from the spoil of the land of Ḫatti.

(39–40) As my brother's greeting-gift, I send you five chariots and five teams of horses.

(41–5) And as the greeting-gift of Kelu-Ḫeba, my sister, I send her one set of golden brooches, one set of golden earrings, one golden mašḫu, *and one flask full of sweet oil.*

(46–50) Herewith I send Keliya, my ambassador, and Tunip-ibri. May my brother dispatch them promptly so that they may report to me promptly, and so that I may hear my brother's greeting and rejoice.

(51–4) May my brother seek friendship with me, and may my brother send me his messengers, so that they bring me my brother's greeting and I hear it.

D. Ḫatti

Toward the end of Akhenaten's reign, Suppiluliuma, king of Ḫatti, opened relations with Egypt. Only four tablets from the correspondence between Egypt and Ḫatti survive among the Amarna letters (EA 41–4), but there must have been more, as is clear from EA 41's discussion of previous amicable exchanges. In EA 41, Suppiluliuma addresses Ḫuriya, king of Egypt, and expounds upon his relations with Ḫuriya's father. The spelling Ḫuriya most likely renders the prenomen of Smenkhkare, who succeeded Akhenaten as pharaoh after (probably) the brief reign of Nefertiti.[13] Thus Suppiluliuma would be referring to exchanges of messengers and gifts, and negotiations for peace and friendship, with Akhenaten. Such negotiations, however, would have proceeded at the same time that Egypt and Ḫatti were edging toward conflict, for not only was Suppiluliuma making progress in his war against Mittanni, his conquests were also encroaching on Egypt's northernmost possessions in the Levant, and probably prompted Akhenaten to undertake a military campaign (see above, introduction to EA 17, and below, introduction to correspondence with Amurru, EA 170 and 165). This scenario should not be seen as self-contradictory: the Hittite ruler's position could only have been enhanced by his presenting a credible military threat to Egypt's empire, for this gave him an advantage in negotiating peace and friendship. Nor should we be fooled by Suppiluliuma's apparent focus on trivialities in EA 41, such as the details of the order for statues that he had placed with the current pharaoh's predecessor, because this discussion of gift exchange was merely one public face of a two-pronged diplomatic and military strategy. The eventual outcome of that strategy was the establishment of the Hittite Empire as the rival "superpower" to Egypt.

Regrettably, the other three surviving letters from Ḫatti to Egypt shed little light on these developments. EA 42 and 43 are so fragmentary that the correspondents' names are missing, as well as most of the content, although what remains of EA 42 testifies to difficulty in the Egypto-Hittite relationship involving a quarrel over relative prestige. EA 44 is a letter from the son of an unnamed Hittite king to an unnamed Egyptian king, whom the Hittite prince addresses as his "father," testifying to a warm phase at some point in the relationship.

97. EA 41: From Suppiluliuma, king of Ḫatti, to Smenkhkare, King of Egypt (von Dassow)

(Address, 1–3) [Thus (says) the Sun,][14] Suppiluliuma, [great] king, [king of the land of] Ḫatti. To Ḫuriya, [king of the land of] Egypt, my brother, speak.

(Salutation, 4–6) [For me all is] well. As regards you, may all be well; [for your wife], your sons, your household, your troops, your chariots, [and for] your country itself, may all be very well.

(7–13) My messengers whom I sent to your father, and the request which your father made, (to wit:) "Between us let us make friendship," I did not withhold. Whatever your father told me, I did it in full. And any request which I made to your father, he withheld nothing; he gave it to me in full.

(14–15) The shipments your father sent to me while he was alive, my brother, why have you withheld them?

(16–22) Now, my brother, you have ascended the throne of your father, and just as your father and I were desirous of mutual greetings, so you and I should now likewise be friendly to each other. And the request which I communicated to your father [I shall communicate] to my brother too. Let us do each other a favor.

(23–8) My brother should not withhold that which [I requested] of your father [. . .] My brother, [send two] statues of gold, one [should be standing and] one should be seated; and two statues of women, [of silve]r(?); and lapis lazuli, a large (piece); and for [. . .], their stand(?), a large one.

(29–38) [(2 lines mostly missing) . . .] bring me, and [. . .]. And if my brother [. . .] let my brother give them. [And if] my brother wishes to give [. . .], when my chariots finish [. . .] . . . then I will return them to my brother.[15] Meanwhile, whatever my brother desires, write to me that I may send it to you.

(39–43) Herewith I send you as your greeting-gift: one silver rhyton (in the form of) a stag, its weight 5 minas; one silver rhyton (in the form of) a ram, its weight 3 minas; two disks of silver, their weight 10 minas; and two big nikiptu-*shrubs.*[16]

II. Vassal Kingdoms

A. Northern Levant

1. Gubla

Among Pharaoh's Levantine vassals, by far the most prolific correspondent was Rib-Hadda, mayor of the coastal city of Gubla (same as Byblos, in later Greek pronunciation). The extant Amarna archive includes nearly 70 letters from Rib-Hadda, addressed to various Egyptian officials as well as to the king. Gubla had enjoyed good relations with Egypt for millennia, literally – there is evidence for commerce between Gubla and Egypt beginning in the early third millennium BCE – and Rib-Hadda often invokes this long-standing relationship when calling on Pharaoh to acknowledge and reward Gubla's loyalty.

About two dozen of Rib-Hadda's letters were written during the reign of Amenhotep III, and the rest during the reign of Akhenaten. Thus his letters cover a considerable span of time, yet they tend to reiterate the same issues throughout that period. Rib-Hadda, the king's loyal servant, and his city Gubla, the king's loyal maidservant, are always hard pressed by war and always in need of royal support which never seems to be forthcoming. In the earlier letters, Rib-Hadda complains about Abdi-Ashirta, the traitorous ruler of Amurru, who makes war on the king's loyal vassals and seizes the king's lands; later, Rib-Hadda complains about Abdi-Ashirta's sons, principally his successor Aziru, who carry on with the same activities. (On the country of Amurru and its leaders, see the introductory remarks about the Amarna letters from Amurru, below.) First Rib-Hadda reports that Abdi-Ashirta has seized the nearby city of Ṣumur and threatens to seize Gubla; later, after Egyptian forces recaptured the city and Abdi-Ashirta met his end, it is Aziru who has seized Ṣumur and threatens to seize Gubla. In almost every letter, Rib-Hadda urgently requests that the king send troops, send provisions, send a commissioner, even just send a reply, because he cannot otherwise defend his city and prevent his people, impoverished due to war, from revolting. Indeed, more than once Rib-Hadda sarcastically asks how the king proposes that he should protect his city: should he guard it with his enemies, or with his peasantry?[17] For, seeing that their ruler gets no support from his Egyptian overlord, Rib-Hadda's destitute and war-weary people are more than ready to defect to the other side.

The other side, according to Rib-Hadda, was the growing coalition of rebels against Egyptian rule, led by the rulers of Amurru and aligned with the people called Ḫapiru. The term "Ḫapiru" denoted persons who had been uprooted from their home communities and, lacking secure positions within the states where they resided, typically subsisted on the fringes of society, sometimes serving as dependent labor or mercenaries, sometimes living as bandits and outlaws. These people did not constitute a single organized group; rather, individual Ḫapiru and bands of Ḫapiru formed a reservoir of available manpower for recruitment into militias such as that assembled by Abdi-Ashirta of Amurru and his sons. As Rib-Hadda tells it, the rulers of Amurru gathered Ḫapiru to the cause of rebellion against Egypt, then persuaded town after town to join their revolt. Inasmuch as they resisted Egyptian domination, Amurru and the Ḫapiru would appear to have engaged in an anti-imperial insurgency, and the modern reader may be encouraged to such a view when Rib-Hadda quotes Abdi-Ashirta urging townsfolk to "kill your prince, then . . . you will be at peace," and reports him conspiring to drive out the mayors appointed by Egypt so that "all the lands" will join the Ḫapiru and have peace (see EA 74: 19–41, below). But the image of Amurru and the Ḫapiru as anti-monarchic "freedom fighters" is largely an artifact of Rib-Hadda's rhetoric. The rulers of Amurru acted less to oppose Egypt than to serve their own interests, and even if the goal of their warfare was liberation from imperial domination, this was not achieved, for when Amurru did eventually break away from Egypt's empire, it was to switch allegiance to Ḫatti. As for the Ḫapiru who fought alongside Amurru, if they sought political freedom they probably found it only in an outlaw existence.

Returning to Rib-Hadda, beleaguered in Gubla, was the situation as dire as he claimed, continually over so many years? Was Egypt really losing control of its territories in the Levant, due to the depredations of Amurru and the Ḫapiru, as well as to the king's neglect thereof? Rib-Hadda rarely mentions that the king of Egypt has addressed the problems of which he complains, but of course the purpose of his letters was to complain and plead for aid, not to convey a balanced report on events and imperial policy. In fact, the constant altercations among Pharaoh's Syro-Canaanite vassals did not upset Egyptian hegemony over them; leaving aside the eventual defection of Amurru, Egypt's hold on its Levantine possessions remained secure. But Rib-Hadda himself did not. Eventually, despairing of help from Pharaoh, he sought alliance with the mayor of Beirut, and while he was visiting there his brother seized control of Gubla. Rib-Hadda's last three letters to Pharaoh were posted from Beirut (EA 136, 137, and 138). Still he implored the king to send troops and restore him to his city; but in vain; he even threw himself upon the mercies of his enemy Aziru of Amurru (according to EA 162: 1–6), to no avail. Rib-Hadda died in exile, and in his place his brother Ili-rapiḫ wrote to Pharaoh to plead Gubla's loyalty and complain of Aziru's crimes. Evidently, the king of Egypt did not much care who occupied the position of mayor in Gubla or any other town, so long as Egypt's interests were served.

There are no ruling lines on Rib-Hadda's tablets; my division of the text into "paragraphs" is based on apparent sense divisions.

98. EA 74: Rib-Hadda, mayor of Gubla, to Amenhotep III, king of Egypt (von Dassow)

(Address, salutation, and prostration, 1–5) Rib-Hadda speaks to his lord, king of all lands, Great King, King of Battle. May the [Lady] of Gubla grant power to [the king], my lord. At the feet of my lord, my Sun, sevenfold seven times I fall.

(5–13) May the lord king know that Gubla, faithful maidservant of the king since the days of his ancestors, is safe. But now, the king has let go his faithful city from his hand. May the king look up the tablets of his father's house, (to check) whether the ruler who is in Gubla has not (always) been a faithful servant! Do not neglect your servant!

(13–19) For the war of the Ḫapiru against me is severe. And, by the gods of your land, our sons and daughters are finished, (as well as) the wood of our house(s), through being sold for our sustenance in the land of Yarimuta. My field, for lack of a ploughman, is like a woman without a husband.[18]

(19–28) All my towns that are in the mountains or on the seacoast have joined the Ḫapiru. (Only) Gubla, together with two towns, is left to me. But now, Abdi-Ashirta has taken Shigata for himself. And he said to the men of Ammiya, "Kill your prince, then you will be like us and you will be at peace," and they acted in accord with his words and became like Ḫapiru![19]

(29–41) Moreover, now Abdi-Ashirta has written to the troops, "Assemble in the temple of NIN.URTA,[20] *and we shall fall upon Gubla. For there is no one who will save it from our hand. Then we shall drive out the mayors from within the lands, and all the lands will join the Ḫapiru, and . . . for all the lands. And our sons and daughters will be at peace forever. Even if the king were to come forth, since all the lands are hostile to him what could he do to us?"*

(42–8) Thus they made an oath between themselves; and thus I am very, very afraid! For there is no one who will save me from their hands. Like a bird that is placed inside a cage, just so am I in Gubla.

(48–57) Why do you neglect your land? I have written like this to the palace, but my words are not heard. Now, Amanappa is with you – ask him! He knows and has seen the trouble that besets me! May the king heed the words of his servant. And may he grant his servant provisions and sustain his servant, so that I may guard his faithful [city], together with our Lady, our goddess, for [you(?)].

(57–65) And may [the king] visit his [land] and [his servant. May he take] thought for [his] land, so that your [land may be pac]ified.[21] *May it please the king, my lord, that he send his man to stay (here) now, so that I myself may arrive before the king, my lord. It is good for me to be with you. What can I do by myself? Accordingly I petition day and night.*

99. EA 137: Rib-Hadda, ex-mayor of Gubla, writes to Akhenaten, king of Egypt, from exile in Beirut (von Dassow)

(Address and prostration, 1–4) Rib-Hadda [speaks] to the king, [his] lord, [the Sun of all countries]. Beneath the feet [of the king, my lord], seven times and seven times [I fall].

(5–14) I wrote repeatedly for [garrison troops], but they were not provided, and the king, my lord, did [not] heed the words [of his servant]. And I sent [my] messenger to the palace, but he [returned] empty-handed; he had no garrison troops. Then the men [of] my [household], seeing that no silver had been provided, wronged(?) me; <they treated?> my brother like (one of) the mayors, and they despised me.

(14–26) Furthermore, when I had gone before Ḫammuniri,[22] my younger brother even estranged Gubla from me, in order to hand the city over to the sons of Abdi-Ashirta! When my brother saw that my messenger had come forth empty-handed, there being no garrison troops with him, he despised me. Thus he committed a crime, and expelled me from the city. May the king, my lord, not be neglectful about this dog's deed!

(27–37) Now, I am not able to come to the land of Egypt myself; I am old, and a terrible sickness afflicts my body. For the king, my lord, knows that the gods of Gubla are powerful(?) and the sickness is great, for I am paying for(?) my sin toward the gods.[23] Thus I cannot enter before the king, my lord. So now I have sent my son, servant of the king, my lord, before the king, my lord.

(38–51) May the king heed the words of his servant, and may the king, my lord, provide a force of archers, that they may seize the city of Gubla, so that the traitorous troops and the [son]s of Abdi-Ashirta do not [en]ter into it – then the archery force of the king would be insufficient to take it. Look, many are the men within the city who love me; few are the traitorous men within it. Once the force of archers comes forth, they will hear of it, and upon its arrival the city will return to the king, my lord.

(52–8) And may my lord know that I would die for him. When I was in the city, I guarded it for my lord, and, my heart being devoted to the king, my lord, I would not give the city to the sons of Abdi-Ashirta. Thus, my brother estranged the city, so as to give it to the sons of Abdi-Ashirta.

(59–65) May the king, my lord, not neglect the city! For lo, very much silver and gold is within it; much is the property of the temple. If the king, my lord, seizes the city, he may do as he likes to his servant, but may he grant (me) the town of Burusilim for my residence.

(65–72) Now, I am staying with Ḫammuniri. Since the cities became hostile, Burusilim (also) became hostile, in fear of the sons of Abdi-Ashirta, so I went before Ḫammuniri – because of the sons of Abdi-Ashirta, since they are stronger than I, and there is no breath of the king's mouth for me.[24]

(73–7) And I said to my lord, "Look, Gubla is his loyal(?) city.[25] There is much property of the king within it, the wealth of our forefathers. If the king neglects the city, all the cities of Canaan will no longer be his!" May the king not neglect this matter!

(78–80) Herewith I send my son before the king, my lord, and may the king dispatch him quickly together with troops that they may take the city.

(81–9) If the king, my lord, would favor me and return me to the city, then I shall guard it for the king, my lord, as before. If the king, my lord, [does not return me] to it, then [. . .] the city from Burusilim [. . .] he may [do] as [he likes to his servant, but may he not] abandon [. . . . . . .] Ḫammuniri [. . .]. Until when [must I stay with him?]

(90–103) [And] may [the king, my lord], heed [the words] of his servant [. . . and send] troops as quickly as possible that they may take the city. May the king, my lord, not neglect this grievous deed that has been done to the lands of the king! And may the king, my lord, rush a force of archers here, that they may take the city as fast as

possible! When it is said before the king, about the city, "The city is strong," it is not strong before the troops of the king, my lord![26]

2. Amurru

We have heard Rib-Hadda's complaints about the misdeeds of Amurru's leaders. What was Amurru's side of the story?

The formation of Amurru as a state, a development that grew out of the extension of Egyptian rule into southern Syria during the early New Kingdom, was in progress in the mid-fourteenth century BCE.[27] The name Amurru was a gentilic denoting the population of lands west of Mesopotamia – the Amorites – hence it also served as the traditional Mesopotamian designation of "the West" (i.e., loosely speaking, the Levant, in modern terminology). This name now became attached to the state that emerged in the region of the Lebanon foothills near the headwaters of the Orontes, with one Abdi-Ashirta as its leader. The origins of Abdi-Ashirta and the processes whereby this region came to be united under his leadership, and under the name Amurru, are matters of speculation, for the extant records contain no information on these points. However he came to power, when we meet Abdi-Ashirta in the Amarna letters, we find him busy expanding his territory at his neightbors' expense and seizing coastal towns, employing Ḫapiru among his armed forces (as we learn from the letters of Rib-Hadda, among others; see the introductory remarks to the letters from Gubla, above). He even dared to attack the city of Ṣumur, which served as the local seat of Egyptian administration and was protected by an Egyptian garrison; once he captured the city, he claimed that he did so to defend it from hostile attack, and, posing as the defender of Ṣumur, he submitted his bid for recognition by Egypt as a vassal ruler. While Egypt may not have cared what trouble Abdi-Ashirta caused for its other Syro-Canaanite vassals, his success at winning their subjects to his side, thereby enlarging his newly created domain, did present a threat. So Abdi-Ashirta's aggression prompted Egypt to send troops to retake Ṣumur, and when they did, they captured Abdi-Ashirta, too. The Egyptians may have allowed Abdi-Ashirta to return to Amurru, under their terms, but soon after he got back there he was murdered; it remains unclear whether he was assassinated by an Egyptian force or by his own people.

Abdi-Ashirta's sons, Aziru chief among them, took up his cause and continued the process of turning Amurru into a kingdom. They recaptured the people's allegiance, as well as coastal towns previously captured by their father. Aziru then recaptured Ṣumur, this time even killing the resident Egyptian official. Somehow, by creating these facts on the ground, Aziru obtained recognition of his rule not only from his subjects, but from Egypt: soon he went to Egypt where he was confirmed as mayor of Amurru. While there, he was kept informed by letters from his brothers and sons, whom he had left in charge of his kingdom's affairs. One of these letters was EA 170, translated below, in which his brother Baʿluya and his son Bet-ili report to him about Hittite troop movements in the region of Amqi, south of Amurru, and Nuḫashe, to the northeast. These Hittite campaigns were part of Suppiluliuma's project to conquer the territories of the soon-to-be-defunct Mittanni Empire (see introductory remarks to EA 17 and 41, above), which threatened Egypt's Levantine empire as well as its tottering ally Mittanni. The contents of EA 170 would therefore have been of great interest to Egypt, and since this letter was found at Amarna, chances are it was confiscated from its addressee, but the information probably reached Aziru anyway. He returned to his kingdom as a vassal of Egypt, provided with Egyptian funds and, no doubt, charged with defending Egypt's northern frontier from Hittite invasion. Under this cover he continued to expand his domain, collaborating with Aitakama, ruler of Qadesh, and ultimately with the Hittites, in doing so. Cities and regions that had formerly belonged to the Mittanni Empire were now in play, and some, including Tunip, Nuḫashe, Niya, and Qatna, sought Egypt's support in resisting the Hittites. The city of Tunip fell to Aziru, and from there Aziru sent a series of letters to Pharaoh and to Egyptian officials, including EA 165, translated below. In these letters he insists on his undying loyalty to Egypt and points to the Hittite military presence in Nuḫashe: the Hittite invasion, right up to Amurru's borders, justifies Aziru's seizure of Tunip – which, like Ṣumur, he must protect on Egypt's behalf – as well as his failure to come to Egypt at Pharaoh's summons; at the same time, he even defends his entertainment of a Hittite envoy, apparently on the grounds that he was obliged to offer hospitality as Egypt's surrogate (EA 164). But Aziru's protestations of loyalty to Egypt, and the spin he put on his actions, were a façade, for he was actually negotiating with Ḫatti. The Egyptians realized what he was up to, and drew up an ultimatum in an attempt to compel their wayward vassal back into submission; this attempt is represented by EA 162, a draft of Pharaoh's ultimatum that remained in the archive at Akhetaten. It was too late – and so was an eventual Egyptian military campaign to Syria. Aziru offered his allegiance to Suppiluliuma, and his position as a Hittite vassal was formalized by treaty.[28] The land of Amurru was lost to Egypt.

100. EA 170: From Baʿluya and Bet-ili (brother and son of Aziru) to Aziru, ruler of Amurru, in Egypt (von Dassow)

(Address, prostration, and salutation, 1–6) To the king, our lord:[29] *Message of Baʿluya, and message of Bet-ili. At the feet of our lord we fall. For our lord may all be well. Here, with the lands of our lord, all is very well.*

(7–13) Our lord, you should not worry about anything; do not distress your heart. As soon as you can, our lord, meet with them, so that they do not delay you there.

(14–18) Another matter: troops of the land of Ḫatti, (under) Lupakku, have captured towns of the land of Amqi, and with the towns they have captured Addumi – our lord should know (about this).[30]

(19–35) Another matter: we have heard as follows: Zitana has come and there are 90,000 footsoldiers who came with him; but we have not checked the report, (to determine) whether they are really there.[31] *Should they arrive in the land of Nuḫashe, then I shall dispatch Bet-ili to him, so that we may meet with them. And I shall quickly dispatch my messenger to you, in order that he may report to you (about) whether it is so or not.*

(36–44) To Rabi-ilu and Abdi-URAŠ, to Bin-Ana and Rabi-ṣidqi: Message of Amur-Ba'la. For you may all be well. Do not distress your hearts, and do not worry about anything. Here, with your households, all is very well. And say hello to Anatu.[32]

101. EA 165: From Aziru, ruler of Amurru, to Akhenaten, king of Egypt (von Dassow)

(Address and prostration, 1–3) To the ki[ng, my lord, my god, my Sun]: Message of [Aziru, your servant. I fall at the feet of my lord] seven times and seven times.[33]

(4–9) My lord, my god, [my sun,] what n[ow do I seek?] The gracious face of the king, my lord, I seek (to see), forever. Both [I] and Ba'luya are your servants.

(10–13) I am guarding the land of the king, my lord, and my intention is (to do) service to the king, my lord, in peace. I would [see] the gracious face of the king, my lord.

(14–17) My lord, now Ḫatip and I are coming, and may my lord know that I shall arrive as soon as possible.[34]

(18–21) The king of Ḫatti is staying [in the land of Nuḫashe], and [I am afraid of him.] Heaven for[fend that he come into the land of Amurru] and the land [of the king, my lord].

(22–7) So, for [this] reason I am staying. Should he [depart] and return to [his own land], then forthwith I shall come, Ḫatip and I. [For I am] a servant of the gracious king, very much so.

(28–41) [My lord, do not wor]ry about anything; I shall come. [Upon the] de[parture(?)] of the king of Ḫatti, [forth]with I shall come [. . .] to see the face of the Sun, [my lord.] My lord, [if I] do not stay in [Amurru], then [the king] of Ḫatti will come into the land of Amurru – the land of the king, my lord – because the king, my lord, does not permit me to guard his land.[35] *And right now he is in the land of Nuḫashe, two days' march from Tunip, and I am afraid of his attacking Tunip. May he depart!*

(42–5) Another matter: my lord, do not listen to trea[cherous] men. [My brothers and] my sons and I are ser[vants of the king, my lord], forever.

B. Southern Levant

During the period of Egyptian rule, the area of central and southern Canaan – corresponding roughly to later Israel, Judah, and Philistia – was divided among a multitude of petty principalities. These tiny vassal states were each ruled by "mayors," appointed or confirmed by Egypt, and they were under the oversight of Egyptian officials based at Gaza, the local seat of imperial administration. In their letters to Pharaoh and his officials, these mayors appear to be constantly fighting with each other while jockeying for royal favor and responding to Egypt's demands for contributions of commodities and personnel. They accuse each other of giving the king's land to the Ḫapiru, and often call each other Ḫapiru, using this term somewhat the way "terrorist" is often used nowadays. They plead for the king to send archers, and they lament the imminent or total loss of the king's lands. Amid these accusations, pleas, and plaints they intersperse declarations of self-abasement, absolute loyalty to the king, and obsequious flattery of him. The perpetual strife among these vassals seems to have suited Egypt, for through making war on each other, coupled with meeting Egypt's exactions, they remained weak – and, in contrast to the situation in the northern Levant, there was no rival superpower to whom Egypt's lands could really be lost. However, the populations and territories over which Egypt exercised effective control, through its officials and vassals, could and did gradually diminish: the southern Levantine vassal states became progressively weaker, and their populations smaller, over the course of New Kingdom imperial rule.

One letter apiece from two of these multitudinous vassal states, Shechem and Jerusalem, are sampled here. Lab'ayu of Shechem seems like a southern counterpart to his contemporary Abdi-Ashirta of Amurru. Through the use of military force, he carved out a mini-empire for himself in central Canaan, and one of his sons even became established across the Jordan, as mayor of Pella. Eventually, despite his protestations of perfect innocence and absolute loyalty, Lab'ayu was called to account by the Egyptian authorities, but escaped being handed over, only to be rubbed out by enemies on his own turf. His sons tried to continue building up his kingdom, with less success than the sons of Abdi-Ashirta. Meanwhile, one of the mayors whom Lab'ayu and his sons antagonized, Abdi-Ḫeba of Jerusalem, resembles Rib-Hadda of Byblos, with similar litanies of complaints against his fellow mayors, constant appeals for the king to send help, and hysterical announcements that all the king's lands are lost, having gone over to the Ḫapiru. One of the interesting features of Abdi-Ḫeba's letters is that he had his scribe append postscripts addressed to the scribe at the Egyptian court, who would – he hoped – read his letters to the king (translating them, of course, into Egyptian). In his postscripts (see, for example, EA 287: 64–70, below), Abdi-Ḫeba begs the receiving scribe to render his letters eloquently and present them to the king in fine words.

1. Shechem

102. EA 254: From Lab'ayu, mayor of Shechem, to the king of Egypt (probably Amenhotep III) (von Dassow)

(Address and prostration, 1–6) To the king, my lord and my sun: Message of Lab'ayu, your servant and the dust of your treading. At the feet of the king, my lord and my sun, sevenfold seven times I fall.

(6–15) I have heard the words that the king wrote to me. And who am I, that the king should lose his land on account of me? Look, I am a loyal servant of the king; I have not transgressed, nor have I committed fault, and I have not withheld my tribute, nor have I withheld any request of my commissioner.

(16–29) Now, he wrongly denounces me, and the king, my lord, does not examine my crime.[36] *Furthermore, is my crime that I entered the city of Gezer and I declared, "The king takes everything of mine, but where is Milk-ilu's property?" He knows the deeds that Milk-ilu (has done) against me!*

(30–7) Another matter: the king sent for my son. I did not know that my son was carrying on with the Ḫapiru. I herewith hand him over to Addaya.

(38–46) Furthermore, even if the king sent for my wife, (heaven forbid) that I should withhold her. Even if the king wrote to me, "Put a bronze dagger in your heart and die," (heaven forbid) that I should not execute the king's command![37]

2. Jerusalem

103. EA 287: From Abdi-Ḫeba, mayor of Jerusalem, to the king of Egypt (Amenhotep III or IV) (von Dassow)

(Address and prostration, 1–3) [To the king], my lord, [speak: Message of] Abdi-Ḫeba, [your] servant. [At the feet of the king], my lord, sevenfold [seven times I fall].

(4–12) [Look at(?) the] entire situation. [Milk-ilu and Tagi(?)] brought [troops(?)] into [the town of Qiltu(?) . . .]. [Look at(?)] the deed that they [did to your servant]. Arrows [. . . (3 lines almost completely missing) . . .] they brought into [Qiltu].[38] *May the king know: all the lands are at peace, (but) for me there is war!*

(13–16) And may the king take thought for his land. Look at the lands of Gezer, of Ashkelon, and of Lachish. They provided them with food, oil, and whatever else they need.

(17–24) May the king also take thought for the archers, and may he send the archers against the men who commit crimes against the king, my lord! If this year there are archers, then the lands and the mayors will belong to the king, my lord. But if there are no archers, the king will have no lands and no mayors!

(25–8) Look at Jerusalem! This neither my father nor my mother gave me, rather, the strong arm of the king gave it to me.[39]

(29–31) Look at this deed, the deed of Milk-ilu and the deed of the sons of Lab'ayu, who have given the land of the king to the Ḫapiru!

(32–7) Look, O king, my lord, right is on my side as regards the Kushites. May the king ask the commissioners whether the house is very strong, yet they attempted a very serious crime. They took their tools, and I sought ref[uge(?) on . . .] the roof![40]

(37–42) And may [the king] send [troops] into [Jerusalem, and the troop]s should come up with [a garrison(?) for (regular)] service. May [the king] take thought for them, that [all(?)] the lands be constrained(?) in their hands [. . .].

(43–52) May the king inquire about them. [May there be] much food, much oil, much clothing, until Pawuru, the royal commissioner, comes up to Jerusalem. Addaya is gone, together with the garrison of soldiers [that] the king provided. May the king know: Addaya [sa]id to me, "[Look], he dismissed me." Do not abandon it![41] *Send me a garrison this [year], right here, [and] send a royal commissioner.*

(53–9) [Caravan]s(?) I sent to the king, my lord: [x] detainees, 5,000 [. . . , and] 8 porters for royal caravans, [but] they were taken in the open countryside of Ayyaluna. May the king, my lord, know that I cannot send a caravan to the king, my lord – for your information.

(60–3) Look, the king has placed his name in Jerusalem, for eternity, and he cannot abandon it, the land of Jerusalem!

(Postscript, 64–70) To the scribe of the king, my lord, speak: Message of Abdi-Ḫeba, your servant. At (your) feet I fall. I am your servant! Convey fine words to the king, my lord: "I am a soldier of the king – I would die for you!"

(Postpostscript, 71–8) And please treat the evil deed as the responsibility of the men of Kush. By a hair's breadth I avoided being killed by the men of Kush, within my own house! May the king [inquire] about them. [Seven] times and seven times [may the king], my lord, [take thought] for me.

Notes

1 In 1907, J. A. Knudtzon published an edition of the 358 Amarna tablets then known (*Die El-Amarna Tafeln*, vol. 1; Leipzig: Hinrichs, 1907), including tablets that are not letters. Knudtzon's numbering of the tablets has become standard; in the case of the letters, he based his numbering on the letters' geographic provenience and hypothetical chronological order. Subsequent to Knudtzon's publication, an additional 24 tablets turned up, and most of these appeared in an edition by A. F. Rainey (*El Amarna Tablets 359–379*, Alter Orient und Altes Testament 8, 2d ed.; Neukirchen: Butzon & Bercker Kevelaer, 1978). All the Amarna letters that are sufficiently preserved for translation are translated by W. L. Moran in *The Amarna Tablets* (Baltimore: The Johns Hopkins University Press, 1992). Moran's book includes a helpful introduction to the entire Amarna corpus, and his annotated translations, which can rarely be improved upon, serve as a point of reference for the present translations.

2 During this period a Kassite dynasty ruled in Babylon, and the Kassite name for their realm, comprising the lands of Sumer and Akkad, was Karduniash; this is the name used for the kingdom of Babylon in the Amarna letters.

3 What connection existed between the daughter and the animals cannot be ascertained due to the break in the tablet. Since Burra-Buriyash later asked Akhenaten to have skilled carpenters make him some lifelike sculptures of land animals or aquatic animals (in EA 10), sculptured animals rather than live ones may be the subject here too. The clause concerning whether Pharaoh will "obtain the seed" of the Kassite king's daughter is not entirely clear; the expression might refer to impregnation (cf. Moran, *Amarna Letters*, 11, who takes the phrase to mean "accept the offspring" of the Kassite princess).

4 The immensity of the amount underscores the absurdity of this declaration: one talent weighed about 60 pounds, so 3,000 talents would be such a gigantic quantity of gold that neither the notion of getting it nor the threat to refuse it would be credible, being rather a rhetorical ploy.

5 Opinions are summarized, with references to earlier literature, by Moran, *Amarna Letters*, 41, n. 16 on EA 16. It should be pointed out that the word "die" was used in exaggeration as much in ancient Near Eastern languages as it often is nowadays in colloquial English.

6 The reading of the addressee's name is uncertain: it should be Napḫurureya, according to the copy of the tablet, though the last sign is incorrect or miscopied, and a different reading has been proposed based on collating the tablet (see Moran, *Amarna Letters*, 39, n. 1 on EA 16). If the name is Napḫurureya, the addressee is Akhenaten, but if the name is read otherwise, the addressee could be one of Akhenaten's successors.

7 Presumably the qualification "of my yoking" (or harnessing, hitching up) means that this chariot and team are of the kind Ashur-uballit uses himself. The better their quality, then, the more Pharaoh would be impressed by the Assyrian king's wealth and military capability.

8 The reference is more likely to Ashur-uballit's grandfather Ashur-nadin-aḫḫe II than to Ashur-nadin-aḫḫe I, who ruled a few decades earlier. Citing past gifts as a standard for the amount of present gifts was common practice, but not necessarily factual; there is no other evidence for relations between Egypt and Assyria prior to Ashur-uballit's reign, and this claim contradicts the statement in EA 15 (above) that there had been no prior contact between the two countries.

9 The Hanigalbatean king, that is, the king of Mittanni, would have been Tushratta (for whom see EA 17, below); his Egyptian counterpart would have been either Amenhotep III, if the addressee of EA 16 was Akhenaten, or Akhenaten, if the addressee was one of his successors (see n. 6, above).

10 The translation of this passage is uncertain. The word here translated "guide" can also mean "pursuer," and how the word "dead" fits into the sentence is unclear (see Moran, *Amarna Letters*, 40, n. 15 on EA 16).

11 The reading of this personal name and the identity of the person so named are uncertain.

12 An exaggeration, surely. The battle to which Tushratta refers may have been fought against Suppiluliuma, or possibly against one of his predecessors, depending on how the chronology of this period is reconstructed; it could have been one of the engagements Suppiluliuma refers to in the historical prologue to his treaty with Tushratta's eventual successor Shattiwaza (see no. 110 "The end of Mittani").

13 Regarding the question of Ḫuriya's identity, see Moran, *Amarna Letters*, xxxviii–xxxix, with n. 137, and 115, n. 2 on EA 41. For the probable reign of Nefertiti as Pharaoh, see William Murnane, *Texts from the Amarna Period in Egypt* (Atlanta: Scholars Press, 1995), 205–8.

14 The opening "Thus (says) the Sun" (*um-ma* ^{d}UTU^{ši}) is restored based on letters from Ḫatti that were found at Ugarit; see Moran, *Amarna Letters*, n. 1 on EA 41, and xxii–xxiii, for the variation on the address formula's usual structure. Like the king of Egypt, the king of Ḫatti was, ideologically, "the sun."

15 Moran's translation of lines 29–36 (*Amarna Letters*, 114) has the Hittite ruler suggesting that his Egyptian counterpart may give something or not, as he likes, which seems a rather unlikely statement to make (albeit true), and which moreover depends heavily on restoring words missing in the breaks.

16 The nature of this last item is unclear (actual plants? representations in silver?), but the penultimate item is surely a pair of disk-shaped silver ingots.

17 E.g., EA 112: 7–12.

18 By this proverb, which Rib-Hadda uses in other letters too (EA 75: 15–17; 81: 37–8; 90: 42–3), he evidently means that his land is so depopulated that no peasants are available to cultivate it. He may mean to imply that too many peasants are

away fighting, leaving no one to till the soil and produce crops, with the result that poverty has become so severe as to necessitate the sale of family members to obtain sustenance. They are sold, he says, in the land of Yarimuta; this was a region on the coast of Lebanon, the exact location of which is not known (RGTC 12/2: 342–3).

19 Shigata was a town that evidently belonged to the territory of Gubla, while Ammiya had its own local ruler; both were located in Lebanon (for their probable sites, see RGTC 12/2: 20 and 270–1).

20 It is uncertain which Canaanite deity's name might be spelled with the logogram NIN.URTA in this instance. The location designated for the troops' assembly, the name of which is written "House of (the god) NIN.URTA," may have been a temple (as rendered in the present translation) or a place with a name formed like that of Bethel, "House of (the god) El" (and analogous ones: Beth-Anath, Beth-Dagon, etc.).

21 The broken verb form could be restored in different ways, and a verbal adjective seems more likely than an imperative addressed to Pharaoh, as in Moran's rendering (*Amarna Letters*, 143). The switch between third and second person in addressing Pharaoh is unexceptional.

22 Ḫammuniri, whose name is also spelled ʿAmmunira, was the mayor of Beirut, presumably the successor of Yapaḫ-Hadda (mentioned in several of Rib-Hadda's letters). Although Rib-Hadda had quarrelled with Yapaḫ-Hadda, he was now forced to take refuge with Ḫammuniri, having been exiled from his own city, Gubla.

23 This tentative rendering is based on reading *kabtu*, "powerful" (*ka*$_4$*-ab-tu*!) instead of *qadšu*, "holy," in l. 32, and reading *ip-dì*, from the root *pdy*, "to redeem" or "ransom," in l. 33 (cf. Moran, *Amarna Letters*, EA 137, with n. 4). Regardless of which readings are correct, the general sense is clear: Rib-Hadda expresses the view that his illness must be divine punishment for a sin he has committed; through his suffering he redeems, thus "pays for," his sin.

24 "Breath of the king's mouth" means the king's provision of troops and resources; Pharaoh's Canaanite vassals had absorbed the Egyptian concept that the breath of life was mediated by the king to his subjects as from a god to his creatures. My rendering of the sequence of clauses in these lines departs somewhat from other treatments (cf. Moran, *Amarna Letters*, 219), on the grounds of the apparent logical relationships among successive statements. Thus, I take "*inūma* I went before Ḫammuniri" as a main clause, instead of a subordinate clause dependent on a later main clause ("when I went before Ḫ., . . . I said to my lord"); this entails rendering the subordinating conjunction *inūma* atypically as a resultative, "so" (*vel sim.*), while in preceding and following clauses *inūma* functions in one of its usual roles as a causative, "since."

25 Reading, tentatively, URU^{lu} *ki-ti*!-*šu*! instead of URU^{lu}.KI-*ši-na*; cf. Moran, *Amarna Letters*, 221, n. 14.

26 The last dozen lines are written on the left edge of the tablet where they are disposed in a rather jumbled fashion. By placing them on the left edge, which was sometimes used rather like the tab on a file folder to indicate a tablet's contents, perhaps the scribe intended to showcase these urgent and repetitive statements, which do not communicate anything of substance not already conveyed elsewhere in the letter.

27 In this brief outline, I have relied on the reconstruction of Amurru's history offered by Itamar Singer, "A Concise History of Amurru," Appendix III in S. Izre'el, *Amurru Akkadian: A Linguistic Study*, vol. 2 (Harvard Semitic Studies, 41; Atlanta: Scholars Press, 1991), 135–95.

28 The treaty establishing the terms of Aziru's vassalage to Suppiluliuma, found in several copies at the Hittite capital, Ḫattusa, is available in an English translation by Gary Beckman, *Hittite Diplomatic Texts* (Society of Biblical Literature Writings from the Ancient World, vol. 7; Atlanta: Scholars Press, 1996), text no. 5.

29 It is Aziru, not the king of Egypt, who is addressed as "king" and "lord" in this letter. While Pharaoh exercised supreme kingship over his vassals, including Aziru, each vassal was king of his own domain, and would be so addressed by his subjects and members of his household.

30 Amqi was the name of the region now called the Beqaa, the valley between the Lebanon and Antilebanon mountain ranges. Amqi lay south of Amurru, and east of Byblos and Beirut across the Lebanon mountains, so the capture of towns in that region by Hittite troops was a significant development, affecting the interests of Egypt no less than Amurru. Lupakku was presumably the general leading these Hittite troops, and Addumi apparently was a local ruler in the Amqu region; the letter does not explain who they were, for this was already known to the addressee.

31 Zitana was evidently another Hittite general, who was reportedly about to arrive at the head of a very large army in Nuḫashe, a region north of Amurru across the Orontes River. The figure given for the number of troops, 90,000, would have been an incredibly large force in this period, and it was probably meant to signify exactly that – "an incredibly large force" – rather than meaning literally 90,000 troops.

32 These lines append to Ba'luya and Bet-ili's letter a message from Amur-Ba'la, perhaps another brother of Aziru, to four men, otherwise unknown to us, who had accompanied Aziru to Egypt. Amur-Ba'la reassures these four that their families are fine, and adds a brief greeting to a fifth man, Anatu, who presumably was not head of a family about whose welfare he needed reassurance.

33 The address and prostration formulae are restored on the basis of Aziru's other letters to Pharaoh (e.g., EA 156: 1–3). The content of this letter is closely comparable to that of EA 164, 166, 167, and 168, making it possible to restore many damaged passages as well as to identify the sender as Aziru.

34 Ḫatip was an Egyptian official, who had arrived in Amurru to convey Pharaoh's summons to Aziru (EA 164), after confiscating funds previously granted to Aziru by the Egyptian king (EA 161).

35 My restoration and translation of this sentence differ somewhat from those of Moran (*Amarna Letters*, 253), who understands it to refer to an event in the past, and of Izre'el (*Amurru Akkadian* 2: 40–3), who understands it as present tense but does not read a negative, nor restore the place name Amurru, in the first clause. Whichever translation is correct, it is clear that Aziru means to indicate that it will be the Egyptian king's fault if Aziru obeys his summons and consequently, thanks to Aziru's absence, the Hittite king invades and takes over Amurru.

36 Who has denounced Lab'ayu – is it Milk-ilu of Gezer, whom Lab'ayu obliquely accuses, in the following lines? This is left unspecified, as are the "crime" of which Lab'ayu has been accused, and Milk-ilu's deeds against him. Lab'ayu's

query about whether it is a crime that he complained about the king's confiscation of his property, when he entered Gezer, is rhetorical.

37 This rendering takes the particle *kī* as a subordinating conjunction introducing an assertory oath, following A. F. Rainey, *Canaanite in the Amarna Tablets*, vol. 3 (Leiden: Brill, 1996), 92. An alternative, adopted by Moran (*Amarna Letters*, 307), is to take *kī* as an interrogative, "how," in which case the following translation results: "how, if the king sent for my wife, how could I withhold her . . ." (etc.). The sense is the same either way.

38 Control of Qiltu, probably biblical Keilah southwest of Jerusalem, is at issue in other letters of Abdi-Ḫeba (EA 289 and 290), as well as in the letters of one of his antagonists, Shuwardata (EA 279 and 280).

39 Abdi-Ḫeba's declaration that he owes his position in Jerusalem to his appointment by Pharaoh does not necessarily mean that he did not inherit that position, only that his tenure of it is dependent on the favor and power of his Egyptian sovereign.

40 Here Abdi-Ḫeba complains of an attack against him by Kushites, who would have been troops assigned by Egypt, presumably to protect Egypt's appointee in Jerusalem; why such troops would use their "tools," and attack the man in their charge, is obscure. The episode is brought up again below, lines 71–8.

41 That is, Jerusalem; the pronominal suffix on the verb "abandon" is feminine, its antecedent being the city. In West Semitic languages, cities are feminine, so, for example, Gubla is the "maidservant" of the king in EA 116: 47, above.

8

Hittite Historical Texts I

Gary Beckman, Petra Goedegebuure, Joost Hazenbos, and Yoram Cohen

An understanding of Hittite history and culture can be derived from thousands of cuneiform texts coming primarily from Ḫattuša, the Hittite capital. The name "Hittite" comes from the Hittite name for central Anatolia, Ḫatti. Although it is not known when and from where the first Indo-European ancestors of the Hittites entered Anatolia, individuals with "Hittite-like" names occur in and the Old Assyrian texts from Anatolian trade centers (ca. 1920–1740 BC). One king mentioned in the Assyrian texts was a certain Anitta who ruled from Kushshar, a city which the early Hittite kings claimed as their city of origin. Anitta (who was probably a Hittite) claims to have destroyed Ḫattuša, although it became the seat of power of the Hittite kings for over five centuries (ca. 1700–1180 BC). The Hittite kings did not, however, claim descent from Anitta. Beginning with Ḫattušili I, approximately 15 kings are known to have ruled from Ḫattuša in the Old Kingdom (ca. 1750–1600 BC). The Hittite state was formed through expansion in this period. During the reign of Ḫattušili I (ca. 1700 BC) the Hittites expanded into northern Syria and west into the land of Arzawa. Mursili I (ca. 1600 BC) raided the city of Babylon (ca. 1595 BC) and ended the First Dynasty of Babylon. However, the Hittites were unable expand into Mesopotamia, and Hittite control of eastern territories seems to have collapsed soon thereafter.

Hittite influence in western Asia Minor and north Syria was reasserted in the period of the New Kingdom by Tudhaliya II (ca. 1420–1370 BC). The greatest expansion took place during the reign of Shuppiliuiluma I and his immediate successors (ca. 1350–1250 BC). The Hittites conquered the powerful Hurrian state of Mitanni, controlled all of Syria north of Damascus, and fought with the Egyptians in Syro-Palestine. In fact, Ḫattušili III (ca. 1250 BC) made a treaty with Rameses II and gave him a Hittite princess in marriage. This treaty stayed in effect until the fall of Hittite power in 1180 BC. However, due to a number of factors, Hittite power began to decline during the reigns of the next three monarchs, Tudahiyah IV, Arnuwanda III, and

Shhuppiliiluma II. The rising power of Assyria in northern Iraq severely truncated Hittite power in Syria. Ahhiyawa (possibly the Hittite term for the Achaeans), a powerful kingdom to the west, threatened Hittite power in western Anatolia. The Hittites also had serious troubles with the rival Hittite kingdom of Tarhuntassha in the south.

What is not certain, however, is what brought about the fall of the Hittite capital, Ḫattuša. Invaders from the west, usually identified in Egyptian sources with the Sea Peoples, may have been the catalyst for its end. Contrary to popular scholarly tradition, Hittite power did not end with the fall of Hattusha; successor dynasties continued at Tarhuntashsha and southeast at Carchemish on the Upper Euphrates. Smaller Neo-Hittite states continued in southeast Anatolia and Syria for at least the next five hundred years (ca. 700 BC). These states were often in conflict with rival Aramean dynasties. Both Aramean and Neo-Hittite states were absorbed into the Assyrian world state. Passages from 2 Sam, and 1–2 Kgs that mention the Hittites most likely refer to the Neo-Hittite states of Syria.

Hittite shares a number of linguistic features with another Indo-European language of Anatolia, Luwian, and distantly resembles other ancient Indo-European tongues, including Sanskrit and Mycenaean Greek. The Hittite language was written for nearly five centuries (ca. 1650–1180 BC) in the cuneiform script developed in southern Mesopotamia. The Hittites either borrowed the script from the Assyrian trade colonies or from the Old Babylonian script used in Syria at Tell Meskene/Emar and elsewhere. The Hittites modified the cuneiform system by giving new phonetic values to certain signs. The Hittite kings also employed a hieroglyphic script to write a dialect of Luwian.

There is an extensive collection of treaty documents in the archives from Ḫattuša that describe Hittite relations with vassal states and other international powers. These documents, which are literary in nature, are structured with six major sections, which include the speaker's introduction, a historical prologue, stipulations, a statement concerning the document, divine witnesses, and a list of curses for recalcitrance and blessings for compliance.

104. The Anitta Text (Beckman)

This Hittite-language text, of which we possess copies on three tablets, is a collection of three inscriptions commemorating the campaigns by which Anitta united central Anatolia under his rule during the middle of the eighteenth century BCE: A (§§1–9), B (§§10–12), and C (§§13–19). The original of the first of these accounts had been displayed in the main gate of Anitta's capital (§9).

Anitta succeeded his father as ruler of Kuššara, a city located somewhere to the southeast of the later Hittite heartland. Inscription A informs us that the divine favor he enjoyed aroused the hostility of the king of Neša (also known as Kaneš), resulting in war. After he had subjugated Neša, Anitta moved the seat of his dynasty to that city, which was of particular significance since it hosted the most important member of the network of Assyrian trading colonies in the region – see Veenhof 1995.

Anitta then undertook a series of campaigns in which he defeated, among other city-states, Zalpuwa/Zalpa, Ḫattuša (the later Hittite capital), Šalatiwara, and Purušḫanda. The latter town had earlier enjoyed preeminence in the area, and the presentation by its ruler of an iron throne and scepter(?) (§19) signified recognition of Anitta's position as the new regional hegemon.

Although later Mesopotamian monarchs often boast of their prowess in the chase, Anitta's hunt (§16) is unparalleled in the historical accounts of Hittite kings.

Inscription A

§1 (A 1–4) Anitta, son of Pitḫana, became king of (the city of) Kuššara. He behaved in a manner pleasing to the storm-god in heaven. And when he was in turn favored by the storm-god, the king of (the city of) Neša was [hostile(?)] to the king of Kuššara.

§2 (A 5–9) The king of Kuššara [came] down from the city with massed forces [and took] Neša by storm at night. He captured the king of Neša but in no way mistreated the inhabitants of Neša. He treated [them] as if they were (his) parents.

§3 (A 10–12) [And] after (the death of) my father Pitḫana, in the same year, I defeated a revolt: Whatever land under the sun rose up – I defeated every last one of them.

§4 (A 13–16) [Then forth] to(?) (the city of) Ullama [I . . .] Later the king of Ḫatti [. . .] I defeated [him] at (the city of) [. . .]tešma. [I sent(?) . . .] to Neša.

§5 (A 17–19) [I took] (the city of) Harkiuna in the heat of midday; I took (the city of) [. . .]ma by storm at night; [I took] (the city of) Wašḫaniya(?) in the heat of midday.

§6 (A 20–6) Then I turned them over to the storm-god of Heaven. [And] we sealed them back up for [. . .] and the storm-god. Whoever should become king after me – out of Neša no one shall resettle [Wašḫaniya(?), . . .]ma, or Ḫarkiuna. (Whoever should do such a thing) shall become the enemy of Neša; he shall become the [enemy] of the entire populace! And like a lion [I fell upon(?)] the land(s).

§7 (A 27–9) But [they shall . . .] to the storm-god whoever somehow [. . .], and settles [. . .] And he, in mind [. . .]

§8 (A 30–2) [And] after (the death of) my father, [. . .] of (the city of) Zalpuwa on the Sea[1] [. . . of Zalpuwa] on the Sea [. . .]

§9 (A 33–5) [I impressed(?)] these words on a tablet in my city gate. In the future no one shall damage this tablet. Whoever damages it shall become the enemy of [Neša].

Inscription B

§10 (A 36–7) Piyušti, king of Ḫatti, [came (for battle)] a second time, and at (the city of) Šalampa [he mustered] the contingent of auxiliaries that he brought.

§11 (A 38–48) All the lands [arose(?)] from the direction of Zalpuwa on the Sea. Long ago, Uḫna, king of Zalpuwa, had carried off our deity[2] from Neša to Zalpuwa, but thereafter I, Great King Anitta, [carried] off our deity back from Zalpuwa to Neša.

I brought Ḫuzziya, king of Zalpuwa, to Neša [alive]. (The city of) Ḫattuša inflicted [evil on me], and I released it. But when later it suffered from famine, their deity Ḫalmašuitt (the throne-goddess) delivered it up, and I took it by storm at night. [I] sowed cress on its grounds.[3]

§12 (A 49–51) May the storm-god of Heaven smite whoever should become king after me and should resettle Ḫattuša.

Inscription C

§13 (A 52–4) I turned my face against (the city of) ~~Šalatiwara~~, and Šalatiwara withdrew its troops [from the city] before (me) [. . .] I brought it(s booty) to Neša.

§14 (A 55–6) And I built fortifications in Neša. Behind the fortifications I built the temple of the storm-god of Heaven and the temple of our deity.

§15 (A 57–8) I furnished the temple of Ḫalmašuitt, the temple of the storm-god, my lord, and the temple of our deity with the goods I brought back from campaign.

§16 (A 59–63) I made a vow, and I [went] hunting. In a single day I brought to my city Neša[4] *2 lions, 70 swine, 60 wild boars, and 120 (other) beasts – leopards, lions, deer, gazelle, and [wild goats].*

§17 (A 64–7) In the same year I went to war against [Šalatiwara]. The ruler of Šalatiwara set out together with his sons and came [against me]. Leaving his land and his city, he took up a position at the Ḫulanna River.

§18 (A 68–72) [But the army] of Neša went off behind [him], set fire to his fortifications, and [. . .] them. The besiegers of the city (Šalatiwara) were 1,400 infantry and 40 horse-drawn [chariots]. He (the ruler of Šalatiwara) gathered up [his treasure] and departed.

§19 (A 73–9) When I went on campaign [against (the city of) Purušḫanda], the ruler of Purušḫanda [brought] me gifts: He brought me a throne of iron and a scepter(?) of iron as presents. When I [came] back to Neša, I brought the ruler of Purušḫanda with me. When he goes into the throne room,[5] *he will sit before me on the right.*

Further reading

On the history of Anatolia at the time of the Assyrian merchant settlements, see T. R. Bryce, *The Kingdom of the Hittites* (Oxford: Clarendon, 1998), ch. 2.

Badalì, E. 1987. Eine neue Lesung im Anfang des "Anitta-Texts." *Die Welt des Orients* 18: 43–4.

Carruba, O. 2001. Anitta res gestae: paralipomena I. In *Akten des IV. Internationalen Kongresses für Hethitologie Würzburg, 4.–8. Oktober 1999*, ed. G. Wilhelm. Wiesbaden: Harrassowitz. Pp. 51–72.

Neu, E. 1974. *Der Anitta-Text.* Wiesbaden: Harrassowitz.

Nowicki, H. 2000. Zum Einleitungsparagraphen des Anitta-Textes (CTH 1,1–4). In *125 Jahre Indogermanistik in Graz*, ed. M. Ofitsch and C. Zinko. Graz: Leykam. Pp. 347–55.

Singer, I. 1995. "Our God" and "Their God" in the Anitta Text. In *II Congresso Internazionale di Hittitologia*, ed. O. Carruba, M. Giorgieri, and C. Mora. Pavia: Gianni Iuculano Editore. Pp. 343–9.

Steiner, G. 1989. Kültepe-Kaniš und der "Anitta-Text." In *Anatolia and the Ancient Near East. Studies in Honor of Tahsin Özgüç*, ed. K. Emre, M. Mellink, B. Hrouda, and N. Özgüç. Ankara: Türk Tarih Kurumu. Pp. 471–80.
——. 1990. How Was the City of Ḫattuša Taken by "Anitta"? In *Uluslararas 1. Hititoloji Kongresi Bildirleri (19–21 Temmuz 1990)* Çorum: Uluslararasi Çorum Hitit Festivali Komitesi Baskanligi. Pp. 170–85.
——. 1993. Acemhöyük = Kãrum Zalpa "im Meer." In *Aspects of Art and Iconography: Anatolia and its Neighbors. Studies in Honor of Nimet Özgüç*, ed. M. Mellink, E. Porada and T. Özgüç. Ankara: Türk Tarih Kurumu. Pp. 579–99.
Veenhof, K. R. 1995. Kanesh: An Assyrian Colony in Anatolia. In CANE, 859–71.

105. Annals of Ḫattušili I (Beckman)

This composition, which was inscribed on a lost statue of gold (§17) as well as on clay tablets excavated at the Hittite capital of Ḫattuša, presents in year-by-year format the military deeds of the first major king of the Hittites, Ḫattušili I, who ruled in the second half of the seventeenth century BCE. It is uncertain whether the five years described here constituted the first portion of his reign or rather particularly significant later years, but it is very likely that the text continued on additional tablets, not yet recovered. The geographic range of Ḫattušili's campaigns is impressive – from Zalpa in northernmost Anatolia, to Arzawa in the southwest of the peninsula, to northern Syria in the south. In addition to narrating the triumphant progress of the Hittite armies, the text details the extravagant booty Ḫattušili carried off from his victims, most notably from the Syrian towns of Ḫaššuwa (§§11–13) and Ḫaḫḫa (§§16–17).

Ḫattušili boasts that in some respects his deeds outshone even those of the great Mesopotamian conqueror Sargon of Akkad (§§19–20) – see Beckman 2001. He attributes this success, particularly in escaping from a situation of peril for both himself and his country, to the favor of the sun-goddess of Arinna (§5). Appropriately, he lavishes the greatest share of his booty upon her temple, and dedicates the population of the city of Ḫaḫḫa to her service (§17). For the repeated use of lion imagery here see Collins 1998.

The document is a Hittite–Akkadian bilingual. This translation is based primarily upon the Hittite version, with divergences in the Akkadian text given in the notes.

First year

§1 (A i 1–8) I, the Great King, the Tabarna,[6] *Ḫattušili, [king of the land of Ḫatti], ruler of (the city of) Kuššar,*[7] *exercised kingship in Ḫatti.*[8] *The brother's son of Tawananna,*[9] *I went to (the city of) Šanaḫuitta, but I did not destroy it; I destroyed its countryside. I left forces in two places*[10] *as garrisons, and I gave whatever sheepfolds there were (in that vicinity)*[11] *to the garrison troops.*

§2 (A i 9–11) [Thereafter] I went to (the city of) Zalpa[12] *and destroyed it. I took its deities and three palanquins and carried them off for the sun-goddess of (the city of) Arinna.*

§3 (A i 12–14) I carried off one golden ox and one golden rhyton in the shape of a fist to the temple of the storm-god. I carried off the deities that remained to the temple of (the goddess) Mezzulla.[13]

Second year

§4 (A i 15–21) In the following year I went to (the city of) Alalaḫ and destroyed it. Thereafter I went to (the city of) Waršuwa,[14] *and from Waršuwa I went to (the city of) Ikakali. From Ikakali I went to (the city of) Tašḫiniya. I destroyed these lands, but I took their(!) goods and filled my palace with goods.*[15]

Third year

§5 (A i 22–34) In the following year I went to the land of Arzawa and took away their cattle and sheep. But in my rear the Hurrian enemy entered the land,[16] *and all the countries became hostile to me; only the single city Ḫattuša remained. I am the Great King, the Tabarna, beloved of the sun-goddess of Arinna. She placed me on her lap, held me by the hand, and ran before me in battle. Then I went in battle to (the city of) Nenašša, and when the people of Nenašša saw me (coming), they opened up (their city).*[17]

§6 (A i 35–45) Thereafter I went in battle to the land of Ulma.[18] *The people of Ulma came against me twice in battle, and I defeated them both times. I destroyed Ulma and sowed [cress] on its territory.*[19] *And I carried off seven deities to the temple of the sun-goddess of Arinna, (including) one golden ox, the goddess Katiti, and Mt. Aranḫapilanni.*[20] *I carried off the deities that remained to the temple of Mezzulla. But when I returned from the land of Ulma, I went to the land of Šalliaḫšuwa. Then the land of Šalliaḫšuwa delivered itself with fire,*[21] *while those persons (its inhabitants) entered my service. Then I returned to my city Ḫattuša.*

Fourth year

§7 (A i 46–52) In the following year I went in battle to (the city of) Šanaḫḫuitta, and I fought Šanaḫḫuitta for five months. [Then] I destroyed [it] in the sixth month.[22] *I, the Great King, was satisfied. The sun-god appeared in the midst of the lands.*[23] *The manly deeds that [I . . .] I took to the sun-goddess of Arinna.*[24]

§8 (A i 53–ii 5) I defeated[25] *the chariotry of the land of Appaya, and I took away the cattle and sheep of (the city of) Takšanaya.*[26] *I went to (the city of) Parmanna. Parmanna was the chief of those kings; it used to smooth out the paths before them.*[27]

§9 (A ii 6–10) And when they saw me coming, they opened up the city gates. The sun-god of Heaven took them by the hand in [that] matter.[28] *(The city of) Alḫa*[29] *became hostile to me, and I destroyed Alḫa.*

Fifth year

§10 (A ii 11–23) In the following year I went to the land of Zaruna,[30] *and I destroyed Zaruna. Then I went to (the city of) Ḫaššuwa.*[31] *The people of Ḫaššuwa came against me in battle, and the troops of the land of Aleppo*[32] *were with them as allies.*[33] *They*

came to me [in battle] and I defeated them.[34] *And in a few days I crossed the Euphrates River.*[35] *I scattered the land of Ḫaššuwa like a lion with its paws.*[36] *When I attacked [it], I piled up dirt [on it]. I took all [of its goods] and I filled Ḫattuša (with them).*[37]

§11 (A ii 24–31) I [took(?) much] silver and gold. Furthermore, [I took] its deities[38]*: the storm-god, Lord of (Mt.) Amaruk,*[39] *the storm-god, Lord of Aleppo, Allatum, (Mt.) Adalur, Lelluri, 2 oxen of gold, 13(!)*[40] *statues of silver and gold, 2 model shrines, and a rear wall. And I plated it with silver and gold; and I plated the door with silver and gold.*[41]

§12 (A ii 32–40) One golden inlaid table, three silver tables, two golden(!)[42] *tables, one golden inlaid throne with arms, a*[43] *. . . of gold, one palanquin of gold, two scepters(?) of stone, plated with gold – these I carried off from Ḫaššuwa*[44] *to the sun-goddess of Arinna. The Young Woman, Allatum, Ḫebat, three statues of silver, and two statues of gold – these I carried off to the temple of Mezzulla.*

§13 (A ii 41–4) One golden lance, [five(?)] golden maces, five silver maces, two double-axes of lapis-lazuli, one double-axe of gold – these I carried off to the temple of the storm-god.

§14 (A ii 45–53) In one year I conquered[45] *Ḫaššuwa. They threw away the spear of the city of Tawannaga.*[46] *I, the Great King, cut off his/its head. I went to (the city of) Zippašna. Indeed, at night I went up*[47] *to Zippašna, and I joined battle with them. I piled up dirt on them, and the storm-god appeared in the midst of the land.*

§15 (A ii 54–iii 5) I, the Great King, the Tabarna, went to Zippašna. Like a lion, I frightened off (the city of) Ḫaḫḫa with menacing gestures,[48] *and I destroyed Zippašna. I took its deities and carried them off to the sun-goddess of Arinna.*

§16 (A iii 6–12) Then I went to Ḫaḫḫa, and at Ḫaḫḫa I gave battle three times in the city gate. I destroyed Ḫaḫḫa. I took its goods and brought them to my city Ḫattuša (two pairs of wagons were loaded with silver):[49]

§17 (A iii 13–24) one palanquin, one silver stag, one golden table, one silver table[50]*; these deities of Ḫaḫḫa: one silver bull,*[51] *one boat with prow inlaid in gold, I the Great King, the Tabarna, brought from Ḫaḫḫa and carried off to the sun-goddess of Arinna.*[52] *I, the Great King, the Tabarna, removed the hands of its slave girls from the grinding stone. I removed the hands of its slaves from the sickle.*[53] *I freed them from compulsory services,*[54] *and I ungirded their loins. I turned them over to the sun-goddess of Arinna, my lady.*[55] *And I made this golden statue of myself*[56] *and set it up before the sun-goddess of Arinna, my lady. And I plated the wall above and below*[57] *with silver.*

§18 (A iii 25–8) The king of (the city of) Timana sent one chariot of silver to (me), the Great King, and I carried (it) off to the sun-goddess of Arinna. I (also) carried off two statues of alabaster to the sun-goddess of Arinna.

§19 (A iii 29–36) No one had crossed the Euphrates River,[58] *but I, the Great King, the Tabarna, crossed it on foot, and my army crossed it on foot behind me. Sargon (of Akkad also) crossed it. [He] fought*[59] *the troops of Ḫaḫḫa, but [he] did not do anything to Ḫaḫḫa. He did not burn it down*[60]*; smoke was not visible to the storm-god of Heaven.*[61]

§20 (A iii 37–42) But I, the Great King, the Tabarna,[62] *destroyed Ḫaššuwa and Ḫaḫḫa, and [burned] them down with fire.*[63] *I showed smoke to the sun-god of Heaven and the storm-god. I hitched the king of Ḫaššuwa and the king of Ḫaḫḫa*[64] *to a wagon.*

Colophon[65]

[First] tablet, [incomplete(?)], of the manly deeds of Ḫattušili.

Further reading

On the history of the early Hittite state, see T. R. Bryce, *The Kingdom of the Hittites* (Oxford: Clarendon, 1998), chs. 3–5. For discussions of Hittite history writing, consult J. Van Seters, *In Search of History* (New Haven: Yale University Press, 1983), 100–26, and the works cited by H. A. Hoffner in the bibliography for texts 115 and 116 in chapter 9 of this volume.

Beckman, G. 2001. Sargon and Naram-Sin in Ḫatti: Reflections of Mesopotamian Antiquity among the Hittites. In *Die Gegenwart des Altertums. Formen und Funktionen des Altertumsbezugs in den Hochkulturen der Alten Welt*, ed. D. Kuhn and H. Stahl. Heidelberg: Edition Forum. Pp. 85–91.

Collins, B. J. 1998. Ḫattušili I, the Lion King. *Journal of Cuneiform Studies* 50: 11–20.

de Martino, S. 2003. *Annali e res gestae antico ittiti*. Pavia: Italian University Press. Pp. 21–79.

Güterbock, H. G. 1964. Sargon of Akkad Mentioned by Ḫattušili of Ḫatti. *Journal of Cuneiform Studies* 18: 1–6.

Haas, V. 1977. Zalpa, die Stadt am Schwarzen Meer und das althethitische Königtum. *Mitteilungen der Deutschen Orient-Gesellschaft* 109: 15–26.

Houwink ten Cate, P. H. J. 1983. The History of Warfare according to Hittite Sources: The Annals of Hattusilis I. Part I. *Anatolica* 10: 91–109.

——. 1984. The History of Warfare according to Hittite Sources: The Annals of Hattusilis I. Part II. *Anatolica* 11: 47–83.

Imparati, F. and C. Saporetti. 1965. L'autobiografia di Ḫattušili I. *Studi Classici e Orientali* 14: 40–85.

Melchert, H. C. 1978. The Acts of Ḫattušili I. *Journal of Near Eastern Studies* 37: 1–22.

Otten, H. 1958. Keilschrifttexte. *Mitteilungen der Deutschen Orient-Gesellschaft* 91: 73–84.

106. The Bilingual Testament of Hattusili I (Goedegebuure)

The edict or testament of Hattusili I (1650–1620 BC),[66] one of the earliest known Hittite kings, provides a lively description of the ~~sometimes desperate internal political situation~~ during Hattusili's reign.

In this Akkadian–Hittite bilingual document, Hattusili describes the schemings of his own family, which have led him to denounce his adopted son and heir to the throne ~~Labarna~~, and to announce his young grandson ~~Mursili~~ as the new crown prince. Most of the attention goes to the dissention caused by the strife in the royal family and the resulting effects of the disregard for the commands and wishes of the king, of which the most serious is civil war. The denouncement of the adopted crown prince is described in §§1–6, followed by the installation of his grandson Mursili as new heir to the throne (§§7–8). The king requires the cooperation of his nobles in raising and educating the young child. He supports his request by the use of a metaphor: Hattusili calls on his subjects and noblemen to act united like a pack of wolves. As is well known, only the alpha-couple breeds, after which the whole pack is involved in raising the pups. Moreover, the pack itself is often the offspring of the alpha-couple. Thus, Hattusili reminds the nobles that they all belong to the (extended) royal family, and therefore have a duty towards Mursili.

Several paragraphs deal with the admonition to remain united and always obey the king's commands and wishes (§§9–11). These instructions are accompanied by the *exemplum* of the highly disloyal behavior of his son Huzziya and an unnamed daughter (§§12–18).

The next paragraphs deal with instructions to Mursili (§19), the first ranking servants (§§20–1), and some closing remarks and personal advice for Mursili (§22) and Hastayar[67] (§23). The last paragraph probably also contains some instructions to Hastayar concerning the burial rites for the king. However, although the king seems to be seriously ill, he probably recovered from his crisis.[68]

The family relationships and order of succession to the throne described in this document and others from the early Hittite Old Kingdom are far from clear and have caused much debate. Labarna, the heir first mentioned (§1) is the nephew and adopted son of Hattusili I; the "snake" and mother of Labarna (§2) is Hattusili's sister. Was nephew Labarna appointed as heir to the throne after the discomfiture of Hattusili's son Huzziya and his daughter (and probably her offspring, §§12–18), or were the succession rules in the Old Hittite period not based on a father–son sequence but on another type of succession? Sürenhagen 1998 chooses the latter option.

According to Sürenhagen 1998, in old Hittite times the Hittite royal family was organized according to the principle of the "avunculate." In such a system the sovereign's sister has priority over the son of the sovereign. The nephew, not the own son, is the heir. The sovereign moreover has authority over his nephew, and is highly involved in his upbringing. This would mean that the nephew and adopted son Labarna, and not one of Hattusili's own sons, is the legitimate heir; for example, Huzziya or the offspring of the unnamed daughter. Indeed, as he states himself, Hattusili is responsible for the upbringing and education of Labarna (§1).

Sürenhagen further explains that the avunculate system is accompanied by certain preferential marriages; that is, between cousins. Thus, the *sister* of the nephew of the king and heir to the throne marries the son of the ruling king, her cousin. The son born from this marriage will then become the next heir to the throne. Summarizing: the son of a ruling king will never become king, but the grandson of the ruling king always will. Besides that, the role of the sister of the future king is important because she will provide the heir.

If we apply this to the family relationships in our text, we see that Mursili, as grandson, is the next legitimate heir in line after Labarna. Moreover, it is possible to see the same order of succession in the past. Hattusili's grandfather, BU.LUGAL-MA, was king when he appointed another Labarna as his heir and adopted son (§20). In disobedience to the king's words however, the nobles enthroned the father of Hattusili, Papahdilmah. In the avunculate system the latter should have never become king, and Hattusili clearly disapproves of the enthronement of his father. With the accession of Hattusili, however, the legitimate order of succession was restored.

In the preceding paragraph two Labarnas are mentioned. Moreover, Hattusili refers to himself as Labarna too (§§21–3). Labarna, and its variant Tabarna, is probably a title by birth, and reserved for the king and the future king; that is, the sister-son of the ruling king.[69]

The preference for the sister-son instead of the own son must at least have been difficult to accept in the patrilinear system of the Hittites. That it often came to strife and murder is not surprising. The Old Hittite king Telipinu therefore introduced a reform of the rules of succession (see "The proclamation of Telipinu," §107 below).

General address to the army and dignitaries

Denouncement of the designated heir, Labarna

§1 (i/ii 1–7) [Gr]eat Ki[ng] Tabarna said to the entire army and the dignitaries:

I have become ill, (so) I introduced young Labarna to you: "He shall be enthroned." I, the king, called him my son, I continually instructed[70] *him, I looked after him constantly. He however showed himself a youth unfit to be seen, he did not cry, he was not kind. Cold he is! He is not kind of heart!*

§2 (i/ii 8–13) I, the king, apprehended him and had him brought to my couch: "Why? Should no one ever again raise his sister's son?"[71] *(But) he did not accept the advice of the king. The advice of his mother, (that) snake, that he accepted! His brothers and sisters sent cold(-hearted) messages to him, and he always listened to their words. However, I, the king heard (of it), and I entered into a lawsuit.*

§3 (i/ii 14–19) Enough (of it)! He is not my son (anymore)! But his mother bellowed like an ox: "They ripped my bull-calf[72] *[from] my living womb, they transferred him, and (now) you will kill him!" Did I, the king, do anything evil to him? Did I not [install him] as priest? I constantly singled him out for good treatment, but he did not show [kindness according to] the king's wishes. How then, could he have fondness for Hattusa out of (some) kindness of his [own heart]?*

Description of horrible future if Labarna becomes king

§4 (i/ii 20–5) His mother is a snake: (so) it will happen that he keeps listening to the words of his mother, his brothers and his sisters. He will approach and he will begin to take vengeance. Concerning [the troops,] dignitaries and servants; that is, those who "are put on" (= protect?) the king, [he will sw]ear: "They will die on account of the king!" Then it will happen that he will finish them off, and he will shed blood, and [he will] have [no] fear.

§5 (i/ii 26–9) And it will happen that he approaches those who are the citizens of Hatti as follows: he will draw near to [take away] cattle (and) sheep of whoever (owns them). [Now,] I [conquer]ed my foreign enemies, and I kept [my country] in peace. It may not happen that in the e[n]d he stirs up [my country]!

Banishment and settlement of Labarna

§6 (i/ii 30–6) But now, [he] shall in no way [go down] just like that (in exile from Hattusa). Hereby I have given my son Labarna an estate, I have given [him man]y [fields], I have given him many cattle, I have given [him man]y [sheep], so let him eat, let him drink. [And if he behaves well], he is allowed to come up from (his estate). [But] if he begins [to cause trouble (?)] or (to spread) some defa[mati]on [or] some [agitat]ion, he may not come up: he must [stay on his estate].

Installation of grandchild Mursili as designated heir and demand to support the young king

§7 (i/ii 37–41) Mursili is hereby my son. [Recognize] him instead. It is him you have to enthrone. [. . .]. [The go]d [installs] a(nother) li[on] in place of the lion. [If at some ti]me the call to arms go[es forth] o[r when] perhaps [a rebellion becom]es [serious], you, my servants and nobles must be [of assistance to my son].

§8 (ii 42–7) [When (it is) the] third [ye]ar, let him go on military campaign. [But already] n[ow] I make [a valiant kin]g [of him]. If, for the moment, (this is) not yet (so), [it will]b[e (so) later]. (Is) he [n]ot[73] *[amon]g the offspring of your king? Raise him (to be) your valian[t king]. Now, [i]f you take [hi]m on a campaign, bring [him] back [safely]. Let your "pack" be [united] like (that) of the wolf[, and] let [it] be [awe-]inspiring.*[74] *The subjects of the "number one"*[75] *(i.e., the alpha-wolf) are born [to one mothe]r.*

§9 (ii 48–52) A single liver, a single set of lungs, and a single [ear] have been allotted [to you]. [Don't] vie with another for preeminence. Let no one be hostile, and let [no]one transgress the command (of the king). Do [not] commit this [deed] of the cities Sinahuwa and Ubariya. May defamation never, ever sit right [with you]. My son will make . . . [. . .]

§10 (ii 53–7) [Let no o]ne say: "The king [will] secretly [do] (what is in) his heart. I will consider it right, whether it is true or not." May defamation never, ever sit right [with you]. You [who yourselves] now acknowledge my words and my wisdom in mind, instruct my son in wisdom!

§11 (ii 58–62) [Let] one [not] shove the other one behind, [let] one [not sho]ve the other one [to the fore (?)]. Let the elders not speak the(se) words: ["You (?)] called [u]s (?)." Let not the elders of Hattusa speak to you (sg.), neither [the lord of Kussar (?)], nor the lord of Hemmuwa, nor the lord of Tamalkiya, [nor the lord of Zalpa (?)], let not one of the population speak to you (sg.).

Exemplum 1: what happens if the royal offspring listens to the advice of others instead of accepting the words of the king

§12 (ii 63–7) [(For) consider] my [so]n Huzziya! I, the king, [appoint]ed him [as lord] over the city Tappassanda. They however got his attention and kept spreading slanders to him. They [act]ed [in a hostile fashion against me]: "Oppose the will of your father.

The [pa]laces that [(are) in Tappassanda], they [are] not [purified]. You must perform the purification."

§13 (ii 6874) But [when] I took hold of [Huzziy]a, the people of Hatti [too]k [up hostility even in Hattusa]. They got the attention of a daughter (of mine). Now, she [had male] offspring, [so] they acted in a hostile fashion [against me]: "[There is no male offspring] of your father [left for the throne]. [So now a serva]nt shall sit on (it), a servant [shall become king"]. Then [she made] Hattusa and the pal[aces disloyal]. [So the nobles] and my palace attendants acted in a hostile fashion [against me]. T[hus] she [in]cited [the entire land].

§14–15 (ii 75–83/iii 1–5) Too broken for translation. What is left of the text makes clear that the daughter caused the death of many inhabitants of Hatti, and that their possessions, such as servants, cattle, fields, gold, and silver, were confiscated.

§16 (iii 6–12a) When [I] hea[rd] [that] she had put the [citizen]s of Hatti to de[ath], I [av]enged your tears. If [I] had not aveng[ed] them, you would have slandered me with the tongue: "He let [his daughter (?)] go." But [I,] the king [. . .] nothing. [(So) she said:] "[Wh]y have you given me this little?" I[f] [I had not given (you) a] litt[le], [if] I [had] given you many cattle, had I given [you many] sheep, [I] would have d[runk] the blood (of the country).

§17 (iii 13–22) Too broken for translation. The lines that can be read descibe how the daughter ignored her father's commands and ravaged the country. It seems that she is expelled from the capital forever and that she has to stay on the countryside.

§18 (iii 23–5) You may [no]t harm [her]. She did harm, [but I] shall do no [harm in retu]rn. (Only this): She [did not call] me father, (so) I do not call her daughter.

Mursili is ordered to observe the words of the king

§19 (iii 26–32) [Until] now nobody [in my family] has accepted my will. [But now you,] Mursili, are [m]y [son], so it is you who must accept it. Observe [the wor]ds [of (your) father]. As long as you observe the words of (your) father, then you will [e]at [bread] and drink water.[76] When young adulthood is in your [heart], eat twice, thrice a day, and take care of yourself. But [when] old age is in your heart, then drink until satisfaction. Then you may discard (your) [father]'s word.

The first-ranking servants are ordered to observe the words of the king, with exemplum 2

§20 (iii 33–45) (And now) you who are my [fir]st-ranking servants: You must [obs]erve my, the king's words: then you will eat bread and drink water, and also Hattusa will stand tall and my country (will be) [peace]ful. But if you do not observe the words of the king, you will not remain alive in [Hattus]a, you will perish! [Anyone who might] contest the words of the king, let him as of right now [no longer be] my [so]n.[77] that one; and let him not [be] a first-ranking servant! They must slit [his throat (?)]. (As for) that (well-known fact): did n[ot] his sons set aside the words of my grandfather [BU.LUGAL-MA]? My grandfather had announced [Laba]rna as his (adopted) son in Sanahuitta. But [afterwards] his servants, the nobles, contested his words, and enthroned my [father] Papahdilmah. How many years have passed, and [how many] have escaped (their fate)? Where are the estates of the nobles? Have they not perished?

§21 (iii 46–54) You must observe my, the Great King Labarna's words. [As long as] you observe [th]em, Hattusa will stand tall and you will make your country [peacefu]l. You will eat bread and drink water. But if you do [not] observe (them), your country shall become another's. You must be reverent in the matter [of the gods]. Let their thick bread, their libation-vessels, and their [ste]w (and) groats stand ready. [Neither] postpone nor fall behind! If you were to [post]pone, evil would result, as in the past. Let it be just so!

Personal address to Mursili

§22 (iii 55–63) [The Gre]at [King] Labarna then turned to Mursili, his (adopted) son:

I have given you my words. Let them read this tablet in your presence every month, so that you will print my words and my wisdom in your heart. You shall reign in justice over my [servant]s and nobles: (If) you notice an offence in anyone, or someone offends before a deity, or someone speaks some (inapproriate) w[ord], (then) consult the advisory body. Let [also] (cases of) slander be turned over to only the advisory body. My son, act according to that which is in [your] heart.

Personal address to Hastayar

§23 (iii 64–73/iv 64–72) The Great King Labarna speaks to Hastayar:

Do not ignore me (that is, my admonitions). May the king not have to speak thus about her: "The palace attendants say: 'Now, this one is constantly consulting the "Old Women."'" Sh[ould] the king speak thus [to her]: "She now still consults the 'Old Women' (saying): I do not know"? Once more, do not ignore me! No! Always consult me, and I shall reveal my words to you.[78]

Wash me well, hold me to your breast, protect me from the earth (lying against) your breast.

(Akkadian colophon:) Tablet of Tabarna, Great King, when the Great King Tabarna fell ill in Kussar, and ordained young Mursili to kingship.

Further reading

Beal, R. H. (1983). "Studies in Hittite History." *Journal of Cuneiform Studies* 35: 115–26.

Beckman, G. (2000). "Bilingual Edict of Ḫattušili I." In COS 2, pp. 79–81.

Bin-Nun, Shoshana R. (1975). *The Tawananna in the Hittite Kingdom*. Texte der Hethiter 5. Heidelberg: Winter.

Bryce, Trevor R. (1983). *The Major Historical Texts of Early Hittite History*. Brisbane: University of Queensland, pp. 99–131.

Carruba, Onofrio (2002). "^{d}UTU^{ši}." In Stefano de Martino and Franca Pecchioli Daddi (eds.), *Anatolia Antica: Studi in memoria di Fiorella Imparati*. Eothen 11. Florence: LoGisma editore, pp. 145–54.

De Martino, S. and F. Imparati (1998). "Sifting through the Edicts and Proclamations of the Hittite Kings." In *Acts of the IIIrd International Congress of Hittitology*. Ankara, pp. 391–400.

De Roos, J. (2001). "Rhetoric in the S. C. Testament of Hattusilis I." In W. H. van Soldt et al. (eds.), *Veenhof Anniversary Volume: Studies Presented to klaas r. Veenhof on the Occasion of His Sixty-fifth Birthday*. Leiden: Nederlands Instituut voor het Nabije Oosten, pp. 401–6.

Goedegebuure, P. M. (forthcoming). "The Hittite Numeral 'one': *šia-*." In T. P. J. van den Hout (ed.), *Acts of the Symposium "The Life and Times of Hattusili III and Tuthaliya IV," Leiden, 12–13 December 2003* (provisional title).

Güterbock, H. G. and H. A. Hoffner (1989–). *The Hittite Dictionary of the Oriental Institute of the University of Chicago*. Chicago: University of Chicago Press.

Haas, V. (1994). *Geschichte der hethitischen Religion*. Leiden: Brill.

Marazzi, M. (1986). *Beiträge zu den akkadischen Texten aus Bogazköy in althethitischer Zeit*. Dipartimento di studi glottoantropologici universita "la sapienza": Rome: Biblioteca di Ricerche Linguistiche, pp. 1–23.

Melchert, H. Craig (ed.) (2003). *The Luwians*. Handbook of Oriental Studies 68. Leiden: Brill.

Sommer, F. and A. Falkenstein (1938). *Die Hethitisch-akkadische Bilingue des Hattušili I*. Abhandlungen der Bayrischen Akademie der Wissenschaften, NF 16. Munich: Verlag der Bayerischen akademie der wissenschaften.

Sürenhagen, D. (1998). "Verwandtschaftsbeziehungen und Erbrecht im althethitischen Königshaus vor Telipinu – ein erneuter Erklärungsversuch." *Altorientalische Forschungen* 25, pp. 75–94.

107. The proclamation of Telipinu (Goedegebuure)

The proclamation of king Telipinu (1525–1500 BC) is the most important source for the history of the Old Hittite Kingdom. The main purpose of the proclamation however is not historiographical but administrative. King Telipinu announces several administrative reforms, concerning, among others, the rules of succession to the throne (§28), judicial procedures (§§29–34), and food storage (§§37–40). The justification for these reforms is provided by the extended historical prologue (§§1–27).

The prologue gives an overview of the reigns and actions of the successive kings, starting with one of the earliest Hittite kings known by name, Labarna, and ending with the reign of Telipinu. It seems that only those actions are presented that support the measures taken by Telipinu as described in the second half of the document. The main lesson Telipinu wants to teach his people is that strife causes disaster, such as attacks from hostile countries, hunger, murder in the royal family, and so forth; whereas unity causes the land to prosper and to become or remain powerful.

One of the most serious threats to the stability of the Hittite kingdom was the repeated assassination of the ruling king or of the heir and his family. One of the most successful kings, Mursili, was assassinated by his brother-in-law Hantili and Hantili's son-in-law Zidanta (§§9–10). Hantili became king, but when he died Zidanta killed Hantili's son (§18) and usurped the throne. Of course, Zidanta did not live long enough to enjoy his position, for he was murdered by his own son Ammuna (§19). After a rather unsuccessful reign,

Ammuna died, leaving behind probably a few sons, who in turn were killed by the supporters of Huzziya, the next usurper (§§21–2). Then we finally arrive at Telipinu, who himself escaped from the murderous plots of Huzziya. After disposing of Huzziya, but not killing him, Telipinu became king.

Given these assassinations and fights for the right to sit on the throne, Telipinu's first reform is the establishment of the rules of succession to the throne (§28). The system he introduces is ~~patrilinear~~; that is, from father to son. This raises the question of how the succession to the throne was regulated in earlier times. An attractive solution is provided by Sürenhagen 1998, who suggests that the Hittite royal family was organized according to the principle of the "avunculate" (for a discussion of this system, see "The bilingual testament of Hattusili I," §106 above).

In short, the royal house consists of two ruling lines. Each ruling king raises his nephew, the son of his sister, to become king, and kingship always skips one generation.

In an otherwise patrilinear society the avunculate system must have been hard to bear, so at least some of the family members must have become quite predatory. This might explain the assassinations by members of the royal family. It seems that Telipinu wanted to adjust the rules of succession to the patrilinear principle. After his reform, however, kingship was taken away forever from the other ruling line. This unpleasant demotion was probably not taken lightly by the former ruling line, so intrigue and usurpation continued after the death of Telipinu.

The historical prologue mostly discusses internal affairs, but there are a few references to foreign countries and peoples. There is, however, only one international synchronism, the destruction of Babylon by Mursili. This raid is mentioned in a Babylonian Chronicle: "In the time of Samsuditana, the Man of Hatti marched against Akkad" (Bryce 1983: 143). This probably took place around 1595 BC (§9) (Beckman 2000: 23).

The importance of the proclamation not only in Old Hittite times but also in the empire period is illustrated by the fact that 10 Hittite copies (and 2 Akkadian copies) from the empire period have been found. It is clear from the sources of that time that the rules of succession to the throne indeed had become patrilinear.

Introduction

§1 (i 1–4) [Thus] (speaks) the Tabarna, Telipinu, Great King.

Historical prologue: Labarna

[O]nce, Labarna was Great King. His [son]s, his [brother]s, and also his in-laws, his kin and his troops were united.

§2 (i 5–6) The country was small but wherever he went on campaign, he held the enemy lands subdued by force.

§3 (i 7–9) He destroyed the lands one by one, he made the lands powerless, and he made them the borders of the sea. And each time he returned from campaign, each of his sons went somewhere to a country.

§4 (i 10–12) Hupisna, Tuwanuwa, Nenassa, Landa, Zallara, Parsuhanta, Lusna[79] *were the countries they each governed, and the great cities made progress.*

Historical prologue: Hattusili

§5 (13–16) Afterwards, Hattusili was king. Also his sons, brothers, in-laws, and his kin and his troops were united. Wherever he went on campaign, he too held the enemy lands subdued by force.

§6 (i 17–20) He destroyed the lands one by one, he made the lands powerless, and he made them the borders of the sea. And each time he returned from campaign, each of his sons went somewhere to a country. Also under his rule the great cities made progress.

§7 (i 21–3) But when later the servants of the princes became corrupt, they began to devour their (i.e. the princes') estates, they began to conspire against their lords and they began to shed their (text: "our") blood.

Historical prologue: Mursili

§8 (i 24–7) When Mursili was king in Hattusa, then also his sons, brothers, in-laws, and his kin and his troops were united. He held the enemy lands subdued by force. He destroyed the lands one by one, he made the lands powerless, and he made them the borders of the sea.

§9 (i 28–31) He went to the city of Halpa.[80] *He destroyed Halpa and brought Halpa's deportees (and) its spoils to Hattusa. Later he went to Babylon, and destroyed Babylon*[81] *and also fought the Hurrian [troops]. He kept the deportees (and) spoils of Babylon in Hat[ti-land].*[82]

§10 (i 31–2) Now, Hanti[li] was a Cupbearer. He had Har[apsi]li, Mursili's sister as wife. – [Zidanta, the . . . , had . . .]a, Hantili's daughter [as wife] –

Historical prologue: Hantili

§11 (i 32–4) Zidanta united with Hantili, and they [ma]de evil cau[se]. They killed Mursili and (thus) committed a crime of blood.

§12 (i 35–8) [Han]tili became afraid: "Will I be [prot]ected?" [The go]ds pro[tect]ed him. Wherever (he) went [on campaign (?)], the populati[on surrendered]: the cities of As[tat]a, [Sukz]iya, Hurpana, (and) Kargami[s[83]*] began to [give troops to Hatt]i (?). [. . .] the troops.*

§13 (i 39–42) But [when H]antili arrived in Tagarama,[84] *[he began . . .] to [say]: "Why have I done this? I hearkened [to the words of] Zidan[ta, m]y [son-in-law!]" [Now, as soon as] he [reign]ed [as king], the gods started to seek (revenge for) the blood [of Mursili].*

§14 (i 43–6)[85] *[The gods s]ummoned the Hurrian [tro]ops, foxes hunting in the bushes. [When the Hurrian enemy (?)] came [t]o the l[and] of Hatti, [. . .]. [The enemy] roamed the [co]untry. [But then the gods (?)]summoned [his (defeat)], and he [ca(me) no more (?)].*

§15 (i 47–52)[86] *(The Hittite text is almost completely lost. The translation is based on the Akkadian text). [Then Hantili said: "Look! The gods (?)] have driven the*

Hurrians away from my country." [. . . brought Harapsil]i and her children to the city of Sugazziya. [But then Hara]psili, the queen, fell ill. [. . .] Ilaliumma, the Pa[lace] Attendant, after her. [. . .] . . . the Palace people of [Suga]zziya [. . .]. [. . .] continually demands [in the city . . .]anda: "Now, [. . . to m]e!"

§16 (i 53–7) [. . . said: "(She is your enemy!) . . .] The queen of [Sukzi]ya [said: ("She is my enemy")]. [The que]en[87] *began [to] die. [Ilal]iuma secretly sent out palace attendants. [He ordered: ("Arrest the queen!)] The queen of Sukziya must die!"*[88] *[They] a[rrested] her [and kil]led [her with her children].*

§17 (58–62) When Hantili inquired (into the case of) the queen of Su[kziya and her children]: "Who kill[ed] them?" the Chief of the Palace Attendants brought word. They gathered [her] family and [brought] them to Taga[laha]. (Then) they chased them into the bushes, and they d[ied].

§18 (i 63–5) Now, when Hantili had become old and started to "become a god" (= to die), Zidanta killed [Piseni],[89] *son of Hantili, together with his sons, and he also killed his first-ranking servants.*

Historical prologue: Zidanta

§19 (i 66–8) So now Zidanta had become king. But the gods started to seek the blood of Piseni. The gods made Ammuna, his (i.e., Zidanta's) son, his enemy, and he killed Zidanta, his father.

Historical prologue: Ammuna

§20 (i 69–71) So now Ammuna had become king. But the gods started to seek the blood of Zidanta, his father. They did not [let prosper (?)] grain, vines, oxen, sheep in his hand. [. . .] in the hand.

§21 (ii 1–7) The land became hostile towards him: the cities of . . . agga, [Mat]ila, Galmiya, Adaniya,[90] *Arzawiya,*[91] *Sallapa, Parduwata and Ahhulla. But wherever (his) troops went on campaign, they did not come back succesfully. Now, when Ammuna had become god (i.e., he died), Zuru, Chief of the Royal Bodyguard, in those same days secretly sent his natural son Tahurwaili*[92] *Man of the Gold Spear, and he killed the family of Titti, together with his sons.*

Historical prologue: Huzziya

§22 (ii 8–12) He also sent Taruhsu, a courier: he killed Hantili together with [his] sons. (Then) Huzziya became king, and Telipinu had Istapariya, his sister of first rank (as wife). Huzziya would have killed them, but the matter became known, and Telipinu chased them away.

§23 (ii 13–15) As for his five brothers, he assigned estates to them: "Let them go settle (there). Let them eat (and) drink!" No o[ne] may harm them! I declare: "They harmed me, but I shall not harm them."

Historical prologue: Telipinu

§24 (ii 16–19) After I, Telipinu, sat down on the throne of my father, I went on campaign against the city of Hassuwa,[93] *and I destroyed Hassuwa. My army was in the city of Zizzilippa as well, and in Zizzilippa a battle took place.*

§25 (ii 20–5) When I, the king came to Lawazzantiya,[94] *Lahha was [hostile to me], and he made Lawazantiya rebellious. [The gods] put him in my hand. Of the first-ranking (ones) there (were) many, the Overseer-of-1,000 [Tarhu- . . .], Karruwa, the Overseer-of-the-Chamberlains Inara, the Overseer-of-the-Cupbearers Kill[a, the Overseer-of-the-X], Tarhumimma, the Overseers-of-the-Staffbearers, Zinwaseli and Lelli, and they sent secretly for Tanuwa, the Staffbearer.*

§26 (ii 26–30) I[, the kin]g did not know (about it). [He killed H]u[zz]iy[a], and his brothers in addition. When I, the king heard (of it), they brought Tanuwa, Tahurwaili [and] Taruhs[u] (up on charges), and the Council condemned them to death. But I, the king, said: "[Wh]y should they die? They shall "hide the eyes" concerning them."[95] *I, the king made them into re[al] farmers: I took their weapons away from their shoulders and gave them a yok[e (?)].*

§27 (ii 31–5) And bloodshed became widespread even within the royal family. Istap[a]riya, the queen, died. Afterwards it came to pass that Ammuna, the prince, died. Also the "Men of the Gods" each said: "Bloodshed has now become widespread in Hattusa." Then I, Telipinu, summoned an assembly in Hattusa. From this moment on in Hattusa, no one shall do evil to a son of the (royal) family and draw a dagger on him.

Reform: ~~succession to the throne~~

§28 (ii 36–9) King shall become a son (who is) a prince of first rank only. If there is no first rank prince, he who is a second rank son, he shall become king. But if there is no prince (among the ranks of) heir(s), then they shall take an in-marrying (son-in-law) for a daughter of first rank, and he shall become king.

Reform: ~~no more disposing of opponents~~

§29 (ii 40–5) In the future, as for the one who will become king after me: let his brothers, his sons, his in-laws, his kin and his troops be united! Thereupon you will hold the countries of the enemies subdued by force. But do not speak as follows: "I will thoroughly 'clean up,'"[96] *for will you not "clean up" yourself, and even bring yourself under siege?*[97] *Do not kill anyone of (your) family for your own purposes, (it is) not right!*

§30 (ii 46–9) Furthermore, whoever becomes king and seeks evil against (his) brother (and) sister, now you are his Council, and you must speak freely to him: "This is a matter of blood." Look at the tablet! "Formerly bloodshed in Hattusa was excessive, and the gods took it out on the royal family."

Reform: ~~fair trial for opponents, protection of their famili~~es

§31 (ii 50–8) Concerning anyone among both brothers and sisters who might do evil and lays eyes on the king's head: you must summon the assembly. If he is found guilty, he shall pay with his head. But they shall not kill secretly, like Zuruwa, Danuwa, Tahurwaili and Taruhsu. They shall not commit evil against his house, his wife (and) his children. So, if a prince sins, he shall just pay with his head, they shall not commit evil against his house and his children. For whatever reason princes might die, (it does) not (concern) their estates, their fields, their vineyards, their male (and) female servants, their cattle (and) their sheep.

§32 (ii 59–65) So now, if some prince sins, he shall just pay with his head, they shall not commit evil against his house and his son. Giving (away) a princes' blade of straw (or) a chip of wood is not right. Those who commit these evil deeds, the Chiefs [of Staff], the Major-Domos, the Chief of the Palace Attendants, the Chief of the Royal Bodyguard and the Chief-of-the-Wine: [if] they desire to take the estates of a prince and [s]ay thus: "I wish that city to be mine," then he commits evil against the lord of the city.

Reform: the Council must arrest renegade Chiefs

§33 (ii 66–73) But now, from this day onward in Hattusa, it is you, palace attendants, royal bodyguards, golden-chariot fighters, cupbearers, ta[ble serv]ers, cooks, staffbearers, horse attendants, commanders of a field batallion, who must remember this matter: let Tanuwa, Tahurwaili, and Taruhsu be a warning to you. If someone commits evil again, either the Major Domo or the Chief of the Palace Attendants, the [Chief-of-the-W]ine, the Chief of the Royal Bodyguard, the Chief of the Commanders of a Field Batallion, be he of lowest (or) of highest rank, now you, the Council, must seize (him) and devour him with your teeth!

Reform: the Chiefs must . . . the subordinates (?)

§34 (iii 1–3) In Hattusa the Chiefs; that is, the Major-Domos, the Chief of the Palace Attendants, the Chief-of-the-Wine, the Chief of the Royal Body[guard], the Chief of the Chariot Fighters, the Overseer of the Military Herald[s], those who are the Chiefs on the [royal e]state, each must take his subordinates [. . .] . . .

Rules concerning the protection of cities

§35 (iii 4–6) Now, in [(the territory of) Hat]tusa the fortified cities (must be) protected. Do (sg.) not leave them! The fortified cities [. . . w]ater, you must divert it 10 times (to) 20 times to the grain.

§36 (iii 7–8) Barely preserved. "Telipinu, Great King" is mentioned.

§36a (iii 9–16). Hardly anything preserved.

Reform: food storage

§37 (iii 17–33) Fragmentarily preserved. Lists 60 + x? cities that contain storage houses.

§38 (iii 34–42) Fragmentarily preserved. Lists 34 cities that contain storage houses for (fodder) mix.

§39 (iii 43–8) I accumulated crops back there. [What fields are assigne]d (??), [let] the farmers . . . [. . .] only those fields[, and] let them seal [the grain (?)]. Only those the population [may] . . . [. . .]. [Let] them [not] contrive deception. Glaringly, they used to tie up either 1 cubits or 2 cubits. They drank out the country's blood. But let them not do (so) now! Whoever does (so), they must give him a frightful death.

§40 (iii 49–54) In the future, whoever becomes king after me, you must always seal the grai[n (stores)] with your (pl.) name. The administrators of the store houses will thereby leave you, and they will speak to you as follows: "[There (is) n]ot [. . .]. Do

not seal ....[98] [......] seal [it (?)]. They will hereby lif[t] you, [...... they shall (?) no]t liv[e ......].

§41 (iii 55–60) Except for a few traces not preserved.

§42 (iii 61–3) Except for a few traces not preserved.

§43 (iii 64–8) Except for a few traces not preserved.

Reform?

§44 (iii 69–75) [Who from n]ow on [becomes king after] m[e . . .] humilia[tes acr]oss (?) [. . . and] says thus to [y]ou: ["...."], now you do not listen! When [you have] harnesse[d] a deportee, you must always compensate the equipment. The troop[s . . .], [you must . . .] him either to your wife or [. . .].

§45 (iv 1–8) Completely lost

§46 (iv 9–14) Too fragmentary to be translated.

Reform: inheritance

§47 (iv 15–20) Too fragmentary to be translated.

§48 (iv 21–6) [Lat]er on, however, when the karpinatti[s] of the mortals took to di[vi]ding [. . .], they [were] oh so disr[espectful], and therefore they were[99] struck by the god(s). But now, [from] now on . . .], if he [so]mehow calls on them; that is, (his) living parents, [because of] (his) share, –whatever he demands to share–, they must cast (him) out of the house, and he must forfeit his own share.

Rules concering murder/manslaughter

§49 (iv 27–9) Now, the procedure in case of bloodshed (is) as follows: whoever commits bloodshed, only (that) which the "lord of the blood" says (will happen). If he says: "He shall die," then he dies, but if he says: "He shall compensate," then he compensates. However, for the king (there will be) nothing.

Rules concerning sorcery

§50 (iv 30–4) (Regarding cases) of sorcery in Hattusa: you must keep cleaning up (all) instances (thereof). Whoever among the members of the royal family is proficient in sorcery, you seize him from the family, and bring him to the palace gate. But [who]ever does not bring him, for that man[100] a frightful end will come.

Colophon

§51 (iv 35–6) First tablet of Telipinu. Finished.

Further reading

Beckman, Gary (2000). "Hittite Chronology." *Akkadica* 119–20: 19–32.

Bryce, Trevor R. (1983). *The Major Historical Texts of Early Hittite History.* Brisbane: University of Queensland, pp. 99–131.

—— (1998). *The Kingdom of the Hittites*. Oxford: Oxford University Press.
Hoffman, Inge (1984). *Der Erlaß Telipinus*. Texte der Hethiter 11. Heidelberg: Winter.
Soysal, O. (1990). "Noch einmal zur Šukziya-Episode im Erlaß Telipinus." *Orientalia* NS, 59: 271–9.
Starke, Frank (1985). "Der Erlaß Telipinus: Zur Beurteilung der Sprache des Textes anläßlich eines kürzlich erschienenen Buches." *Die Welt des Orients* 16: 100–13.
Sürenhagen, D. (1998). "Verwandtschaftsbeziehungen und Erbrecht im althethitischen Königshaus vor Telipinu – ein erneuter Erklärungsversuch." *Altorientalische Forschungen* 25: 75–94.
Van den Hout, T. P. J. (1997). "The Proclamation of Telipinu." In William W. Hallo (ed.), COS 1, 194–8.

108. CTH 40: Manly Deeds of Shuppiluliuma (excerpts) (Hazenbos)

The narration of the exploits of the Hittite king Shuppiluliuma I, called "Manly Deeds of Shuppiluliuma" by the Hittites, was not written in the days of Shuppiluliuma himself. It is his son and indirect successor Murshili II who is the narrator of this text. The first person in the narration therefore is Murshili, Shuppiluliuma being referred to as "my father."

Shuppiluliuma (reign about the third quarter of the fourteenth century BC), the founding father of the New Hittite Empire, had become king by violence. He had to dispose of his brother Tudkhaliya the Younger before he could ascend the throne in Khattusha. His reign was a powerful one. Shuppiluliuma was able to reestablish Hittite power in Anatolia and even add new territory to the empire. He succeeded in making the Hurrian kingdom of Mittani (in northern Mesopotamia and Syria) and various kingdoms in Syria subordinate to Khattusha. In doing so, he increased the strategical and economical strength of the Hittite Empire, which by now had become a notable political power of the Near East, a rival to Egypt, Assyria, and Babylonia.

As we have seen, the work "Manly Deeds of Shuppiluliuma" was not composed until after Shuppiluliuma's death, during the reign of Murshili II. Its author or authors could rely on earlier sources, however. Fragments of another historiographical work on Shuppiluliuma have been preserved. They are to be ascribed to Arnuwanda II, who reigned a short period between Shuppiluliuma I and Murshili II. It is quite possible that Shuppiluliuma himself also had a work on his reign written, but if this work existed, we don't have any fragments of it.

One of the colophons of the "Manly Deeds" mentions that the text had to be laid down on a bronze tablet. This piece seems to be lost forever, but numerous clay tablet fragments belonging to the text survive. The composition as a whole, which according to the colophons must have consisted of more than seven tablets, is far from being totally preserved. Yet, in the first comprehensive edition of the "Manly Deeds" (1956, see "Further reading") H. G. Güterbock could reconstruct many, often large, fragments, many of them preserved in various manuscripts. This edition is still seminal, and in referring to parts of the "Manly Deeds" we still use Güterbock's fragment count.

The parts presented here in translation describe how Shuppiluliuma pacified Anatolia by defeating the Gashgaeans (whom the Hittites never succeeded in defeating entirely), and how he undertook an expedition to Syria against the Hurrians. The last part contains the famous episode of the Egyptian queen asking Shuppiluliuma for a son of his to become her husband.

Fragment 1 (introduction in manuscript F)

(F I 1) [These are the words of His Majesty, Great King Murshili, king of the country of Khattusha, h]e[ro(?), son of Shuppiluliuma, king of the country of Kh]attusha, h[ero, grandson of Tudkhaliya, k]ing of the country of Khatt[usha, hero].

From Fragment 28

(Line count after manuscript A) *(A I 1) Then he went back to Mount Zukkuki and fortified two towns: Atkhulishsha and Tukhupurpuna. While he was fortifying these towns, the enemy was boasting: "We shall let him come down into the country of Almina in no way!" Yet, when he had finished fortifying the towns and had come into Almina, no enemy offered him further resistance in battle.*

(A I 9) He went and began fortifying Almina. In the rear, in the army an epidemic broke out. My father took a stand on Kuntiya Mountain, Chief Commander Khimuili held a position at the Shariya river, and Marshal Khanutti held a position in the town of Parparra, whereas the engineering corps kept on fortifying Almina. Now, because the country of the Gashga had been entirely pacified, the Hittite population in the towns of the Gashga partly held their inn in the towns again, and partly had returned to their town.

(A I 18) When the Gashgaeans had seen there was an epidemic in the army, they seized the population that had gone back into their towns. And they killed one part of them, the other part they seized. The enemy now arrived at night and split up: they went for battle to all the forts that were being held by the lords. And to whichever forts they went for battle, the gods of my father ran before the lords, so that they defeated them all. The enemy died in large numbers. No one resisted the [f]o[r]t of my father. W[h]en [m]y fath[er] had slain the enemy, the Gashgaean enemy in their entirety feared him.

(A I 31) And while he was fortifying the town of Almina, he sent out Urawanni and [Chi]ef of the Herdsmen Kuwal[anaziti] to attack the country of Kashula. The gods of my father ran before them, and they conquered the country of Kashula completely. They brought its inhabitants, oxen and sheep before my father. The deporte[es] t[hey] brought amounted to one thousand.

(A I 37) My father conquered the country of Tumanna completely. He rebuilt and reestablished it, and made it part of the country of Khattusha again.

(A I 40) Then he came back to Khattusha to pass the winter there. But as soon as he had finished celebrating the Festival of the Year, he went to the country of Ishtakhar[a]. Since the Gashgaean enemy [had] taken Ishtakhara, [Hi]ttite territory, [my father] drove the enemy out of it. Then he rebuilt the town of x[- . . .], the town

of Manaziya[na(?)], the town of Kalimuna and the town of [. . .]-x-da. [. . .]. He reestablished them, and [m]ade them part o[f the country of Khattusha] again. And as he had [ree]stablished the [country of Ishtakhara], he came back to Khatt[usha] to [pass the wint]er there.

(Rest of column I in manuscript A blank.)

(A II 1) Tribal troops now arriv[ed] in great numbers and [made] an incursion on his army at night. The gods of my father now ra[n] before my brother,[101] *so that he conquered the enemy tribal troops and [slew] them. And as he had conquered the tribal troops, and [the count]ry o[f the enemy] saw him, they became afraid. The countries of Arz[iy]a and Kargamish, all of them, made peace with him, and the town of Murmuriga made peace with him. In the country of Kargamish, only one town, the town of Kargamish, did not make peace with him. The Priest, my brother, left six(?) hundred men of the infantry and horse-troops, as well as the army's Overseer of Ten Lupakki in the country of Murmuriga. The Priest came to Khattusha with the intention of meeting my father. But my father was in the town of Uda to celebrate festivals. So he met him there.*

(A II 15) Now, as the Hurrians had seen the Priest leaving, the Hurrian infantry and horse-troops – and the Amumikuni[102] *Takukhli was among them – came and surrounded Murmuriga. They held the infantry and horse-troops that were Hittite in check.*

(A II 21) The Egyptian infantry and horse-troops now came, and they attacked the country of Kadesh, that my father had conquered. A message was brought to my father: "The Hurrians hold the infantry and horse-troops surrounded, which are up in Murmuriga." So my father mobilized infantry and horse-troops, and marched against the Hurrians. As soon as [he had] arrived in the country of Tegarama, he held a review of his infantry and horse-troops in the town of Talpa. Then he sent his son Arnuwanda and the Chief of the Body Guard Zit[a] in advance from Tegarama to the Hurrian country. And as [Arnuwa]nda and Zita arrived down there in the country, [the enemy] came against them in a battle. [The gods] of my father now ran in front of Zita and Arnuwanda, so that they [defeated the enemy]. But the enemy [. . .] below the town, and he now went [t]o [escape from below the town(?)]. [. . . the mounta]ins(?) of the country of Tegarama. [. . .] Now, [a]s [my father he]ard: "[He] is already [go]ing(?), and he will escape from below the town." – [a]s my father [c]ame down to the country, he did [n]ot come upon the enemy from the Hurrian country. So he went [dow]n to the town of Kargamish and surrou[nd]ed it. (The text now becomes fragmentary.)

(A III 1) While he was down in Kargamish, my father sent out Lupakki and Tarkhuntazalma to the country of Amka. They went and attacked Amka, and brought deportees, oxen and sheep back before my father. And when the Egyptians had heard about the attack on Amka, they became afraid. As their lord Nipkhururiya had died just then, the queen of Egypt (who was Dakhamunzu) sent a messenger to my father and wrote to him in the following way: "My husband has died, and I have no son. People often say that you have a lot of sons. If you would give me one son of yours, he would become my husband. I do not intend to select a servant of mine in order to make him my husband. I am afraid of a stigma(?)!" As soon as my father had heard this message, he invited the Great Ones to a meeting, and said: "Such a thing has never happened to me before!" Finally my father sent out the chamberlain Khattushaziti

with this order: "Go and bring a reliable report back to me! Maybe they are setting a trap for me. Maybe they do have a son of their lord. You bring a reliable report back to me!"

(The text now describes the victory of Shuppiluliuma in Kargamish before it takes up the Egyptian affair again.)

(E3 III 24) And as it ha[d] become spring, Khattushaziti [came back] from Egypt, and an Egyptian messenger, Lord Khani, came together with him. Now my father had given Khattushaziti the following instructions while sending him to Egypt: "Maybe they do have a son of their lord, they are setting a trap for me and are not wishing a son of mine for kingship." Therefore the Egyptian queen now wrote back to my father on a clay tablet: "Why have you spoken to me like that: 'They are setting a trap for me.'? If I would have had a son, would I then have written to another country about the humiliation of myself and of my country? You did not trust / believe(?) me, and you have even spoken to me like that. The man, who was my husband, has died. I have no son, and I do not intend to take a servant of mine in order to make him my husband. I have not written to any other country, to you I have written. People often say that you have a lot of sons. Give me one son of yours. He will be my husband, and king in Egypt!" And since my father was a kind man, he complied with the word of the woman, and concerned himself with the matter of a son.

(Manuscript A has colophon [A IV 16–18] *"Seventh tablet; not finished. Not yet written on a bronze tablet." After a gap continued in manuscript E3.*)

(E3 IV 1) (Shuppiluliuma is speaking to Khani) *". . . [I] was friendly. [Y]ou suddenly treated [me] badly. You [. . .]. You attacked the man of Kadesh, whom I had [taken away] from the king of the country of Khurri. [As soon a]s I heard this, I became angry. I [sent] out my infantry, chariotry and Lords. They came and attacked the country of Amka, your [count]ry. [May]be you got afraid because they attacked your [country of Amk]a, and for that reason you keep on asking for a son of mine, so that [h]e will become a hostage somehow. But you will not make him your [kin]g!" [Kh]ani said to my father: "My lord! That [. . .] the humiliation of [o]ur country. Would we have come to [a]n[o]ther country and have kept on asking for a lord of ours, if a prince of ours had existed? Nipkhururiya, who used to be our lord, has died. He had no so[n]. Our lord's wife is a [w]idow. We keep on asking for a son of you, our lord, to assume kingship in Egypt, and we keep on asking for him to become husband to the woman, our lady. Up till now we haven't gone to any other country, we have come only here! Give us a son of yours, our lord!"*

(E3 IV 25) Now for them my father concerned himself again with the matter of a son. He asked again for the tablet with the treaty, describing how formerly the storm-god had taken people of the city of Kurushtama, Hittites, had carried them to Egypt, and had made them Egyptians; how the storm-god had concluded a treaty between the countries of Egypt and Khattusha, and how they cherished a long-lasting friendship between them. And then, as they had read aloud the tablet in their presence, my father said to them: "In [o]ld times Khattusha and Egypt cherished a friendship between them. Now this, too, has [happ]ened between us. The countries of Khattusha [and] Egyp[t] will furthermore cheri[sh] a [long]-lasting friendship between them!"

Further reading

Bryce, T., *The Kingdom of the Hittites* (Oxford: Clarendon, 1998), 168–205 (ch. 7).
Cancik, H., *Grundzüge der hethitischen und alttestamentlichen Geschichtsschreibung. Abhandlungen des deutschen Palästinavereins* (Wiesbaden: Harrassowitz, 1976), 151–84.
Güterbock, H. G., "Hittite Historiography," in H. Tadmor and M. Weinfeld (eds.), *History, Historiography and Interpretation: Studies in Bibliography and Cuneiform Literatures* (Jerusalem: Magnes, 1983), 21–35.
Güterbock, H. G., "The Deeds of Šuppiluliuma as Told by His Son, Mursili II," *Journal of Cuneiform Studies* 10 (1956): 41–68, 75–98, 107–30.
Hoffner, H. A., Jr., "Deeds of Šuppiluliuma," in COS 1, 185–92.
Hoffner, H. A., Jr., "Histories and Historians of the Ancient Near East: The Hittites," *Orientalia* 49 (1980): 283–332.
Hout, T. P. J. van den, "Der Falke und das Küken: der neue Pharao und der hethitische Prinz?" *Zeitschrift für Assyriologie und Vorderasiatische Archäologie* 84 (1994): 60–88.
Klengel, H., *Geschichte des hethitischen Reiches*. Handbuch der Orientalistik 1/34 (Leiden: Brill, 1999), 135–68 (ch. IV.1).

109. The tribute agreement between Šuppiluliuma of Ḫatti and Niqmaddu of Ugarit (Cohen)

The Hittite kingdom saw a decline of its power during the sixteenth and the fifteenth centuries, as it was eclipsed by the rise of the Hurrian state of Mittanni. However, it was to regain its status, with the ascendancy of a young and energetic Hittite king, Šuppiluliuma I, on the onset of the fourteenth century. Šuppiluliuma brought about the demise of Mittanni, and advancing into North Syria, displayed his might, enough to intimidate the local principalities. These principalities, such as Nuḫašše, which was under the sway of Mittanni, or Amurru, under the Egyptian sphere of power, were all eventually to fall under Hittite rule. Each of those signed a treaty with the Hittites that acknowledged the rule of the Hittite king, and promised loyalty to the Hittite royal house for generations to come.

The city of Ugarit, a wealthy emporium on the Syrian coast, also received its own treaty of stipulations, following its surrender before the Hittite king (see Beckman 1999: 34–6). Ugarit's treaty was supplemented by the Tribute Agreement between Šuppiluliuma of Ḫatti and Niqmaddu of Ugarit. This agreement opens with an historical prologue, which relates how the king of Ugarit, Niqmaddu, refrained from opening hostilities against Šuppiluliuma, despite the pressure from the neighboring kings, thus winning the Hittite king's good favor. The document continues by detailing the exact amount of tribute that Niqmaddu has to deliver to the Hittite king and his queen, to the crown prince, and finally, to various top officials. The agreement closes with a description of Niqmaddu's willful capitulation in the presence of the Hittite king. The thousand gods (of Ḫatti) bear witness to the contents of the tablet, while the major deities of both Ugarit and Ḫatti ensure that it will not be changed in the future.

(1–2) Thus says His Majesty, Šuppiluliuma, Great King, King of Ḫatti, the Brave.

(3–6) When all the kings of Nuḫašše and the king of Mukiš were hostile to His Majesty, the Great King, their lord, Niqmaddu, the king of Ugarit, was at peace, and not hostile to His Majesty, his lord. (7–11) Then the kings of Nuḫašše and the king of Mukiš put pressure on Niqmaddu, king of Ugarit, saying so: "why are you not hostile to His Majesty, along with the rest of us?" (12–14) However, Niqmaddu refused to become hostile to His Majesty, the Great King, his lord. (14–20) Then His Majesty, the Great King, saw the loyalty of Niqmaddu; so Šuppiluliuma, Great King, King of Hatti, thus concluded a treaty with Niqmaddu, king of Ugarit, saying Your tribute to His Majesty, the Great King, your lord, is (as follows):

(21–4) 12 talents and 20 "big" shekels of gold, one gold vessel, its weight a talent, are the principal part of the tribute; 4 linen cloths, 1 big linen cloth, 500 (shekels) of blue wool, 500 (shekels) of red wool for His Majesty, the Great King, his lord.

(25–6) One gold vessel, its weight 30 (shekels), 1 linen cloth, 100 (shekels) of blue wool, [100 (shekels)] of red wool for the queen.

(27–8) [One] gold vessel, its weight 30 (shekels), 1 linen cloth, 100 (shekels) of blue wool, 100 (shekels) of red wool for the crown prince.

(29–30) One silver vessel, its weight 30 (shekels), one linen cloth, 100 (shekels) of blue wool, 100 (shekels) of red wool for the chief scribe.

Here the tribute list continues, detailing the quantities Niqmaddu has to give to additional Hittite top officials. Then Šuppiluliuma assures that no additional demands will be put toward Niqmaddu, once the tribute is delivered.

(38–42) No one among the dignitaries of His Majesty, the Great King, his lord, will extract from Niqmaddu anything else in addition to his payment, on the day when Niqmaddu delivers his tribute.

(43–6) And so, His Majesty, the Great King, saw the loyalty of Niqmaddu when Niqmaddu came up to him and groveled at the feet of His Majesty, the Great King, his lord.

(46–8) Then His Majesty, the Great King, his lord, gave him this treaty.

(48–50) May the thousand gods (of Ḫatti) know about the contents written on this tablet.

(50–3) May the sun-god of the sky, the sun-goddess! of Arinna, the storm-god of the sky, (and) the storm-god of Ḫatti, recognize (and inflict punishment on) him who will have the contents of this tablet changed.

Bibliography

Sources: CTH 47 (= RS 17.227, RS 17.373, RS 17.330+, RS 17.300)
First edition: Nougayrol 1956: 40–4.
Literature: Beckman 1999: 166–7; Dietrich and Loretz 1964–6; Lackenbacher 2002: 73–5; van Soldt 1990; Singer 1999.

Beckman, G. 1999. *Hittite Diplomatic Texts*. 2nd ed. Atlanta.
Dietrich, M. and Loretz, O. 1964–6. Der Vertrag zwischen Šuppiluliuma und Niqmandu: Eine philologische und kulturhistorische Studie. *Die Welt des Orients* 3: 206–45.
Lackenbacher, S. 2002. *Textes Akkadiens d'Ugarit*. Paris.
Nougayrol, J. 1956. *Le Palais Royal d'Ugarit IV: Textes accadiens des archives sud*. (Mission de Ras Shamra 9 = PRU IV). Paris.

Singer, I. 1999. A Political History of Ugarit. In W. G. E. Watson and N. Wyatt (eds.) *Handbook of Ugaritic Studies*. Handbuch der Orientalistik 39. Leiden: Brill, 603–733.
van Soldt, W. 1990. Fabrics and Dyes at Ugarit. *Ugarit Forschungen* 22: 321–57.

110. The end of Mittani (CTH 51.I) (Hazenbos)

The Hurrian kingdom of Mittani, situated in the northern parts of Syria and Mesopotamia, probably came into existence in the first half of the sixteenth century BC. Before that, Hittite texts already report on contacts with Hurrians in Syria, who seem not to be united in a single empire yet. Late seventeenth-century texts from North-Syrian Tikkunani, a town with a strongly Hurrian-flavored population, confirm this impression. With the unification of small entities into the Mittani Empire a new Ancient Near Eastern superpower had entered the stage. It would not take long before the Hittites would sense the consequences of this development.

During the sixteenth century, Mittanian influence grew gradually stronger. The South Anatolian district of Kizzuwatna made itself independent from the Hittite Empire, and in Syria the once powerful city of Khalab/Aleppo, conquered by the Hittite king Murshili I during his raid on Babylon, became part of the Mittani Empire. In the fifteenth century and the first half of the fourteenth century the Hittites were mostly absent from the Syrian front. Egypt and Mittani had divided Syria among themselves: the southern parts of Syria fell under Egyptian rule, whereas North Syria was dominated by Mittani. The coexistence of Egypt and Mittani was often violent, but in the first half of the fourteenth century the two empires were linked through dynastic marriages, and established peaceful contacts between them.

With the accession of Shuppiluliuma I to the throne a long period of Hittite weakness on the international scene came to an end. Shuppiluliuma was a successful conqueror, and thanks to a combination of military successes and the building-up of a strong diplomatic network the Hittites soon acquired a firm hold on North Syria. One of Shuppiluliuma's victims was the Mittani Empire, which went through a period of weakness at the very same time the Hittite Empire increased its power. Shuppiluliuma aptly made use of the Mittanian weaknesses: by intrigue he strengthened the inner-dynastic strifes in Mittani. The flight of the Mittanian prince Shattiwaza to Khattusha finally offered a welcome excuse to invade Mittani. The Hurrians became part of the Hittite sphere of influence. By giving him one of his daughters in marriage Shuppiluliuma bound Shattiwaza to the Hittite court. This was the end of the independence of Mittani.

The text translated here narrates the final phase of the Mittani Empire from the Hittite point of view. It is taken from the Akkadian version of a treaty Shuppiluliuma made with Shattiwaza.[103] The treaty is one between unequal partners: Shuppiluliuma dictates the rules his son-in-law Shattiwaza has to obey. As is usual in Hittite treaties, the beginning of the text is a historical introduction. This introduction is one of our foremost sources for the end of Mittani. The treaty is in Akkadian, because this was the international language of the Late Bronze Age.

It should be noted that the names of the Mittanian protagonists in our text (the royal names Artatama, Tushratta, and Shattiwaza) are not of a Hurrian, but of an Indo-Iranian character; the same is true of the word for an elite class in Mittani, *mariyannu*. This phenomenon has fascinated scholars from the time of its discovery, and has led to many hypotheses. One of the possibilities is that an Indo-Iranian group of elite warriors supported the creation of the Mittani Empire, but the details of the contacts between Indo-Iranians and Mittanians remain obscure. The presence of Indo-Iranian elements in the Mittanian lexicon still is one of the unsolved problems in Ancient Near Eastern history.

(A Obv. 1) When Art[ata]ma, king of the country of Khurri, together with My Majesty Shuppiluliuma, great king, hero, king of the country of Khattusha, beloved of the storm-god, had concluded a treaty between them, Tushratta, king of the country of Mittani, drew attention(?) from the [great] king, the king of Khattusha. Then I, great king, hero, king of Khattusha, turned my attention(?) to Tushratta, king of Mittani: I p[lu]ndered the lands on this river bank,[104] *and I made Mount Lebanon part of my territory again. King Tushratta appeared boastful before me a second time and spoke thus: "Why are you plundering on yonder bank of the Euphrates?"*[105] *King Tushratta said: "You are plundering the lands on the opposite bank of the Euphrates. I too will plunder the lands on the opposite bank of the Euphrates!" – king Tushratta was keen on annexing it – "If you are plundering them, what am I to do with them? Thus I will cross this bank of the Euphrates. Just take away either a lamb or a billy-goat belonging to my country!" I, great king, king of the country of Khattusha, appeared mighty before him. In the reign of the father of the king of Khattusha the country of Ishuwa became hostile. Troops of the country of Khattusha entered the country of Ishuwa. Troops of Gurtalishsha, troops of Arawanna, of the country of Zazzisha, of the country of Kalashma, of the country of Timna, of Mount Khaliwa, of Mount Karna, troops of Durmitta, of the country of Alkha, of the country of Khurma, of Mount Kharana, half of the country of Tegarama, troops of Tapurziya, troops of Khazga and troops of the country of Armatana became hostile during the reign of my father. My Majesty Shuppiluliuma, great king, hero, king of the country of Khattusha, beloved of the storm-god, slew them. Now the troops who had escaped from my hand, these troops entered the country of Ishuwa. All these troops and these countries became hostile during the reign of my father. They were living across(?) the country of Ishuwa among the enemy.*

(Obv. 17) I, My Majesty Shuppiluliuma, great king, king of the country of Khattusha, hero, beloved of the storm-god, went against the presumptuousness of king Tushratta. I crossed the Euphrates and went to the country of Ishuwa. I overpowered the country of Ishuwa for the second time, turned its inhabitants into my servants for the second time. The troops and countries that had entered the country of Ishuwa during the reign of my father – the troops of Gurtalishsha, the troops of Arawanna, of the country of Zazzisha, of the country of Tegarama,[106] *of the country of Timmina, of Mount Khaliwa, of Mount Karna, the troops of Durmitta, of the country of Alkha, of the country of Khurma, of Mount Kharana, half of the country of Tegarama, the troops of Tepurziya, the troops of Khazga, the troops of Armatana, – these troops and those countries I overpowered. I made them return to the country of Khattusha. I released the countries*

that I had taken; they lived in their own regions. All the people that I had released, returned to their own people; the country of Khattusha took their regions.

(Obv. 25) I, My Majesty Shuppiluliuma, great king, king of the country of Khattusha, hero, beloved of the storm-god, reached the country of Alshe. I overpowered the district of Kutmar and gave it as a gift to Antaratli of the country of Alshe. I invaded the district of Shuta, and p[lundere]d it. While plundering I reached Washshukkanni.[107] *I brought the people of the country of Shuta to the country of Khattusha together with their oxen, their sheep, their horses, their [p]ossessions and their deportees. Ki[ng] Tushratta [we]nt away. He didn't come to confront me in battle.*

(Obv. 30) I returned and [crossed] the Euphrate[s]. I overpowered the countries of Khalpa and Mukish. Takuwa, king of Niya, came to meet me in Mukish to offer peace. After Takuwa his brother Akiteshshub made the country of Niya and the town of Niya hostile. And [Agiteshshub], this man united their mariyannu-men:[108] *Khishmiya, Aziri, Zulkiya, Khabakhi,*[109] *[. . .], B[irriy]a and Niruwabi together with their chariots and their troops bec[am]e(?) one with Agiya, king of Arakhti. They occupied Arakhti and became hostile. They said: "Let us fight against the great king of Khattusha!" I, great king of Kha[ttus]ha, overpowered Arakhti. I captured Agiya, king of Arakhati, Takuwa's brother Agiteshshub, and all their mariy[a]nnu-men, together with [every]thing they possessed, and brought them to the country of Khattusha. I brought the city of Qatna with their property and all their possessions to the country of Khattusha.*

(Obv. 38) As I went to the country of Nukhashshe, I took all the countries. Sharrupshi lept aside.[110] *I captured his mother, his brothers and his sons, and brought them to the country of Khattusha. I installed Tagibsharri, Sharrupshi's servant, in kingship in the city of Ugulzat, and went to the country of Abina. I didn't try to defeat the country of Kinza.*[111] *Shutatarra came with his son Aitakkama and his chariots to confront me in battle. I defeated him and they went into the city of Abzuya. I surrounded Abzuya. I [cap]tured Shutatarra together with his sons, his maryannu-men, his brothers, and all his [possessions], and brought them to the country of Khattusha. I went to the country of Abina. Ariwana, king of Abina, and his noblemen Wambadura, [A]kparu and Artaya came to confront me in battle. These I brought [al]together, with their country and all their possessions to the country of Khattusha. Because of the presumptuousness of king T[u]shratta I plundered all of these countries in one year, and brought them to the country of Khattusha. From Mount Lebanon to yonder bank of the Euphrates I brought them to my territory.*

(Obv. 48) Then his son conspired with his servants, and killed his father, king Tushratta. After king Tushratta had died, the storm-god decided the case of Artatama and revived his[112] *dead son Artatama. The Assyrian country and the Alshean country had divided among them the country of Mittani, which had been entirely ravaged. Until then the great king, hero, king of the country of Khattusha had not crossed the river to the other bank, and had not taken litter and wood chips*[113] *belonging to the country of Mittani. Then, as the great king, king of the country of Khattusha, heard about the poverty of the country of Mittani, he let palace servants bring oxen, sheep and horses. The Hurrians were confused among themselves. Shuttarna*[114] *together with the mariyannu-men tried to kill Shattiwaza, the king's son. He escaped and came to My Majesty Shuppiluliuma, king of the country of Khattusha, hero, beloved of the storm-god. The great king spoke thus: "The storm-god has decided his case: After I have taken Shattiwaza, son of king Tushratta, in my hand, I let him sit on his father's throne, so that the country of Mittani, the great country, will not perish. The great king, king of the country of Khattusha, has revived the country of Mittani for his*

daughter's sake. I took Shattiwaza, son of Tushratta, in my hand and gave him a daughter as his wife."

Further reading

Beckman, G., *Hittite Diplomatic Texts*. 2d ed. Society of Biblical Literature Writings from the Ancient World Series 7 (Atlanta: Scholars Press, 1997), 41–54 (complete translation of both treaties of Shuppiluliuma I and Shattiwaza).

Kühne, C., "Imperial Mittani: An Attempt at Historical Reconstruction," in D. I. Owen and G. Wilhelm (eds.), *Studies on the Civilization and Culture of Nuzi and the Hurrians*, vol. 10 (Bethesda: CDL, 1999), 203–21.

Wilhelm, G., *The Hurrians* (Warminster: Aris & Phillips, 1989).

111. The Hittite–Egyptian treaty (Cohen)

When the Hittite king Šuppiluliuma extended his empire into North Syria, Egypt saw how its vassal kingdoms, notably Amurru, quickly fell under Hittite control. A few decades later, in an attempt to stop Hittite expansionism and to regain its lost territories, Egypt confronted the Hittites outside the Syrian city of Qadesh. The Hittite king Muwattalli and the Egyptian pharaoh, Ramses II, raged a fierce battle, which, while giving no clear-cut victory to the Hittites, certainly did not result in the Egyptians regaining their lost territories. The period of hostilities between the two countries was finally brought to an end in Ramses's twenty-first year, some 15 years later, when Ḫattušili III reigned in Ḫatti. The two kings signed the "silver treaty," which was to bring a full, if somewhat cautious, cooperation between the two superpowers of the Late Bronze Age, culminating in a diplomatic marriage between Ramses II and Ḫattušili's daughter (see Bryce 1998: 255–63; 304–15; and Klengel 2002).

The treaty was originally inscribed onto silver tablets, now lost. It was written in Akkadian, employing the diplomatic jargon of the period (see Liverani 1990 and Zaccagnini 1990). Its aim was to establish the relations, or the understanding (*ṭēmu*), between the two kings. This was to ensure the preservation of their peaceful brotherhood (*salāmu aḫḫuttu*), and the prevention of enmity (*nukurtu*) between the two nations in the future. Such conduct was the appropriate behaviour (*parṣu*) that was dictated by the gods and required of civilized nations at peace (see Cohen 2002).

The treaty is preserved in two versions. The version written in Ḫatti was brought by international delegates to Egypt, where it was translated into Egyptian and inscribed in hieroglyphs onto the walls of Ramses' temples. The version written in Egypt was sent to Ḫattuša, the Hittite capital, and there copied (and perhaps modified) onto clay tablets, which are the main source of this translation. The clay tablets' degree of preservation is rather poor, therefore, the Akkadian text itself has to be reconstructed on the basis of the Egyptian Hieroglyphic version, as has been done expertly by Edel 1997 (and see further Rainey and Cochavi-Rainey 1990; Spalinger 1981).

This means that parts of the restored text are conjectural, and no more (see Liverani 1999–2000).

The treaty opens with the introduction of the two parties, the Egyptian and Hittite kings. The historical prologue, typical of the Hittite treaties, is missing in the Akkadian version, although preserved in the Egyptian one. There, it tells us of a glorious (if somewhat mythical) past of the two nations, only briefly mentioning the Battle of Qadesh. In the Akkadian version, the relations that the two countries had had in the past are only referred to obliquely, as we read that Ramses is renewing them by means of the present treaty. Both kings are then made to promise not to raid each other's territories, but no claim is forwarded by Egypt regarding its lost territories. Hence, the treaty implicitly acknowledges Hittite sovereignty over North Syria.

(1–3) [The treaty which] Ramses, [Beloved] of Amon, Great King, King of [Egypt, made upon a tablet of silver] together with Ḫattušili, Great [King], King of Ḫatti, his brother, for (the benefit of) [Egypt and Ḫatti], in order that there will be great peaceful [brother]hood among them forever.

(3–7) Thus (speaks) Ramses, Beloved of Amon, Great King, King of the Egypt, the Brave one of all the lands, son of Minmuarea (Seti I), Great King, King of Egypt, the Brave, grandson of Minpahtare[!] (Ramses I), Great King, King of Egypt, the Brave, to Ḫattušili, Great King, King of Hatti, the Brave, son of Muršili, Great King, King of Ḫatti, the Brave, grandson of Šuppiluliuma, Great King, King of Ḫatti, the Brave.

(7–13) Behold, I have enabled the being of good peaceful brotherhood between us forever, so that there will (also) be good peaceful brotherhood a[mong] Egypt and Ḫatti forever. Behold, the age-old understanding that was between the Great King, King of the Land of Egypt [and the Great King], King of Ḫatti – the god never did enable (it) to fall into a state of enmity by [means of] a [treaty]. Behold, (now) Ramses, Beloved of Amon, Great King, King of Egypt, is enabling (by means of the present treaty) the (re)-creation of the understanding that [the sun-god] and the storm-god had created for Egypt and Hatti, so that, following their! age-old understanding, [no] enmity will be possible between them ever.

(13–17) So now, Ramses, the Beloved of Amon, Great King, King of [Egypt] is (re)-creating (that understanding) by means of a treaty (inscribed) upon a tablet of silver with [Ḫattuši]li Great King, King of Ḫatti, his brother, as to this very day – so that there will be good peaceful brotherhood between [them for]ever. As he is [my] brother, so am I his brother, as <he is at peace with me>, so am I at peace with him for[ever].

(17–21) [Behold], we will create our [peace]ful brotherhood, far better than the peaceful brotherhood of Egypt and Hatti from old times. Behold, Ramses, [Great] King, King of Egypt, is in good peaceful brotherhood with [Ḫattušili], Great King, King of Ḫatti. Behold, the children of Ramses, Beloved of Amon, <Great King>, King of Egypt, will (also) be in peaceful brotherhood with the children of Ḫattušili, Great King, King of Ḫatti, forever. Following our understanding of peaceful brotherhood, they, along with Egypt and Ḫatti, will be peaceful brothers like us, forever.

(22–4) Ramses, Beloved of Amon, Great King, King of Egypt, shall never attack Ḫatti for the purpose of taking anything from it. So shall Ḫattušili, Great King, King of Ḫatti, never attack Egypt for the purpose of taking anything from it.

(24–7) Behold, the appropriate behaviour for eternity, which the sun-god and the storm-god had created, (is for) peaceful brotherhood, (and for) prohibiting enmity between them. Behold, Ra[mses], Beloved of Amon, Great King, King of Egypt, has seized it (the appropriate behaviour) for creating peace as to this very day (onward). Behold, Egypt and Ḫatti are peaceful brothers for eternity.

As in non-parity treaties, a pact of mutual defense against external and internal enemies was formulated. Here both kings promise to aid each other by sending their army when the need arises.

(27–30) Now if an external enemy comes against Ḫatti, then Ḫattušili, <Great King>, [King of Ḫatti], will write to me, saying: "Come to my aid against him." Then R[amses Be]loved of Amon, Great King, King of Egypt, will send his army and chariotry, and they will kill [his enemy], avenging Ḫatti.

(31–3) And if Ḫattušili, Great King, King of Ḫatti will be [angry] with his very own subjects, after they committed an offense against him, he (var. you) will write to Ramses, Great King, King of Egypt, about this. Ramses, Beloved of Amon, will send his army and chariotry, and they will destroy all with whom he (Ḫattušili) was angry.

(33–6) And if an external enemy comes against Egypt, then Ramses, Beloved of Amon, [King] of Egypt, your brother, will write to (you) Ḫattušili, King of Ḫatti, his brother, saying: "Come to my aid against him." So Ḫattušili, King of Ḫatti, will send his army and chariotry, and he will kill my enemy.

(36–9) And if Ramses, Beloved of Amon, [King] of Egypt, becomes angry with his very own subjects, after they committed an offense against him, then I (Ramses) will write to Ḫattušili, Great King, King of Ḫatti, my brother, about this. So Ḫattušili, [Great King, King] of Ḫatti, my brother will send [his] troops and chariotry, and they will destroy all [with whom] I was angry.

King Ḫattušili, whose hold on the Hittite throne is illegitimate, may have feared that when he dies, a dynastic struggle in Ḫatti will ensue. Therefore, the purpose of this stipulation is to ensure that in case internal revolts arise, Ramses will protect the future Hittite king upon his ascendancy.

(40–3) Behold, the son of Ḫattušili, King of Ḫatti, will become king over Ḫatti instead of Ḫattušili, his father, following the many years of Ḫattušili [(as) King of] Ḫatti. But if the citizens of Ḫatti will commit an offense against him, [Ramses], Beloved of Amon, will send his troops and chariotry <to his aid>, and avenge him.

The stipulations in the following section deal with fugitives fleeing from Ḫatti to Egypt and vice versa. In the non-parity Hittite treaties, the vassal king is obliged to hand the escaping party from Ḫatti back to the Hittite king, while the Hittite king reserves the right to keep all fugitives in Ḫatti. In this treaty, however, the obligation to return the fugitives to their country of origin falls on both parties. This detailed section has led scholars to believe that it was formulated as a result of the Egyptians giving political asylum to the fugitive Urḫi-Teššub, who was the legitimate Hittite crown prince deposed by Ḫattušili during the struggle for the Hittite crown. The implicit objective of this section, then, was to pressure the Egyptians to extradite Urḫi-Teššub to the hands of Ḫattušili, with the promise that no harm would befall him or his family. (Indeed, Hittite customary law prohibits the execution or maltreatment of political fugitives.) As we learn from extraneous sources, Urḫi-Teššub was yet at large after the treaty was signed, but whether he was a guest at the Egyptian court remains unclear.

(43–6) [If a dignitary fl]ees Ḫatti, [or] if a town's population situated in the lands belonging to the King of Ḫatti (flees), and co[mes] to Ramses, Beloved of Amon, Great King, King [of Egypt, then] Ramses, [Beloved of Amon, Great King, King of Egypt], will seize them, and deliver [them to the hands of Ḫattušili, Great King, King of Ḫatti, their lord].

(46–8) [And] if one or two [anonymous men] come [to Ramses, Beloved of Amon], in order to serve somebody else (other than Ḫattušili), then Ra[mses, Beloved of Amon, will seize them and deliver them to the hands of] Ḫattušili, king of Ḫatti.

(49–51) Now [if a dignitary flees Egypt and comes to some vassal king, or if] a town's population c[omes to some vassal king, then he will seize them], and have them sent to the King of Ḫatti, [his] lord, [and Ḫattušili, Great King, King of Ḫatti, will deliver them to Ramses, Beloved] of Amon, Great King, King of Egypt.

(52–4) And if [one or two anonymous men flee the land of the King of Egy]pt, and they are not [willing to be at his (the King of Egypt's) service, then Ḫattušili, Great King, King of Ḫatti], will deliver them to the hands of <his> brother, and [he will not settle them down in] Ḫatti.

(54–7) [And if one or two nobles flee Ḫatti], and they are not [willing to be at the service of Ḫattušili and they flee the land of the Great King, King of] Ḫatti, for not [being at his service, then Ramses, Beloved of Amon, will seize them], and have them sent to [Ḫattušili, Great King, King of Ḫatti, his] brother, [and he will not settle them down in Egypt].

(57–60) And if one or [two] nobles flee [Egypt and] they come to [Ḫatti], then Ḫattušili, [Great King, King of Ḫatti, will seize them and] have them sent over to Ra[mses, Beloved] of Amon, [Great King, King of Egypt, his brother].

(60–3) [And if] one, two, or [three] men flee [Ḫatti and they come to] Ramses, Beloved [of Amon, Great King, King of] Egypt, [then Ramses], Beloved of Amon, Great King, [King of Egypt, will seize them and have them sent] to Ḫattušili, his brother, because they are brothers.

(63–4) The (fugitives) [will not be punished] for their offenses. [Their tongues (or) eyes will not] be torn out, and their ears (or) feet [will not be chopped off, and their houses will not be destroyed together with their wives and to]gether with their sons.

(65–8) And if [one], two, or three men flee [the land of Ramses, Great King, King of Egypt], and [they come to Ḫattušili, Great King], King of Ḫatti, my brother, [then Ḫattušili, Great King, King of] Ḫatti, my brother, will seize them and have [them sent over to Ramses, Beloved of Amon, Great King, King] of Egypt, because Ramses, Great King, King of [Egypt, and Ḫattušili are brothers].

(68–70) [The (fugitives) will not be punished for their offenses. Their tongues (or)] eyes will not be torn out and [their ears (or) feet will not be chopped off, and their houses will not be destroyed] along with their wives and their sons.

The Akkadian version becomes rather fragmentary at this point, as the issue of fugitives is concluded. The Egyptian version includes a list of the deities witnessing the signing of the treaty, curses and blesses, and a unique verbal description of the impressions of the royal seals on the original silver tablet.

Bibliography

Sources: CTH 91 (= KBo 1.7+ and KBo 1.25+).
Edition: Edel 1997.
Translations: Beckman 1999; Edel 1983; and Kitchen 1996 (Egyptian version).

Beckman, G. 1999. *Hittite Diplomatic Texts*. 2d ed. Atlanta, 96–100.

Bryce, T. 1998. *The Kingdom of the Hittites*. Oxford.

Cohen, Y. 2002. *Taboos and Prohibitions in Hittite Society: A Study of the Hittite Expression natta āra*. Texte der Hethiter 24. Heidelberg.

Edel, E. 1983. Der ägyptisch-hethitische Friedensvertrag zwischen Ramses II. und Hattusili III. In O. Kaiser (ed.), *Rechts- und Wirtschaftsurkunden: historisch-chronologische Texte*. (*TUAT*, Band 1, 2.) Aachen, 135–53.

Edel, E. 1997. *Der Vertrag zwischen Ramses II. von Ägypten und Ḫattušili III. von Hatti*, Berlin.

Kitchen, K. A. 1996. *Ramesside Inscriptions Translated and Annotated: Translations*. Vol. 2. Oxford: OUP, 79–85.

Kitchen, K. A. 1999. *Ramesside Inscriptions Translated and Annotated: Notes and Comments*. Vol. 2. Oxford, 136–45.

Klengel, H. 2002. From War to Eternal Peace: Ramesses II and Khattushili III. *The Canadian Society for Mesopotamian Studies Bulletin* 37: 49–56.

Liverani, M. 1990. *Prestige and Interest: International Relations in the Near East ca. 1600–1100 B.C.* Padua: Sargon, 1990.

Liverani, M. 1999–2000. Review of Edel 1997. *Archiv für Orientforschung* 46–7: 341–2.

Rainey, A. F. and Cochavi-Rainey, Z. 1990. Comparative Grammatical Notes on the Treaty between Ramses II and Hattusili III. In S. Israelit-Groll (ed.), *Studies in Egyptology Presented to Miriam Lichtheim*. Vol. 3. Jerusalem, 796–823.

Spalinger, A. 1981. Considerations on the Hittite Treaty between Egypt and Hatti. *Studien zur altägyptischen Kultur* 9: 299–358.

Zaccagnini, C. 1990. The Forms of Alliance and Subjugation in the Near East of the Late Bronze Age. In L. Canfora et al. (eds.), *I trattati del mondo antico: forma, ideologia, funzione*. Rome, 37–79.

Notes

1 See note 6, text 105, "The Annals of Ḫattušili I."

2 This god is not mentioned by name, but only by his or her appellation "our deity." The interest shown by both Neša and Zalpuwa in this divinity suggests that the two cities belonged to a single cultural group, almost certainly that of the Indo-European immigrants into Anatolia.

3 See note 19, text 105, "The Annals of Ḫattušili I."

4 Text C: to Neša, for each of my gods.

5 Text B: to Zalpa = Zalpuwa.
6 A title of the Hittite monarch, which probably meant "The Powerful One" in the Luwian language.
7 The dynasty of the Old Hittite period had its origins in Kuššar, the same city in which Anitta began his career – see the "Anitta Text." It is unlikely, however, that the Hittite rulers continued the earlier line of kings, and in any case, more than a century separated Anitta and Ḫattušili.
8 Akkadian version abbreviates the titulary: "I, the Great King, the Tabarna, exercised kingship in Ḫatti."
9 Here Ḫattušili indicates his relationship to the previous generation of rulers in Ḫatti: He was the nephew of the earlier queen, Tawananna.
10 Akkadian: "twice."
11 Akkadian: "whatever goods were to be had."
12 There were two, or perhaps even three, cities with this name in the area within which Ḫattušili was active. Meant here is probably the northern Zalpa/Zalpuwa, located somewhere in the valley of the Kızıl İrmak near the Black Sea coast, a city with which Ḫattuša and the early Hittite dynasty had a long and bitter rivalry. See V. Haas, Zalpa, die Stadt am Schwarzen Meer und das althethitische Königtum. *Mittlilungen der Deutschen Orient-Gesellschaft* 109 (1977): 15–26.
13 Akkadian: "I dedicated one golden ox to the temple of the storm-god and its nine deities to the temple of Mezzulla."
14 The Akkadian version employs the form Uršu for this town.
15 Akkadian: "When I returned I destroyed Uršu and filled the palace with goods."
16 Akkadian: "the enemy from Ḫanigalbat entered my land."
17 Akkadian: "I(!) went to the . . . of Nenašša, and they opened before me(!)."
18 Akkadian: "Ullumma."
19 Akkadian: "I cultivated cress(!) on its territory and expropriated it." The scattering of the seed of wild cress on the ruins of a conquered city symbolically returned the precincts to their natural state. This action was accompanied by a curse upon anyone who might resettle the grounds.
20 Akkadian: "one ox, the female Katiti, and Mt. Aranḫapila." The Hittites considered some topographical features, including rivers, springs, and mountains, to be divine.
21 Akkadian: "Šalliaḫšuwa set itself afire." This probably indicates that the city demonstrated its submission through the destruction of its own fortifications.
22 Akkadian: "They gave battle for five months; I destroyed Šanaḫut in the sixth month."
23 Akkadian: "The sun-god stood behind the lands."
24 Akkadian: "Whatever I brought I dedicated to the sun-goddess of Arinna."
25 Akkadian: "I(!) overturned."
26 Akkadian: "the foreign inhabitants(?) of Takšanaya, (together with) its cattle and its sheep."
27 Akkadian: "[And] Parmanna was the head; it used to organize those rulers."
28 Akkadian: "Parmanna opened its city gate before me. The sun-god took its hand." I.e., the deity brought the people of Parmanna to realize that discretion was the better part of valor.
29 Akkadian: "Alaḫḫa."
30 Akkadian: "(the city of) Zarunti."
31 Akkadian: "Ḫaššu."

32 At this time the city of Aleppo, center of the country of Yamḫad, was the most powerful polity in northern Syria.
33 Akkadian: "They took a stand before it, and the troops of Aleppo were with them."
34 Akkadian adds: "at Mt. Adalur."
35 Akkadian: "In a matter of days I, the Great King, crossed the Euphrates River like a lion."
36 Akkadian: "As for Ḫaššuwa – I poured out earth upon it like a lion with its paws."
37 Akkadian: "And I filled Ḫattuša with its possessions."
38 Akkadian: "There was no end of its silver and gold."
39 So Akkadian; Hittite corrupt.
40 Text: 3, but duplicate and Akkadian have 13.
41 Akkadian has only gold in both instances.
42 So duplicate and Akkadian.
43 Akkadian adds: "royal."
44 Akkadian: "of."
45 Akkadian: "they cut off."
46 So Akkadian; Hittite text gives this name the personal determinative. In any event, the gesture of casting down the weapon presumably indicates that the enemy surrendered without resistance.
47 Akkadian: "entered."
48 Akkadian: "kept glaring at."
49 Akkadian: "two wagons of silver."
50 Akkadian: "two palanquins of silver, one table of gold, one table of silver."
51 Akkadian: "one . . . silver ox."
52 The scribe of the Hittite version incorrectly omitted the latter portion of this sentence; it has been restored from the Akkadian text.
53 Akkadian: "I removed . . . from the hands of its slaves."
54 Akkadian: "I established their freedom under Heaven."
55 Akkadian: "I installed them in the temple of the sun-goddess of Arinna."
56 Akkadian: "I made a golden statue."
57 Akkadian: "the exterior wall above the exterior gate."
58 So the Akkadian text; the Hittite version names the Mala River, probably a tributary of the Euphrates.
59 Akkadian: "led off (into captivity)."
60 Akkadian: "He did not set fire."
61 Akkadian: "He did not show smoke to the storm-god."
62 Duplicate: "king of Ḫ[atti]."
63 Akkadian: "I destroyed the king of Ḫaḫḫa and Ḫaḫḫa; I(!) set fire."
64 The Akkadian version mentions only this ruler.
65 Present only in the Hittite version.
66 The text, *KUB* 1.16 + *KUB* 40.65, is originally old Hittite (and Akkadian), but only survived in a much later copy (thirteenth century BC).
67 The identity of Hastayar is not clear (see Further Reading section pages 227–8 for the full citations of references mentioned in this section of the notes). Beal 1983: 123 and Sürenhagen 1998: 88 fn. 56 assume that she is the daughter-in-law of Hattusili and the mother of Mursili. On the other hand, Sommer and Falkenstein 1938: 188–9, followed by for example Bin-Nun 1975: 71, Bryce 1983: 108, Haas 1994: 15, 217 and De Martino and Imparati 1998: 393 take her to be Hattusili's wife.

68 Beckman in COS, 2000: 79.
69 See Sürenhagen 1998: 77 with n. 5 (with references); pp. 85, 87. "Labarna" is also a personal name (*CHD* L p. 41ff.). For *tabarna* as a Luwian word meaning "(the) powerful (one)," see Melchert 2003: 19.
70 The translation of *te-/tar-* as "instruct" follows Beckman in COS, 2000: 79, with n. 3.
71 For the direct speech as a rhetorical question see Sürenhagen 1998: 86 n. 54.
72 Following Beckman in COS, 2000: 79 n. 4 who reads i 15 as GUD *bi-ri* "bull-calf."
73 For this interpretation see Carruba 2002: 151 n. 26 [*na-a*]*t-ta-aš-ša-an* "non è (egli) [. . .]?"
74 I suggest restoring in ii 47 [*na-at mu-*]*u-wa-an e-eš-du*. The lexeme *muwa-* indicates an awe-inspiring quality (*CHD* L-N p. 314).
75 The meaning of the Hitttite stem *šia-* as the numeral "one" (instead of "this, that" or the like) is established in Goedegebuure's forthcoming work.
76 Eating bread and drinking water is a sign of abundance, not of scarcity.
77 I prefer to read in iii 39 [DU]MU-*la-aš-mi-iš*. If this reading is correct, then we can identify the first-ranking servants with the "sons of the king"; that is, the princes. These princes are not necessarily the king's own sons but may also belong to the extended royal family.
78 The exact interpretation of the preceding lines is quite difficult, and allows different translations. It seems to me that the king describes a future situation in which he confronts Hastayar with information from the palace attendants concerning her consultation of the "Old Women," a class of diviners and practitioners of magic, while all she had to do was to turn to the king for information and consultation. Again Hattusili stresses the main point of this edict: that the persons involved should only turn to the king for guidance, and never heed the words of others, be it members of the royal family, the elders of a city, the population, or diviners. For translations different from each other and from the one presented here, see among others Bryce 1983: 107; *CHD* P: 378; Beckman 2000: 81.
79 These cities are all located in southern Anatolia, south of Tuz Gölü, and north of classical Cilicia.
80 Modern Aleppo in northern Syria.
81 1595/4 BC, middle chronology.
82 Restoration follows Van den Hout 1997.
83 All located in northern Syria.
84 Possibly modern Gürün in Turkey.
85 The Akkadian text is more elaborate. The restorations based on the Akkadian text are placed between brackets. Still, the reconstruction of §§14–16 is quite difficult.
86 The reconstruction and translation basically follows O. Soysal in *Orientalia* NS, 59: 271–9, 1990.
87 I.e., Harapsili.
88 Probably as revenge for the death of Harapsili, or *jus talionis*: "an eye for an eye . . ."
89 The name can also be read as "Kasseni."
90 Possibly modern Adana.
91 Country in southwestern Anatolia.
92 Literally "a son of his begetting." Tahurwaili is Ammuna's son by a prostitute.

93 In northern Syria.

94 Near Hassuwa.

95 I.e., "They will further ignore them completely," following Van den Hout in COS 1, 1997: 196, with n. 44.

96 Disposal of the enemy, possibly within the royal family. See the last clause of the paragraph.

97 The translation and interpretation of these lines is quite difficult, and one will find different interpretations that sometimes even contradict each other. To start with, Inge Hoffmann, *Der Erlaß Telipinus*, Texte der Hethiter 11, Heidelberg: Winter, 1984: 33 (translated from German): "'I will clean (it) up.' But you will clean nothing. On the contrary, you will oppress"; *CHD* P: 173: "'I will thoroughly clean up,' while you yourself (*-za*) clean nothing up, but you yourself (*-za*) rather oppress"; T. R. Bryce, *The Major Historical Texts of Early Hittite History*. Brisbane: University of Queensland (1983): 137: "'I grant absolution.' You must grant no such absolution. You must press (him; i.e., the offender) all the more"; Van den Hout in COS 1997: 197: "'I will clean (it) out,' for you will not clean anything. On the contrary, you will get involved yourself." The latter clause is a methaphorical rendering of the more litteral "you will close yourself in" (l.c., n. 51). I more or less follow Van den Hout in the interpretation of the final clause, but take it as a rhetorical question. The reason is that I do not emend *kuit* "for, because, why, what" to *kuitki* "nothing, anything." Combined with the negation and Van den Hout's interpretation of the last clause, this has to lead to a question: "for you will not 'clean up' yourself," meaning something like "you will not dispose of yourself" is meaningless. A rhetorical question on the other hand would indicate that disposal of the enemy would eventually lead to disposal of the king, as has been described in the preceding paragraphs. The expression *anda hatkisnu-* is also used for oppressing cities; that is, for besieging them. Hence my translation: "and even bring yourself under siege?"

98 The transliteration of the beginning of iii 52 as *nu-wa-at-ma-az* (*nu=wa=at=ma=az*) "and-particle-it-but-self" is impossible for two reasons. First, *-ma* cannot appear after the enclitic pronoun. Secondly, in front of an enclitic pronoun beginning with a vowel the direct speech particle should take the form *-war-*, not *-wa-*.

99 Text has singular verb form.

100 A duplicate has "for that man (and) for his house."

101 Shuppiluliuma's son Telipinu, who as Priest of Khalab/Aleppo was one of the most important representatives of Hittite power in Syria.

102 Unknown Hurrian title.

103 In early scholarly literature also called Kurtiwaza or Mattiwaza.

104 The west bank of the Euphrates, as seen from a Hittite viewpoint.

105 The west bank of the Euphrates, as seen from a Hurrian viewpoint.

106 Probably a scribal error for Kalashma.

107 This town probably was the capital of the Mitanni Empire.

108 An elite group in Mittani and related Hurrian kingdoms.

109 The same name as Khalpakhi?

110 I.e., fled.

111 Kinza is the Hittite name for Kadesh.

112 I.e., Tushratta's.

113 I.e., not even the smallest thing.

114 A son of Artatama.

9

Hittite Historical Texts II

Kathleen R. Mineck, Theo van den Hout, and Harry A. Hoffner, Jr.

112. The Ten Year Annals of Muršili II: excerpts (Mineck)

The Hittite kings, unlike their neighbors, did not date their texts by regnal years, by lists of significant events or officials' names, and there is no known Hittite king list. This greatly hinders our understanding of Hittite royal chronology. However, the Hittites often included historiographical information in letters, edicts and treaties and there are a few texts outlining military campaigns on a year-to-year basis such as this one, known as Muršili's Ten Year Annals. There is also a second annals text that provides at least 10 more years of Muršili's reign known as the Comprehensive Annals.

Throughout the text Muršili attributed all of his military accomplishments to divine favor and protection. His first act as king was to celebrate the neglected festivals for the sun-goddess of Arinna. And he was careful to repeatedly name the sun-goddess of Arinna along with the other deities he believed "ran before him in battle." They legitimized his reign and made him victorious.

We are told early in this text that Muršili was young when he came to the throne and was not given due respect from other polities. The Kaška people (just to the northeast of the Hittite capital city Hattuša) were in the habit of raiding Hittite territories, and Muršili was compelled to campaign vigorously to keep them at bay. Muršili's usual argument and justification for initiating the campaigns was that his opponents refused to provide him with troops or they had in their possession certain displaced persons that he claimed (translated here as civilian captives). The civilian captives were an important issue for the Hittites, and typically, the Hittite treaties included provisions concerning their extradition.

This is a well-organized text that summarizes Muršili's year-to-year military activities back and forth throughout Anatolia. The end of each year is summarized by the phrase "This I did in one year" and the next paragraph begins with "In the next year . . ." Muršili ends his annals by stating that all these accomplishments were achieved in his first 10 years as king.

Text: CTH 61 (KBo 3.4 + KUB 23.125)[1]

§1 Thus (says) My Majesty Muršili, Great King, King of Hatti-land, Hero, the son of Šuppiluliuma, Great King, Hero:

§2 When I had not yet sat on the throne of my father, all the surrounding enemy lands had (already) begun hostilities. When my father became a god (i.e., he died) Arnuwanda, my brother, sat on the throne of his father. But later, he also became ill.[2] And when the enemy lands heard of the illness of Arnuwanda, my brother, they began to make war.

§3 But when my brother Arnuwanda became a god, the enemy lands who were not (yet) making war, those enemy lands also became hostile. The surrounding enemy lands said the following: "His father who was the king of Hatti was a heroic king. He held the enemy lands subjected. But he has become a god. His son who sat on his father's throne, he also was already a grown man. But he became ill, and he also became a god."

§4 "The one who now has sat on the throne of his father is young. He will not sustain Hatti-land or the border territories of Hatti."

§5 Because my father was continually garrisoned in the land of Mittanni (Hurrian territory to the east) and he lingered in garrison, the festivals of the sun-goddess of Arinna, my lady, were uncelebrated.

§6 But when I, My Majesty, sat on the throne of my father, before I went to any of those neighboring enemy lands whatsoever that had made hostilities against me, I reestablished and I performed the regular festivals for the sun-goddess of Arinna, my lady. I raised my hand to the sun-goddess of Arinna, my lady, and I said the following: "O sun-goddess of Arinna, my lady! The neighboring enemy lands who have called me a child, they have belittled me. And they have begun to try to take your borderlands. O sun-goddess of Arinna, my lady, stand with me, and destroy before me those surrounding enemy lands." The sun-goddess of Arinna heard my word and stood with me. And when I sat on the throne of my father, I overcame these surrounding enemy lands in ten years and I destroyed them.

Year 1

§7 The Kaška of the land of Turmitta, began hostilities against me, and [fought me]. Furthermore (other) Kaška also came and began to attack the land of Turmitta. I, My Majesty, went to them, [to Halil]a and Dudduška which were the primary cities of the Kaška lands, and I attacked them. I took up from them civilian captives, cattle and sheep, and I brought them away to Hattuša, and I burned down Halila and Dudduška.

§8 [But whe]n the Kaška [he]ard of the destruction of the cities of Halila and Dudduška, the entire Kaška land came in support. [It] came in battle against me and I, My Majesty, fought it. The sun-goddess of Arinna, [my lady], the mighty storm-god, my lord, Mezzulla and all the gods ran before me. And I overcame the auxiliary Kaška troops and destroyed them. The Kaška [of] Turmitta were subjected a second time and they began to send [troops to me].

§9 [Then I, My Majesty] returned and because the Kaška of Išhupitta [fought me] and were not giving me troops, I, My Majesty [went] into Išhupitta. I attacked [. . .] –]humešša. And I [took up] from it deportees, cattle and sheep. And I brought them away to Hattuša. I [burned] down the city [. . .]. I recaptured the Kaška city of Išhupitta a second time and they [gave me troops]. I did this in one year.

Year 2

The text for year 2 and the beginning of year 3 is only partially preserved.

Year 3

§15 Then I went [up into] Išhupitta and I attacked Palhuišša. The Pišhuruan [enemy] approached behind me in Palhuišša for battle and I fought him. The sun-goddess of Arinna, my lady, the mighty storm-god, my lord, Mezzulla and all the gods ran before me and I destroyed the Pišhuruan enemy in Palhuišša. Then I burned the city down.

§16 Afterwards I returned to Hatti from Palhuišša. I mobilized the infantry and horse-troops and in that same year I proceeded to the land of Arzawa (a powerful Luwian territory to the west southwest). I sent a messenger to Uhhaziti and I wrote to him (as follows): "My servants who have gone over to you that I requested back from you, you have not given them back to me. You have been calling me a child and you have been belittling me. Now, come! We will battle! May the storm-god, my lord, judge our case!"

§17 But when I had set out and I reached Mt. Lawaša, the mighty storm-god, my lord, revealed his divine power. He shot a thunderbolt. My armies saw the thunderbolt and the land of Arzawa saw it. The thunderbolt went and struck Arzawa. It struck Apaša, Uhhaziti's city (probably Ephesus). Uhhaziti fell to his knees[3] and he became ill. As Uhhaziti was ill, he did not then come against me in battle. He sent forth his son Piyama-LAMMA together with troops and horse-troops against me. He approached me for battle at the Aštarpa River at Walma. And I, My Majesty, fought him. And the sun-goddess of Arinna, my lady, the mighty storm-god, my lord, Mezzulla and all the gods ran before me. I overpowered Piyama-LAMMA, son of Uhhaziti together with his troops and his horse-troops. I slaughtered them. Still I pursued him. I crossed into Arzawa and I went into Apaša, Uhhaziti's city. Uhhaziti did not resist me. Rather he fled from me! And he crossed the sea. He went by ship (?). And he remained there.

§18 The entire land of Arzawa fled. There were civilian captives who went to Mt. Arinnanda and occupied Mt. Arinnanda, civilian captives who went to Puranda and occupied Puranda, and civilian captives who went across the sea with Uhhaziti. I, My Majesty, went after the civilian captives in Mt. Arinnanda and I battled (the land of) Mt. Arinnanda. The sun-goddess of Arinna, my lady, the mighty storm-god, my lord, Mezzulla and all the gods ran before me. And I conquered Mt Arinnanda. There were fifteen thousand five hundred captives that I, My Majesty, brought for the royal estate. There was no counting the captives that the lords, troops and horse-troops of Hattuša brought for themselves. Subsequently I sent the captives forth to Hattuša and they led them away.

§19 When I had conquered Mt Arinnanda, then I returned to the Aštarpa River. I built a walled fortification at the Aštarpa River. And I celebrated the monthly festival there. I did this in one year.

Year 4

§20 [But wh]en it became spring, because Uhhaziti was ill, and was in the sea (on an island?), his sons were with him. Uhhaziti died in the sea. Then his sons split up. One of them was still in the sea, but one of them, Tapalazunauli, came out from the sea. Because all of the [rest of the] land of Arzawa had gone up into Puranda, Tapalazunauli went up to Puranda.

§21 But when I completed the yearly festival, I went to Puranda for battle. Tapalazunauli came against me in battle with the troops and horse-troops from Puranda. He approached me in battle on his cultivated lands. I, My Majesty, fought him. The sun-goddess of Arinna, my lady, the mighty storm-god, my lord, Mezzulla and all the gods ran before me. I conquered Tapalazunauli together with his troops and horse-troops and I destroyed him. Then I seized him and I proceeded to surround Puranda and I besieged it. I diverted its water.

§22 When I was besieging Puranda, because Tapalazunauli, son of Uhhaziti was up in Puranda, he became afraid and he fled down from Puranda at night. Further he gathered his sons and captives in haste? and led them down from Puranda.

§23 But when I, [My Majesty, h]eard: "Tapalazunauli had fled [by night] and had gathered his wife, his children and civilian captives in haste? and had led them down from Puranda," [I, My Majesty], sent [troops] and horse-troops after him, and they overtook Tapalazunauli on the road and they took his wife, his children and his civilian captives away from him and they led them back. One person, Tapalazunauli, escaped. The aforementioned troops and horse-troops took the civilian captives that they o[vertook] on the road for themselves.

§24–5 It is most unfortunate that the next paragraphs are broken because after a fragmentary section regarding the conquest of and booty taken from Puranda, the top of column three mentions the son of Uhhaziti (Piyama-LAMMA) in association with the king of Ahhiyawa (a reference to Achaeans) and possibly a ship.

§26 [But when] I returned to the Š[eha River Land where Manapa-Tarhunta was lord], I would have fought him. When [Manapa-Tarhunta he]ard of me: "The king of Hatti is coming!" he [became af]raid. He did [not come] against me, rather he sent his mother and the old men and women forth [to] me. They came to me and [bowed] at my feet. And because the women came and bowed at my feet, I gave in for the sake of [the women] and then I did [not g]o into the Šeha River Land. They sent me the Hittite civilian captives who were [in] the Šeha River Land. There were four thousand civilian captives that they sent me. I sent them forth to Hattuša and they led them away. I took Manapa-Tarhunta and the Šeha River Land in servitude.

§27 Then I went to the land of Mira. I gave the land of Mira to Mašhuiluwa. I gave the Šeha River Land to Manapa-Tarhunta. I gave the land of Hapalla to Targašnalli. I subjected these lands on the spot. I levied troops from them and they began to send me troops. Because I wintered in the land of Arzawa, in two years the sun-goddess of Arinna, my lady, the mighty storm-god, my lord, Mezzulla and all the gods ran before me and I conquered the land of Arzawa. Some (of the people) I sent away to Hattuša and some I subjected on the spot. I levied troops on them and they began to send them to me. Because I conquered the entire land of Arzawa, there were 66,000 civilian captives all together that I, My Majesty, conducted to the royal house. There

was no counting the civilian captives, cattle and sheep that the lords, troops and horse-troops of Hattuša brought for themselves. When I had conquered the entire land of Arzawa, I returned to Hattuša. And because I had spent the winter in Arzawa, I did this in one year.

Year 5

§28 The following year I went to Mt. Ašharpaya. The Kaška that had occupied Mt. Ašharpaya had cut off the roads of the land of Paya. I fought the aforementioned Kaška of Mt. Ašharpaya. The sun-goddess of Arinna, my lady, the mighty storm-god, my lord, Mezzulla and all the gods ran before me and I conquered the Kaška that had occupied Mt. Ašharpaya and I destroyed them. I emptied Mt. Ašharpaya and then I left. When I arrived in Šammaha, I entered Ziulila.

§29 While my father was in the land of Mittani, the Arawannean enemy that was continually attacking the land of Kiššiya had severely hurt it. I, My Majesty went into the land of Arawanna and I fought the land of Arawanna. The sun-goddess of Arinna, my lady, the mighty storm-god, my lord, Mezzulla and all the gods ran before me and I conquered the entire land of Arawanna. There were 3,500 civilian captives that I conducted to the royal house. And there was no counting the civilian captives, cattle and sheep that the Hittite lords, troops and horse-troops brought for themselves. And when I had conquered the land of Arawanna, I then returned to Hattuša. This I did in one year.

Year 6

§30 The following year I went into the land of Zimurriya. In my grandfather's time, the Kaška who had occupied Mt. Tarikarimu by force then became a problem for Hattuša. They attacked Hattuša and they did much damage. I, My Majesty went and I attacked the Kaška that had occupied Mt. Tarikarimu. The sun-goddess of Arinna, my lady, the mighty storm-god, my lord, Mezzulla and all the gods ran before me and I conquered the Kaška of Mt. Tarikarimu and I destroyed them. I emptied Mt. Tarikarimu and I burned out the entire land of Zimurriya. Then I returned to Hattuša. I did this in one year.

Year 7

§31 The next year I went to the land of Tipiya. While my father had been in the land of the Mittani, Pihhuniya, the ruler of Tipiya, proceeded to attack the Upper Land. He advanced as far as Zazziša and he took up (looted) the Upper Land and he brought it down into the land of the Kaška. He took the entire land of Ištitina and made it his place of pasturing.

§32 Afterwards Pihhuniya did not rule in a Kaška manner. Suddenly, when there was (normally) no foremost ruler in the Kaška city, that Pihhuniya ruled like a king. I, My Majesty, went to him and I sent him a messenger. I wrote to him, saying: "My servants whom you took and led down to the Kaška, send them out to me." Pihhuniya wrote back to me as follows: "I will give you back nothing. If you come to me in battle, I will in no way fight you on my cultivated lands. I will come against you on your land. I will approach in battle in the midst of your land." When Pihhuniya replied so

to me, and he would not return my servants, I went to him in battle. I attacked his land. The sun-goddess of Arinna, my lady, the mighty storm-god, my lord, Mezzulla and all the gods ran before me and I conquered the entire land of Tipiya. And I burned it out. I seized Pihhuniya and I led him away to Hattuša. Then I returned from the land of Tipiya and I refortified the land of Ištitina that Pihhuniya had taken. And I made it a land of Hatti again.

§33 Then when I conquered the land of Tipiya, I sent a messenger to Anniya, king of Azzi. I wrote to him (saying): "My servants who went to you while my father was in the land of Mittani, [return them to me]."

The rest of the narration for years seven, eight, and the beginning of year nine is lost in a break. For an extensive restoration based on Muršili's Comprehensive Annals see Beal, *COS* II, 88–90, which includes the death of Muršili's beloved brother Šarri-Kušuh, king of Carchemesh, in his ninth year.

§36 But when I, My Majesty, came up from Kizzuwatna (ancient Cilicia), [it was well into] the year. So I did not go further into the land of Azzi. But because Yahrešša had been hostile to me and was not sending me troops, and it was continually fighting [. . .] I, My Majesty, [went] to Yahrešša and I attacked Yahrešša. The sun-goddess of Arinna, my lady, the mighty storm-god, my lord, Mezzulla and all the gods ran before me and I conquered the city Yahrešša. Then I burned (it) out. I went forth [to the la]nd of Piggainarešša. And I fought the Kaška of Piggainarešša. I conquered it and I burned [ou]t the land of Piggainarešša. I took up from it civilian captives, cattle and sheep and I brought them away to Hattuša. When I had conquered Yahrešša and the land of Piggainarešša, I returned to Hattuša. This I did in one year.

Year 10

§37 In the following year I went to the land of Azzi. The troops and horse-troops of Azzi did not stand against me in (open) battle. They occupied all the fortified cities of the land. I fought only two fortified cities: Aripša and Dukkamma. The sun-goddess of Arinna, my lady, the mighty storm-god, my lord, Mezzulla and all the gods ran before me. I took Aripša and Dukkamma down in battle. And the civilian captives that I, My Majesty, brought for the royal house were 3,000. But this (number) did not include (the number of) the civilian captives, cattle and sheep that the lords, troops and horse-troops of Hattuša brought for themselves.

§38 I have already been king for 10 years since I sat on the throne of my father. I have conquered these enemy lands in 10 years by my (own) hand. The lands that the princes and lords were conquering are not in (this account). What the sun-goddess of Arinna, my lady, extends to me I will accomplish it and I will set it down (i.e., in words on a tablet).

Further reading

For the text edition see Albrecht Götze, *Die Annalen des Muršiliš*, Leipzig, Hinrichs Buchhandlung (1933); and Jean-Pierre Grélois, "Les annales decennales de Muršili II (CTH 61, I)," *Hethitica* 9 (1988): 17–145. For a previous English translation see Richard H. Beal, "The Ten Year Annals of Great King Murshili II of Hatti (2.16)," in COS, vol. 2, William W. Hallo and K. Lawson Younger, eds., Boston, Brill (2000), 82–90. For the history of the period see Trevor Bryce, *The Kingdom of the Hittites*, Oxford, Clarendon (1998), ch. 8. On the Ahhiyawa question see Bryce, *Kingdom*, 59–63, 321–4, 342–4. On Hittite historiography see Harry A. Hoffner, Jr., "Histories and Historians of the Ancient Near East: The Hittites," *Orientalia* 49 (1980): 283–332. On Hittite treaties see Gary M. Beckman, *Hittite Diplomatic Texts*, 2nd ed., Biblical Writings from the Ancient World 7, Atlanta, Scholars Press (1999).

113. Muršili II's "First" Plague Prayer (van den Hout)

Around the year 1325 BC the Hittite Great King Suppiluliuma I campaigned in Syria and laid siege to the city of Karkemish in the late summer. Meanwhile, he sent two of his generals to raid Amqa, the Egyptian controlled territory to the south of Karkemish. With this, Suppiluliuma violated a century old Egyptian–Hittite treaty. In Karkemish he then received a letter from the Egyptian queen, informing him of her husband's death and asking him for a son to marry, knowing, as she wrote, that he had many sons. The identity of the Pharaoh and his queen is still a matter of debate, but most scholars tend to identify them as Tutankhamun and Ankhesenamun.

After some initial hesitation and the dispatch of embassies to verify the sincerity of the queen's request, Suppiluliuma finally sent his son Zannanza. By the spring or early summer of the following year, it was already too late: adherents of the traditional Amun religion had again seized power and the Hittite prince was killed. Thereupon Suppiluliuma ordered another son, Arnuwanda, to carry out a punitive raid into the same area. Although Arnuwanda returned victorious, by Muršili's own account an epidemic of some kind developed among the thousands of prisoners and deportees whom the Hittites brought with them into Hatti-Land (the Hittite kingdom).

This epidemic, or "plague" as it is usually referred to, exacted a high toll among the deportees as well as the Hittite population. Among the most notable casualties were Suppiluliuma himself and his son and first successor Arnuwanda II. When Suppiluliuma's youngest(?) son, Muršili II, finally ascended the throne around 1318 BC, it took him 10 years to restore order in Hatti-Land. All the while, the epidemic kept taking lives until Muršili, after two decades of "plague," decided to take action (ca. 1300 BC). Even though he had described the rise of the epidemic among the deportees from Egypt as the immediate cause for the present predicament, this was not the true cause in the mind of the Hittites. Soul-searching by Muršili and archival research turned up three more fundamental causes that had angered the gods and caused them to send the plague. These were then confirmed by oracular inquiry and with that the process of healing could start. The three causes were the murder of Tudhaliya the Younger, briefly king and a close relative of Suppiluliuma (who was closely involved with his death), the violation of the Egyptian–Hittite treaty by Suppiluliuma mentioned earlier, and the neglect by the Hittites to bring regular offerings to the river Mala (Euphrates?). The murder of Tudhaliya is the topic of the so-called "First Plague Prayer"

(PP1), while the other two are dealt with in the "Second" (PP2) one. The "plague" is mentioned in at least four more prayers from the time of Muršili. The "Fourth" and "Fifth Plague Prayer" both mention the incursion into Egyptian-controlled territory in Syria as a cause, while the preserved part of the "Third" speaks only of a plague in general terms. The same is true of the well-preserved Prayer to the sun-goddess of Arinna. Although the traditional numbering of these prayers might suggest a chronological sequence, we have no way of establishing such an order. The fact that three prayers (PP1 §2, PP2 §1, and the Third Prayer) mention that the epidemic had already lasted 20 years, suggests a more or less simultaneous creation for them.

The first of the prayers translated here is addressed to the totality of Hittite gods and goddesses, while the second is addressed to the Hittite storm-god and other gods. Both are classic examples of the relation between god and man as seen through Hittite eyes. A bond exists between them very much like a treaty between a Hittite Great King and his vassals. There are mutual rights and duties, with the rights dependent upon the fulfillment of duties. In exchange for regular cult offerings the gods offer their protection and benefits. Since this relation resembles a legal one (or was felt as such), the prayers take the form of pleading before a court of law. While Muršili shows all the reverence and genuine humility due to the gods in the "First Plague Prayer," unquestioningly accepting full responsibility for what happened, the tone of the "Second" is distinctly different, almost defiant. He presents his arguments to convince the gods that they should withdraw the plague from Hatti-Land. He points out that all causes date to the days of his father's reign and that as a consequence he cannot be blamed for them (PP2 §9). He almost accuses the gods of supporting his father (PP2 §4). The "First Prayer" contains the same element (PP1 §4) but immediately acknowledges that Suppiluliuma ultimately faced the consequences when he fell victim to the plague himself. This is absent in the preserved part of the "Second." Yet, in a very modern way, Muršili is prepared to take responsibility for and acknowledges the mistakes made by his predecessors (PP2 §§6, 9). Also, he confronts the gods with the ultimate consequence of their policy; in the end there will be no people left to bring them their daily offerings of bread and wine (PP1 §8; less explicit PP2 §9). Finally, he appeals to an unwritten law of moral conduct: a master will forgive his servant, if the latter steps forward voluntarily and confesses his wrongdoing.

The "First Plague Prayer" has come down to us in only two exemplars, the second of which (B) is just a small fragment with traces of eight lines. The main copy (A) stems from the storerooms surrounding the main temple ("Temple 1") in the Lower City of Hattusa, the Hittite capital. The latter is a relatively small, single column tablet with just over 50 lines on each side. It was probably written in the (later?) thirteenth century and thus in all probability postdates Muršili's reign. In view of the very many erasures and the still remaining mistakes, it is a rough copy, perhaps even the work of a junior scribe. Exemplar B, duplicating §2 only, is too small for a reliable dating. Given the practically equal line length, this may have been a single-column tablet as well.

§1 [A]l[l] you [God]s (and) all you Goddesses [of Hatti-Land] . . . [. . .], a[l]l you [Oath Go]ds (and) al[l] you Oath Goddesses, [. . .] all you [pr]imeval Gods (and) Goddesses, [w]ho have been call[ed upon] to con[vene] in tha[t matter] to witness the [o]ath, you Mountains, Rivers, Springs, Underground Streams, now I, Muršil[i, Great King], your [prie]st, your servant, plead with you. On behalf of what [c]ause I make a plea to you, you, O Gods, my lords: [listen] to my w[o]rds!

§2 O Gods, [my] lords, [i]n Hatti-Land a plague has risen: Hatti-Land is being oppresse[d] by the plague and it [is being] severely pun[ished]. This is (already) the twentieth year! And since dying continues in [Hatti] – Land on a large scale, the affair of Tudaliya the Younger, son of Tudali[ya], started to weigh on [m]e and I conducted an oracle investigation through the god [and] the affair of Tudaliya the Younger was confirmed also by the god. Since for Hatti-Land Tuth[aliya] the Younger was their lord, [Hat]tusa's princes, commanders, chiefs-of-thousand, officers (and) [officials] as well as [troops] and chariots, everybody had sworn an oath to him. My father too [had] sworn an oath to him.

§3 [But when m]y [father] punished Tudaliya, Hattusa's [princes, commander]s, chiefs-of-thousand (and) officers, all of [them joine]d my father and the Oath [Deities seized] Tuthaliya [and they ki]lled [Tudaliya]! Moreover, his brothers who [. . . , them too they k]illed. [. . . others, who . . .], they sent them to Alasiya and [. . .] he was their [. . .], but they/them to him . . . [. . .] and the lords had broken the oath!

The gist of the passage is that Tudaliya was killed by the Oath Deities, implying that he had broken a certain oath himself. This, however, did not justify the murder by Suppiluliuma and his fellow conspirators: not only did they break their oath to him, but killing one's own relative is one of the severest taboos in Hittite society, which inevitably will lead to divine repercussions.

§4 [. . . O Gods,] my [lord]s, you have protected my father [. . .] . . . [. . .] . . . and since Hattusa [had been . . .] by the [. . .] and the enemy had taken Hatti-Land's [territories, my father thereupon] started [attac]king [the enemy land]s. He destroyed them and each of Hatti-Land's te[rritories he took back], but he (also) took from them (their) territories and re[settled] them. And further, other foreign countries during his reig[n he conquered]. Hatti-Land flourished and [he took] territories everywhere. During his reign all of Hatti-Land made progress: [people,] cattle (and) sheep multiplied in his time, even the displaced persons who had been [deported] from the en[emy] country, prospered. Nothing perished. Then the moment came that you, O Gods, after [the fact], sought revenge for that matter of Tudaliya the Younger from my father: my father [died] because of the bloodshed of Tudaliya, and the princes, commanders, chiefs-of-thousand (and) officials who had joined [my father,] th[ose too] died for [that] reason. That same matter affected Hatti-Land too and [Hatti-L]and began to die for [that] reason. Hatti-Land . . . [. . .], but then the plague became even worse and Hatti-Land was [severely] punished. It [has beco]me small and I, Muršili, [your] ser[vant], cannot overcome the agony [in my heart], cannot [overcome] the anguish in my body.

According to the above description the epidemic initially affected a small group among the ruling elite and then spread under the population at large.

§5 [. . . Gods,] my [lord]s, you who . . . [. . .], since [you] were c[alled] to witness the oath, . . . everybody had sworn an oath on [. . .] and [. . .], but since it came to pass that they had [. . . -ed] lord[ship(?)] of the oath, [you, O Gods,] my lords, did not [. . .] in that lawsuit. In no way [did you] s[eek revenge from them(?)] for the bloodshed [of Tudhaliya, but now, O Gods,] my lords [you are] prevailing [over me.]

Two unpublished fragments possibly contain up to four or five lines more of a new paragraph extending to the lower edge of the obverse. Depending on whether this new paragraph continued on the reverse or formed a paragraph by itself, the next paragraph should be §6 or §7. To avoid confusion with the numbering of paragraphs in Goetze's edition, the next one will be numbered §6′. The first eight lines of the reverse are too fragmentary to translate, towards the end of the paragraph the text becomes better preserved again.

§6′ [. . .] For that reason my father la[ter brought] an offering for the bloodshed but [H]attusa did not [do] anything. Thereupon I too performed [an offering for the bloodshed] but the people did [no]t d[o] anything, [no]thing they did [fo]r the sake of the country.

§7′ But since Hatti-Land is being heavily oppressed now by the p[lag]ue and Hatti-Land keeps on dying, the affair of Tuthaliya started to weigh on the people and through [the god] was it confirmed for me. So I conducted an oracle investigation [concerning i]t. Before yo[u, O Gods], my lords of the oath, they (i.e., the people of Hatti) are carrying out the offerings, that were determined for you, O Gods, my lords, for your temples in connection with the oath, the country (and) the plague. [Before] y[ou] they are clearing (the matter/themselves?) and to you, O Gods, my lords, I offer compensation and propitiation for the p[lagu]e in the land.

§8′ Now that you, O Gods, my lords, seek revenge for the bloodshed of Tudaliya: those who killed Tudaliya, [have] pa[id] for the bloodshed. And that bloodshed [has] further finished off Hatti-Land as well, so that Hatti-Land too has already paid for it. And now that it has come to me, I too with my house will start paying with compensation (and) propitiation. May your mind, O Gods, my lords, be satisfied! Have mercy on me again, O Gods, my lords, and let me appear before yo[u]. Listen to my plea to you: since I myself did not do anything evil, (and since) nobody of those days, (that is,) of the ones, who sinned and did do evil, is alive any longer and they have long since died, now that my father's doing has come to me, right now to you, O Gods, my [lord]s, for the land because of the plague I will start giving (and) paying propitiation. And since I will start paying propitiation and compensation, O Gods, my lords, [have] mercy on me again and let me appear before you. Since the plague punished Hatti-Land, [it] has become [s]mall but to you, O Gods, my lords, they have [offe]red bread and libations. The plague has heavily oppressed them and because of the plague they have [di]ed out. While the plague does not take (them) away entirely, they do keep dying and when the few that (still) offer bread and bring libations, perish, n[o]body will give bread and libatio[ns] to you any longer.

§9′ [O Gods, my lords,] for the sake of bread and libations have mercy on m[e], whom . . . [. . .] and let me appear before you! [B]an the plag[ue from Hatti-Land]. Do no longer let these few left to offer you bread [and libations], be punished(!?) and do not let them d[ie]! Let them offer to yo[u bread and liba]tions. C[ome], you Gods, my lords, [tur]n the plag[ue away]. And whatever evils happened in Hatti-Land [beca]use of Tu[daliya]'s death, ban them, O Gods . . . [. . .]! Ban them to an enemy country but have mer[cy again] on Hatti-Land! Let [the plag]ue stop and [let] me, your priest (and) servant, appear before you. Have mercy [on me] and ba[n] the agony from my heart and take the anguish from my [b]ody!

On Manuscript A's left edge there is a colophon:

[First tablet;] finished: "When Muršili ma[de] his plea [. . .]."

114. Muršili II's "Second" Plague Prayer (van den Hout)

Three exemplars or fragments exist of the "Second Plague Prayer," each preserving large parts of the composition. We know the findspot only of B, as it stems from the storerooms surrounding the main temple ("Temple 1") in the Lower City of Hattusa, the Hittite capital. Copy A is a single column tablet with about 75 lines per column. Judging by the ductus of the cuneiform script it might be a contemporary copy. Both copies B and C were of approximately equal length as A but had two columns on each side. B shows a number of erasures and probably dates to the (later?) thirteenth century, while C is even older. The division in paragraphs differs slightly among the three copies; the present division follows that of Goetze's edition.

§1 Storm-god of Hatti, my lord, [and you, Gods of Hatti], my [lor]ds, Murš[ili, Great King,] your servant, has sent me (saying): "Go, speak as follows to the [sto]rm-god of Hatti, my lord, and to the Gods, my lords: 'Concerning this that you have done: you have allowed a plague into Hatti-Land and Hatti-Land has been very heavily oppressed by the plague. During my father('s and) brother('s reign) people started to die, and even now that I became priest to the Gods, people continue to die in my days!'" This is (already) the twentieth year, that the dying continues in Hatti-Land, and still the plague is not lifted from Hatti-Land. I cannot overcome the agony in (my) heart nor can I overcome any longer the anguish in my body!

The quote in the first paragraph makes sense only if understood as a quote within a quote: Muršili sends someone else (a priest?) to speak to the gods the prayer that he, Muršili himself, has composed. The grammatical marker for direct speech is correctly used for a few lines and then dropped. The final quotation marks in the translation above are meant only to indicate the end of the grammatical direct speech.

§2 Then, also when I celebrated the festivals, I went back and forth to all the gods, not a single temple did I leave aside. Because of the plague I made pleas to all the gods,

[while] making vows to them (saying): ["Now you, O Gods,] my [lord]s, listen [to me] and [ban] the plague [from Hat]ti[-Land] . . . [Why Hatti-Land] keeps [dying,] let it [either be determined by oracle] or [let me see] it [through a dream or] let [a pro]phet tell [it!"] But the gods [did not listen] to me and the plague [in] Hatti[-Land] did not [st]op, [and Hatti-Land was very heavily oppress]ed.

§3 Also those [few], that were [lef]t of the ones who offer bread [and wine] to the gods, s[tarted to] die. [Then the matte]r [of . . .] started to weigh [on me] again and I made the go[ds' . . . the subject of an oracle inquiry.] Two [o]ld tablets [I found.] One tablet ab[out an offering to the River Mala: . . .] . . . for[me]r kings [had] brought the offering to the river Mala, but [now], for as long as since the days of my father [people have] d[ied] in Hatti-Land, we had never made [the offering] to the River Mala.

The mentioning of a festival for the River Mala by Muršili himself in his Extensive Annals for his nineteenth regnal year can be taken as a *terminus ante quem* for the composition of this prayer and fits well the overall period of 20 years that the plague has raged since Arnuwanda's raids into Syria.

§4 The second tablet is about the town of Kurustamma: how the storm-god of Hatti brought the people of Kurustamma to Egypt and how the storm-god of Hatti made a treaty for them with the people of Hatti, (and how) they were then put under oath by the storm-god of Hatti. Now that the people of Hatti and Egypt were put under oath by the storm-god, it happened that the people of Hatti turned away and suddenly broke the divine oath: my father sent troops and chariots and they attacked Egyptian territory, the land of Amqa. And again he sent them and again they attacked. When the Egyptians became frightened, they came and even asked my father for a son of his for kingship! When my father had given them a son of his and when they had escorted him away, they killed him! My father burst out in rage, he went to Egypt, attacked it and destroyed Egypt's troops and chariots. Even then the storm-god of Hatti, my lord, let my father prevail in the lawsuit: he defeated Egypt's troops and chariots and destroyed them. When they brought back home to Hatti-Land the prisoners of war that they had captured, a plague developed among the prisoners and they s[tarted] to die.

§5 When they had brought the prisoners into Hatti-Land, the prisoners carried the plague with them into Hatti-Land and from that day onwards people in Hatti-Land started to die. Now, when I had found that tablet about Egypt, I made it the object of a divine oracle inquiry (as follows): "Concerning that thing done by the storm-god of Hatti, if it has become a reason for anger for the storm-god of Hatti, my lord, because the people of Egypt and the people of Hatti are under oath (and) because the Household Deities are in the temple of the storm-god of Hatti, my lord, while it was the people of Hatti who suddenly broke (the oath)." That was confirmed.

The prayer quotes here directly from an oracle tablet, which explains the anakolouthon. Normally, the "if" clause should be followed by an expression of an expected oracle result ("then let the oracle be favorable/unfavorable"). Instead, the result ("That was confirmed") is given in the narrative of the prayer outside the quote. Note that at the moment of the oracle Muršili considered the Hittites as still being under oath. The

Household deities can be compared to the Roman Penates who also played a role in oath ceremonies.

§6 Also, I made an oracle inquiry in connection with the plague about the offering to the Ri[ver Mala] and in that case, too, it was determined for me to present myself to the storm-god of Hatti, my lord. So, her[e it is,] I confessed my [si]n [to the storm-god]: It is (true), we have done [it]. [That it did not] happen in my days, that [it happened] in my father's days, [. . .] I know all too well . . .

Approximately 30 lines in A are lost at this point. How many paragraphs those lines contained cannot be determined, but Goetze's paragraph numbering will be followed.

§7′ [. . . O storm-god of Hatti, my lord,] listen [to me] ! [Let] the plague [be] lifted [from Hatti-Land].

§8′ I will start [paying] for the things that were determined, [when] I made the oracle inquiry. [. . . I will start p]aying. Since it was [determined by the go]d [in connection] with the plague, I brought an offering [. . .] to the storm-god of Hatti, [to . . . of Hatt]i(?) . . . I made an offering . . . Concerning the off[ering] to the River Mala that was determined for me in con[nection with the plague], since I am now going to the river Mala, let me off the hook, O storm-god of H[atti], my lord, (and) Gods, my lords. I want to make the offering to the River [Mala] and I want to provide for it, because of the plague, that's why! O Gods, my lords, have mercy on me and let the plague in Hatti-Land stop!

§9′ Storm-god of Hatti, my lord, Gods, my lords, as it happens, people sin. My father too sinned. He broke (his) word to the storm-god of Hatti. I, on the other hand, did not sin at all, but as it happens, a father's sin passes down to his son. To me too my father's sin passed down. So now before the storm-god of Hatti, my lord, and before the Gods, my lords, I have confessed it: it is true, we have done it. Since I have confessed my father's sin, so let the storm-god, my lord's, and the Gods, my lords', their mind be satisfied again. Have mercy on me again, and ban the plague from Hatti-Land again. Do not let those few remaining, who take care of the bread offerings and libations, die on me!

§10′ To the storm-god, my lord, I make a plea now because of the plague: listen to me, O storm-god of Hatti, my lord and save me! The fo[llowing I give] you [to consider:] a bird seeks refuge in its cage and the cage sa[ves] it. Or if something weighs heavily on a servant, he will make a plea with his lord, his lord will listen to him and [will have merc]y on him. Whatever weighed on him, he will set it right for him. Or if some servant has sinned, but confesses the sin to his lord, his lord will have his way with him as he wishes, but since he confesses to his lord, the lord's mind will be satisfie[d and] his [lord] will not punish that servant. Now it is me confess[ing] my father's sin: it is true, I did it. If there are amends to be made: the many things that earlier too through th[at plag]ue (Hatti-Land paid), that is, the deportees from Egypt, [the pris]oners of war they brought home and the deportees [they . . . , tha]t which Hattusa has paid through the plague, it is thus happening twentyfold already, and yet the mind of the storm-god of Hatti, my lord, and of the Gods, my lords, is not satisfied! Or if on [m]e, however, you separately impose some kind of amends, tell it to me in a dream and I will give it to you.

§11′ Now I keep pleading [with y]ou, storm-god of Hatti, my lord: save me! [I]f for this reason perhaps people are dying, do not let those remaining of the people who take care of the gods' bread offerings and libations, die any longer, until I start setting it straight again. If, furthermore, for some other reason people keep dying, let me either see it in a dream or let it be [ascert]ained through an oracle or let a prophet tell it or the priests will sleep holily concerning that which I ordered [a]ll of them. O storm-god of Hatti, my lord, save me! And let the gods, my lords, show their guidance and let someone then see it in a dream. It must be found out, why people keep dying! We are dangling from the point of a needle! Storm-god of Hatti, save me and lift the plague off Hatti-Land again!

The literally translated phrase of the priests sleeping "holily" in all likelihood refers to the practice of incubation, where a priest would try to induce dreams that would then be interpreted as a divine message.
A colophon concludes copy C.

First tablet, finished: "[When] Muršili[. . .] because of the plague [made a pl]e[a].

Further reading

The basic edition for the above prayers is still Albrecht Goetze's "Die Pestgebete des Muršili," *Kleinasiatische Forschungen* 1 (1929): 161–251. A French edition with translation and commentary is available in René Lebrun, *Hymnes et prières hittites* (Louvain-la-neuve, 1980), 192–239. Further translations exist in German, French, and Spanish. The most recent English translation is that by Itamar Singer in *Hittite Prayers*, Writings from the Ancient World, Atlanta, 2002), 47–69. For Hittite prayers in general see Johan de Roos, "Hittite Prayers," in J. Sasson et al. (eds.), *Civilizations of the Ancient Near East*, vol. 3 (New York, 1995), 1997–2005.

115. The Apology of Ḫattušili III (Hoffner)

The "Apology" of Ḫattušili – so called because the first three-quarters of the text reads like an autobiographical defense of the man's usurpation of the imperial throne from his nephew, Muršili III (also known as Urḫi-Teššub) – covers a period from the last half of the reign of his father Muršili II (1321–1295 BC), through the entire reign of his older brother Muwatalli II (1295–1272 BC), and that of Muwatalli's son Muršili III (1272–1267 BC). But because the final portion of the text consists of a royal decree establishing temple estates for the goddess Ištar of the city Šamuḫa, it is generally thought that the long "historical" section is meant to serve as a prologue to the edict proper, much as the Hittite state treaties were always introduced by historical prologues. As with the latter, so Ḫattušili's text is highly tendentious and serves to justify his actions at every turn. The text must be used with caution as a historical source, but it is of great interest as a sample of royal propaganda. It has no exact parallel among either Hittite or other ancient Near Eastern royal texts. In some respects it resembles the so-called Court History of King David of Israel, which tells of his rise to the throne in spite of persecution by King Saul. Although it attempts to justify Ḫattušili's usurpation of the throne, evidence points to a date toward the end of his reign for its composition (1267–1237 BC).

> *Thus speaks the Tabarna, Ḫattušili, Great King, King of Ḫatti, son of Muršili, Great King, King of Ḫatti, grandson of Šuppiluliuma, Great King, King of Ḫatti, descendant of Ḫattušili (I), King of Kushshar.*

With these words the king introduces his text. Tabarna is a royal title of uncertain translation. The words "Great King" were not used lightly, as a kind of boast, but constituted a specific exalted rank among the kings of the Near East. Only the most powerful of kings, commanding a string of dependent ("vassal") states, could employ this title for themselves: Egypt, the Hittites, the Assyrians, the Babylonians, and the Mycenaean Greeks (the kingdom of Aḫḫiyawa). The king skips his two immediate predecessors, his brother Muwatalli II and the latter's son Muršili III, enumerates his own father Muršili II and his grandfather Šuppiluliuma I, both of whom qualified as "Great Kings," and then skips all the way back to the beginning of the Old Kingdom to his eponymous ancestor Ḫattušili I (1650–1620 BC). In the process the king also skips Muršili II's older brother and predecessor Arnuwanda II, since he is only interested in his own direct royal ancestors. Then begins the text proper with a statement of purpose.

> *I will celebrate Ištar's divine providence. Let (every) man hear it, and may in the future my son, grandson, and further royal descendants honor Ištar among (all) the gods.*

The purpose is twofold: to praise the king's patron goddess for raising him to the throne and to obligate his own successors on the throne of Ḫatti to the perpetuation of the cult of this goddess. "Ištar" is just the Akkadian reading of the cuneiform sign used to designate this goddess. Her Hittite name has been claimed to be Enzili and her Hurrian name Šawuška. The provisions for the perpetuation of her cult will be taken up again at the end of the text. The king then describes his place among the legitimate children of his father, king Muršili II. Of course, he also had children by harem women, but only the children of the first wife were eligible to succeed to the throne.

> *My father Muršili had four children: (three sons) Ḫalpašulupi, Muwatalli and Hattušili, and a daughter Maššanauzzi. Of all these I was the youngest child.*

As the youngest male child, Hattušili followed Ḫalpašulupi and Muwatalli in eligibility. The former apparently predeceased Muršili, and the latter succeeded his father on the throne. One significant event from Ḫattušili's childhood is singled out, for it bears upon his eventual rise to kingship and to the special role played by Ištar of Šamuḫa.

Ištar, my lady, sent Muwatalli my brother to Muršili my father by means of a dream (saying): "The years (of his life) are few for Ḫattušili: he will not live (long). But hand him over to me, and let him be my priest, and he will live." So my father put me in the (priestly) service of the goddess while I was yet a child, and as a priest I brought offerings to the goddess. At the hand of Ištar my lady I experienced prosperity. Ištar my lady took me by the hand and was my guide.

In the following paragraphs Ḫattušili tells of events in the reign of his older brother Muwatalli II: how he rose step by step in military service to the high rank of Chief of the Royal Bodyguard, a post often held by younger brothers of the reigning monarch. Along the way Ḫattušili was met with jealous relatives who brought false charges against him, from which he was exonerated by the intervention of his patron goddess. When Muwatalli II moved the imperial capital from Hattusha south to Tarḫuntašša, just north of the Mediterranean coast, Ḫattušili was left to command the northern armies in protection of the old capital. So successful was he that Muwatalli also made him King of the dependent city-state of Ḫakpiš to the northeast of the old capital. When it finally came to a pitched battle between Muwatalli of Ḫatti and Ramses II of Egypt at Kadesh on the Orontes, Ḫattušili commanded troops in the Hittite expeditionary force. After the battle, which the Hittites considered themselves to have won, as Ḫattušili returned home via the kingdom of Kizzuwatna-Kummanni, he contracted a marriage with the daughter of a very influential priest of Kizzuwatna. Her name was Puduḫepa, and she ruled as queen long after the death of her husband. He describes the strategic marriage as another of the events comprising Ištar's providential guidance.

At the command of the goddess (Ištar) I took Puduḫepa, daughter of the priest Pentipšarri, as my wife. We joined (in matrimony), and the goddess gave us the love of husband and wife. We had sons and daughters. On this occasion the goddess my lady appeared to me in a dream (saying): "Serve me with your household!" So I served the goddess together with my household. The goddess was there with us in the household which we made, and our household thrived. This (too) was (a sign) of Ištar's honoring me.

The text proceeds next to tell of the death of Muwatalli and his succession by his son Muršili III (here called by his other name Urḫi-Teššub). According to the tendentious account of Ḫattušili, he was then persecuted by Muršili III, whom he claimed was jealous and afraid of him. Ḫattušili offered no resistance until the persecution became unbearable.

Out of respect for my brother (Muwatalli) I did not resist at all. And I submitted for seven years. He (i.e., Muršili III), however, sought to kill me with the help of (his) gods and men. He also took away from me (my kingdom of) Ḫakpiš and Nerik. Now I no longer submitted.But when I took up arms against him, I did not commit a moral offense by surreptitiously revolting against him in (his) chariot or within his own house. Rather in a manly way I declared to him: "You have disrespected me. You are a Great King, whereas I am king of the single fortress town that you have left to me. come! Let Ištar of Šamuḫa and the storm-god of Nerik judge our case (in the ordeal of battle)!"

Writing this years after the events, and knowing what accusations he had to counter after defeating and deposing his nephew Muršili, Ḫattušili counters the accusations of immoral behavior with arguments that justify his actions and portray him as a virtuous, god-fearing man acting completely in self-defense. He then describes the key events in the battle that led to his defeat of Muršili. After he ascended the throne, he claims that none of the states allied with Ḫatti during the previous kings' reigns defected, but all continued to send ambassadors to his court with gifts. Finally, he turns to the edict that this narrative was intended to introduce.

O Ištar, my lady! How many times have you helped me! You installed me in "The High Place," in kingship over the Ḫatti Land. I, then, gave Ištar the estates of (my opponent) Arma-Tarḫunta, withdrawing it (from the private sphere) and handing it over to her . . . Ištar is my goddess, and (my descendants) will worship her as Ištar the Exalted One. The mausoleum which I made for myself I also dedicated to the goddess. And I dedicated my son Tudḫaliya to you (O goddess) as well. Let Tudḫaliya, my son, Administer the temple of Ištar. As I am the servant of the goddess, so also let him be the servant of the goddess . . . Whoever in the future seeks to take away the descendants of Hattušili and Puduhepa from service to Ištar, or who seeks to take from her storehouse and threshing floor so much as a blade of straw or a chip of wood, let him be Ištar of Šamuḫa's enemy in court . . . Whatever son, grandson or descendant of Ḫattušili and Puduḫepa arises in the future, may he venerate Ištar of Šamuḫa.

With these words Ḫattušili concludes his great Apology and edict in favor of Ištar of Šamuḫa, who remained a highly honored goddess in the reigns of his descendants Tudḫaliya IV, Arnuwanda III, and Šuppiluliuma II.

Further reading

For the history of the period covered by this text see Trevor R. Bryce, *The Kingdom of the Hittites* (Oxford: Clarendon, 1998), chs. 8–11; and Theo van den Hout, "Khattushili III, King of the Hittites," in Jack M. Sasson (ed.), *Civilizations of the Ancient Near East*, vol. 3 (New York: Scribners/Macmillan, 1995), pp. 1107–20. An English translation of the text can be found in W. W. Hallo and K. Lawson Younger (eds.), *The Context of Scripture*, vol. 1 (Leiden: Brill, 1997), 199–204. On Hittite historiography and this text in particular as "history" see the following works: Alfonso Archi, "The Propaganda of Hattusilis III" *Studi Micenei ed Egeo-Anatolici* 14 (1971): 185–216, Hans Gustav Güterbock, "Hittite Historiography: A Survey," in *History, Historiography and Interpretation: Studies in Bibliography and Cuneiform Literatures*, edited by Hayim Tadmor and Moshe Weinfeld (Jerusalem: Magnes, 1983), 21–35; Harry A. Hoffner, Jr., "Histories and Historians of the Ancient Near East: The Hittites," *Orientalia* NS 49 (1980): 283–332; J. Gregory McMahon, "History and Legend in Early Hittite Historiography," in

Faith, Tradition, and History. Old Testament Historiography in Its Near Eastern Context, edited by Alan R. Millard, James K. Hoffmeier, and David W. Baker (Winona Lake, Ind.: Eisenbrauns, 1994), 149–58; Herbert M. Wolf. "The Historical Reliability of the Hittite Annals," in *Faith, Tradition, and History*, 159–64.

116. The treaty with Kurunta of Tarḫuntašša (Hoffner)

When Muwatalli II (r. 1295–1272 BC) moved his capital from Ḫattuša to Tarḫuntašša shortly before the Battle of Kadesh, he established a new center, which persisted after the capital was returned to Ḫattuša as the capital of a new allied state called Tarḫuntašša. According to which of two theories are followed, either the first king of that state was Ulmi-Teššub, who was succeeded by Kurunta, or the two names represent the same ruler. Either way, it is agreed that Ḫattušili III (r. 1267–1237 BC) made a treaty with Ulmi-Teššub, and Tudḫaliya IV (r. 1237–1209 BC) revised and renewed it with Kurunta. It is this second treaty that is presented here.

Kurunta was a son of Muwatalli II and a younger brother of Muršili III / Urḫi-Teššub (r. 1272–1267 BC). The latter may have been almost as old as his uncle Ḫattušili, while Urḫi-Teššub's younger brother Kurunta was closer in age to Ḫattušili's son Tudḫaliya. Eventually, as king of Tarḫuntašša, Kurunta had himself depicted on a rock relief near present-day Konya. On this relief he is styled "Great King," a title not accorded him in this treaty.

Indications in colophons had long ago informed scholars that the Hittites of the New Kingdom inscribed the original copies of especially important treaties on metal tablets: either silver as in the case of the treaty with Egypt, or bronze as in the case of this treaty. But before the discovery of the Kurunta treaty in July of 1986 no example of a metal tablet of the Hittites had ever been recovered. According to the wording of the colophon, seven copies of this treaty – all apparently metal tablets – were prepared.

> *This (treaty) was made into seven tablets and sealed with the seals of the sun-goddess of Arinna and the storm-god of Ḫatti. One tablet was placed before the sun-goddess of Arinna, one before the storm-god of Ḫatti, one before the goddess Lelwani, one before the goddess Ḫebat of Kizzuwatna, one before the storm-god of Lightning, and one in the king's house before the god Zitḫariya. And Kurunta, king of Tarḫuntašša keeps one in his house.*

By *"before (the god)"* is meant keeping the copy in the temple of that deity. Six of the copies were intended for deities and one for Kurunta. We do not know which of the seven copies was the one found in 1986. Its location, under the Hittite pavement, suggests an intentional burial, perhaps indicating that it was no longer valid. The tablet was in perfect condition, with not a single cuneiform sign on its engraved surface illegible.

Like all New Kingdom Hittite treaties the Kurunta treaty exhibits a conventional form: royal titulary, historical prologue, stipulations and obligations, divine witnesses, and sanctions ("blessings" and "curses"). But the special circumstances of the treaty partners called for modifications: consideration of and modification of terms in the preceding treaty by Ḫattušili, modifications to the borders of the kingdom, which after all directly abutted the kingdom of Ḫatti, addition of a section not adjacent to the "historical prologue" detailing the special close relationship of Tudḫaliya and Kurunta from childhood, and the comparative status of the Tarḫuntašša and Carchemish cadet branches of the Hittite royal family.

On the Kurunta treaty Tudḫaliya's royal titulary, as was customary, extended back three generations (father Ḫattušili III, grandfather Muršili II and great-grandfather Šuppiluliuma I) after which it jumps back to a remote namesake king, in this case Tudḫaliya I/II (1400–1360 BC). In this titulary only the currently reigning king Tudḫaliya is styled "Tabarna," while all the rest are "Great King" and "Hero."

The first two paragraphs of the historical prologue must because of their importance be given in translation.

When my father Ḫattušili made war on Urḫi-Teššub son of Muwatalli, he deposed him from kingship, but no treason (literally "sin") was proven against Kurunta. Kurunta was in no way involved in whatever treasonous acts the men of Hatti committed. Even before this King Muwatalli had entrusted him to my father Ḫattušili to raise, and . . . my father raised him. But when my father had deposed Urḫi-Teššub from kingship, he took Kurunta and installed him in kingship in the land of Tarḫuntašša. My father made treaty tablets for him concerning the obligations my father imposed on him and how he had set boundaries for him. Kurunta still has these.

Following a long section delineating boundaries and Hittite enclaves within Tarḫuntašša, Tudḫaliya turned to a sensitive subject: Kurunta's access to the Eternal Rock Mausoleum. the wording of this section does not make clear what was entailed in "approaching" or "going up" to this mausoleum. One assumes that, since Muwatalli never returned to the old capital, he was buried in this mausoleum, and that access by Kurunta was considered by Ḫattušili III's advisor Maraššanta to constitute a threat to his and Tudḫaliya's status as the legitimate emperors in Ḫattuša. The section reads:

With respect to the matter of the Eternal Rock Mausoleum, my father (Ḫattušili III) took it from the mouth of Maraššanta (who had said): "Kurunta should not approach the Eternal Rock Mausoleum." My father (once) made a tablet for Maraššanta, which Maraššanta (still) has. But my father did not yet know how the wording of the Eternal Rock Mausoleum inside the sanctuary of Teššub was inscribed: how from now on the Eternal Rock Mausoleum will never be taken away from Kurunta. Now when he came to hear the wording, my father reversed his ruling. And when I, Tudḫaliya, Great King, succeeded to the throne, I sent a man who saw how the word of the Eternal Rock Mausoleum inside the sanctuary of Teššub was inscribed: "From now on the Eternal Rock Mausoleum will never be taken away from Kurunta." Therefore if Maraššanta ever brings the tablet which he has, let it not be accepted.

Tudḫaliya takes great pains to tell the entire story and to explain the existence of a tablet that might take the opposite position. He had to protect himself from the accusation that he as well as his father were violating the wording of the inscription, which most likely was accompanied by a curse on whatever king thereafter violated its terms.

The next section again deals with boundaries, but its detachment from the earlier systematic boundary description is due to its focusing upon a significant natural resource of the Ḫulaya River Land, which formed the northernmost extension of Tarḫuntašša and directly adjoined Ḫatti. This natural resource was the deposit of salt in the cliff faces of that region. Tudḫaliya cedes this resource entirely to Kurunta. No Hittite may enter this region either to use it for summer pasture of flocks or to harvest the salt.

> *No goatherd may go into the Ḫulaya River Land, which is the boundary (area) of the land of Tarḫuntašša. And if they drive up from the Ḫulaya River Land to the Great Saltlick Rock, let them not take from him (i.e., Kurunta) the saltlick rights. They are given to the king of Tarḫuntašša, and he may regularly take the salt. My father Ḫattušili gave to Kurunta, king of Tarḫuntašša, the towns of Šarmana, Pantarwanta and Maḫrimma together with their fields, grounds, meadows, sheep pastures, the whole saltlick, and the whole salt deposit. I too, My Majesty, Tudḫaliya the Great King, have given them to him. Therefore let no other person encroach upon the salt of the town Šarmana.*

After a short section on Hittite contributions to the cult of Tarḫuntašša, Tudḫaliya returns to the subject of his longstanding friendship with Kurunta. This is a sensitive matter, since everyone was aware that Tudḫaliya's father Ḫattušili had wrested the kingship from Kurunta's brother, and that after that the childless brother Kurunta himself was in line to succeed to the throne. It was important therefore for Tudḫaliya to establish the fact that Kurunta had once in effect given his loyalty to him as the future emperor.

> *Before I, Tudḫaliya the Great King, had become king, the god had already brought Kurunta and me together in friendship. Already we were dear and good to each other. We even were parties to an oath: "Let each be loyal to the other." But at that time my father had placed an older brother in the rank of Crown Prince. At that time (my father) had not yet decided that I should become (the next) king. But even at that time Kurunta was loyal to me and swore allegiance to me personally as follows: "Even if your father does not install you in kingship, in whatever place your father puts you I will be loyal to you only. I am your servant." I too swore my allegiance to Kurunta: "I too will be loyal to you."*

In this passage Tudḫaliya consciously uses technical terms for treaty partners, even though he is describing an informal relationship formed during childhood. The god "bringing together" the two echoes the language his father and Ramses II of Egypt had used in their treaty. The terms "dear" and "good" also find frequent employment in the language of state treaties. And the existence of an oath had special significance, since treaties were always enforced by oaths. Furthermore, the verb "be loyal" (translatable also as "protect") is the standard term of choice used to describe the primary obligation of the partners to a treaty. And finally, by putting in Kurunta's mouth the words "I am your servant" he establishes that Kurunta consented in advance to a subordinate position, in effect disavowing any claim to the imperial throne of Ḫatti. The use of direct quotes here raises the question of whether Tudḫaliya had this in writing or was just quoting from memory. If this was an event of his childhood, the latter would almost have to be the case. If it was an event of his young adulthood, there is a possibility that the two young men actually put it in writing and solemnized the vow with a ceremony of some kind. Compare the oath between David and Jonathan in 1 Samuel 23: 15–18, and the earlier symbolic transfer of Jonathan's garment and weapons to David in 1 Samuel 18: 1–4.

To further prove Kurunta's commitment to him Tudḫaliya cites how Kurunta immediately recognized him as legitimate successor upon the death of Ḫattušili, thus acknowledging the existence and validity of the oaths of subordination and loyalty he had earlier taken to Tudḫaliya:

> *But when my father died, although (some) lands adopted a wait-and-see policy (of recognizing me), at that time too Kurunta put his life on the line for me. He was loyal to me and broke none of the oaths he had sworn. And when the deity took me, and I became king, I made this treaty with Kurunta. I gave even cities which were not mentioned on the treaty tablet of my father . . . to be subjects of Kurunta . . . I redrew the boundaries in a manner favorable to him. I gave the Eternal Rock Mausoleum back to him. In the future let no one take the Eternal Rock Mausoleum away from a descendant of Kurunta.*

After a short section obligating both sides and their descendants to keep the terms of this treaty Tudḫaliya addresses the question of the relative ranking of the important states of Tarḫuntašša and Carchemish:

> *Let the protocol of the king of the land of Carchemish be allowed to him with respect to the Great Throne (i.e., the imperial kingship of Hatti). Let only the crown prince (of Hatti) be greater than the king of the land of Tarḫuntašša; let no one else be higher in rank than he. What royal insignia (or protocol) is allowed to the king of the land of Carchemish, let it also be allowed to the king of the land of Tarḫuntašša.*

Both of these states survived the fall of the imperial capital at Ḫattuša, and we know that the kings of Carchemish continued for a time to use the title "Great King."

In his earlier treaty with Tarḫuntašša, Ḫattušili III had included a clause to the effect that the Hittite empress Puduḫepa had the right to choose a wife for Kurunta, and that only a child of that wife could succeed to the throne. Tudḫaliya now revokes that clause.

Whatever son of his Kurunta prefers, whether the son of his (first) wife or the son of some other woman, whatever son is the choice of Kurunta, whatever son Kurunta prefers, let him place him in kingship in the land of Tarḫuntašša. Let no one overrule Kurunta in this matter.

On the same subject of the future of Kurunta's line Tudḫaliya added:

Let this treaty be valid for Kurunta, his son and his grandson. I, My majesty, will not throw out your son. I will not accept (in your son's place) your brother or anyone else. Your descendant alone will possess the land of Tarḫuntašša which I have given to you.

The text further stipulates, following almost identical wording in the earlier treaty of Ḫattušili with Tarḫuntašša, that if a descendant of Kurunta commits treason against the emperor, he will be tried, and if convicted might even be executed. But the direct line of Kurunta's descendants would not be abandoned and another line substituted. This commitment is even guaranteed by a separate oath and curse invoked upon whatever successor of Tudḫaliya might do such a thing:

Let the storm-god of Ḫatti and the sun-goddess of Arinna destroy whoever does that thing.

The next sections deal with Kurunta's obligation to ensure the succession and permanence of Tudḫaliya's descendants and Tarḫuntašša's obligation to provide troops for major military campaigns of Hittite emperors.

The divine witnesses to the treaty include the usual groupings found in New Kingdom treaties:

The Thousand gods have now been called to assembly for (attesting the contents of) this treaty tablet that I have just executed for you. Let them see, hear and be witnesses thereto.

There follow the sun-god of Heaven, the sun-goddess of Arinna and the storm-god of Heaven, who are the three preeminent gods of the state pantheon, followed by a large group of localized storm-gods, then a large group of localized "Patron Gods," localized Ḫebat-goddesses, and Ištar-Šawuška-goddesses. These categories are followed by various deities not belonging to a specific class of deities. The list concludes with the standard enumeration of "nature deities":

Heaven and earth, the great sea, the mountains, rivers and springs of the land of Hatti and of the land of Tarḫuntašša.

Since the function of these divine witnesses is to prosper those who keep the treaty terms and punish violators, there follows a statement to this effect, with the blessings of obedience preceding the curses upon violation.

Finally, the names of the scribe and the human witnesses are given, which include over 20 Hittite royal princes, some identified as kings of small states rather than as "prince."

> *Ḫalwa-ziti the scribe, the son of Lupakki of Ukkiya, inscribed this tablet in the city of Tawa in the presence of the following witnesses: Prince Nerikkaili, (Prince) Ḫuzziya Chief of the Royal Bodyguard, Prince Kurakura, Ini-Teššub king of Carchemish, Mašturi king of the Šeḫa River Land, Šawuška-muwa the king's son-in-law, Uppara-muwa the anduwašalli, Tattamaru the Chief of the Guard of the Left Side, Prince Eḫli-Šarruma, Prince Taki-Šarruma, Prince En-Šarruma, Alalimi Chief of the military tribunes, Alantalli king of the land of Mera, Bentešina king of the land of Amurru, Šaḫurunuwa Chief of the Wood Scribes, Field Marshall Ḫattuša-Kurunta, GAL-[d]U Chief of the Chariot Drivers, Field Marshall Ḫuršaniya, Zuzuḫḫa Chief of the Chariot Warriors, Šalikka Chief of the Guards of the Right Side, Tapa-ziti the Decurio, Tuttu Commander of the Royal Storehouses, Walwa-ziti Chief of the Scribes, Kammaliya Chief Scribe of the Kitchen Staff, Nana-zi Chief of the Scribes and Overseer of the food-servers – and all sorts of military commanders, magistrates and all the royal family.*

Such a gathering in the city of Tawa was a major occasion, with kings from as far west as Mera on the Aegean Coastland as far southeast as Amurru in southern Syria convening. All of these important political figures swore their compliance with the terms of this treaty and acted as human guarantors of its commitments. In some respects only the treaty of Ḫattušili III with Ramses of Egypt equaled this treaty in importance. In the final decades of the Hittite imperial throne in Ḫattuša the cohesiveness of this vast network of kings and military figures was vital to the survival of the empire. It was presumably the failure of that cohesion that led to the fall of Ḫattuša 40 years later in 1190 BC.

Further reading

For the historical background of this treaty see Trevor R. Bryce, *The Kingdom of the Hittites* (Oxford: Clarendon, 1998), chs. 11–12. On the line of kings at Tarḫuntašša see Itamar Singer, "Great Kings of Tarhuntassa," in *Studi Micenei ed Egeo-Anatolici* 38 (1996): 63–71. On the rock relief of Kurunta see Ali M. Dinçol, "The Rock Monument of the Great King Kurunta and Its Hieroglyphic Inscription," in *Acts of the IIIrd International Congress of Hittitology. Çorum, September 16–22, 1996*, edited by Sedat Alp and Aygül Süel (Ankara: Grafik, Teknik Hazirlik Uyum Ajans, 1998), 159–66. For English translations of other Hittite treaties see Gary M. Beckman, *Hittite Diplomatic Texts*. 2d ed. Writings from the Ancient World 7 (Atlanta: Scholars Press, 1999).

117. A letter from the Hittite King Hattušili III to Kadašman-Enlil II, King of Babylonia, in Akkadian (Mineck)

When corresponding with persons outside Hittite territory, the Hittites wrote in Akkadian, the *lingua franca* of the ancient Near East. But even in their own language, in letter writing they adopted the standard Akkadian introductory formula used in this text: thus (says) X, say to Y. This shows us that letters were dictated to one scribe and then read aloud to the addressee by another scribe, and that the Hittite court maintained scribes conversant with Akkadian. The introduction is typically followed by greetings that are also formulaic. They are equivalent to our "I am fine – I hope you are fine." This text also makes extensive use of the epithet "My Brother," which was routinely used to address other members of this international brotherhood of royal peers, even though they had never actually met.

Letters are by nature one-sided. But in this letter from Hattušili III of Hatti to his much younger contemporary, Kadašman-Enlil II of Babylonia, Hattušili quotes extensively from previous correspondence, a common practice among the Hittites, which helps to fill in the historical background. Hattušili begins the letter (par. 4) with a historical prologue recounting his relationship with Kadašman-Enlil's father with protests of good intentions. He then (par. 5) earnestly cajoles the younger king to stand up to the (unnamed) Assyrian king who apparently would not allow Babylonian messengers to pass through to Hittite territory. Free passage for messengers was, of course, a major diplomatic concern for allies, indicating here that Hattušili would like to strengthen their previously strained political ties in the face of increasing Assyrian power.

Throughout the rest of the letter, Hattušili comments paragraph by paragraph on the previous correspondence he has received from Kadašman-Enlil, concerning other matters of political importance such as the mistreatment of merchants, the control of vassals, and the exchange of trained experts. The last seven paragraphs are quite broken but they concern greeting-gifts that were luxury goods exchanged by the royal families of this time period by means of their messengers. These include requests from Hattušili for a sculptor, Babylonian horses, lapis lazuli, and gold plating. This is followed by a list of the greeting gifts Hattušili will be sending Kadašman-Enlil and the promise to send anything else he might ask of the Hittite king.

Text: CTH 172 (KBo 1.10 + KUB 3.72 with KUB 4 Nachträge)

§1 (obv 1–2) [Thus] (says) Hattušili, Great King, King of Hatti-Land: Sa[y to] Kadašman-Enlil, Great King, King of [Kar]anduniyaš (Babylonia), my brother:

§2 (obv 3–4) [With] me, it is well. With my house, my wife, my children, my troops, my horse-troops, my chariot-troops and within my entire land, everything is exceedingly well.

§3 (obv 5–6) With you, may it be well! With your house, your wives, your children, your troops, your horse-troops, your chariot-troops and within your entire land, may it be exceedingly well!

§4 (obv 7–24) When your father and I concluded friendship and we turned into loving brothers (became allies), we did not become brothers for just one day. Did we not conclude brotherhood and friendship forever? [And together] we issued an [agree]ment as follows, saying: "We are mortal. S[hould one of us] go to his fate, may the survivor protect his sons." And while the gods made [long years] for me, your father went to his fate. Like a brother I wept for him. Your father's[. . .] that I repaid, washed away my

tears. Then I [se]nt a messenger [to Babylonia]. To the [officials] of Babylonia, I sent a message as follows, [saying: "If] you do not protect [the progen]y of my brother in lordship, I will become your enemy. I will proceed to invade Babylonia. (Otherwise) if some enemy rises up against you, or if some matter is an obstruction for you, send a message to me, so that I may come to your aid." But in those days, my brother was young, so they did not recite the tablets to you. Now are those scribes no longer alive? Are there no tablets deposited? (i.e., there should be a record of Hattušili's correspondence). Let them recite those tablets to you. I sent them these words as an appropriate gesture. But Itti-Marduk-Balātu, whose (life) the gods have prolonged for countless (years), in whose mouth ugly words never come to an end- my heart became cold at his words, (namely) with the words that he wrote to me, saying: "You do not correspond with us as brothers (i.e., as equals). You treat us like your servants."

§5 (obv 25–35) Thus to my brother: how did I treat them like my servants? Did the people of Babylonia ever mistreat the people of Hatti? When have the people of Hatti in any way mistreated the people of Babylonia? I had written to them with good intentions, saying they should protect the progeny of my brother Kadašman-Turgu. Then Itti-Marduk-Balātu wrote this to me! What evil word did I send them that Itti-Marduk-Balātu can write these (evil words) to me? I did indeed write to them as follows, saying: "If you do not protect the son of your lord as ruler, then if an enemy rises against you, I will in no way come to your aid." But I have not held the words of Itti-Marduk-Balātu anywhere in my heart. In those days my brother was young and Itti-Marduk-Balātu, the evil man, spoke at will. How could I take his word (seriously)?

§6 (obv 36–54) Thus to my brother: concerning the message that my brother sent to me, saying: "I stopped sending my messengers. As the Ahlamu (Arameans) are hostile, I have stopped sending my messengers." How is it that as my brother, you have cut off your messengers because of the Ahlamu? My brother, is the extent of your kingship reduced, or perhaps, Itti-Marduk-Balātu has said unpleasant things to my brother (about me), and my brother has stopped sending messengers because of these (words)? In my brother's land, the horses hang as much as straw (i.e., they are plentiful). Should I have brought one thousand chariots and met your messenger in Tuttul? Could the hand of the Ahlamu have made difficulties for you? If my brother [says] thus: "The king of Assyria will not give my messengers [passage] in his land" – in troops and chariots, the King of Assyria is not equal to [those] of your land. But your messenger with force [. . .] your l[and? . . .]. What is the King of Assyria that he holds back your messenger? My envoys continually pass through, yet the King of Assyria detains your messengers [so that] you cannot cross [into] my la[nd]. My brother, you are a Great King, you have [. . . attai]ned old age. My brother, see how I [continually send my messenger] for the love of my brother, but my brother does not send his messenger. [. . .] they do not know. But I will retain the word that my brother sent me. [If two parties are] hostile, their messengers do not continually travel back and forth together. [My brother,] why have you stopped sending [your messengers]?

§7 (obv 55–75) [Thus to my brother concerni]ng the messenger of the King of Egypt that my brother wrote about to me: [concerning] this, the King of Egypt's [messenger], I sent a message as follows to my brother [saying: When] yo[ur father] and I concluded friendship and then became brothers, w[e spo]ke [as follows], saying: "We are brothers. With an enemy [let us be hostile] together [and with] an ally let us be at peace together." And when the King of Egypt [and I were fur]ious [with each other], I sent a message to your father, Kadašman-Enlil, [saying: "The King of Egypt] has become hostile with me." Then your father sent me the following message [saying:

"If your troops] go to Egypt, I will come with you. [If you go to Egypt, I will send] those troops and chariot-troops (here) with me that are ready to go." [N]ow, my brother, question your officials and may they tell you [about the tr]oops and chariot-troops as much as he said would accompany me. [. . .] what did I accept? The enemy lord of mine (Urhi-Teššub) who [has fled] to another land, has gone to the King of Egypt. As I wrote to him [saying: "Deliver my enemy lord to me!"] But he did not deliver my enemy lord to me. [And because of this, I and the King of Egy]pt became angry with each other. Then [I wrote] to your father [saying: "The King of Egyp]t comes to the aid of my enemy lord." [Then your father] cut off [his messenger from the King of E]gypt. And when my brother [became king], you sent [your messengers to the King of Egy]pt and the affair of the messenger [. . . the King of Egy]pt your [gifts he accepted and you acc]epted [his gifts]. Now [if you s]end [your messengers to the King of Egypt] – would I wish to detain you?

A large portion of the next few paragraphs at the bottom of the tablet are broken away making translation difficult. Paragraph 10 deals with the murder of Babylonian merchants in Hittite territory. Translation resumes here with paragraph 11.

§11 rev 26–33) [Th]us to my brother concerning Bentešina of whom my brother wrote to me, saying: "He continually curses my country." When I questioned Bentešina, he spoke as follows to me, saying: "The Akkadians (i.e., Babylonians) owe 3 talents of silver" (approximately 200 pounds / 91 kilograms). And now, herewith, a servant of Bentešina is coming that my brother may judge his case. And regarding the curses of my brother's land, in the presence of Adad-šar-ili, your messenger, Bentešina swore by the gods. And if my brother doesn't believe (this), let your servant who heard as Bentešina continually cursed my brother's land come to me and judge him. And I will put pressure on Bentešina. Bentešina, he is my servant. If he has cursed my brother, did he not curse me?

§12 rev 34–41) Thus to [my brother] concerning the physician that my brother sent me: when they took delivery of the physician, he performed fi[ne work]s (medical cures). And when illness confined him, I exerted myself for him and I repeatedly performed divinations for him, but when the day [of his fate] arrived, he died. And herewith, my messenger is in receipt of his servants. My brother [should quest]ion them that they may tell my brother the works he performed. And I[f the gifts] I gave [to] their lord have disappeared, they will be afraid and they will conceal the matter. My brother [should know] that the chariot, the wagon, the horses, the silver and the linen which I have given to the physician are writt[en down]. I will send the tablet to my brother that my brother may hear it. [The physician], when [his time] came, he died. Am I liable to have detained the physician?

§13 rev 42–8) [Thus to my brother]: when in (the reign of) my brother Muwatalli, they received an exorcist and a physician, and they detained them [in the land of Hatti], I spoke with him saying: "Why have you detained them? It is not customary to detain [foreign specialists]." And now should I detain your physician? [Concerning the] form[er specialists] that they received, perhaps the exorcist did die [but the physician] is living. The woman he married, she is my relative and he is the owner of a fine house. [And if he sa]ys: "I will go away to my country." Let him set out and go [to his

country. Should I] have detained the physician Raba-ša-Marduk? (This is either his name or his title.)

§14 rev 49–55) [Thus to my brother: I have hea]rd that my brother has grown into a man and he regularly goes hunting. [. . .] the storm-god has exalted the name of my brother Kadašman-Turgu! [. . .] go thus and plunder an enemy country that I may hear of it. [. . .] he struck. Thus to my brother- they say you are a king who puts down weapons and who sits (around). Do they not say thus of him? [. . . . My] brother, do not sit (around)! Go to an enemy country and strike the enemy! [. . . has go]ne, go to a land you outnumber three or four times!

Further reading

For the edition of this letter see A. Hagenbuchner, *Texte der Hethiter* 16, Heidelberg, Winter (1989), 281–300. For previous translations in English see A. Leo Oppenheim, *Letters From Mesopotamia*, Chicago, University of Chicago Press (1967), 139–49; and Gary M. Beckman, *Hittite Diplomatic Texts*, 2d ed., Atlanta, Scholars Press (1999), 138–43. For the Hittite history of this period see Trevor Bryce, *The Kingdom of the Hittites*, Oxford, Clarendon (1998), chs. 10–11.

Notes

1 This is the main text. For a list of the other text copies and numerous fragments go online to the Konkordanz der hethitischen Texte at <www.orient.uni-wuerzburg.de/>.

2 Both Šuppiluliuma and Arnuwanda succumbed to a plague brought into Hatti by Egyptian prisoners-of-war.

3 Another possible interpretation is literally "It struck Uhhaziti, namely his knees." A celestial sign like a meteor would have been considered a very bad omen.

10

Neo-Assyrian and Syro-Palestinian Texts I

Sarah C. Melville, Brent A. Strawn, Brian B. Schmidt, and Scott Noegel

I. Neo-Assyrian Texts I

A. *Adad-nirari II (Melville)*

At the turn of the second millennium BC Assyria, like so much of the Near East, suffered grievously from Aramean incursions and repeated attacks of other nomadic peoples. During this period, Assyrian territories shrank drastically and formidable enemies bordered the country on all sides. In the tenth century BC, Ashur-dan II set about restoring Assyria's sphere of influence; consequently historians attribute the start of the Neo-Assyrian period to the reign of this king. Ashur-dan's son, Adad-nirari II, who ruled Assyria for 21 years, successfully continued his father's efforts to reassert Assyria's control of the areas to the west and north. A vigorous campaigner, Adad-nirari also succeeded in extending Assyrian hegemony south toward Babylonia. Few inscriptions belonging to Adad-nirari have survived, but one nearly intact text (translated here) and two fragmentary copies found at Ashur, narrate the campaigns of his first 18 years (Grayson 1991: 142).

Our text begins with an invocation of the most important deities and continues with a section of self-praise, followed by a long, grammatically inconsistent summary of military achievements, a year-by-year campaign narrative, an account of hunting exploits, the restoration of the Gula temple at Ashur, and finally, blessings and curses, and the date of the text (893 BC). In general, the content and structure of the text are in keeping with the early tradition of Assyrian annals developed by Adad-nirari's predecessors, in which we find the fundamental portrait of the ideal Assyrian king – the virile military leader, mighty hunter, shepherd of his people, and pious devotee of the gods, who is concerned with public works and temple building. This ideal representation of the king persists (with some latitude for variation) in Assyrian royal inscriptions, and develops its most sophisticated form under the Sargonid kings (721–612 BC). In his royal inscriptions, Adad-nirari established himself as a legitimate Assyrian king, who fulfilled the requirements of his job, not just adequately, but better than former kings. Hence he was careful to point out that he had been able to reconquer territory lost by Tiglath-pileser II and reimpose tribute on peoples who had withheld it since the time of Tukulti-Ninurta I. Although his self-praise seems extravagant, exaggerated, and hyperbolic, he essentially had to earn the right to use his epithets and was careful to substantiate his claim to them by detailed accounts of his exploits.

The main military narrative of the text gives a full account of Adad-nirari's campaigns from 901 to 894 BC, carefully dating each one by the year's eponym. Adad-nirari's military strategy was aimed primarily at the subjugation of the Habhu and the Nairi lands to the north, the Aramean tribes to the west in Hanigalbat (the Syrian Jezirah), and the extension of Assyrian influence south (Grayson 1982: 249). The king campaigned eight times against the Arameans in Hanigalbat and finally penetrated across the Balikh River into the territory of Bit-Adini, from which tribe he received the exotic present of two apes. Adad-nirari's tenacious pursuit of success against the Arameans eventually brought victory, and the Assyrians were able to make a triumphant and unopposed sweep through the region in 894 BC to display their might and collect their due. The campaigns to the Nairi lands and into Babylonia are not narrated in great detail in this text, perhaps because they were not quite as fruitful.

Aside from making territorial gains, Adad-nirari's army successfully executed at least one new siege tactic when they encircled the enemy fortifications with their own defensive works, although exactly what form these took is not at all clear and, consequently, we cannot be sure that modern military terms such as "bulwark" or "redoubt" accurately describe the Assyrian innovation. In any case, the king's new tactic seems to have been a success. Adad-nirari was also adept at military logistics, for he designated a series of supply depots, which enabled him to move his army swiftly through the new territory without need of constant foraging for supplies (Grayson 1991: 142). Here we see not only the basis for the later Assyrian provincial system, but one of the primary reasons for Assyrian military success – the ability to field an army for long periods and supply it with adequate food and gear. Adad-nirari was also acutely aware of the strategic importance of certain areas and took care to promote an Assyrian presence in them. For example, he rebuilt the ancient city Apku, which lay to the north of Assyria, and "built palaces in the districts of my land," presumably as administrative centers and supply depots.

In addition to his obvious interest in Assyrian military achievements, Adad-nirari, like most other Assyrian kings, expressed a fascination for exotic fauna. Success in the hunt was one of the requirements of Assyrian kingship and Adad-nirari took care to play his part to the hilt. He not only killed a wide range and vast number of animals, but he collected live specimens and took them to Ashur, perhaps for display in one of the world's first zoos. Lastly, Adad-nirari, as the dutiful custodian of Assyria's temples and public works, restored the Gula temple and the quay wall at Ashur (the latter is described in another text). Adad-nirari II's rule helped lay the foundation of the Neo-Assyrian empire and brought the country closer to realizing its imperial goals.

118. Text

[The gods Ashur . . . Enlil . . . Sin] lord of radiance, [Shamash, judge of] heaven and the underworld, ruler of everything, Marduk, sage of the gods, lord of omens, Ninurta [warrior of] the Igigu- and Annunaku-gods, Nergal, perfect king of battle, Nusku, the one who carries the pure scepter, deliberate god, Ninlil, wife of Enlil, mother of the great gods, Ishtar, pre-eminent in heaven and the underworld, who is perfect in the rites of combat:[1]

The great gods, who finalize decisions, who decree (fate), they righteously created me, Adad-nirari, reverent prince, [. . .]. They changed my physique to lordly physique; they properly made my outward appearance perfect and filled my lordly body with wisdom. After the great gods decreed (my fate) and filled my hand with the scepter which constantly tends the people, raised me above those crowned kings, crowned me with royal radiance, they made my illustrious name greater than (those of) all lords, they called me the significant name Adad-nirari, king of Assyria. Strong king, king of Assyria, king of the four quarters, sun of all the people am I. Son of Ashur-dan, appointee of Enlil, viceroy of Ashur, who conquered all his enemies, son of Tiglath-pileser, king of Assyria, pure progeny of Ashur-resha-ishi, aggressive king, who tramples evildoers. At that time, at the command of the great gods, my kingship and lordship were revealed; they called me to plunder the property of all the lands. I am king, I am lord, I am powerful, I am important, I am splendid, I am strong, I am all-powerful, I am exceedingly radiant, I am a hero, I am a warrior, I am a potent lion, I am first, I am supreme, I am very fierce.

Adad-nirari, strong king, king of Assyria, king of the four quarters, the one who conquers his enemies, I, the king, powerful in battle, flattener of cities, the one who burns the mountains of the lands, I, manly hero, the one who encircles his opponents, inflamed against the villainous and evil, like the god Girru I burn, I destroy like the flood [. . .], I have no subduer, I am aggressive like [. . .], I smite the wicked like a furious dagger, I blow like the assault of winds, I am ferocious like a tempest, like a [. . .] of skin, I tear out (my enemies), I envelop like a battle net, I encase like a bird-snare. At the mention of my powerful name, the princes of the four quarters bend like reeds in a storm; at the start of my campaign their weapons melt as if in a kiln; heroic man who marched with the aid of Ashur his lord from the opposite bank of the lower Zab, the district of the lands of Lullumu, Habhu, Zamua to the passes of the land of Namru, and subjugated the wide land of Qumanu, to the lands of Mehru, Salua and Uratri; (who) ruled over the entire district of Katmuhu and returned it to the border of his land; conqueror of the entire district of Karduniash; who accomplished the defeat of Shamash-mudammiq, king of Karduniash from Mt. Ialman to the river Turan, (the area) from the city Lahiru to Ugar-sallu was included in the boundaries of Assyria; I conquered the entire district of the city of Der; I returned the cities Arrapha, Lubdu, the forts of the land of Karduniash (Babylonia), to the territory of Assyria, and marched a fourth time to the Nairi lands and conquered the interior of Habhu, the cities Nahur and Ashnaku; and (who) constantly crossed the great mountains; (who) conquered the cities of the land of Natbu and verily I (who) overwhelmed Alzi in its entirety like ruin hills of the flood; I (who) seized hostages from them and imposed tribute and tax on them; (I who) accomplished the defeat of the ground troops of the land of Ahlamu, land of the Arameans; I (who) received tribute of the Suhu; (who) brought into the borders of his land the cities Idu and Zaqqu, forts of Assyria (and) the cities Arinu, Turhu, Zaduru conquests which Shubria had torn away from Assyria; the old city Apku which kings who went before me built, had become run-down and turned into ruin heaps. I rebuilt that city anew and I constructed it from its foundation to its parapet. I made (it) perfect, I made (it) appropriately splendid (and) I made (it) better than before. Inside, I built my supreme lordly palace.

In the eponymy of Dur-mati-Ashur I marched to the wide land of Hanigalbat. Nur-Adad, the Temannite, mustered his troops (and) we drew up our battle lines at the city Pauza at the foot of Mt. Kashiari; we fought with each other. I accomplished his defeat from the city Pauza to the city Naṣibina. I destroyed his many chariots.

In the eponymy of Ili-emuqaia, I marched against Hanigalbat for the second time. I fought with him at Naṣipina. I dyed the ground red with the blood of his warriors. I entered the city Iaredu. I harvested the crops of his land; I considered the city Saraku as my own and inside (it) I laid up the barley and grain.

In the eponymy of Ninualia I marched against Hanigalbat for the third time. I seized the city Huzirina. I encircled the wall all around. The cities at the foot of Mt. Kashiari which Mamli the Temannite, had seized, submitted to me. His palaces I considered as my own. At that time, I received a large female ape and a small female monkey, a consignment from the land of Bit-Adini, which is set on the banks of the Euphrates River.

In the eponymy of Likberu, I marched against Haniglabat for the fourth time. At that time Muquru the Temannite, broke the oath of the great gods and was hostile to me in order to do combat. He put trust in his fortified city, his powerful bow and his vast army and the Arameans and he revolted against me. I mustered my chariots and my troops and marched to the city Gidara, which the Arameans call Raqammatu, (and) which the Arameans took away by force from Tiglath-pileser, son of Ashur-resha-ishi, king of Assyria, a prince who came before me. In the wisdom of my heart, I laid down a bulwark all around it, which (tactic) did not exist among the kings, my fathers. He dug a moat all around his city (but) they became afraid in the presence of my furious weapons, my fierce battle and my powerful forces, and I entered with force and strength into the city Raqammatu. That one I lead out from inside his palace. I reviewed his property, valuable stones of the mountains, chariots, horses, his wives, his sons, his daughters, his heavy plunder. That one, together with his brother, in bronze fetters I fastened them (and) I brought to my city Ashur. I have constantly established the power and strength of Ashur, my lord, over it, the land of Hanigalbat.

In the eponymy of Adad-aha-iddina, governor of Ashur, I marched to Hanigalbat a fifth time. I received the tribute of the lands.

In the eponymy of Adad-dan with the fury of my strong weapons, I marched to Hanigalbat a sixth time. I enclosed Nur-Adad, the Temannite, in Naṣibina; I laid down seven bulwarks all around it. I made Ashur-dini-amur, the Turtan (general), take position inside it. He (Nur-Adad) dug a moat, which did not exist before, in firm bedrock. He made it nine cubits wide (and) caused it to reach ground water. The wall was adjacent to the moat. I made my warriors surround his moat like a flash of fire and they (the enemy soldiers) howled about it like little children. [. . .] traps for him as strong as the devastating flood. I deprived him of grain. At the command of Ashur my great lord, I plundered from his city his [. . .], his gold, his possessions, valuable mountain stones, his gods, chariot teams, [. . .], a scepter, battle equipment, gold thrones, shiny gold dishes, inlaid [. . .], weapons, arrows, a gold tent at the value appropriate for his kingship, [. . .] whose weight I did not grasp, and vast property of his palace. [. . .] . . . sat on his lordly throne. Inside his sanctuary, he slaughtered pure sacrifices, offered oxen, made a libation of ritual beer (and) he finished with pure sweet mountain wine. He established his offerings and glorified himself with grand praise. "The kings of all the lands are in dire straits! The mountains quake!" The king speaks [. . .] to his nobles, "The man of Ashur praise of his heroism is vaunted; his deeds are the god Dagan's, the king who makes great his praise!" I brought Nur-Adad with his vast army into my presence as captives. I presented them – cities with people – (to) Assyria and I counted them (among the Assyrians).

In that same eponymy on my campaign (in) which I returned Nur-Adad and his vast army to my presence as captives, I brought him to my land (and) made him enter Nineveh. I levied the chariots and troops (and) marched narrow roads (and) mountain tracks which were not fit for the passage of my chariots and troops, near to which none of the kings, my fathers, had advanced, and (even) the flying birds of the air did not approach. I went to the city Sikkur, the city Sappanu, which since the time of Tukulti-Ninurta, king of Assyria, son of Shalmaneser, likewise king of Assyria, a prince who went before me, had held back tax and tribute from Ashur, my lord; I encircled the cities Sikkur and Sappanu and I fought with them. I massacred them. I brought their plunder, their possessions, property, cattle and flocks of sheep to my city Assur. I conquered the cities of the province in the environs of the cities Sikkur and Sappanu. Those remaining who had fled in the face of my strong weapons, came down and seized my feet (i.e., formally submitted). I received from them tribute and set for them increased tribute and taxes.

In the fifteenth day of Siwan, the eponymy of Ina-iliia-allak, I went to help the city Kummu. I made sacrifices before the god Adad of the city Kummu, my lord. I burned with fire the cities of the land Habhu, enemies of the city Kummu. I gathered the harvest of his land. I set for them increased tribute and taxes.

In the month Nisan, the eponymy of Shamash-abuia, I went to help the city Kummu a second time. The cities Satkurru, Iasaddu, Kunnu, Tabsia, cities of the land of Habhu, in the vicinity of Kummu, withheld (their tribute of) my chariot teams. Those cities I defeated, burned with fire (and) demolished. At the command of Ashur, great lord, my lord, and Ishtar, lady of battle and war, the one who goes before my vast army, in the month Siwan, in the same eponymy, I marched a fifth time to Hanigalbat. I received the tribute of Hanigalbat, above and below. I ruled the broad land Hanigalbat to the borders of its totality. I brought it within the limit of my land. I assigned to them one commander. I crossed the Habur River and entered the city Guzana which Adi-Salamu, a member of (the tribe) Bit-Bahiani held. I entered the city Sikkanu, which is located at the source of the Habur River. By the supreme force of Shamash, lord of my diadem, who loves my priesthood, I received from him many chariots, chariot teams, silver, gold, the property of his palace, I imposed tribute on him. On my (same) campaign I took (the road) along the banks of the Habur River. I stayed overnight in the city Arnabanu. I departed from the city Arnabanu (and) stayed overnight in the city Ṭabitu. I departed from Ṭabitu and entered the city Shadikannu. I received tribute, payment, chariots, (and) gold. I departed from the city Shadikannu. I stayed overnight in the city Kisiru. I departed from the city Kisiru. I entered the city Qatnu. I installed Amil-Adad, a man of Qatnu, as my vassal. I received from him the property of his palace, chariots, horses, wagons and cattle. I imposed tribute on him.

From Qatnu I departed (and) stayed the night in the land Buṣu, set on the banks of the Habur River. I departed the mountains and entered Dur-aduklimmu. I considered the city Dur-aduklimmu as my own. I departed from Dur-aduklimmu and went to the land of Laqu, to the city Zurih (which) Bartara, the Halupian, held. I received from him tribute and tax. I proceeded to the city of the man of Haran (and) received tribute and tax. I went to the city Sinqu, which is set on that bank of the Euphrates, which Mudadda the Laqaian held. I received tribute, tax, property of his palace, cattle, agalu-donkeys, tribute, and tax of the land Laqu to its entire limit above and below. I received tribute of the city Hindanu. I brought (it) to my city Ashur. I built palaces in the districts of my land. I readied plows in the districts of my land (and) stored up more grain than ever before. I hitched teams of horses for the forces of my land more than ever before.

Ninurta (and) Nergal, who love my priesthood, gave me the beasts of the steppe and ordered me to hunt. I killed 360 lions from my open chariot with the combat of my manhood (or) on my nimble feet with a javelin; 240 bulls I killed; I took alive 9 strong, wild, potent bulls, those with horns. I killed 6 elephants in a fight. I set a trap for 4 elephants and took (them) alive. I took 5 (more) in a snare. I collected herds of lions, wild bulls, elephants, stags, wild goats, onagers, roe deer, and ostrich inside (my) city.

When the earlier temple of Gula, my lady, which formerly Tukulti-Ninurta, my ancestor, viceroy of Ashur made, that temple became run-down, I dismantled its ruins and I reached its foundation platform. That temple I greatly extended more than previously and I made (it) large. From its foundation to its parapet I completed it and set up my stele. May a future prince restore its ruins; may he return my inscribed name to its place. Ashur and Gula will hear his prayers. The one who erases my inscription and my name, may Ashur and Gula overthrow his kingship (and) make his name and his seed disappear from the land.

In the month of Ab, seventeenth day, eponymy of Ili-napishti-uṣur, eunuch of Adad-nirari, king of Assyria.

B. Ashurnasirpal II (Strawn)

Ashurnasirpal II (Akkadian: *Aššur-naṣir-apli*, "the god Ashur guards the son") ruled Assyria 883–859 BCE as the son and successor of Tukulti-Ninurta II. Ashurnasirpal left more numerous and more detailed inscriptions than any of his predecessors (Grayson 1976: 113) and this fact cannot be explained simply as the chance circumstances of discovery or preservation. On the contrary, it is additional testimony to this king's energy and industriousness (Kuhrt 1995: 483) and well suits both the length and importance of his reign (Grayson 1976: 114).[2] Ashurnasirpal's annals recount 14 major campaigns prior to 866, including several to the northern (Anatolia) and eastern (the Zagros) parts of the empire. Subsequently, he went west where he says he washed his weapons in the Mediterranean Sea.[3]

The extensive military exploits of Ashurnasirpal II are what produced the formidable Neo-Assyrian empire of the ninth and early eighth centuries, and he bequeathed both this empire and his military legacy to his son, Shalmaneser III (see that entry). Ashurnasirpal's campaigns, and the inscriptions that bear witness to them, testify to the ruthless manner in which he dealt with acts of disloyalty. His harsh policy included public acts of cruelty and mass executions as well as the razing of whole cities. The annals are replete with such actions, mentioning on numerous occasions how he made piles of decapitated heads; impaled, skinned, or burnt people alive; or dyed the landscape red with the blood of his enemies. Given this iron fist – what some have called "the calculated frightfulness of Ashurnasirpal" (see Millard 2000: 38) – most countries chose to placate the king, knowing that such a move was to their own benefit and self-preservation.[4] The success of Ashurnasirpal's tactics was not lost on those who ruled after him, and they continued in his imperialistic footsteps.

The text that is translated here is selected from what is typically thought to be the definitive edition of Ashurnasirpal's annals.[5] This text comprises one of the most extensive and important Assyrian royal inscriptions ever discovered. It was inscribed on large stone reliefs that lined the temple of Ninurta at Calah (Nimrud). It recounts many of the king's campaigns from his accession through the eighteenth year of his reign in great and often gory detail (see above).

In addition to his military prowess, Ashurnasirpal was an energetic builder. The capstone of his building career was the work done at Calah, which transformed that site into a thriving metropolis and his capital city (Grayson 1991: 189). Not only did the king forcibly settle people there, but he also dug a canal; planted gardens; constructed a large palace (the "Northwest Palace," more than 656 feet × 394 feet [200 × 120 meters]); erected the temples of Adad and Šala, Šarrat-nipḫi, Ea and Damkina, Gula, Kidmuru, Nabû, Enlil and Ninurta, the Sibitti, and Sin; and built a wall around the city (Grayson 1991: 189–90). The so-called "Banquet Stele" describes the king's inauguration of sorts and offers a detailed description of the building of Calah. In the text the king claims to have entertained 69,574 people from around the empire and from Calah itself for 10 straight days (see *ANET*, 558–60; Kuhrt 1995: 2: 486–7).

In addition to the massive efforts at Calah, which must have extended over most of his reign, Ashurnasirpal also undertook construction projects at Nineveh, Ashur, Imgur-Enlil (modern-day Balawat), and Apqu (Tell Abu Marya) (see Grayson 1991: 190). Leick is certainly correct, then, when she states that Ashurnasirpal "presents a high point of the might of Assyria, an indefatigable campaigner, but also resourceful diplomat, able to inspire loyalty as well as fear, and not least a cultivated patron of arts and letters" (1999: 31).

119. Calah Annals Text[6]

Invocation (i: 1–9a)

To divine Ninurta:[7] the strong (one), the mighty (one), the exalted (one), first among the gods, splendid-perfect warrior, whose attack in battle is unrivaled, first son, gatherer of battle, child of divine Nudimmud,[8] *warrior of the Igigi-gods,*[9] *capable (one), prince of the gods, offspring of Ekur,*[10] *holder of the bond of heaven and earth, opener of springs, the one who walks the wide world, god without whom no decision in heaven or earth is made, swift (one), ferocious (one), whose oral command is not changeable, first in the (four) quarters (of the world), giver of scepter (rule) and decision (law) to each and every city, furious canal-inspector, whose spoken utterance cannot be altered, widely capable, sage of the gods, noble (one), divine Utulu,*[11] *lord of lords, whose hands are entrusted with the perimeter of heaven and earth, king of combat, powerful (one) who boasts in battles, triumphant (one), perfect (one), lord of springs and seas, angry (one), merciless (one), whose attack is a flood, who flattens enemy lands, who ruins the evildoer, splendid god who does not change even once, light of heaven and earth, enlightener of the midst of the apsû,*[12] *destroyer of evil, who subjects the incompliant, annihilator of enemies, whose command no god in the divine assembly can change, giver of life, merciful god, whose prayer is good,*[13] *who inhabits Calah, great lord, my lord (listen):*

Royal epithets (i: 9b–17a)[14]

(I am) Ashurnasirpal (II), strong king, king of the world, king without rival, king of all of the four quarters (of the world), divine sun[15] *of all the people, favorite of divine Enlil and divine Ninurta, beloved of divine Anu and divine Dagan, divine weapon of the great gods, reverent (one), beloved of your heart,*[16] *the prince, darling of divine Enlil, whose priesthood is pleasing to your great divinity and whose reign you established,*[17] *heroic (young) man who moves about with the help of (the god) Ashur, his lord, and who has no rival among the princes of the four quarters (of the world), wonderful shepherd, who is fearless (in) combat, high flood-wave that has no opponent, king who subjects those not submissive to him, who rules each and every person, strong male, the one who walks upon the necks of his foes, who tramples all enemies, who scatters the band of the arrogant, who moves about with the help of the great gods, his lords, and whose hand has conquered all lands; who rules the entirety of the highlands*[18] *having received their tribute, seizer of hostages, establisher of victory*[19] *over all lands.*[20]

Expedition to Carchemish and Lebanon (iii: 56–92a)

On the eighth of (the month of) Iyyar, I set out from Calah. After I crossed the Tigris river, I journeyed to the city of Carchemish which (is in) the land of Hatti. I drew near to Bīt-Baḫiāni. I received the tribute of the king of Baḫiāni:[21] *harnessed chariots, horses, silver (items), gold (items), tin (items), bronze (items), (and) bronze vessels. I took the chariots, cavalry, (and) infantry-men of the king of Baḫiāni with me.*[22]

I set out from Bīt-Baḫiāni. I drew near to the land of Azallu. (After which time), I received the tribute of Adad-ʾime, the (A)zalluite: harnessed chariots, horses, silver (items), gold (items), tin (items), bronze, bronze vessels, oxen, sheep, (and) much wine. I took the chariots, cavalry, (and) infantry-men with me.

I set out from the land of Azallu. I drew near to Bīt-Adini. The tribute of Aḫunu, the king of Adini[23] *(was as follows): silver (items), gold (items), tin (items), bronze, bronze vessels, ivory dishes, ivory couches, ivory chests, ivory thrones plated (with) silver (and) gold, gold bracelets, gold rings with inlays, gold necklaces, a gold dagger, oxen, sheep, (and) much wine. I received his tribute. I took the chariots, cavalry, (and) infantry-men of Aḫunu with me.*

At that time, I received the tribute of Ḫabinu of the city Tīl-abni: four minas of silver (and) 400 sheep. I imposed upon him 10 minas of silver as his annual tribute.

I set out from the land Bīt-Adini. In truth, I crossed the Euphrates river at its flood in rafts of (inflated) goatskins. I drew near to the land of Carchemish. I received the tribute of Sangara, king of the land of Hatti, (objects) indicative of his royalty: 20 talents[24] *of silver, a gold ring, a gold bracelet, gold daggers, 100 talents of bronze, 250 talents of iron, bronze cauldrons, bronze buckets, bronze washbasins,*[25] *a bronze oven, many utensils from his palace, the weight of which could not be ascertained, boxwood beds, boxwood thrones, boxwood dishes plated (with) ivory, 200 adolescent girls, multicolored linen garments, purple wool, red-purple wool, gišnugallu-alabaster, ivory of elephants (i.e., tusks), a polished (gold) chariot, (and) a gold couch with inlays. I took the chariots, cavalry, (and) infantry-men of the city of Carchemish with me. The kings of all the lands came down to me. They submitted to me. I took hostages from them (who) were kept before me (as) they marched to Mt. Lebanon (Lab-na-na).*

I set out from the land of Carchemish. I journeyed in between Mt. Munzigānu (and) Mt. Ḫamurga. I passed Mount Aḫānu on my left. I drew near to the city of Ḫazazu of (king) Lubarna, the Patinu(ite). I then received gold (items) (and) linen garments. I then passed through (and) crossed the Aprê river. I pitched camp (and) spent the night (there).

I set out from the Aprê river.[26] *I drew near to the city of Kunulua, the royal city of Lubarna, the Patinu(ite). He was terrified at the sight of my raging weapons (and) my fierce battle (abilities) and (so) he submitted to me in order to save his life. I received as his tribute (the following): 20 talents of silver, one talent of gold, 100 talents of tin, 100 talents of iron, 1,000 oxen, 10,000 sheep, 1,000 multicolored linen garments, boxwood couches with plated inlays, boxwood beds, beds with plated inlays, many dishes of ivory (and) boxwood, many utensils from his palace, the weight of which could not be ascertained, 10 female singers, his niece with her rich dowry, a large female monkey, (and) large birds. As for (the king) him(self), I showed him mercy. I took the chariots, cavalry, (and) infantry-men of the Patinu(ite)*[27] *with me. I (also) took hostages from him.*

At that time, I received the tribute of Gūsu of the land of Iaḫānu: silver, gold, tin [. . .], oxen, sheep, (and) multicolored linen garments.

I set out from the city of Kunulua, the royal city of Lubarna, the Patinu(ite). I then crossed the [Oron]tes river. I pitched camp (and) spent the night by the Orontes river.

I set out from the Orontes river. I journeyed in between Mt. Iaraqu (and) Mt. Iaḫturu. I then traversed Mt. [. . .]ku. I pitched camp by the Sangurru river.

I set out from the Sangurru river. I journeyed in between Mt. Saratinu (and) Mt. Qalpānu. I pitched camp by [the . . .]bamesh [river].[28] *I entered into the city of Aribua, the fortified city of Lubarna, the Patinu(ite). I seized the city for myself. I harvested the barley and straw of the land of Luḫutu; I stored (it) inside. I held a celebration in his palace. I settled people from Assyria in the midst (of the city). While I was in the city of Aribua, I conquered the cities of the land of Luḫutu. I killed many of them (i.e., the inhabitants). I demolished; I destroyed; I burnt with fire. I captured soldiers alive by hand. I impaled (them) on stakes in front of their cities.*

At that time, in truth: I journeyed to the slopes of Mt. Lebanon, went up to the great sea of the land of Amurru,[29] *washed my weapons in the great sea, (and) performed sacrifices to the gods. I received the tribute of the kings of the seacoast – namely, the lands of the peoples of Tyre, Sidon, Byblos, Maḫallatu, Maizu, Kaizu, Amurru, and the city Arvad which is (an island) in the middle of the sea: silver (items), gold (items), tin (items), bronze (items), a bronze vessel, multicolored linen garments, a large female monkey, a small female monkey, ebony (items), boxwood (items), (and) ivory of naḫiru sea creatures.*[30] *They submitted to me. (Then), in truth: I went up to Mt. Amanus; cut down beams of cedar, cyprus, daprānu-juniper, (and) burāšu-juniper; (and) performed sacrifices to my gods. I made a memorial to my valor. I erected (it) thereon. I carried cedar beams from Mt. Amanus. I brought (them) to Ešarra, to my temple – the shrine,*[31] *a joyful temple – to the temple of the divine Sin and Shamash,*[32] *the holy gods. I went to the land of the meḫru-trees. I conquered the entirety of the land of the meḫru-trees. I cut down beams of meḫru-trees. I brought (them) to the city of Nineveh. I gave (them) to Ishtar, lady*[33] *of Nineveh, my lady.*[34]

C. Shalmaneser III (Strawn)

Shalmaneser III (Akkadian: *Šulmānu-ašarēdu*, "the god Shulman is preeminent") was the son and successor of Ashurnasirpal II; he ruled Assyria from 858 to 824 BCE. No king left more royal inscriptions and annals than Shalmaneser III (Leick 1999: 146). Moreover, the practice of summarizing military campaigns in order of the king's regnal year was apparently initiated by this important Assyrian king.

Shalmaneser inherited the large and powerful kingdom established by his father, but he immediately faced growing unrest across the empire.[35] The result was the need to campaign almost constantly with a grand total of 34 campaigns recorded for his reign.[36] A number of these trips were to the west,[37] where he first faced a north Syrian coalition under the leadership of Bit-Adini. After several attempts, the Assyrian king defeated this group and annexed Bit-Adini to his empire. Slightly later, Shalmaneser faced another coalition in the west, this one under the leadership of Hadadezer (Adad-idri) of Damascus, Irḫulēni of Hamath, and Ahab of Israel (*a-ḫa-ab-bu KUR sir-ʾi-la-a-a*).[38] The forces clashed at Qarqar in Shalmaneser's sixth regnal year (853) and the fullest account of the battle is found in the Kurkh Monolith (see *COS* 2.113A: 261–4; *ANET*, 278–9; Luckenbill 1989: 1: 211–24). The Assyrian king claimed a victory, saying he killed 25,000 people, but the fact that he pushes no further west at this time and that he had to face the same group again three more times in subsequent years indicates that the situation was not as decisive as the king would have it seem. This north Syrian coalition eventually broke, however, partly due to changes in leadership in its partner states (Kuhrt 1995: 2: 488), and, in 841, Shalmaneser was able to triumph over them, receiving tribute from its constituent groups. The tribute reception is described and depicted in several of the 20 panels on the Black Obelisk, where the king of Israel[39] is among those shown bringing gifts and doing obesience to the Assyrian monarch.[40]

Shalmaneser also conducted military operations on the northern frontier, against the kingdom of Urartu, and played an important role in Babylonian politics at several key junctures. In addition to this impressive military resume,

Shalmaneser undertook numerous building projects, including, at Calah (Nimrud), the construction of or completion of the ziggurat, the temples of Ninurta and Nabu, and a large fortress (some 12 acres [5 hectares]) called "Fort Shalmaneser" by its excavators. He devoted even more time and energy at Ashur, reconstructing walls and gates and restoring the temples of Ashur and Anu-Adad there (Grayson 1996: 5). He was also active at other sites with smaller building projects (see Grayson 1996: 5–6).

The text translated below is selected from Shalmaneser's Black Obelisk – so called because of its shape and its material (black alabaster) – which was discovered by A. H. Layard at Calah in 1846.[41] The obelisk is over 6 feet [2 meters] tall with four sides, each of which is inscribed. Each of the four sides also has five pictures that are meant to be "read" laterally around the four sides of the obelisk; each row has its own epigraph. The top of the obelisk is in the shape of a ziggurat or step-pyramid structure. After an introduction, which invokes the gods and identifies Shalmaneser (lines 1–21), the body of the text runs from the king's accession down to his thirty-first year (828). The information for each regnal year is relatively concise and mostly concerns the king's military campaigns,[42] often across the Euphrates, sometimes with additional data regarding what the king did in these foreign locales. After the thirty-first year, there is no space left on the obelisk, and, since there are no concluding formulae or building descriptions, the scribe probably ran out of space and simply stopped (Grayson 1996: 63). Despite its somewhat inconclusive nature, however, the inscription is often thought to be the final or definitive edition of Shalmaneser's annals (McCarter 1996: 21). Whatever the case, the last dated regnal year on the monument allows one to fix the date of the execution of the monument to late 828 or 827 (Grayson 1996: 63).

The reliefs on the Black Obelisk have been of particular interest to scholars insofar as they provide visual data that accompanies the inscription. The second frieze depicting the king of Israel is especially intriguing since it is the only contemporary depiction of an Israelite king known from antiquity. But it is not only *that* such personages as the Israelite king are artistically represented on the obelisk that is of importance; equally important is *how* these figures are portrayed. The first frieze portrays the tribute of Sūa, the Gilzānean;[43] the second depicts the Israelite king. He, like Sūa, is clearly dominated, down on hands and knees, but – unlike Sūa whose face is up – the Israelite king has his nose to the floor. He dare not even look up at the Assyrian king who stands above him holding a bowl of some sort, perhaps an item of tribute that he is admiring. Directly above both kings in the first two friezes, surmounting these climactic scenes, are the winged disk and star symbols that represent the gods Ashur and Ishtar.[44] The juxtaposition of these two tribute receptions also communicates something important. Gilzānu was probably in the far (north)east of the empire;[45] Israel belonged to the far (south)west. The combination thus "creates a pictorial merism stressing the gigantic extent of Shalmaneser's Assyrian empire" (Younger 2000: 269;

cf. Green 1979; Porada 1983; Lieberman 1985; Marcus 1987). There is also a chronological merism of sorts, since not all of the friezes depict the same time period.[46]

120. Black Obelisk[47]

Invocation (1–14)

(O) divine Ashur, great lord, king of all of the great gods; (O) divine Anu, king of the Igigi-gods[48] and the Anunnaki-gods,[49] (O) divine Enlil, sovereign, exalted (one), father of the gods, creator of everythi[ng; (O) divine] Ea, king of the apsû,[50] decider of destinies; (O) divine [Sin, the wise], king of the crown,[51] exalted in radiance; (O) divine Adad, powerful, awesome, lord of plenty; (O) divine Shamash, judge of heaven and earth, governor of all; [(O) divine Mardu]k, sage of the gods, lord of omens; (O) divine Ninurta, warrior of the Igigi-[gods] and the Anunnaki-gods, mighty god; (O) divine Nergal, [perf]ect one, king of battle; (O) divine Nusku, bearer of the holy scepter; god of deliberation; (O) divine Ninlil, spouse of Enlil, mother of the [great] gods; (O) divine Ištar, first (in) heaven and earth, who is perfect in the rites of battle: (O all you) great gods, deciders of destinies, who have made my sovereignty great, (listen).

Royal epithets (15–21)

(I am) Shalmaneser (III), king of all peoples, prince, ruler of Ashur, strong king, king of all of the four quarters (of the world), divine sun[52] of all the people, ruler of all lands, son of Ashurnasirpal (II), exalted priest whose priesthood was pleasing to the gods and who made all lands bow at his feet, pure progeny of Tukulti-Ninurta (II), who killed all his enemies and wiped (them) out like a flood.[53]

Year 1

(26b–31) In the first year of my reign: I crossed the Euphrates at its flood; I marched to the western sea;[54] I washed my weapons in the sea;[55] I performed sacrifices for my gods (there); I climbed the Amanus mountain range; I cut cedar and juniper logs (there); I climbed Mount Lallar; I set up my royal statue (ṣalmu)[56] thereon.[57]

Year 6

(54b–66) In the sixth year of my reign: I approached the cities that are on the banks of the Baliḫ river – they (had?) killed Giammu, the lord of their cities – I entered the city of Tīl-Turaḫi; I crossed the Euphrates at its flood; I received the tribute of [all] the kings of the land of Hatti. (Now), at that time Hadadezer (Adad-idri) [of] the land of Damascus (and) Irḫulēni (of) the land of the Hamathites, along with the kings of the land of Hatti and (of) the coast(al areas), trusting in (their) combined forces, came against me in order to make war and battle. At the command of Ashur, the great lord, my lord, I fought with them. I accomplished their defeat. Their chariots, their cavalry, (and) their battle equipment I took away from them. I put 20,500 of their fighting men to the sword.[58]

Year 11

(87–89a) In the eleventh year of my reign: I crossed the Euphrates for the ninth time; I captured countless cities; I descended to the cities of the land of the Hamathites; I captured 89 cities (there). (Now) Hadadezer (Adad-idri) (of) the land of Damascus (and) 12 kings of the land of Hatti stood in (their) combined forces. I accomplished their defeat.[59]

Year 14

(91b–92a) In the fourteenth year of my reign: I mustered the country; I crossed the Euphrates; 12 kings[60] *came against me; I fought <with them>; I accomplished their defeat.*[61]

Year 18

(97b–99a) In the eighteenth year of my reign: I crossed the Euphrates for the sixteenth time; Hazael of the land of Damascus came to do battle; I took away from him 1,121 of his chariots (and) 470 of his cavalry along with his camp.[62]

Year 21

(102b–104a) In the twenty-first year of my reign: I crossed the Euphrates for the twenty-first time; I marched to the cities of Hazael of the land of Damascus; I captured four of his cities; I received tribute from the land of the Tyrians, the land of Sidonians, (and) the land of Byblians.[63]

Epigraph 1[64]

I received the tribute of Sūa, the Gilzānean: silver (items), gold (items), tin (items), bronze vessels, the staffs of the king's hand,[65] *horses, camels with two humps.*

Epigraph 2

I received the tribute of Jehu (Ia-ú-a),[66] *the son*[67] *of Omri: silver (items), gold (items), a gold bowl, a gold goblet, gold cups, gold buckets, tin (items), a staff of the king's hand, spears.*[68]

Epigraph 3

I received the tribute of Egypt (Muṣri): camels with two humps, a river ox,[69] *a rhinoceros, an antelope, female elephants, female monkeys, apes.*[70]

Epigraph 4

I received the tribute of Marduk-apla-uṣur, the Suḫean: silver (items), gold (items), gold buckets, ivory, spears,[71] *byssus, clothes with colored trim, and linen (items).*

Epigraph 5

I received the tribute of Qarparunda, the Patinean: silver (items), gold (items), tin (items), bronze compound,[72] *bronze vessels, ivory (items), ebony (items).*

D. Eponym lists (Melville)

Past events play a vital role in the way every culture forms, evolves and maintains its identity. And of course, without a proper chronological context, economic transactions, tax schedules, military musters, and administrative records, as well as cultic accounts and private records quickly become useless. In order to administer their present and discuss their past in a meaningful way, the ancients needed a coherent, widely understood means of establishing the sequence of events; that is, a dating system. In the ancient Near East three different methods were used (at different times and in different places) to distinguish years:

1. Years were named after an important event (year names)
2. The years of a king's reign were numbered consecutively (regnal years)
3. Each year was named after a high official called a *limmu* (eponym)

The Assyrians favored eponym dating and used the system from (at least) the nineteenth century BC (Millard 1994: 1). Obviously, in order to keep track of the eponym sequence it was essential for master lists to be widely available for consultation. In Assyria, two types of lists recorded the eponyms; simple lists naming only the eponym and occasionally his title (known as Type A lists), and lists which enumerate the eponyms, their titles and specific information for each year. The latter are known as Type B lists or Eponym Chronicles. The two types of Assyrian eponym lists have thus far been found only in Assur, Nineveh and Sultantepe, but it is probable that they existed at every important Assyrian administrative center (Millard 1994: 4–5). For convenience, the eponym table produced here combines information from both types of eponym text. Column 1 provides the modern Julian date (which of course does not appear on the original documents); column 2, reproducing both Type A and Type B texts, gives the eponyms; and column 3 includes the titles and historical information found only in the Type B/Eponym Chronicle tablets. Space limitations prohibited the inclusion of the whole list, therefore (with a few exceptions) the entries are confined to kings and the five officials following them.

There are 19 extant eponym lists (nine Type A; ten Type B) in various states of preservation, the most complete of which begin in 910 BC with the reign of Adad-nirari II. No list extends past 649 BC (Millard 1994: 4). In addition to the lists, there are hundreds of texts that are dated by eponym. Eponym dates appear most commonly on administrative and economic documents, which have survived from all periods of Assyrian history, especially the eighth and seventh centuries BC, but some Royal Inscriptions use eponyms to identify each yearly campaign (see the inscriptions of Adad-nirari II, for example). Other documents, such as literary texts, also occasionally include colophons with the scribes name and the eponym. Since the lists are incomplete, but documents with eponym dates relatively common, we know the names of many more eponyms than appear on the lists, and scholars have often attempted, with varying results, to place the "unlisted" eponyms in order. The eponyms from the period 649–612 BC, known as post-canonical, have presented a particularly intriguing and complex riddle. There are too many of these post-canonical eponyms for the 37-year period (up to 50, depending on which are accepted) and there is little evidence to elucidate their order, although recent efforts have produced some plausible results (see Whiting 1994: 72–8; Radner 1998: xviii–x; and Reade 1998: 255–65). The lists themselves contain some errors and inconsistencies. If an eponym died before taking office, internecine strife prevented his appointment, or a scribe simply did not know the name of the current *limmu,* then he could date a document by the previous eponym, writing *ina limme ša arki* (in the eponymy after) to mark the lapse (Larsen 1974; Millard 1994: 67–8).

While there remain various problems concerning the Assyrian eponyms, the eponym lists, together with king lists, royal inscriptions and other documents have been essential in establishing the relative chronology (putting events in general order) of the ancient Near East. Additionally, information gleaned from the eponym chronicles and assorted ancillary evidence has allowed scholars to determine the absolute chronology (actual dates) for much of Assyrian history. The eponym chronicles mention that in the eponymy of Bur-saggile, during the reign of Ashur-dan III, a solar eclipse occurred in the month of Siwan (June). Because solar eclipses are periodic, astronomers can calculate precisely when they occurred. As a result, we can securely date the Bur-saggile eclipse to 763 BC, and by extension, establish a firm chronology for the entire period of the lists (910–649 BC), which can then be used in concert with other evidence to extend our absolute chronology even further.

In addition to their chronological value, the eponym lists provide some interesting information about court organization, the status of different officials, and important events, especially military campaigns. For example, it is apparent that at least from the time of Shalmaneser III the eponymy rotated among certain top officials, though not invariably in the same order. After the king held the office, normally in his second regnal year, he was followed by the *turtan* (commander-in-chief of the army), the *rab shaqe* (chief cupbearer), *nagir ekalli* (palace herald) *masennu* (treasurer), and *shakin mati* (governor of Ashur), and then by the governors of different cities (Millard 1994: 9–11). If the king ruled for 30 years (something of a rarity in Assyria) he became eponym a second time. Originally, the eponym may have been chosen by lot, but eventually the order was more or less predetermined and the lot-taking became ceremonial (see Finkel and Reade 1995). Whether the office of *limmu* was initially associated with cultic duties or something more mundane remains uncertain.

The Eponym Chronicles are noteworthy for being forthright about politically sensitive issues such as rebellion, plague, and military defeats, that royal inscriptions and other official documents carefully avoid. The entry for 705 BC, for example, recounts the fact that Sargon II was killed in a skirmish against northern tribes. In contrast, Sargon's son and successor, Sennacherib, nowhere mentions the fate of his father in his inscriptions, since officially admitting to such a defeat would have been contrary to Assyrian royal ideology. The events noted in the Eponym Chronicles typically state the location of the king and his army at the beginning of the year, hence the preponderance of the phrase "to GN." When there was internal disorder in the realm caused by rebellion or plague, no location is given because the king and his troops stayed "in the land." After Shalmaneser III's second eponymy, for instance, the chronicle records seven years of rebellion during which the army was obviously needed at home. Although the Chronicles seem to highlight military events, other incidents such as the commencement of new construction projects are sometimes included as well. Unfortunately we do not know who chose the information to be entered and what criteria, if any, they followed in making entries.

121–2. Assyrian Eponym Lists (= Type A) and Chronicles (= Type B) (Melville)

Modern date	*Eponym officials type A and type B*	*Historical information, type B only*
910	Adad-nirari (Adad-nirari II)	
909	She'I-Ashur	Governor of Kilizi
908	Ashur-da''inanni	
907	Ashur-deni-amur	
906	Barmu	
905–890 omitted		
889	Tukulti-Ninurta, king (Tukulti-Ninurta II)	
888	Taklak-ana-belia	
887	Abu-ilaya	
886	Ilu-milki	
885	Na'id-ilu	
884	Yari	
882	Ashur-naṣir-apli, king (Ashurnaṣirpal II)	
881	Ashur-iddin	
880	Miqti-adur	
879	Sha-ilima-damqa	

Modern date	*Eponym officials type A and type B*	*Historical information, type B only*
878	Dagan-belu-naṣir	
877	Ninurta-piya-uṣur	
876–858 omitted		
857	Shulmanu-ashared (Shalmaneser III)	King of Assyria
856	Ashur-belu-ka''in	Commander-in-chief
855	Ashur-bunaya-uṣur	Chief cupbearer
854	Abi-ina-ekalli-lilbur	Palace herald
853	Dayan-Ashur	Commander-in chief
852	Shamaš-abua	Governor of Naṣibina
851–828 omitted		
827	Shulmanu-ashared (Shalmaneser III, second eponymate)	King of Assyria, to Mannea
826	Dayan-Ashur	Revolt
825	Ashur-bunaya-uṣur	Revolt
824	Yahalu	Revolt
823	Bel-bunaya	Revolt
822	Shamshi-Adad (Shamshi-Adad V)	King of Assyria, revolt
821	Yahalu	revolt
820	Bel-dan	Palace herald, revolt
819	Ninurta-ubla	To Mannea
818	Shamash-ilaya	[to . . .]shumme
817	Nergal-ilaya	Governor of [. . . , to] Tille
816–810 omitted		
809	Adad-nirari (Adad-nirari III)	King of Assyria, to Media
808	Nergal-ilaya	Commander-in-chief, to Guzana
807	Bel-dan	Palace herald, to Mannea
806	Ṣil-beli	Chief cupbearer, to Mannea
805	Ashur-taklak	Treasurer, to Arpad
804	Ilu-issiya	Governor of the land, to Hazazu
803–782 omitted		
781	Shulmanu-ashared (Shalmaneser IV)	King of Assyria, to Urartu
780	Shamshi-ilu	Commander-in-chief, to Urartu

Modern date	*Eponym officials type A and type B*	*Historical information, type B only*
779	Marduki-remanni	Chief cupbearer, to Urartu
778	Bel-lesher	Palace herald, to Urartu
777	Nabu-ishdeya-ka"in	Treasurer, to Itu'a
776	Pan-Ashur-lamur	Governor of the land, to Urartu
775–772 omitted		
771	Ashur-dan (Ashur-dan III)	King of Assyria, to Gananati
770	Shamshi-ilu	Commander-in-chief, to Marad
769	Bel-ilaya	Of Arrapha, to Itu'a
768	Aplaya	Of Zamua, in the land
767	Qurdi-Ashur	Of Ahizuhina, to Gananati
766	Mushallim-Ninurta	Of Tille, to Media
765	Ninurta-mukin-nishi	Of Habruri, to Hatarikka; plague
764	Sidqi-ilu	Of Tushhan, in the land
763	Bur-Saggile	Of Guzana, revolt in the citadel; in Siwan the sun was eclipsed
762–754 omitted		
753	Ashur-nirari (Ashur-nirari V)	King of Assyria, in the land
752	Shamshi-ilu	Commander-in-chief, in the land
751	Marduk-Shallimanni	Palace herald, in the land
750	Bel-dan	Chief cupbearer, in the land
749	Shamash-kenu-dugul	Treasurer, to Namri
748	Adad-belu-ka"in	Governor of the land, to Namri
747–744 omitted		
743	Tukulti-apil-Esharra (Tiglath-pileser III)	King of Assyria, in Arpad, defeat of Urartu made
742	Nabu-da"inanni	Commander-in-chief, to Arpad
741	Bel-Harran-belu-uṣur	Palace herald, to Arpad, within three years taken
740	Nebu-eṭiranni	Chief cupbearer, to Arpad
739	Sin-taklak	Treasurer, to Ulluba, citadel captured
738	Adad-belu-ka"in	Governor of the land, Kullani captured
737–724 omitted		
723	Shalmanu-ashared (Shalmaneser V)	King of Assyria

Modern date	*Eponym officials type A and type B*	*Historical information, type B only*
722	Ninurta-ilaya	
721	Nabu-tariṣ	
720	Ashur-nirka-da"in	
719	Sharru-kenu (Sargon II)	King of Assyria
718	Zeru-ibni	Governor of Rasappa, to Tabal
717	Ṭab-shar-Ashur	Treasurer, [Dur-Sharru]ken founded
716	Ṭab-ṣil-Esharra	Governor of the citadel, to Mannea
715	Taklak-ana-beli	Governor of Naṣibina, [. . .] governors appointed
714	Ishtar-duri	Governor of Arrapha, to Urartu, Musasir, Haldia
713–706 omitted		
705	Nashur-bel	Governor of Amedi, the king [. . .] against Qurdi the Kulummaean, the king was killed, the camp of the king of Assyria [. . .], on 12th Ab, Sennacherib [was made] king
704	Nabu-deni-epush	Governor of Nineveh, [. . .] Larak, Sarabanu, the palace of Kilizi was built, [. . .] the nobles against [. . .]
703	Nuhshaya	Governor of Kilizi [. . .]
702	Nabu-le'i	Governor of Arbela
701	Hananu	Governor of Til-Barsip, from Halzi- [. . .]
700–688 omitted		
687	Sin-ahhe-eriba (Sennacherib) No further kings appear as eponyms	After 700, no further event information included King of Assyria
686–651 omitted		
650	Bel-Harran-Shadua	Governor of Tyre
649	Ahu-ilaya	Governor of Carchemish

Source: after Millard SAAS II, 1994

II. Syro-Palestinian Texts I

123. Treaty of Ktk and Arpad (Strawn)

The Treaty of Ktk and Arpad, often called the Sefire Inscription(s), is extant on three fragmentary basalt stelae. The precise find spot of the first two stelae, recovered in 1930, is not known, but was probably at or near the village of Sefire, a town 14 miles (23 kilometers) southeast of Aleppo. These two stelae are in the shape of a truncated pyramid, each having three faces. A third inscription was acquired by the Beirut Museum in 1956 and was published quickly thereafter, along with a new and improved edition of the first two (Dupont-Sommer and Starcky 1956; 1960; cf. Ronzevalle 1930–1). The third stela, unlike the others, is flat and two-sided. The relationship of the three texts is debated: it is possible that one or two are copies of another[73] but certainty is precluded due to the fragmentary and incomplete state of the inscriptions and the fact that there is no clear overlap between them (Layton 1988: 179).[74]

The inscriptions are written in Old Aramaic and comprise the longest Aramaic epigraphic text yet discovered. The inscriptions date to the middle of the eighth c. BCE[75] and recount the treaty between Bar-Ga'yah, the king of a location named Ktk, and Mati'el, the king of Arpad. There is little debate about the latter person: Arpad lies about 18 miles (29 kilometers) north of Aleppo and its king, Mati'el, is also listed in a treaty of Aššur-nirari V (754–745 BCE), where his name is spelled by its Akkadian equivalent Mati'-ilu (see *RANE*, 101 and *ANET*, 532–3). The facts about Bar-Ga'yah, however, are deeply vexed. There is no consensus as to the identification of Ktk or its king.[76] Lemaire and Durand (1984: 3–58) argued that Bar-Ga'yah (literally, "son of majesty") was a title referring to Šhamši-ilu, an Assyrian high official (*turtanu*) of northern Syria in the early eighth century, and that Ktk is thus to be identified with Kit(t)aka (or Kit[t]ika or Kit[t]uka) – a GN preserved in an inscription of Shalmaneser III and that they think is an alternative name for Til-Barsip.[77] But one might well wonder why an important, public, and political document such as a treaty would cipher not one but two important names – especially that of one of (perhaps the most important of) the treaty partners and his land (cf. *TSSI*, 2: 22). Moreover, the identification of Ktk with Kitaka (or the like) was challenged by von Soden (1985), who argued that the GN was, instead, Kiski, a place mentioned in a campaign of Adad-nirari III in 786.[78] But this identification is also not without problems (Layton 1988; Dion 1997: 131 n. 87), so both the GN and PN remain unknown – at least with any degree of certainty.

Even though some of the historical facts surrounding the treaty will probably remain debated for some time, the text still contains valuable information for students of the ancient Near East. Perhaps most important in this regard is that the Sefire inscriptions provide the only extensive example of a treaty-form from the first millennium, in parts west (in this case, Syria), and in a Northwest Semitic language. As such, it can be profitably compared with other treaties from elsewhere in the Near East, many of which are from roughly contemporaneous Assyria or which are from second millennium Hatti (see McCarthy 1981: esp. 86–105; Parpola and Watanabe 1988; Fitzmyer 1995: 162–6). The following points are significant.

1. *The Nature of the Treaty.* The treaty seems to be one of unequal partners – that is, if Mati'el is not a vassal to Bar-Ga'yah, the king of Arpad is at least the weaker party, conceding greater status to the king of Ktk and bearing the brunt of the obligations himself (*NERT*, 257; Fitzmyer 1995: 165; contrast *TSSI* 2: 20).[79] The significance of this depends in part on the identification of Ktk and Bar-Ga'yah: if the latter is associated with Assyria, the treaty becomes one of loyalty to the Assyrian empire; if Ktk and Bar-Ga'yah are not Assyrian, then the treaty may actually belie an alliance against Assyria, especially given the potential threat to Arpad from that empire as attested in the reigns of both Aššur-nirari V and Tiglath-pileser III (see below).
2. *The Structure of the Treaty.* The treaty-structure as recorded in Stela I – in its standard order and with comparable sections from the other stelae – can be outlined as follows:

I.A: 1–7a	*Introduction* identifying the parties involved in the treaty
I.A: 7b–14a	List of *gods who are witnesses* to the treaty
I.A: 14b–42	*Curses* if Mati'el violates the treaty *with accompanying rites* (cf. II.A: 1–14)
I.B: 1–11	The *sacred nature* of the treaty
(I:B: 12–20	broken or lost)
I.B: 21–45	*Stipulations* that Mati'el must keep (cf. II.B: 1–21; III: 1–29)
I.C: 1–9a	*Conclusion*
(I.C: 9b–14	broken or lost)
I.C: 15–16a	*Blessings* if the treaty is maintained
I.C: 16b–24	*Additional Curses* if the treaty is broken (cf. II.C: 1–17)

This ordering has been challenged, however. Van Rooy (1989: 138), followed by Fitzmyer (1995: 19–20), made the case that the original order of Sefire I was A, D (which is now lost), B, and C; the order of Sefire II was A, C, B, D. This produces the following structure:

Introduction I.A: 1–7a
List of gods I.A: 7b–14a
Curses I.A: 14b–42 (cf. II.A: 1–14; II.C: 1–17)
[Document clause] *not extant* (I.D?)
Stipulations I.B: 1–45 (cf. II.B: 1–21; III: 1–29)
[Addendum] I.C[80]

This structure is similar to Assyrian treaties of the first millennium (Parpola and Watanabe 1988), but the precise sequence is distinct, perhaps given the

West Semitic context. Yet even this structural outline is not without problems and is contingent on the proper reconstruction of the inscriptions' ordering and placement.

3. *The Political Context of the Treaty*. The historical and political facts regarding the treaty are dependent, in no small degree, on the identification of Ktk and Bar-Ga'yah. Since certainty regarding those entities is not forthcoming, one must proceed cautiously. It should be stressed that the treaty's most important contributions may be those already mentioned above: the date, location, and language of the treaty along with its nature and structure. Nevertheless, some historical data can be discussed. According to a stela of Tiglath-pileser III, Mati'el was an important player in an anti-Assyrian coalition that also involved Sarduri II of Urartu (Leick 1999: 103). Mati'el was defeated by Tiglath-pileser III in this matter ca. 740. Prior to this, perhaps ca. 754, Mati'el was the lesser party in a treaty with Aššur-nirari V. It is not possible to say if the Sefire inscriptions predate the treaty with Aššur-nirari V or follow it.[81] Even so, it is tempting to locate the inscriptions *between* these two dates of Assyrian dominance. If so, they would reflect *a response to* (specifically, *against*) Assyrian political dominance under Aššur-nirari V, reflecting Arpad's interest in an anti-Assyrian coalition, either with Urartu or one of its satellite states (cf. *TSSI*, 2: 21–2).[82] If so, the inscriptions would also provide *a motivation and explanation for* the subsequent campaign of Tiglath-pileser III and his defeat of Arpad. The data are meager enough, however, that a definitive judgment seems impossible, even while they are sufficient enough to provide a window onto the complex political situation in northern Syria in the middle of the eighth c. BCE.

Introduction (I.A: 1–7a)[83]

(These are) the treaty-stipulations[84] of Bar-Ga'yah, the king of Ktk, with Mati'el, the son of 'Attarsamak,[85] the king of [Arpad; and the treaty-stipulati]ons of the sons of Bar-Ga'yah with the sons of Mati'el; and the treaty-stipulations of the grandsons of Bar-Ga'yah and] his [descendants] with the descendants of Mati'el, the son of 'Attarsamak, the king of Arpad; and the treaty-stipulations of Ktk with [the treaty-stipulations of] Arpad; and the treaty-stipulations of the lords of Ktk with the treaty-stipulations of the lords of Arpad; and the treaty stipulations of one al[ly with another][86] and with all Aram and with Mṣr[87] and with his sons who will arise in [his] place, and [with the kings of] all Upper and Lower Aram and with everyone who enters or [leaves] the house of the king. They have set up these treaty-stipulations [on th]is [stela].

Divine witnesses (I.A: 7b–14a)

And these are the treaty-stipulations that Bar-Ga'[yah] has made[88] [in the presence of (the god) Ashur] and Mullesh[89] and before Marduk and Zarpanit,[90] in the presence of Nabu and T[ashmet,[91] in the presence of Ir and Nus]k,[92] in the presence of Nergal and Laṣ,[93] in the presence of Shamash and Nur,[94] in the presence of S[in and Nikkal . . .[95]

in the pre]sence of Nikkar and Kadi'ah,[96] *in the presence of all the gods of Raḫbah and Adam,*[97] *[in the presence of Hadad of A]leppo, in the presence of (the) Seven,*[98] *in the presence of 'El and 'Elyon,*[99] *in the presence of Hea[ven and Earth,*[100] *in the presence of (the) A]byss and (the) Springs, and in the presence of Day and Night.*[101] *All (you) g[ods of Ktk and (you) gods of Arpad] are witnesses! Open your eyes to see the treaty-stipulations of Bar-Ga'yah [with Mati'el king of Arpad]!*

Curses for violation of the treaty with accompanying rites (I.A: 14b–42)[102]

(Curses for treaty violation) *Now if Mati'el, the son of 'Attarsamak, the kin[g of Arpad], is unfaithful [to Bar-Ga'yah, the king of Ktk, and i]f the descendants of Mati'el are unfaithful [to the descendants of Bar-Ga'yah . . . and if the sons of] Gush*[103] *[are unfaithful] (. . .)*[104] *[. . .] a ewe, then may it not conceive;*[105] *and (even if) seven [nurs]es anoin[t their breasts and] nurse a child, then may it not be satisfied; and (even if) seven mares suckle a colt, then may it not be sati[sfied; and (even if) seven] cows suckle a calf, then may it not be satisfied; and (even if) seven ewes suckle a lamb, then [may it not be satis]fied; and (even if) seven hens go looking for food, then may they not kill.*[106] *And if Mati'[el] is unfaithful [to] his (i.e., Bar-Ga'yah's) son*[107] *or to his descendants, (then) may his kingdom become like a kingdom of sand – a kingdom of sand! – as long as Ashur rules. [(And) may Ha]dad pour (upon it) every kind of evil (there is) on earth and in heaven along with every kind of trouble and may he pour out [ha]il-[stones] on Arpad. And (for) seven years may the locust(s) devour, and (for) seven years may the worm(s) devour, and (for) seven [years may] lament*[108] *[come] over the face of his (i.e., Mati'el's)*[109] *land. And may the grass not sprout so that no green is seen, nor may (any of) its vegetation b[e seen]. And may the sound of the lyre not be heard in Arpad, but (instead) the sound of sickness and the tum[ult of out]cry*[110] *and lamentation among his people. And may the gods send every type of devourer on Arpad and on his people: [May the mou]th of a snake, the mouth of a scorpion, the mouth of a bear,*[111] *and the mouth of a leopard [devour]. And [may] a moth, a louse, and a [. . . become] the throat of a serpent against it.*[112] *[May] its vegetation be completely [de]stroyed and may Arpad become a ruin*[113] *to [(serve as a) house of desert animal(s) and] gazelle(s) and fox(es) and hare(s) and wild-cat(s) and owl(s)*[114] *and [. . .] and magpie(s). And may [this] ci[ty] not be discussed (any more), nor Mdr', nor Mrbh, nor Mzh, nor Mnlh, nor Sharun, nor Tu'im, nor Bethel, nor Bynn, nor [. . . nor Ar]neh, nor Ḥazaz, nor Adam.*[115]

(Accompanying rites) *Just as this wax is burned with fire,*[116] *thus may Arpad and [her gr]eat [daughters]*[117] *be burned. May Hadad sow in them salt*[118] *and weeds and may it (Arpad) not be discussed (any more). This gnb'*[119] *and [this . . .] (are) Mati'el – it is his life. Just as this wax is burned with fire, thus may Ma[ti'el] be burned [with fi]re. Just as the bow and these arrows are broken, thus may Inurta and Hadad break [the bow of Mati'el] and the bow of his lords.*[120] *And just as the man of wax is blinded, thus may Mati'e]l be blinded.*[121] *[And just as] this calf is cut up, thus may Mati'el and his lords be cut up.*[122] *[And just as the prost]it[ute is stripped], thus may the wives of Mati'el and the wives of his descendants and the wives of [his] no[bles] be stripped.*[123] *[And just as this wax woman is taken] and one strikes her face, thus may [the wives of Mati'el] be taken [and struck on their face . . .]*

The sacred nature of the treaty (I.B: 1–11)[124]

[(These are) the treaty-stipulations of Bar-Ga'yah, the king of Ktk, with Mati'el, the son of 'Attarsamak, the king of Ar]pad; and the treaty-stipulations of the sons of Bar-Ga'yah with the sons of Mati'el; and the treaty-stipulations of [the grandsons of Bar-]Ga'yah with the descendants of Mati'el and with the descendants of any king who [arises and rules] in his place and with the sons of Gush[125] and the House of Ṣilul[126] and with [all] Ar[am; and the treaty-sipulation]s of Ktk with the treaty-stipulations of Arpad; and the treaty-stipulations of the lords of Ktk with the tre[aty stipulations of the lords of A]rpad and with its people; and the treaty-stipulations of the gods of Ktk with the treaty-stipulations of the g[ods of Arpad]. These are the treaty-stipulations of the gods which the gods themselves have made.

Blessed [for]ever is the reign of [Bar Ga'yah], (the) great king, and from thes[e] tre[aty-stipulation]s [. . . and heaven]. And [all the gods] will guard [these] treaty-stipulations. Not one of the words of thi[s] inscription should be (kept) silent; [rather, let them be heard from] 'Arqu unto Ya'd[i and] Bz, from Lebanon unto Yab[rud, and from Damasc]us unto 'Aru and (. . .), [and fr]om Bq't unto Ktk.[127] [. . . the Ho]use of Gush[128] and its people with their worship-sites,[129] the[se] treaty-stipulations [. . .] (gap)[130]

Stipulations (III: 1–29)[131]

[. . .] or to your son or to your descendants or to one of the kings of Arpad and s[peak]s [agai]nst me or against my son or against my grandson or against my descendants, in the manner of any man who is angry,[132] and speaks evil words against me, [you] will [not] receive such words from his hand. (Instead), you must hand them (any such persons) over to me with dispatch,[133] and your son will hand (them) over to my son, and your descendants will hand (them) over to my descendants, and the descendants of [one of the k]ings of Arpad will hand (them) over to me. I will then do to them whatever seems good to me.[134] Otherwise, you have been unfaithful[135] to all the gods of the treaty-stipulations which are in [this] inscription.

If a fugitive flees from me, (whether it is) one of my officials, or one of my brothers, or one of my eunuchs, or one of the people who are in my control, and they go to Aleppo,[136] you must not gi[ve] food [to] them and you must not say to them "Stay quietly in your place," and you must not stir up their spirits against me. (Instead), you must pacify them carefully[137] and (then) must return them to me. And if they are not [dwelling] in your land, (nevertheless) pacify them there until I myself come and I pacify them.[138] But if you stir up their spirits against me and give food to them and say to them "Stay in yo[ur] place and do not turn (back) to his region," you have been unfaithful to these treaty-stipulations.

Now (as for) all the kings of my vicinity or any one who is my friend, when I send my messenger [t]o him for peace or for any business of mine or (when) he sends his messenger to me, the road must be open for me. You will not be superior to me in this (matter) and you will not protest to me about [it. Ot]herwise, you have been unf[ait]hful to these treaty-stipulations.

If someone – (whether) one of my brothers or one of the house of my father or one of my sons or one of my officers or one of my [of]ficials or one of the people who are in my control or one of my enemies – seeks my head so as to kill me or to kill my son or my descendants, if they do (in fact) kill m[e], (then) you yourself must come and you must avenge my blood from the hand of my enemies. And your son will come: he will avenge the blood of my son from his enemies. And your grandson will come: he will avenge the blo[od of] my [gr]andson. And your descendants will come: they will avenge the blood of my descendants. And if it is a town (that conducted the assassination), you will strike it hard[139] *with the sword. And if it was one of my brothers or one of my servants or [one of] my officials or one of the people who are in my control, you will strike h<i>m and his descendants and his nobles*[140] *and his friends hard with the sword.*[141] *Otherwise, you have been unfaithful to all the gods of the [treat]y-stipulations which is on this inscription.*

If (it) should come into your mind[142] *and you make plans*[143] *to kill me, or (if it) should come into the mind of your grandson and he makes plans to kill my grandson, or if (it) should come into the mind of your descendants and they make plans to kill my descendants, or if (it) should come into the [m]ind of the kings of Arpad – however someone might die*[144] *– you have been unfaithful to all the gods of the treaty-stipulations that are in this inscription.*

If [my] son, who sits upon my throne (after me), contends <with> one of his brothers and he (the latter) would depose him (the former), you must not send your tongue between them[145] *and say to him "Kill your brother" or "Imprison him and do [not] let him go free." [Instead], if you mediate*[146] *between them, he will not kill and will not imprison (him). But if you do not mediate between them, you have been unfaithful to these treaty-stipulations.*

Now (as for) the [k]ings [who are in] my [vicini]ty, if a fugitive from me flees to one of them or a fugitive from them flees and comes to me, if he has returned the one who is mine, I will restore [the one who is his. And] you yourself must [n]ot hinder me (in this). Otherwise, you have been unfaithful to these treaty-stipulations.

You will not send (your) tongue among my house or my grandsons or neph[ews or the sons of] my [desc]endants or the sons of my people and say to them, "Kill your lord and become his successor, because he is no better than you." (If so, be assured) someone will avenge [my blood. And if you] act treacherously towards me or towards my son or towards [my] descendants, you have been [unfa]ithful to all the gods of the treaty-stipulations that are in thi[s] inscription.

[Tal'ay]im[147] *and its villages and its lords and its territory belonged to my father and to [his house from] ancient times. But when the gods struck the house [of my father, it be]came another's (possession). Now, however, the gods have restored the hou[se of my father and the house of] my father [has become great]. Tal'ayim has returned to [Bar-Ga'y]ah and to his son and to his grandson and to his descendants forever. So, [if my son or] my [grands]on or my descendants contends [with your descendants conce]rning Tal'ayim or its villages or its lords, whoever lifts up [. . .] the [ki]ngs of Arpad [. . .] (. . .) you have been unfaithful in these treaty-stipulations.*

If [. . .] and they bribe in any way a king who (. . .) [. . . everything th]at is beautiful and everything that is go[od . . .]

Conclusion (I.C: 1–9a)[148]

Thus we have spoken [and thus] we have [wr]itten. What I, [Mati'‘]el have written (is) for a reminder to my son [and to] my grand[son] who will arise in my [place], for (their) goo[d].[149] *May [they] act [under] the sun [for (the sake of) my] ro[yal hou]se [so] that [no]thing ev[il is done against] the house of Ma[ti‘el or his son or his [grand]son for[ever . . .] (gap)*[150]

Blessings (I.C: 15–16a)[151]

(. . .) may the gods keep [all evils?] from his time and from his house.[152]

Additional curses (I.C: 16b–24)[153]

But whoever does not guard the words of the inscription that is on this stela, but says (instead) "I will efface some of its words" or "I will overturn the good (circumstances) and I will turn (them) [into] evil (ones)," on the day that he doe[s] this, may the gods overturn [th]at ma[n] and his house and everything that is [in] it. May they turn it completely [up]side down![154] *And may his offsp[ring] not inherit a name.*

124. Tel Dan stele inscription (Schmidt)

The Tel Dan stele inscription mainly comprises a basalt stone fragment inscribed with 13 surviving or partially surviving lines discovered in July of 1993 (fragment A) with two smaller, additional fragments recovered in June of 1994 (fragments B1 and B2). Both discoveries were made during excavations of the Hebrew Union College expedition to Tel Dan in the upper Galilee (biblical Dan and Laish?). Although the authenticity, date, and unity of these three inscribed fragments have been vigorously challenged, they are provisionally treated here as representative of a single, larger royal monumental or memorial inscription. They were found in secondary context in the remains of a wall (fragment A in 1993), in an adjacent flagstone pavement of a piazza (B1) and in nearby debris (B2). The wall has been dated to the beginning of the eighth century BCE based on the dating of pottery beneath the wall to the end of the ninth / beginning of the eighth centuries. This along with the paleographic analysis of the inscriptions has rendered a date for the larger hypothetical stele in the second half of the ninth century BCE. The language of the inscriptions is Early or Old Aramaic. The fragments were originally housed in the Hebrew Union College Museum in Jerusalem, but are now on display in the Israel Museum, Jerusalem.

Commentary

Of particular historical interest is (1) the clear reference to "the king of Israel" or *mlk yšr'l* in line 8 and (2) the phrase in line 9, *bytdwd*, most likely a reference to "the house of David." Citing various lines of support, interpreters have offered alternative proposals for *bytdwd*: "the house of the beloved," or "Bethdod," a place name (even as a reference to Jerusalem), or "a temple of (the god) Dod." The authors of the *editio princeps* of the inscribed fragments, A. Biran and J. Naveh, having accepted a significant degree of congruence between this inscription and the biblical traditions in 2 Kgs, suggested the possible mention of kings Jehoram of Israel and Ahaziah of Judah in lines 7–8. In their opinion, the stele was erected by king Hazael of Aram, a usurper of one Ben-Hadad (I or II). King Hazael erected the stele following his campaign in the region and his defeat of Jehoram of Israel and Ahaziah of Judah around 835 BCE (cf. also 2 Kgs 8: 25–9). It may have been subsequently smashed by king Jehoash of Israel who in 2 Kgs 13: 25 is portrayed as having recovered regions of Israel from the Arameans. A piece of the stele (fragment A) was then reused by those responsible for later rebuilding the city.

The text, unfortunately, is incompletely preserved where the royal names Jehoram and Ahaziah have been reconstructed in lines 7–8 (three of the five, and three of the six letters that make up these proposed names are present and the names Ahab and Jehoram, a king of Judah, both enclosed in brackets "[xxx]" in the following translation of these same lines, are entirely reconstructed). In fact, the name of another king, Jehu of Israel, has been suggested as a more fitting reconstruction in place of Ahaziah in line 8 since 2 Kgs 9: 24–7 ascribes the deaths of these two kings to Jehu and not to Hazael. According to this view, the inscription describes Hazael as defeating Jehoram who was killed by Jehu, the vassal of Hazael or "son of the king" (cf. the end of line 8 where "son" is clearly present, Aramaic *br*, and "king" can be partially restored [*ml*]*k*). An alternative reconstruction for the name of the father of Hazael has also been suggested for the space at the very beginning of line 2, immediately preceding and completing the phrase "[. . . -]el my father . . ." that is, "[Baraq]el, my father. . . ." Another viewpoint identifies Jehu, instead of Hazael, as the author of the inscription who refers to himself in the first person ("I," cf. lines 5–6). In this rendition, the name Hazael is reconstructed at the beginning of line 2 immediately preceding and completing the phrase "[. . . -]el my father . . . ," or "[Haza]el, my father . . . ," i.e., Jehu's "father"(politically speaking that is). In the final analysis, the currently available fragments of the text impede any attempt to advance beyond such interpretative possibilities to the historically probable.

If the phrase *bytdwd* is to be interpreted as "the house of David," then the Tel Dan inscription provides the earliest extra-biblical reference to the name David and to a dynasty thereof (but see now the Mesha inscription no. 126 for another possible occurrence of this phrase). It also indicates that with the passage of time, the dynastic line in Judah had attained some regional notoriety, just as the northern dynasty had earlier (cf. the roughly contemporary Mesha inscription and Assyrian texts where the dynasty of Omri is so recognized, Akkadian *bīt humrî*, "the house of Humrî," and cf. *mār* [*bīt*?] *humrî*, "the man of [the house of] Humrî"). Nevertheless, it confirms significant Aramean military victories over Israel and its ally (or satellite?), Judah, in the second half of the ninth century BCE. Granting for the sake of argument its unity and authenticity (there remain, for some, significant questions) the Tel Dan inscription provides new historical information, some of which may differ at points with details in the biblical traditions. Yet such royal memorial records might have functioned as archival sources for the later southern writers and editors from Judah who produced the bulk of the multifarious accounts that comprise 2 Kgs.

Translation

1. *[..................................] and cut [. . . a treaty?]*
2. *[. . .]el, my father we[nt up against him when] he fought at [. . .]*
3. *And my father lay down, he went to his [.......]. And the king of I[s-]*
4. *rael entered previously my father's land. [And] it was I Hadad made king.*
5. *And Hadad went in front of me[and] I went forth from [the] seven[. . . -]*
6. *s of my kingdom, and I slew [seve]nty kin[gs] who harnessed thou[sands of cha-]*
7. *riots and thousands of horsemen. [I killed Jeho]ram, son of [Ahab,]*
8. *king of Israel and [I] killed [Ahaz]iahu, son of [Jehoram, kin-]*
9. *g of the house of David. And I set [their towns into ruins and turned]*
10. *their land into [desolation..]*
11. *other [..and Jehu ru-]*
12. *led over Is[rael..and I laid]*
13. *siege upon [..]*

125. Zakkur Inscription (Noegel)

The basalt stele of Zakkur, king of Hamath and Lu'ash, was discovered by Henri Pognon in 1903 at Afis in Syria. Little remains of the figure that once stood atop the stele, but most of its Old Aramaic inscription has survived, with the exception of some lacunae and about 30 lines. Though the date of the stele is debated (dates range from 805 to 775 BCE), it constitutes an important source of evidence for the Aramean kingdom, and permits a rare portrait into the frequent border skirmishes that preoccupied Aramaea in the early eighth century BCE.

The inscription offers an autobiographical account of Zakkur's annexation of Hazrach (the biblical Hadrach [Zech 9: 1]), and a battle against 17 city-states[155] that ensued because of it. Zakkur describes the battle only in the most general terms. He says nothing of the context or causes that may have led to the war or of envoys or previous contacts with these kings. He cites no specific campaigns and gives no bloody details or lists of booty. He appears far more interested in portraying himself as a man saved by the gods from near certain annihilation because of his piety.

After asserting that the god Baal-shamayin (lit. "Lord of the Heavens") placed him on the throne of Hazrach, Zakkur immediately describes the insurmountable odds that he faced; a powerful confederation of city-states led by "Bar-Hadad, son of Hazael, king of Damascus" (796–770 BCE). The list of coalition forces is partially broken but includes the kings Bar-Gush, the king of Arpad, and the unnamed kings of Quwe, 'Umq, Gurgum, Sam'al, and Meliz, and if restorations are correct, also of Tubal, Kittik, and Amurru (Lipínksi 2000: 254). Far from being a dry roster of players in the arena, the list of kings serves to build suspense by slowing down the narrative and diminishing the likelihood of victory. The reader waits with anticipation to hear what transpired next.

It is at this point that Zakkur, realizing that the attack was imminent, looked not to his generals and chariotry for salvation, but to Baal-shamayin:

> *But I raised my hands to Baal-shamayin, and Baal-shamayin answered me, and Baal-shamayin spoke to me by the hand of seers and by the hand of diviners; and Baal-shamayin said to me: "Fear not! For it was I who made you king, and [I will rise] with you. I will rescue you from all of [these kings] who have forced the rampart upon you." And Baal-shamayin said to me: "[I will strike] all these kings who forced [the rampart upon you] . . . and this wall wh[ich they have raised . . .]."*

The account employs a literary motif well known to students of ancient Near Eastern literature in which a leader receives divine salvation from an imminent battle after praying for help (e.g., Gen 15: 1; 1 Kgs 8: 33–52; Isa 7: 4–9; 2 Chr 20: 1–30). The inscription's mention of seers and diviners is of particular importance to historians of religion since it attests to the existence of the institution of prophecy in Aramaea, and to the access of mantics in the Aramean royal house (Zobel 1971).

Equally important is the fact that Zakkur attributes his victory to the storm god Baal-shamayin, apparently the Aramaic name for Ilu-wer, to whom the stele is dedicated. Though Ilu-wer has a long history that originates not in Syria, but in Mesopotamia, Baal-shamayin appears to have been a local god, though his cult in Hamath may suggest Phoenician influence (Lipínski 2000: 254).

Zakkur's recourse to mantics, the divine promise of victory, and the dedication of the stele to Ilu-wer are all meant to underscore the king's piety. By depicting Zakkur as a man who seeks and receives divine guidance, the stele demonstrates that he has the support of the gods, and thus also of the religious establishment upon whom his legitimacy may in part depend.

Following the divine promise, the stele immediately lists a number of building projects which Zakkur's victory allowed him to achieve.

> *[. . .] Hazrach [. . .] for chariot [and] horseman [. . .] his king in its midst. I [built up] Hazrach and [I] added [to it] all the territory of [. . .] and I established it [. . .] fortresses on every side. I [bui]lt temples for the gods through[out] my [land], and I built [. . .] Apish and [. . .] temple.*
>
> *[and] I established before [Ilu-Wer] this (very) stele, and [I] inscrib[ed upon] that which my hands [accomplished].*

Since such projects, especially those that strengthened the cult of the city god, were deemed acts of piety, this list of projects similarly served to bolster the portrait of Zakkur as a king whose heart is in the right place when it comes to worship. It is he who erected his stele in Apish (modern Afis), perhaps the name of a sacred precinct in Hazrach (Lipínski 2000: 257).

The stele then concludes with a fragmentary series of curses against anyone who might remove it from its place. The curses reaffirm the role of the divine world in protecting the inscription even as they recall the protection of the king from his enemies.

[Who]ever removes th[at which was (accomplished) by the hands of] Zakkur, king of Hama[th and Lu'ash] from the stele, and who[ever re]moves this stele from [befo]re Ilu-wer and carries it off fr[om] its [place], or whoever casts [it] in [. . .]. May Baal-shamayin and Ilu-[wer], and Shamash and Shahar, [. . .] and the gods of heav[en and the go]ds of earth, and Baal[. . .] the man and [. . .] the name of Zakkur and the name of [. . .].

We know precious little about Zakkur. He appears to have been a native of 'Ana on the Euphrates River, a place well within Assyrian influence (Millard 1990). He also appears to have been the founder of the Aramean dynasty at Hamath, and a usurper, since the kings who ruled Hamath in the ninth century BCE bear Luwian (neo-Hittite) names (Hawkins 1982).

We know little more about his enemy Bar-Hadad III (or II). When he came to the throne, sometime before 800 BCE, he had inherited a powerful kingdom from his father Hazael, who both the Bible (2 Kgs 8: 15) and records of Shalmanezer III (858–824 BCE) call a usurper. The extent of Hazael's power can be seen in that Shalmanezer tried twice (in 841 and 838) to take Damascus, but failed. It also can be seen by the fact that inscriptions discovered in Greece at Etruria and Samos refer to Hazael as "our Lord" (Dion 1995: 1285). Moreover Hazael's name was still attached to Damascus in Assyrian records more than a century after his death.

The biblical record is somewhat ambivalent about Hazael. The prophet Elijah anointed him king of Damascus (1 Kgs 19: 15), but recognized nevertheless that his kingdom would spell disaster for Israel (2 Kgs 8: 12). Indeed, according to the Bible, Hazael and his son Bar-Hadad would eventually extend their power not only to the border of Judah in the south, but to the Arnon River in the Transjordan. It would not be until the reign of Amaziah (800–783 BCE) when Hamath would again be within Israelite control (2 Kgs 14: 25), a border created first under Solomon (1 Kgs 8: 65).

Despite the useful background that such biblical texts provide, attempts to clarify the historical context of Zakkur's battle have met mostly with frustration. Some have suggested that the coalition may have retaliated against Zakkur for uniting Hamath and Lu'ash. Others have argued that though Assyria is nowhere mentioned on the stele it must have played a role in deciding the victor since it was the major power of the day. Indirect evidence for this comes from the Assyrian Eponym Chronicle, which tells us that Adad-nirari III's (810–783 BCE) campaign in 796 BCE reached Mansuate (Millard 1994). If Mansuate is to be connected with the modern town of Masyaf, southwest of Hamath by 28 miles (Lipinski 1971: 396; 2000: 303–10), then the Assyrian campaign of 796 under Adad-nirari III might be connected to the liberation of Zakkur at Hazrach. This also would fit well the record of Assyria's continued interest in the region. The Eponym Chronicle, for example, also lists a later Assyrian attack against Damascus in 773 BCE and several campaigns to Hazrach in 772, 765, and 755 BCE.

Additional evidence of Assyrian involvement comes from a Neo-Assyrian stele now in the Museum at Antakya that describes an Assyrian attempt to settle a border dispute between Zakkur of Hamath and Atarshumki I of Arpad sometime around 807–806 BCE (Donbaz 1990). The context of the event, in which Adad-nirari III gives cessions to the king of Arpad, demonstrates a close Assyrian involvement in the region and appears to be connected to the western campaign of Adad-nirari III in 796 BCE mentioned in the Assyrian Eponym Chronicle. Some also have opined that Zakkur may even have allowed Adad-nirari III passage through his kingdom in order to besiege Damascus (Puech 1992: 329–34; Lipínski 2000: 285). If this view is correct, and there is some tangential archaeological evidence to support an Assyrian presence at Hamath at this time, then Zakkur and Adad-nirari III may have shared something of an alliance. This would then help to explain an Assyrian intervention to save Zakkur at Hazrach.

Additional, albeit weaker, evidence comes from a broken bas-relief, now in the British Museum, that illustrates a capped man raising a bowl and that contains the name Zakuri in cuneiform characters. If this figure is indeed our only portrait of Zakkur of Hamath, it may depict him paying tribute to Adad-nirari III (Lipínski 2000: 302).

It is also possible that the section of Zakkur's stele that describes his building activities does reference Assyrian involvement, though this is debated. There are several gaps in the inscription at this point, but one can make out the name Hazrach, the mention of troops (lit. a chariot and horseman), and the phrase "his king in its midst." Since it is unlikely that Zakkur would refer to himself in the third person, some see it as a reference to the Assyrian monarch, though "his" might also be read "its" and reference something now lost (Lipínksi 2000: 310; cf. Millard 2000: 155).

We will perhaps never know for certain whether the Assyrians intervened on Zakkur's behalf. Moreover, even if an intervention did occur, one would not necessarily expect to find the Assyrian king credited on Zakkur's stele. Such a reference would detract from Zakkur's own glory and would not suit its purpose as a memorial to the god Ilu-wer.

Indeed, the Zakkur Inscription is a literary account of a historical event whose ideological purpose forces us to exercise caution when using it as a historical source. Its literary nature is demonstrated by a number of features, some of which already have been mentioned, such as the text's autobiographical monologue, and the literary motif of a god answering a pious king in time of crisis. Others might be less obvious (Tawil 1974). For example, when describing how the enemy besieged Zakkur the stele employs merism, a device in which opposites express a totality.

And all the kings erected a rampart upon Hazra[ch],
and they raised a wall higher than the wall of Hazrach,
and they dug a trench deeper than its trench.

Zakkur also uses merism when asserting that Baal-shamayin spoke to him through seers and diviners. The word for seer (which is cognate with the term for "seer, prophet" in biblical Hebrew) suggests someone, perhaps a non-professional, who randomly receives divine messages depending on the deity's will, whereas the diviner represents an expert who solicits oracles from the divine. The merism thus demonstrates that Baal-shamayin communicated his intention to Zakkur through every possible means.

In the series of curses quoted above one also finds examples of parallelism: for example, "removing what Zakkur has accomplished" and "removing what is before Ilu-wer." One also sees literary coupling in the section containing the curses: for example, Zakkur and Ilu-wer, Hamath and Lu'ash, Baal-shamayimn and Ilu-wer, Shamash and Shahar, and the gods of heaven and the gods of earth (perhaps also examples of merism).

In addition, the stele uses the same verb for "to establish" with three different meanings, a literary device known as antanaclasis. It first appears in connection with the stele that Zakkur "erected." It then appears in conjunction with the siege rampart that the coalition of kings "raised up." Finally, it is used for Hazrach itself which Zakkur "established." The subtle repetition of this verb in this relatively short inscription draws the three events into contrast and allows readers to connect cause and event. In essence, the erection of the stele and the successful establishment of Hazrach itself remind us of the unsuccessful siege.

The inscription's literary aspects, coupled with other details, have led some scholars to theorize that the stele reworked an older textual source that featured Zakkur's military victory against coalition forces into a new context in order to emphasize the king's piety. Others have observed that the inscription resembles more of a thanksgiving psalm than a chronicle (Greenfield, 1972: 178–84). Still others have found typological parallels in biblical texts such as 2 Kgs 3: 4–27; 6: 24–7: 20; 18: 13–19: 37.

Regardless of how we define its genre, and barring any new discovery that might alter the picture we now possess, the Zakkur Inscription will continue to be one of our most important sources of information for the Aramean kingdom in the eighth century BCE.

126. Moabite Stone (Schmidt)

There is a general consensus that Frederick A. Klein, a German born, Alsatian missionary working in Palestine in the service of the Anglican church, was the first westerner to see the monument upon which was incised the now famous inscription of king Mesha of Moab. On August 19, 1868, while on a journey to several planned missionary stops on the east side of the Jordan, Klein was unexpectedly shown an inscribed black basalt stone monument by a local Bedouin tribe, the Banî Ḥamîda who were encamped at Dibon. The monument once stood over a meter in height and was more or less, 2 feet (a half meter) in width and in thickness (measurements taken by Klein and subsequent estimates by others such as the French scholar C. Clermont-Ganneau vary somewhat).

In any case, the accompanying inscription had to have been comprised of more than the 34 existing lines as the end of the monument is broken off and irretrievably lost. Owing to several contingencies, transporting the monument from its location was out of the question and Klein was able to sketch only a handful of inscribed letters before his departure (accounts differ as to the exact number). Soon after Klein's return to Jerusalem, news spread of the discovery and various local European authorities, British, French, Prussian as well as Ottoman, thus began a 15-month battle to acquire the stone. In reaction to all this unwanted interest on the part of foreigners, it seems that the local Bedouin broke the monument into pieces with only some major portions subsequently recovered in 1870 (approximately two-thirds of the original). Fortunately, Clermont-Ganneau had commissioned three Arabs to make squeezes (or facsimile impressions on wetted paper) of the inscription prior to its destruction. He subsequently published the inscription on the basis of these squeezes and remaining fragments. The fragments were sent to Paris and pieced together in the Louvre. Gaps in the monument and its accompanying inscription were provisionally completed on the basis of the squeezes.

The inscription remains to this day the longest and most informative Iron age inscription ever recovered from the southern Levant. It provides our major evidence for the Moabite language, which is closely related to Phoenician and northern Hebrew, and constitutes a unique epigraphic source for the Iron age geopolitical history and religion of the region. The events narrated in the Mesha inscription should probably be dated to ca. 855–830 BCE. The actual inscription on the stele and perhaps some of the events it preserves might date several decades later depending on the length of Mesha's reign. While the inscription's words are separated by dots . . . there appears an additional technique of broader segmentation comprising vertical lines that displace the dots where they occur. These lines have been interpreted as demarcating whole coordinate lines or sentences. Others have identified still larger levels of segmentation in the text of the inscription based on content or discourse (e.g., Parker 1997; and cf. now Routledge 2004).

Translation

1. *I am Mesha, son of Kemosh[yatti], the king of Moab, the Daybonite.*
2. *My father ruled over Moab 30 years, and I ruled*
3. *after my father. And I made this high place for Kemosh in Qarho, a high place*
4. *of salvation, because he has saved me from all the kings and because he caused me to prevail over all my enemies. Now Omr[i],*

5. *king of Israel oppressed Moab many days, for Kemosh was angry with his land.*
6. *And his son succeeded him, and he also said, "I will oppress Moab." In my days he spoke this,*
7. *but I prevailed over him and over his house. Now Israel utterly perished forever. Now Omri had taken possession of the land*
8. *of Madaba. And he dwelt in it his days and half the days of his son, 40 years, but*
9. *Kemosh restored it in my days. And I built Ba'al-Ma'on and I made in it a water reservoir and I built*
10. *Qiryaten. Now the men of Gad had dwelt in the land of Ataroth from of old and the king of Israel had built for them*
11. *Ataroth. And I fought against the city and took it, and I slew all the people of*
12. *the city as a spectacle(?) for Kemosh and Moab. And I brought back from there "the lion statue of its Beloved (i.e., the city god?)" and I*
13. *hauled it before Kemosh in Qiryat. And I settled in it the men of Sharon and the men of Meharoth(?).*
14. *And Kemosh said to me: "Go take Nebo from Israel," so I*
15. *went by night and fought against it from the break of dawn until noon, and I*
16. *took it and slew all, seven thousand male citizens and foreign men seven thousand men, female citizens, foreign*
17. *women and female slaves. For Ashtar-Kemosh I had it put to the ban. And I took from there the vessels*
18. *of Yahweh, and I hauled them before Kemosh. Now the king of Israel had built*
19. *Jahaz and dwelt in it while fighting against me. But Kemosh drove him out from before me and*
20. *I took from Moab two hundred men, its whole division, and I led it up against Jahaz and captured it*
21. *to add it to Daybon. Now I built Qarho, the parkland walls and the walls*
22. *of the acropolis; and I built its gates and I built its towers, and I built*
23. *the palace, and I made the retaining walls of the reservoir for the water supply inside*
24. *the city. Now there was no cisterns inside the city at Qarho so I said to all the people: "Make your-*
25. *selves one cistern each in his house;" and I dug the trenches for Qarho with the prisoners*
26. *of Israel. I built Aroer and I made the highway through the Arnon.*
27. *And I built the temple of Bamoth, for it had been destroyed. And I built Beṣer, for [it was] in ruins*
28. *[And] the men of Daybon stood in military array, for all of Daybon was [now] obedient. And I ruled.*
29. *over the hundreds in the cities that I had added to the land. And I built*
30. *[Mada]ba and the temple of Diblaten and [the temple of Ba'al-Ma'on. And I took up there*
31. *sheep of the land . . . Now [as for] Hawronen, the Ho[use of Da]vid dwelt in it and.....*
32. *Kemosh said to me: "Go down, fight against Hawronen," so I went down and....*
33. *Kemosh [retur]ned it in my days And I brought up from there ten...*
34. *[..........] And I [. . .]*
35.

The Mesha Inscription and the religions of Moab and Israel

The Mesha Inscription is recorded on a royal memorial stele and as such, celebrates Mesha's victory over Israel. In that capacity, it attributed Moab's victory to the benevolent inclination of Kemosh, Moab's principle deity and, by all appearances, Mesha commissioned the inscription on the occasion of his dedication of the high place he constructed in honor of Kemosh.

Kemosh and related compound names appear some 12 times in the Mesha inscription. Not only was he the patron deity of Moab, but given the more generally recognized henotheistic orientation that characterized the regional cults at the time, he was also considered the highest-ranking god of the Moabite pantheon. In fact, the Mesha inscription makes clear that it was Kemosh who possessed the power both to grant military victories to his king and his people. Moreover, as indicated in line 5, he, like Israel's god Yahweh, also exercised the alternative to wreak havoc on his people, even subjugating them to a foreign power as an expression of his divine displeasure or anger. Another element these religious traditions share is the possible attribution of a female deity or consort-wife to both male deities. In the case of Kemosh, that would feasibly be the goddess (?) Ashtar-Kemosh mentioned in line 17, while Yahweh's consort, Asherah, is unequivocally documented as such in the recent Iron age finds from Kuntillet ʻAjrud and Khirbet el-Qom.

The Hebrew Bible mentions Kemosh by name eight times and in all but one case, he is recognized as the patron deity of Moab (Num 21: 29; Judg 11: 24 [note: Kemosh here is curiously identified with the Ammonites]; 1 Kgs 11: 7,33; 2 Kgs 23: 13; Jer 48;7, 13, 46). Particularly worthy of mention is the fact that in Judg 11: 24, the biblical writer acknowledges Kemosh's active involvement in history and, in particular, in the disposition of land. Based on these and related data, scholars have also proposed that Kemosh is alluded to in 2 Kgs. 3: 27. Though he is not explicitly mentioned in this text, Kemosh is the most obvious or likely source for the outpouring of divine wrath against the Israelite army mentioned in the text. Even though commanded by Yahweh to undertake the military campaign against Moab, Israel is forced to retreat from its siege of the Moabite city following the Moabite king's sacrifice of his son on the wall of the city. This ritual killing of a human was viewed by the author of 2 Kgs 3 as genuinely initiating the "great wrath" that so overwhelmed the Israelite army it was forced to abandon its offensive against Moab in retreat. The accounts of Kemosh's intervention and specific guidance in times of war as highlighted in the Mesha inscription find their close parallels in the biblical accounts of Yahweh. Yet, what may surprise many readers is the fact that the power of Kemosh to intervene in history was also recognized by some biblical writers who evidently viewed him as a worthy rival of Yahweh.

In lines 3–4 of the Mesha inscription, Mesha is depicted as having built a "high place" which he dedicated to Kemosh as an act of gratitude for the military victories over Israel that Kemosh had granted Mesha (this also is most likely the rationale for the erection of the very stele upon which our inscription was incised). The term employed for high place is the exact cognate to that used in biblical Hebrew to refer to the same, namely a "bamah" (Heb. *bāmâ*)." While the exact meaning of the term high place or bamah is itself a point of continuing discussion (e.g., was it an altar or a sanctuary or both?), the Hebrew Bible mentions that Solomon built just such a high place to Kemosh in 1 Kgs 11: 7 and 2 Kgs 23: 13.

Another point of comparison relevant to biblical studies is the inscription's use of the concept of the "ban" (or *ḥerem*) or oath of destruction in which a defeated people was slaughtered in response to a divinely ordained mandate. Lines 14–18 of the Mesha inscription find a close parallel in Josh. 8: 18–29 as both include an oracle, the army's departure, a battle, the capture of a city, the slaying of its people, the "ban" itself, and the taking of booty. In lines 17–18, the Mesha inscription refers to the outcome of the "ban" on the city of Nebo. Following the ritual slaughter of the people (who were dedicated in this instance to Ashtar-Kemosh, possibly a female goddess and consort of Kemosh), Mesha looted a heretofore unattested Yahweh shrine at Nebo. He then presented the captured objects to Kemosh. The reference to Yahweh here is the oldest unequivocal occurrence of the name Yahweh outside the Hebrew Bible. The mention of the capture of the "vessels of Yahweh" has invited much speculation as to what might have been included in that booty. In view of the known practice of capturing, displaying and transferring cult images that represented the gods of defeated populations to the temples of the victorious gods, among other captured accoutrements, was perhaps the cult image of Yahweh.

A variety of interpretations have been proposed for the phrase "the *ʿ-r- ʿ-l* (ariel?) of its d·w·d" in line 12 including among others, the "the lion statue of its beloved (i.e., the city god)." But now with the widely accepted reading of "the house of David" in the Tel Dan inscription (no. 124), the presence of the name David in line 12 of the Mesha inscription has regained some popularity; for example, "the lion figure of (its) David." Yet, a stronger case has been made for identifying the name David in line 31 where the reading "ho[use of Da]vid" creates far fewer complications and has much more comparative support. Besides, the item or object referred to in line 12 has its closest analogy to "the vessels of Yahweh" in line 17, for both lines contain references to the booty which Mesha carried off. It is more likely that a cultic object of some sort is in view in line 12. While the configuration of beliefs and practices in these respective traditions sufficiently differed so that each can be understood on its own terms as reflective of distinct Iron age cultural traditions, many of those associated with Kemosh worship in the Mesha inscription are remarkably paralleled by those concerning Yahweh as attested in the Hebrew Bible.

The Mesha Inscription and local history

In addition to the possible mention of "the ho[use of Da]vid" in line 31, the Mesha inscription also preserves a reference to king Omri of Israel in lines 4–5 and another to Omri's "son" in line 6. Scholars have identified the last as either Ahab or more likely his later descendent, Jehu, since there appears to be some discrepancy between the length of the reigns of Omri and his son in the inscription and their reigns in the Hebrew Bible. In 2 Kgs 1: 1 and 3: 5, the biblical writer states that Moab, under Mesha revolted on the death of Ahab, son of Omri, but in lines 7–8 of the Mesha inscription Omri conquered the land of Madaba all his days and half the days of his son, 40 years in total.

It should be kept in mind that at the time of the events recorded in the Mesha inscription, major historical transformations of the region were already underway. The Assyrian king Shalmaneser III conducted six campaigns in southern Syria in the mid-ninth century BCE. These advances were initially met by a coalition made up of various polities from the southern Levant including Israel, Damascus, and Hamath, but also involving Kedarite Arabs, Egypt and Phoenicia. This marked the initial demise of localized control of the region by the indigenous powers and yet, at the same time, it exemplified an attempt by all parties with vested interests to maintain the status quo in the region both politically and economically.

These developments also mark the beginning of Assyrian expansion into the Mediterranean littoral of ancient West Asia. Assyria's consolidation of various north Syrian polities as provinces in the ninth century contributed to the eighth century formation of new frontier polities farther south and west; polities that laid outside the boundaries of the northern provinces. While these new polities likewise became the eventual targets of further Assyrian expansion, Assyria's domination of the wider region was not always continuous and without interruption. During one period when Assyria appears all but absent from the local scene (ca. 830–803 BCE), various local powers such as Aram (Damascus), Israel (Samaria), and even Moab (Dibon) made (re?-)newed expansionistic attempts at subjugating their neighbors. It is within this broader historical backdrop that one should view the events narrated in the Mesha inscription as well as those only partially legible in the Tel Dan inscription.

Bibliography (I A)

For a full edition of the inscriptions of Adad-nirari II, see RIMA and further bibliography included there. For historical assessments of Adad-nirari's reign, see W. Schramm, *Einleitung in die assyrischen Königsinschriften, Zweiter Teil: 934–722 v. Chr.* Handbuch der Orientalistik Ergänzungsband V/1/2 (Leiden: Brill, 1973), 3–6; J. N. Postgate, "Some Remarks on Conditions in the Assyrian Countryside," *Journal of the Economic and Social History of the Orient* 17 (1974), especially pages 233–6; A. K. Grayson, "Assyria: Ashur-dan II to Ashur-Nirari V (934–745 BC)," in *The Cambridge Ancient History*, vol. 3

(Cambridge: Cambridge University Press, 1982), 249–51; and Amélie Kuhrt, *The Ancient Near East c. 3000–330* BC, vol. 2. (London: Routledge, 1995), 478–83.

Bibliography (I B)

ANET, 275–6; 558–60.

Black, Jeremy and Anthony Green. *Gods, Demons and Symbols of Ancient Mesopotamia: An Illustrated Dictionary*. Austin: University of Texas Press, 1992.

Grayson, A. Kirk. "CI Ashur-nasir-apli II." In idem, *Assyrian Royal Inscriptions*, 2 (1976): 113–211. 2 vols. Wiesbaden: Otto Harrassowitz, 1972–6.

——. "Ashurnasirpal II: A.0.101." In idem, *Assyrian Rulers of the Early First Millennium* BC *I (1114–859)*. RIMA 2, Pp. 189–393.

Kuhrt, Amélie. *The Ancient Near East c. 3000–330* BC. 2 vols. Routledge History of the Ancient World. London: Routledge, 1995.

Leick, Gwendolyn. *Who's Who in the Ancient Near East*. London: Routledge, 1999.

Luckenbill, Daniel David. *Ancient Records of Assyria and Babylonia*. 2 vols. London: Histories and Mysteries of Man, 1989. Esp. 1: 269–96.

Millard, Alan R. "Ashurnasirpal." In *Dictionary of the Ancient Near East*. Ed. Piotr Bienkowski and Alan Millard. Philadelphia: University of Pennsylvania Press, 2000. Pp. 38–9.

Roth, Marth T. *Law Collections from Mesopotamia and Asia Minor*. 2d ed. Atlanta: Scholars Press, 1997.

Bibliography (I C)

ABAT2, 42, Taf. 54–5 (figs. 121–4).

ANEP, 120–1, 290–1 (figs. 351–5).

ANET, 276–81.

Black, Jeremy and Anthony Green. *Gods, Demons and Symbols of Ancient Mesopotamia: An Illustrated Dictionary*. Austin: University of Texas Press, 1992.

DOTT, 46–50 (and Pl. 3).

Elat, M. "The Campaigns of Shalmaneser III Against Aram and Israel." *Israel Exploration Journal* 25 (1975): 25–35.

Grayson, A. Kirk. *Assyrian Rulers of the Early First Millennium* BC *II (858–745* B.C.*)*. RIMA, 1996. Esp. 62–71 (Black Obelisk).

Green, A. R. "Sua and Jehu: The Boundaries of Shalmaneser's Conquest." *Palestine Exploration Quarterly* 111 (1979): 35–9.

Kelle, B. E. "What's in a Name? Neo-Assyrian Designations for the Northern Kingdom and Their Implications for Israelite History and Biblical Interpretation." *Journal of Biblical Literature* 121 (2002): 639–66.

Kuhrt, Amélie. *The Ancient Near East c. 3000–330* BC. 2 vols. London: Routledge, 1995.

Leick, Gwendolyn. *Who's Who in the Ancient Near East*. London: Routledge, 1999.

Lieberman, S. J. "Giving Directions on the Black Obelisk of Shalmaneser III." *Revue d'Assyriologie* 79 (1985): 88.

Luckenbill, Daniel David. *Ancient Records of Assyria and Babylonia*. 2 vols. London: Histories and Mysteries of Man, 1989. Esp. 1: 200–52.

Marcus, M. I. "Geography as an Organizing Principle in the Imperial Art of Shalmaneser III." *Iraq* 49 (1987): 77–90.

McCarter, P. Kyle, Jr. *Ancient Inscriptions: Voices from the Biblical World.* Washington, DC: Biblical Archaeology Society, 1996.

Millard, Alan R. "Shalmaneser." In *Dictionary of the Ancient Near East.* Ed. Piotr Bienkowski and Alan Millard. Philadelphia: University of Pennsylvania Press, 2000. Pp. 262–3.

Porada, E. "Remarks About Some Assyrian Reliefs." *Anatolian Studies* 33 (1983): 13–18.

RANE, 144–5.

Yamada, Shigeo. *The Construction of the Assyrian Empire: A Historical Study of the Inscriptions of Shalmanesar III (859–824* B.C.*) Relating to His Campaigns to the West.* Leiden: Brill, 2000.

Younger, K. Lawson, Jr. "Shalmaneser III (2.113)." In *COS* 2 (2000): 261–72.

Bibliography (I D)

For a complete publication of the extant Assyrian eponym lists and detailed commentary, see Alan Millard, *The Eponyms of the Assyrian Empire 910–612* BC State Archives of Assyria Studies 2 (Helsinki: Helsinki University Press, 1994). An earlier treatment of the eponym texts can be found (in German) in Ungnad, "Eponymen" *Reallexikon der Assyriologie* 2 (1938): 412–57. For Middle Assyrian eponyms, see Claudio Saporetti, *Gli eponimi medio-assiri.* Bibliotheca Mesopotamica 9 (Malibu: Undena, 1979); On the post-canonical eponyms see M. Falkner, "Die eponymen der spätassyrische Zeit," *Archiv für Orientforschung* 17 (1954): 100–120; R. Whiting, in Alan Millard, *The Eponyms of the Assyrian Empire 910–612* BC State Archives of Assyria Studies 2 (Helsinki: Helsinki University Press, 1994): 72–8; K. Radner, *Prosopography of the Neo-Assyrian Empire,* vol. 1, part 1 (Helsinki: University of Helsinki Press, 1998): xi–xxviii; and J. E. Reade, "Assyrian Eponyms, Kings and Pretenders 648–605 BC," *Orientalia* 67 (1998): 255–65. For other aspects of the eponym lists, see M. T. Larsen, "Unusual Eponymy-Datings from Mari and Assyria," *Revue d'Assyriologie* 68 (1974): 15–24; A. Millard, "Observations from the Eponym Lists," in S. Parpola and R. Whiting eds., *Assyria 1995 Proceedings of the tenth Anniversary Symposium of the Neo-Assyrian Text Corpus Project, Helsinki, September 7–11, 1995* (Helsinki: the Neo-Assyrian Text Corpus Project, 1997): 207–16; and I. L. Finkel and J. E. Reade, "Lots of Eponyms," *Iraq* 57 (1995): 167–72.

Bibliography (II: 123)

ANET, 659–61.

Barré, Michael L. "The First Pair of Deities in the Sefîre I God-List." *Journal of Near Eastern Studies* 44 (1985): 205–10.

Black, Jeremy and Anthony Green. *Gods, Demons and Symbols of Ancient Mesopotamia: An Illustrated Dictionary.* Austin: University of Texas Press, 1992.

Dion, P.-E. *Les Araméens à l'âge du fer: Histoire politique et structures socials.* Paris: Gabalda, 1997.

Dupont-Sommer, André and Jean Starcky. "Les inscriptions araméennes de Sfiré (Stèles I et II)." *Mémoires présentés à l'Académie des Inscriptions et Belles-Lettres* 15 (1960; appeared in 1958): 197–351.

——. "Une inscription araméenne inedited de Sfiré," *Bulletin du Musée de Beyrouth* 13 (1956; appeared in 1958): 23–41.

Fitzmyer, Joseph A. "Sefire Aramaic Inscriptions." In *Oxford Encyclopedia of Archaeology in the Near East* 4 (1997): 512–13.

——. *The Aramaic Inscriptions of Sefire*. Rev. ed. *Bibliotheca orientalis* 19/A. Roma: Pontifical Biblical Institute, 1995.

——. "The Inscriptions of Bar-Ga'yah and Mati'el from Sefire (2.82)." In *COS* 2.82 (2000): 213–17.

Fitzmyer, Joseph A., and Stephen A. Kaufman. *An Aramaic Bibliography Part I: Old Official, and Biblical Aramaic*. Baltimore: The Johns Hopkins University Press, 1992. Esp. 17–19.

KAI, 222–4 (vol. 1: 41–5; vol. 2: 238–74; vol. 3: Tafeln xv–xxiii).

Kaufman, S. A. "Reflections on the Assyrian-Aramaic Bilingual from Tell Fakhariyeh." *Maarav* 3 (1982): 137–75.

Layton, Scott C. "Old Aramaic Inscriptions." *Biblical Archaeologist* 51 (1988): 172–89. Esp. 178–80.

Leick, Gwendolyn. *Who's Who in the Ancient Near East*. London: Routledge, 1999.

Lemaire, André and Jean-Marie Durand. *Les inscriptions Araméennes de Sfiré et l'Assyrie de Shamshi-ilu*. Geneva: Librairie Droz, 1984.

Lipinski, Edward. "Re-reading the Inscriptions from Sefire." In idem, *Studies in Aramaic Inscriptions and Onomastics I*, 24–57. Orientalia Lovaniensia analecta 1. Leuven: Leuven University Press, 1975.

McCarthy, Dennis J. *Treaty and Covenant: A Study in Form in the Ancient Oriental Documents and in the Old Testament*. New ed. Analecta biblica 21A. Rome: Biblical Institute Press, 1981.

NERT, 256–66.

Parpola, Simo and Kazuko Watanabe. *Neo-Assyrian Treaties and Loyalty Oaths*. State Archives of Assyria 2. Helsinki: Helsinki University Press, 1988.

RANE, 101–3.

Ronzevalle, Sébastien. "Fragments d'inscriptions araméennes des environs d'Alep." *Mélanges de l'Université Saint-Joseph* 15 (1930–1931): 237–60.

Rooy, H. F. van. "The Structure of the Aramaic Treaties of Sefire." *Journal of Semitics* 1 (1989): 133–9.

Rosenthal, Franz, ed. *An Aramaic Handbook Part I/1–2: Texts and Glossary*. Wiesbaden: Harrassowitz, 1967.

Segert, S. "Zur Schrift und Orthographie der altaramäischen Stelen von Sfire." *Archiv Orientalni* 32 (1964): 110–26.

TSSI, 2: 18–56 (nos. 7–9).

TUAT, 1: 178–86.

Von Soden, W. "Das Nordsyrische *Ktk*/Kiski und der Turtan Šamšī-ilu: Erwägungen zu einem neuen Buch." *Studi epigrafici e linguistici sul Vicino Oriente antico [Sel]* 2 (1985): 133–41.

Bibliography (II: 124)

Athas, G., *The Tel Dan Inscription*. Sheffield: Sheffield Academic Press, 2003 (cf. reviews by W. Schiedewind in *Review of Biblical Literature* 10/5 [2003] and N. Naaman, *Review of Biblical Literature* 10/16 [2004]).

Biran, A. and Naveh, J. "An Aramaic Stele Fragment from Tel Dan," *Israel Exploration Journal* 43 (1993): 83–98.

——, "The Tel Dan Inscription: A New Fragment," *Israel Exploration Journal* 45 (1995): 1–18.

Dion, P., *Les Araméens à l'âge du fer: Histoire politique et structures sociales*. Paris: Gabalda, 1997. Pp. 191–5.

Puech, E., "La stèle araméenne de Dan: Bar Hadad II et la coalition des Omrides et la maison de David," *Revue Biblique* 101 (1994): 215–41.

Schniedewind, W. M. and Zuckerman, B., "A Possible Reconstruction of the Name of Haza'el's Father in the Tel Dan Inscription," *Israel Exploration Journal* 51 (2001): 88–91.

Wesselius, J.-W., "The Road to Jezreel: Primary History and the Tel Dan Inscription" *Scandinavian Journal for the Old Testament* 15 (2001): 83–103.

Bibliography (II: 125)

Dion, Paul E. 1995. "Aramean Tribes and Nations of First-Millennium Western Asia." In CANE 2, Pp. 1281–94.

Donbaz, V. 1990. "Two Neo-Assyrian Stelae in the Antakya and Kahramanmaraş Museums," *Annual Review of the Royal Inscriptions of Mesopotamia Project* 8: 5–24.

Greenfield, J. C. 1972. "The Zakir Inscription and the Danklied." In Pinchas Peli and Avigdor Shin'an, eds., *Proceedings of the Fifth World Congress of Jewish Studies I*. Jerusalem: World Congress of Jewish Studies. Pp. 174–91.

Hawkins, J. D. 1982. "The Neo-Hittite States in Syria and Anatolia." In John Boardman, ed., *Cambridge Ancient History*. 2d ed. Vol. 3. London: Cambridge University Press, Pp. 372–441.

KAI.

Kaiser, O. (ed.) 1984. *Texte aus der Umwelt des Alten Testaments*. Gütersloh: Mohn.

Layton, S. C. 1988. "Old Aramaic Inscriptions." *Biblical Archaeologist* 51: 172–89.

Lipínski, Edward. 1971. "The Assyrian Campaign to Manṣuate, in 796 B.C., and the Zakir Stele." *Annali dell' Istituto Universitario Orientale di Napoli* 21: 393–9.

——. 2000. *The Arameans: Their Ancient History, Culture, Religion*. Orientalia Lovaniensia Analecta 100; Leuven: Peeters.

Millard, Alan. 1990. "The Homeland of Zakkur." *Semitica* 39: 47–52.

——. 1994. *The Eponyms of the Assyrian Empire 910–612 BC*. State Archives of Assyria Studies 2; Helsinki: University of Helsinki, Neo-Assyrian Texts Corpus Project.

Otzen, B. 1990. "The Aramaic Inscriptions." In P. J. Rijs and M.-L. Buhl, eds., *Hama II.2. Les objets de la période dite Syro-Hittite (Age du fer)*. Copenhagen: Nationalmuseet. Pp. 267–318.

Puech, É. 1992. "La stèle de Bar-hadad à Melqart et les rois d'Arpad." *Revue Biblique* 99: 311–34.

Sader, H. 1987. *Les états araméens de Syrie depuis leur fondation jusqu'a à leur transformation en provinces assyriennes*. Beiruter Texte und Studien, 36; Beirut: Steiner.

Tawil, H. 1974. "Some Literary Elements in the Opening Sections of the Hadad, Zakir, and the Nerab II Inscriptions in the Light of the East and West Semitic Inscriptions." *Orientalia* NS 43: 40–65.

TSSI.

Zobel, H.-J. 1971. "Das Gebe um Abwendung der Not und seine Erhörung in den Klagiedern des Alten Testaments und in der Inschrift des Königs Zakir von Hamath." *Vetus Testamentum* 21: 91–9.

Bibliography (II: 126)

Bordreuil, Pierre, "A propos de l'inscription de Meshac deux notes," in *The World of the Arameans III: Studies in Language and Literature in Honour of Paul-Eugène Dion.* Ed. P. M. Michèle Daviau, John W. Wevers and Michael Weigl. Sheffield: Sheffield Academic Press, 2001. Pp. 158–67.

Dearman, Andrew (ed.), *Studies in the Mesha Inscription and Moab.* Atlanta: Scholars Press, 1989.

Emerton, J. A., "The Value of the Moabite Stone as an Historical Source," *Vetus Testamentum* 52 (2002): 483–92.

Parker, S. B., *Stories in Scripture and Inscriptions.* New York: OUP, 1997. Pp. 44–58.

Routledge, B., *Moab in the Iron Age.* Philadelphia: University of Pennsylvania Press, 2004.

Thompson, T. L., *The Mythic Past.* New York: Basic, 1999. Pp. 11–15.

Notes

1 The restorations in square brackets follow Grayson.

2 For overviews of Ashurnaṣirpal II's reign, see Grayson 1976: 113–17; 1991: 189–91; Leick 1999: 30–1; Kuhrt 1995: 2: 483–7; Millard 2000: 38–9. Collected texts are found in Grayson 1976: 113–211 (translation only); 1991: 189–393 (text and translation).

3 See the text translated below.

4 Kuhrt 1995: 2: 485 notes that not all of the interactions between Assyria and its neighbor-states were "marked by aggression, destruction and plunder – [instead,] careful decoding of the rhetoric of the royal inscriptions reveals that several states were anxious to establish mutually profitable relations, and so share in Assyria's growing glory and power by linking themselves to the Assyrian court via precious gifts, military aid and perhaps marriage."

5 See Grayson 1991: 189, 191; 1976: 114, 117 for a discussion of how the annals are actually of mixed type, including display narratives. The main difference between annals and display texts is that the annals arrange the campaigns in chronological order, whereas the display texts do not, opting instead (usually) for a geographical presentation.

6 For the full text, see Grayson 1991: 193–223. The selected materials are from pp. 193–5 and 216–19.

7 A war god who was long worshiped in the ancient Near East and, especially, by the Assyrian kings. Ashurnaṣirpal II built a temple to Ninurta adjacent to the ziggurat in Calah. See Black and Green 1992: 142–3.

8 Another name for the god Enki/Ea (see Black and Green 1992: 75).

9 A term originally used for the (10) "great gods," but later used to refer to the heavenly deities collectively. One text says there are as many as 300 Igigi-gods. See Black and Green 1992: 106.

10 Lit. "Mountain House"; the name of the temple of Enlil at Nippur (Black and Green 1992: 74).
11 Another name for Ninurta (Grayson 1991: 194).
12 The primordial and subterranean ocean that was the home and realm of the god Enki/Ea (Black and Green 1992: 27).
13 I.e., with Grayson 1991: 194, "to whom it is good to pray."
14 Note how the king's attributes echo that of his god; in some places the same words or constructions are employed. Additional royal epithets are found in the lines that follow this section – namely, i: 18b–37a (but also elsewhere; see, e.g., iii: 113b–118a). Indeed, the introduction to this text "includes one of the lengthiest passages of royal epithets of any Assyrian royal inscription" (Grayson 1976: 117 and n. 474 for an analysis).
15 Lit. "divine Shamash."
16 I.e., Ninurta's heart, as it is Ninurta that is addressed in the invocation (see i: 1 above).
17 For the second person forms, see the previous note.
18 Lit. "the mountain(s') border/district."
19 In Akkadian, "hostages" and "victory" are a wordplay (*līṭu* and *lītu*, respectively).
20 After this section and additional introductory items (i: 17b–43a) comes a treatment of the campaigns from the accession through the fifth regnal year (i: 43b–ii: 125a). After that is a section that corresponds to display-type inscriptions (ii: 125–35; see n. 5 above), which is then followed in iii: 1–112 by an extended complex recounting campaigns from Years 6 to 18 (see the selection below). The descriptions are too detailed and the various locales mentioned too numerous to adequately summarize here. See Grayson 1991: 196–214; 1976: 120–47 for a translation.
21 Lit. "of the son of Baḫiāni" (DUMU *ba-ḫi-a-ni*); contrast Grayson 1991: 216: "from Bīt-Baḫiāni." Note later locations (including the next) which have Ashurnasirpal receiving tribute from a named individual, presumably the king. The son of the dynastic house (the name of which typically derived from the founder) was its leader or king. This casts significant light on the designation of Jehu as "the son of Omri" in the Black Obelisk of Shalmaneser III (see there).
22 See previous note.
23 See note 21 above.
24 Approximately 66 pounds (30 kilograms) (Roth 1997: xvi).
25 The two preceding items were used for taking a bath in the ancient Near East. See *ANET*, 275 n. 2.
26 The contemporary river Afrîn (see *ANET*, 276 n. 9).
27 Probably a reference to the king Lubarna.
28 Or, perhaps, "I pitched camp by [the lak]es." See Grayson 1991: 218; 1976: 143 n. 621; *ANET*, 276.
29 I.e., the Mediterranean.
30 Perhaps walruses. See *ANET*, 276 and n. 17.
31 Following Grayson's interpretation and translation of the form (1991: 219). Cf. also *ANET*, 276 n. 20.
32 The moon- and sun-gods, respectively. Grayson 1991: 219 believes there are two temples involved: Ešarra and the temple of Sin and Shamash.

33 I.e., female "lord" (Grayson 1991: 219: "mistress").
34 After this section is additional material relating to Years 6–18, followed by a conclusion that also corresponds to the display-text type (see notes 5 and 20 above), culminating in a description of Ashurnasirpal's building at Calah.
35 For overviews of Shalmaneser's reign, see briefly Grayson 1996: 3; Leick 1999: 145–6; Kuhrt 1995: 2: 487–90; Millard 2000: 262–3. More extensive work is found in Yamada 2000 with collected texts in Grayson 1996: 5–179.
36 Shalmaneser III may thus be seen as the principal architect of what would become the Assyrian masterplan to dominate the west (see McCarter, 1996: 22).
37 The indispensable study of Shalmaneser III's inscriptions, especially his western campaigns, is Yamada 2000.
38 The Kurkh Monolith credits Ahab with 2,000 chariots and 10,000 soldiers. This is by far the largest brigade of chariotry in the coalition, equal to that of Assyria itself (see Kelle 2002: 641–6).
39 Probably Jehu (or his envoy); see further below.
40 See further below, along with note 46.
41 The translated portions focus on Shalmaneser's western campaigns against the second of the north Syrian coalitions described above.
42 Note that, according to the inscription, the last few campaigns (years 27–31) were led, not by the king himself, but by his general, Daiiān-Aššur.
43 This person is called Asu in other annals of Shalmaneser III. See Grayson 1996: 148; Younger 2000: 269 n. 5.
44 See Black and Green 1992: 169–70, 185–6. They would attribute the disk to the sun god Shamash (Utu).
45 See Younger (2000: 265 n. 6), who notes that Gilzānu may have been on the western shores of Lake Urmia (in northeast Iran).
46 The tribute from Sūa belongs to Shalmaneser's accession year (Grayson 1996: 148) and that of the Israelite king to ca. 841 (cf. note 66 below); while the occasions for the tribute from Egypt and from Mardu-apla-uṣur, friezes 3 and 4, are unknown (see Grayson 1996: 149–50). (Note that the tribute of Egypt does not seem to be associated with their role in the battle of Qarqar – the only reference to Egypt in Shalmaneser's annals. See Grayson 1996: 149; Younger 2000: 270 n. 10.) Finally, the tribute from Qarparunda of Patinu may be dated to 857, 853, or 848, since the annals record tribute from the ruler of Patinu in each of these years. Grayson (1996: 150) thinks 853 is the most likely date.
47 For the Akkadian text, see Grayson 1996: 62–71, 148–51.
48 See note 42 above.
49 A term used to refer collectively to the gods of the underworld; one text indicates there are 600 Anunnaki gods (Black and Green 1992: 34, 106).
50 The primordial and subterranean ocean that was the home and realm of the god Ea/Enki (Black and Green 1992: 27).
51 Either as a symbol of the god's rule or as a reference to the corona of a solar body, here the moon. Grayson 1996: 63: "king of the lunar disk."
52 Lit. "divine Shamash."
53 Following this is a brief section on Shalmaneser's accession year and his capture of the city of Aridu.
54 I.e., the Mediterranean Sea. Lit. "sea of the sunset [divine Shamash]."
55 A ritual act.

56 Some scholars have connected the Mesopotamian royal statue to the image of God mentioned in Genesis 1: 26–7, especially as the Hebrew term used there (*ṣelem*) is cognate with the Akkadian term used for the statue.

57 Following this is a treatment of Years 2–5, which included multiple campaigns against Bit-Adini and locations in Hatti.

58 Following the sixth year, years 7–10 record campaigns against the cities of Ḫabinu (and environs), of Sangara in Carchemish (and environs), and against rebels in Babylonia.

59 After year 11, years 12–13 depict the king waging war against the lands of Paqaraḫubunu and Matiētu.

60 Although not certain, it seems likely that the 12 kings mentioned in Year 14 are related to (or identical with) those of Year 11.

61 Following this year, years 15–17 recount trips to the sources of the Tigris and Euphrates, eastward against Namri, and westward to the Amanus mountain range to get timber.

62 After year 18, in his nineteenth and twentieth regnal years, Shalmaneser returned to the Amanus mountain range for more timber and then marched against the land of Que.

63 Following this, years 22–31 recount various campaigns to various locations, especially to the east and west. Recall that the campaigns of years 27–31 were led by Shalmaneser's general, Daiiān-Aššur.

64 The epigraphs are located above the five rows of pictures, as described above in the introduction.

65 See Elat 1975: 33–4 (cf. Younger 2000: 270 n. 8) for a discussion of this item(s). He argues that giving this kind of staff to the Assyrian king symbolized the desire of the subjugated monarch to be protected by Assyria.

66 There has been some debate about the person depicted in the obelisk. Jehu's name would probably have been pronounced something like **Yaw-hū'* ("he is Yahweh") in the ninth century (McCarter 1996: 22). The main problem, however, is that the person in the obelisk is called "the son of Omri" (DUMU [*mār*] ᵐ*ḫu-um-ri-i*). (See 1 Kgs 16: 15–28 for a biblical resumé of the Israelite king, Omri.) According to the Bible, Jehu was not the son of Omri, but, instead, a usurper who killed the entire house of Omri (see 2 Kgs 9: 2; 10: 1–17). In the light of this, it has been argued that it is not Jehu but Joram who is mentioned and depicted in the Black Obelisk. If so, the Akkadian *Ia-ú-a* does not stand for Jehu, but for J(eh)oram (**Yaw-rām*, "Yahweh is exalted"). If so, this would have significant ramifications, especially for Israelite chronology. Most scholars are agreed, however, that Jehu, not Joram, is the king in question (Yamada 2000: 192–3 n. 400; Kelle 2002: 646–7 and nn. 21–2). The "son" language is probably employed loosely, not genealogically, and denotes, perhaps as a gentilic, "little more than 'Israelite'" (*Documents from Old Testament Times*, 49) or, geopolitically, "the man/king of Bīt-Humri" (Yamada 2000: 193; Kelle 2002: 648 and nn. 28–30). Cf. Younger's (2000: 270) and Grayson's (1996: 149) translations – "(the man) of Bīt-Ḫumrî" and "of the house of Omri," respectively – which, without explanatory notes, are potentially misleading.

67 See previous note.

68 The translation is uncertain; see Younger 2000: 270 n. 9.

69 I.e., a water buffalo.

70 Several of the last terms are uncertain; see Grayson 1996: 149–50.

71 See note 68 above.

72 Following Grayson 1996: 151; literally, "fast bronze."

73 See, e.g., the remarks (sometimes tentative) in Segert 1964: 111; Dupont-Sommer (in Rosenthal 1967: 3); Gibson (*TSSI* 2: 20–1); van Rooy 1989: 133; Lemaire and Durand 1984: 56–8; but this has been disputed (e.g., Fitzmyer 1995: 121; 2000: 215). Stelae I and II seem more closely related than either is to Stela III (Fitzmyer 1995: 121). Further complicating the issue is the question of paleography. Gibson (*TSSI* 2: 19) discerns no fewer than four scribal hands; Fitzmyer (1995: 18) argues for just one.

74 Note the following data (Fitzmyer 1995; 1997: 512; 2000: 213–16):

Stela I (reconstructed height: 52 inches [131 centimeters] high × 14 inches [35 centimeters] wide)
- A = 42 lines (text on left side is broken; at least three lines missing from middle)
- B = 45 lines (text on right side is broken; at least three lines missing from middle)
- C = 25 lines (at least three lines missing from middle)
- D = lost

Stela II (similar shape as Stela I; 35 centimeters wide; reconstructed from ca. 12 fragments).
- A = 14 lines (very fragmentary)
- B = 21 lines
- C = 17 lines
- D = lost

Stela III (28 inches [72 centimeters] high × 40 inches [102 centimeters] wide; reconstructed from 9 fragments)
Reverse = 29 fragmentary lines (beginning and end lost)

75 Prior to 740 when Tiglath-pileser III conquered Arpad (*NERT*, 256–7; *TUAT*, 178; *COS* 2.82: 213; Fitzmyer 1997: 512).

76 For a survey of options regarding the land of Ktk, see Fitzmyer 1995: 167–74, who lists no fewer than 11 different possibilities.

77 Cf. Gibson (*TSSI* 2: 20), who observes that most, but not all, of Bar-Ga'yah's gods, who are listed first, are Mesopotamian.

78 Von Soden argued that Bar-Ga'yah was a son of Adad-nirari III.

79 Note that there are only two clear instances in the treaty where Bar-Ga'yah has obligations (II.B: 6–7; III: 19–20). On the other hand, the language of "the treaty-stipulations of Ktk with the treaty-stipulations of Arpad" (e.g., I.A: 3–4; I.B: 4) could imply a more equitable relationship (*TSSI*, 2: 20, 35).

80 Van Rooy does not believe I.C was an original or integral part of the treaty-structure. This significantly impacts the reconstruction of the inscriptions. See further below note 148.

81 Indeed, scholars sometimes date the three stelae independently. That is, Sefire I (or some of its faces) might predate II and III. The relative chronology of the inscriptions, therefore, is not firmly known or fixed.

82 Dupont-Sommer (in Rosenthal 1967: 3 n. 3) thinks that the diverse origins of the gods listed in I.A: 7–12 "corresponds to the diversity of the countries in the coalition" led by Bar-Ga'yah.

83 The translation here follows the text established by Fitzmyer (1995) with some of the restorations following those of Lipinski (1975). Readers should be advised that the stelae do not include word dividers and, subsequently, differences in word division and interpretation sometimes vary widely. Note also that the fragmentary sections of I.B: 12–45 and II.A–C have not been included here. See further notes 102, 131, 148, and 153 below.

84 The Aramaic term used here (*ʿdy*) is related to (perhaps the origin of) the Akkadian term commonly used for vassal treaties (*adê*). Both forms are technically plural (often in construct) though most translations treat them as (complex) singulars: "treaty." The present translation retains the plural insofar as it helps specify the nature and content (esp. the stipulations) of the document.

85 Called Ataršumki in Assyrian inscriptions.

86 So Lipinski 1975: 24–5; cf. Fitzmyer 1995: 42–3, 64–5: "Ḫa[bur]u." An earlier interpretation (see, e.g., *TSSI* 2: 28–9, 35) produced "Treaty of the confederacy of [Urart]u" but that restoration is uncertain and depends on a particular historical reconstruction that is debated (Fitzmyer 1995: 64–5; 2000: 213 n. 5).

87 This may be a shortened form of a Hittite personal name (*NERT*, 257 n. j). If so, the person mentioned may be a Hittite ruler of some sort, and this has some importance for the historical value of the inscription. Alternatively, it could be a GN (cf. Aram earlier in the line).

88 Literally: "cut." The same idiom (with a different word) appears in biblical Hebrew: "to cut a covenant." The Aramaic term used here is also used to describe the cutting of a calf in the next section. Compare the story in Genesis 15.

89 The chief god of Assyria and his consort (Black and Green 1992: 37–9, 140–1). For the restoration, see Barré 1985.

90 The chief god of Babylon and his consort (Black and Green 1992: 128–9, 160).

91 The god of Borsippa and his consort (Black and Green 1992: 133–4).

92 This is the god of plague, Erra, and his companion, the fire god Nusku (Black and Green 1992: 135–6, 145). They are also mentioned in the treaty between Matiʿel and Aššur-nirari V.

93 The god of the underworld and his consort (Black and Green 1992: 135–6).

94 The sun god and his consort, who is named Aya, but is here called "light" (Akkadian *nūru*; Black and Green 1992: 182–4).

95 The moon god and his consort (Black and Green 1992: 135, 138), both of whom had an important cult center in Harran in the latter part of the first millennium. There may have been room in the lacuna for an epithet of Nikkal; perhaps "of Gurat" or "of Nuban" (*NERT*, 258 n. r; Lipinski 1975: 26, 49).

96 These gods are not otherwise known. They may belong to the local pantheon of Ktk.

97 So Fitzmyer (1995: 43; 2000: 213 and n. 9). *NERT* (258) and *TSSI* (2: 29) take the words as common nouns: "the desert and cultivated land." In favor of the place name is the context and the fact that Adam is mentioned in I.A: 35.

98 The seven gods (*Sebittu*) are known from Mesopotamian texts. They may be the children of Išhara, who is sometimes presented as the wife of Dagan or equated with Inanna, and are astrologically associated with the Pleiades (Black and Green 1992: 110, 162).

99 Cf., perhaps, the asyndetic compound designation *ʾēl ʿelyôn* ("God Most High") in the Old Testament/Hebrew Bible (e.g., Gen 14: 18–20, etc.; cf. Ps 57: 2).

100 This dyad may not be intended as gods proper though their inclusion here is a divinization of sorts and at least includes these entities as witnesses to the treaty. Similar language is found in the Bible: e.g., Deut 4: 26; 30: 19; 31: 28; 32: 1; Isa 1: 2.

101 On the last two pairs, cf. the previous note.

102 Sefire II.A: 1–14 is extremely broken but contains some passages that are quite similar to I.A: 14b–42. Indeed, I.A: 21–5 is often used to restore II.A: 1–4. It is not certain, however, that the two sections are identical (i.e., that II is a copy or version of I) and other treaties also have more than one set of curses (see J. C. Greenfield, *Journal of Biblical Literature* 87 [1968]: 240–1, who drew attention to the different curses in the vassal treaties of Esarhaddon, lines 414–93 and 518–688). See Fitzmyer 1995: 126, and, further below, the additional curses at the end of Sefire I.C. In any event, II.A is not included here, see Fitzmyer 1995: 122–3; 2000: 215 for a translation.

103 Gush was an ancestor of Arpad's ruling family. "Sons of Gush" and "House of Gush" (see below) are ways to refer to the royal dynasty or its constituents. Akkadian records know of the entity as *Bīt Agusi.*

104 Apart from the mention of Gush in line 16, lines 16–21a are lost or too broken for translation.

105 This and the following lines contain futility curses – even if such-and-such happens, the desired result will be frustrated, the attempt futile. The main issues concern fertility, productivity, and satiety.

106 The interpretation and meaning of this line is both difficult and debated. The translation above follows Fitzmyer (1995: 81–3; 2000: 214), who is following Dupont-Sommer and Starcky (1960). The best alternative is that of Kaufman (1982), who, on the basis of a similar line in the Tell Fakhariyeh inscription, translates the line as follows: "and may his seven daughters bake bread in an oven (?) but not fill (it)." This may suit the futility-context better, but Fitzmyer rightly notes the literary progression of animals which could lead one to expect a small-sized farm animal of some sort. He also cites some evidence of chickens killing worms, larvae, and bugs (1995: 81 and n. 24), though "kill" (*hrg*) still seems inappropriate with reference to hens.

107 Fitzmyer 1995: 44–5 and 83 thinks that the scribe has omitted "to Bar-Ga'yah" and so he corrects the text to include it. He also argues that "and" was present in the break, which would make the mistake virtually certain. Also pertinent is Sefire II.A: 3, a line that is quite similar, where Bar-Ga'yah's name is extant.

108 So *NERT*, 259 and n. b; cf. Lipinski 1975: 28–9. Fitzmyer 1995: 45 leaves the term untranslated.

109 The governing subject here and in the lines that follow could be Arpad. If so, read: "its land," "its people," etc.

110 The term can evoke social injustices as well as physical maladies.

111 "Bear" is oddly spelled here; it may be an error. *NERT*, 259 and n. c; Lipinski 1975: 29 translates "bear of woe."

112 Following Fitzmyer (1995: 89; 2000: 214), though the line is difficult. Fitzmyer paraphrases the sentiment: "a wish is probably being expressed that even small insects may become far more voracious toward Arpad than was ordinary." *ANET*, 660 and *TSSI* 2: 30–1 divide the words differently, taking the clause to refer to

defoliation of the land, a possibility that has significant merit giving the preceding mention of insects and the following clauses regarding the land's desolation.

113 Literally: "a Tell."

114 The terms are technically singular, though they may be functioning as collectives.

115 Of this list of 12 (one in the break) towns, Sharun, Tu'im and Ḥazaz are known from Assyrian documents. The location and pronunciation of the towns without vowels is not certain. Whatever the case, the list may contain locations dependent on Arpad (*ANET*, 660 n. 8). For Adam, see above (I.A: 10).

116 At this point, the inscription refers to rites that were performed along with the treaty and that involved wax (*šʿwtʾ*) models of various sorts. (Perhaps the closest contemporary parallel would be common conceptions of "voodoo dolls.") In the case of Sefire I, the wax models were evidently thrown into the fire.

117 I.e., her satellite cities.

118 The sowing of salt was a practice that is known from both biblical (Deut 29: 22–3; Judg 9: 45; Jer 17: 6; etc.) and Akkadian texts (e.g., Tiglath-pileser I). It was thought to render the soil unproductive. See Fitzmyer 1995: 93; *NERT*, 259 n. g.

119 This section is difficult. The word *gnbʾ* normally means "thief, bandit." Some think that a thief (or wax model thereof?) was used in the ritual at this point. See Fitzmyer 1995: 94, *NERT*, 259–60 and n. h for further discussion.

120 Inurta (Ninurta), the war god, and Hadad (Adad, Iškur), the storm god, are militant deities often depicted with bows and arrows. "Breaking the bow and arrows" has obvious military connotations – specifically, *de*-militarizing connotations – but it is also a phrase sometimes used in sexual contexts, which would imply a loss of potency in areas other than physical combat proper.

121 Cf. 2 Kgs 25: 7; Jer 39: 7; 52: 11 for Zedekiah being blinded after political disloyalty.

122 See note 88 above.

123 Note the following biblical passages that also speak of stripping as a form of punishment and public disgrace: Jer 13: 26; Ezek 16: 37; Hos 2: 3; Nah 3: 5.

124 This section, which seems to comprise a second introduction of sorts, has caused problems for interpreters. Calling this section "the sacred nature" of the treaty follows Fitzmyer (1995: 47; cf. Lipinski 1975: 50: "Firmness of the Treaty") who is attempting to account for why the introductory formulae would be repeated – namely, to emphasize the gravity of the agreement (*TSSI*, 2: 20–1). One might note that scholars have discerned two introductions to Deuteronomy (1: 1–4: 40; 4: 44–11: 32). Other reasons could also explain the repeated introduction; cf. the discussion regarding the order of the stelae above.

125 See note 103 above.

126 The vocalization of the PN is based on Akkadian texts, where it appears as Ṣilulu. Apparently Ṣilul and/or his house were prominent in Arpad. See *NERT*, 260 n. n; Lipinski 1975: 32.

127 See *NERT*, 260 n. o and Fitzmyer 1995: 103, for the possibility that these sites, all from Syria, are listed in a particular order and demarcate the area over which the treaty is operative. This also has bearing on the size and extent of Matiʿel's kingdom. For example, he had evidently annexed the kingdom of Ya'di in the north.

128 See note 103 above. If the reconstruction is correct (it is fairly certain), the Aramaic here (Bêt Guš) is equivalent to the Akkadian designation (*Bīt Agusi*).

129 The meaning of this term (*'šrthm*) is unclear. It may be related to the name of the goddess Asherah (*'šrh*).

130 I:B: 12–20 are too broken (or lost) for translation.

131 Although intact, the stipulations portion of Sefire I.B (lines 21–45) is damaged. Stipulations similar to what is found there are also found in the fragmentary lines of Sefire II.B: 1–21. Since Sefire III also contains similar material and since it is in good condition, offering a fairly continuous text, it is presented at this point in the translation. Again, it is not certain that Sefire I–III are truly copies of each other and this may be especially true of Sefire III, which was found later and has a different shape than Sefire I–II. Note that the proper name of Bar-Ga'yah must be reconstructed in line 25 and this is by no means certain. For translations of I.B: 21–45 and II.B: 1–21, see Fitzmyer 1995: 48–53; 2000: 214–15; and 1995: 122–5; 2000: 215–16, respectively.

132 Lit. "who causes the breath of his nostrils to boil." See Fitzmyer 1995: 143; 2000: 216 n. 18, who compares Lam 4: 20; Prov 1: 23; and Isa 11: 15.

133 An emphatic construction; literally, "you will certainly hand them over."

134 Lit. "what is good in my eyes."

135 The situation described is hypothetical and technically future. Hence, "you will have been unfaithful" is an acceptable translation. This also holds true for the other instances of this phrasing in the lines below.

136 Aleppo may have been a place of refuge of some sort, perhaps because there was a shrine to Hadad there (*TSSI*, 2: 53). Cf. I.A: 10–11.

137 Another emphatic construction. There is some debate over the meaning of the verb used here. It could be the same as III: 18–19 below, where it must mean "to pacify, placate, be conciliatory" or the like; but some have argued that a different verb is used here, one that means "to capture," which might fit the context better (see Fitzmyer 1995: 148 for a discussion). A bit of double entendre, perhaps accidental but nevertheless operative, may also be at work, especially in the following sentence.

138 See previous note.

139 An emphatic construction; literally, "you will certainly strike it."

140 The term is uncertain; see Fitzmyer 1995: 139, 154. *NERT*, 265: "relatives"; *TSSI* 2: 49: "members of his clan."

141 See note 139.

142 Lit. "come upon your heart." The same clause is repeated several times in this sentence.

143 Lit. "take (it) upon your lips." The same clause is repeated several times in this sentence.

144 I.e., be killed. *TSSI*, 2: 49 translates temporally: "*when* someone dies." Contextually, a causative verb would suit the context ("however one might kill someone"), but the morphology seems to preclude that (unless the *h* elided or there is an error in the text). *NERT*, 265 interprets the line quite differently, understanding the Aramaic *br 'nš* – literally, "(a) son of (a) man" (above: "someone") – to be a royal designation. "[I]f a son of man [i.e., a prince or king] dies in any way . . ." Whatever the case, Sefire III: 16 is the earliest occurrence of a phrase in Aramaic that becomes quite famous in later literature (e.g., Dan 7: 13).

145 I.e., encourage the contention by exacerbating the problem. Fitzmyer captures the basic sense by his periphrastic translation "interfere."

146 Another emphatic construction; literally, "if you indeed mediate."

147 This place may be in the Khabur region or, further west, in the Balikh area; Akkadian documents call the place Talḫayum (Fitzmyer 1995: 159).

148 Several scholars argue that I.C was written by Mati'el himself in light of the first-person plural forms in line 1 and the first-person singular forms in lines 2–4 (see, e.g., van Rooy 1989). In this perspective, I.C is an addendum to the treaty in which Bar-Ga'yah is not mentioned, probably because this addition is not an integral part of the treaty structure (see, e.g., McCarthy 1981: 104). To find corresponding text where both treaty-parties are included, these scholars believe, one must turn to II.C: 1–17, which does not contain first-person forms referring to the treaty-parties. This argument may well be correct and could warrant that II.C be translated here instead of I.C. However, one should note that the first-person forms referring to Mati'el are dropped after line 6 and he is subsequently spoken of in the third person (lines 7–9; cf. also 15–16a?). Moreover, the final lines of I.C (lines 16b–24) are very similar to portions of II.C: 1–17, containing similar language, formulae, and – most important for the point at hand – an absence of first-person forms relating to the treaty-parties.

149 Contrast the translations in Fitzmyer 1995: 53; *NERT*, 262. But see Deut 6: 24.

150 I.C: 9b–14 are too broken (or lost) for translation.

151 Some of the preceding lines would have probably contained additional blessings.

152 Or, perhaps, "may the gods guard him (the treaty-keeper?) with regard to his day and his house," meaning his life and posterity (*ANET*, 660 n. 9; similarly *TSSI*, 2: 33).

153 Sefire II.C: 1–17 contain material that is similar to this section of I.C. The existence of additional curses may reflect the traits of later first-millennium treaties (Fitzmyer 1995: 164); cf. note 102 above. But recall that van Rooy 1989 argued that the final element of the Sefire treaty structure was the stipulation section.

154 Lit. "may they make its bottom-part (i.e., its foundation?) [into] its [up]per-part (its ceiling?)."

155 The exact number is broken (only one letter remains), but suggests the reading "16" or "17." Shortly after this section there is a lacuna also containing a broken number which can be read as "17" or "7". It is unclear whether the latter number is meant to be an exact total of the previous list of kings or a reference to a separate group, perhaps "the [7] kings of Amurru" (Lipinski 2000: 254). Gaps in the list of kings do not allow us to tally them with certitude.

11

Neo-Assyrian and Syro-Palestinian Texts II

Brent A. Strawn, Sarah C. Melville, Kyle Greenwood, and Scott Noegel

I. Neo-Assyrian Texts II

A. *Tiglath-pileser III (Strawn)*

Tiglath-pileser III (Akkadian: *Tukulti-apil-Ešarra*: "My help is the son of Ešarra"[1]) ruled Assyria from 745 to 727 BCE. The Assyrian King List states that he was the son of Ashur-nirari V, but most scholars think he was an usurper who took the throne during a rebellion in Nimrud ca. 746 (Leick 1999: 165; Tadmor 1994: 212–13). The only official monument to mention Tiglath-pileser's parentage is an enameled brick, which states that he is "the son of Adad-nirari" III (810–783),[2] though this presents chronological problems.[3] Whatever the case, after a series of three somewhat weak rulers (Kuhrt 1995: 2: 490–3, 496), Tiglath-pileser returned Assyria to its full vitality by means of vigorous expansion and a number of new conquests that reestablished Assyrian domination in the western regions of the empire. It is no exaggeration to say that, in many ways, it was under his rule that Assyria attained the pinnacle of its power and influence as preeminent ancient Near Eastern superpower.

It is not surprising, then, to hear from Tiglath-pileser's inscriptions that he invested heavily in Assyrian military endeavors. Indeed, unlike some kings, Tiglath-pileser marched out with his army every year of his reign, save one (year 16). Nor is it surprising to learn that his military exploits were brutal. As foremost example of these, mention should be made of Tiglath-pileser's significant innovations in repopulation strategies. Assyrian kings such as Ashurnasirpal II before him engaged in the practice of forced deportation and importation of subjugated peoples, but Tiglath-pileser made it a systematic and regular habit as did those who followed him on the throne. This practice resulted in large-scale population shifts, the most famous of which is probably the fall of the capital city of the northern kingdom of Israel, Samaria, and its correlate deportation(s) ca. 722 BCE (see Becking 1992).

Upon taking the throne, Tiglath-pileser moved first against Babylon to the south before turning his attention northward toward Urartu. There he faced the king of Urartu, Sarduri II, who was in league with the king of Arpad, Matiʿ-ilu (cf. the Sefire Inscriptions). After an extended siege, Tiglath-pileser took Arpad in 740. He came west again in 738, this time against a Syrian coalition headed by Azriyau.[4] At this time he received tribute from Damascus and Samaria. By 735, he had effectively eliminated any future threats from Urartu. So, having secured his borders to the south, north, and west, Tiglath-pileser set his eyes toward Egypt. He marched through the Levant, taking Gaza in 734. During this campaign, he again received tribute from nearby locales, including Hamath, Damascus, and Tyre. The next year he conquered Damascus and its king, Rezin, and turned the region into a province in 732.[5] Thereafter, the Assyrian turned his attention to the eastern frontier of his empire and, following an uprising in Babylon, marched south where he put down the rebellion and took the throne, being called in Babylonian (and Hebrew) king "*Pul(u)*."[6]

127. Calah Annals

In the latter years of Tiglath-pileser's reign, a final edition of his annals was composed, comprising 17 regnal years (*palûs*). These annals were inscribed on stone slabs in the palace at Calah (Nimrud), but the palace was never completed, and Esarhaddon later dismantled and reused some of the slabs in his southwest palace. This, along with the fact that many of the slabs were lost, damaged, or destroyed in antiquity or in the early excavations of Nimrud, means that the reconstruction of the texts and their chronological arrangement is notoriously complicated.[7] As might be expected, most of the annals concern the king's military campaigns, but the summary (non-annalistic) inscriptions also include treatments of the building projects he undertook, notably his palace at Nimrud (see Tadmor 1994: 25, 117–204).[8]

Introduction

(. . .)[9]

(Royal epithets [Ann. 1a+b: 1–7]) (. . .)[10] *precious descendant of Baltil,*[11] *beloved of the god [. . .] a creation of divine Ninmenna,*[12] *who for the dominion of the lands [. . .] he grew up for kingship [. . .] governor [. . .] mighty male, light (for) all his people [. . .] (the one who) knocks his enemies away, heroic (young) man, (who) overwhelms [(his foes?)*[13] *. . .] I cut straight through jagged mountains*[14] *and [. . .]*[15]

Year eight

(Ann. 19*: 1–12)[16] *(. . .) [. . .] Azriyau*[17] *[. . . I] seized and [. . .] (. . .) [. . .] tribute like that of [. . .] the city (of) [. . .] his reinforcement(s) the city of El[. . .] the city of Usn]u, the city of Siannu, the city of Ma[. . .], the city of Kaspuna, [which (are) on the coast] of the sea, including the cities [. . .] as far as Mt. Saue, which* *adjoins the Lebanon, (Mt.) Baal-Sapon, as far as (Mt.) Ammanana, boxwood mountain, all of Mt. Saue, the province of Kar-Adad,*[18] *the city of Hatarikka, the province of Nukudina, [Mt. Hasu? incl]uding, the cities of its surroundings, the city of Ara [. . .], both of them, the cities of their surroundings, all of Mt. Sarbua, the city of Asḫani, the city of Yatabi, all of Mt. Yaraqu (. . .) the citi of Ellitarbi, the city of Zitanu, as far as the city of Atinni (. . .), the city of Bumame: 19 regions of Hamath, including the cities of their surroundings which (are) on the coast of the western sea, which in rebellion and sin were taken*[19] *for Azriyau, I annexed to Assyrian territory. Two of my eunuchs I placed over them as provincial governors. [. . .] I settled 83,000 [people . . .] from those cities (in) the province of Tuš[ḫan]. I settled 1,223 people in the province of Ulluba (. . .)*[20]

(Ann. 13*: 10b-Ann. 14*: 5a)[21] *I received the tribute of Kushtashpi of Kummuḫ,*[22] *Rezin (Ra-ḫi-a-nu) of Damascus,*[23] *Menahem (Me-ni-ḫi-im-me) of Samaria, Hiram of Tyre, Sibitti-bi'il of Byblos, Urikki of Que, Pisiris of Carchemish, Eni-il of Hamath, Panammu of Sam'al,*[24] *Tarḫulara of Gurgum, Sulumal of Melid, Dadi-ilu of Kaska, Uassurme of Tabal, Usḫitti of Tuna, Urballa of Tuḫana, Tuḫamme of Ishtunda, Urimme of Hubishna, (and) Zabibe, the queen of the land of Arabia: gold, silver, tin, iron, elephant hides, elephant tusks (i.e., ivory), multi-colored garments, linen garments, blue-purple (dyed) wool, red-purple (dyed) wool, ebony, boxwood – whatever (was) valuable (enough for a) royal treasure – (also) live sheep whose wool is dyed red-purple, flying birds of the sky whose wings are dyed blue-purple,*[25] *horses, mules, cattle and sheep, camels, (and) female camels*[26] *along with their young.*[27]

Year thirteen

(Ann. 23*: 1'-17') *(. . .) [of] Rezin (Ra-ḫi-a-ni) [of Damascus . . . he]avy [spoil? . . .] his advisor [. . . the blood of his] war[rriors], the river [. . .] furious, [I d]yed (like) a [re]d flo[wer . . .] his cour[tiers], charioteers and [. . .] their weapons, I destroyed, and (. . .) their horses (. . .) [. . .] I capt[ur]ed his [fig]hters, archers, (and) shield and lance [be]arers and [I disp]ersed their battle. In order to save his life, he (i.e., Rezin) fled alone and entered the gate of his city [like] a mongoose. I impaled his foremost men (i.e., officials) alive [on] stakes and made his land watch. For 45 days I set up my camp [aro]und his city*[28] *and enclosed him like a caged bird.*[29] *I cut down his gardens [. . .] countless orchards. I did not leave one (standing).*[30] *I besieged and captured [. . .]ḫadara,*[31] *the ancestral home*[32] *of Rezin (Ra-ḫi-a-ni) of Damascus (and) [the p]lace of (his) birth. I took 800 people together with their property, their cattle, (and) their sheep as spoil. I took 750 captives of the cities of Kuruṣṣa (and) Sama (as well as) 550 captives from the city of Metuna as spoil. I destroyed 591 cities from the 16 districts of Damascus like ruins*[33] *from the Flood.*[34]

B. Sargon II (Melville)

Sargon II took the Assyrian throne upon the death of Shalmaneser V in 722 BC. Whether Sargon murdered Shalmaneser or simply took advantage of his (half) brother's death is not known, but his accession appears to have been violent and it took him well over a year to quell opposition in Assyria and solidify his position as king. As a usurper, it was vital for the new king to address the issue of his legitimacy. Although he was a son of Tiglath-pileser III, Sargon did not make use of that connection and did not include his patrimony in his inscriptions as was customary. Instead, he established a new order by boldly adopting the illustrious name Sargon (Akkadian Sharru-kenu meaning "true king" – obviously not a name bestowed on a child at birth). This name not only forcefully declared the king's legitimacy, but perhaps invited comparison to the early Assyrian king of that name or even the ancient legendary hero/king, Sargon of Akkad. In political terms, however, Sargon seems to have continued his father's expansionist policies. A capable administrator and exceptional military leader, Sargon II campaigned throughout his seventeen year reign. In spite of almost ceaseless warring, Sargon undertook various building activities, the most ambitious of which was a new capital called Dur-Sharruken (Fort Sargon), completed just a year before his death in battle in 705 BC.

The most elaborate and literary of Sargon's surviving inscriptions is his "Letter to Ashur," which narrates the events of his eighth military campaign. In 714 BC, Sargon personally led his army north and northeast of Assyria into the mountainous lands in and around Urartu. Addressed to the god Ashur, the gods and people of Ashur, and the city itself, the "Letter to Ashur" was probably read aloud as part of a ceremony celebrating the successful conclusion of the campaign (Oppenheim 1960: 143). Other examples of Assyrian letters to gods have survived (Esarhaddon and Ashurbanipal wrote such letters) but they are too fragmentary to tell us much either about the literary conventions of the genre or its purpose (Ibid.: 133). Hence, any discussion of the eighth campaign narrative is of necessity limited to the text itself; we can only speculate about why Sargon chose this genre, what he hoped to accomplish by doing so, how common or uncommon his use of it was, or why he apparently singled out the city of Assur for his attentions. The text itself does not elucidate any of these questions. Nevertheless, Sargon's "Letter to Ashur" has received a great deal of scholarly attention for it is not only a rich source of literary language, references and wordplay, but it also offers an unusually detailed account of a single campaign (albeit one still shrouded in royal rhetoric) and is informative about the historical geography of the area as well (Foster 2005: 790; Levine 1977).

The "Letter to Ashur" assumes the narrative stance typical of Assyrian royal inscriptions; the invincible and valorous king successfully leads his army against a host of evil and cowardly enemies. Nonetheless, Sargon is careful to state his objectives clearly. He has launched the campaign in order to avenge the wrongs done to his vassals by neighboring municipalities. Thus, the eighth campaign was not undertaken at a whim or for personal glory but as the fulfillment of royal duty. In this way, Sargon shows himself to be a serious, dutiful and legitimate king. In some respects, however, the "Letter to Ashur" is atypical for a royal inscription. It not only includes interesting information about foreign cultures and details of geographical features unknown in Assyria, but it emphasizes the ability of the Assyrian troops (not just the king) to overcome serious obstacles such as impossibly steep ascents, impenetrable forests, deep gorges, and raging mountain torrents. Although soldiers are described as leaping rivers effortlessly, they also put in back-breaking work with picks as they literally cut a road through the mountains. Sargon celebrates the agility, perseverance and fearlessness of his men as he boasts of his own; what they accomplish they accomplish together. In the eighth campaign narrative we get a rare glimpse of an Assyrian king as a genuine military commander, someone who leads his troops personally. At one point, just before a pitched battle with Rusa, king of Urartu (passage not included here), Sargon laments the fact that he cannot provide food, water, or any adequate encampment for his men who are exhausted. While this scene may have been included to enhance the dramatic appeal, it nonetheless reveals the very real logistical difficulties of supplying the Assyrian army during campaigns in inhospitable territory. By mentioning the crisis, Sargon acknowledges both the quality of his troops and his bond with them. This passage would not be out of place in any commander's memoir, and reminds us to look beyond the monolithic image of the king that is normally portrayed in Assyrian Royal Inscriptions.

The true focus of Sargon's "Letter to Ashur" is, however, his sack of the Urartian cult center, Musaṣir. For reasons not stated (possibly lack of supplies), Sargon sends the bulk of his army home and, with only 1,000 of his best troops, turns aside to besiege and sack Musaṣir. At this point in the text, Sargon lists numerous omens, including an eclipse of the moon, as testament to the gods' support for his actions. It is possible, as many scholars believe, that by sacking an important cult center Sargon risked public disapproval, and anticipating this, sought to justify his actions. However, it is equally likely that the omens themselves, particularly the widely visible celestial events, motivated Sargon to take action, and he simply included them in the text in order to explain what happened. In any case, Sargon and his men successfully captured Musaṣir and took home a great deal of booty, including statues of the gods, Haldi and his wife. The Letter closes with an acknowledgement of the campaign's casualties; only six men from the army's different units. The same list of dead ("one charioteer, two riders and three infantry") is given at the end of Esarhaddon's letter to a god and is obviously meant to be taken symbolically, rather than literally. Lastly, we are introduced to Ṭab-shar-Ashur, Sargon's chief treasurer and governor of the northern provinces, who was apparently given the honor of reading the tablet out and then depositing it in the temple. The many personal features of the text, such as the tacit recognition of the soldiers and even war dead, coupled with the mention of individual Assyrians by name, gives strong support to the supposition that the "Letter to Ashur" was composed in commemoration of what Sargon considered to be his most exceptional military venture.

In addition to the remarkable "Letter to Ashur" Sargon's scribes produced more conventional royal inscriptions that fall naturally into two groups:

those found at Dur-Sharruken (modern Khorsabad) and those from other cities (namely Ashur, Nimrud, and Nineveh). The so-called Display Inscriptions from Khorsabad, selections of which are translated here, were written on the walls, pavements, and foundation tablets of the palace and offer an official, somewhat abbreviated account of the first 15 years of Sargon's reign (Fuchs 1994). The excerpt included here deals with Sargon's activities in Babylonia where he confronted Marduk-apla-iddina II (known as Merodach-baladan in the Bible), who confounded the Assyrians off and on for nearly 20 years. Although the situation in Babylonia had been fairly stable under Sargon's predecessors, the strife in Assyria occasioned by Sargon's accession provided Marduk-apla-iddina with the opportunity to seize the Babylonian throne. In 720 BC, the Assyrians battled the Babylonians and their allies at Der; both sides claimed victory but Sargon probably suffered a defeat since he was unable to do anything to oust Marduk-apla-iddina for another 10 years, a fact that attests both to the strength of the Babylonian opposition and to the many pressing problems that Sargon faced elsewhere. In the Display Inscriptions, Sargon's scribes deal with the embarrassment of Marduk-apla-iddina's lengthy, uninterrupted rule in a couple of ways. First, the text is structured to enhance our appreciation of Marduk-apla-iddina's final defeat and Sargon's glory rather than to explicate events chronologically. Thus the text begins by emphasizing Sargon's restoration of the privileged status of many Babylonian cities, something he obviously couldn't have done while Marduk-apla-iddina ruled. This preface also includes a long summary enumeration of Sargon's many military accomplishments. All of these deeds then appear in stark contrast to the blasphemous and underhanded activities of Marduk-apla-iddina, who broke his oath to the great gods and seized the throne under false pretences. In this way, the length of Marduk-apla-iddina's reign simply becomes symbolic of the depths of his depravity, and, by defeating him, Sargon not only rids Assyria of an enemy, but reestablishes the order of the gods in Babylonia. Animal imagery that appears in the account of the Assyrian siege of Dur-Iakin serves to underscore the sharp contrast between the opposing forces: Marduk-apla-iddina is variously compared to a fleeing bat and a skulking cat, his men to roosting birds and helpless sheep; while Sargon's troops are compared to soaring eagles. Sargon's victory is so complete that he can "grasp the hands of Marduk" and take his rightful place as king of Babylon. He neatly finishes this portion of the text by briefly describing his pious good works for the first three years of his reign, a reference not to his rule of Assyria, but to his new reign in Babylonia as a truly Babylonian king.

Having begun his reign in violence and under a cloud of illegitimacy, Sargon II went to great lengths to establish himself, his dynasty and his empire. His royal inscriptions and his military achievements reveal that Sargon was a clever tactician who took advantage of every means to promote his policies, although, like other Assyrian monarchs, he doubtlessly subscribed wholeheartedly to conventional Assyrian royal ideology.

128. Sargon's Letter to Ashur

May it be exceedingly well with Ashur, father of the gods, great lord, who dwells in Ehursaggalkurkurra, his temple! May it be exceedingly well with the gods of destinies and the goddesses, who dwell in Ehursaggalkurkurra, their great temple! May it be exceedingly well with our gods of destinies and the goddesses who dwell in the city of Ashur, their great temple! May it be well with the city and its people, may it be well with the palace and the ones who dwell inside. It is exceedingly well with Sargon, the high priest, the servant who fears your great divinity, and his camp.

In the month of Dumuzi (July), the one that makes firm the regulations of mankind, the month of the powerful, foremost son of Enlil, the overpowering one of the gods, Ninurta, wherefore the lord of wisdom, Ninshiku wrote on a venerable tablet for the gathering of the army and setting the camp in order, I set out from the city of Kalhu, the city of my kingship and I impetuously crossed the upper Zab in full flood. On the third day, in order to muzzle the mouth of the arrogant, to shackle the legs of the adversary, I prostrated myself devoutly to Enlil and Ninlil. I caused the armies of Shamash and Marduk to jump over like a ditch the lower Zab whose crossing is difficult. I entered into the passes of the Kullar mountains, steep mountains of the Lullubeans which they call the land of Zamua. In the district of the land Sumbi I inspected my army and checked the number of horses and chariots. With the great encouragement of Ashur, Shamash, Nabu and Marduk, for the third time I arranged the march into the mountains. Against the lands of Zikirtu and Andini I guided the (chariot) yoke of Nergal and Adad, whose standards precede me. I passed between the land of Nikappa and the land of Upa, high mountains covered with impenetrable trees, whose interiors are labyrinthine and whose passes are frightful; a shade is cast over their region as if it were a cedar grove and the one who goes on their paths cannot see the shining sun. The River Puia, (in) the gully between them, I crossed as many as 26 times and my army in its might did not fear the flood water. The mountain, Simirriu, the highest peak of the mountains which lunges up like the point of a spear, raising its head above the mountains, the dwelling of the mistress of the gods, whose summit leans up to heaven, whose root reaches down in the midst of the underworld, and (where) like the backbone of a fish, there is no going side by side, its ascent on all sides is difficult, on whose sides gullies and mountain ravines are deeply cut and the act of looking at it is shrouded in terror, unfit for the ascent of chariots or for horses to show their mettle, its access was too difficult for foot soldiers, through the understanding and wide knowledge which Ea and the mistress of the gods decreed for me, they enabled me (lit. opened my knees) to destroy the land of my enemy. I had my soldiers carry strong copper picks and they cut off the jagged parts of the steep mountain like limestone and they raised a path. I took (my place) at the front of my army and I caused my chariots, cavalry, battle troops, the ones who accompany me, to fly over its loftiness like valiant eagles. I made the corvée troops and scouts follow them. Camels and pack donkeys like mountain-bred goats leaped its height. I caused the huge army of Ashur to rise up the laborious ascent safely and I organized my camp on that mountain. Sinahulzi, Biruatti, barren mountains whose vegetation was leeks and the fragrant Sumlalu plant, Turtan, Sinabir, Ahshuru, Shuia, seven mountains I crossed with difficulty, (likewise) the river Rapaa, the river Aratta, rivers whose cascades I crossed in their floods as if they were irrigation ditches. I descended against Surikash the border district of the regions of Karalli and Allabria. Ullusunu, the Mannaean, because, year in and year out, I did not stop planning to avenge him, he heard of my expedition's coming, and that one, together with his princes, elders, advisors, the seed of his father's house, the governors and followers, who govern his land, with a joyous heart and a happy face, from the midst of his land he came to me quickly without hostages. From Izirti, the city of his kingship, to Sinihini, a border fortress of his land, he came before me. He brought before me his tribute: horses, broken to the yoke together with their harnesses, cattle and sheep, and he kissed my feet.

(Sargon proceeds and receives more tribute.)

From Parsuash I descended, I drew close to Missi, a region of Mannea. Ullusunu, having set his heart to do service, together with the people of his land, waited for my force in Sirdaku, his fortress. Like my officials or the governors of Assyria, he piled up grain and wine for the provisions of my army. He delivered his eldest son with peace presents to me and he set up his stele (before me) in order to make his kingship firm. Large draft horses, cattle, sheep and goats I received from him as his tribute, and so that I might wreak vengeance (on his enemies), he prostrated himself. To bar the feet of the land of Kakmui, the evil enemy, from inside his land, to repulse Ursa in open battle, to turn the scattered Mannaeans to their place, to stand in might over his enemy, to do what he wants, that man, together with his nobles, the governors of his land, entreated me, crawling before me on their four limbs like dogs. I took pity on them, I paid attention to their prayers, I heard their words of entreaty and spoke to them truly! Because of the surpassing greatness that Ashur and Marduk gave to me, causing my weapons to be great over all princes of the world, I ordered for them the defeat of Urartu, to return their boundaries, to restore the distressed people of Mannea, and their heart was quieted.

Of Ullusunu, their lord, I spread an honored banquet table before him and exalted his throne above that of Iranzi, the father who engendered him. Those people with the people of Assyria, I caused to sit down at a joyous table; before Ashur and the gods of their land, they blessed my majesty. Zizi of Appatar, Zalaia of Kitpata, the city rulers of the region of Gizilbundi, who live in faraway mountains, a distant place in the area of the Mannaeans and the Medes, blocking the way like a barricade – the people who dwell in these cities trusted in their own strength, they knew no lord – none of the kings who preceded me saw their dwellings, heard their name or received their tribute. At the great command of Ashur, my lord, who gave me as a gift the subjugation of the princes of the mountains and the receipt of their presents, they heard the approach of my force and fear of my radiance covered them. In the midst of their land terror afflicted them. They sent their tribute: draft horses without number, cattle, sheep, and goats from the cities Appatar and Kitpat. In Zirdiakka of the land of Mannea they brought it before me. They prayed to me to spare their lives and kissed my feet so that their fortresses would not be destroyed, and for the safety of their land, I appointed the officials over them. I place them in the hand of my officers and the governor of Parsuash. From Zirdiakka, the fort of the land of Mannea, I departed.

(Sargon defeats Rusa in battle and decides to invade Urartu.)

On my return journey, Urzana of Musaṣir, doer of wrong and crimes, breaker of the oath of the gods, who did not submit to my lordship, the dangerous mountain man who sinned against the loyalty oath of Ashur, Shamash, Nabu, and Marduk and revolted against me, he interrupted the advance of my return journey and my expedition by (withholding) his ample gifts; he did not kiss my feet. He withheld tribute, gifts and his presents and not once did he send his messenger in order to ask about my health. In the anger of my heart, I caused all of my chariots, my abundant cavalry and my whole camp to take the road to Assyria. In his great trust in Ashur, father of the gods, lord of the land, king of all of heaven and the underworld, begetter, lord of lords, to whom from distant days Marduk, the Enlil of the gods, gave the gods of the land and the mountains of the four quarters, so that not one should avoid making him great, with their treasuries heaped up in order to make delivery to Ehursaggalkurkurra; at the exalted command of Nabu and Marduk who set in motion the position of the stars signifying a good omen for the taking up of my weapons, and favorable signs which mean the gaining of power, Sin, lord of the crown, remained eclipsed for more than one watch, (a portent) for the Guti to be wiped out. At the valuable consent of the hero, Shamash, who caused the entrails to be inscribed with favorable omens, which means going at my side, with one chariot alone at my feet, and one thousand of my furious horsemen, soldiers, bowmen, shield-bearers and spearmen, my fierce heroes, trained for the heroism of battle, I took the road to Musaṣir, a difficult road. I caused my army to go up the mountain, Arsiu, a strong mountain whose gradient like the rungs of a ladder has no ascent.

(Description of the arduous journey and further action.)

Because Urzana, the king, their prince, did not fear the command of Ashur, threw off the yoke of my lordship and forgot to serve me, I planned to carry off the people of that city and I ordered that the god, Haldi, the protector of Urartu, be brought out. Triumphantly, I caused him to take his seat by his city gate; his sons, his daughters, his people, seeds of his father's house, I plundered. With 6,110 people, 12 mules, 380 donkeys, 525 cattle, 1,235 sheep I counted (them) and I made them enter inside the wall of my camp. I entered triumphantly into Musaṣir, the dwelling of Haldi, as a lord I dwelled in the palace, the abode of Urzana. The storerooms, piled up with abundant riches, I opened the sealings of their treasure.

(Here follows a long inventory of booty.)

The property of the palace of Rusa and Haldi, together with their bountiful possessions which I took up from inside Musaṣir, I laid alongside the mass of my wide army and caused them to drag to Ashur. I counted the people of the region of Musaṣir together with the people of Assyria, I imposed ilku-service and compulsory labor on them as upon the Assyrians. Rusa heard and fell to the ground. He ripped his garments and bared his limbs. His headgear was thrown to the ground, he tore out his hair and beat his breast with his fists. He threw himself on his stomach. His heart stood still, his insides burned, in his mouth were painful lamentations. In the whole region of Urartu, I caused mourning to be spread, I caused wailing to be established in the Nairi lands forever. In the sublime strength of Ashur, my lord, in the might and strength of Bel, Nabu, the gods of my aid, at the favorable oracle of Shamash, the great judge of the gods who opened my way and established the protection of my army. In the greatness of Nergal, strongest of the gods, the one who goes at my side, the one who protects my camp, from the region of Sumbi between the lands of Nikippa and Upa, the inaccessible mountains, I entered the land of Urartu. In Urartu, Zikirtu, the lands of the Mannaeans, Nairi and Musaṣir like a wild lion who is lordly with frightfulness, I went and I did not see an adversary to overwhelm me. I defeated the many armies of Rusa, the Urartian, Metatti, the Zikirtian, on the battlefield. 430 cities of the 7 regions of Rusa the Urartian, all of it I subjugated and lay waste to his land. From Urzana, the Musaṣiran, Haldi, his god, Bakbartu, his goddess, together with the abundant property of his temples, with 6,210 people, 12 mules, 380 asses, 525 cattle, 1,285 sheep, his wife, his sons, and his daughters, I carried off. Through the pass of Andarutta, an inaccessible mountain opposite Hipparna, I went out and returned in health to my land. 1 charioteer, 2 riders and 3 infantry were killed. I had the best orator, Ṭab-shar-Ashur, the chief treasurer, bring (the tablet) into the presence of Ashur, my lord.

129. The display inscription from the palace of Sargon at Dur-Sharrukin (Khorsabad)

Palace of Sargon, the great king, the mighty king, king of the world, king of Assyria, governor of Babylon, the king of Sumer and Akkad, beloved of the great gods, to whom Ashur, Nabu, and Marduk entrusted an incomparable rule and have brought my good name to preeminence.

I continually made provisions for Sippar, Nippur, Babylon, and Borsippa, whose exempt people, as many as there were, I recompensed for damage (suffered). I eliminated their forced labor. I calmed the people of Der, Ur, Uruk, Eridu, Larsa, Kullaba, Kisik, and Nemed-Laguda. Ashur and Haran, whose freedom was for many days forgotten, I restored their interrupted privileges. The great gods looked on me with their loyal hearts; among all the princes they gave me the strength of manhood and made my form massive. In the days of my rule, there was no rival prince. I saw no adversary who could subdue me in making war and battle. I smashed all the enemy lands like pots and I cast the nose-rope on the rebels of the four (regions). Distant mountains, whose passes were difficult and without number, I opened. Again and again I passed over steep, inaccessible paths whose locations were extremely frightening. I continually crossed all watercourses. With the power and strength of the great gods, my lords, who set my weapons in motion and smote all my enemies, from Iadnana in the midst of the sea of the setting sun, to the border of the lands of Egypt and Mushki, the wide land of Amurru, Hatti in its entirety, all of Gutium, Mada on the border of the Bikni mountains, to the lands of Ellipi, Rashi, which is on the border of Elam on the banks of the Tigris; the people of Itu'u, Rubu'u, Hatallum, Labdudu, Hamranu, Ubulum, Ru'ua, Li'taya on the banks of the Surappi and Uqni rivers, the Gambulu, Hindaru, Puqudu, Sute, the desert people of Iadburi, as many as there are, up to the cities of Sam'una, Bab-duri, Dur-Teliti, Hilimmu, Pillatum, Dunni-Shamash, Bube, Til-Humba on the border of Elam, Karduniash (Babylonia) north and south, Bit-Amukkani, Bit-Dakkuri, Bit-Shilani, Bit-Sa'allu, all of Chaldea, as much as there was, Bit-Iakin on the shores of the Sea up to the border of Dilmun, altogether I ruled. I set my eunuchs, my governors over them and imposed on them the yoke of my lordship.

Marduk-apla-iddina, member of the Iakin tribe, King of Chaldea, seed of a murderer, scion of an evil demon, who did not fear the name of the lord of lords, who trusted in the Sea's surging swell and who overthrew the oath of the great gods and withheld his tribute, he turned to Humbanigash, the Elamite, for help and the whole of the Suti, the desert people, he caused to rebel against me. He prepared for battle and made straight for Sumer and Akkad. Twelve years, against the will of the gods, he ruled over and administered Babylon, the city of Enlil and the gods. At the command of Ashur, father of the gods, and the great lord Marduk, I got my (chariot) team ready, organized my camp and ordered the advance against Chaldea, the brazen enemy. That Marduk-apla-iddina heard of the coming of my campaign and panic for himself befell him. From Babylon to Iqbi-Bel, he fled like a bat in the night. His cities, inhabitants and the gods who dwell in them, he gathered as one and made them enter Dur-Iakin, and he strengthened its enclosure wall. The people of the tribes Gambulu, Puqudu, Damunu, Ru'ua, and Hindaru he made his auxiliary forces and made them enter and (so) he made battle preparations. He took a measuring rope from its great wall 200 cubits distance and caused a moat to be dug one and a half nindan deep and reached ground water. He cut a channel from the Euphrates and flooded its meadows; the flood plain of the city, the battle zone, he filled with water and broke the bridges. That one, together with his auxiliary troops and battle troops, set his lordly tent and prepared his camp in the midst of the canals like pelicans. I sent my warriors over his ditches like eagles and they accomplished his defeat. With the blood of his soldiers they dyed the water of his canals red like red wool. The Suteans, his reinforcements, who turned to his side and came to his aid, together with the Marsane, I slaughtered like sheep and I sprinkled the remaining surviving people with the poison of death. That one left his royal tent, golden throne, golden couch, golden scepter, silver chariot, golden sun-shade and the ornament on his neck inside his camp and fled alone. Like a cat, sneaking along its wall, he entered his city. I besieged and I sacked Dur-Iakin. That one, together with his wives, his sons, his daughters, gold and silver goods, property, the treasure of his palace, as much as there was, with the heavy plunder of his city and the survivors, the remainder of his people who fled before my weapons, I took as if they were a single thing, and counted them as booty. Dur-Iakin, his strong city, I burned with fire, I demolished, I destroyed its enclosure wall. I tore out its foundation and I made it become like a mound (left after) a flood. The citizens of Sippar, Nippur, Babylon, and Borsippa who were imprisoned inside it without their being guilty, I destroyed their prison and showed to them the light (of day). The fields which from distant days, the Suti had taken away during the confusion in the land, I restored to them. The Suti, desert people, I felled with the sword. Their neglected border territory which was abandoned during the disturbances in the land, I transferred to them.

For Ur, Uruk, Eridu, Larsa, Kullaba, Kissik, and Nemed-Laguda, I established their freedom and returned their plundered gods to their shrines. I restored their regular offerings. I renewed their disused places. The land of Bit-Iakin, north and south, together with the cities of Samuna, Bab-duri, Dur-Telitim, Bube, and Til-Humba which were in the region of Elam, I ruled completely. The people of Kummuhi which is near the land of Hatti, who, with the help of the great gods, my lords, my hand captured, I made them take up residence there, and so made its wasteland inhabited. Along the border of Elam, at the city Sagbat, I had Nabu-damiq-ilani build a fort in order to block the way of the enemy Elamites. That land I divided equally; I entrusted it to my official, the governor of Babylon and to my official, the governor of Gambulu. To Babylon, the cult center of Enlil of the gods, I entered joyfully with a rejoicing heart and shining face. I grasped the hands of the great lord, Marduk, and I completed the procession to the Bit Akiti. 154 talents, 26 minas, 10 shekels of shining gold, 1,604 talents, 20 minas of pure silver, bronze and iron without number, obsidian, lapis-lazuli, agate, (four unidentified) precious stones in quantity, purple and azure cloth, multicolored clothing and linen, boxwood, cedar and cypress, everything aromatic, products of the Amanus mountains, whose scent is sweet, from my accession year to my third year I gave as presents to Bel, Sarpanitum, Nabu, Tashmetum, and the gods who dwell in the cult centers of Sumer and Akkad.

C. *Sennacherib (Melville)*

After Sargon II was killed in battle while on campaign in the northwest in 705 BC, Sennacherib, his long-standing Crown Prince, acceded to the Assyrian throne without any challenge from within the regime. Whenever the Assyrian throne changed hands, rebellions frequently broke out among Assyria's vassals and Sargon's death proved no exception. Within a year of his accession, Sennacherib was faced with a serious rebellion in Babylonia. In fact, finding a way to rule Babylonia successfully proved to be the greatest difficulty Sennacherib faced during his 24-year reign. In terms of imperial policy it seems that Sennacherib aimed to consolidate his father's empire rather than expand it, but Sennacherib's plans to implement imperial peace were repeatedly thwarted by his enemies, who spurred each other on to open rebellion whenever possible.

Sennacherib followed the Assyrian tradition of writing annalistic accounts of his military exploits and these have survived in many recensions and multiple copies. Although only certain selections are included here, it is important to remember that numerous versions of the Annals were composed throughout Sennacherib's reign and their contents vary according to the political circumstances and ideological concerns that were relevant at the time of writing. Like all Assyrian kings, Sennacherib had to act expediently in the political and military sphere, while also making sure that his actions could be explained according to accepted notions of Assyrian kingship and divine interaction with the mundane world. As a result, the royal inscriptions of Sennacherib must be seen both as factual reports of specific events, and as the official ideological interpretations of those events. In addition to his annals, Sennacherib produced a number of building inscriptions of a strongly ideological nature, such as the text commemorating the construction of the new Akitu House (temple of the New Year's feast) at Ashur. The selections under discussion here were chosen because they are particularly interesting examples of the methods Assyrian scribes used to put the right ideological "spin" on historical events.

It is fairly rare for us to be able to compare the historical narrative of Assyrian inscriptions with information from other types of sources. However, Sennacherib's third campaign of 701 BC against Judah offers just such an opportunity. The Assyrian account of this campaign is written in the standard prose style of most royal inscriptions; there is nothing very original or unusual about it. At the behest of his national deities, especially Ashur, the king marches against vassals who have dared to rebel. In typical Assyrian fashion, Sennacherib treats his foes, depending on the situation, with a combination of ruthlessness and mercy. He is unerringly victorious. Negative or unsuccessful events are rarely included in Assyrian inscriptions and the king gets credit for all military and political accomplishments. What is particularly interesting about the third campaign is the exceptional amount of corroborating evidence that has survived concerning it. Archaeological excavations at Lachish (one of the cities in Judah taken by Sennacherib, albeit with nary a mention in his annals) uncovered the siege ramp constructed by the Assyrians as well as artifacts such as armor and weaponry (Ussishkin 1982). In an exciting and unusual correlation between art and artifact, sculptured reliefs from Sennacherib's palace at Nineveh depict the Lachish siege right down to the siege ramp (BMWAA 124904–124915). We also have an account of the siege of Jerusalem from the opposing side in Bible verses 2 Kings 18.3–19.36, 2 Chronicles 32 and Isaiah 36–37 of the Old Testament. According to the biblical version, which includes a wonderfully vivid speech of the Assyrian Rab Shaqe (chief cupbearer/commander of the northern army) to the citizens of Jerusalem, the Assyrian army eventually falls prey to a plague sent by the Angel of the Lord: 185,000 soldiers are killed in a single night, and Sennacherib retreats to Nineveh where he is murdered by his sons. The discrepancies between the two accounts (was there a plague? why does the biblical story seem to indicate that Sennacherib's murder took place immediately upon his return to Nineveh instead of 20 years later?) have given rise to much speculation, but the fact remains that both versions agree on at least three points: the Egyptians ultimately failed their allies; Hezekiah paid Sennacherib a great deal; and the Assyrians retained control of the area. Not surprisingly, both the Assyrian and biblical sources interpret events according to their own particular ideologies.

While the Mediterranean vassals caused Sennacherib only minimal difficulty, Babylonia and her ally, the Elamites, proved to be a constant, nagging problem. Because the Assyrians shared their language, religion and basic culture with the Babylonians, they seem to have given Babylonia special status in the empire. In general, the Assyrians held Babylonian cities in high regard and made every effort to maintain their institutions, especially religious ones. Sargon II ruled Babylonia as a traditional king of Babylon, taking care to respect and participate in many of the country's royal customs including the Akitu festival, and it appears that initially Sennacherib planned to do the same. However, soon after his accession, Assyria's long-time foe, Marduk-apla-iddina, having secured Elamite aid once again, put himself on the throne in Babylon. Sennacherib defeated the combined Elamite Babylonian forces in battle and Marduk-apla-iddina was forced to flee into exile again. After the rebellion of 704 BC, Sennacherib diverged from his father's Babylonian policy and chose to install a puppet-king, Bel-ibni, who had been raised as a hostage at the Assyrian court. This was only the first attempt at finding a satisfactory way to rule Babylonia, but Bel-ibni proved to be a poor choice and after only three years, it was necessary for Sennacherib to take the field against Mushezib-Marduk and Marduk-apla-iddina. Although he was again victorious on the battlefield, Sennacherib did not capture the rebels who were able to elude him. In a second attempt to solve the problem of Babylonian rule, Sennacherib removed Bel-ibni from office and placed his eldest son, Ashur-nadin-shumi on the throne of Babylon. Things were relatively peaceful in Babylonia for the next six years, but eventually Sennacherib launched a campaign against Elam, ostensibly to go after fugitives from Assyrian justice and punish the Elamites for harboring them. The sixth campaign of 694 was an ambitious undertaking in which Sennacherib attacked Elam by sea. Unfortunately, some Babylonians at Ashur-nadin-shumi's court availed themselves of the absence of the Assyrian army to take their king captive and turn him over to the Elamites. Ashur-nadin-shumi was never heard of again and probably died a horrible death in Elam. The loss of his son was the last straw for Sennacherib, who from 693 until Babylon fell in 689, focused all his attention on eradicating Babylonian resistance once and for all.

Assyria's religious and cultural ties to Babylonia, coupled with prevailing notions of the parallelism between mundane and divine events and the king's role in connecting them, made it essential that Sennacherib carefully prepare his subjects for the violent destruction of his enemy and express all his actions in the correct ideological terms. It is therefore no surprise that the narration of the eighth campaign and the battle of Halule in particular, displays certain literary characteristics and takes on an almost mythical quality (Weissert 1997: 190ff). The battle of Halule itself took place in 691 between Sennacherib's army and a huge coalition of enemy forces consisting of the Babylonian and Elamite armies and their allies. Sennacherib claims to have enjoyed an overwhelming victory but the *Babylonian Chronicle*, a document that tersely lists important events in Babylonia year by year, reports that the Assyrians suffered a defeat (Grayson 1965: 342). Although the Assyrians gained no ground as a result of the battle, they lost none, and because they were subsequently able to follow through with their plans in Babylonia, it would probably be wrong either to accept the *Babylonian Chronicle*'s not unbiased assessment or to suggest that the hyperbole of the Assyrian account is merely a poor attempt at a public cover-up. On the contrary, the high literary language and innovative phraseology of the narrative of the battle of Halule seem rather to be preparatory propaganda designed to pave the way for the destruction of Babylon. By using obscure language and rare words alluding to such important works as *Enuma Elish*, the Babylonian creation epic, the author elevates the narrative to a heroic level (see Weissert 1997: 200–2). In this way, Sennacherib's talented scribe not only created an atmosphere of overwhelming heroism but also demonized the Babylonians and encouraged his audience to pursue a complete and devastating victory. Once Babylon was destroyed, the need for such manipulation ceased to exist and the extended account of the battle was dropped from the Annals.

Just how complete Sennacherib's destruction of Babylon was remains uncertain, but his descriptions both stress the finality of the devastation, and carefully place the blame on the blasphemous Babylonians, who used funds from the temple of Marduk to fund their rebellions. Even though Sennacherib emphasized that he was always carrying out the will of the gods, the destruction of Babylon was not accomplished without the need for further ideological justification. According to Assyrian understanding of the cosmic order, what kings accomplished on earth was the reflection of events in the divine sphere. As the sacker of Babylon and conqueror of the whole of Babylonia, Sennacherib was clearly the most powerful king, therefore his god, Ashur, must be the most powerful god, more powerful even than Marduk, the chief god of Babylon. In order to establish Ashur's promotion over Marduk in the pantheon, Sennacherib made a number of religious reforms including the construction of a new Akitu (New Year's) temple in Assur. Although practiced in other cities for other deities (some even in Assyria), the Akitu festival was a quintessentially Babylonian rite whose enactment both renewed Marduk's supremacy in the pantheon and legitimized his earthly representative, the Babylonian king (Frahm 1997: 282–8). When Sennacherib commandeered the festival for Ashur he thus made some radical alterations in the theology of the day. Since his purpose was to replace Marduk with Ashur at the head of the divine pantheon, Sennacherib depicted Ashur, rather than Marduk, in the heroic fight with the primeval monster Tiamat in narrative scenes from the Creation epic decorating the bronze doors of his new temple. Sennacherib's Akitu inscription also describes in detail how he took the very soil of Babylon and put it in the new temple as a symbol of his and Ashur's invincibility. It has often been suggested that Sennacherib's destruction of Babylon was regarded as sinful heresy by at least some of his subjects and possibly contributed to his later murder, but since there is no hard evidence to substantiate this, it is better to see his actions as being right in line with other Assyrian kings, who always took pains to justify their policies in religious/ideological terms, not only in answer to opposition, but simply because they their understanding of cosmic reality required it.

130. Oriental Institute Prism: campaigns in Babylonia and Judah

On my first campaign, in the environs of Kish, I brought about the defeat of Marduk-apla-idinna, king of Karduniash (Babylonia), together with the army of Elam, his ally. In the midst of that battle he abandoned his camp, fled alone and saved his life. Chariots, horses, wagons, donkeys which he left behind at the beginning of battle, my hands conquered. I joyously entered his palace, which is inside Babylon, and I opened his treasury. Gold, silver, equipment of gold and silver, precious stones, anything at all, property and possessions without number, heavy tribute, his palace women, his courtiers, his nobles, his male and female musicians, all of the workforce, as many as there were, the servants of his palace, I made go out and I counted as booty. By the strength of Ashur, my lord, 75 of his heavily fortified cities of Chaldea and 420 small towns of their environs, I besieged, I destroyed, I carried off their plunder. Arabs, Aramaeans and Chaldeans who were inside Uruk, Nippur, Kish, Hursagkalamma, Kutha, Sippar, together with the citizens, criminals, I made go out and I counted them as booty.

Bel-ibni, son of a building inspector, descendant of Shuanna (Babylon), who grew up in my palace like a young puppy, I set over them as king of Sumer and Akkad. (This passage added from the Bellino cylinder, not the Oriental Institute prism.)

On my third campaign I duly went against Hatti. Luli, king of Sidon, fear of the radiance of my majesty overwhelmed him and he escaped far away in the middle of the sea and he disappeared. Great Sidon, small Sidon, Bit-Zitti, Zasribtu, Mahalliba, Ushu, Akziba, Akku, his strong cities, fortresses where there were pastures and watering places for his garrisons, the terrifying weapon of Ashur, my lord, overwhelmed them and they bowed down at my feet. I sat Tuba'lu on the royal throne over them and I imposed tribute, payment for my majesty yearly without interruption. From, Tuba'lu of Sidon, Abdili'ti of Arvad, Uru-milki of Byblos, Mitinti of Ashdod, Pudu-ilu of Beth-Ammon, Kammusu-nadbi of Moab, Ayarammu of Edom, kings of Amurru, all of them, for the fourth time they brought before me extensive gifts, their heavy tribute, and they kissed my feet. But Sidqa, king of Ashkelon, who did not submit to my yoke, the gods of his father's house, himself, his wife, his sons, his daughters, his brothers, the seed of his father's house, I uprooted and brought to Assyria. Sharruludari, son of Rukibtu, their former king, I placed over the people of Ashkalon. I imposed on him the payment of tribute, gifts to my majesty. He pulled my harness.

In the course of my campaign, Beth-Dagan, Joppa, Bainabarka, Asuru, cities of Sidka, who did not bow to my feet quickly, I surrounded, I conquered, I carried off their spoil. The governors, officials, and people of Ekron, who threw Padi, their king, (then) under oath and allegiance to Assyria, in iron shackles and turned him over to Hezekiah, the Judaean; they confined him like an enemy. On account of their villainous act, their heart feared. They got help from the kings of Egypt, troops, archers, chariots and cavalry of the king of Nubia, a force without number, and they came to their assistance. In the vicinity of Elteka, battle lines were drawn in front of me. They sharpened their weapons. With the help of Ashur, my lord, I fought with them and brought about their defeat. The charioteers and princes of Egypt together with the charioteers of the king of Nubia, my hands took alive in the midst of battle. Elteka and Timnah I besieged, I defeated and I carried off their plunder. I approached Ekron. I killed the governors and officials who caused the crimes. Their bodies I hung on the enclosure walls of the city. Citizens of the city who committed sin and sacrilege, I counted as plunder. The remainder, who did not bear sin and contempt, who were not guilty, I ordered their release. Padi, their king, I brought out from the midst of Jerusalem and I made him sit on the royal throne over them and I imposed on him my royal tribute.

As for Hezekiah, the Judaean, who did not submit to my yoke, 46 heavily fortified cities and small cities of their environs, which were countless, with siege ramps, and siege engines drawn close, combat infantry, mines, breaches and scaling ladders, I surrounded (and) conquered 200,150 people, small and great, male and female, horses, mules, donkeys, camels, cattle and sheep without number, I took out from their center and counted as booty. Him, like a caged bird I confined inside Jerusalem, his royal city. I constructed siege walls against him and the one coming out of his city gate I turned back to his misfortune. His cities that I plundered I took from his country and gave to Mitinti, king of Ashdod, Padi, king of Ekron, and Silli-Bel, king of Gaza and I reduced his land. I assigned more than the former tribute and I increased payment of gifts to my lordship. I set the nose-rope on him. That Hezekiah, fear of the radiance of my majesty overwhelmed him and the Arabs and auxiliary soldiers whom he had brought into Jerusalem in order to make it strong, they withheld (their service). With

30 talents of gold, 800 talents of silver, precious stones, antimony, daggassu stone, ivory couches, high-backed ivory chairs, elephant hide, elephant tusks, ebony, boxwood, all that heavy treasure (along with) his daughters, his concubines, male and female musicians, he caused them to bring back to me to Nineveh, the city of my sovereignty, and in order to pay tribute and make obeisance, he sent his messenger.

In my fourth campaign, Ashur, my lord, encouraged me and I levied my troops in their great numbers and I ordered (them) to march against Bit Iakin. During the course of my campaign I brought about the defeat of Mushezib-Marduk, the Chaldean who dwelled in the midst of the marshes at Bitutu. That one, terror of my battle fell upon him and his heart became dark. He fled alone like a lynx and his location was not found. The front of my yoke I turned and I took the road to Bit Iakin. That Marduk-apla-iddina, whose defeat I brought about in the course of my first campaign, I broke up his gang. He feared the cacophony of my weapons and the onslaught of my furious battle. He gathered the gods of his entire land in their dwellings and loaded (them) into ships, and he fled like a bird to Nagiterakki, which is in the midst of the sea. His brothers, the seed of his father's house, whom he abandoned on the sea-shore, together with the remaining people of his land, I caused to go out from Bit Iakin, the midst of swamp and marsh, and I listed (them) as booty. I turned and carried off and demolished his cities. I caused them to change into ruin mounds. I poured out awe-inspiring radiance on his ally, the king of Elam. On my return, I set Ashur-nadin-shumi, my first born son, the offspring of my loins, on the throne of his lordship and I handed over to him the wide lands of Sumer and Akkad.

In my sixth campaign, the remaining people of Bit Iakin who groveled before my great weapons like calves and gathered the gods of their entire country in their dwellings, crossed the great sea of the East and they positioned their dwellings in Nagitu of Elam. In Hittite ships I duly crossed the sea. Nagitu, Naitu-dib'bina together with Himu, Billatu and Hupapanu, districts of Elam, I destroyed. The people of Bit Iakin, together with their gods and the people of the king of Elam, I plundered; not an evildoer escaped. I loaded (them) inside ships and I caused them to cross over to this side and I made them take the road to Ashur. The cities that were in those districts I demolished, I destroyed, I burned with fire. I turned them into ruin mounds and heaps. On my return, Nergal-ushezib, a Babylonian who took over the rule of Sumer and Akkad during a period of confusion in the land, I brought about his defeat in a pitched battle. I seized his life in my hands. I threw tethers and iron fetters on him and brought him to Assyria. The king of Elam who turned to his side and went to his aid, I accomplished his defeat, I scattered his band and broke up his gathering.

In my eighth campaign, after Mushezib-Marduk revolted and the citizens of Babylon, evil demons, closed the gates of the city, their hearts schemed to do battle. Mushezib-Marduk, the Chaldean, the low-life, impotent man, the servant who obeys the governor of Lahiru, gathered to him the fugitive Arameans, the runaway, the killer, the criminal, and they went down into the midst of the marshes and made rebellion. I surrounded him and I constricted his life. From misdeed and hunger he fled to Elam. When conspiracies and schemes were created against him there, he hurried from Elam and entered into Babylon. Inappropriately for him, the people of Babylon made him sit on the throne and they handed over to him the rule of Sumer and Akkad. They opened the treasury of Esagil and the gold and silver of Marduk and Sarpanitum, the property of the temples of their gods, they brought out and delivered to Umanmanu, king of Elam, who did not have either judgment or intelligence, (and they said) "Collect your army, raise your camp, hasten to Babylon and stand by our side. Be our encouragement."

That Elamite whose cities I conquered and turned into ruin mounds on my previous campaign against Elam, his heart did not ponder (and) he accepted bribes from them. He collected troops and his camp and he prepared his chariots and wagons. He checked the horses and mules (for) his chariot teams.

The lands of Parsua, Anzan, Pasheru, Ellipi, the men of Yazan, Lakabra, Harzunu, Dummuku, Sulai, Samuna, the lands of Bit-Adini, Bit-Amukkani, Bit-Sillana, Bit-Salatutu-akki, the city of Lahiru, the men of Bukudu, Gambulu, Halatu, Ru'ua, Ubulum, Malahu, Rapiku, Hindaru, Damunu, great reinforcements he called up to his side. Their hosts took the road to Akkad. They went off to Babylon, (and) together with Mushezib-Marduk, the Chaldean, king of Babylon, they brought about their assembly. Like the onslaught of swarms of locusts of the springtime, they were rising up against me in order to do battle. The dust of their feet like a heavy fog in the depths of winter covered the face of the wide heavens. The battle line was drawn up before me in the city of Halule, on the banks of the Tigris, and they sharpened their weapons. But I, I appealed to them, to Ashur, Bel, Nabu, Nergal, Ishtar of Nineveh, Ishtar of Arbela, the gods who are my support, in order to conquer my strong enemies. They quickly heard my prayer and came to my assistance. Like a lion I rampaged. I put on my mail coat, I put on my helmet, symbol of combat. In the rage of my heart, I speedily mounted my splendid war chariot that crushes the enemy. I seized in my hands the strong bow that Ashur bestowed on me. The arrow that slices through throats, I grasped in my hands. Against the entire armies of the evil enemy I roared loudly like a storm. Like Adad, I bellowed. At the command of Ashur, the great lord, my lord, on the flank and front I assaulted the enemy like the onslaught of a furious storm. With the weapons of Ashur, my lord, and the onset of my furious attack, I put them to flight and I effected their retreat. I pierced the enemy soldiers with the points of arrows and I perforated all their bodies like a storm (?). Humbanindasha, the herald of the king of Elam, a prudent man, the commander of his armies, his trusted official, together with his nobles, who wear the golden sword-belt, whose wrists were accoutered with red gold bracelets, like fat bulls who are tethered, I quickly slaughtered them and brought about their defeat. I slit their throats like sheep. I cut their precious lives like threads. Like the swollen flood waters of seasonal rains, I caused their blood to flow over the broad earth. My fleet war horses, my chariot team, were immersed in the flood of their blood like the river-god. The wheels of my war chariot that crushes the villainous and wicked were drenched with blood and muck. With the corpses of their warriors I filled the plain like grass. I hacked off their lips and I destroyed their pride (?). Like the sprout of a cucumber at just the right time, I cut off their hands. I took the bracelets of bright gold which hung on their wrists. With sharp swords I cut through their belts and deprived them of the gold and silver dagger belts that were round their middles. Those remaining of his officials, together with Nabu-shum-ishkun, son of Marduk-apla-idinna, who took fright before my battle and had shifted to their side, my hands grasped them alive in the midst of the battle. The chariots, together with their horses, whose riders were killed at the start of the mighty battle, and who were left to themselves, ran amuck until the last double-hour of the night passed, I put a stop to their fight. That Umanmenanu, king of Elam, with the king of Babylon and the leaders of Chaldea, the ones who had gone to his side, the terror of my battle overwhelmed their bodies like a bull. In order to save their lives they trampled the corpses of (their) soldiers. They fled, their hearts fluttering like a pursued hatchling dove. They painfully discharged their long-held urine (and) released their excrement in their chariots. In order to catch them, I sent my horse-drawn chariots after them. Those fugitives who did escape with their lives, they will smite with weapons whenever they locate (them).

131. The Bavian inscription: the destruction of Babylon

In my next campaign, I moved swiftly against Babylon whose destruction I strove for, and like the onset of a storm I attacked. Like a mist I enveloped it. I filled the city square with their corpses. Mushezib-Marduk, king of Babylon, together with his family I carried off alive to my country. The property of that city – silver, gold, precious stones, goods, possessions – I delivered into the hands of my people and they made it their own. The gods that dwell inside, the hands of my people acquired them and they broke them up and they took their goods and property . . . The city and its houses, from its foundations to its parapets, I swept away, I demolished, I burned with fire. The wall and the outer wall, the temples and the gods, the ziggurat of mudbrick and earth, as many as there were, I tore down and deposited them in the Arahtu canal. In the midst of that city I dug ditches and flooded its ground with water. The form of its foundations I destroyed and I caused its devastation to exceed that of (any) flood so that in later days the ground of that city, (its) temples, and (its) gods would be forgotten. I caused it to be covered with water and I finished it off like river flats.

132. The Akitu inscription from Ashur

Sennacherib, great king, mighty king, king of the world, king of Assyria, king of the four quarters, the one who makes widespread people obey, maker of the image of Ashur and the great gods, the one who completes the forgotten rituals of Esharra, who, by oracle and by order of Shamash and Adad, makes great their purification rites, the one who returns the abandoned Lamassu of Esharra to its place, who fears the gods of heaven and who greatly knows the gods of Assyria, who enriches the great gods in their dwellings, who makes great their symbols, the maker of Assyria, the one who makes its shrines perfect, the one who subjugates the enemy lands, the destroyer of their villages, who causes canals to be dug, who, releasing the waters, causes canal water to flow, who establishes abundance and plenty in the broad meadows of Assyria, who firmly establishes irrigation water for the meadowland of Assyria – ditches and installations that no one had seen in Assyria from earlier days, that no one knew, and that those before did not make – the one who lays the foundation of the work of Libittu, from the work of the living to the tombs, proper symbols of the dead, with limestone of the mountains which none of the kings of Assyria who came before me did; prudent prince whose rule is attentive above (all) kings who sit on daises, protector of his land, trustworthy in battle and war, I am the protection of its armies. At that time after I made the image of Ashur, the great lord, my lord, and the images of the great gods and I had them occupy their peaceful dwellings, in the month Nisan, the primary month of the father, Enlil, the month of the visibility of the plough star, (the month) of the feast of the banquet of the king of the gods, Ashur, which, from distant days, on account of political disorder and rebellion, the rites of the king of the gods, Ashur, were (then) being practiced in the Bit Akiti inside the city, (but) were forgotten in open country; my heart moved me for the making of the Bit Akiti with that design and I came to know the decision of Shamash and Adad and they gave to me their true consent; they ordered me to build. In a good month on a favorable day, with the craft of purification priests (and) the skill of incantation priests, I laid its foundations of mountain limestone. I raised its top from its foundation to its parapet, I completed it in limestone and I built it up like a mountain. Two canals I had dug at its sides and a garden of plenty, a fruit orchard, I made surround it; I encircled its sides with appealing gardens. After I destroyed Babylon, the gods of which I shattered, I overwhelmed its people with weapons. So that the ground of that city not be identified, I took its earth away and I had it carried to the Euphrates, to the sea. Its soil arrived at Dilmun and the people of Dilmun saw. Terror of the fearsomeness of Ashur fell upon them and they brought their audience gifts to me. With their presents, craftsmen – a levy of their land, corvée labor – copper spades, copper nails, tools of the work of their country, they sent to me on account of the destruction of Babylon. To quiet the heart of Ashur, my lord, that people sing the praises of his might (and) for the inspection of posterity, I took away the dirt of Babylon and stored it in heaped up mounds in that Bit Akitu.

D. Esarhaddon (Melville)

Esarhaddon ruled only 11 years (680–669 BC), but in his short reign he accomplished a great deal: he successfully imposed the *pax Assyriaca* on most of the empire, brought lasting peace and prosperity to Babylonia and extended Assyrian territory to include, albeit briefly, Egypt. In spite of the generally positive circumstances of his reign, Esarhaddon had to deal with a number of problems that threatened not only the stability of the empire, but the life of the king himself. Esarhaddon's brothers, who had murdered their father, Sennacherib, remained at large and thus posed a continuing threat to the throne, while the fact that Esarhaddon himself had a number of sons undoubtedly made the king mindful of the potential for future upheaval. Ill health plagued Esarhaddon from the beginning of his reign and apparently drove him to pay particular attention to omens and divination. Circumstances also required that the king take action in Babylonia, which languished in the aftermath of Sennacherib's destruction. Using every means at his disposal from military action to prognostication and written propaganda, Esarhaddon not only managed to rule effectively, but he implemented a succession policy that would avoid the internecine strife that had erupted at the end of his father's reign. The excerpts from the royal inscriptions and succession treaty translated here reflect Esarhaddon's many concerns and show us how he and his scribes made the king's policies palatable to his subjects.

One of the first things Esarhaddon did as king was to order the reconstruction of the city of Babylon and the economic rebuilding of Babylonia. His reasons for so abruptly and completely reversing Sennacherib's policies are not well known, but economic and political concerns coupled with what the omens said, probably played a greater role in his decision than any personal desire to oppose his father. Esarhaddon spent his entire reign working to establish an Assyrian rule over Babylonia that would be acceptable to the inhabitants of both countries. Such was the history of antagonism between the two countries by the time Esarhaddon became king that he had to act with great political insight and diplomatic agility in order to implement his plans successfully. To this end, the inscriptions concerning the reconstruction of Babylon are masterpieces of ideological manipulation presented in a number of recensions which were carefully modified for different audiences (some Assyrian, some Babylonian), in different places, at different times (Cogan 1983: 84; and Porter 1983: 6–8). The excerpts included here are mostly restricted to the text Babylon A (written in 680 BC), but occasionally include some composite elements from other versions.

In these inscriptions Esarhaddon's Babylonian policies are always revealed as divinely sanctioned and ordained. In no text does he mention his father by name or identify him as the source of destruction. Rather, the blame is put (with greater or lesser severity depending on the text's intended audience) squarely on the shoulders of the Babylonians for their iniquity against the gods, especially Marduk, who abandons and punishes his people. Esarhaddon's scribes explain the time period of the abandonment by cleverly manipulating the cuneiform writing system; 70 turns into a passable 11 when turned upside down. Once Marduk is mollified, he chooses Esarhaddon as the instrument whereby Babylon and Babylonia may be restored to their former greatness. Esarhaddon takes special care in these texts to justify his reconstruction of Babylon by repeatedly referring to celestial omens and other types of divination. For example, the unusually detailed observation of Jupiter included in several recensions of the text (and translated here) quotes the canonical omen literature, probably the series *Enuma Anu Enlil* ("When Anu and Enlil"). The fact that the ominous meaning of Jupiter's observed position could be verified in the canonical omen series thus validated Esarhaddon's actions and gave credence to his other claims. It also took the responsibility for the decision out of his hands; he was only doing the gods' will. In order to demonstrate his respect for the culture and traditions of Babylonia, Esarhaddon also makes a point of describing how he takes part in the ritual carrying of the head basket (Porter 1993: 44ff). At the start of any large (temple) construction project, Babylonian kings would ceremoniously do labor in much the same way we have groundbreaking ceremonies. By doing this, Esarhaddon reveals his intention to be a proper Babylonian monarch. Evidence shows that Esarhaddon's careful attention to public relations paid off and his Babylonian policies were largely, if not always enthusiastically, accepted in both countries.

Esarhaddon told the story of his own accession in a text (designated Nin A by Borger 1956) which survives in at least 20 copies and dates to 673/672 BC (Porter 1993: 18 n 29). Interestingly, the text does not name either Esarhaddon's father or his brothers, nor does it actually state that murder occurred. Esarhaddon waited nearly eight years to give an account of the events leading to his unorthodox accession and there are several likely reasons for his delay. Aside from a reluctance to describe regicide in an official document, he probably did not want to bring up the subject of his legitimacy until his authority as king was well established, but once his position was firm and he wished to settle the succession, then questions about the past needed to be addressed. The inscription seems to have been timed to prepare for the announcement of Esarhaddon's chosen successors (Tadmor 1983: 45). By emphasizing the fact that he was Sennacherib's youngest son, Esarhaddon prepared his audience to accept Ashurbanipal, also a younger son, as his heir in Assyria while he designated the elder son, Shamash-shum-ukin, as crown prince of Babylon. The reasons for this unusual move remain obscure, but the king may have been prompted to repeat his father's actions (i.e., choosing a younger son) by a desire to establish the legitimacy of such a choice and therefore his own legitimacy. Nin A also reminds Esarhaddon's subjects of the loyalty oath Sennacherib exacted on his behalf which in turn sets up the loyalty oath he would impose in aid of Ashurbanipal.

One of Esarhaddon's paramount concerns was the succession which he went to great lengths to settle. Not only did he broach the subject subtly as in the accession account discussed above, but he attempted to secure his successors by imposing an empire-wide loyalty oath on their behalf. The Succession Treaty of Esarhaddon has been reconstructed from hundreds of pieces belonging to at least eight copies, which were found in the Nabu temple at Nimrud (Parpola and Watanabe 1988: xixx–xxx). It is the best preserved and longest of the surviving Neo-Assyrian treaties and has a complex organization which was probably standard for such agreements (Ibid.: xxxv). Of the treaty's 11 sections (preamble, seal impressions, divine witnesses, oath section, historical introduction, treaty stipulations, violation clause, traditional curses, vow, ceremonial curses, and colophon) only parts of the stipulation, violation sections and the colophon are included here. The text enumerates in detail the treasonous activities that the oath-takers must reject and it is easy to see how Esarhaddon's previous trials and tribulations could have influenced the treaty's content. For example, the oath takers are adjured not to tell any lies that would cause a rift between the king and the crown prince, which according to Nin A, is exactly what Esarhaddon's own brothers had done to him. Likewise, there are injunctions in the treaty against aiding any of the brothers of the crown prince in rebellion. The elaborate preparations for the oath-taking, which was concluded in several separate ceremonies that took place in Iyyar (May) 672, are described in a number of letters from officials to the king and attest to the importance with which Esarhaddon invested the procedure (Parpola and Watanabe 1988: xixx). In spite of his careful plans, however, Esarhaddon had to quell an attempted *coup d'état* in 670, and after his death later that year, his mother, Naqia/Zakutu, imposed yet another loyalty oath on the Assyrians on behalf of Ashurbanipal, who took the throne without incident.

Far from being a weak, superstitious, or vacillating king as historians have sometimes called him, Esarhaddon proved himself to be politically adept, sensitive to the ideologies of his various constituents, and able to identify and then deal with threats to the throne.

133. Nin A: Esarhaddon's accession

Palace of Esarhaddon, the great king, the mighty king, king of the world, king of Assyria, governor of Babylon, king of Sumer and Akkad, king of the four quarters, the true shepherd, favorite of the great gods, whose name from his youth Ashur, Shamash, Bel and Nabu, Ishtar of Nineveh, and Ishtar of Arbela, pronounced for the kingship of Assyria, son of Sennacherib, king of Assyria, son of Sargon, king of Assyria, who, with the help of Ashur, Sin, Shamash, Nabu, Marduk, Ishtar of Nineveh, and Ishtar of Arbela, the great gods, his lords, constantly roams from east to west without having an equal.

Of my older brothers, I was their younger brother. At the command of Ashur, Sin, Shamash, Bel, Nabu, Ishtar of Nineveh, and Ishtar of Arbela, the father who created me truly raised my head among my brothers with the words, "This is my son and heir." He consulted Shamash and Adad by divination and they answered (with) their true consent, "He is your successor." He was attentive to their important words and he gathered together the people of Assyria, big and small, and my brothers, the seed of my father's house, and he caused them to swear a solemn oath before Ashur, Sin, Shamash, Nabu, and Marduk, the gods of Assyria, the gods who dwell in heaven and earth, in order to protect my princeship.

In a favorable month, on a propitious day, according to their exalted command, I joyfully entered the succession palace, the awe-inspiring place wherein the nature of kingship exists. True conduct was poured out on my brothers, but they abandoned the gods and trusted their own insolent deeds and they plotted evil. Evil rumors, calumny they started against me, against the will of the gods they were constantly repeating evil, incorrect and hostile (rumors) behind my back. They alienated from me, against the gods, the open heart of my father, (though) at the bottom of his heart there was love and his intentions were that I should become king.

I considered with my heart and deliberated in my gut. "Their deeds are insolent and they have trusted in their own initiatives. What blasphemous thing will they do?" I prayed to Ashur, king of the gods (and) merciful Marduk, to whom slander is an abomination, and I bowed to them in submission, and they granted my prayer concerning the judgment of the great gods, my lords, about the evil machinations. They caused me to dwell in a secret place and they extended their good shadow over me and protected me for kingship.

Afterwards my brothers went mad and did something not good against the gods and mankind. They plotted evil and drew weapons in the midst of Nineveh, contrary to (the will of) the gods. Like kids, they butted against each other over the exercise of kingship. Ashur, Sin, Shamash, Bel, Nabu, Ishtar of Nineveh, and Ishtar of Arbela looked askance on the deeds of the usurpers, who acted against the will of the gods, and did not stand at their side, but incapacitated their forces and caused them to kneel in obeisance to me. The people of Assyria, who swore the oath of the great gods with water and oil to protect my kingship, did not come to their assistance.

I, Esarhaddon, who, with the aid of the great gods his (sic!) lords, did not retreat in the midst of battle, learned of their evil deeds and cried, "Woe!" I tore my princely garments and I raised a wail of lamentation. I raged like a lion and my liver started to boil with fury. In order to assume the kingship of my father's house, I clapped my hands (in prayer). To Ashur, Sin, Shamash, Bel, Nabu, Nergal, Ishtar of Nineveh, and Ishtar of Arbela, I raised my hands and they reacted favorably to my words. With their true consent they kept sending me a helpful oracle, "Go without holding back. We will constantly be at your side and we will strike down your enemy." I did not delay one day or even two days. I did not wait for my army. I did not look back. I did not organize the care of the horses, the binding of the teams or my battle equipment. I did not heap up provisions for my campaign. I did not fear the snow and frost of the month of Shabat, the depth of winter. Like a winged eagle, I attacked in order to scatter my enemies. With difficulty, I struck out quickly on the road to Nineveh. Before me, in the land of Hanigalbat, all their splendid warriors blocked my progress and brandished their weapons. Fear of the great gods, my lords, overwhelmed them. They saw the fierce onslaught of my battle and they became frenzied. Ishtar, lady of war and battle, who loves my priesthood, stood beside me, smashed their bows and broke up their battle order. Together they cried out, "This is our king!" At her exalted command, they kept turning themselves to my side and they gamboled after me like lambs. They appealed to my rule. The people of Assyria who had sworn an oath before me by the great gods, came into my presence and kissed my feet. As for those usurpers, who had fomented rebellion and revolt, when they heard of the coming of my troops, they abandoned their trustworthy troops and escaped to an unknown land.

In the month of Adaru, a good month, on the eighth day, a feast day of Nabu, I joyfully entered into Nineveh, the city of my government, and I happily sat on the throne of my father.

134. Babylon A-G: Esarhaddon's reconstruction of Babylon

Previously, during the reign of an earlier king, evil omens appeared in Sumer and Akkad. The inhabitants continually answered one another "yes" and "no." They spoke falsehoods.

On the possessions of Esagila, the palace of the gods, an inaccessible place, they laid their hands on gold, silver, and precious stones, which they released to Elam as the market price (for help against Assyria). Marduk, the Enlil of the gods, became enraged. In order to overwhelm the land and destroy the people he contrived something evil. All around heaven and earth there were constantly numerous evil signs concerning the destruction of mankind. The path of the star of Enlil, the path of the star of Anu, and the path of the star of Ea, their positions became unfavorable and they exhibited ruinous signs. They kept changing simultaneously. The Arahtu, a river of plenty, a swift flood, a furious wave, a massive high-water, the very likeness of the Deluge, washed over the city of his dwelling and his shrine and turned it into a ruin. The gods and goddesses who dwelled there flew up to heaven like birds. The people who lived there escaped somewhere else and took refuge in an unknown land.

Seventy years, the appointed time of his abandonment, he wrote (on the Tablet of Destiny), but merciful Marduk, as soon as his heart quieted, he turned (the Tablet) upside down and ordered his sojourn for (only) 11 years.

Me, Esarhaddon, you truly summoned from among my older brothers in order to redress these deeds, and you put your good protection on me. All my enemies you overwhelmed like a flood and my opponents you killed. You caused me to achieve my desire. To quiet the heart of your great divinity, to calm your temper, you entrusted me with the shepherdship of Assyria.

At the beginning of my reign, in my first regnal year, after I sat in majesty on the throne, there were good omens in heaven and earth. Concerning the reconstruction of the city and the renewal of its temples, he (Marduk) continually sent his signs. Bright Jupiter, the one that passes a verdict on the land of Akkad, drew near in Siwan and stood where the sun repeatedly flared up. It was exceptionally bright and its features were red. Its rising was effective like the rising of the sun. Angry gods were reconciled with the land of Akkad. There were abundant rains and regular inundation in Akkad. It repeated and in the month of "the opening of the gate" it reached its culmination point and was stationary in its position. He (Marduk) ordered the work to get started for the completion of the cult-room, the renewal of the shrine and to put in order the ordinance of Esagila, palace of the gods. Month after month, by their appearance, Sin and Shamash confirmed with one another their true consent that the land of Akkad be set right.

I levied all my workers, the whole of Karduniash and they cut down trees and marsh reeds with axes. They tore out the roots. The waters of the Euphrates' swamp I drained from its (Babylon's) center and caused it to flow back to its previous course. I collected my workers and the people of Karduniash (and its) environs. I caused them to handle the pickaxe and I placed the earth basket on them. With good oil, honey, ghee, kurunnu-beer, choice wine, and pure mountain wine, I smeared the slope of the earth heap. In order to reveal to the people his (Marduk's) great godship and to cause them to be reverent of his lordship, I lifted the kudurru-basket onto my head and I made myself carry it. I had bricks made in brick molds of ivory, ebony, boxwood, and wood from the Makan tree.

Esagila, the palace of the gods, together with its sanctuaries, from its foundation to its battlements, I built anew. I made it greater, higher, and more splendid than before. Like celestial writing, I made it beautiful. To the wonderment of all the people, I filled it with splendor. The Babylonians, who had been brought to slavery and separated into gangs and riffraff, I collected and counted them as Babylonians. I established their exempt status anew.

135. The Succession Treaty of Esarhaddon

§4 Oath that Esarhaddon, king of Assyria, has established with you in the presence of the great gods of heaven and earth on behalf of Ashurbanipal, crown prince of the succession house, son of Esarhaddon, king of Assyria, your lord, whose name he has called and whom he has appointed to the crown princeship of the succession house.

When Esarhaddon, king of Assyria, goes to his fate, you will sit Ashurbanipal, crown prince of the succession house, on the royal throne and he will exercise kingship and lordship over you. In the fields and the city, you will guard him. You will fall and die for him. You will talk with him in the truth of your heart and you will give him good council whole-heartedly. You will make his way easy for him.

You will not become hostile to him or seat one of his brothers, older or younger, on the throne of Assyria instead of him. You will not change or alter the word of Esarhaddon, king of Assyria, but you will obey Ashurbanipal, the crown prince of the succession house, whom Esarhaddon, king of Assyria, your lord, has shown to you, and he will exercise the kingship and lordship of Assyria over you.

§6 If you hear any bad, improper, or incorrect word concerning the exercise of kingship, that is incorrect or wrong, either from the mouth of his brothers, his uncles, his cousins, the kin of his father's family; or from the mouth of his officials and governors; or from the mouth of his advisors; or from the mouth of any person at all,

you will not conceal it but will go and tell it to Ashurbanipal, the crown prince of the succession house.

§7 If Esarhaddon, king of Assyria, goes to his fate when his sons are small, you will help Ashurbanipal, crown prince of the succession house, take the throne of Assyria, and you will help Shamash-shum-ukin, his equal brother, the crown prince of Babylon, sit on the throne of Babylon. You will hold for him the kingship over all Sumer, Akkad and Karduniash. He will take with him all the gifts that Esarhaddon, king of Assyria, his father gave to him; do not withhold even one!

§14 If an Assyrian, or an Assyrian vassal, or a bearded man, or a eunuch, or a citizen of Assyria, or the citizen of another country, or a living being, as many as there are, confines Ashurbanipal, crown prince of the succession house, in the fields or in the city, and carries out conspiracy and rebellion, you shall stand with Ashurbanipal, crown prince of the succession house, and you shall protect him, and with all of your heart beat the men who made rebellion against him, and you shall save Ashurbanipal, the crown prince of the succession house, and his brothers, sons of the same mother.

§26 If anyone carries out conspiracy and rebellion against Esarhaddon, king of Assyria and sits himself on the royal throne, you shall not be joyful about his kingship but you shall seize him and kill him. If you are not able to seize him and kill him, you shall not consent to his kinship or swear an oath of service to him, but you shall rebel against him, and wholeheartedly do battle with him. You shall cause other lands to be hostile to him, you shall plunder booty from him, and you shall utterly defeat him. You shall abolish his name and seed from the land and you shall help Ashurbanipal, crown prince of the succession house, to take the throne of his father.

§27 If you, together with his brothers, his uncles, his cousins, or with the kin of his father's family, or the descendants of a former king, or an official, governor, eunuch, or with a citizen of Assyria, or the citizen of another land, they cause you to scheme, saying to you, "Slander Ashurbanipal, the crown prince of the succession house, in the presence of his father. Say negative and improper words." You shall not sow discord between him and his father, creating hatred between them.

§29 If someone gets you involved in a scheme, whether his brothers, his uncles, his cousins, seeds of his father's house, a eunuch, or a bearded man, an Assyrian or the citizen of some other country, or one of the totality of the black-headed people, as many as there are, (and) says, "Slander his brothers, sons of his mother, before him. Cause a fight between them. Separate his brothers, sons of his mother, from him." You shall not listen or speak evil about his brothers in his presence. Nor will you separate him from his brothers. The ones who speak of such matters, you will not allow them to leave. You shall come to Ashurbanipal, great Crown Prince of the Succession House (and) you shall speak thus: "Your father imposed a treaty on us and made us swear an oath concerning it."

§33 You shall not abrogate or rescind the oath . . . You shall not think of or do (anything) to abrogate or rescind the oath. You and your sons born in future days, you shall be bound by this oath concerning Ashurbanipal, great Crown Prince of the Succession House, son of Esarhaddon, your Lord, from this day until what happens after this treaty.

§107 Month of Iyyar, eighteenth day, the eponymy of Nabu-bel-usur, governor of Dur-Sharrukin. Treaty of Esarhaddon, king of Assyria, established on behalf of Ashur-banipal, crown prince of Assyria and Shamash-shum-ukin, crown prince of Babylon.

E. Naqia/Zakutu (Melville)

Naqia (Zakutu in Akkadian) joined Sennacherib's household when he was still Crown Prince under Sargon II, in about 713 BC. Although Naqia was not Sennacherib's queen, she bore him Esarhaddon, the youngest of his 11 (or more) sons (Melville 1994). As far as we know, neither Naqia nor her son was prominent during Sennacherib's reign until ca. 683 BC when the king bypassed his older sons and chose Esarhaddon to become Crown Prince. It has often been assumed that Naqia was responsible for Sennacherib's unconventional choice, having somehow managed to manipulate him with her "feminine wiles," but there is absolutely no evidence to support such a contention, and it is far likelier that other, more compelling factors inspired Sennacherib's decision. Nonetheless, the promotion touched off a series of events that culminated in Sennacherib's murder by the disaffected sons in 681 BC. Only after Esarhaddon decisively defeated (but did not capture) his brothers and became king, did Naqia achieve truly elevated status. Significantly, almost all of the evidence concerning her dates to Esarhaddon's reign.

The circumstances of his accession made Esarhaddon particularly eager to avoid internecine strife and settle the succession. Understandably, he did not wish to fall victim to a rebel plot or allow anyone but his own chosen Crown Prince to succeed him. Because he could not entirely trust his officials (some of whom would eventually rebel against him in 670 BC) or even his own wives and children, who might plot against him for their own ends, he turned to the only person he could rely on, his mother, who had no other male children and depended entirely on her son for her position and well-being. Together, Esarhaddon and Naqia contrived to establish her as an authority figure, who could help to secure the throne for Esarhaddon's chosen successor, Ashurbanipal, when Esarhaddon died. Publicizing Naqia's status was not a simple task, however. Esarhaddon could not afford to offend courtiers or make himself look weak by allowing a woman to have too prominent a position. Nonetheless, with subtlety and careful attention to protocol, they established Naqia's rank. She wrote to and received letters from officials, donated to temples, was depicted on monuments, undertook at least one building project, and administered her private estates. Much of what Naqia did reflected, but did not reproduce or impinge upon, the king's actions. Thus, when he reconstructed a temple, she donated to the venture; when he built at Nineveh, she built there.

In Assyria, one of the most common ways for the king to prove his status and power was to sponsor a building program and to commemorate it with inscriptions. This was a privilege reserved for kings, however. Naqia's construction of a palace for her son was unprecedented in Assyria, but it certainly proclaimed her status publicly. Her building inscription has survived in three fragmentary copies which are translated here as a composite (Borger 1956: 115–16). The text is written exactly like a royal building inscription, but is purposely much shorter and less grand. All the normal components are present: titles/genealogy, report of labor and materials, location of the building, list of furnishings, sacrifice for the gods, banquet, and description of the building's lavish splendor and purpose. Naqia must have been very well off to undertake such a project, but it is noteworthy that Esarhaddon supplied the labor and some of the materials. Circumstantial evidence indicates that the building was constructed between 677 and 673 BC, and although Naqia claims that she built the palace for her son, it is likely that if anyone lived there, it was she (Melville 1999: 38). In building a palace and making a dedicatory inscription, Naqia had effectively declared her status, but at the same time, the relatively modest claims of the inscription emphasize her restraint and desire not to flout convention too much.

In 672 BC, Esarhaddon publicly proclaimed Ashurbanipal Crown Prince, while also naming another son, Shamash-shum-ukin, Crown Prince of Babylon. During the next few years Esarhaddon took pains to promote his heirs and see to it that his mother developed enough political clout to help them when he died. Planning paid off, and when Esarhaddon passed away in 669 BC, Naqia implemented a loyalty oath on behalf of Ashurbanipal. The Zakutu treaty is unique. It is the only extant Neo-Assyrian treaty to have been imposed by anyone other than the king. This fact has often led to the mistaken assumption either that Naqia was inordinately powerful, or that the situation was so critical that only her intervention could avoid disaster. Neither position is tenable, however. In 669 BC the political situation in Assyria and the relationship between the two Crown Princes was stable, and remained so for the next 17 years. The treaty itself, which is of modest length and wording compared to the Succession Treaty, seems to have been hastily drawn up and summarily imposed. It acted as a reminder of all that the Succession Treaty adjured, rather than as a principal loyalty pact. Naqia and the treaty were, in effect, Esarhaddon's insurance policy. Having seen Ashurbanipal safely on the throne, Naqia, duty done, disappeared from public life. We do not know when she died, but she probably did not long outlive her son.

As a woman, Naqia/Zakutu enjoyed an unusually exalted position at the court of her son, but this seems to have been the result of a deliberate plan, implemented by Esarhaddon in order to safeguard the succession, rather than the byproduct of a domineering mother's influence over a weak and easily manipulated son. Naqia was undoubtedly an intelligent and dynamic woman, but it is essential to remember that she did not act on her own behalf; she never wielded power independently, but always acted in support of a man, whether son or grandson.

136. Building Inscription

[Naqia/Zakutu], wife of Sennacherib, king of the world, king of Assyria, daughter-in-law of Sargon, king of the world, king of Assyria, mother of Esarahaddon, king of the world, king of Assyria; Ashur, Sin, Shamash, Nabu, Marduk, [Ishtar of Nineveh,

Ishtar of Arbela] were pleased (and) they happily put Easrhaddon, (my) son, my offspring, on the throne of his father. From the top of the upper sea to the lower sea, they constantly went [. . .] no rival. They overwhelmed [his enemies] and they put the nose-rope on the kings of the four quarters. People of all the lands, his enemy prisoners of war he gave as my lordly portion. I caused them to carry the pickaxe and the dirt basket and they made bricks. A piece of empty land in the midst of Nineveh behind the Sin and Shamash temple, as a royal [dwelling] for Esarhaddon, [my beloved son . . .]

. . . I stretched [across it]. Door leaves of cypress, a gift of my son, I hung side by side on its gates. That house, I built it, completed it (and) filled it with splendor. Ashur, Ninurta, Sin, Shamash, Adad, Nabu, and Marduk, the gods who dwell in Nineveh, I invited inside (and) [I made before them] pure, extravagant offerings.

The king . . . on . . . whatever . . . the one who dwells . . . may the shedu and lamassu (protective deities) care for its interior and constantly watch over (it) . . . I had set . . . Esarhaddon, king of Assyria, my beloved son, I invited inside and held [a banquet . . .]

Everything valuable, furnishings of a palace, symbols of kingship, for Esarhaddon, [my beloved son . . .]

137. The Zakutu Treaty

Treaty of Zakutu, wife of Sennacherib, king of Assyria, mother of Esarhaddon, king of Assyria, [likewise (grand)mother of Ashurbanipal, king of Assyria] with Shamash-shum-ukin, his equal brother, with Shamash-metu-uballit and the remainder of his brothers, with the royal relatives, with the nobles and the governors, with the bearded and the eunuchs, courtiers, with the exempted people and all those who enter the palace, with the citizens of Assyria, small and the great:

Whoever (takes part in) this treaty which Zakutu, the queen dowager, has imposed on all the people of the country on behalf of Ashurbanipal, her favorite (grand)son, whoever should [. . .] lie, carry out a deceitful or evil deed or revolt against Ashurbanipal, king of Assyria, your lord; devise an evil scheme (or) speak slander in your hearts against Ashurbanipal, king of Assyria, your lord; discuss an evil suggestion (or) speak of a wicked plan for rebellion (and) uprising in your hearts against Ashurbanipal, king of Assyria, your lord; [. . .] (or) plot with another concerning the murder of [Ashurbanipal] king of Assyria, your lord, [may . . .] Jupiter, Venus, Saturn, Mercury [. . .]

(break in text . . .)

[And if] you from this day on (hear) an evil [word] of rebellion (and) uprising spoken against Ashurbanipal, king of Assyria, your lord, you shall come to Zakutu, his (grand)mother and Ashurbanipal [king of Assyria], your lord and reveal (it); and if you hear (a plot) to kill or destroy Ashurbanipal, king of Assyria, your lord, you shall come (and) reveal (it) to Zakutu, [his (grand)mother] and Ashurbanipal, king of Assyria, your lord; and if you hear an evil [plan] being plotted against Ashurbanipal, king of Assyria, your lord, you shall speak before Zakutu, his (grand)mother and Ashurbanipal, king of Assyria, your lord; and if you hear (or) know that there are men who instigate and agitate (rebellion) among you – whether they are bearded men or eunuchs, his brothers or royal relatives or your brothers or your friends – should you hear or [know],

you will seize them and [. . .] them and bring them to Zakutu [his (grand)mother and to] Ashurbanipal, [king of Assyria, your lord].

F. Ashurbanipal (Melville)

Ashurbanipal, the last great king of Assyria, ascended the throne when his father died unexpectedly in 669 BC while on campaign to Egypt. Ashurbanipal reigned for over thirty years, but since few texts survive from the later part of his reign, the date of his death is not known. Surviving editions of Ashurbanipal's annals were all written on prism-shaped tablets, also known as cylinders. Seven different editions have survived: cylinders E, B, D, K, C, F, and A and these range in date from about 666 to 639 BC (Gerardi 1987: 49). Their internal organization tends to be more geographical than chronological, which sometimes makes it difficult to determine the order events really occurred. Campaigns are given numbers, but these seem to be artificial designations, not precise indicators of a sequence of distinct military operations. Ashurbanipal's scribes made some narrative innovations that not only resulted in chronological ambiguities, but also represent developments in the expression of Assyrian ideology. The selections translated here, from Cylinder A (also known as the Rassam Cylinder, written ca. 639) and Cylinder B (written ca. 649), deal with some of the major events of Ashurbanipal's reign, but like other royal inscriptions, the narrative omits political/economic explanations and couches everything in highly ideological terms.

Cylinder A belongs to a category of text known as "autobiographical apology" because it emphasizes the personal experiences and character of the king in order to justify his rule (Tadmor 1983: 47–51). Not only does Ashurbanipal stress his relationship to his father (Esarhaddon) and grandfather (Sennacherib), but he tells the story of his childhood in the *bēt-rēdûti*, and gives a detailed account of his education as Crown Prince. This personal touch is carried throughout the text, where Ashurbanipal often refers to Esarhaddon as "the father, my creator." Such attention to personal relationships is no accident, nor does it simply reflect family feeling and a happy childhood, although those elements are certainly present. By continually referring to Esarhaddon as his biological father, Ashurbanipal highlights his own legitimacy. All the language of this text is subtly aimed at inviting the audience to see political and military actions as entirely justifiable responses to both current and past events. Cylinder A ends with a description of the rebuilding of the *bēt-rēdûti* (passage not included here) which suggests that the text was written at the time Ashurbanipal settled his own succession, but since there is no corroborating evidence, this remains conjecture (Tadmor 1983: 51).

In 667, nearly two years after his accession, Ashurbanipal finally sent an army to quell the rebellion that had started in Egypt before his father's death. Rather than ignore the lengthy delay, Ashurbanipal's scribes emphasize the situation in Egypt under Esarhaddon in order to demonstrate what a good son and king Ashurbanipal is. Not only is Ashurbanipal acting on his own behalf, but as his father's loyal son, he exacts revenge on Esarhaddon's former subjects. On several occasions, Ashurbanipal mentions the officials appointed by Esarhaddon and how he exceeds his father's benevolence in dealing with them. According to the accounts of the first and second campaigns, Ashurbanipal successfully reconquered Egypt. Yet the conquest of Egypt by Assyria was not a practical undertaking and probably would not have been attempted by Esarhaddon in the first place had he not needed new revenue (plunder and tribute) to fund the reconstruction of Babylon. Most of the lenience Ashurbanipal shows the Egyptian officials is the result of expedience, rather than a soft heart. What the text fails to admit is that Ashurbanipal could not hope to maintain control of Egypt from such a distance, nor, because of insufficient troops and supplies, could he control it by force. He had to rely on native Egyptians to rule in his stead, but they were unreliable and by about 655 BC Egyptian forces effected an Assyrian withdrawal. Cylinder A, written after Egypt gained its freedom, neglects to mention the fact.

Assyria's relationship with Babylonia and Elam under Ashurbanipal proved to be as fraught with difficulty as his immediate predecessors'. Like Sennacherib, Ashurbanipal faced a serious challenge to his authority from Babylonia and Elam. While Esarhaddon had not needed to fight a major campaign against either country, he certainly devoted a great deal of time and resources to establishing and maintaining order in the south. When Esarhaddon settled the succession he designated two heirs: Ashurbanipal to be king of Assyria; and Shamash-shum-ukin to be king of Babylonia. There is no evidence explaining the relationship the two kingdoms were to have, but it is clear from Ashurbanipal's texts that he understood Shamash-shum-ukin to be subordinate to him (Frame 1992: 109ff). The arrangement worked for 16 years, but eventually frustration over real or imagined slights, and (probably) pressure from local Babylonian factions drove Shamash-shum-ukin to seek freedom from Assyrian hegemony. With the aid of the Elamites, Shamash-shum-ukin was able to keep the war going for four years (652–648 BC), which proved to be a serious drain on Assyrian resources. In the end Ashurbanipal was victorious, but his brother was dead and his father's plans for a double kingship were wrecked. Special care was needed to explain these events to the people of Assyria, and more importantly, to the gods. Ashurbanipal and/or his scribes came up with a brilliant interpretation that not only showed Ashurbanipal in a good light, but also proved that he was actually avenging his father and grandfather.

The predominance of Babylonia and Elam in recent political and military affairs was not lost on Ashurbanipal, and when it came time for him to write about his own actions in these regions he took full advantage of the past. The fact that Sennacherib was murdered by a son (or sons) who were then defeated by their brother, Esarhaddon, provided Ashurbanipal with a convenient and highly symbolic parallel: Ashurbanipal, the good son and faithful brother, would defeat Shamash-shum-ukin, the bad son and evil brother, thus symbolically avenging his father and grandfather and restoring cosmic order. In his account of the Egyptian campaigns, Ashurbanipal emphasizes his relationship to his father and describes himself almost as the custodian of Esarhaddon's policies. By the time we get to the fifth and sixth campaign narratives we have been well prepared to view Ashurbanipal not only as the legitimate king, but as the "good son," always mindful of his heritage. In Babylonia Ashurbanipal once again claims to have done even more than his father, but he has shown his brother the utmost generosity only to be met with deceit and subterfuge. Shamash-shum-ukin and the rebels further demonstrate their iniquity by preventing Ashurbanipal from carrying out his cultic duties in Babylonia. In response, the gods throw Shamash-shum-ukin into the fire, proving their support of Ashurbanipal and relieving him of the guilt of fratricide. When Ashurbanipal has some of the rebel prisoners killed at the site of Sennacherib's murder "as a funerary offering" and then symbolically feeds their remains to wild animals, his revenge is complete. Graphic descriptions of rebel suffering, the result of divine wrath, are offset by Ashurbanipal's attention to reestablishing cult centers and public institutions.

According to Cylinder A, Ashurbanipal fought his fifth, seventh and eighth campaigns against Elam, whose throne changed hands a bewildering number of times during this period (e.g. Frame 1992: 123–4). There were at least five claimants (occasionally simultaneously), some of whom (Tamaritu, for example) were supported by the Assyrians for as long as it suited either side. Ashurbanipal's description of the brutal and complete destruction of Elamite lands, cities and temples (not all of which is included here) surpasses even Sennacherib's portrayal of the destruction of Babylon in ferocity and finality. While Sennacherib flooded Babylon, Ashurbanipal spread salt on the ground of Elam. Not content to destroy Elam and her allies materially, he subjects his enemies to all sorts of terrible punishments: the brothers, Nabu-na'id and Bel-eṭir, are compelled to commit sacrilege by publicly grinding up the bones of their father, while Nabu-qate-ṣabat must wear the severed head of his brother around his neck (episode not included here). In other respects the description of Elam's destruction is reminiscent of the narrative of Sargon's eighth campaign against Urartu (see §128, "Sargon's Letter to Ashur") during which he destroyed the cult center of the Urartian god, Haldi. The similarities between the texts of these three kings may arise from the fact that they were written to justify particularly brutal campaigns in which cult centers and divine statues were destroyed. However in the process of making such a justification Ashurbanipal found it extremely useful to refer, sometimes openly, to his ancestors. We should not think, however, that Ashurbanipal himself (or any other Assyrian king, for that matter) did not buy into his own ideology. There is every reason to believe that Ashurbanipal truly saw his wars with Egypt, Babylonia and Elam as opportunities to avenge his father and grandfather.

The short selection from Cylinder B is included here as a comparison to Cylinder A. Cylinder B, written before the conclusion of the Shamash-shum-ukin rebellion and the final campaign against Elam, is quite different from the later text, Cylinder A. For example, in Cylinder B the eighth campaign is focused on the officials of Teumam, king of Elam, who, according to Cylinder A, was killed during the fifth campaign. The eighth campaign is completely different in the two cylinders. The discrepancies between the two texts illustrate how the Assyrians sometimes compressed episodes, narrated them out of order, or omitted them altogether, depending on the focus of the text. Far more than simple narrative history, the Assyrian Royal Inscriptions were written in fulfillment of a complex (and ever-changing) set of ideological imperatives.

138. Apology and Egyptian campaigns

I, Ashurbanipal, creation of Ashur and Ishtar, great crown prince of the succession palace, whom Ashur and Sin, lord of the crown, from distant days named for kingship and created while in the womb of his mother for the shepherdship of Assyria, Shamash, Adad, and Ishtar spoke their firm verdict to make my kingship. Esarhaddon, king of Assyria, the father, my creator, extolled the word of Ashur and the great gods, his support, who ordered him to establish my kingship. In Ajaru, the month of Ea, lord of mankind, on the twelfth day, a favorable day, a feast-day of Gula, by the noble word that Ashur, Ishtar, Sin, Shamash, Adad, Bel, Nabu, Ishtar of Nineveh, queen of Kidmuru, Ishtar of Arbela, Ninurta, Nergal, and Nusku commanded, he gathered the people of Assyria, small and great from the upper (to) the lower sea, he made them swear an oath on the life of the gods in order to guard my princeship and later the kingship of Assyria; he strengthened the contract. With joy and celebration I entered the Bit Riduti, the sophisticated place, the center of royalty in which Sennacherib, the father of the father, my creator, practiced princeship and kingship; the place in which, Esarhaddon, the father, my creator, was born and grew up (and) practiced the lordship of Assyria, controlled all the princes, extended the family, gathered (his) relatives and family; and wherein I, Ashurbanipal, learned the wisdom of Nabu, laid hold of scribal practices of all the experts, as many as there are, examined their instructions, learned to shoot the bow, ride horses and chariots, and hold the reigns. By the command of the great gods whose names I invoked, I spoke their praise, they ordered that I exercise kingship, they entrusted me to be the provider of their shrines, they destroyed my enemy on my behalf, they struck my opponents. I am a valiant hero, beloved of Ashur and Ishtar, descendant of royalty. After Ishtar of Nineveh, queen of Kidmuri, Ishtar of Arbela, Ninurta, Nergal, and Nusku caused me to sit joyfully on the throne of the father who created me, Adad sent rains, Ea released his blessing, the grain reached 5 cubits in its stalk, the ear 5/6 of a cubit. Successful harvests, plentiful grain, caused the pastureland to flourish constantly. The fruit of the orchards was very luxuriant and cattle gave birth easily. During my reign there was abundance and plenty. During my years there was surplus and bounty.

On my first campaign I went against Magan (Egypt) and Meluhha (Ethiopia?). Taharqa, king of Egypt and Kush (Nubia) whom Esarhaddon, king of Assyria, the father, my creator, defeated, whose land he ruled over, he, Taharqa forgot the might of Ashur and Ishtar and the great gods, my lords, and trusted in his own strength. Against the kings, the officials whom the father, my creator, appointed in Egypt, he went in order to kill, rob and plunder Egypt. He entered behind them and took up residence inside Memphis, a city which the father, my creator, destroyed and annexed to the territory of Assyria. A courier came into Nineveh and reported to me. My heart became furious over these doings and my liver boiled with rage. I lifted my hands and prayed to Ashur and the Assyrian Ishtar. I gathered my mighty troops with whom Ashur and Ishtar filled my hand. I made them take the road to Egypt and Nubia. In the course of my campaign, 22 kings of the seaside, of the midst of the sea, and of the dry land, my subjects, carried their heavy gifts before me and kissed my feet. Those kings, together with their troops and their boats, on the sea and on dry land with my army, I made them take the course and path. In order to hasten aid to the kings, officials who were in Egypt, my subjects, I quickly marched, going as far as Kar-Banti. Taharqa, king of Egypt and Kush, heard of the coming of my army in the midst of Memphis, and in order to do battle and combat with me, he levied his battle troops. With the aid of Ashur, Bel, Nabu, the great gods, my lords, who go at my side, I defeated his army in battle on the wide plain. Inside Memphis Taharqa heard of the defeat of his army. The awe-inspiring radiance of Ashur and Ishtar overwhelmed him and he became frenzied. The fearsome brilliance of my majesty, with which the gods of heaven and earth provisioned me, covered him. He abandoned Memphis and in order to save his life, he fled to the middle of Thebes. I took that city, I caused my army to enter and occupy it. Nikku, king of Memphis and Saa, Sharru-lu-dari, king of Si'inu, Pishanhuru, king of Nathu, Paqraru, king of Pishaptu, Bukkunanni'pi, king of Hathiribi, Nahke, king of Hininshi, Putubishti, king of Sa'nu, Unumunu, king of Nathu, Harsiaeshu, king of Sabnuti, Buama, king of Pintiti, Susinku, king of Pushiru, Tabnahti, king of Punubu, Bukkunani'pi, king of Ahni, Iptiharteshu, king of Pihattihurnunpiki, Nahtihuruansini, king of Pishabdi'a, Bukurninib, king of Pahnuti, Siha, king of Shiautu, Lamentu, king of Himuni, Ishpimatu, king of Taini, Mantimeanhe, king of Thebes, these kings, officials, representatives whom the father, my creator, appointed in Egypt, who gave up their posts before Taharqa's attack, filled the plain. I restored their posts, I let them do their service. Egypt and Nubia which the father, my creator, conquered, I took anew. I made the outposts stronger than in former days and I concluded an agreement. With much plunder, heavy booty I returned in safety to Nineveh.

Later those kings, as many as I appointed, they sinned against my oath. They did not preserve the oath of the great gods, forgot the good deeds I did for them and their hearts plotted evil. They made false reports and they advised unprofitable counsel for themselves thus, "They are expelling Taharqa from Egypt. How can we dwell here?" To Taharqa, king of Kush, they dispatched their messengers in order to establish a treaty and amity, saying, "Let us establish peace between us; let us help each other. Let us divide the land among ourselves, let there not be another lord among us." Against the troops of Assyria, my lordly force, which I had caused to come to their aid, they repeated evil talk. My officials heard the plans and they seized their messengers together with their messages, and saw their criminal deeds. I seized those kings and I bound them hand and foot in iron fetters and iron handcuffs. The curse of Ashur, king of the gods, came over them for they sinned against the oath of the great gods. Their hands swept away the good things I did for them, and the people of Sais, Pindidi, and Si'I, and those remaining cities, as many as were present with them (when they) plotted evil, small and great, they felled with weapons. No single man escaped. Their bodies they hung up on stakes. They flayed their skins and clad the city wall with (them). These kings who planned evil against the armies of Assyria, they brought before me alive to Nineveh. From among them, I showed compassion to Niku and I allowed (him) to stay alive. I imposed an oath on him that I made exceed the previous one. I clothed him in multicolored garments and I gave him a gold hoe, symbol of (Egyptian) kingship. I put gold rings on his hand, I gave him an iron dagger, the belt of which I inlaid with gold. I wrote my nomenclature on it. I gave him chariots, horses and donkeys for his lordly vehicle. I sent with him my officials, governors, as his help. I returned him to his residence in Sais, where the father, my creator, had appointed him as king. Nabushezibani, his son, I appointed at Hathariba. I did good deeds for him that exceeded those of the father, my creator.

The place where Taharqa fled, the terrifying appearance of the weapon of Ashur, my lord, overwhelmed him and he died. Afterwards, Urdamane, son of Shabaku, sat on the royal throne. He established Thebes and Heliopolis as his fortresses. He gathered his troops in order to fight my soldiers, citizens of Assyria, who were in Memphis. He prepared his battle. He confined those people (in the city) and seized their escape route. Messengers came quickly to Nineveh and told me (about it).

On my second campaign I made straight for Egypt and Kush. Urdamenani heard of the coming of my army and that I had crossed the border of Egypt. He abandoned Memphis and fled to Thebes in order to save his life. The kings, officials, representatives whom I established in Egypt, came before me and kissed my feet.

139. Civil war and Elamite campaigns

On my fifth campaign I marched right to Elam. At the command of Ashur, Sin, Shamash, Adad, Bel, Nabu, Ishtar of Nineveh, queen of Kidmuri, Ishtar of Arbela, Ninurta, Nergal and Nusku, in the month of Ullulu, the work of goddesses, the month of the king of the gods, Ashur, father of the gods, Enlil, like the onset of a furious storm I covered Elam completely. I cut off the head of Teumam, their king, the arrogant one who planned evil. I killed his soldiers without number. I took his soldiers alive in my hands and, like thornbushes and camelthorn, I filled the environs of Susa with their corpses. I caused their blood to flow into the river Ulai; I dyed its waters like red wool. Ummanigash, son of Urtak, king of Elam, who had fled before Teumam to Assur, seized my feet. I brought him with me to Elam and I set him on the throne of Teumam. Tamaritu his third brother, who had escaped with him, I set him as king in Hidalu.

In those days, Shamash-shum-ukin, false brother, to whom I did good and established as king of Babylon, whatever gold ornaments, appropriate symbols of kinship (he wanted), I made and gave him, I collected and filled his hands with soldiers, horses and chariots. I increased cities, fields, orchards, people who dwell within and I gave him more than the father, my creator, had ordered, but he forgot those good deeds I did for him and he plotted evil. Aloud, with his lips he avowed goodwill (but) underneath his heart plotted murder. The citizens of Babylon whom I saw in Ashur, my subjects, he deceived. He spoke falsehoods to them. Deviously, he sent them before me to Nineveh in order to ask about my health. I, Ashurbanipal, king of Assyria, for whom the great gods decreed a good fate, whom they created with truth and justice, I caused those citizens of Babylon to be present at a table of hospitality. I wrapped them in multicolored linen garments, I put gold rings on their fingers. While those Babylonians were present in Assyria they obeyed my command, but that Shamash-shum-ukin, false brother, who did not keep my oath, incited the people of Akkad, my subjects, against me, and Ummanigash, the refugee, who seized the feet of my majesty, whom I had appointed for the kingship of Elam, and the kings of Guti, Amurru and Meluhha, whom my hands had installed at the command of Ashur and Ninlil, all of them he caused to be enemies with me. They reached an agreement with him. The gates of Sippar, Babylon, and Borsippa, he bolted and he broke (our) brotherhood. He made his fighters go up on the walls of those cities and they continually made war against me. He prevented me from making my sacrifices before Bel, son of Bel, light of the gods, Shamash, and the warrior Erra, and he caused me to abandon giving my food offerings. In order to take away the temples, dwellings of the great gods whose shrines I supplied copiously and loaded up with gold and silver – I adorned their interiors appropriately – he plotted evil. At that time one dream interpreter, while he slept at night, he saw a dream as follows: on the surface of the pedestal of Sin was written, "who plots evil against Ashurbanipal, king of Assyria, and starts a fight, I will give an evil death. By means of a swift stab from an iron dagger, (by) fire, famine, (or) plague, I will destroy their lives." I heard these things and heeded the word of Sin, my lord.

On my sixth campaign I levied my troops and went right to Shamash-shum-ukin. Inside Sippar, Babylon, Borsippa, and Kutha, I confined him and his fighting men and I blocked their way out. In the city and the plain I accomplished their defeat without mercy. The remainder lay down their lives from plague, famine and starvation.

In those days the people of Akkad who put in with Shamash-shum-ukin, plotted evil. On account of hunger, they ate the flesh of their sons and their daughters; they chewed on straps. Ashur, Sin, Shamash, Adad, Bel, Nabu, Ishtar of Nineveh, queen of Kidmuri, Ishtar of Arbail, Ninurta, Nergal, and Nusku, who go before me striking my opponents, they threw down Shamash-shum-ukin, enemy brother who attacked me, into the raging conflagration. They destroyed his life. But the people who came up with these plans for Shamash-shum-ukin (and who) did evil, who feared death and who valued their lives (more than his), they did not fall into the fire with Shamash-shum-ukin, their lord. Those who escaped the cut of the iron dagger, famine, starvation, and the conflagration and took refuge, the net of the great gods, my lords, which cannot be escaped, enveloped them. No one got away. No survivor escaped from my hands; my hands counted (them all). Chariots, palanquins, sunshades, concubines, property of his palace, they brought before me. Those people, their insolent mouths which spoke iniquity against Ashur, my lord, and me, the prince who fears him, who plotted evil, I tore out their tongues and I massacred them. Those remaining alive, by the Shedu and Lamassu where they overwhelmed Sennacherib, father of the father my creator, now I destroyed them there as his funerary offerings. I fed their dismembered flesh to dogs, pigs, jackals, vultures, eagles, the birds of heaven and fish of the deep. After I did those deeds, I calmed the hearts of the great gods, my lords. The corpses of the people whom Erra (the plague god) caused to fall, and who from famine and starvation lay down (their) lives, the remainder of the food of dogs and pigs that blocked the streets and filled the precincts, I had their remains removed from Babylon, Kutha, and Sippar. I cast (them) outside. Through the work of the purification priests, I cleansed their sanctuaries, I purified their filthy streets. Their furious gods and their angry goddesses I quieted with offerings and prayers. I restored their regular offerings which had become too little, as in distant days. The rest of the citizens of Babylon, Kutha, and Sippar, who escaped plague, slaughter, and starvation, I had mercy on them. I ordered the preservation of their lives (and) I caused them to dwell in Babylon. People of Akkad, as well as those of Chaldea, Aramu, and the Sea Land, who helped Shamash-shum-ukin unanimously (lit. turned to one mouth), they became hostile to me on their own. At the command of Ashur, Ninlil, the great gods, my help, I trampled them everywhere. The yoke of Ashur which they cast off, I imposed on them. Governors and officials, appointments of my hand, I put over them. Regular offerings of Ashur, Ninlil, and the gods of Assyria I established for them. I imposed on them tribute, payment of my lordship yearly without ceasing.

In my eighth campaign at the command of Ashur and Ishtar, I levied my troops and went straight against Ummanaldash, king of Elam. [large gap] *For a march of one month and twenty days I caused devastation in the entire territory of Elam. I scattered salt and cress over them. Daughters of kings, the sisters of kings, together with the older and younger families of the kings of Elam, officials, mayors of those cities as many as I conquered, chiefs of bowmen, governors, chariot drivers, cavalry, archers, eunuchs, craftsmen, all the army, as many as there were, people, male and female, small and great, horses, mules, donkeys, cattle, and sheep, which were more numerous than grasshoppers, I carried away to Assyria. The soil of Susa, Madaktu, Hatemash, and the rest of their towns I collected and took to Assyria. In a month I ransacked Elam everywhere. The cries of men, the tracks of cattle and sheep, the singing of a happy song, I cut off from its pastures; I abolished its harvest. Onagers, gazelles, animals of the steppe, as many as there are, I caused to lie among them in the meadow.*

Nana, who was angry for 1,635 years, went (and) dwelled in the midst of Elam, an improper place for her. But in these days, she and the gods, her fathers, called my name for the rulership of the lands. She waited for me to return her divinity (and spoke) thus: "Ashurbanipal will bring me out from the midst of evil Elam and he will make me enter Eanna." The word of the command of their divinity, which from distant days they spoke, now they made apparent to people of later (days, and) I gripped the hand of her great divinity. She took the direct road to Eanna with a heart made joyful. On the first day of Kislimu, I made her enter into Uruk and take up residence in Ehileanna, the eternal shrine which she loves.

140. Elamite campaign

Umbadara (and) Nabu-damiq, the envoys of Teumam, king of Elam, in whose hands Teumam sent correspondence, whom I detained in my presence (while) they waited for the imposition of my decision, they saw the severed head of Teumam, their lord, in Nineveh and madness seized them. Umbadara tore out his beard (and) Nabu-damiq pierced his stomach with the iron dagger of his belt. I presented the severed head of Teumam as an offering opposite the central gate of Nineveh so that the severed head of Teumam, king of Elam, would reveal to the people the might of Ashur and Ishtar, my lords. Shumaya, son of Nabu-ushalim, grandson of Marduk-apla-iddina, whose father fled to Elam before the father of the father, my creator; after I set Ummanigash for the kingship of Elam, he seized Shumaya, son of Nabu-ushalim and brought him before me. Dunanu, Samgunu, sons of Bel-iqisha of Gambulu, whose fathers harassed the kings, my fathers and also upset the exercise of my kingship, I brought them to Ashur and Arba'il in order to show reverence (to me) in the future. Mannuki-ahhe . . . Dunanu and Nabu-usallim, men who were over Gambulu, who spoke great lies against my gods, I tore out their tongues in Arba'il and flayed their skin. They threw Dunanu down on a slaughtering block and slaughtered him like a sheep. I killed the remaining brother of Dunanu and Shumaya. I dismembered his flesh and had it carried around as a lesson for all the lands. Nabu-na'id, Bel-eṭir, sons of Nabu-shum-eresh, the chief accountant, whose father, their creator, Urtak incited for battle with

Akkad, the bones of Nabu-shumu-eresh which I took from Gambulu to Ashur, those bones I made his sons crush opposite the gate in Nineveh.

G. *Assyrian King List (Greenwood)*

As its name implies, the Assyrian King List (AKL) is a register of royal names who ruled in Ashur from the early second millennium BCE through the middle of the first millennium. With few exceptions, the format is rather repetitious: "Royal Name, the son of Royal Name, ruled *X* years." Some historical (or at least, etiological) commentary is interspersed throughout.

The list has been preserved in three copies: the Nassouhi List, the Khorsabad List, and the Seventh-Day Adventist Theological Seminary (SDAS) List. The oldest copy, named after the Frenchman Essad Nassouhi, who first published the text in 1927, is of unknown provenance. It is housed in the Archaeological Museum of Istanbul. Of the three copies, it is the most poorly preserved. The list from Khorsabad was unearthed during the Oriental Institute excavations of 1932–3. Khorsabad, ancient Dur-Sharrukin, was founded by Sargon II (721–705 BCE) on the outskirts of modern Mosul in Iraq. Like the Nassouhi List, the SDAS List is also of unknown provenance, having been purchased from residents of Mosul during the waning years of Ottoman control. The tablet now resides with the Seventh-Day Adventist Theological Seminary in Washington, DC. In addition to these three major copies, there are two small fragments, one from Assur and one from Nineveh.

At least two of the tablets, the Khorsabad List and the SDAS List, were in the shape of an amulet. The top of the Nassouhi tablet has been broken to the extent that making any conclusive determination about its shape is impossible. It has been surmised that the top tab served as a hinge through which a pin could fit horizontally. The tablet could then be read much like a student's legal pad in which notes have been taken on both the front and back.

Each side of the tablet was ruled with both horizontal and vertical lines. Double vertical lines divided the tablet into two columns. Each column was then subdivided into left and right sides with another double vertical rule. Horizontal lines separated individual entries. From Erishu I onward, each king has his own entry.

Like its predecessor, the Sumerian King List, the original purpose of the AKL was apologetic in nature. Its original objective was to demonstrate Shamshi-Adad I's legitimate right to the throne of Assur. Having established a working template on which to build, future kings were then able to add their names and defend their own claims to legitimacy. A logical consequence of this system was the concept of hereditary monarchy.

For historians, the AKL has its benefits and its limits. One of the benefits is that it provides a systematic ordering of Assyrian monarchs. Another benefit is that it rather reliably indicates the length of each reign. A third benefit is the occasional mention of an eponym year, allowing for more precise dating.

With respect to its limitations, the Assyrian King List is not concerned with co-regencies or dual claimants. As a result, the genealogical record is less than accurate at times and presents a one-sided, sanitized history of the Assyrian monarchy. Finally, there are occasional errors in the regnal lengths, but most of these can be attributed to scribal errors.

Due to space considerations, the entire AKL has not been reproduced here. Instead, the following translation includes only those excerpts that are pertinent to other texts treated in this volume, as well as a few other notable sections. However, those portions which have been omitted will be described in brief.

141. Text

(i)26–(ii)7 Erishu (I), the son of Ilu-shuma, [whose . . .] ruled 30 years.
Ikunu, the son of Erishu, ruled [x years].
Sargon (I), the son of Ikunu, ruled [x years].
Puzur-Ashur (II), the son of Sargon, ruled [x years].
Naram-Sin, the son of Puzur-Ashur, ruled [x] + 4 years.
Erishu (II), the son of Naram-Sin ruled [x years].
Shamshi-Adad (I), the descendent of Ilu-kabkabu, went to Karduniash in the time of Naram-sin. In the eponym year of Ibni-Adad, Shamshi-Adad went up from Karduniash. He seized Ekallatum and occupied it for 3 years. In the eponym year of Atamar-Ishtar, Shamshi-Adad went up from Ekallatum. He even dethroned Erishu, the son of Naram-Sin, and seized it for himself. He ruled 33 years.
Ishme-Dagan (I), the son of Shamshi-Adad, ruled 40 years.

(ii)8–12 Ashur-dugul, the son of a nobody, with no authority to the throne, ruled 6 years.
In the time of Ashur-dugul, the son of a nobody, Ashur-apla-idi, Nasir-Sin, Sin-namir, Ipqi-Ishtar, Adad-salulu, Adasi – 6 kings who were sons of nobodies – ruled during the same eponym year.

(iii)5–(iii)14 Ashur-uballit (I), the son of Eriba-Adad, ruled 36 years.
Enlil-nirari, the son of Ashur-uballit, ruled 10 years.
Arik-den-ili, the son of Enlil-nirari, ruled 12 years.
Adad-nirari (I), the son of Arik-den-ili, ruled 32 years.
Shalmaneser (I), the son of Adad-nirari, ruled 30 years.
Tukulti-Ninurta (I), the son of Shalmaneser, ruled 37 years.
While Tukulti-Ninurta was alive, his son Ashur-nadin-apli seized the throne for himself. He ruled 3 years.
Ashur-nirari (III), the son of Ashur-nadin-apli, ruled 6 years.
Enlil-kudurri-usur, the son of Tukulti-Ninurta, ruled 5 years.

(iii)15–(iii)36 Ninurta-apil-Ekur, the son of Ili-hadda, descendant of Eriba-Adad, went up to Karduniash. He came up from Karduniash and seized the throne. He ruled 3 years.
Ashur-dan (I), the son of Ninurta-apil-Ekur, ruled 46 years.
Ninurta-tukulti-Ashur, the son of Ashur-dan, ruled during the same eponym year.
Mutakkil-Nusku, his brother, fought against him and deported him to Karduniash.

During the same eponym year Mutakkil-Nusku took control of the throne, then he died.
Ashur-resh-ishi (I), the son of Mutakkil-Nusku, ruled 18 years.
Tiglath-pileser (I), the son of Ashur-resh-ishi, ruled 39 years.
Ashared-apil-Ekur, the son of Tiglath-pileser, ruled 2 years.
Ashur-bel-kala, the son of Tiglath-pileser, ruled 18 years.
Eriba-Adad (II), the son of Ashur-bel-kala, ruled 2 years.
Shamshi-Adad (IV), the son of Tiglath-pileser, came up from Karduniash, dethroned Eriba-Adad, the son of Ashur-bel-kala, and seized the throne for himself. He ruled 4 years.

(iv)10–27 Ashur-dan (II), the son of Tiglath-pileser (II), ruled 23 years.
Adad-nirari (II), the son of Ashur-dan, ruled 21 years.
Tukulti-Ninurta (II), the son of Adad-nirari, ruled 7 years.
Ashurnasirpal (II), the son of Tukulti-Ninurta, ruled 25 years.
Shalmaneser (III), the son of Ashurnasirpal, ruled 35 years.
Shamshi-Adad (V), the son of Shalmaneser, ruled 13 years.
Adad-nirari (III), the son of Shamshi-Adad, ruled 28 years.
Shalmaneser (IV), the son of Adad-nirari, ruled 10 years.
Ashur-dan (III), the brother of Shalmaneser, ruled 18 years.
Ashur-nirari (V), the son of Adad-nirari, ruled 10 years.
Tiglath-pileser (III), the son of Ashur-nirari, ruled 18 years.
Shalmaneser (V), the son of Tiglath-pileser, ruled 5 years.

SDAS Colophon (1)

It was written and checked against its original. A tablet of Bel-shum-iddin, an incantation priest from Ashur. Whoever takes it away, may Shamash take him away.

Commentary

The first three entries to the list have been omitted. The first entry contains "17 kings who lived in tents." The second comprises "10 ancestral kings," who are listed in reverse chronological order. The third entry lists "6 kings whose eponyms are destroyed." The dates of these 33 kings are unknown.

(i)30–(ii)6 It has been suggested that the missing phrase preceding Erishu I's regnal length should read "whose father and eponym is known." Erishu I is the first king for whom a regnal year is given, but it has been preserved as "30 years" in the SDAS list and "40 years" in the Khorsabad list.

The precise history of Shamshi-Adad's origins are unknown. According to best estimates, he ruled in Ekallatum until Naram-Sin of Eshnunna invaded Ashur and Ekallatum, forcing Shamshi-Adad to flee to Karduniash. Circa 1808 BCE, upon Naram-Sin's death, Shamshi-Adad returned from Babylon, deposed Naram-Sin's son Erishu, and reclaimed Ashur and Ekallatum. To legitimate his place on the throne of Ashur, he incorporated his lineage into the list of city-rulers through the ancestry of Ilu-kabkabu.

While Shamshi-Adad was still alive, he appointed his eldest son Yasmah-Adad as ruler over Mari and Ishme-Dagan as ruler over Ekallatum. This effectually solidified control over all of northern Mesopotamia for Shamshi-Adad. In the south, however, Rim-Sin conquered Isin, thus seizing control of southern Mesopotamia. After Shamshi-Adad's death, Zimri-Lim conquered Mari, leaving Ishme-Dagan as the sole Assyrian monarch in 1775. By 1760, however, Ashur went the way of the rest of Mesopotamia and fell to the Amorite, Hammurapi.

(ii)7–12 The term "son of a nobody" indicates that not all kings were as fixated with absolute, hereditary lineage as Shamshi-Adad. A king having unknown progeny did not necessarily lose his royal privilege, as long as his own progeny could be defended. The fact that these 6 kings ruled within the same eponym year suggests an unstable transfer of power following the death of Ishme-Dagan and the subsequent domination of Hammurapi. It should be noted that there are no known inscriptions from any of these 6 or the next 11 kings.

Lines (ii)13–28 have been omitted. The entirety of this section consists of the formula, "RN, son of RN, ruled *X* years." It covers the period from ca. 1760 to 1363 BCE, although the sum of the known regnal years adds up to only about 300 years.

(ii)29–(iii)14 With the accession of Ashur-uballit I ca. 1363 BCE, Assyria emerged as a prominent force in the ancient Near East, as attested by the Amarna Letters. His reign marks the beginning of what is called the Middle Assyrian period, which thrives off and on until its formal conclusion in 935 BCE, at the conclusion of the reign of Tiglath-pileser II.

The Middle Assyrian Empire was at its strongest during the reigns of Adad-nirari I, Shalmaneser I, and Tukulti-Ninurta I, who collectively reigned for virtually all of the thirteenth century. However, as the king list recounts, this long-standing stability came to an abrupt end with the demise of Tukulti-Ninurta. It is known from one of the chronicles that Ashur-nadin-apli assumed the throne after leading a band of rebels in the dethronement, imprisonment, and ruthless assassination of his father. However, the three main copies of the AKL are unclear regarding the circumstances surrounding the *coup d'état*. The two oldest copies read, "While Tukulti-Ninurta was alive." With the simple transposition of two cuneiform signs, however, the SDAS list reads, "When Tukulti-Ninurta became disturbed," perhaps commenting on the attitude that led to his dethronement, which is also reflected in the chronicle.

(iii)15–(iii)36 Tukulti-Ninurta's assassination led to a period of considerable instability. By the time Ninurta-apil-Ekur seized control of the throne, no detectable royal lineage could be traced without going back to Eriba-Adad, who ruled two hundred years prior. Although Ninurta-apil-Ekur's reign was brief, his son Ashur-dan I had the longest rule of any Assyrian king.

Upon Ashur-dan's death, but before a new eponym year had begun his son, Ninurta-tukulti-Ashur, succeeded him. Within that same year, however, Mutakkil-Nusku ousted his brother and imposed some sort of corvée labor or other taxation on the land, though the reading is not entirely clear.

With Ashur-resh-ishi and Tiglath-pileser I a temporary renaissance was launched in Assyria. After Tiglath-pileser died in 1076, however, instability resumed and the Aramean threat that he had so adeptly controlled and defeated became an ever-present and encroaching nuisance. The omitted lines (iv)1–9 round out the kings of the Middle Assyrian period.

(iv)10–27 Ashur-dan II inherited a kingdom in disarray. When he assumed power in 934 BCE he set about shoring up the national economy, which had taken a beating under the exploits of his predecessors. Rather than attempting to emulate the grandiose military visions of Tiglath-pileser I, he constructed administrative buildings and provided ploughs for agricultural productivity, although his inscriptions do mention at least one campaign. Under his rule Assyria re-emerged as a world power, giving rise to what is called the Neo-Assyrian period.

This new empire really began to flourish with Ashur-dan's great-grandson, Ashur-nasirpal II (883–859), whose military successes rivaled those of Tiglath-pileser I.

By 853 BCE Assyria's strength became such a concern for Syria-Palestine that Adad-idri (biblical Ben-Hadad) of Damascus, Ahab of Israel, and "the 12 kings of the west (Hatti) and the seashore" joined forces against Shalmaneser III at the Battle of Qarqar on the Orontes River. Although the outcome of the battle can be debated, within 13 years Shalmaneser had defeated Hazael of Damascus and subjugated Jehu of Israel, as depicted in the famous Black Obelisk.

Once again, Assyria fell into a period of decline until Tiglath-pileser II (744–727) raised her up into an international superpower, receiving tribute from the Taurus Mountains to the border of Egypt. The final king in the king list, Shalmaneser IV, is credited with besieging Samaria in an effort to put down a Phoenico-Palestinian revolt, although his son Sargon II takes personal credit for its fall.

SDAS Colophon (2)

The colophon provides insightful information on the transmission process of the list, indicating that the text had a particular *Vorlage* from which the scribe worked. This particular colophon comes at the end of the reign of Shalmaneser IV, whereas the colophon from the Khorsabad List appears after Ashur-nirari V, demonstrating that it is older than the SDAS List. The Nassouhi List does not contain a colophon, but its registry stops with the reign of Tiglath-pileser II, thus being the oldest of the three major copies.

II. Syro-Palestinian Texts II (Noegel)

142. Ekron inscription

The Ekron dedicatory Inscription was discovered at Tel Miqne (ancient Ekron) in 1996. It was discovered *in situ* in the cella of a sanctuary firmly dated to ca. 680–655 BCE. Though it contains only five lines, it holds a singular importance since it represents the most complete Philistine text in existence.

The Philistines are perhaps best known as the arch-enemies of Israel's early kings. However, archaeological remains at Ekron and other Philistine sites reveal that they were hardly the one dimensional warrior people portrayed in the Bible, much less "Philistine" in the modern sense of the term. Instead, nearly everything they have left behind suggests that they were also extremely adept at farming, building, metallurgy, and the production of olive oil. Situated on the western flank of the coastal plain that divided Philistia from Judah, Ekron also played an important commercial, and thus, political role in the region. According to the Bible, Ekron was one of five capital cities belonging to the Philistines, along with Ashdod, Ashkelon, Gath, and Gaza. Hence, the importance of this brief inscription.

The script used to record the dedication at Ekron contains a mixture of Phoenician and Hebrew features, suggesting that it was a local development (Gitin, Dothan, and Naveh, 1997: 13), but the inscription's format follows a Phoenician model. The inscription's contents recognize the piety of Ekron's ruler for building the sanctuary and dedicating it to his goddess.

> *The temple that he built, Akhayus, son of Padi, son of Yasad, son of Ada, son of Ya'ir, ruler of Ekron, for Ptgyh his Lady. May she bless him, and protect him, and lengthen his days, and bless his [l]and.*

Assyrian records from the time of kings Esarhaddon (680–669 BCE) and Assurbanipal (668–627 BCE) inform us that Akhayus (called Ikausu in these texts) was a ruler of Ekron, as was Padi, his father. Unlike the name Padi, however, and the other names in this inscription, all of which are Semitic, Akhayus appears to be an Aegean name. This has led some to read Akhayus as equivalent to the Greek word *Axaios* meaning "Achaean" or "Greek" (Gitin, Dothan, and Naveh 1997: 11; Naveh 1998: 35–337). The name is related to that of Akish, the Philistine king of Gath in the Hebrew Bible (1 Sam 21: 11–16; 1 Sam 27: 1–29: 9; 1 Kgs 2: 39–40), though the two figures cannot be identical because the biblical Akish ruled during the early tenth century BCE.

Assyrian records characterize Ekron as a vassal of Assyria. An inscribed prism of Esarhaddon lists Akhayus as one of 12 rulers from the seacoast who provided him with the raw materials for building his palace at Nineveh. In 667 BCE, Assurbanipal ordered Akhayus to support his military campaign to Egypt and Cush.

Akhayus' father Padi appears in another brief dedicatory inscription from Ekron that reads "for Baal and for Padi," and in a monumental inscription of Sennacherib (704–681 BCE). According to the latter text, when Phoenicia and Israel refused to pay tribute in 701 BCE, Sennacherib brought his armies to their gates. When confronted with the Assyrian threat, some kings fought and were defeated, and others fled or recapitulated. It is in this context that Sennacherib tells us about Padi.

> *The officials, the nobles, and the people of Ekron who had thrown Padi, their king, (at that time) under oath and allegiance to Assyria, into iron fetters, and handed him violently to Hezekiah, the Judean, became afraid (of me) because of the treason they committed.*

The people of Ekron then called upon the Egyptians for help, but Sennacherib intercepted the Egyptian army and defeated them at Timnah and Eltekeh. Sennacherib then attacked Ekron and executed the culprits behind the rebellion, hanging their corpses on the city's towers. Sennacherib ordered Padi released from Jerusalem and installed him once again as ruler of Ekron. He also put him in charge of lands formerly belonging to Hezekiah of Judah (715–687 BCE). Shortly afterwards, in 699 BCE, Padi is again delivering tribute to Assyria. The other royal names in the inscription (i.e., Yasad, Ada, and Ya'ir) are not known from other sources.

It is unclear to what extent peoples outside of Assyria viewed Akhayus and his line as kings in their own right, or whether the rulers of Ekron considered themselves at times autonomous from Assyria, though the latter is doubtful. The word translated "ruler" in the Ekron inscription, while equivalent to a Hebrew word meaning "ruler" (i.e., non-king) in the Bible (e.g., Judg 3: 3; 1 Sam 29: 1),[35] may have meant "king" to the Philistines. Alternatively, the term could have signified rulers under the suzerainty of Assyria or under another Philistine "king," like the biblical Akish of Gath in 1 Sam 21: 11.

The goddess named Ptgyh has proven difficult to identify. Some view Ptgyh as a local name for the Semitic goddess Asherah (Gitin et al. 1997: 12), who is referenced elsewhere, albeit briefly, in other inscriptional remains at Ekron. Others propose to read it as the Greek title *potnia* meaning "lady," and equate it with the Greek Artemis or Athena, or the Semitic goddess Asherah (Demsky 1997: 1–5; 1998: 53–8). However, this reading poses two problems. First, it requires that we read the inscription as containing an "n" and not a "g," which now appears unlikely. Second, it would suggest that the inscription contains a Semitic gloss on the foreign term, meaning something like, "*potnia* (that is to say in the Semitic tongue), his lady." The reasons for such a gloss would be difficult to explain. Complicating this reading also is the fact that in antiquity the title *potnia* was associated with many other goddesses besides Artemis or Athena, making any certain identification impossible (Thomas and Wedde 2001). Others suggest that we read the name as Ptryh, a goddess known from Ugaritic texts (Görg 1998), but the match is not exact, and in any event, it again seems clear that the name contains the letter "g" (and not "n" or "r"). Perhaps the most tantalizing suggestion has been to read Ptgyh as Pythogaia. This would connect the goddess to the Delphic sanctuary of Pytho, where the earth-goddess Gaia was worshiped (Schäfer-Lichtenberger 1998: 64–76).

The Aegean origin of the goddess and the identification of Akhayus as "Achaean" or "Greek" support the already considerable evidence for the Aegean origins of the Philistines. A relief at Medinet Habu in Egypt, depicts

Ramses III (1187–1156 BCE) in a sea battle against the Sea Peoples, among whom are the Philistines (Sandars 1978). The evidence also correlates with what we know from the material remains of Philistine settlements at Ekron and elsewhere in the Levant, especially their megaron-type structures with circular hearths, and their pottery.

It is difficult to know to what extent the Aegean elements in the Ekron inscription represent an ethnic continuity reaching back to the twelfth century BCE. Indeed, according to the archaeological record, Ekron appears to have been a multicultural city in the seventh century BCE with a highly hybrid urban culture. This can be seen in the inscription itself, which employs a hybrid script, and in Ekron's material, especially cultic remains, which demonstrate Egyptian, Israelite, and Mediterranean influences. Moreover, biblical narratives about Philistines nowhere record a need for an interpreter, demonstrating again, that whatever their origins, they adapted quite easily to their new environment. The Aegean elements in the inscription, therefore, might be less of an indicator of ethnic continuity than of the preservation of the Philistines' Aegean origins in the collective memory of the Ekronites. After all, according to the inscription, the earliest rulers of Ekron bore Semitic names.

Bibliography (I A)

ANET, 282–4.

Becking, Bob. *The Fall of Samaria: An Historical and Archaeological Study*. Leiden: E. J. Brill, 1992.

Black, Jeremy and Anthony Green. *Gods, Demons and Symbols of Ancient Mesopotamia: An Illustrated Dictionary*. Austin: University of Texas Press, 1992.

Brinkman, J. A. *A Political History of Post-Kassite Babylonia 1158–722 B.C.* Analecta orientalia 43. Rome, Pontifical Biblical Institute, 1968.

DOTT, 53–8.

Kuhrt, Amélie. *The Ancient Near East c. 3000–330 BC*. 2 vols. Routledge History of the Ancient World. London: Routledge, 1995.

Leick, Gwendolyn. *Who's Who in the Ancient Near East*. London: Routledge, 1999.

Luckenbill, Daniel David. *Ancient Records of Assyria and Babylonia*. 2 vols. London: Histories and Mysteries of Man, 1989, esp. 1: 269–96.

Millard, Alan R. "Tiglath-pileser." In *Dictionary of the Ancient Near East*. Ed. Piotr Bienkowski and Alan Millard. Philadelphia: University of Pennsylvania Press, 2000, 289–91.

Na'aman, N. "Sennacherib's 'Letter to God' on his Campaign to Judah." *Bulletin of the American Schools of Oriental Research* 214 (1974): 25–39.

——. "Tiglath-Pileser III's Campaigns Against Tyre and Israel (734–732 BCE)." *Tel Aviv* 22 (1995): 268–78.

RANE, 145.

Tadmor, Hayim. *The Inscriptions of Tiglath-Pileser III King of Assyria: Critical Edition, with Introductions, Translations and Commentary*. Jerusalem: Israel Academy of Sciences and Humanities, 1994.

Younger, K. Lawson, Jr. "Tiglath-Pileser III (2.117)." In COS 2: 284–92.

Bibliography (I B)

For the most recent edition of Sargon's "Letter to Ashur," see Walter Mayer, "Sargon's Feldzug gegen Urartu – 714 v. Chr." *Mitteilungen der Deutschen Orient-Gesellschaft* 115, 63–132. A complete English translation and literary commentary appear in Benjamin R. Foster, *Before the Muses: an Anthology of Akkadian Literature*. 3d ed. (Bethesda: CDL, 2005): 790–813. For a new publication of Sargon's Khorsabad inscriptions see A. Fuchs, *Die Inschriften Sargons II. aus Khorsabad* (Göttingen: Cuvillier, 1994). For different interpretations of the "Letter to Ashur" A. L. Oppenheim, "The City of Assur in 714 BC," *Journal of Near Eastern Studies* 19 (1960): 133–47; L. D. Levine, "Sargon's Eighth Campaign," in T. Cuyler Young, Jr. (ed.), *Mountains and Lowlands: Essays in the Archaeology of Greater Mesopotamia* (= Bibliotheca Mesopotamica 7) (Malibu: Undena, 1977), pp. 135–51; C. Zaccagnini, "An Urartean Royal Inscription in the Report of Sargon's Eighth Campaign," in *Assyrian Royal Inscriptions: New Horizons in Literary, Ideological and Historical Analysis*. Edited by F. M. Fales (Rome: Istituto per L'Oriente, Centro per le antichità e la storia dell-arte del vicino Oriente, 1981); F. M. Fales, "Narrative and Ideological Variations in the Account of Sargon's Eighth Campaign," in M. Cogan and I. Eph'al (eds.), *Ah, Assyria . . . Studies in Assyrian History and Ancient Near Eastern Historiography Presented to Hayim Tadmor* (= Scripta Hierosolymitana 33) (Jerusalem: Magnes, 1991), pp. 129–47; and K. F. Kravitz, "A Last-Minute Revision to Sargon's Letter to the God," *Journal of Near Eastern Studies* 62 (2003): 81–95.

Bibliography (I C)

For the most recent and in-depth study of Sennacherib's inscriptions, see E. Frahm, *Einleitung in die Sanherib-Inschriften*. Archiv für Orientforschung 26. Vienna: Institut für Orientalistik der Universität, 1997. But see also the rather out-of-date English translations in D. D. Luckenbill, *The Annals of Sennacherib*, Oriental Institute Publications 2 (Chicago: Oriental Institute Press, 1924). For recent analyses of Sennacherib's campaign in Judah and further bibliography, see William R. Gallagher, *Sennacherib's Campaign to Judah: New Studies* (Leiden: Brill, 1999); Walter Mayer, "Sennacherib's Campaign of 701 BCE: the Assyrian View," *Journal for the Study of the Old Testament Supplement Series* 363 (2003): 168–200 and D. Ussishkin, The Conquest of Lachish by Sennacherib. Tel Aviv: Tel Aviv University, 1982. For different views of Sennacherib's activities in Babylonia and further bibliography, see the following: J. A. Brinkman, "Sennacherib's Babylonian Problem: An Interpretation," *Journal of Cuneiform Studies* 25 (1973): 89–95; L. D. Levine, "Sennacherib's Southern Front: 704–689 B.C.," *Journal of Cuneiform Studies* 34 (1982): 28–48; G. Frame, *Babylonia 689–627 B.C.: A Political History*. Istanbul: Nederlands Historisch-Archaeologisch Institut, 1992. For the literary characteristics of battle of Halule narrative, see E. Weissert, "Creating a Political Climate: Literary Allusions to *Enuma Elish* in Sennacherib's Account of the Battle of Halule," in *Assyrien im Wandel der Zeiten*, ed. H. Waetzoldt and H. Hauptmann. Heidelberg: Heidelberger Orientverlag, 1997, 191–202. For a different view of the battle, see A. K. Grayson, "Problematical Battles in Mesopotamian History," in *Studies in Honor of Benno Landsberger on His Seventy-fifth Birthday, April 21, 1965*, ed. H. G. Güterbock and T. Jacobsen. Assyriological Studies 16. (Chicago: University of Chicago Press, 1965): 337–42.

Bibliography (I D)

For the transliterations and complete translations (in German) of Esarhaddon's royal inscriptions see R. Borger, *Die Inschriften Asarhaddons Königs von Assyrien*. Archiv für Orientforschung Beiheft 9. Graz: E. Weidner, 1956. The complete transliteration and translation (in English) of the Succession Treaty is published in S. Parpola, and K. Watanabe, *Neo-Assyrian Treaties and Loyalty Oaths*. State Archives of Assyria II. Helsinki: Helsinki University Press, 1988. B. N. Porter, *Images, Power and Politics: Figurative Aspects of Esarhaddon's Babylonian Policy*. Memoirs of the American Philosophical Society, vol. 208. Philadelphia: American Philosophical Society, 1993, offers a thorough discussion of Esarhaddon's Babylonian texts. A somewhat different view is given in M. Cogan, "Omens and Ideology in the Babylon Inscription of Esarhaddon," in *History, Historiography and Interpretation: Studies in Biblical and Cuneiform Literatures*. Ed. H. Tadmor and M. Weinfeld. Jerusalem: Magnes, 1984. Pp. 76–87. For an interpretation of Esarhaddon's accession account see H. Tadmor, "Autobiographical Apology in the Royal Assyrian Literature," in *History, Historiography and Interpretation: Studies in biblical and Cuneiform Literatures*. Edited by H. Tadmor and M. Weinfeld. Jerusalem: Magnes, 1984. Pp. 36–7. For a general history of the Neo-Assyrian period and further bibliography see Amélie Kuhrt, *The Ancient Near East c. 3000–330 BC*. Vol. 2. London: Routledge, 1995.

Bibliography (I E)

For Naqia's building inscription, see R. Borger, *Die Inschriften Asarhaddons Königs von Assyrien*. Archiv für Orientforschung Beiheft 9. Graz: E. Weidner, 1956, 115–16; and R. Borger, "König Sanheribs Eheglück," *Annual Review of the Royal Inscriptions of Mesopotamia Project* 6 (1988): 5–11. For other editions of the Zakutu treaty, see S. Parpola, "Neo-Assyrian Treaties from the Royal Archives of Nineveh," *Journal of Cuneiform Studies* 39 (1987): 161–89; and S. Parpola and K. Watanabe, *Neo-Assyrian Treaties and Loyalty Oaths*. State Archives of Assyria 2. Helsinki: Helsinki University Press, 1988, #8. E. Frahm, *Einleitung in die Sanherib-Inschriften*. Archiv für Orientforschung 26. Vienna: Institut für Orientalistik der Universität, 1997, offers some interesting insights on Naqia as Sennacherib's wife. For a complete treatment of Naqia's life plus further bibliography, see S. C. Melville, *The Role of Naqia/Zakutu in Sargonid Politics*. State Archives of Assyria S 9. Helsinki: Helsinki University Press, 1999.

Bibliography (I F)

For the inscriptions of Ashurbanipal, see M. Streck, *Assurbanipal und die letzten assyrischen Königs zum Untergans Nineveh's*. Leipzig: Hinrichs, 1916 (in transliteration and German translation – still an important work in spite of its age); R. Borger, *Beiträge zum Inschriftenwerk Assurbanipals: die Prismenklassen A*. Wiesbaden: Harrassowitz, 1996 (new transliteration and some translation in German); D. D. Luckenbill, *Ancient Records of Assyria and Babylonia*, vol. 2. London: Histories and Mysteries of Man, 1989. For the history of Ashurbanipal's reign see the following and further bibliography contained therein: G. Frame, *Babylonia 689–627 B.C.: A Political History*. Istanbul:

Nederlands Historisch-Archaeologisch Institut, 1992; S. S. Ahmed, *Southern Mesopotamia in the Time of Ashurbanipal*. The Hague and Paris: Mouton, 1968; A. Spalinger, "Assurbanipal and Egypt: A Source Study," *Journal of the American Oriental Society* 94 (1974): 316–28. For interpretation of the texts and chronological problems, see H. Tadmor, "Autobiographical Apology in the Royal Assyrian Literature," in *History, Historiography and Interpretation: Studies in Biblical and Cuneiform Literatures*. Ed. H. Tadmor and M. Weinfeld. Jerusalem: Magnes, 1984. Pp. 36–7; A. K. Grayson, "The Chronology of the Reign of Ashurbanipal," *Zeitschrift für Assyriologie* 70 (1981): 227–45; and P. Gerardi, "Assurbanipal's Elamite Campaigns: A Literary and Political Study." PhD dissertation, University of Pennsylvania, 1987.

Bibliography (I G)

For a complete translation of the entire list see Alan Millard, "Assyrian King Lists," in *The Context of Scripture I: Canonical Compositions*, edited by W. W. Hallo and K. L. Younger, Jr. (Leiden: Brill, 1997), 463–5; and A. Leo Oppenheim, "The Assyrian King List," in ANET, 564–6. A helpful diagram of the genealogy of Assyrian kings from the Middle Assyrian period to the end of the kingdom has been produced in Marc van de Mieroop, *A History of the Ancient Near East ca. 3000–323 BC* (London: Blackwell, 2004), 294–6. Photographs of the Khorsabad and SDAS exemplars have been published by I. J. Gelb in "Two Assyrian King Lists," *Journal of Near Eastern Studies* 13 (1954), pls. 14–17. Photographs of the Nassouhi List are available in E. Nassouhi, "Grande liste des rois d'Assyrie," *Archiv für Orientforschung* 4 (1927): pls. 1–2.

Bibliography (II)

Demsky, Aaron. 1997. "The Name of the Goddess of Ekron: A New Reading." *Journal of the Ancient Near Eastern Society* 25: 1–5.

——. 1998. "Discovering a Goddess: A New Look at the Ekron Inscription Identifies Mysterious Deity." *Biblical Archaeology Review* 24: 53–8.

Dothan, Trude. 1982. *The Philistines and Their Material Culture*. New Haven: Yale University Press; Jerusalem: Israel Exploration Society.

——. 1990. "Ekron of the Philistines, Part 1: Where They Came From, How They Settled Down and the Place They Worshiped in." *Biblical Archaeology Review* 18: 28–38.

Dothan, Trude, and Moshe Dothan. 1992. *People of the Sea: The Search for the Philistines*. New York: Macmillan.

Gitin, Seymour, and M. Cogan. 1999. "A New Type of Dedicatory Inscription from Ekron." *Israel Exploration Journal* 49: 193–202.

Gitin, Seymour, Trude Dothan, and Joseph Naveh. 1997. "A Royal Dedicatory Inscription from Ekron." *Israel Exploration Journal* 48: 1–18.

Görg, M. 1998. "Die Göttin der Ekron-Inschrift." *Biblische Notizien* 93: 9–10.

Naveh, J. 1998. "Achish-Ikausu in the Light of the Ekron Dedication." *Bulletin of the Schools of Oriental Research* 310: 35–7.

Sandars, Nancy K. 1978. *The Sea Peoples: Warriors of the Ancient Mediterranean, 1250–1150* B.C. London, Thames & Hudson.

Sasson, Victor. 1997. "The Inscription of Achish, Governor of Ekron, and Philistine Dialect, Cult, and Culture." *Ugarit Forschungen* 29: 627–39.

Schäfer-Lichtenberger, C. 1998. "PTGJH–Göttin und Herrin von Ekron." *Biblische Notizien* 91: 64–76.

Thomas, Carol, and Michael Wedde. 2001. "Desperately Seeking Potnia." In R. Laffineur and R. Hagg, eds., *Potnia: Deities and Religion in the Aegean Bronze Age*. Austin, TX: University of Texas Press. Pp. 3–14.

Notes

1 Ešarra was the name of a temple in Ashur.

2 *apil* ^{m}*Adad(x)*-ÉRIN.TÁḪ *(nērāri)*. This inscription is labeled Misc. III.1 by Tadmor (1994: 212–13).

3 See Tadmor 1994: 212–13 and 40–1 for further discussion and data, including a royal edict from the time of Adad-nirari III or Ashur-dan III (772–755), which mentions a Tiglath-pileser who may have been an official of some sort under this king. Tadmor thinks it is possible that Tiglath-pileser was Adad-nirari's grandson.

4 See note 17 below.

5 During this period, the Assyrian threat also exercised significant influence on Israelite and Judean politics. See, e.g., Summary Inscriptions 4: 14′–19′; 9: 4, 9 (Tadmor 1994: 140–1; 186–7) for mentions of Israel (Bit-Humri) and its annexation.

6 The Babylonian regnal dates are 728–727. *Pul(u)* – literally, "limestone, limestone block" – may have been the king's official throne name, but others have argued that it was either: a) the king's original name; b) a quasi-hypocoristic for the middle element of his full name (*apil* > *pil/pul*); or c) a folk nickname of some sort (see Brinkman 1968: 61–2 n. 317; 240–1 n. 1544; Younger 2000: 284 n. 21; Tadmor 1994: 280).

7 The most thorough study to date is Tadmor 1994 (note esp. his introduction to the annals: pp. 27–39). Tadmor's reconstruction has not gone without criticism, but it is the most extensive, exhaustive, and careful treatment now available and the present translation is based on his text with the caveat that further discoveries or work may involve changes to what is presently known and possible to know given the unfortunate nature of the annals' preservation.

8 For the text see Tadmor 1994. See also the previous note.

9 The beginning of the introduction, which would have invoked the gods is unfortunately lost.

10 See previous note.

11 Another name for the city of Ashur, perhaps its most ancient part (*libbi āli*). See Erich Ebeling, "Baltil," *Reallexikon der Assyriologie* 1: 395; Tadmor 1994: 40.

12 Lit. "lady of the crown" – a mother goddess, of whom little is known. See Black and Green 1992: 132–3; Tadmor 1994: 41.

13 The restoration is hypothetical and uncertain, but follows Tadmor 1994: 41; cf. *CAD* S, 159.

14 The meaning of the term is uncertain. It literally means "intertwined" or the like (see *CAD* I/J, 295). The translation follows Tadmor 1994: 41.

15 The latter portion of the prologue and the beginning of Year 1 are preserved on a slab (NA 9/76) which was unpublished and thus unavailable to Tadmor (see 1994: 37, 40). The first regnal year apparently ennumerates a list of east Aramaean tribes conquered by Tiglath-pileser (see ibid., 272 n. 10) – a list paralleled in his Summary Inscription 7: 5–6 (see ibid., 158–9 for text and translation). Years 2–7, not all of

which are extant in the Calah annals, were concerned with campaigns against Media, Urartu and Arpad (the latter fell in 740, at which time Bit-Agusi was annexed to the empire; see Summary Inscription 9: 24′–25′ [ibid., 186–7]), and Ulluba. For a synopsis of Tiglath-pileser's campaigns, see Tadmor 1994: 232–7.

16 With restorations from Ann. 22+26. See Tadmor 1994: 58–63.

17 There has been considerable debate regarding the identification of this person. Some have argued that he is the same as Azariah, the given name of King Uzziah of Judah (see 2 Kgs 15: 1), who reigned ca. 783–742. This identification was possible given the existence of another fragmentary tablet that seemed to indicate that this person was king of a place called *Ia-u-da-a-a*. Although a few scholars supposed that this GN was Y'dy/Sam'al, this supposition was proven erroneous since that GN is always written KUR/URU *Sam'al(la)* in Neo-Assyrian records (Tadmor 1994: 274 n. 3). The GN *Ia-u-da-a-a* (*Yaūdu/i*) must be Judah, then, since this is how it was written at this time. However, Na'aman (1974) made the case that the fragmentary tablet containing this GN actually belonged to another text (the Azekah inscription; see *COS* 2.199D: 304–5). This means that there is no longer any clear indication of Azriyau's land and so any identification of that land and its king, along with correlate reconstructions, must remain extremely tentative in the absence of additional evidence. Na'aman (1995) himself argued that Azriyau was the king of Hatarikka, a state bordering Hamath. For further discussion see Younger 2000: 285 n. 10 and Tadmor 1994: 273–6.

18 Perhaps Aleppo (Halab), which was a cult-center for the storm-god Adad/Hadad. Cf. the Sefire inscriptions.

19 *e-ki-i-mu*. The translation follows Tadmor 1994: 63; see there for discussion.

20 Following this, the annals go on to describe further activities in Year 8, including: battles with Aramaean tribes and other entities, how the spoil from these battles was brought to the king who was then in Hatti, and subsequent repopulations.

21 With restorations from Anns. 3, 4, and 27. See Tadmor 1994: 68–71. The translation here follows that of Tadmor (ibid.) and Younger 2000: 285–86. Since Ann. 14*: 5b begins the ninth regnal year, the preceding lines obviously belong to Year 8. For the impact of this on the chronology of Menahem's tribute, see Tadmor 1994: 274–6.

22 All of the GNs in this listing could be translated as gentilics; e.g. "Kushtaspi, the Kummuḫite, Rezin, the Damascene," and so forth (so Younger 2000: 285–6).

23 See further below. Rezin is also mentioned in Misc. I,2: 9 (Tadmor 1994: 208–9).

24 See the Panamuwa inscription (*COS* 2.37: 158–9), executed by his son Bar-Rakib, perhaps to memorialize his father after his death during Tiglath-pileser's campaign against Damascus.

25 An earlier interpretation took these to be stuffed and decorated animals (see *ANET*, 283 n. 7), a possibility eliminated by a newer reading that indicates that the sheep (at least) were "alive" (see Tadmor 1994: 69–70).

26 The words for female camels and their young are loan words from West Semitic, attesting "to a familiarity with the pastoral nomadic milieu" (Tadmor 1994: 70).

27 Following the eighth year, Years 9–12 (not all of which are preserved in the annals) describe campaigns against Media, Urartu, and Philistia as far as the Egyptian border. See Tadmor 1994: 234–5.

28 Tadmor 1994: 79 notes that the text does not indicate that Tiglath-pileser directly attacked the city but, instead, concerns his devastation of the surrounding countryside. Cutting the city off from external resources was a common military tactic. For the fall of Damascus and the execution of Rezin, see 2 Kgs 16: 9, which is the only surviving reference to these events.

29 This same simile is used in the famous description of Sennacherib's siege of Jerusalem. Tadmor (1994: 79) thinks that the construction, first attested here, is hyperbolic and "employed as a face-saving device to cover for a failure to take the enemy's capital and punish the rebellious king."

30 Another technique and "face-saving device" due to an unsuccessful siege (so Tadmor 1994: 79). Whatever the case, contrast Deut 20: 19–20: "If you besiege a town for a long time, making war against it in order to take it, you must not destroy its trees by wielding an ax against them. Although you may take food from them, you must not cut them down. Are trees in the field human beings that they should come under siege from you? You may destroy only the trees that you know do not produce food; you may cut them down for use in building siegeworks against the town that makes war with you, until it falls" (NRSV).

31 Perhaps this should be restored as *Bīt-Hadara* which might be identified with Hadar, a site 33 miles (53 kilometers) southwest of Damascus (see Tadmor 1994: 80).

32 Lit. "the house of his father."

33 Lit. "Tell."

34 Years 14–19, not all of which are preserved in the annals, recount campaigns against Damascus (732, when the city fell and the Galilee and Transjordan were annexed), Shapiya, and Nabu-Mukin-zeri of Babylonia (after which Tiglath-pileser ascended the Babylonian throne). See Tadmor 1994: 234–7.

35 The word (Hebrew *seren*) may be of Indo-European derivation and related to the Greek word for ruler *turanos*.

12

Neo-Babylonian Period Texts from Babylonia and Syro-Palestine

Benjamin Studevent-Hickman,
Sarah C. Melville, and Scott Noegel

I. Texts from the Neo-Babylonian Period: 626–539 BCE

The Neo-Babylonian kings brought the locus of cuneiform culture back to its homeland. Indicative of the event is the conspicuous effort they made to relive the golden days of Babylonian independence. The kings frequently boast of resurrecting the religious and political agendas of their forebears, and in many cases their inscriptions are written in an archaizing script and language. To be sure, this doctrine was greatly facilitated by the artifacts they discovered during their many building projects (see Winter 2000).

Neo-Babylonian royal inscriptions provide relatively little information concerning historical events. Most commemorate monumental building projects, above all the renovation of temples. Like all Mesopotamian royal inscriptions, they are written in a language that is heavily theological and propogandistic, so they do offer considerable insight into the social and religious ideology of the crown. In structure they are fairly simple. They open with the royal titulary then proceed to describe the setting for the event commemorated. After narrating the event, the inscriptions generally conclude with a prayer to the appropriate deity; the consistency of this last feature distinguishes them from other royal inscriptions from Mesopotamia. Nevertheless, given their limited values for historical reconstruction, one must supplement these inscriptions with other contemporary sources, above all administrative texts (mostly from temples) and the Neo-Babylonian Chronicle Series, which details the major military campaigns of the kings year by year.

Bibliography

Winter, I. J. "Babylonian Archaeologists of the(ir) Mesopotamian Past." In *Proceedings of the First International Congress of the Archaeology of the Ancient Near East: Rome, May 18th–23rd 1998*. Ed. P. Matthiae et al. Rome: Università degli studi di Roma "La Sapienza" 2000, 1785–1800.

A. *Nabopolassar 626–605 BCE (Studevent-Hickman)*

143. The restoration of the Babylonian inner wall named Imgur-Enlil ("Enlil has consented")

Nabopolassar acceded to the throne of Babylon amidst the chaos that followed the death of Kandalanu, the Assyrian puppet-king in Babylon. Almost nothing is known about his background, but within 10 years he successfully united Babylonia and expelled the Assyrians. With the help of the Medes, his forces dealt the final blow to the Assyrian empire in 609 BCE.

One of the most interesting monumental inscriptions from Nabopolassar's reign describes his restoration of the inner city wall of Babylon, the wall Imgur-Enlil ("Enlil has consented"). The restoration likely took place between 622 and 612 BCE (al-Rawi 1985: 2); the commemoration begins with the king's requisite epithets:

Nabopolassar, the king of justice;
the shepherd called (to rulership) by Marduk;
the one fashioned by Ninmenna, the exhalted princess, the queen of queens;
the one (to whom) Nabu and Tashmetu stretched their hands;
the prince, the beloved of Ninshiku.

Nearly all royal inscriptions invoke the divine realm for the royal titulary, but it is not always clear why specific deities are selected and presented the way they are. Their personal relationship to the king, tradition, the context of the inscription, and other factors were certainly at play. In the above case, the presence of Marduk; Nabu, his son; and Tashmetu, Nabu's wife; is understandable: alongside Zarpanitu, Marduk's wife, these are the chief deities of the Babylonian state. But the mention of Ninmenna and Ninshiku (a manifestation of the god Ea) is more puzzling. Both of these deities are from cities in Babylonia's deep south, which may suggest that Nabopolassar was from that region (Beaulieu 2003: 307 nn. 3, 5). It cannot be excluded, however, that their presence reflects other agendas.

The inscription turns to an autobiographical sketch of the king and the setting for the building of the wall. Although the section says little about Nabopolassar's background – he claims to be a native Babylonian from the humblest origins – it does refer to his ousting of the Assyrians and the context for the rebellion.

When, in my childhood – I was the son of a no one – I would seek out the shrines of Nabu and Marduk, my lords; (when) my mind was focused on establishing their rites and completing their cultic procedures; when my attention (lit. "my ears") was on truth and justice; Shazu, the lord who knows the hearts of the gods of heaven and the netherworld,[1] *who constantly examines the behavior of humankind, examined my heart and appointed me, the meek one who was undiscovered among the people, to (a position of) prominence in the country in which I was born. He did indeed call me to the lordship of the land and the people and caused the benevolent Lamassu*[2] *to walk beside me. He fulfilled whatever I undertook. He made Nergal, the mightiest of the gods, walk beside me. He killed my adversaries, felled my enemies.*[3] *As for the Assyrian who ruled the land of Akkad because of the anger of the gods and harassed the people of the land with his heavy yoke, I, the feeble one, the wretched one, the one who seeks out the lord of lords, with the mighty strength of Nabu and Marduk, my lords, eliminated their footsteps from the land of Akkad and caused (the people) to cast off their yoke.*

The switch from singular to plural in reference to the Assyrian(s) is interesting. It is possible that the former refers to a specific king: likely Sennacherib, whose complete destruction of Babylon was seen almost universally as an afront to the cosmic order (*History* 237–8). Also worth noting is the issue of divine abandonment. The text clearly states that the Assyrian ruled the people "because of the anger of the gods." It was a common belief in ancient Mesopotamia that foreign occupation or destruction of a city was a function of divine punishment, the patron deity having abandoned the city because of some transgression by the population or the king. In any event, it is well established that Nabopolassar ousted the Assyrians, and it is in the context of this expulsion that he receives his commission for the city wall.

At that time, I, Nabopolassar, the king of Babylon, the one who pleases Nabu and Marduk – because Imgur-Enlil, the great wall of Babylon . . . had grown decrepit and fallen down, (because) its wall had eroded from rain and heavy downpours, (and because) its base had piled up and become a mound of ruins – mustered the troops of Enlil, Shamash, and Marduk (and) made them bear the hoe, imposing corvée duty (upon them).[4]

Babylon had clearly fallen into a state of disrepair under the Assyrians, and the "time of troubles" that followed the death of Kandalanu surely contributed to its decay. The amount of labor needed for the project is in fact suggested. The inscription states that Nabopolassar mustered "the troops of Enlil, Shamash, and Marduk," clearly a reference to the populations of Nippur, Sippar, and Babylon itself, the respective cities of these deities.

After defining the borders of the area to be excavated, the inscription connects the project to its past, even to its cosmic foundations.

I removed the dirt that had accumulated and checked and inspected its (i.e., Imgur-Enlil's) old base. I verily laid its brickwork in the original location. Indeed, I established its foundation on the edge of the netherworld.

Cosmic descriptions of temple architecture are well attested in ancient Mesopotamia (see, e.g., Edzard 1987). For the Neo-Babylonian kings this imagery is often connected specifically to the region's history. An example of this is found in the section dealing with the burial of the foundation deposit.[5]

I, Nabopolassar, the obedient, the submissive, (the one) who reveres Nabu and Marduk, the shepherd who pleases Ṣarpanitum (Marduk's wife), who inspects the old foundations of Babylon, who discovers the original brickwork,[6] who reveals the original eternal ground, who takes the hoe of the Igigi, who bears the corvée basket of the Anunaki, who built Imgur-Enlil for Marduk, my lord – so no future king should revoke my precious words, so no future matter should be brought up against my pronouncement, (I swore) by the life of Marduk, my lord, and Shamash, my god: "(Woe to me) if my words are not true but false." On that day I found a royal statue of (a king) who had gone before me, who had restored this wall, (so) I indeed placed it with my statue in a secure place in the great foundation platform for all eternity.

As noted by Beaulieu (2003: 308 n. 17), the oath formula is very similar to those used by the Sargonic kings (see Chapter 2, the Old Akkadian period texts, in this volume). It is therefore possible that the statue found by Nabopolassar contained the very oath that he is now taking. Unfortunately, we do not know the identity of the king whose statue he found.

The conclusion of this inscription is unique. Instead of a prayer it contains instructions to a future ruler, drawn from the Akkadian wisdom literature, particularly legends concerning the Sargonic king Naram-Sin.

To the king of the land – be he a son or a grandson – who follows me and whom Marduk calls for rulership of the land: You should not concern yourself with might and power. (Instead) seek out the shrines of Nabu and Marduk in your heart that they may slay your enemies. Marduk, the lord, keeps check of utterances and inspects the heart. The foundations of the one who is loyal to Bel (i.e., Marduk) will be firmly established. The one who is loyal to the son of Bel (i.e., Nabu) will last forever. When this wall grows old and you remove its decay, just as I found an inscription of a king who preceded me and did not alter its location, (so should you) find the inscription (bearing) my name and set it in the (same) place as your inscription. By the command of Marduk, the great lord, whose pronouncement cannot be changed, may the utterance of your name be established forever.

Bibliography

al-Rawi, F. N. J. "Nabopolassar's Restoration Work on the Wall Imgur-Enlil at Babylon." *Iraq* 47 (1985): 1–13 and pl. 1.

Beaulieu, P.-A. "Napopolassar's Restoration of Imgur-Enlil, the Inner Defensive Wall of Babylon." In COS 2: 307–8 no. 2.121.

Edzard, D. O. "Deep-Rooted Skyscrapers and Bricks: Ancient Mesopotamiam [*sic*] Architecture and Its Imagery." In *Figurative Language in the Ancient Near East*. Ed. M.

Mindlin, M. J. Geller, and J. E. Wansbrough. London: University of London, School of Oriental and African Studies, 1987, 13–24.
Ellis, R. S. *Foundation Deposits in Ancient Mesopotamia.* New Haven: Yale University Press, 1968.

B. Nebuchadnezzar II: 604–562 BCE (Studevent-Hickman)

Nebuchadnezzar II – hereafter Nebuchadnezzar – is by far the most famous Neo-Babylonian king. According to classical sources he is the architect of the "Hanging Gardens of Babylon" (one of the ancient wonders of the world), for which there is very little contemporary evidence. He is best-known for his destruction of the temple in Jerusalem and deportations of the Judean population (see, e.g., 2 Kgs 24–25). Together these represent one of the defining events of the biblical tradition; indeed, the Babylonian Exile fundamentally transformed the role of law and textual interpretation in ancient Jewish life.

The basic historicity of the biblical account is corroborated by native Babylonian sources. The similarities between 2 Kgs 24: 10–17 and the Neo-Babylonian Chronicle Series are quite remarkable. The latter places the siege of Jerusalem and the largest wave of deportations in Nebuchadnezzar's seventh regnal year. (See Arnold Chronicle 5 below.)

Judah had been a problem for the Babylonian kings for years, so the siege of Jerusalem was important enough to be the only event recorded for this year. The identifications of the deposed king and his replacement are not provided by the chronicler; however, from the biblical account the two may be identified as Jehoiachin and Mattaniah respectively, the latter renamed Zedekiah by Nebuchadnezzar (2 Kgs 24: 17). These identifications are secured by several Neo-Babylonian administrative texts.

144. Administrative texts from Babylon concerning King Jehoiachin of Judah

Among the thousands of administrative tablets from the Neo-Babylonian period are four texts discovered in the vaults of king Nebuchadnezzar's palace in Babylon (Weidner 1939: 924). These texts record disbursements of oil to captives from various nations. Among them are Jehoiachin, the exiled king of Judah; several members of his family (cf. 1 Chr 3: 17–18); and other functionaries from Jerusalem.

32 pints (15 liters) (of sesame oil) for Jehoiachin king of Judah
5 pints (2.5 liters) (of sesame oil) for [the 5] sons of the king of Judah
8 pints (4 liters) (of sesame oil) for 8 men of Judah: 1 pint (1/2 liter) each

Although not historical texts proper, these records are clearly indispensable for reconstructions of both Mesopotamian and biblical history. Without these texts we would have no extra-biblical evidence of Jehoiachin's life in exile – indeed, of his being in exile at all. Along with the others, Jehoiachin was clearly cared for by Nebuchadnezzar's administration. He receives 30 times as much oil as his sons and the "men of Judah"; this discrepancy has generated considerable discussion. Since, according to the Bible, Jehoiachin was 24 years old at the time,[7] some have suggested that his sons would have been very young and thus received considerably less. Others have argued that Jehoiachin received favorable status in Nebuchadnezzar's palace. It is impossible to resolve these issues with the evidence now available.

All other details concerning Jehoiachin's activities in exile are found exclusively in the Bible (see Berridge 1992: 663 for a list of attestations and discussion).

Bibliography

Berridge, J. M. "Jehoiachin." In *Anchor Bible Dictionary*. 6 vols. New York: Doubleday, 1992, 3: 661–3.

Weidner, E. F. "Jojachin, König von Juda, in Babylonischen Keischrifttexten." In *Mélanges Syriens offerts a Monsieur René Dussaud*. Vol. 2. Paris: P. Geuthner, 1939, 923–35.

145. The court and state document of Nebuchadnezzar II

One of the most remarkable texts from the Neo-Babylonian period is an eight-sided prism found in the central palace of Nebuchadnezzar. The only known example of a Neo-Babylonian prism, it summarizes the major renovations conducted during Nebuchadnezzar's reign and the establishment of cultic procedures for various deities. It dates to his seventh regnal year, the same year in which he took Jerusalem. The text has been restored extensively by Unger; his suggestions are followed for this translation.

As for the Ezida, I adorned its form.
As for Nabu and Nanaya,
in joy and celebration,
I made them dwell within it.
Daily, one fattened sacrificial bull, a blemishless bull,
(and) 16 choice sacrificial lambs,
for (the statues) of the gods of Borsippa;
an allocation of fish, fowl . . .
the finest from the marshland;
honey, butter, milk without fat,
beer, and pure wine;
at the offering table of Nabu and Nanaya,
my lords, I provided more lavishly than before.

The proper offerings for Nergal
and the goddess Laṣ, the gods of Emeslam, I established.
The regular provisions of the great gods I made abundant,
increasing their proper offerings from the earlier offerings.

A list of the temples that Nebuchadnezzar renovated follows. The entirety of these measures are summarized in a section that introduces Marduk, whose role in the establishment of the empire is made very clear. Extensive offerings to Marduk in his temple Esagila[8] are then listed, as is a brief note concerning the renovation of a fortifying wall around the palace. The section concludes with a prayer to Marduk.

I then raised my hand; to the lord of lords,
to Marduk, the merciful, my supplications went forth:
"O lord of the lands, Marduk, hear the utterance of my mouth!
Let me be fully content in my palace, which I built!
Let me reach old age within Babylon!
Let me enjoy a ripe old age!"

The most interesting aspect of this text, at least with respect to the Judean exile, is its conclusion. Immediately following the prayer to Marduk is a basic wish for the lands to undertake corvée labor for the building of Nebuchadnezzar's palace. The text provides a remarkable list of the officials "whom Nebuchadnezzar had commissioned" for his works, namely the high court officials, the "great ones of the land of Akkad (i.e., Babylonia)," and priests and governors from various cities. The first high court official listed is Nabu-zer-iddinam, the chancellor. He is the very Nebuzaradan who purportedly burned the entire city of Jerusalem and deported the remainder of the population when Zedekiah rebelled (see 2 Kgs 25: 8).

Direct matches with the biblical narrative, such as those offered here, are extremely rare. They provide an exciting insight into the ways each may be used for the reconstruction of history.

C. *Nabonidus: 556–539 BCE*

The last king of the Neo-Babylonian dynasty – indeed, the last ruler of an independent Mesopotamian state – was Nabonidus. Very little is known about his background, but his blatant exhaltation of the moon-god Sin, the patron deity of Ur, which included the installation of his daughter En-nigaldi-Nanna; his relationship to his mother; and his sojourn in the Arabian peninsula all make him an extremely colorful character in Mesopotamian history. He was clearly not related to Nabopolassar's dynasty but may have served as an official under these kings. He usurped the throne from Labaši-Marduk, the son of Neriglissar, in 556 BCE.

Bibliography

Unger, E. *Babylon: Die heilige Stadt nach der Beschreibung der Babylonier*. 2d ed. Berlin: De Gruyter, 1970.

146. The autobiography of Adad-guppi (Melville)

Adad-guppi was the mother of Nabonidus, the sixth and last king of the relatively short-lived Neo-Babylonian dynasty, which had been founded by Nabopolassar upon the expulsion of the Assyrians from Babylonia in 626 BC. The first two kings of the dynasty, Nabopolassar and Nebuchadnezzar II, established the Babylonian Empire, but were followed by a quick succession of three weak rulers, the last of whom, Labaši-Marduk, was deposed and presumably murdered in 556 BC after ruling a scant month. At this time, Nabonidus, who was not of royal descent, managed to seize the throne and garner enough support to keep it. As a usurper, Nabonidus needed both to establish himself as a *bona fide* Babylonian king in the eyes of his subjects, and also to justify his actions in theological terms. He could explain away his non-royal origins and usurpation by insisting that the gods chose him – a pious and just man – to reestablish a true Babylonian kingship because the ruling dynasty had become weak and irreverent. Many of Nabonidus' royal inscriptions are, therefore, "apologies," designed to represent him and his actions in the best possible light (Kurht 1994: 598). Although the Adad-guppi inscription is written in the first-person as an autobiographical account of her long, one hundred and four year life, there is little doubt that it was, in fact, composed *after* the remarkable lady's death. Therefore, it is in the context of Nabonidus' self-promotion (Longman 1991: 101; Beaulieu 1989: 209) that we must first consider the autobiography of Adad-guppi. The text is not only a thinly veiled political justification, however, but also functions as a didactic literary work, promulgating pious behavior and devotion to the gods, especially Sin.

Two fragmentary copies of the Adad-guppi text survive: Pognon published a first, badly preserved exemplar in 1907, and Gadd published a second, more complete copy in 1958. The text was originally inscribed on two stelae displayed at the temple of Sin in Harran, presumably to commemorate its rebuilding by Nabonidus, and it contains our most explicit information about Nabonidus' origins and family history. The beginning of the inscription includes an oblique reference to the destruction of Harran, the last Assyrian hold-out, in 610 BC: "In the sixteenth year of Nabopolassar, king of Babylon, Sin, king of the gods, became angry with his city and his temple and went up to heaven. The city and the people in it went to ruin." Since it was the Babylonians who sacked Harran and its temples, the author of our text tactfully omits mention of the human perpetrators, instead attributing the city's downfall to Sin, its patron deity, who abandoned his city in anger. According to this view, the city's sad state was the natural outcome of divine abandonment rather than the result of war. In the aftermath of Harran's ruin, Adad-guppi claims to have made every effort to maintain Sin's cult and to appease his anger. When the Ehulhul (the temple of Sin in Harran) was destroyed, it is likely that the statues of Sin and his coterie of gods (Ningal, Nusku, and Sardannunna) were removed to Babylon, the capital of the Neo-Babylonian dynasty,[9] and that among the spoils of war, Adad-guppi (and possibly her son) were also taken south at this time, though it is not clear in what capacity. It has often been assumed that Adad-guppi was the high priestess of Sin at the Ehulhul in Harran, but there is no evidence to support this, and the text itself only claims that she was a devotee of this god (Longman 1991: 98; Beaulieu 1989: 68–75).

If we follow the chronology included in the text and do a little math, we see that Adad-guppi was born in 649/648 BC and would have been at least 39 years old – therefore, almost certainly already a mother – when Harran was destroyed. She died in 547 BC (the ninth year of her son's reign) and so must have been a whopping 95 when he took the throne. Nabonidus himself would have been in his sixties when he became king – an old man by Mesopotamian reckoning. Adad-guppi's official position at the Babylonian court is never stated, nor is her husband identified, although several of Nabonidus' inscriptions identify him as someone named Nabu-balatsu-iqbi (possibly an Assyrian official in Harran?) (Beaulieu 1989: 68). According to our text, Adad-guppi served three Babylonian kings and was responsible for introducing her son to their service. Both mother and son were apparently favored by these kings, whom they served wholeheartedly. The text makes a point of Adad-guppi's pious attention to the kings' funerary cults, in spite of the negligence shown by their less worthy successors, Amel-Marduk and Labaši-Marduk. The emphasis on piety in Adad-guppi's autobiography serves two purposes: first, it validates Nabonidus' kingship through his mother and her relationship to Sin; second, it disseminates the social message that all people should revere the gods. Good behavior may be rewarded; Adad-guppi attained extreme old age because she earned it through devotion to her gods.

Over the course of his 17-year reign, Nabonidus made major theological changes, perhaps attempting to shift cultic prominence, and thereby political power, from Marduk (historically the head of the Babylonian pantheon) and his temple, to Sin. Scholars have struggled to interpret this huge change, but it seems most probable that Nabonidus was motivated by political expedience as well as religious belief. On the one hand, his mother had a long-standing connection to the god, at least as a lay-devotee, and may truly have passed on her reverence to her son. On the other hand, the Sin-connection provided Nabonidus with a convenient and completely fresh means to explain and promote his rule. Since Nabonidus usurped the throne, it was in his best interest to establish his own power base, and by promoting Sin and his cult, Nabonidus aimed to do just that. At the same time, it is probable that he actually recognized his good fortune as originating with his mother's personal god, Sin. According to Adad-guppi, she and Nabonidus promised to repay their success by (among other things) rebuilding the Ehulhul in Harran. In spite of the text's claim that Adad-guppi lived to see the reconstruction of the temple accomplished, other evidence indicates that the Ehulhul was not repaired until at least the fifteenth or sixteenth year of Nabonidus' reign, thus a good six or seven years after Adad-guppi's death (Beaulieu 1989). What appears to us as a glaring contradiction is nonetheless fully in keeping with Mesopotamian literary conventions and the royal practice of dating events to suit situational requirements.

In spite of the political, theological and moral lessons to be found in Adad-guppi's autobiography, there is little to evoke the woman herself, yet she could certainly claim to have achieved more than most. Having come from a modest (or at least non-royal) background, she eventually served in some official capacity at the Babylonian court, subsequently became queen mother, and managed to retain all her faculties into extreme old age. Reaching such a venerable age, while not unheard of in ancient Mesopotamia, would have been a rarity nonetheless. The indomitable Adad-guppi remains one of the only women in Mesopotamian history (as far as we know) to have received such public recognition.

I am Adad-guppi, mother of Nabonidus, king of Babylon, who reveres Sin, Ningal, Nusku and Sardannunna my gods, who from my childhood sought their divinity. In the sixteenth year of Nabopolassar, king of Babylon, Sin, king of the gods, became angry with his city and his temple and went up to heaven. The city and the people in it went to ruin. I sought after the shrines of Sin, Ningal, Nusku, and Sardanunna, worshiped their divinity and took hold of the robe of Sin, king of the gods. Night and day, all day without stopping, I continuously sought their great divinity, so that as long as I lived I was the devotee of Sin, Shamash, Ishtar, and Adad in heaven and earth. The good things that they gave to me I gave back to them day and night (for) months and years. I took hold of the robe of Sin, king of the gods, night and day my eyes were fixed on him. In prayers and veneration I bowed before them praying thus, "May your return to your city happen so that the black headed people may worship your great divinity." In order to calm the heart of my god and my goddess, I would not wear a fine wool dress, gold or silver jewelry, a new garment, nor would I let perfume or sweet oil touch my body, (but) I wore a torn garment and my clothing was sackcloth. I sang their praises; the veneration of my city and my goddess were established in my heart. I kept their watch; I did not leave out anything good that I could bring before them.

From the twentieth year of Ashurbanipal, king of Assyria, in which I was born, until the forty-second year of Ashurbanipal, the third year of Assur-etil-ilani, his son, the twenty-first year of Nabopolassar, the forty-third year of Nebuchadnezzar, the second year of Amel-Marduk, the fourth year of Neriglissar, for 95 years I kept seeking after the shrine of the great divinity of Sin, king of the gods of heaven and the netherworld. He looked happily on me (for) my good deeds. He heard my prayers, consented to my words, (and) the rage of his heart was appeased. To Ehulhul, the temple of Sin in the midst of Harran, his favorite dwelling, he became reconciled and decided to return. Sin, king of the gods, looked upon me and called Nabonidus, my only son, for the kingship. The kingship of Sumer and Akkad from the border of Egypt on the upper sea to the lower sea, all the lands he entrusted (to him). I lifted up my hand to Sin, king of the gods, reverently in prayer and prayed thus, "You called him to the kingship and you pronounced his name. By order of your great divinity, may the great gods go at his side, may they cause his enemies to fall. May you not forget Ehulhul and the completion of its perfect foundation." When in my dream, his hands were set on (me?), Sin, king of the gods, spoke thus to me, "With you, I will place the return of the gods and the habitation of Harran in the hands of Nabonidus, your son. He will build Ehulhul and he will complete its work. He will make Harran more perfect than it was before and he will restore it. He will grasp the hand of Sin, Ningal, Nusku, and Sardanuna and cause them to enter Ehulhul." The word of Sin, king of the gods, which he spoke to me, I paid heed to and I myself saw (it done). Nabonidus, my only son, my offspring made perfect the forgotten rites of Sin, Ningal, Nusku, and Sardanunna. He built anew Ehulhul and completed its fabric. Harran he made more perfect than it was before and he restored it. He took the hands of Sin, Ningal, Nusku, and Sardanunna from Babylon, his royal city and made them dwell in the midst of Harran, in Ehulhul, their favorite abode with joy and delight. What previously Sin, king of the gods, had not done and had not given to anyone, he did for love of me, who revered his divinity and seized the hem of his robe. Sin, king of the gods, raised my head and established for me a good reputation in the country. Long days, years of contentment he multiplied for me. From the time of Ashurbanipal, king of Assyria, until the ninth year of Nabonidus, king of Babylon, (my) son, my offspring, Sin, king of the gods, made me live one hundred and four good years in the awe which he set in my heart. I myself, the sight of my two eyes is sharp and my comprehension is excellent, my hands and feet are healthy and my words are well chosen, food and drink agree with me, I am in good health, my heart is full. My descendants to the fourth generation, I have witnessed their existence and I am replete with extreme old age. Sin, king of the gods, you looked upon me with favor and you have made my days long, (therefore) let me entrust (to you) Nabonidus, king of Babylon, my son. As long as he lives he shall not sin against you. Appoint to him the good protective spirits that you appointed to me and who caused me to attain old age, and do not tolerate sin and transgression against your great divinity, but may he revere your great divinity.

During the 21 years, the 43 years, and the 4 years in which Nabopolassar, king of Babylon, Nebuchadnezzar, the son of Nabopolassar, and Neriglissar, king of Babylon, ruled; during the 68 years I behaved respectfully towards them and I served them. I introduced Nabonidus, (my) son, my offspring to Nebuchadnezzar, son of Nabopolassar, and Neriglissar, king of Babylon. Day and night he served them and did whatever made them happy. He established my good name before them and they promoted me as if I had been their daughter, their (own) offspring.

Later they (Nabopolassar, Nebuchadnezzar and Neriglissar) died. No one among their sons and no one among their people or their nobles, whose goods and properties they increased when they promoted them, established incense offerings for them. I, every month without stopping, (wearing) my good clothes, made for them all the funerary offerings: [. . .], fattened sheep, bread, high quality beer, [. . .], oil, honey, and fruit, and I fixed for them regular, sweet-scented, luxuriant offerings and continuously set them before them.

(The last part of the text, which is very fragmentary, describes Adad-guppi's funeral and ends with an exhortation to future readers. Possible restorations are in brackets.)

In the ninth year of Nabonidus, king of Babylon, she died (lit. went to her own fate) and Nabonidus, king of Babylon, (her) son, her offspring . . . interred her body . . . fine [garments], a . . . mantle, gold, fine ṣtones, [valuable] stones, precious stones, fine oil, her body . . . they put in a hidden place. He slaughtered fattened sheep before it. He assembled [the people] of Babylon, Borsippa with [the people] living in distant areas, [kings, princes], and governors from [the border] of Egypt, the Upper Sea, to the Lower Sea. He [had them] mourn and . . . they made lamentation. They cast [dust?] on their heads for 7 days and 7 nights; they murmured; their clothes were cast off. On the seventh day, the people of the entire land cut their hair. Their clothes . . . their clothes boxes in their places(?) . . . in a meal . . . He accumulated filtered perfumes. He poured fine oil on [their] heads. He caused their hearts to rejoice, he made their minds . . . They went back to their homes.

You, whether a king or a prince . . . Sin, king of [the gods], lord of the gods of heaven and earth . . . Day and night (seek) his great divinity. Shamash, Adad, and Ishtar, lords [of heaven and earth] who . . . the ones who dwell in Esagila and [Ehulhul] . . . and pray (to the gods) in heaven and earth . . . the command of Sin and Ishtar, the one who saves . . . keep your descendants safe [forever and ever].

Bibliography

The two exemplars of the Adad-guppi text are published in H. Pognon, *Inscriptions sémitique de la Syrie, de la Mésopotamie, ed de la region de Mossoul* (Paris: Gabalda, 1907); and C. J. Gadd, "The Harran Inscriptions of Nabonidus," *Anatolian Studies* 8 (1958): 35–92. For other translations of the text and/or further discussion of Adad-guppi, see E. Dhorme, "La mère de Nabonide," *Revue d'Assyriologie* 41 (1947): 1–22; A. L. Oppenheim, "The Mother of Nabonidus," in ANET, 104–8; Paul-Alain Beaulieu, *The Reign of Nabonidus King of Babylon 556–539* BC (New Haven: Yale University Press, 1989); Tremper Longman III, *Fictional Akkadian Autobiography* (Winona Lake, Ind.: Eisenbrauns, 1991), 97–103 (commentary), 225–7 (translation); and (in Italian) F. D'Agostino, *Nabonid, Adda Guppi, il deserto e il Dio luna: storia, ideologia e propaganda nella Babilonia del 6.sec. a.C.* (Pisa: Giardini, 1994).

147. The installation of En-nigaldi-Nanna, daughter of Nabonidus, as high priestess of Nanna at Ur (Studevent-Hickman)

In conjunction with Nabonidus' exhaltation of Sin came a major religious and political move. In the second half of his second regnal year, Nabonidus renovated the Egipar, the residential quarters of the *entu*-priestess of Nanna in Ur, and installed his daughter En-nigaldi-Nanna in the office. The procedure, specifically the latter step, is most often associated with Sargon, the founder of the Akkadian empire, who installed his daughter En-hedu-ana to the same position (*History* 62). However, *entu*-priestesses are attested as late as the Post-Kassite period, suggesting that at least the office was perpetuated whenever possible.

The installation of En-nigaldi-Nanna took place in the second half of Nabonidus' second regnal year. Of particular interest is the use of provoked and unprovoked omens in the process. The inscription, interestingly enough, skips the royal titulary and goes directly to the setting.

> *When Nanna desired an entu-priestess, the son of the prince (i.e., Nanna) revealed his sign (to) the world. Namra-ṣit*[10] *made manifest his firm decision; to Nabonidus, the king of Babylon, caretaker of the Esagila and the Ezida, the reverent shepherd, who continually seeks out the sanctuaries of the great gods; Nanna, the lord of the tiara, who bears the portent for the inhabited world, made his sign known. Because of the desire for an entu-priestess, in the month of Ululu, on the thirteenth day of the month "the work of the goddesses,"*[11] *the Fruit (i.e., Nanna) was eclipsed and set while eclipsed. "Sin desires an entu-priestess" was thus his sign and decision.*

The eclipse of the moon described here is critical to the date of the event and the chronology of Nabonidus' reign in general. It took place on September 26, 554 BCE (hence the latter half of the year).[12] The meaning of the eclipse was either supplied or confirmed by the omen series *Enuma Anu Enlil*, but not without considerable discussion between Nabonidus and the scholars of his day.[13] Suffice it to say that the installation of En-nigaldi-Nanna met with some opposition, so Nabonidus was quick to confirm Nanna's request.

> *I, Nabonidus, the shepherd, the one who worships him (lit. "his divinity"), did revere his firm command and become attentive. Because of the desire for an entu-priestess I sought out the sanctuaries of Shamash and Adad, the lords of divination (i.e., extispicy), and Shamash and Adad answered me with a firm "yes". In my divination they wrote a favorable omen,*[14] *an omen (concerning) the desire for an entu-priestesses, the desire of the gods. I repeated (the inquiry) and checked the message, and they answered me with an omen more favorable than before.*
>
> *I (then) performed an omen concerning the daughters of my relatives, but they answered me with a no. A third time I made an extispicy concerning a daughter of my (own) issue, and they answered me with a favorable omen.*[15] *I was attentive to the word of Sin, the exhalted lord, the god who fashioned me, and the command of Shamash and Adad, the lords of divination, and installed a daughter of my own issue in the office of high priestess and named her En-nigaldi-Nanna.*

Just as Nabopolassar discovered a statue of an Akkadian king during his restoration of Imgur-Enlil (see above), Nabonidus discovered several artifacts during his restoration of the Egipar. Yet, again, the objects prove both informative and appropriate for the task at hand.[16]

> *Since the rites of the entu-priestess were forgotten a long time ago and their (lit. "its") application was not known, I sought counsel daily. The appointed time arrived and the gates were opened to me.*[17] *I discovered an old stele of Nebuchadnezzar (I), son*

of Ninurta-nadin-shumi, a former king, which had an image of the entu-priestess fashioned on it. Moreover, her insignia, her clothing, and her jewelry were recorded[18] *(on it) and brought (these texts) into the Egipar. I brought out the ancient tablets and writing boards and restored the panels as they were (restored) in the past.*[19] *I fashioned a stele, her insignia, and the utensils of her residence anew. I inscribed it (lit. "wrote on it") and set it up before Sin and Ningal, my lords.*

The passage has several linguistic difficulties, but the general sense is clear. A more comprehensive account of the Egipar's condition before its restoration follows.

At that time the area of the luxurious foundation in the midst of the Egipar, the pure cella, the place of the rites of the office of high priestess, had become a heap of ruins. Wild date palms (and) a fruit orchard were growing in its midst. I cleared the trees and removed the dirt that had collected.[20] *I looked over the structure and discovered its foundation platform. I looked at the writing of the names of the kings of the ancient past in its midst. I looked at an old inscription of En-ane-du, the entu-priestess of Ur, the daughter of Kudur-Mabuk, the sister of Rim-Sin, the king of Ur, who renovated the Egipar and restored it, who surrounded with a wall the resting place of the ancient entu-priestesses alongside the Egipar. (Thus) I built the Egipar anew as (it was) in the past.*

The text then goes on to iterate the consecration of Nabonidus' daughter and the extensive increase of offerings to Sin and Ningal (cf. the text of Nebuchadnezzar above). The section is indeed valuable, for it mentions the offices associated with the the household. It is important to remember that temple households in Mesopotamia were economic households as well. It also reminds us that the Egipar was part of a larger structure, the Egishnugal, the temple of Nanna in Ur.

The text concludes with a typical prayer.

May Sin, the gleaming deity, the lord of the tiara, the light of humankind, the exhalted god, whose utterance is true rejoice in my accomplishments and love my kingship. May he grant me a lasting life and ripe old age as a gift. Let him raise no one to rival me. With each new month may propitious signs be revealed. May the crown of kingship remain firmly on my head forever. Establish the throne of my lordship for days to come. When you renew yourself each month let me let repeatedly see your propiscious sign. May Ningal, the exhalted mistress, speak well of me before you. May En-nigaldi-Nanna, (my) daughter, the beloved of my heart, come before you that her utterance may be true. May her deeds be pleasing; she will be a true entu-priestess. May she have no sin.

Bibliography

Beaulieu, P.-A. *The Reign of Nabonidus, King of Babylon 556–539* BC. Yale Near Eastern Researches 10. New Haven: Yale University Press, 1989.

Clay, A. T. *Miscellaneous Inscriptions in the Yale Babylonian Collection.* Yale Oriental Series 1. New Haven: Yale University Press, 1915.
Lewy, H. "The Babylonian Background of the Kay Kaûs Legend." *Archiv Orientalni* 17 (1949): 28–109.
Reiner, E. *Your Thwarts in Pieces, Your Mooring Rope Cut: Poetry from Babylonia and Assyria.* Ann Arbor: Horace H. Rackham School of Graduate Studies at the University of Michigan, 1985, 2–5 (cf. 1–16).
Schaudig, H. *Die Inschriften Nabonids von Babylon und Kyros' des Großen.* AOAT 256, Münster: Ugarit-Verlag, 2001, 373–7.

II. Syro-Palestinian Documents

148. Samaria Ostraca (Noegel)

A total of 102 ostraca (inscribed potsherds) have been discovered at Samaria (modern Sabaste), the northern capital of ancient Israel (ca. 870–722 BCE), most of them during G. Reisner's excavations in 1910. The archaeological context in which they were found and paleographic analysis of the Hebrew script in which they were written suggest that they date to the second quarter of the eighth century BCE (Kaufman 1982: 231–4), thus roughly 50 years before the Assyrian destruction of the city. Of the 102 ostraca, only 63 are legible enough to provide useful information.

The documents are of two basic types, but both types appear to have been written in Samaria in roughly the same period, and both served as means of recording the transmission of luxury goods. The first type contains the date of the shipment based on the king's reign (invariably years 9 or 10), the clan or district from which it came, the person or persons to whom it was intended, and the item that was transmitted. There is some variation in this group in terms of the number of goods or people named or the order in which the information appears, but all ostraca contain the same basic elements. A few examples include:

In the ninth year (of the king): from (the district of) Qosah, to Gediyahu: a jar of aged wine. (Ostracon 6)

In the tenth year (of the king): from (the district of) Seper, to Gediyahu: a jar of fine oil. (Ostracon 16a)

In the tenth year (of the king): to Shemaryahu, from (the district) of Be'erayim: a jar of aged [wine]. Raga' (son of) Elisha' – 2, 'Uzza (son of) Qadbes – 1, 'Eliba' – 1. (Ostracon 1)

The second group of ostraca also begins with the date (invariably year 15 of the king), but adds the clan from which the item came, the person to whom the item is intended (often with a patronymic), a second personal name, and the name of the town within the clan or district. Another important feature that distinguishes this group, though undetectable in translation, is its method of dating, which employs a hieratic numerical system developed first in Egypt. Two examples of the second group include:

> *In the fifteenth year (of the king): from (the district of) Heleq to 'Asa' (son of) 'Ahimelekh, Heles from (the district of) Haserot. (Ostracon 22)*
>
> *In the fifteenth year (of the king): from (the district of) Shemyada' to Heles (son of 'Epsah), Ba'ala' (son of) Zakkur (Ostracon 31a)*

The differences between the two groups of ostraca and the ambiguities inherent in such brief documents make it difficult for scholars to attribute to them a precise function. Scholars concur that the ostraca served as an accounting system, but there is some disagreement concerning the role of the individuals named on the dockets. Three different theories have been proposed. The first sees the individuals as officials or land owners who had been given land from the king, and who were sending the produce from these lands to Samaria as a form of in-kind tax. This view rests on reading the arguably ambiguous preposition preceding the person's name (Hebrew *le-*) as "from" or "to be credited to." The second theory understands the individuals named on the ostraca as tax officials "to" whom the merchandise was delivered as a form of in-kind tax. The third view sees the figures on the documents as important officials or nobles resident at Samaria who were providing for their own subsistence at the royal court from fields and vineyards they had received from the king. In essence they were "eating at the king's table," to use a biblical idiom (e.g., 1 Sam 8: 14; 22: 7; 2 Sam 9: 9–10; 1 Kgs 18: 19).

Of the three theories, the last has received the widest acceptance. It also makes sense given the types of fine products mentioned in the document, such as aged wines and body oil, which befit the niceties of a courtier's lifestyle. Judging by the words of the Israelite prophet Amos, a contemporary of the ostraca, these luxury goods must have appeared to the average Israelite as the extravagance of the idle rich (Amos 6: 4–6).

In addition to providing insights into such biblical texts, the ostraca provide scholars with a great deal of information on Israelite topography, clan systems, methods of distribution, and administrative practices. The topographical data they contain constitute the largest number of Israelite place names found outside the Bible, and are invaluable for locating a number of cities surrounding Samaria, some of which appear in the Bible. All of the clan names given in the second group of ostraca belong to the tribe of Manasseh. That all but one of them appear in clan lists found in the Bible (Num 26: 29–34; Josh 17: 2–3) demonstrates the longevity of ancient tribal divisions and their administrative purposes.

The amounts of oil and wine delivered and the amounts received by the people named in the documents also suggest that the ostraca represent the transactions of at least three different socio-economic classes.

Insight into ancient scribal practices comes from the ostraca as well. It is of note that typically the ostraca that document the transmission of oil were written on gray ware while those documenting the arrival of wine were written on red ware. This suggests a method of sorting the documents based on their appearance; probably a device for facilitating organization.

As valuable as such information is, however, it does not help a great deal in elucidating the most significant problem posed by the ostraca; namely, their precise date. Unfortunately for us, the documents never name the king because the scribes who wrote them took this information for granted. The archaeological and paleographic evidence suggests the second quarter of the eighth century BCE, but there are several Israelite kings who fit into this period, and the chronology of the Israelite kings generally is much debated. Moreover, though the existence of two distinct groups of ostraca at Samaria could be interpreted as representing a change in administration, and thus be attributed to two different kings, they could just as well represent an administrative change during a single reign. In addition, one of the ostraca (n. 63) provides the longest reign mentioned in the documents, but the hieratic numerical system employed to write it has been variously interpreted as 12, 14, 16, and 17. One cannot use it, therefore, to narrow the field of possible kings whose reigns lasted at least 17 years.

The inability to offer a more precise date for the dockets has led to a number of widely divergent proposals concerning which king or kings are referenced in them (e.g., Maisler 1948; Yadin 1961; and Shea 1977). Despite a plethora of proposals, two primary theories have emerged.

The first is based on what is felt to be a paleographic consistency between the two groups of documents, and on an interpretation of the archaeological data (both groups of ostraca were found mixed together in the same spot). This theory holds that both groups of ostraca date to the reign of Jeroboam II.

The second theory, is really a set of two related theories, each of which has in common the recognition that Israelite kings sometimes placed their sons on the throne as co-regents. They also share the view that the two groups of ostraca represent a change in administration brought about by the co-regency. The two theories in this group diverge, however, when it comes to the specific kings who served as co-regents, whether Jehoahaz and Jehoash, or Joash and Jeroboam II.

Of the two theories, the second appear to have become scholarly consensus. It attributes the first group of documents (referencing years 9 and 10) to Jeroboam II (793–752 BCE), and the second group (referencing year 15) to the reign of his father Joash (798–782 BCE). It adopts a well-established chronological reconstruction, and calculates that, according to the biblical text, Joash had installed his son Jeroboam II as co-regent in 793 BCE just before the battle against Amaziah of Judah at Beth-Shemesh (2 Kgs 14: 11–14; 2 Chr 25: 21–4). This places the date of first group of ostraca at 785/784 (year 9) and 784/783 (year 10 of Jeroboam II), and the second group at 783/782 (year 15 of Joash). Since the first group of ostraca contains no clan names associated with the Manasseh tribe, the change in administrative practice is taken to suggest that when Jeroboam II came to the throne that he went outside the traditional clan distribution system when allotting land to his courtiers. As intriguing as these suggestions are, they are nevertheless unprovable, and until further evidence comes to light, it will perhaps be most useful merely to recognize the likelihood that at least some of the Samaria Ostraca date to the reign of Jeroboam II.

Bibliography

Aharoni, Y. 1962. "The Samaria Ostraca – An Additional Note." *Israel Exploration Journal* 12: 67–9.

Israel, Felice. 1975. "L'olio da Toeletta Negli Ostraca di Samaria." *Rivista degli studi Orientali* 49: 17–20.

Kaufman, Ivan T. 1966. "The Samaria Ostraca. A Study in Ancient Hebrew Paleography. Texts and Plates." Unpublished doctoral dissertation; Cambridge, Mass.: Harvard University.

——. 1982. "The Samaria Ostraca: An Early Witness to Hebrew Writing." *Biblical Archaeologist* 45: 229–39.

Maisler (Mazar), B. 1948. "The Historical Background of the Samaria Ostraca." *Journal of the Palestine Oriental Society* 21: 117–33.

O'Doherty, E. 1953. "The Date of the Ostraca of Samaria." *Catholic Biblical Quarterly* 15: 24–9.

Poulter, A. J. and G. I. Davies. 1990. "The Samaria Ostraca: Two Onomastic Notes." *Vetus Testamentum* 40: 237–40.

Rainey, A. F. 1962. "Administration in Ugarit and the Samaria Ostraca." *Israel Exploration Journal* 12: 62–3.

——. 1970. "Semantic Parallels to the Samaria Ostraca." *Palestine Exploration Quarterly* 102: 45–51.

——. 1967. "The Samaria Ostraca in the Light of Fresh Evidence." *Palestine Exploration Quarterly* 99: 32–41.

——. 1979. "The *Sitz im Leben* of the Samaria Ostraca." *Tel Aviv* 6: 91–4.

——. 1988. "Towards a Precise Date for the Samaria Ostraca." *Bulletin of the Schools of Oriental Research* 272: 69–74.

Rosen, Baruch. 1986–7. "Wine and Oil Allocations in the Samaria Ostraca." *Tel Aviv* 13–14: 39–45.

Sasson, Victor. 1981. "Šmn Rḥṣ in the Samaria Ostraca." *Journal of Semitic Studies* 26: 1–5.

Shea, William H., 1977. "The Date and Significance of the Samaria Ostraca." *Israel Exploration Journal* 27: 16–27.

——. 1985. "Israelite Chronology and the Samaria Ostraca." *Zeitschrift des Deutschen Paleastina-Vereins* 10: 9–20.

Yadin, Y. 1959. "Recipients or Owners: A Note on the Samaria Ostraca." *Israel Exploration Journal* 9: 184–7.

——. 1959–60. "Tax-Payers or Tax-Collectors (On the Problem of the *Lamed* in the Samaria Ostraca)." *Bulletin of the Jewish Palestine Exploration Society* 24: 17–21. (Hebrew)

——. 1961. "Ancient Judaean Weights and the Date of the Samaria Ostraca." *Scripta Hierosolymitana* 8: 9–25.

——. 1962. "A Further Note on the Samaria Ostraca." *Israel Exploration Journal* 12: 64–6.
——. 1968. "A Further Note on the *Lamed* in the Samaria Ostraca." *Israel Exploration Journal* 18: 50–1.

149. Lachish Ostraca (Noegel)

This collection of 22 inscribed postsherds (ostraca) were discovered between 1935 and 1938 at Tell ed-Duweir,[21] a site that most scholars have identified as ancient Lachish, an Israelite military outpost west of Jerusalem. Two of the ostraca contain lists of names, perhaps of those entering the gates of Lachish, and some of them refer to food rations. The most significant among them, however, are 12 letters, several of which are too fragmentary to provide useful historical information.

Though the ostraca were not the only inscriptions discovered at the site, nor the last to be discovered there, they are among the most important. At the time of their discovery they represented the only Hebrew inscriptions that antedated the exilic period, hence their early publication received immediate attention. Though the ostraca no longer hold this distinction, they are still valuable for the light they shed on the classical Hebrew language and its grammar and epistolary formulae, as well as on Israelite military history, administration, and intelligence. Based on archaeological and internal data found in the ostraca, scholars date them to the early summer of 589 CE, thus, just three years before the Babylonian destruction of Jerusalem.

It is debated whether the letters represent copies of originals that were sent to Jerusalem or elsewhere from Lachish. The letters preserve the military correspondence between an individual of higher rank (named Yaush), presumably the commander of Lachish, and one of lower rank (named Hoshiyahu), who was apparently stationed not far from Lachish. It is unclear, however, whether Yaush is the intended recipient of all the letters, or if Hoshiyahu initiated all of them. Sixteen of the letters were found in a room located in the city's entrance gate, where the military headquarters was stationed, and five of these were stored in the same vessel. Nevertheless, many of the ostraca appeared to have been authored by different hands. What is clear, however, is that all of them were written over a relatively short period of time.

It is difficult to reconstruct a single historical context for the letters based on such a limited sample, especially since they were discovered alongside hundreds of other potsherds, which may or may not have originally contained letters. Nevertheless, one can glean something of their original context from clues in the letters themselves. One learns, for example, that the Babylonian invasion of Judah had not yet begun since one could travel in some safety from Lachish to Jerusalem, and harvesting crops in the Lachish's environs was still possible. Thus one letter concludes:

> *May Yahweh allow my lord to witness a good harvest today. Is Ṭobiyahu going to send royal grain to your servant? (Ostracon 5)*

Communication between cities also appears unhindered. Indeed, letters appear to have been received at Lachish on a daily basis, as we see in the following letter.

> *May Yahweh let my lord hear a report of well being and [goodness].*[22] *[And] now, supply ten bread-loaves and two (measures) of w[in]e. Return word [to] your servant by the hand of Shelemyahu concerning that which we should do tomorrow. (Ostracon 9)*

Despite the ability to carry out daily activities, the threat of Babylon was certainly looming on the horizon for one letter tells us that a smoke signal system was being tested, much like those found in the Bible (e.g., Jer 6: 1; Judg 20: 38; 20: 40).

> *May Yahwe[h] let my l[ord] hear a good report at this very moment!*[23] *And now according to all (the orders) that my lord sent, so has your servant done. I have written on a writing board according to all that [you] sen[t m]e to do. Regarding that which my lord sent concerning the matter of Beth-Haraphid: there is no one there. Concerning Semakyahu–Shemayahu has seized him and has taken him up to the city (i.e., Jerusalem). And (as for) your servant, I cannot send the witness there [. . .], unless he [comes (to you)] with the morning (inspection) round. One will (then) know that we are observing the smoke signals of Lachish according to the codes that my lord gave us, for the code of Azekah has (indeed) not been seen.*[24] *(Ostracon 4)*

The orders received by the subordinate infer a previous context that makes any reconstruction of events impossible. The place Beth-Harapid is unknown and one cannot tell if the words "no one there" refer to a specific group mentioned in his original orders (now lost to us), or to the population of the city, perhaps in reference to an evacuation or invasion. As for Semakyahu and Shemayahu; we have no idea who they were, or why the latter arrested the former. We are similarly ignorant as to why a witness would be required. Perhaps Semakyahu's crime was related in someway to the smoke-signal system; the witness appears to be. In any event, a legal proceeding was being arranged, but that is about all we can infer. The mention of the smoke signal system as an issue of serious concern, however, does suggest that tensions in Lachish were high.

Indeed, news of emerging political factions in Jerusalem had reached the military commander of Lachish, which he in turn relayed to one of his officers. Alarmed by the news, the officer wasted no time in alerting his superior to the damage that such news would cause to troop morale.

> *To my lord Yaush. May Yahweh cause my lord to see this moment (in) well being. Who is your servant (but) a dog,*[25] *that my lord has sent the king's [lett]er [and] the office[rs'] letters [say]ing "Please read (them)!"? And behold the words of the [officers] are not good! (They) weaken [your] hands and cause the hands of the m[en] to go sl[ack. And now] My lord, will you not write to them saying "Why are you doing this, and [in Jeru]salem?! Beh[ol]d [y]ou have done this thing against the king [and against*

his house]. As Yahweh your God lives, s[inc]e your servant read [the] letter[s], your serv[ant has had no peace]." (Ostracon 6)

This was not an imagined crisis, for Jerusalem was severely divided over whether to become a Babylonian vassal or to rebel and seek Egyptian help (Jer 38: 1–5) and the wrong decision would spell certain disaster. The soldiers knew, of course, that the cities and garrisons surrounding Jerusalem, like Lachish, would be the first to experience the disaster. Indeed, Egypt and Babylon were engaged in a colossal tug of war and the entire Levant was in the middle of it.

Just a few years earlier in 605 BCE, the Babylonians had defeated the Egyptian army in Syria at Carchemish and then again at Hamath. In 601 BCE the Babylonian king Nebuchadnezzar (604–562 BCE) brought his troops to the very border of Egypt. Though the battle that ensued forced Nebuchadnezzar to return home and regroup, the reprieve was only temporary. A year later he again entered the Levant, and by 597 had taken Jerusalem, deported its king (Jehoiachin) to Babylon, and installed a king of his own choosing over Jerusalem named Zedekiah (597–587). Nebuchadnezzar must have thought him a good choice because his brother Jehoahaz had been dethroned earlier by the Egyptian Pharaoh Neco II (610–595 BCE) who had held influence over Jerusalem at that time. In any event, Zedekiah's advisors and officers wielded considerably more power than he, and in 589 BCE they convinced him to withhold tribute from Babylon and side with Egypt (Jer 27: 8–11; 37: 6–8).[26]

It is in this context that another letter informs us of an Israelite military commander who was sent to Egypt, probably to obtain military support from Pharaoh Apries (589–570 BCE) in the imminent war against Babylon.

Your servant Hoshayahu has sent (this letter) to report to my lord Yaush: May Yahweh let my lord hear a report of well being and a report of goodness.

And now, please open the eye(s) of your servant as to (the purpose of) the letter that he sent to your servant last night, for the heart of your servant has been sick since you sent (it) to your servant. For my lord said: "You don't know how to read it!" As Yahweh lives, nobody has ever attempted to read for me a letter! And moreover, every letter that comes to me, when I have read it, afterwards I can repeat it (in) detail!

Now your servant has received (a report) saying (that) the military general Koniyahu son of ʿElnatan has gone down to enter Egypt. Concerning Hodavyahu son of ʿAhiyahu and his men, he has sent (word) to take them from here. And (as for) the letter of Ṭobiyahu,[27] servant of the king (that) came to Shallum son of Yadaʿ from the prophet[28] saying "Beware," your servant is sending it to my lord. (Ostracon 3)

Though the letter's contentious tone reflects something of its author's brusque, if not defensive, personality,[29] it also illustrates an authority structure weakened by the Babylonian crisis. Hoshayahu's defiant remarks to his superior border on insubordination. We are bereft of the context for Yaush's accusation of Hoshayahu's illiteracy, but it is difficult to take his reprimand literally, as Hoshayahu apparently took it. Perhaps Yaush was criticizing Hoshayahu for not grasping the intent of his words, that is, for not reading "between the lines." It is likely that the concluding content of the letter was also connected to Yaush's accusation, but one cannot tell in what way.

The identity of the unnamed prophet in this letter has intrigued scholars for some time. Some see him as the same figure referenced in Lachish Ostracon 16, a very poorly preserved letter: "[the le]tter of the sons of [-ya]hu the prophet [. . .]." The latter text informs us that the prophet's name ended with the element -yahu (a shortened form of Yahweh). This, in turn, has led some to identify him as one of the biblical prophets of the period whose names contain the same ending, especially Uriah (Jer 26: 20) or Jeremiah. However, as tantalizing as these identifications may appear, they are by no means certain. Indeed, the two prophets mentioned in the ostraca might be different individuals, and even if we possessed their entire names they might be unknown to us from the Bible. Nevertheless, it is still of general value to know that the words of prophets were taken seriously by the military elite of Lachish, either because they represented divinely sanctioned advice or unwanted interference in political affairs.

The ostraca unfortunately do not tell us more as to what transpired in Lachish before the Babylonian attack, but we can reconstruct some of the events from the Bible and from Nebuchadnezzar's own records. Relying on Egyptian support, as it turned out, was not wise. Though the Egyptian army did mount an attack against the Babylonians in the south, Nebuchadnezzar quickly routed them (Jer 34: 21; 37: 5–11), and by 588 BCE Nebuchadnezzar had possession of many of Judah's cities including Lachish (Jer 34: 6–7). In the heat of July of 587 BCE Jerusalem too was finally taken and reduced to ruins. King Zedekiah tried to flee Jerusalem but was captured near Jericho and dragged back to Riblah in Syria, where he was forced to watch the murder of his sons before being blinded (Jer 39: 1–9). He, his officials, and many other Jerusalemites then were taken to Babylon in fetters as exiles. One can only assume that the soldiers at Lachish experienced a similar grizzly fate.

Bibliography

Aharoni, Y. 1975. *Investigations at Lachish: The Sanctuary and the Residency (Lachish VI)*; Tel Aviv: Gateway Publishers. Pp. 22–4.

Albright, W. F. 1936. "A Supplement to Jeremiah: The Lachish Ostraca." *Bulletin of the Schools of Oriental Research* 61: 10–16.

——. 1938. "The Oldest Hebrew Letters: The Lachish Ostraca." *Bulletin of the Schools of Oriental Research* 70: 11–17.

Birnbaum, S. 1939. "The Lachish Ostraca." *Palestine Exploration Quarterly* 71: 20–8, 91–110.

Cross, F. M. 1956. "Lachish Letter IV." *Bulletin of the Schools of Oriental Research* 144: 24–6.

——. 1985. "A Literate Soldier: Lachish Letter III." In A. Kort and S. Morschauser, eds., *Biblical and Related Studies Presented to Samuel Iwry*. Winona Lake, Ind.: Eisenbrauns. Pp. 41–8.

Diringer, D. 1953. "Early Hebrew Inscriptions." In Olga Tuffnell, et al., eds. *The Iron Age (Lachish III)*. London: Oxford University Press. Pp. 331–59.

Dussaud, R. 1938. "Le prophète Jérémie et les lettres de Lakish." *Syria* 19: 256–71.

Ganor, N. R. 1967. "The Lachish Letters." *Palestine Exploration Quarterly* 99: 74–9.

Goldwasser, Orly. 1991. "An Egyptian Scribe from Lachish and the Hieratic Traditions of the Hebrew Kingdoms." *Tel Aviv* 18: 248–53.

Lemaire, A. 1976. "A Schoolboy's Exercise on an Ostracon at Lachish and the Hieratic Tradition of the Hebrew Kingdoms." *Tel Aviv* 3: 109–10.

Michaud, H. 1957. "Les Ostraca de Lakis conserves a London." *Syria* 34: 39–60.

Parker, S. B. 1994. "The Lachish Letters and Official Reactions to Prophecies." In L. M. Hopfe, ed., *Uncovering Ancient Stones. Essays in Memory of H. Neil Richardson*. Winona Lake, Ind.: Eisenbrauns.

Peuch, Émile. 1986–7. "The Canaanite Inscriptions of Lachish and Their Religious Background." *Tel Aviv* 13–14: 13–25.

Thomas, D. Winton. 1946. "Jerusalem in the Lachish Ostraca." *Palestine Exploration Quarterly* 78: 86–91.

Torczyner, H. (= Tur-Sinai). 1938. *The Lachish Letters. Lachish I.* London: Oxford University Press.

——. (= Tur-Sinai). 1940. *Lachish Ostraca: Letters from the Days of Jeremiah the Prophet.* Jerusalem: Jewish Palestine Exploration Society (republished in 1987 by the Bialik Institute and the Israel Exploration Society). (Hebrew)

Yadin, Y. 1981. "The Lachish Letters – Originals or Copies and Drafts?" In H. Shanks, ed., *Recent Archaeology in the Land of Israel.* Washington, DC: Biblical Archaeology Society. Pp. 179–86.

Notes

1 This description of Shazu (i.e., Marduk) follows the literal meaning of his name, composed of logograms for "heart" and "to know."

2 A protective deity or genius.

3 The Akkadian terms behind "adversaries" and "enemies" are largely synonymous, which makes it difficult to translate them precisely. Such phrases are common in Mesopotamian literature.

4 The term for corvée duty, one's basic work-obligation to the state in return for sustenance or parcels of land, uses the Akkadian word that can mean more specifically "carrying basket" or "brickmold."

5 As their name implies, foundation deposits were objects deposited in the foundations of monumental structures (see Ellis 1968), although the term has come to refer more generally to objects buried in walls or floors. A foundation deposit usually bears an inscription commemorating the project and an address to future kings who may discover it in the course of their own renovations. In the Neo-Babylonian period, these objects were generally cylinders such as the one bearing this inscription. Statues, tablets, and prisms were also used in ancient Mesopotamia.

6 The sentence may require a slight emendation to justify this translation. See Beaulieu in COS 2003: 308 n. 16 for discussion.

7 One of these administrative texts is dated to Nebuchadnezzar's thirteenth regnal year, which would place it 6 years after the siege of Jerusalem, when Jehoiachin was 18 years old (see 2 Kgs 24: 8).

8 The name means "house whose head is raised"; cf. Gen 11: 4.

9 The removal of cult statues after the sack of a city was customary. See, e.g., the many instances of this practice in the Neo-Assyrian Royal Inscriptions.

10 An epithet of Nanna, literally "Light Emission."

11 This phrase is a translation of the Sumerian name of the month.

12 H. Lewy "The Babylonian Background of the Kay Kaûs Legend." *Archiv Orientalni* 17 (1949): 50 n. 105, cited P.-A. Beaulieu "The Reign of Nabonidus King of Babylon 556–539 BC" (New Haven: Yale University Press, 1989: 23). The event is also placed in Nabonidus's second year by the Royal Chronicle, a text resembling the Neo-Babylonian Chronicle Series but dealing exclusively with this reign.

13 See Beaulieu 1989: 128–9 for discussion.

14 Literally "a favorable flesh," hence extispicy.

15 See previous note.

16 Citing other literature, Reiner considers the whole episode "fictitious, created solely for this purpose" (*Your Thwarts in Pieces, Your Mooring Rope Cut: Poetry from Babylonia and Assyria*. Ann Arbor: University of Michigan, 1985: 6). A discussion of the issue is beyond the scope of this translation.

17 The meaning of the phrase in this context is not entirely clear.

18 Lit. "they had written." Plural verbs with unspecified subjects are commonly used for passive construction in Akkadian.

19 Following Beaulieu 1989: 130 n. 36.

20 Lit. "the dust of its ruin heap."

21 One ostracon, probably not a letter, also was discovered in 1966. Four other inscriptions (not ostraca) found during the earlier excavation apparently did not appear in published form until Diringer. More inscriptions were discovered again in 1973. Other finds at Lachish include several Proto-Canaanite inscriptions, a number of seals and bullae (Y. Aharoni "The Samaria Ostraca – An Additional Note." *Israel Exploration Journal* 12, 1968: 165–7), an Aramaic inscription on an altar, and several Egyptian inscriptions.

22 Idiomatic for "the best possible news."

23 The frequent mention of the sacred name Yahweh in the letters suggests that the practice of substituting the title Adonai "Lord" for the name Yahweh, as is done in later Judaism, was not yet in place.

24 The final clause is often rendered "we cannot see Azeqah," or the like.

25 Addressing a figure of higher rank apparently required a protocol of self-abasement for the sender always refers to his superior as "lord" and himself as his "servant," sometimes even as a dog, as in this letter. The latter is an idiom attested in the Bible (e.g., 2 Sam 9: 8) and elsewhere in the ancient Near East.

26 Two jar inscriptions dating to the same level as the ostraca contain dates that most take as referring to the regnal years of Zedekiah.

27 It is unclear whether Ṭobiyahu is the same figure referenced in Ostracon 5 above.

28 Just how this letter was transmitted between the named individuals is ambiguous.

29 In the light of the charge of literary leveled at him by his superior, one wonders whether Hoshiyahu's expanded salutation ("May Yahweh let my lord hear a report of well being [*shalom*] and a report of goodness [*ṭob*]," is intended to show his mastery of the language by means of word plays on the names Shallum and Ṭobiyahu, who figure prominently in the text. As such Hoshiyahu's letter would constitute a rhetorical form of one upmanship.

13

Achaemenid Period Historical Texts Concerning Mesopotamia

Bill T. Arnold and Piotr Michalowski

I. The Neo-Babylonian Chronicle Series (Arnold)

These Babylonian chronicles provide most of the information we have on historical and military events in the Neo- and Late-Babylonian periods because we lack royal annals from Babylonia, such as we have among Neo-Assyrian sources. We have 15 tablets or fragments of Babylonian chronicles, which are conventionally divided into the Neo-Babylonian Chronicle Series (Chronicles 1–7) and the Late Babylonian Chronicle Series (Chronicles 8–13a). The first group is presented here in translation.[1]

We glean here a broad outline of the series of events, although the Series is far from complete and the information is often terse. The tradents who produced the Series were interested almost exclusively in Babylonia and the military exploits of the king. Besides reconstructing to some degree the broad outline of events in the period, the chronicles can sometimes be correlated to extra-Babylonian sources, especially events in the southern Levant; for example, the capture of Jerusalem in 597 BCE, and again in 587 BCE. It is often observed that the tradition that produced these texts represents the greatest achievement of the Babylonian historians when it comes to reliable and objective historiography.[2]

150. Chronicle 1[3]

The best copy we have of this chronicle was written in Babylon during the twenty-second year of Darius (500 BCE), as the colophon attests (iv 43). It chronicles events in Babylonia, Assyria, and Elam, from Nabu-nasir (747–734 BCE) to Shamash-shum-ukin (668–648 BCE). It covers a more comprehensive period of history than Chronicles 2–7, although in less detail.

After a broken beginning, this chronicle picks up with the accession year of Tiglath-pileser III and therefore illumines Assyro-Babylonian relations during the period. The text includes activities from a list of Babylonian rulers and usurpers during Tiglath-pileser's reign: Nabu-nasir, Nabu-nadin-zeri, Nabu-shuma-ukin II, and (Nabu)-Mukin-zeri. None is able to sustain success against him, and eventually he united the thrones and ruled Babylonia himself (i 19–23). After the interlude that was Shalmaneser V, Sargon II rose to the throne of Assyria, and the Babylonian throne returned to native hands in the person of Merodach-baladan II. The latter's 12-year reign is chronicled in some detail. Eventually Sargon drove him from Babylonia and resumed control of the royal city himself (ii 1–5). The chronicle records events from Sargon's rule, and after a gap in the text, his son and successor Sennacherib is on the throne. An extended portion of the chronicle is devoted to the rule of Sennacherib and his son, Ashur-nadin-shumi (ii 19–iii 38). There were intermittent Babylonian rulers during this time (Nergal-ushezib and Mushezib-Marduk), and a time when "there was no king in Babylon" (iii 28). The remainder of the chronicle covers the reign of the Assyrian monarch, Esarhaddon, and his son, Shamash-shum-ukin, who assumed the throne in Babylon while his brother ruled in Assyria.

(i1–8) . . . [Year 3: Nabu-nasir,] king of Babylon. Tiglath-pileser III ascended the throne in Assyria. That year, [the king of Assyria] went down to Akkad,[4] *plundered the cities Rabbilu and Hamranu, and took away the gods of Shapazza. At the time of Nabu-nasir, Borsippa rebelled against Babylon, but the campaign that Nabu-nasir conducted against Borsippa is not recorded.*

(i9–10) Year 5: Nabu-nasir. Humban-nikash I ascended the throne in Elam.

(i11–13) Year 14: Nabu-nasir became ill and died in his palace. Nabu-nasir exercised kingship in Babylon for 14 years. Then Nabu-nadin-zeri, his son, ascended the throne in Babylon.

(i14–18) Year 2: Nabu-nadin-zeri was killed in a rebellion. Nabu-nadin-zeri exercised kingship in Babylon for two years. Nabu-shuma-ukin II, provincial governor and chief of the rebellion, ascended the throne. Nabu-shuma-ukin exercised kingship in Babylon for one month and [x] days.[5] *Then Mukin-zeri,*[6] *son of Amukani,*[7] *deposed him and seized the throne.*

(i19–23) Year 3: Mukin-zeri. When Tiglath-pileser III went down to Akkad, he plundered Bit-Amukani and defeated Mukin-zeri. Mukin-zeri exercised kingship in Babylon for three years. Then Tiglath-pileser III ascended the throne in Babylon.

(i24–8) Year 2: Tiglath-pileser III died in the month of Tebet. Tiglath-pileser exercised kingship in Akkad and Assyria for <18> years.[8] *He exercised kingship for two years in Akkad itself. On the twenty-fifth day of the month of Tebet, Shalmaneser V ascended the throne in Assyria <and Akkad>. He plundered the city of Samaria.*[9]

(i29–32) Year 5: Shalmaneser V died in the month of Tebet. Shalmaneser V exercised kingship in Akkad and Assyria for five years. On the twelfth day of the month of Tebet, Sargon II ascended the throne in Assyria. In the month of Nisan, Merodach-baladan II ascended the throne in Babylon.

(i 33–7) Year 2: Merodach-baladan II. Humban-nikash I, king of Elam, conducted a campaign in the province of Der against Sargon II, king of Assyria. He put Assyria to flight,[10] *and inflicted a very great defeat on them. Merodach-baladan II and his*

forces, who had gone to the assistance of the king of Elam, did not reach the battle so he withdrew.

(i38–42) Year 5: Merodach-baladan II. Humban-nikash I, king of Elam, died. Humban-nikash I exercised kingship in Elam for 26(?)] years. [Shutruk-Nahhu]nte, his sister's son, ascended the throne in Elam. From the beginning of the kingship of Merodach-baladan II until the tenth year, [Assyria/Sargon] was hostile toward Merodach-baladan II.

(i43–4) Year 10: Merodach-baladan II destroyed Bit-[. . .], he plundered it.

(ii1–5) Year 12: Merodach-baladan II. Sargon II went down [to Akkad] and conducted a campaign against [Merodach-bala]dan II. Merodach-baladan II [took flight] before [him] and became a fugitive in Elam. Merodach-baladan II exercised kingship in Babylon for 12 years. Sargon II ascended the throne in Babylon.

(ii1′–2′)[11] *Year 13: Sargon II seized the hand of Bel (i.e., Marduk). He conquered Dur-Yakin.*

(ii3′) Year 14: The king stayed in the land (i.e., Babylonia).

(ii4′–5′) Year 15: On the twenty-second day of the month of Tishri, the gods of the Sea Land returned to their former places. There were plagues in the land of Assyria.

(ii6′) [Year 17(?): Sarg]on II [marched] to the land of Tabalu.

(broken text)

(ii19–23) He [Sennacherib(?)] did not scatter the Babylonians. He pursued(?) [Merodach-baladan II(?)] to the border, but Merodach-baladan II [. . .]. He [Sennacherib(?)] plundered his land. [. . .] The cities of Larak and Sarrabanu [. . .] When he withdrew, he (Sennacherib) placed Bel-ibni on the throne in Babylon.

(ii24–5) First year of Bel-ibni. Sennacherib destroyed the cities Hirimma and Hararatum.

(ii26–31) Third year of Bel-ibni. Sennacherib went down to Akkad and plundered Akkad. He took Bel-ibni and his overseers into exile in Assyria. Bel-ibni exercised kingship in Babylon for three years. Then Sennacherib placed Ashur-nadin-shumi, his son, on the throne in Babylon.

(ii32–5) First year of Ashur-nadin-shumi. With regard to Shutruk-Nahhunte II, king of Elam – Hallushu-Inshushinak I, his brother, seized him and imprisoned by him. Shutruk-Nahhunte II exercised kingship in Elam for 18 years. Then Hallushu-Inshushinak I, his brother, ascended the throne in Elam.

(ii36–45) Sixth year of Ashur-nadin-shumi. Sennacherib went down to the land of Elam and destroyed the cities of Nagitum, Hilmi, Pillatum and Hupapanu. He plundered them. Afterwards, Hallushu-Inshushinak I, king of Elam, went to the land of Akkad and entered Sippar at the end of the month of Tishri. He killed its people. Shamash did not come forth from E-babbar. Ashur-nadin-shumi was captured and taken away to Elam. Ashur-nadin-shumi exercised kingship in Babylon for six years. Then the king of Elam placed Nergal-ushezib on the throne in Babylon. He put Assyria to flight.

(ii46–iii 8) First year of Nergal-ushezib. On the sixteenth day of the month of Tammuz, Nergal-ushezib captured Nippur. He plundered it, and carried away the booty. On the first day of the month of Tishri, the army of Assyria entered Uruk. They plundered the gods of Uruk and its people. As for Nergal-ushezib – after the Elamites had come and taken away the gods of Uruk and its people[12] *– on the seventh day of the month of Tishri, he conducted a campaign against the army of Assyria in the province of Nippur. He was captured during pitched battle and led away to the land of Assyria. Nergal-ushezib exercised kingship in Babylon for one year (i.e., six months of*

a regnal year[13]). On the twenty-sixth day of the month of Tishri, the people of Hallushu-Inshushinak I, king of Elam, rose up against him. They imprisoned him and killed him. Hallushu-Inshushinak I exercised kingship in Elam for six years.

(iii9–12) Kudur-Nahhunte ascended the throne in Elam. Afterwards, Sennacherib went down to the land of Elam and destroyed it from the land of Rashi to Bit-Burnaki. He plundered it. Mushezib-Marduk ascended the throne in Babylon.

(iii13–18) First year of Mushezib-Marduk. On the seventeenth[14] day of the month of Ab, Kudur-Nahhunte, king of Elam, was captured during an insurrection and killed. Kudur-Nahhunte exercised kingship in Elam for 10 months. Humban-nimena ascended the throne in Elam. In a year not known, Humban-nimena called up the armed forces of Elam and Akkad, and conducted a campaign against the land of Assyria in the city of Halule. He put Assyria to flight.

(iii19–27) Year 4: Mushezib-Marduk. On the fifteenth day of the month of Nisan, Humban-nimena, king of Elam, was struck with paralysis and his mouth was so affected that he was unable to speak. In the month of Kislev, on the first day of the month, the city was captured. Mushezib-Marduk also was captured and taken away to Assyria. Mushezib-Marduk exercised kingship in Babylon for four years. In the month of Adar, on the seventh day of the month, Humban-nimena, king of Elam, died. Humban-nimena exercised kingship in Elam for four years. Then Humban-haltash I ascended the throne in Elam.

(iii28–38) During the eighth year, in which there was no king in Babylon, on the third day of the month of Tammuz, the gods of Uruk came from Elam to Uruk. In the month of Tishri, on the twenty-third day of the month, Humban-haltash I, king of Elam, was wounded at midday, and died at sunset. Humban-haltash I exercised kingship in Elam for eight years. Then Humban-haltash the second, his [son], ascended the throne. In the month of Tebet, on the twentieth day of the month, Sennacherib, king of Assyria, was killed by his son during an insurrection. Sennacherib exercised kingship in Assyria for [x] years. From the twentieth day of the month of Tebet until the second day of the month of Adar, insurrection continued in the land of Assyria. In the month of Adar, on the twenty-eighth[15] day of the month, Esarhaddon, his son, ascended the throne in Assyria.

(iii39–48) First year of Esarhaddon. When Nabu-zer-kitti-lishir, governor of the Sea Land, had gone upstream, he encamped against Ur, but he did not [capture] the city. He became a fugitive before the officials of Assyria and went to the land of Elam. In the land of Elam, the king of Elam captured him and killed him with weapons. In a month not known, the governor in Nippur . . . In the month of Elul, Ishtaran[16] and the gods [of Der] went [from . . .] to Der. [. . .] went to Dur-Sharrukin [. . .] In the month of Adar . . . [. . .] Second year: the palace supervisor . . . [. . .]

(iv1–2) [Third year. X-ahhe]-shullim, the governor of Nippur and [Shamash-ibni, son of Dakk]uri,[17] were led away to the land of Assyria, and in the land of Assyria, they were executed.

(iv3–4) Fourth year. The city of Sidon was captured and turned into booty. In that same year, the palace supervisor levied troops in the land of Akkad.

(iv5–8) Fifth year. On the second day of the month of Tishri, the army of Assyria captured Bazza. In the month of Tishri, the head of the king of Sidon was cut off and carried to the land of Assyria. In the month of Adar, the head of the king of Kundu and Sisu was cut off and carried to the land of Assyria.

(iv9–15) Sixth year. The king of Elam entered Sippar; a massacre ensued. Shamash did not come forth from E-babbar. The Assyrians <went> to the land of Milidu. On

the seventh day of the month of Elul, Humban-haltash II, king of Elam, died in his palace without becoming ill. Humban-haltash II exercised kingship in Elam for five years. Then Urtaki, his brother, ascended the throne in Elam. In a month not known, Shuma-iddina, the governor of Nippur and Kudurru, son of Dakkuri, were led away to Assyria.

(iv16–18) Seventh year. On the fifth day of the month of Adar, the army of Assyria was defeated in the land of Egypt. In the month of Adar, Ishtar of Akkad and the gods of Akkad came from the land of Elam and entered Akkad on the tenth day of the month of Adar.

(iv19–22) Eighth year of Esarhaddon. On the (text broken) day of the month of Tebet, the land of Shubria was captured and turned into booty. In the month of Kislev, its booty entered Uruk. On the fifth day of the month of Adar, the wife of the king died.

(iv23–8) Tenth year. In the month of Nisan, the army of Assyria went to Egypt. (text broken) Three times – the third, sixteenth, and eighteenth days of the month of Tammuz – a massacre ensued in Egypt.[18] *On the twenty-second day (of Tammuz), Memphis, the royal city, was captured and its king abandoned. His son and bro[ther were cap]tured.(?) (Memphis) was turned into booty; its people taken as plunder; and its property carried off.*

(iv29) Eleventh year. The king in Assyria killed his many officials with weapons.

(iv30–3) Twelfth year. The king of Assyria went to the land of Egypt. He became ill during the campaign and on the tenth day of the month of Arahsamni, he died. Esarhaddon exercised kingship in Assyria for 12 years. Then his two sons ascended the throne, Shamash-shum-ukin in Babylon and Ashurbanipal in Assyria.

(iv34–8) Accession year of Shamash-shum-ukin. In the month of Iyyar, Bel (i.e., Marduk) and the gods of Akkad came out from the city of Libbi-ali (i.e., Ashur), and on the fourteenth [or twenty-fourth(?)] day of the month of Iyyar, they entered Babylon. In that same year, the city of Kirbitu was ca[ptured] and its king defeated. On the twentieth day of the month of Tebet, Bel-etir, the judge of Babylon, was captured and killed.

(iv39–43) The first section was written according to its original, and checked and properly executed. Tablet of Ana-Bel-erish, son of Liblutu, son of Kalbi-Sin. Handwritting of Ea-nadin, son of Ana-Bel-erish, son of Kalbi-Sin. In Babylon, on the sixth[19] *[day of the month of x], the twenty-second year of Darius, king of Babylon and the lands.*

151. Chronicle 2[20]

The beginning of the chronicle is entirely lost, and the start of each line at the beginning of the text is also missing. Enough remains to illuminate more of the Assyro-Babylonian hostilities, ending eventually in Babylonian victory and the accession of Nabopolassar to the throne (14–17). However, hostilities continued between the two countries after he became king, with each inflicting inconclusive defeats upon the other (18–41).

(1–17) [. . .] . . . when he [they(?)] sent during the night [to] Babylon . . . they conducted a campaign against the city during the day. [. . .] of Sin-shar-ishkun became a fugitive in the land of Assyria. [. . .] he appointed officials for the city. On the twelfth day of the month of Elul, the army of Assyria entered [. . .] the city of Shaznaku. They burned the temple with fire.[21] *[. . .] in the month of Tishri, the gods of Kish came to Babylon. The [army of] Assyria came to Nippur, and Nabopolassar took flight*

before them. [The army of Assy]ria and the Nippurians followed after him as far as Uruk. At Uruk, they conducted a campaign against Nabopolassar but they took flight before Nabopolassar. In the month of Iyyar, the army of Assyria came down to the land of Akkad. On the twelfth day of the month of Tishri, the army of Assyria – when they had come toward Babylon – on that same day, the Babylonians came forth from Babylon. They conducted a campaign against the army of Assyria, and they inflicted a very great defeat on the army of Assyria. They plundered them. For one year there was no king in the land. On the twenty-sixth day of the month of Marchesvan, Nabopolassar ascended the throne in Babylon. Accession year of Nabopolassar. In the month of Adar, the gods of the land of Susa – which Assyria had brought and settled in Uruk – their gods Nabopolassar sent back to the city of Susa.

(18–24) First year of Nabopolassar. On the seventeenth day of the month of Nisan, terror fell on the city.[22] *Shamash and the gods of the city of Shapazzu went to Babylon. On the twenty-first day of the month of Iyyar, the army of Assyria entered the city of Sal[lat]. They brought out the possessions. On the twentieth day <of the month of Sivan or Tammuz(?)>*[23]*, the gods of Sippar went to Babylon. On the ninth day of the month of Ab, Nabopolassar and his army [went to the city of Sal]lat, and conducted a campaign against Sallat. He did not capture the city. Rather, the army of Assyria arrived, and he took flight before them and withdrew.*

(25–8) [Second year] of Nabopolassar. At the beginning of the month of Elul, the army of Assyria came down [to Akkad] and encamped by the Banitu Canal.[24] *They conducted a [campaign against Nabo]polassar, but they did not carry off anything. [. . .] and they withdrew.*

(29–41) [Third year.] On the eighth day [of the month . . .], Der rebelled against the land of Assyria. On the fifteenth day of the month of Tishri, [. . .] the king of Assyria and his army came down to Akkad, and . . . , and [stationed troops] in Nippur.[25] *Afterwards, Itti-ili [. . .] . . . and posted a garrison in Nippur. [. . .] he marched upstream*[26] *[against] the Transeuphrates (i.e., Syria) and against [. . .] he destroyed [. . .] and set his face towards Nineveh.*[27] *[. . .] . . . who had come for battle against him [. . . when] they saw him, they bowed down in submission before him. [. . .] . . . the rebel king [. . .] one hundred days [. . .] . . .*

152. Chronicle 3[28]

The chronicle covers events from Nabopolassar's tenth to his eighteenth years (616–609 BCE), including the fall of Nineveh. During the intervening years between the end of chronicle 2 and this one, the Babylonians have greatly increased in military strength. The campaigns of Nabopolassar now engaged the Assyrians further from the homeland and with increasing victory. Eventually they overcame the Assyrians within their own territories and together with Cyaxares the Mede, Nabopolassar participated in the capture of the Assyrian capital cities (16–30 and 38–52). This chronicle is important for the light it sheds on the fall of Assyria as well as the gradual rise of Babylonian military power.

(1–15) Tenth year of Nabopolassar. In the month of Iyyar, he called up the armed forces of the land of Akkad, and went to the bank of the Euphrates. The lands of Suhea and Hindanea did not conduct a campaign against him. Rather their gifts they

placed before him. In the month of Ab, the army of Assyria gathered at the city of Gablini, and Nabopolassar went upstream against them. On the twelfth day of the month of Ab, he conducted a campaign against the army of Assyria. The army of Assyria took flight before him, and he inflicted a very great defeat on Assyria. He plundered them thoroughly. They captured the land of Mannea, which had come to their help, and the officials of Assyria. On that same day, he captured the city of Gablini. In the month of Ab, the king of Akkad and his army went upstream to the cities of Mane, Sahiri, and Balihu. They plundered them. They carried off very much booty; they hauled off their gods. In the month of Elul, the king of Akkad and his army turned back. On his journey back, he also carried off the city of Hindanu and its gods to Babylon. In the month of Tishri, the army of Egypt and the army of Assyria pursued the king of Akkad as far as the city of Gablini, but they did not reach the king of Akkad, so they withdrew. In the month of Adar, the army of Assyria and the army of Akkad conducted a campaign against each other in the city of Madanu, that is Araphu. The army of Assyria took flight before the army of Akkad, and they[29] *inflicted a very great defeat on them. They drove them back to the Zab River. They captured their chariots and their horses. They plundered them thoroughly. [. . .] . . . they brought across the Tigris many things with them, and brought them into Babylon.*

(16–23) [Eleventh year. The king] of Akkad called up his army and went to the bank of the Tigris. In the month of Iyyar, he encamped against Baltil.[30] *[On the . . . day] of the month of Sivan, he conducted a campaign against the city, but he did not capture the city. Rather the king of Assyria called up his army and pushed the king of Akkad back from Baltil. Then he pursued him as far as the city of Takritain, a city which was on the bank of the Tigris [. . .]. The king of Akkad posted his army in the fortified outpost of Takritain. The king of Assyria and his army encamped against the army of the king of Akkad, which was posted in Takritain. For 10 days, he [the Assyrian king] conducted a campaign against them [the Babylonians], but he did not capture the city. The army of the king of Akkad, which he had posted in the fortified outpost inflicted a very great defeat upon Assyria. The king of Assyria and his army [withdrew(?)] and he returned to his land. In the month of Marchesvan, the land of Medes went down to the land of Arraphu and [. . .].*

(24–30) Twelfth year. In the month of Ab, the Medes, when [they had set out (?)] against Nineveh [. . .] they rushed quickly, and they captured the city of Tarbisu, a city of the province of Nineveh. [. . .], they came down to the [Tig]ris and encamped against Baltil. They conducted a campaign against the city, and [. . .] tore (it) down. They greatly defeated a mighty people. They plundered them, and carried away the booty. The king of Akkad and his army, who had gone out to the assistance of the Medes, did not reach the battlefield. The ci[ty . . .] . . . [The king of Akka]d and Cy[ax]ares[31] *met*[32] *one another beside the city. They established an alliance of good will and good relations [i.e., peace].*[33] *[Cyax]ares and his army returned to his land; the king of Akkad and his army returned to his land.*

(31–7) [Thirteenth year. In the month of Iy]yar, the land of the Suheans revolted against the king of Akkad, and acted with hostility. [The king of Akkad] called up his armed forces and went to Suhu. On the fourth day of the month of Sivan, he conducted a [campaign against] Rahilu, a city (on an island) in the middle of the Euphrates,[34] *and at that time, he captured the city. He built his [. . .] The men of the bank of the Euphrates came down to him. [. . .] he encamped against the city of Anati. The siege-tower [he brought over (?) from the op]posite bank on the west. [. . .] . . . he brought the siege-tower up to the city wall. He conducted a campaign*

against the [city,] and [captured it (?) . . . The king of] Assyria and his army came down, and the king of Akkad and his army . . . [. . .] . . .

(38–52) [Fourteenth year.] The king of Akkad called up his armed forces [and went to the land of xxx]. The king of the Umman-manda [came down (?)] towards the king of Akkad. . . . [. . .] . . . they met one another . . . the king of Akkad . . . [Cy]axares . . . brought across and they went to the bank of the Tigris, and . . . [they encamped] against Nineveh. From the month of Sivan until the month of Ab – for three [months . . .] – they conducted a rigorous campaign against the city. [On . . . day] of the month of Ab, [. . .] they inflicted a great [defeat upon] a mighty [people.] At that time, Sin-sharra-ishkun, king of As[syria . . .] . . . [. . .] . . . they carried away heavy spoils from the city and the temple. [They turned] the city into a ruin heap. [. . .] of Assyria escaped from the enemy, and . . . the king of Akkad . . . [. . .] On the twentieth day of the month of Elul, Cyaxares and his army returned to his land. Afterwards, the king of Akk[ad and his army(?)] went to the city of Nasibini. Plunder and exile . . . [. . .] and they brought [the people of (?)] the land of Rusapu before the king of Akkad in Nineveh. On [the . . . day of the mo]nth of [X . . . Ashur-uballit II] ascended the throne of kingship over Assyria in the city of Harran. Until the [. . . day of the] month [of . . .] in Nineveh, [. . .] from the twentieth day of the month of [. . .] the king of [. . .] took away, and in the city of [. . .].

(53–7) Fifteenth year. In the month of Tam[muz, the ki]ng of Akkad [called up his armed forces and . . .] went to the land of Assyria. [. . .] triumphantly [. . .] . . . of the land of . . . [. . .] and he conquered the land of Shu-[. . .]. They plundered them; they carried away heavy spoils. In the mon[th of Marchesv]an, the king of Akkad [took] the lead of his army and [went ag]ainst the land of Rug[gulitu(?)]. He conducted a campaign against the city and on the twenty-eighth day of the month of Marcheswan, he captured the city [. . .] . . . He did not [leave behind] a single man alive [. . .] He returned [to his land].

(58–65) Sixteenth year. In the month of Iyyar, the king of Akkad called up his armed forces and went to the land of Assyria. Fro[m the month of . . .] until the month of Marchesvan, they marched around triumphantly[35] *in the land of Assyria. In the month of Marchesvan, the land of Umman-mand[a, who had come to the assis]tance of the king of Akkad, joined their troops together and went to the land of Harran, [against Ashur-uballit II(?)], who had ascended the throne in the land of Assyria. As for Ashur-uballit II and the army of the land of Eg[ypt, who] had come [to his aid] – terror of the enemy fell upon them, and they gave up the city, and [. . .] crossed over. The king of Akkad reached the city of Harran and [. . .] captured the city. He carried away heavy spoils from the city and the temple. In the month of Adar, the king of Akkad abandoned their [. . .] and returned to his land. And the Umman-manda, who had come to the assistance of the king of Akkad, withdrew.*

(66–75) <Seventeenth year.> In the month of Tammuz, Ashur-uballit II, king of Assyria, the large army of Egypt [. . .] He crossed the river and went to the city of Harran in order to conquer it [. . . they cap]tured it. They defeated the garrison, which the king of Akkad had posted in it. When they defeated it, they encamped against the city of Harran. Until the month of Elul, they conducted a campaign against the city. They did not [carry off] anything, but neither did they withdraw. The king of Akkad went to the aid of his army, and [. . .] he went up to [the land] of Izalla, and [. . .] . . . the many towns of the mountains [. . .] burned their [. . .] with fire. At the same time, the army [of . . .] went as far as the province of the city of Urartu. In the land of [. . .] they plundered their [. . .]. The garrison, which the king [. . . had

posted inside it, he remo]ved,(?) and they went up to the city of [. . .] . . . the king of Akkad returned to his land.

(76–8) In the [eighteenth ye]ar, [during the month of El]ul, the king of Akkad called up his armed forces and [went . . .] . . .[36] *[Whoever] loves Nabu and Marduk, guard (this tablet); may it not be turned over to other hands!*

153. Chronicle 4[37]

The chronicle covers events from later in Nabopolassar's reign (608–606 BCE), picking up where chronicle 3 ended (notice the catch-line at the end of 3 and beginning of 4). These years saw the Babylonian armies conducting campaigns in Urartu and regions in the northern Euphrates. In Nabopolassar's nineteenth year, the Babylonian army is divided into two, with the crown prince, Nebuchadnezzar II leading one and his father leading the other (5–15). However, Nabopolassar soon returned home and left Nebuchadnezzar to win his own victories on the field of battle.

(1–4) Eighteenth year of Nabopolassar. In the month of Elul, the king of Akkad called up his armed forces, and went down to the bank of the Tigris and to the mountain of Bit-Hanunya, in the province of Urartu. He burned the cities with fire; he plundered them thoroughly. In the month of Tebet, the king of Akkad returned to his land.

(5–15) Nineteenth year. In the month of Sivan, the king of Akkad called up his armed forces and Nebuchadnezzar – his eldest son, the prince of the crown-prince's palace[38] *– also called up his armed forces, and they went to the mountains of the land of Za-[. . .]. The king of Akkad left the prince and the army behind in the country and returned to Babylon during the month of Tammuz. Afterwards, Nebuchadnezzar conducted a campaign against the city of Biranatu of the mountains*[39] *and captured it. He burned it with fire; he plundered the mountains thoroughly. He conquered all of the mountains as far as the province of the land [of . . .]. [In the mon]th of Elul, the prince returned to Babylon and in the month of Tishri, the king of Akkad called up his armed forces and went to the land of Kimuhu, which is on the bank of the Euphrates. He crossed the river and conducted a campaign against the city. In the month of Kislev, he captured the city. He carried away its booty; he posted his garrison in its midst. In the month of Shebat, he returned to his land.*

(16–26) Twentieth year. The army of the land of Egypt went to the city of Kimuhu, against the garrison there, which the king of Akkad had posted in it, and conducted a campaign against the city for four months. They captured the city; they defeated the garrison of the king of Akkad. In the month of Tishri, the king of Akkad called up his army and went to the bank of the Euphrates, and pitched his camp at the city of Quramati, which is on the bank of the Euphrates. He made his army cross the Euphrates, and captured the cities of Shunadiru, Elammu, and Dahammu, cities of the Transeuphrates. He plundered them. In the month of Shebat, the king of Akkad returned to his land. The army of Egypt, which was in the city of Carchemish, crossed the Euphrates and went against the army of Akkad, which was encamped in the city of Quramati. They drove the army of Akkad back, and so they withdrew.

(27–8) Twenty-first year. The king of Akkad remained in his land. Nebuchadnezzar – his eldest son, the prince of the crown-prince's palace – called up the armed forces of Akkad, and . . .[40]

154. Chronicle 5[41]

The chronicle covers events from the early years of Nebuchadnezzar II (605–595 BCE), picking up where chronicle 4 ended (notice the catch-line at the end of 4 and beginning of 5). This chronicle records the historically important battle at Carchemish, where the Babylonians thoroughly defeated Egypt and gained control of the important city of Hamath (obv 1–8). In the same year, Nabopolassar died and Nebuchadnezzar ascended the throne (obv 9–11). In the first three years of Nebuchadnezzar's reign, the chronicle records repeated victories in the west (obv 12–23, rev 2–4). In the fourth year, they fought Egypt to a draw and found it necessary to stay home with no campaign during the fifth year (rev 5–8). After successes against the Arabs of the west in the sixth year (rev 9–10), the chronicle records the Babylonian capture of the "city of Judah" in 597 BCE, the capture of Jehoiachin and appointment of Zedekiah (rev 11–13). The rest of the chronicle is poorly preserved, but appears to record more campaigns in the west, mostly successful, and occasional rebellion at home. Unfortunately, the chronicles for the rest of Nebuchadnezzar's reign, the years of Evil-Merodach's, and the early years of Neriglissar's are lost.

(obv 1–11) [Twenty-first year.] The king of Akkad remained in his land. Nebuchadnezzar – his eldest son, [the pri]nce of the crown-prince's palace – called up [the armed forces of Akkad]. He took his army's lead and went to the city Carchemish, which is on the bank of the Euphrates. He crossed the river [against the army of Egypt(?)], which was encamped at Carchemish. [. . .] They struck each other, and the army of Egypt took flight before him, and he inflicted a defeat upon him. He finished them off until none were left. As for the remnant of the army of [Egypt], which had escaped the defeat without serious injury[42], – the army of Akkad conquered them in the province of the land of Hamatu. They inflicted such a defeat upon them that no man returned to his land. At that time, Nebuchadnezzar conquered Hamatu completely.[43] For twenty-one years, Nabopolassar exercised the kingship of Babylon. On the eighth day of the month of Ab, he died. In the month of Elul, Nebuchadnezzar returned to Babylon, and on the first day of the month of Elul, he ascended the royal throne in Babylon.

(obv 12–14) In the accession year of Nebuchadnezzar, he returned to the land of Hatti,[44] and until the month of Shebat, he marched around triumphantly in Hatti. In the month of Shebat, he took the heavy tribute of Hatti to Babylon. In the month of Nisan, he grasped the hands of Bel and of the son of Bel. He observed the akītu-festival.[45]

(obv 15–20) First year of Nebuchadnezzar. In the month of Sivan, he called up his armed forces and went to the land of Hatti, and marched around triumphantly in Hatti until the month of Kislev. All the kings of the land of Hatti came before him, and he received their heavy tribute. He went to the city of [. . .]-illunu and captured it in the month of Kislev. He caught up with its king, plundered it and [carried away] the booty. He turned the city into a ruin heap. In the month of Shebat, he left and returned to Babylon.

(obv 21–3) [Second ye]ar. In the month of Iyyar, the king of Akkad gathered his main body of troops, and [went to the land of Hatti(?)]. He encamped [. . .]. He

brought large siege-towers acro[ss . . . From the month of Iy]yar until the mon[th of . . . he marched around triumphantly in Hatti(?)]

[. . . lacuna of indefinite length . . .]

(rev 2–4)[46] *[Third year. On the] thirteenth [day of the month of . . .], Nabu-shumu-[lishir . . . In the month of . . . , the king of Akk]ad called up his armed forces and [went] to the land of Hatti. [. . .] . . . he brought into Akkad the vast [spoils(?)] of Hatti.*

(rev 5–7) Fourth year. The king of Akkad called up his armed forces and went to the land of Hatti. [He marched around trium]phantly in Hatti. In the month of Kislev, he took the lead of his army and went to the land of Egypt. When the king of Egypt heard it, he ca[lled up(?)] his armed forces. They fought in close battle on the open battlefield,[47] *and inflicted a very great defeat on one another. The king of Akkad and his army turned around and [returned] to Babylon.*

(rev 8) Fifth year. The king of Akkad remained in his land. He gathered a great many chariots and horses.

(rev 9–10) Sixth year. In the month of Kislev, the king of Akkad called up his armed forces and went to the land of Hatti. He sent his army off from Hatti and directed them into the desert. They thoroughly plundered the vast land of Arabia – their goods, their livestock, and their gods. In the month of Adar, the king returned to his land.

(rev 11–13) Seventh year. In the month of Kislev, the king of Akkad called up his armed forces and went to the land of Hatti. He encamped against the city of Yahudu.[48] *On the second day of the month of Adar, he captured the city and defeated its king. He appointed a king of his own choosing in it. He to[ok away] its heavy tribute and brought it into Babylon.*

(rev 14–15) Eighth year. In the month of Tebet, the king of Akkad [went . . .] to the land of Hatti as far as the city of Carche[mish . . .]. In the month of Shebat, [the king returned] to his land.

(rev 16–20) Ninth year. [In the month of . . . , the king of Akk]ad and his army [went . . .] the bank of the Tigr[is . . .]. The king of the land of [. . .] . . . the king of Ak[kad . . .] . . . he pitched his camp at [. . . a city(?)], which is on the bank of the Tigris. Between them was the distance of a day's journey. . . . he feared the king of E[lam(?)] and terror fell on him, so he re[turned(?)] to his land.

(rev 21–4) Tenth [year. The king of Akk]ad remained in his land. From the month of Kislev until the month of Tebet, there was rebellion in the land of Akkad . . . He killed his many [officials][49] *with weapons. He defeated his enemy with this own hands.*[50] *. . . he went [to the la]nd of Hatti, and . . . The kings and . . . [. . . He received] their heavy tribute and returned [to Babyl]on.*

(rev 25–6) [Eleventh year]. In the month of Kislev, the king of Akkad [called up] his armed forces, and went [to the land of H]atti.[51]

155. Chronicle 6[52]

The chronicle covers events from the third year of Neriglissar (557 BCE). It records a campaign against one Appuashu of Pirindu in Anatolia, who had conducted a raid into Syria and then attempted to ambush the Babylonian troops. Appuashu appears to have escaped although Neriglissar can claim a modest victory.

(1–14) Third year. Appuashu, king of the land of Pirindu, called up his [numerous] armed forces and set [his face] towards the Transeuphrates for purposes of plunder and spoils. Neriglissar called up his armed forces and went against him in the land of Hume. Prior to this,[53] *Appuashu had placed his army and the mounted couriers that he had gathered in position for ambush in a mountain gorge. When Neriglissar reached them, he inflicted a defeat upon them. He defeated the large army; he captured his troops and many horses. He pursued Appuashu over a 15-mile (24-kilometer)*[54] *distance in difficult mountainous terrain, in which men had to march in single file, as far as his royal city, Ura. He caught up with him, captured the city of Ura, and carried away his spoils.*

[. . . erasure . . .]

(15–27) (He continued on) from Ura as far as the city of Kirshi, the royal city of his fathers, over a 6-mile (10-kilometer) distance in severe mountainous terrain and difficult passes. When he came to Kirshi, he captured the strong city, his royal city. He burned its wall, its palace, and its people with fire. He captured in boats the city of Pitusu, a mountain (on an island) in the middle of the (Mediterranean) Sea and the 6,000 combat troops who had gone up inside it. He carried off its city and captured its people. In that same year, he burned with fire (everything) from the entrance of the city of Sallune as far as the border of the city of Ludu.[55] *Appua[shu] became a fugitive, so he did not ca[tch up] with him. In the month of Adar, the king of Akkad returned to his [land].*

156. Chronicle 7[56]

The chronicle covers events from the reign of Nabonidus (556–539 BCE), and is therefore sometimes known as the "Nabonidus Chronicle." It is especially interested in the king's neglect of the *akītu*-festival, which is not unlike the Hebrew Chronicler's interest in the Israelite kings' attitude toward the feasts of the priestly calendar (e.g., 2 Chr 30; 31: 3; 35: 1). The first several years of Nabonidus' reign recorded here are poorly preserved, leaving only traces of campaigns in the west but few details (all of column 1). The conflict between Astyages and Cyrus II is preserved for the sixth year of Nabonidus (ii 1–4). The seventh year is the first in which it is reported that the king stayed in the city of Tema, and the *akītu*-festival "did not take place" (ii 5–8), a theme repeated for years 9, 10, and 11. The lines for the next several years are poorly preserved, but in the seventeenth year of the king, the festival was finally celebrated again (iii 5–12). In the same year, the city fell to the Persians and Nabonidus was captured (iii 12–16). The chronicle records the peace that ensued, and the joy with which all Babylonians received Cyrus (iii 17–20).

(i1–8)[57] *[First year(?). . . .] . . . he carried. The king . . . [. . .] carried off the [. . .] of their land to Babylon. . . . [. . .] . . . they were terrified, and he did not carry [. . .] . . . all their families. [. . .] . . . the king called up his armed forces and [went] to Hume.*

(i9–10) [Second year(?). . . .]. In the month of Tebet, [. . . .] to the land of Hamatu . . .[58] *[. . .].*

(i11–22) [Third year(?). . . . On the . . . day of the mon]th of Ab, [. . .] the land of Ammananu, the mountains [. . .] . . . orchards, fruit of all kinds [. . .] . . . from them into the center of Babylon. [. . . the king(?) be]came ill, but survived. In the month of Kislev, the king [called up] his armed forces . . . and to Nabu-tattan-uṣur[59] *[. . .] . . . of the land of Amurru, to [. . ., and] he/they encamped [against E]dom.*[60] *[. . .] . . . and numerous troops [. . . the g]ate of the city of Rugdini(?). [. . .] . . . he defeated him [. . .] . . . the troops . . .*

(ii1–4) [Astyages[61]*] called up [his armed forces and] went against Cyrus,*[62] *the king of Anshan for purposes of con[quest]. As for Astyages, his army rebelled against him, and he was taken into custody. [They presented him(?)] to Cyrus [. . .]. Cyrus <went> to the land of Ecbatana, the royal city, and the silver, gold, goods, and property, which he carried away as spoils from Ecbatana, he took to Anshan. The goods and property of the army [. . .].*

(ii5–8) Seventh year. The king remained in the city of Tema. The king's son, his officials, and his army remained in the land of Akkad. [In the month of Nisan, the king] did not come to Babylon. Nabu did not come to Babylon. Marduk did not come out, and the [akītu]-fest[ival did not take place].[63] *The offerings were given to the gods of Babylon and Borsippa in Esagil and Ezida as [in more prosperous times*[64]*]. The šešgallû-priest poured out (libations) and cared for the temple.*

(ii9) Eighth year. [blank space][65]

(ii10–18) Ninth year. Nabonidus, the king, remained <in> the city of Tema. The king's son, the officials, and the army remained in the land of Akkad. In the month of Nisan, the king did not come to Babylon. Nabu did not come to Babylon. Marduk did not come out, and the akītu-festival was neglected. The offerings were given to the gods of <Babylon> and Borsippa in Esagil and Ezida as in more prosperous times. On the fifth day of the month of Nisan, the king's mother died in Dur-Karashu, which is on the bank of the Euphrates upstream from Sippar. The king's son and his army were disconsolate[66] *for three days, and a mourning-ritual was performed. In the month of Sivan, a mourning-ritual was performed for the king's mother in the land of Akkad. In the month of Nisan, Cyrus, king of the land of Persia, called up his armed forces, crossed over the Tigris downstream from the city of Arba'il, and in the month of Iyyar [he went to(?)] the land of Lu[uddi*[67]*(?)]. He killed its king, took its goods, and posted a garrison (in it) for himself [. . .] Afterwards, the king and his garrison remained in its midst [. . .]*

(ii19–22) Tenth year. The king remained in the city of Tema. The king's son, the officials, and his army remained in the land of Akkad. In the [month of Nisan], the king [did not come to Babylon]. Nabu did not come to Babylon. Marduk did not come out, and the akītu-festival was neglected. The offerings were given to the gods of Babylon and Borsippa in E[sagil and Ezida] as in more prosperous times. On the twenty-first day of the month of Sivan, [. . .] of the land of Elammya, in the land of Akkad . . . [. . .] the governor of Uruk [. . .]

(ii23–5) Eleventh year. The king remained in the city of Tema. The king's son, the officials, and his army remained in the land of Akkad. [In the month of Nisan, the king did not come to Babylon. Nabu] did not come [to Baby]lon. Marduk did not come out, and the akītu-festival was neglected. The offer[ings] were given [to the gods of Baby]lon and Borsippa [in Esagil and Ezida as in more prosperous times].

(iii1–28) [. . .] . . . the Tig[ris] River [. . .] . . . Ishtar of Uruk [. . .] . . . [the gods] of Pa[rsu[68] *returned to their former places(?)] . . . [. . .]*

[Seventeenth year(?).] Nabu [came] from Borsippa for the processional of [Marduk. Marduk came out . . . in the month of] Tebet, the king crossed into Etur-kalamma. In . . . [. . .] . . . he poured out a libation of wine . . . [. . .] . . . Marduk came out. They performed the akītu-festival as in more prosperous times. In the month of [. . .] . . . [. . . and the gods] of Marad, Zababa[69] *and the (other) gods of Kish, Ninlil [and the (other) gods of] Hursagkalamma*[70] *entered Babyon. Until the end of the month of Elul, the gods of the land of Akkad [. . .] while those above the IM*[71] *and those below the IM were entering Babylon. But the gods of Bosippa, Cuthah, and Sippar did not enter. In the month of Tishri, when Cyrus conducted a campaign at Opis on [the bank(?)] of the Tigris against the army of the land of Akkad, the people of Akkad took flight. He made off with plunder and killed the people. On the fourteenth day, Sippar was captured without a fight. Nabonidus became a fugitive. On the sixteenth day, Ugbaru, the provincial governor of the land of the Gutium and the army of Cyrus entered Babylon without a fight. Afterwards, when Nabonidus had withdrawn, he was captured in Babylon. Until the end of the month, the shield-bearers of the Gutium surrounded the gates of Esagil. There was no interruption of any kind in Esagil or the temples, and no festival-period was missed. On the third day of the month of Marchesvan, Cyrus entered Babylon. They filled bags before him(?).*[72] *Peace was established in the city. Cyrus sent greetings to all of Babylon. Gubaru, his provincial governor, appointed (additional) provincial governors for Babylon. From the month of Kislev until the month of Adar, the gods of the land of Akkad, which Nabonidus had taken into Babylon, returned to their shrines. On the eleventh day of the month of Marchesvan, Ugbaru died during the night. In the month of [. . .], the king's wife died. From the twenty-seventh (day) of the month of Adar until the third day of the month of Nisan, a mourning-ritual was performed in Akkad. All the people uncovered their heads. On the fourth day, when Cambyses, the son of Cyrus, entered Egidrikalammasummu, the temple official(?)*[73] *of Nabu who [. . .] When he came [. . .] because of his Elamite garments(?),*[74] *the hands of Nabu . . . [. . .] . . . [Lan]ces and quivers from [. . .] . . . the king's son(?) to the corvée [labor . . .] Nabu to Esagil . . . before Marduk and the son of Mar[duk . . .]*

(iv1–9) [. . .] . . . Babylon, water [. . .] . . . burned incense [. . .] . . . the gate was demolished [. . .] . . . Eanna of . . . [. . .] . . . he went out of the sculptor-workshop[75] *[. . .] . . . [. . .] . . . into Babylon . . . [. . .] Babylon, he depicted (on bas-relief*[76]*), and . . .*

Bibliography

Arnold, Bill T. *Who Were the Babylonians?* Atlanta: Society of Biblical Literature, 2004.

Beaulieu, Paul-Alain. *The Reign of Nabonidus, King of Babylon, 556–539 B.C.* Yale Near Eastern Researches 10. New Haven: Yale University Press, 1989.

Becking, Bob. *The Fall of Samaria: An Historical and Archaeological Study.* Leiden: Brill, 1992.

Black, Jeremy A. "The New Year Ceremonies in Ancient Babylon: 'Taking The Hand of Bel' and A Cultic Picnic." *Religion* 11 (1981): 39–59.

Black, Jeremy A., and Anthony R. Green. *Gods, Demons, and Symbols of Ancient Mesopotamia: An Illustrated Dictionary.* Austin: University of Texas Press, 1992.

Brinkman, John A. *A Political History of Post-Kassite Babylonia, 1158–722 B.C.* Rome: Pontifical Biblical Institute, 1968.

——. *Prelude to Empire: Babylonian Society and Politics, 747–626 B.C.* Occasional publications of the Babylonian Fund 7. Philadelphia, Pa.: Distributed by Babylonian Fund, University Museum, 1984.
——. "Ur: 721–605 B.C.," *Orientalia* NS 34 (1965): 241–58.
Delitzsch, Friedrich. *Die babylonische Chronik nebst einem Anhang über die synchronistische Geschichte P.* Abhandlungen der philologisch-historischen Klasse der Königl. Sächsischen Gesellschaft der Wissenschaften 25. Leipzig: Teubner, 1906.
Glassner, Jean-Jacques. *Chroniques mésopotamiennes.* Paris: Les belles Lettres, 1993.
Grayson, A. K. *Assyrian and Babylonian Chronicles.* Texts from cuneiform sources 5. Winona Lake, Ind.: Eisenbrauns, 2000.
——. *Assyrian Royal Inscriptions.* Records of the ancient Near East 1/2. Wiesbaden: Harrassowitz, 1972–.
——. 1982. "Königslisten und Chroniken, B: Akkadisch." *Reallexikon der Assyriologie* 6: 86–135.
Kuan, Jeffrey K. *Neo-Assyrian Historical Inscriptions and Syria-Palestine: Israelite/Judean-Tyrian-Damascene Political and Commercial Relations in the Ninth–Eighth Centuries B.C.E.* Jian Dao dissertation series, Bible and Literature 1.1. Hong Kong: Alliance Bible Seminary, 1995.
Kuhrt, Amélie. "Usurpation, Conquest and Ceremonial: From Babylon to Persia." In *Rituals of Royalty: Power and Ceremonial in Traditional Societies.* Edited by David Cannadine and S. R. F. Price. Cambridge: Cambridge University Press, 1987, 20–55.
Mellink, M. 1982. "The Native Kingdoms of Anatolia." *Cambridge Ancient History* 2 3/2: 619–65.
Oates, Joan. 1982. "The Fall of Assyria (635–609 B.C.)." *Cambridge Ancient History* 2 3/2, 172–84.
Oppenheim, A. Leo. 1969. "The Neo-Babylonian Empire and Its Successors." *Ancient Near Eastern Texts Relating to the Old Testament,* 301–7.
Wiseman, D. J. *Chronicles of Chaldaean Kings (626–556 B.C.) in the British Museum.* London: Trustees of the British Museum, 1961.
——. " 'Is it Peace?' – Covenant and Diplomacy." *Vetus Testamentum* 32 (1982): 311–26.
——. *Nebuchadrezzar and Babylon.* Schweich Lectures 1983. Oxford: Published for the British Academy by Oxford University Press, 1985.
Young, T. Cuyler, Jr. "The Early History of the Medes and the Persians and the Achaemenid Empire to the Death of Cambyses." *Cambridge Ancient History* 2 4, 1–52.
Zawadzki, Stefan. *The Fall of Assyria and Median-Babylonian Relations in Light of the Nabopolassar Chronicle.* Poznan: Adam Mickiewicz University Press, 1988.
——. "The First Year of Nabopolassar's Rule according to the Babylonian Chronicle BM 25127: A Reinterpretation of The Text and Its Consequences." *Journal of Cuneiform Studies* 41 (1989): 57–64.

Notes

1 The Late-Babylonian Chronicle Series is preserved only very fragmentarily; for introduction to the material generally, see A. K. Grayson, "Königslisten und Chroniken, B: Akkadisch," *Reallexikon der Assyriologie* 6: 86–135, esp. 86–7.

2 E.g., A. K. Grayson, *Assyrian and Babylonian Chronicles,* Texts from cuneiform sources 5 (Winona Lake, Ind.: Eisenbrauns, 2000), 8.

3 This chronicle has been the focus of scholarly attention for well over a century, having been copied, translated, and studied numerous times. For copy, see *CT* 34, plate 47. For translations, besides that of Grayson, see A. L. Oppenheim, "The Neo-Babylonian Empire and Its Successors," *ANET* 301–7, esp. 301–3; Jean-Jacques Glassner, *Chroniques mésopotamiennes* (Paris: Les belles Lettres, 1993), 179–84; and Friedrich Delitzsch, *Die babylonische Chronik nebst einem Anhang über die synchronistische Geschichte P* (Abhandlungen der philologisch-historischen Klasse der Königl. Sächsischen Gesellschaft der Wissenschaften 25; Leipzig: Teubner, 1906). For more bibliography prior to 1975, see Grayson, *Assyrian and Babylonian Chronicles*, 70.

4 "Akkad" in this series of chronicles will refer to "Babylon" and "Babylonia." Thus, the many occurrences of "king of Akkad" refer to a king of Babylonia.

5 Evidence from Babylonian King List A suggests Nabu-shuma-ukin ruled either 1 month, 2 days or 1 month, 13 days; see Grayson, *Assyrian and Babylonian Chronicles*, 72.

6 The full personal name may be Nabu-mukin-zeri; see John A. Brinkman, *A Political History of Post-Kassite Babylonia, 1158–722 B.C.* Analecta Orientalia 43 (Rome: Pontifical Biblical Institute, 1968), 235, n. 1492.

7 That is, from the Chaldean tribe known as Bit-Amukani; see John A. Brinkman, *Prelude to Empire: Babylonian Society and Politics, 747–626 B.C.* Occasional publications of the Babylonian Fund 7 (Philadelphia, Pa.: Distributed by Babylonian Fund, University Museum, 1984), 14–15.

8 The number of years has been omitted, probably because the author did not have the information at the time of composition; see Grayson, *Assyrian and Babylonian Chronicles*, 72–3.

9 Earlier scholars debated whether this geographical name (^{uru}*Šá-ma-ra-ʾ-in*) should be identified with Samaria, because the cuneiform signs *ma* and *ba* are so similar (thus ^{uru}*Šá-ba-ra-ʾ-in* was possible). The issue has long since been resolved in favor of such an identification; Bob Becking, *The Fall of Samaria: An Historical and Archaeological Study*, Studies in the History of the Ancient Near East 2; Leiden: Brill, 1992), 23; Jeffrey K. Kuan, *Neo-Assyrian Historical Inscriptions and Syria-Palestine: Israelite/Judean-Tyrian-Damascene Political and Commercial Relations in the Ninth-Eighth Centuries B.C.E.* Jian Dao dissertation series, Bible and Literature 1.1 (Hong Kong: Alliance Bible Seminary, 1995), 195, n. 9.

10 On the likelihood of this meaning for *nabalkattu* + geographical name [Assyria] + *šakānu*, see *AHw* 694b, *CAD* N/1: 10. See also Grayson, *Assyrian and Babylonian Chronicles*, 73–4; and see chronicle 1: ii,45.

11 Lines of text with apostrophes are taken from a different text tradition, because the main textual exemplar is broken; Grayson, *Assyrian and Babylonian Chronicles*, 75.

12 The chronology is anticipatory, since this event is found in iii, 29 below.

13 John A. Brinkman, "Ur: 721–605 B.C.," *Orientalia* NS 34 (1965): 241–58, esp. 245, note 1.

14 Variant, "eighth day"; see Grayson, *Assyrian and Babylonian Chronicles*, 80.

15 Or, perhaps only 18.

16 The city god of Der, a city on the border with Elam; Jeremy A. Black and Anthony R. Green, *Gods, Demons, and Symbols of Ancient Mesopotamia: An Illustrated Dictionary* (Austin: University of Texas Press, 1992), 111.

17 I.e., from the Chaldean tribe known as Bit-Dakkuri; see Brinkman, *Prelude to Empire: Babylonian Society and Politics, 747–626 B.C.*, 14–15.

18 Another copy (text C) adds at this point, "It (Egypt) was plundered and its gods were abducted."
19 The break on the tablet obscures whether it should be "sixth," "sixteenth," or "twenty-sixth."
20 For copy, see D. J. Wiseman, *Chronicles of Chaldaean Kings (626–556 B.C.) in the British Museum* (London: Trustees of the British Museum, 1961), plates vii and viii; and for bibliography prior to 1975, Grayson, *Assyrian and Babylonian Chronicles*, 87. See also Glassner, *Chroniques mésopotamiennes*, 191–3.
21 Lit. "they threw fire down upon the temple."
22 The city, according to Zawadzki was not Babylon, but rather Shapazzu; see Stefan Zawadzki, "The First Year of Nabopolassar's Rule according to The Babylonian Chronicle BM 25127: A Reinterpretation of The Text and Its Consequences," *Journal of Cuneiform Studies* 41 (1989): 57–64, esp. 59.
23 Or, the month Iyyar, again according to Zawadzi; Ibid.
24 A principal waterway near Kish; see Erich Ebeling, "Banîtu," *Reallexikon der Assyriologie* 1: 397.
25 Presumably the idiom intended by the Š-stem of erēbu(m); *CDA* 77; *AHw* 236, Š, #b.
26 For *šaqû*, "move upstream," see *CAD* Š/2: 21.
27 Common Semitic idiom for determination or intent to do something; *CDA* 263.
28 For copy, see Wiseman, *Chronicles of Chaldaean Kings (626–556 B.C.) in the British Museum*, ix–xii; and for bibliography prior to 1975, Grayson, *Assyrian and Babylonian Chronicles*, 90. See also Glassner, *Chroniques mésopotamiennes*, 193–7.
29 I.e., the Babylonians.
30 "Baltil" in this series of chronicles will refer to "Ashur"; Erich Ebeling, "Baltil," *Reallexikon der Assyriologie* 1: 395.
31 The name made immortal by Herodotus, although the spelling in this chronicle is "Umakishtar." See Joan Oates, "The Fall of Assyria (635–609 B.C.)," *Cambridge Ancient History 2* 3/2: 172–84; Stefan Zawadzki, *The Fall of Assyria and Median-Babylonian Relations in Light of The Nabopolassar Chronicle* (Poznan: Adam Mickiewicz University Press, 1988), 114–31.
32 For *amāru* #8, "meet," see *CAD* A/2: 27.
33 D. J. Wiseman, "'Is it Peace?' – Covenant and Diplomacy," *Vetus Testamentum* 32 (1982): 311–26.
34 Lit. "a city of the middle Euphrates"; Grayson, *Assyrian and Babylonian Chronicles*, 93.
35 "March around triumphantly" in these chronicles (*šalṭāniš ittallak*) is a general expression, which may have less to do with combat operations than with maintaining a Babylonian presence in conquered territories in order to establish law and order; Donald J. Wiseman, *Nebuchadnezzar and Babylon*, Schweich Lectures 1983 (Oxford: Published for the British Academy by Oxford University Press, 1985), 21–2.
36 A catchline, being substantially the same line as that at the beginning of the next chronicle.
37 For copy, see Wiseman, *Chronicles of Chaldaean Kings (626–556 B.C.) in the British Museum*, plates xiii–xiv; and for bibliography prior to 1975, Grayson, *Assyrian and Babylonian Chronicles*, 87. See also Glassner, *Chroniques mésopotamiennes*, 197–8.
38 Lit. "prince of the house of legitimate succession", or "succession house" (*AHw*, 134, #23). All references to Nebuchadnezzar in this text refer to Nebuchadnezzar

II (604–562 BCE), as distinct from Nebuchadnezzar I (1125–1104 B.C.E.) of the Second Dynasty of Isin; see Bill T. Arnold, *Who Were the Babylonians?* Society of Biblical Literature Archaeology and Biblical Studies 10 (Atlanta: Society of Biblical Literature, 2004), 79; 91–9.

39 Grayson observes that this may simply be "fortresses" in the mountains rather than a specific place name, although the determinative for "city" occurs both here and in the next line; Grayson, *Assyrian and Babylonian Chronicles*, 97.

40 A catchline related to the first line of chronicle 5.

41 For copy, see Wiseman, *Chronicles of Chaldaean Kings (626–556 B.C.) in the British Museum*, plates xiv–xvi; and for bibliography prior to 1975, Grayson, *Assyrian and Babylonian Chronicles*, 87. See also Glassner, *Chroniques mésopotamiennes*, 198–200.

42 Lit. "no weapon had reached them."

43 Lit. "to the border of its entirety," *AHw*, 852; *CAD* G: 77.

44 "Hatti" or "Hittite" in this chronicle will generally refer to Syria-Palestine in the west.

45 The 12 days of the *akītu*-festival were celebrated at Babylon in Nisan around the time of the vernal equinox. Similar New Year festivals were celebrated at the city of Ur as early as the Neo-Sumerian period, but assumed new religious significance during the early Neo-Babylonian period, around the time of the ascendancy of Babylon's god Marduk (Bel). The ritual for the festival called for prayers to Marduk on behalf of the city of Babylon, a ritual cleansing of his temple, a symbolic enthronement of Marduk ("grasping the hands of Bel" as here), as well as a symbolic recitation of the *Enūma Eliš* on the fourth day of the festival. Thus the festival represented a convergence of power and authority in the sole personhood of Marduk, his city Babylon, and the king of Babylon; Jeremy A. Black, "The New Year Ceremonies in Ancient Babylon: 'Taking the Hand of Bel' and A Cultic Picnic," *Religion* 11 (1981): 39–59; Amélie Kuhrt, "Usurpation, Conquest and Ceremonial: From Babylon to Persia," in *Rituals of Royalty: Power and Ceremonial in Traditional Societies*, eds. David Cannadine and S. R. F. Price (Cambridge: Cambridge University Press, 1987), 20–55.

The religious and symbolic significance of the festival in Babylonian culture during the Neo-Babylonian period is best illustrated by the way these Chronicles (especially Chronicle 7 below) carefully note times when the festival was suspended due to political weakness.

46 Line rev 1 has only illegible traces.

47 For this idiomatic use of *irtu*, "breast, chest," see *CAD* I–J: 185.

48 The siege of Jerusalem (the "city of Judah") began in November/December (Kislev) and culminated in the fall of the city on the second of Adad (March 15/16, 597 BCE). The captured king was Jehoiachin, and the king of Nebuchadnezzar's own choosing was Zedekiah; 2 Kgs 24: 10–17; 2 Chr 36: 9–10; Jer 22: 24–30; 24: 1; Ezek 17: 12.

49 Grayson restores "army" here instead, but I am assuming a parallel with Chronicle 1, iv: 29; Grayson, *Assyrian and Babylonian Chronicles*, 102; and see also Wiseman, *Nebuchadrezzar and Babylon*, 34.

50 The Chronicle suggests that the king himself captured the culprit in person; Wiseman, *Nebuchadrezzar and Babylon*, 34.

51 Apparently a catchline for the next tablet, now lost.

52 For copy, see Wiseman, *Chronicles of Chaldaean Kings (626–556 B.C.) in the British Museum*, plates xvii–xviii; and for bibliography prior to 1975, Grayson, *Assyrian*

and Babylonian Chronicles, 87. See also Glassner, *Chroniques mésopotamiennes*, 200–201.

53 The preposition *lāma* plus possessive suffix indicates anterior action, in this case; *AHw* 531; *CAD* L: 53. Thus Appuashu stationed troops for an ambush before Neriglissar's advance.

54 The *bēru* is a linear measure of a double-hour, and often translated simply "mile," perhaps approximating 10,800 meters; CDA 43. For *bēru* A, "mile" plus *qaqqari*, see *CAD* B: 209–10.

55 The Iron Age kingdom of Lydia was in western Anatolia, west of Phrygia; M. Mellink, "The Native Kingdoms of Anatolia," *Cambridge Ancient History 2* 3/2: 619–65, esp. 643–55.

56 For bibliography prior to 1975, Grayson, *Assyrian and Babylonian Chronicles*, 104. See also Glassner, *Chroniques mésopotamiennes*, 201–4; Oppenheim, "The Neo-Babylonian Empire and Its Successors," esp. 305–7.

57 Presumably, this portion chronicles events from Nabonidus' accession year and first year.

58 Grayson restores ŠED7 (*kaṣû*), "it was cold." However, without the context of line 10, it is impossible to be confident; Grayson, *Assyrian and Babylonian Chronicles*, 105.

59 The personal name is problematic in form and meaning; Oppenheim, "The Neo-Babylonian Empire and Its Successors," 304; Glassner, *Chroniques mésopotamiennes*, 202; Grayson, *Assyrian and Babylonian Chronicles*, 282.

60 Reading *[u]-du-um-mu* for *[a]-du-um-mu*; see Paul-Alain Beaulieu, *The Reign of Nabonidus, King of Babylon, 556–539 B.C.* (Yale Near Eastern Researches 10; New Haven: Yale University Press, 1989), 166.

61 The name made immortal by Herodotus, although the spelling here is "Ishtumegu." Astyages probably came to the throne of Media in 585 BCE; T. C. Young, Jr, "The Early History of the Medes and the Persians and the Achaemenid Empire to the Death of Cambyses," *Cambridge Ancient History 2* 4: 1–52, esp. 16–17.

62 The name familiar from biblical and classical sources is spelled here "Kurash"; ibid., esp. 24–46.

63 For *baṭālu*, "to stop, interrupt an activity, to cease regular deliveries, to come to an end," see *CAD* B: 174–6. On the *akītu*-festival, see note 45 above. The implication of this chronicle is that the king was expected to be present in Babylon during Nisan, the appointed time for the festival. An important part of the festival was the processional in which Marduk "came forth" [(w)āṣû(m)] from his shrine, Esagil.

64 The meaning of the phrase, restored from a similar expression in Chronicle 17, ii: 4, is uncertain. For this proposal, see Grayson, *Assyrian and Babylonian Chronicles*, 106.

65 The events of the eighth year were unavailable to the scribe for some reason. A blank space was left to be filled in later, but the scribe either forgot to return to this point or never found the pertinent information.

66 For *adāru* #5, *šu'duru* "to cause annoyance," see *CAD* A/1: 103–5; *AHw* 11.

67 Lydia.

68 Grayson, *Assyrian and Babylonian Chronicles*, 282.

69 The local deity of Kish, Zababa a warrior god attested from Early Dynastic times; Black and Green, *Gods, Demons, and Symbols of Ancient Mesopotamia: An Illustrated Dictionary*, 187.

70 Twin city of Kish in northwestern Babylonia.

71 The interpretation of the logogram IM is still not resolved satisfactorily. For attempts, see A. K. Grayson, *Assyrian Royal Inscriptions,* Records of the ancient Near East 1/2 (Wiesbaden: Harrassowitz, 1972–), 1: 71, note 140.

72 Bags of gold, perhaps; *ḫarinnu,* cf. *AHw* 326. The line is in question, see Grayson, *Assyrian and Babylonian Chronicles,* 110.

73 For questions about the [lú]É.PA of line 25, see Grayson, *Assyrian and Babylonian Chronicles,* 111.

74 As difficult as this line is, Grayson's reconstruction remains an improvement over Oppenheim's; compare Grayson, *Assyrian and Babylonian Chronicles,* 111 and Oppenheim, "The Neo-Babylonian Empire and Its Successors," 307, n.16.

75 For *bīt mummu,* as a workshop used to make and repair ritual objects, see CAD M/2: 197–8; *AHw* 672.

76 This interpretation of *eṣēru* may be preferable in light of the mention of the *bīt mummu* in the preceding context.

II. The Cyrus Cylinder (Michalowski)

Beginning in 614 BC, the Medes and Babylonians laid waste to Assur, Nineveh, and all the major urban centers of the Assyrian Empire, culminating with the conquest of the Syrian city of Harran in 610. The center of power in Mesopotamia shifted south, and the Neo-Babylonian state took over many of the areas previously governed by Assyria. Some historians have stressed the differences between the two Mesopotamian states, but others have focused on the similarities, on continuity rather than change. The Neo-Babylonian state lasted less than a century; its last king, Nabonidus, came the throne in 555 and was to reign only 18 years.

Nabonidus is one of the most enigmatic figures in Mesopotamian history. He reclaimed, or rather reinvented, ancient traditions, spent 10 years living far away from Babylon in Arabia, and revered the moon-god Sin, celebrating and rebuilding his cult centers in Mesopotamian Ur and Syrian Harran. It is difficult to understand both his motivations and contemporary reactions to his actions because although documents and inscriptions from his time have survived, later opinions about him were formed on the basis of the words of his enemies.

Nabonidus returned from Arabia and had to face a new threat from Iran: the Persians under the leadership of Cyrus, having consolidated power in Iran, had outflanked the Babylonians in Anatolia by defeating Sardis in 541. Eight years later they swept down into Babylonia from the east through the Diyala valley and after brutal fighting approached the capital city of Babylon. The city fell to Cyrus in October 539; some sources claim that the end came without a battle, but there is no contemporary evidence to support this suspicious claim. Thus ended the last independent ancient Mesopotamian state. Babylonia was now one of the provinces of a huge new territorial state – the Persian Empire.

Our knowledge of these events is based primarily on three one-sided texts, written by scribes working for the conquerors, known by their modern names as The Nabonidus Chronicle, The Persian Verse Account, and the Cyrus Cylinder. We cannot judge just how representative these texts are, since they were preserved by accident and undoubtedly provide only partial documentation of the polemics of the times. However, most biblical and Greek sources that relate or allude to the Persian takeover of Babylonia echo similar sentiments and seem to take inspiration from likeminded ideological claims of the new masters of the land.

The Babylonian text of the Cyrus Cylinder is inscribed an a barrel-shaped clay cylinder that was discovered out of context in Babylon in 1879 and deposited in the British Museum. An additional piece of the same object made its way to the antiquities market and ended up in the Yale Babylonian Collection in New Haven, Connecticut. Objects of this shape were usually inscribed with dedicatory inscriptions and were buried in foundation deposits under walls or buildings and were not addressed to contemporary audiences but to future readers and to the gods. The "Cylinder" was written by someone familiar with the language of Assyrian and Babylonian royal inscriptions, and it is possible that it was written in conjunction with the rebuilding of Imgur-Enlil, the city wall of Babylon, which had previously been worked on by Assurbanipal (668–627), the last great king of Assyria, as well as by Nabopolassar (626–605), the founder of the Neo-Babylonian dynasty.

The first few lines are broken, but it would appear that the first section is an attack on the cultic actions of Nabonidus, aiming to portray him as an enemy of Marduk, the chief god of Babylon. If the translation offered here is correct, and it does gloss over a grammatical difficulty, Cyrus criticized an event that the Babylonian ruler had described with pride in his own inscriptions: the elevation of his daughter to be the high priestess of the moon-god, thus turning his own words against him. It should be noted however, that the sentence in question could also be translated as "an incompetent (i.e., Nabonidus) had been appointed to rule in his land," perhaps an allusion to his usurpation of power. The author then uses an old Mesopotamian ideological turn, ascribing a king's downfall to divine withdrawal of favor. Marduk then searched throughout the world for a new king to take his place; this again is an old motif that goes back more than a millennium. With the god at his side, Cyrus marched upon Babylon, which surrendered without a battle; the Persians entered in peace and without resorting to the customary plunder and pillage that customarily accompanied such events.

The stress on a peaceful entry – it is repeated for emphasis – contains a clear message: Cyrus was different from previous conquerors of the city, notably the Assyrians under the kings Tukulti-Ninurta I (1245–1208) and Sennacherib (704–681), who had sacked the sacred city. Other literary patterns demonstrate that the scribe who composed it wanted to provide allusions to the language of the inscriptions of Assurbanipal and to a foundation cylinder of Nabopolassar that celebrated the rebuilding of Imgur-Enlil. The fragmentary ending provides a more concrete connection to the deeds of the Assyrian king, whose earlier foundation deposit was apparently found during the renovations of the wall. Such archaeological links with the past were characteristic of writings composed in the name of Nabonidus, who also attempted to portray himself as a successor to the legacy of Assurbanipal and the Assyrian state. The author of the Cyrus Cylinder clearly wanted to combine all of these elements in the name of Cyrus, making him the true king of Babylon not only by Marduk's choice, but also by displacing the ignominious Nabonidus, turning his words and deeds upside down and making his own claim as the cultural and literary heir to the legacy of both Assyria and Babylonia.

The Cyrus Cylinder is therefore primarily a legitimation text that provides us with some insight into the kind of claims that were made by Cyrus as he sought to bring to his side Babylonian elites and to convince them to back his claims to the throne of Babylon. Generically, it belongs with other foundation deposit inscriptions; it is not an edict of any kind, nor does it provide any unusual human rights proclamation as is sometimes claimed.

157. Text

[When . . .] his . . . [. . .] the regions . . . , an insignificant (candidate) was installed as high priestess (of the Moon) in his land, and [. . .] he imposed upon them. He made a replica of the Esaggil, [. . . established] improper rites for Ur and the remaining cult centers as well as [unclean offer]ings; daily he continuously uttered unfaithful (prayers); furthermore he maliciously suspended the regular offerings and upset the rites. He plotted to end the worship of Marduk and continuously perpetuated evil against his city. Daily [he . . .] brought all his [people] to ruin by (imposing) toils without rest.

Hearing their complaints, the Enlil of the Gods was terribly angry [and left] their territory; the gods living amongst them abandoned their abodes. (Nabonidus) brought them into Babylon, to (Marduk's) fury. Marduk, ex[alted one, the Enlil of the God]s, roamed through all the places that had been abandoned, (and upon seeing this) reconciled his anger and showed mercy to the people of Sumer and Akkad who had become (as) corpses.

He sought and looked through all the lands, searching for a righteous king whose hand he could grasp. He called to rule Cyrus, king of Anshan, and announced his name as the king of the universe. He made the Guti-land and all the Medes (Ummanmanda) bow in submission at his feet and so (Cyrus) assiduously looked after the justice and well-being of the Black-Headed People over whom he had been made victorious (by Marduk). And Marduk, the great lord, leader of his people, looked happily at the good deeds and steadfast mind of Cyrus and ordered him to march to his own city Babylon, set him on the road to Babylon, and went alongside him like a friend and companion. His teeming army, uncounted like water (flowing) in a river, marched with him fully armed. (Marduk) allowed him to enter Babylon without battle or fight, sparing his own city of Babylon from hardship, and delivered Nabonidus, who had not worshiped him, into his hands.

All the people of Babylon, the entire land of Sumer and Akkad, rulers and princes, bowed down to him, kissed his feet, and rejoiced at his rule, filled with delight. They happily greeted him as the lord, by means of whose trust those who were as dead were revived and saved from all trial and hardship; they praised his name.

I am Cyrus, king of the world, great king, mighty king, king of Babylon, king of the lands of Sumer and Akkad, king of the four quarters of the universe, son of Cambyses, great king, king of Anshan, descendant of Teispes, great king, king of Anshan, from an ancient royal lineage, whose reign is beloved by (the gods) Marduk and Nabu, whose kingship they desired to make them glad.

After entering Babylon in peace, amidst joy and jubilation I made the royal palace the center of my rule. The great lord Marduk, who loves Babylon, with great magnanimity, established (it) as (my) destiny, and I sought to worship him each day. My teeming army paraded about Babylon in peace, and I did not allow any trouble in all of Sumer and Akkad. I took great care to peacefully (protect) the city of Babylon and its cult places. (And) as for the citizens of Babylon . . . whom (Nabonidus) had made subservient in a manner (totally) unsuited to them against the will of the gods, I released them from their weariness and loosened their burden. The great lord Marduk rejoiced in my deeds. Kindly he blessed me, Cyrus, the king, his worshiper, Cambyses, the offspring of my loins, and all of my troops, so that we could go about in peace and well-being.

By his lofty command, all enthroned kings, the whole world, from the Upper Sea to the Lower Sea, inhabitants of distant regions, all the kings of the West, tent dwellers, brought their heavy tribute to me in Babylon and kissed my feet. From [Babylon] to Aššur and Susa, Agade, Eshnunna, the cities of Zamban, Meturnu, Der as far as the borders of the Gutians – I returned to these sanctuaries on the other side of the Tigris, sanctuaries founded in ancient times, the images that had been in them there and I made their dwellings permanent. I also gathered all their people and returned to them their habitations. And then at the command of Marduk, the great lord, I resettled all the gods of Sumer and Akkad whom Nabonidus had brought into Babylon to the anger of the lord of the gods in their shrines, the places which they enjoy. May all the gods whom I have resettled in their sacred cities ask Marduk and Nabu each day for a long life for me and speak well of me to him; may they say to Marduk, my lord that Cyrus, the king who worships you, and Cambyses, his son . . . their . . . I settled all the people of Babylon who prayed for my kingship and all their lands in a peaceful place. Daily I supplied (the temple) [with offerings of x gee]se, two ducks, and ten turtledoves above the former (offerings) of geese, ducks, and turtledoves. The wall Imgur-Enlil, the great (city) wall of Babylon, I strove to strengthen its fortifications [. . .] the baked brick quay on the bank of the city moat, constructed by an earlier king, but not completed, its work [I . . . thus the city had not been completely surrounded], so [to complete] the outside, which no king before me had done, it troops, mustered in all the land, into Babylon [. . .]. I made it anew with bitumen and baked bricks and [finished the work upon it. . . . I installed doors of] mighty [cedar] clad with bronze, thresholds and door-opening[s cast of copper in all] its [gates. . . . I saw inside it an in]scription of Assurbanipal, a king who came before [me . . . for e]ver.

Bibliography

Sources: The first edition of the British Museum piece was published in H. C. Rawlinson and T. G. Pinches, *The Cuneiform Inscriptions of Western Asia V*. London: R. E. Bowler, 1880–4, no. 35. A drawing of the Yale fragment was first published in J. B. Nies and

C. E. Keiser, *Historical, Religious and Economic Texts and Antiquities*, Babylonian Inscriptions in the Collection of J. B. Nies II, New Haven: Yale University Press, 1920, no. 32; and the two were joined and edited together by P.-R. Berger, "Der Kyros-Zylinder mit dem Zusatzfragment BIN II Nr. 32 und die Akkadischen Personenamen in Danielbuch," *Zeitschrift für Assyriologie* 64 (1975): 192–234. A new edition, with improvements of the text based on inspection of the originals has now been provided by Hanspeter Schaudig, *Die Inschriften Nabonids von Babylon und Kyros' des Großen samt den in ihrem Umfeld entstandenen Tendenzschriften. Textausgabe und Grammatik.* Altes Orient und Altes Testament 256. Münster: Ugarit Verlag, 2001, 550–6.

Further reading

The life of Nabonidus has been studied by Paul-Alain Beaulieu, *The Reign of Nabonidus, King of Babylon 556–539* BC. New Haven: Yale University Press, 1989. See also Piotr Michalowski, "The Doors of the Past," *Eretz-Israel* 27 (2003): 136–52. On the historical and ideological ramifications of the conquest of Babylon by the Persians see (with further bibliography) Pierre Briant, *From Cyrus to Alexander: A History of the Persian Empire*. Winona Lake, Ind.: Eisenbrauns, 2002. The structure and message of the Cyrus Cylinder has been analyzed in Janos Harmatta, "The Literary Patterns of the Babylonian Edict of Cyrus," *Acta Antiqua* 19 (1971): 217–31; Amélie Kuhrt, "The Cyrus Cylinder and Achaemenid Imperial Policy," *Journal for the Study of the Old Testament* 25 (1983): 83–97. See also Amélie Kuhrt, "The Achaemenid Empire: a Babylonian Perspective," Proceedings of the Cambridge Philological Society 34 (1988). Older translations into English are by A. Leo Oppenheim in ANET, 315–16; and by A. K. Grayson in A. K. Grayson and D. B. Redford, *Papyrus and Tablet* (Englewood Cliffs: Prentice-Hall, 1973), 124–6.

Index